Oracle® SQL
by Example

Oracle® SQL
by Example

ALICE RISCHERT

PRENTICE
HALL

Upper Saddle River, NJ • Boston • Indianapolis • San Francisco • New York •
Toronto • Montreal • London • Munich • Paris • Madrid • Cape Town • Sydney •
Tokyo • Singapore • Mexico City

Many of the designations used by manufacturers and sellers to distinguish their products are claimed as trademarks. Where those designations appear in this book, and the publisher was aware of a trademark claim, the designations have been printed with initial capital letters or in all capitals.

The author and publisher have taken care in the preparation of this book, but make no expressed or implied warranty of any kind and assume no responsibility for errors or omissions. No liability is assumed for incidental or consequential damages in connection with or arising out of the use of the information or programs contained herein.

The publisher offers excellent discounts on this book when ordered in quantity for bulk purchases or special sales, which may include electronic versions and/or custom covers and content particular to your business, training goals, marketing focus, and branding interests. For more information, please contact:

U.S. Corporate and Government Sales
(800) 382-3419
corpsales@pearsontechgroup.com

For sales outside the United States please contact:

International Sales
international@pearson.com

Visit us on the Web: informit.com/ph

Library of Congress Cataloging-in-Publication Data:

Rischert, Alice.
  Oracle SQL by example / Alice Rischert.
     p. cm.
  ISBN 978-0-13-714283-5 (pbk. : alk. paper) 1. SQL (Computer program language) 2. Oracle (Computer file) I. Title.
  QA76.73.S67R57 2009
  005.13'3—dc22
                                    2009022733

ISBN-13: 978-0-137-14283-5
ISBN-10: 0-137-14283-8
Text printed in the United States on recycled paper at Edwards Brothers in Ann Arbor, Michigan
First printing August 2009

Editor-in-Chief: Mark Taub
Acquisitions Editor: Trina MacDonald
Development Editor: Michael Thurston
Managing Editor: Kristy Hart
Technical Editors: Oleg Voskoboynikov
                   Robert Vollman
Project Editors: Julie Anderson
                 Jovana San Nicolas-Shirley
Copy Editor: Kitty Wilson
Indexer: Alice Rischert
Proofreader: Sheri Cain
Publishing Coordinator: Olivia Basegio
Interior Designer: Gary Adair
Cover Designer: Anne Jones
Compositors: Nonie Ratcliff
             Gloria Schurick

To my daughter, Kirsten, and my parents, Albert and Hilde

Contents

CHAPTER 5   Date and Conversion Functions   189

CHAPTER 15   Security   **661**

CHAPTER 16   Regular Expressions and Hierarchical Queries   695

CHAPTER 17   Exploring Data Warehousing Features   741

FOREWORD

The Ancient Problem

The year was 1680; the place was the Levant—a region on the eastern shores of the Mediterranean. The political climate was stable enough to support peaceful trade among nations, and seaports were bustling with merchants from many countries. These merchants found trade outside their native land profitable, but they faced many challenges in travel, as well as in adapting to foreign cultures and seemingly strange customs. One major challenge was communication. As a seller of goods, a key sales technique is verbally extolling the virtues of your product to a potential customer, but how do you market to a target audience whose language you have not mastered? Sign language and written symbols can be quite effective but are not nearly as personal and understandable (and beneficial to sales) as well-chosen words. The problem with spoken language in a melting pot like the Levant is that there are many languages to master.

The Ancient Solution

The solution that emerged to this problem nearly a half century ago has been used by people of many lands throughout history: When gathered in a multilingual environment, speak a common language. In the Levant, the common language that evolved was a combination of Italian, Spanish, French, Greek, Arabic, and Turkish. This language, called *Lingua Franca*, became a standard in many ports, as merchants used it to successfully communicate with their customers and fellow traders. Those who learned and mastered this language became the most effective and successful businesspeople. Although Lingua Franca is now extinct, the term *lingua franca* is still applied to any common language used for communication between people of diverse native languages.

The Lingua Franca of IT

Today's information technology (IT) industry uses the concept of *lingua franca*. Businesses solve their data management requirements by using relational databases. The challenges that companies face when using relational databases are mainly in creating flexible and efficient human interfaces. Developing customized user interfaces often takes much in the way of effort and resources if it is to properly fulfill the requirements of the business.

IT professionals who are tasked with creating modern database systems must rely on their training and expertise, both in designing the proper database storage objects and in programming the most efficient application programs. In the recent past, developers of relational database systems have created application programs using procedural programming languages such as COBOL, Fortran, and C. Regardless of the procedural language used, there is an additional language embedded in these procedural programs. This language offers a standard way to define and manipulate the data in a relational database and is, therefore, the lingua franca of database technology: Structured Query Language (SQL).

With SQL, developers using diverse programming languages, database software, hardware, and operating systems can effectively communicate with the database in a completely standard way.

A standard language means that the written code is understood easily and can be supported fully and enhanced quickly. This is the promise of SQL, and this promise has been fulfilled successfully for decades, in countless relational database application programs.

The Modern-Day Problem

The problem today is not the lack of a common language, as was the case in the days before a lingua franca. SQL is the common language. The problem today is in the assimilation and proper use of this language. As the computer industry continues its logarithmic growth, the number of application developers increases similarly. Each new developer who writes programs that need to access a relational database must be trained in the lingua franca. In the past, with a small number of new developers, this was a manageable feat for most organizations. When a new developer was in training, she or he would learn both a procedural programming language and the database language embedded in it—SQL.

Today, IT solutions are leaning toward object orientation. Object-oriented analysis, design, and programming have come of age and, according to popular opinion, are now the best tools for creating computer systems. As a result, object-oriented languages, such as Java, C#, and C++, are replacing the traditional procedural languages for building new systems. From the perspective of a database management system, this is merely a shift in the main programming language that the developer uses to create the application's user interface. The core database language, SQL, is still required and is of key importance.

However, something fundamental has been lost in this paradigm shift to object orientation. That something is a solid background in SQL. This problem persists for many reasons. Unfortunately, IT management professionals everywhere are employing object-oriented programmers who do not have a solid grasp of SQL. This arrangement works up to a point, but there is, eventually, a collision with a brick wall. In many situations, as a consultant, I have had to break into the SQL code used in a Java program and found inefficient or incorrect use of SQL. Misunderstanding or misuse of SQL can have adverse effects on the program's efficiency and can drag down the performance of production data systems, which are critical to the functioning of the business. On the other hand, proper use of SQL results in application programs being simpler to create and maintain and being most efficient in data storage and data access.

The Modern-Day Solution

The solution to the problem of misunderstanding the lingua franca of databases is simple: an increased focus on learning the foundations and abilities of SQL and the correct methods for coding SQL programs. Time and money spent for training on the basics of SQL are time and money well spent. There are many ways to learn a subject like SQL. In my experience of over 25 years as a trainer in the IT and other industries, the best learning experience results from a multifaceted approach. Human beings learn in different ways, and using different approaches to present the same subject ensures that the subject will be understood and assimilated. In addition, the repetition of concepts and material in different formats ensures mastery of the subject. Research has proven that repetition and variety are key learning techniques.

What Ms. Rischert has accomplished in this book is the epitome of the solution for the correct understanding of SQL. This book will be useful for seasoned IT professionals who need to study the language more completely or who just need a refresher on the concepts and thought processes of using SQL. It will also be useful for those who are new to the subject and are interested in learning it thoroughly and in the right way.

The author applies the key teaching principles of variety and repetition in a multifaceted approach to the subject. This approach allows the student of the subject to fully grasp the basics as well as the best ways to use the language. All core SQL subjects are treated with this approach, which includes a brief description of the concept followed by simple and easy-to-grasp examples. Examples that you can try using an Oracle database make the concepts real and allow you to quickly grasp the subject. In addition, exercises and quizzes make you think about the concepts you just learned and therefore help you assimilate them.

The very best way to learn the concepts of any technology is to be tasked with an application development project that uses that technology. However, a project in the real-world workplace is not the right place to learn; the stakes are too high and the pressure too great. This book gives you a taste of real-world application development needs and processes by assigning workshops where you further apply the knowledge gained from the conceptual discussions, examples, exercises, and quizzes. The book then provides the solutions to all questions presented so that you can check your work. Proper use of these follow-up sections will lead you to a solid mastery of the language and give you the ability to use this lingua franca successfully to solve real-world business problems. This type of mastery will serve you well in whatever type of database programming environment you find yourself.

Peter Koletzke
Quovera
San Carlos, California
May 2009

PREFACE

SQL is the de facto standard language for relational databases, and Oracle's database server is the leading relational database on the market today. *Oracle SQL by Example,* 4th edition, presents an introduction to the Oracle SQL language in a unique and highly effective format. Rather than being a reference book, it guides you through basic skills until you reach a mastery of the language. The book challenges you to work through hands-on guided tasks rather than read through descriptions of functionality. You will be able to retain the material more easily, and the additional exercise and quiz questions reinforce and further enhance the learning experience.

Who This Book Is For

This book is intended for anyone requiring a background in Oracle's implementation of the SQL language. In particular, application developers, system designers, and database administrators will find many practical and representative real-world examples. Students new to Oracle will gain the necessary experience and confidence to apply their knowledge in solving typical problems they face in work situations. Individuals already familiar with Oracle SQL but wanting a firmer foundation or those interested in the new Oracle 11g features will discover many useful tips and tricks, as well as a wealth of information.

The initial audience for the book was the students of the Oracle SQL class at Columbia University's Computer Technology and Applications program. The student body typically encompassed a wide-ranging level of technology experience. Their questions, learning approaches, and feedback provided the framework for this book. Many students cited the hands-on exercises as critical to their understanding of database technology and SQL and continuously asked for more examples and additional challenging topics. This book shares much of the material presented in the classroom and looks at the various angles of many solutions to a particular issue.

The book begins with the basic concepts of relational databases, the SQL Developer and SQL*Plus tools, and SQL; it then gradually deepens the knowledge. Whether you already have some fundamental understanding of SQL or not, you will benefit from reading this book as it allows you to gain insight into writing alternative SQL statements. After performing the exercises in this book, you will harness the power of SQL and utilize much of Oracle's SQL functionality.

What Makes This Book Different

This book encourages you to learn by doing, to actively participate by performing the exercises, quizzes, and Workshop exercises. Ultimately, the reward is a thorough understanding of SQL and a high level of comfort dealing with real-world Oracle SQL topics. Performing the exercises aids in retention of the material, and the quizzes and Workshop sections further test your understanding and offer additional challenges. The companion Web site, located at www.oraclesqlbyexample.com, provides solutions to the Workshop exercises and includes additional exercises and answers.

The book's focus is on providing examples of how the SQL language is commonly used, with many exercises supporting the learning experience. Unlike other SQL books, this book discusses Oracle's specific implementation of the language. Learning the language alone is not enough. The book also teaches you how to adopt good habits and educates you about many Oracle-specific technology features that are essential to successful systems development. The examples are based on a sample database that takes you through the typical tasks you will encounter when working with an Oracle database.

This book is not a reference book; rather, it teaches SQL by illustrating its use through many examples. Take advantage of the index to look up concepts and refer to certain topics. The best way to learn the SQL language is to perform the exercises and compare your answers with the sample answers and accompanying explanations. Additional teaching points are part of the answers; the idea is that after you have performed an exercise, you are ready for additional, more advanced material.

This book does not cover the entire Oracle SQL syntax but emphasizes the essentials of the most frequently used features, with many examples to reinforce your learning. Some of Oracle's syntax options are too numerous, and many are very infrequently used; including them all would make the book swell by several hundred additional pages. Instead, I have concentrated on those that you will use most. After performing the exercises, you will also have gained sufficient knowledge to read up and understand the Oracle documentation, if needed. I hope that you will enjoy this learning experience and come away with the knowledge you hoped to gain.

How This Book Is Organized

Each chapter of this book is divided into labs covering particular topics. The objective of each lab is defined at its beginning, with brief examples that introduce you to the covered concepts.

Following the lab's introductory examples are exercises, which are the heart of the lab. They reinforce and expand your knowledge of the subject. Each exercise consists of a series of steps to follow to perform specific tasks or particular questions that are designed to help you discover the important aspects of the SQL language. The answers to these questions are given at the end of the exercises, along with more in-depth discussion of the concepts explored.

After you perform the exercises and compare the answers with the sample queries, answers, and explanations, you can move on to the multiple-choice quiz questions. These are meant to test your understanding of the material covered in the lab. The answers to these questions appear in Appendix A, "Answers to Quiz Questions." There are additional quiz questions at the book's companion Web site, located at www.oraclesqlbyexample.com.

At the end of each chapter, the Workshop section reinforces and combines all the topics learned in labs and helps you solidify your skills. The answers to these questions are provided on the companion Web site for this book.

Each chapter is laid out as follows:

     Chapter introduction

         Lab

              Exercises

              Exercise Answers (with detailed discussion)

              Quiz

         Lab

         …

         Workshop

The chapters should be completed in sequence because concepts covered in earlier chapters are required for the completion of exercises in later chapters.

What You Need

To complete the exercises, you need the following:

- ▶ The Oracle database software
- ▶ Oracle's SQL Developer or SQL*Plus software
- ▶ Access to the Companion Website

ORACLE 11G

Oracle 11g is Oracle's latest version of the relational database software and its flagship product. To follow along with this book, you can use either the Standard Edition or Enterprise Edition. The Enterprise Edition of Oracle version 11.1.0.6.0 was used to create the exercises for this book.

If you have a previous version of the Oracle database, you will be able to complete a large majority of the exercises; however, some syntax options and features are available only in Oracle 11g.

If you do not have the latest release of the Oracle software available, you can obtain a trial copy from Oracle's Web site, at www.oracle.com. You have the option of either downloading the Standard Edition or Enterprise Edition or purchasing a CD media pack from the Oracle store (https://oraclestore.oracle.com) for a nominal fee.

ORACLE SQL DEVELOPER AND SQL*PLUS

You can perform most of the exercises in this book with Oracle's SQL Developer or SQL*Plus software. Both software tools are included with the Oracle database and are part of the default installation.

SQL Developer is easier to use and offers a superior display of results. Because SQL Developer is a relatively new product and independent of the Oracle database release, you may find later versions of the software on Oracle's Web site, as a separate product download.

The book's screenshots and described functionality are based on SQL Developer 1.5.3. This tool sets the future product direction and has many useful features to improve your productivity and enhance your SQL knowledge and skill set.

This book is not intended as a comprehensive SQL Developer book. Rather, the focus is SQL. You use SQL Developer as part of your interaction with the Oracle database. Oracle's intended target audience for the SQL Developer tool is not only SQL users but also PL/SQL programmers. Therefore, you'll find that menu options in this tool are related to PL/SQL. The purpose of this book is not to describe and point out every menu option but to teach you the SQL language. SQL Developer is a useful tool for executing SQL statements and helping you understand the effects of the commands. The coverage of SQL Developer's core functionality is intended within the context of SQL.

Using the SQL Developer graphical user interface does not eliminate the need to know and understand the SQL language. SQL Developer is a productivity tool that makes you a more effi- cient and proficient user of the language. You still need to know and understand your actions, and the tools can eliminate some basic mistakes and alleviate some frustrations for a beginning user.

SQL*Plus has been part of Oracle since its early beginnings and will continue to be shipped with every installation and platform. It has such a long history and defined purpose in Oracle's strat- egy that you cannot ignore SQL*Plus altogether. Therefore, you will gain some basic knowledge of this tool as part of the exercises in this book. This book points out the relevant differences between SQL Developer and SQL*Plus, and you will gain an appreciation for each tool's inher- ent benefits. You can choose to perform most of the exercises in either tool, depending on your preference. Because the book cannot comprehensively cover both tools and the SQL language, it focuses on the SQL Developer and SQL*Plus features you will use most.

Instead of executing your statements in SQL Developer or SQL*Plus, you can also use other SQL execution environments; a list of such environments is provided in Appendix H, "Resources."

Access to the Companion Web Site

The companion Web site, located at www.oraclesqlbyexample.com, provides the following.

- ▶ Installation files you need to download before you begin reading the book

- ▶ Answers to the Workshop questions

- ▶ Additional Quiz questions

- ▶ Additional resources, such as links, tips, and errata

INSTALLATION FILES

All the exercises and quiz questions are based on a sample schema called STUDENT. You can download the required files to install the STUDENT schema and the installation instructions from the companion Web site. (The sample database is identical to the companion book of this series, *Oracle PL/SQL by Example*, 4th Edition, by Benjamin Rosenzweig and Elena Silvestrova Rakhimov; Prentice Hall, 2008.)

WORKSHOP

The answers to the Workshop sections are provided at the companion Web site.

ADDITIONAL QUIZ QUESTIONS

The Web site provides many other features, such as additional quiz questions and periodically updated information about the book.

 Visit the companion Web site and download the required files before starting the labs and exercises.

About the STUDENT Schema

Throughout this book, you access data from a sample schema called STUDENT, which contains information about a computer education program. The schema was designed to record data about instructors, courses, students, and their respective enrollments and grades.

After you download the installation files to create the schema within your Oracle database, you will be able to follow the exercises in the book. Chapter 1, "SQL and Data," introduces you to the relational concepts necessary to read a schema diagram. Appendix D, "STUDENT Database Schema," shows a graphical representation of the schema, and Appendix E, "Table and Column Descriptions," lists descriptive information about each table and column.

Conventions Used in This Book

Several conventions used in this book help make your learning experience easier. These are explained here.

 This icon denotes advice and useful information about a particular topic or concept.

 This icon flags tips that are especially helpful tricks to will save you time or trouble—for instance, a shortcut for performing a particular task or a useful method.

Warnings are provided to warn you about any potential issues regarding the safety of your database or to save you headaches in the long run.

Errata

I have made every effort to make sure there are no errors in the text and code. However, to err is human. At the companion Web site (www.oraclesqlbyexample.com), you will find corrections as they are spotted. If you find an error that has not been reported, please let me know by contacting me at ar280@yahoo.com. Your comments and suggestions are greatly appreciated.

ACKNOWLEDGMENTS

As soon as the research and writing for this fourth edition started, it quickly became apparent that coverage of Oracle's new SQL Developer tool was an important topic to be included.

This book includes revisions of a number of topics and the addition of new exercises. Because each new version of the Oracle database adds new valuable features, the goal was to include as many practical and real-world scenarios as possible.

I am privileged to acknowledge a number of individuals who contributed along the way by offering suggestions, corrections, guidance, ideas, comments, and advice. In particular, I would like to express my appreciation for the tremendous efforts of Oleg Voskoboynikov and Robert Vollman. They reviewed all chapters for accuracy to ensure that the functionality worked exactly as described. Their excellent comments and suggestions are reflected in the book.

A number of readers and past students sent in comments, corrections, and suggestions. There are too many individuals to acknowledge individually, but all their contributions were extremely helpful and very much appreciated.

I am particularly grateful to Trina MacDonald at Prentice Hall for initiating and believing in this project and putting up with inevitable delays, due to family, work, and life in general. Michael Thurston, the development editor of this book, offered many terrific suggestions that helped organize the material in a more accessible and readable format. He meticulously combed through the manuscript and ensured consistency and readability. Olivia Basegio kept track of the different chapters, edits, and readers to make certain nothing was missed. Thank you to Kitty Wilson for her detailed copy edits and Julie Anderson for smoothly coordinating the production process.

Thanks to the clients and my colleagues at Vitech who unwittingly provided some of the material. Their questions, problems, and challenges provided some of the framework of the book.

I would like to thank those individuals who helped with the earlier editions of the book, as many of their contributions continue to be reflected in this work. Thank you, Ben Rosenzweig, Elena Silvestrova, Dan Diaz, Bernard Dadario, and Alex Morrison.

Douglas Scherer has offered his continued encouragement and insight with each edition of the book. Peter Kolezke has been a dear friend and supporter for so many years, and his enthusiasm and encouragements once again helped me see the light at the end of the tunnel.

The Garcia family, my parents, my sisters, Irene and Christa, and my brother, Guenter, deserve a great deal of thanks for their tremendous advice and encouragement. And thanks to Spooky, our kitty, for keeping me company during long nights and weekends spent writing and entertaining me with her antics. Finally, I owe most of my thanks to my lovely daughter, Kirsten. Thanks for your understanding, love, and doing so well in school. You continue to amaze me with your talents every day!

Alice Rischert

ABOUT THE AUTHOR

Alice Rischert, former chair of Columbia University's Database Application Development and Design program, has taught classes in Oracle SQL, PL/SQL, and database design to hundreds of students. Ms. Rischert's wide-ranging technology experience encompasses systems integration, database architecture, and project management for a number of companies in the United States, Europe, and Asia. Ms. Rischert has presented on SQL and PL/SQL topics at Oracle conferences and has worked with Oracle since version 5.

CHAPTER 1

SQL and Data

CHAPTER OBJECTIVES

In this chapter, you will learn about:

- ▶ Relational Databases
- ▶ Data Normalization and Table Relationships
- ▶ The STUDENT Schema Diagram

Before getting started writing SQL statements, it is beneficial to introduce some basic database concepts and review the history of databases.

What Is SQL?

SQL (pronounced "*sequel*") is an acronym for *Structured Query Language,* a standardized language used to access and manipulate data. The history of SQL corresponds closely with the development of a relational databases concept published in a paper by Dr. E. F. Codd at IBM in 1970. He applied mathematical concepts to the specification of a method for data storage and access; this specification, which became the basis for relational databases, was intended to overcome the physical dependencies of the then-available database systems. The SQL language (originally called "System R" in the prototype and later called "SEQUEL") was developed by the IBM Research Laboratory as a standard language to use with relational databases. In 1979 Oracle, then called Relational Software, Inc., introduced the first commercially available implementation of a relational database incorporating the SQL language.

The SQL language evolved with many additional syntax expansions incorporated into the American National Standards Institute (ANSI) SQL standards developed since. Individual database vendors continuously added extensions to the language, which eventually found their way into the latest ANSI standards used by relational databases today. Large-scale commercial implementations of relational database applications started to appear in the mid- to late 1980s, as early implementations were hampered by poor performance. Since then, relational databases and the SQL language have continuously evolved and improved.

Why Learn SQL?

Today, SQL is accepted as the universal standard database access language. Databases using the SQL language are entrusted with managing critical information affecting many aspects of our daily lives. Most applications developed today use a relational database, and Oracle continues to be one of the largest and most popular database vendors. Although relational databases and the SQL language are already over 30 years old, there seems to be no slowing down of the popularity of the language. Learning SQL is probably one of the best long-term investments you can make for a number of reasons:

- SQL is used by most commercial database applications.

- Although the language has evolved over the years with a large array of syntax enhancements and additions, most of the basic functionality has remained essentially unchanged.

- SQL knowledge will continue to be a fundamental skill because there is currently no mature and viable alternative language that accomplishes the same functionality.

- Learning Oracle's specific SQL implementation allows you great insight into the feature-rich functionality of one of the largest and most successful database vendors.

An Introduction to Databases

Before you begin to use SQL, you must know about data, databases, and relational databases. What is a database? A *database* is an organized collection of data. A *database management system (DBMS)* is software that allows the creation, retrieval, and manipulation of data. You use such systems to maintain patient data in a hospital, bank accounts in a bank, or inventory in a warehouse.

A *relational database management system (RDBMS)* provides this functionality within the context of the relational database theory and the rules defined for relational databases by Codd. These rules, called "Codd's Twelve Rules," later expanded to include additional rules, describe goals for database management systems to cope with ever-challenging and demanding database requirements. Compliance with Codd's Rules has been a major challenge for database vendors, and early versions of relational databases complied with only a handful of the rules.

Understanding relational database concepts provides the foundation for understanding the SQL language. Those unfamiliar with relational concepts or interested in a refresher will receive an overview of basic relational theories in the next two labs. If you are already familiar with relational theory, you can skip the first two labs and jump directly to Lab 1.3, which teaches you about the organization of a fictional university's student database called STUDENT. This database is used throughout the exercises in this book.

LAB 1.1
The Relational Database

LAB OBJECTIVES

After this lab, you will be able to:

▶ Understand Relational Database Concepts

▶ Define *SQL*

▶ Name the Components of a Relational Database

This lab introduces you to the terminology of relational databases. You will appreciate some of the inherent advantages of relational database design and gain an overview of SQL language commands.

What Is Data?

Data is all around you; you make use of it every day. Your hair may be brown, your flight leaves from gate K10, you try to get up in the morning at 6:30 A.M. Storing data in related groups and making the connections among them are what databases are all about.

You interact with a database when you withdraw cash from an ATM, order a book from a Web site, or check stock quotes on the Internet. The switch from the information processing society to the knowledge management society will be facilitated by databases. Databases are a major asset to any organization. They contain information that helps run the business, and the information and technology employed in these database systems represent the backbones of the many technological advances we enjoy today.

Before the availability of relational databases, data was stored in individual files that could not be accessed unless you knew a programming language. Data could not be combined easily, and modifications to the underlying database structures were extremely difficult. The relational model conceived by E. F. Codd provided the framework to solve a myriad of these and many other database problems.

How Is Data Organized?

Relational databases offer *data independence*, meaning a user does not need to know on which hard drive and file a particular piece of information is stored. The RDBMS provides users with *data consistency* and *data integrity*. For example, if an employee works in the finance department, and we know that he can work for only one department, then there should not be duplicate department records or contradicting data in the database. As you work through this lab, you will discover many of these useful and essential features.

A relational database stores data in tables, essentially a two-dimensional matrix consisting of columns and rows. Let's start with a discussion of the terminology used in relational databases.

TABLES

A table typically contains data about a single subject. Each table has a unique name that signifies the contents of the data. A database usually consists of many tables. For example, you may store data about books you read in a table called BOOK and store details about authors in the AUTHOR table.

COLUMNS

Columns in a table organize the data further, and a table consists of at least one column. Each column represents a single, low-level detail about a particular set of data. The name of the column is unique within a table and identifies the data you find in the column. For example, the BOOK table may have a column for the title, publisher, date the book was published, and so on. The order of the columns is unimportant because SQL allows you to display data in any order you choose.

ROWS

Each row usually represents one unique set of data within a table. For example, the row in Figure 1.1 with the title "The Invisible Force" is unique within the BOOK table. All the columns of the row represent respective data for the row. Each intersection of a column and row in a table represents a value, and some do not, as you see in the PUBLISH_DATE column. The value is said to be *null*. Null is an unknown value, so it is not even blank spaces. Nulls cannot be evaluated or compared because they are unknown.

BOOK_ID	TITLE	PUBLISHER	PUBLISH_DATE
1010	The Invisible Force	Literacy Circle	
1011	Into The Sky	Prentice Hall	10/2008
1012	Making It Possible	Life Books	08/2010

← Row

↑ Column

FIGURE 1.1
The BOOK table

PRIMARY KEY

When working with tables, you must understand how to uniquely identify data within a table. This is the purpose of the *primary key*. This means you find one, and only one, row in the table by looking for the primary key value. Figure 1.2 shows an example of the CUSTOMER table with CUSTOMER_ID as the primary key of the table.

CUSTOMER_ID	CUSTOMER_NAME	ADDRESS	PHONE	ZIP
2010	Movers, Inc.	123 Park Lane	212-555-1212	10095
2011	Acme Mfg, Ltd.	555 Broadway	212-566-1212	10004
2012	ALR Inc.	50 Fifth Avenue	212-999-1212	10010

Primary Key

FIGURE 1.2
Primary key example

At first glance, you might think that the CUSTOMER_NAME column can serve as the primary key of the CUSTOMER table because it is unique. However, it is entirely possible to have customers with the same name. Therefore, the CUSTOMER_NAME column is not a good choice for the primary key. Sometimes the unique key is a system-generated sequence number; this type of key is called a *synthetic*, or *surrogate, key*. The advantage of using a surrogate key is that it is unique and does not have any inherent meaning or purpose; therefore, it is not subject to changes. In this example, the CUSTOMER_ID column is such a surrogate key.

It is best to avoid any primary keys that are subject to updates as they cause unnecessary complexity. For example, the phone number of a customer is a poor example of a primary key column choice. Though it may possibly be unique within a table, phone numbers can change and then cause a number of problems with updates of other columns that reference this column.

A table may have only one primary key, which consists of one or more columns. If the primary key contains multiple columns, it is referred to as a *composite primary key*, or *concatenated primary key*. (Choosing appropriate keys is discussed further in Chapter 12, "Create, Alter, and Drop Tables.") Oracle does not require that every table have a primary key, and there may be cases in which it is not appropriate to have one. However, it is strongly recommended that most tables have a primary key.

FOREIGN KEYS

If you store customers and the customers' order information in one table, each customer's name and address is repeated for each order. Figure 1.3 depicts such a table. Any change to the address requires the update of all the rows in the table for that individual customer.

CUSTOMER_ID	CUSTOMER_NAME	ADDRESS	PHONE	ZIP	ORDER_ID	ORDER_DATE	TOTAL_ORDER
2010	Movers, Inc.	123 ParkLane	212-555-1212	10095	100	12/23/2007	$500
2010	Movers, Inc.	123 ParkLane	212-555-1212	10095	102	7/20/2008	$100
2010	Movers, Inc.	123 ParkLane	212-555-1212	10095	103	8/25/2008	$400
2010	Movers, Inc.	123 ParkLane	212-555-1212	10095	104	9/20/2008	$200
2011	Acme Mfg, Ltd.	555 Broadway	212-566-1212	10004	105	9/20/2008	$900
2012	ALR Inc.	50 Fifth Avenue	212-999-1212	10010	101	1/5/2008	$600

FIGURE 1.3
Example of CUSTOMER data mixed with ORDER data

If, however, the data is split into two tables (CUSTOMER and ORDER, as shown in Figure 1.4) and the customer's address needs to be updated, only one row in the CUSTOMER table needs to be updated. Furthermore, separating data this way avoids the possibility of data inconsistency, whereby the data differs between the different rows. Eliminating redundancy is one of the key concepts in relational databases, and this process, referred to as *normalization*, is discussed shortly.

Primary Key   **CUSTOMER**

CUSTOMER_ID	CUSTOMER_NAME	ADDRESS	PHONE	ZIP
2010	Movers, Inc.	123 Park Lane	212-555-1212	10095
2011	Acme Mfg, Ltd.	555 Broadway	212-566-1212	10004
2012	ALR Inc.	50 Fifth Avenue	212-999-1212	10010

Foreign Key   **ORDER**

ORDER_ID	CUSTOMER_ID	ORDER_DATE	TOTAL_ORDER
100	2010	12/23/2007	$500
102	2010	7/20/2008	$100
103	2010	8/25/2008	$400
104	2010	9/20/2008	$200
105	2011	9/20/2008	$900
101	2012	1/5/2008	$600

FIGURE 1.4
Primary and foreign key relationship between CUSTOMER and ORDER tables

Figure 1.4 illustrates how the data is split into two tables to provide data consistency. In this example, CUSTOMER_ID becomes a *foreign key* column in the ORDER table. The foreign key is the column that links the CUSTOMER and ORDER table together. You can find all orders for a particular customer by looking for the particular CUSTOMER_ID in the ORDER table. The CUSTOMER_ID corresponds to a single row in the CUSTOMER table that provides the customer-specific information.

The foreign key column CUSTOMER_ID happens to have the same column name in the ORDER table. This makes it easier to recognize the fact that the tables share common column values. Often the foreign key column and the primary key have identical column names, but it is not required. You will learn more about foreign key columns with the same and different names and how to create foreign key relationships in Chapter 12. Chapter 7, "Equijoins," teaches you how to combine results from the two tables using SQL.

 You connect and combine data between tables in a relational database via common columns.

Overview of SQL Language Commands

You work with tables, rows, and columns using the SQL language. SQL allows you to query data, create new data, modify existing data, and delete data. Within the SQL language you can differentiate between individual sublanguages, which are a collection of individual commands.

For example, *Data Manipulation Language* (DML) commands allow you to query, insert, update, and delete data. SQL allows you to create new database structures such as tables or modify existing ones; this subcategory of SQL language commands is called the *Data Definition Language* (DDL). Using the SQL language, you can control access to the data using *Data Control Language* (DCL) commands. Table 1.1 shows you different language categories, with examples of their respective SQL commands.

TABLE 1.1   Overview of SQL Language Commands

DESCRIPTION	SQL COMMANDS
Data Manipulation	SELECT, INSERT, UPDATE, DELETE, MERGE
Data Definition	CREATE, ALTER, DROP, TRUNCATE, RENAME
Data Control	GRANT, REVOKE
Transaction Control	COMMIT, ROLLBACK, SAVEPOINT

One of the first statements you will use in the exercises is the SELECT command, which allows you to query data. For example, to retrieve the TITLE and PUBLISHER columns from the BOOK table, you may issue a SELECT statement such as the following:

```
SELECT title, publisher
  FROM book
```

The INSERT command lets you add new rows to a table. The next command shows you an example of an INSERT statement that adds a row to the BOOK table. The row contains the values Oracle SQL as a book title, a BOOK_ID of 1020, and a publish date of 12/2011, with Prentice Hall as the publisher.

```
INSERT INTO book
        (book_id, title, publisher, publish_date) VALUES
(1020, 'Oracle SQL', 'Prentice Hall', '12/2011')
```

To create new tables, you use the CREATE TABLE command. The following statement illustrates how to create a simple table called AUTHOR with three columns. The first column, AUTHOR_ ID, holds numeric data; the FIRST_NAME and LAST_NAME columns contain alphanumeric character data.

```
CREATE TABLE author
        (author_id    NUMBER,
        first_name   VARCHAR2(30),
        last_name    VARCHAR2(30))
```

You can manipulate the column definitions of a table with the ALTER TABLE command. This allows you to add or drop columns. You can also create primary and foreign key constraints on a table. Constraints enforce business rules within the database. For example, a primary key constraint can enforce the uniqueness of the AUTHOR_ID column in the AUTHOR table.

To grant SELECT and INSERT access to the AUTHOR table, you issue a GRANT command. It allows the user Scott to retrieve and insert data in the AUTHOR table.

```
GRANT SELECT, INSERT ON author TO scott
```

Starting with Chapter 2, "SQL: The Basics," you will learn how to execute the SELECT command against an Oracle database; Chapter 11, "Insert, Update, and Delete," describes the details of data manipulation and transaction control; and Chapter 12 introduces you to the creation of tables and the definition of constraints to enforce the required business rules. Chapter 15, "Security," discusses how to control access to data and the various Oracle database security features.

▼ LAB 1.1 EXERCISES

a) What is SQL, and why is it useful?

b) Try to match each of the SQL commands on the left with a verb from the list on the right.

    1. CREATE   a. manipulate

    2. UPDATE   b. define

    3. GRANT   c. control

c) Why is it important to control access to data in a database?

d) How is data organized in a relational database?

e) Is it possible to have a table with no rows at all?

f) Figure 1.5 displays an EMPLOYEE table and a DEPARTMENT table. Identify the columns you consider to be the primary key and foreign key columns.

g) Would it be possible to insert into the EMPLOYEE table an employee with a DEPT_NO of 10?

EMPLOYEE

EMPLOYEE_ID	FIRST_NAME	LAST_NAME	SALARY	DEPT_NO
230	Kyle	Hsu	$80,000	40
231	Kirsten	Soehner	$130,000	50
232	Madeline	Dimitri	$70,000	40
234	Joshua	Hunter	$90,000	20

DEPARTMENT

DEPT_NO	DEPARTMENT_NAME
20	Finance
40	Human Resources
50	Sales
60	Information Systems

FIGURE 1.5
EMPLOYEE and DEPARTMENT tables

▼ LAB 1.1 EXERCISE ANSWERS

a) What is SQL, and why is it useful?

ANSWER: SQL, the Structured Query Language, is a standardized relational database access language. It is useful because it allows a user to query, manipulate, define, and control data in an RDBMS.

SQL is sanctioned by ANSI, which determines standards on all aspects of SQL, including data types. However, most relational database products, including Oracle, have their own extensions to the ANSI standard, providing additional functionality within their respective products by further extending the use of SQL. By learning SQL, you will be able to use the language on other non-Oracle databases with some minor syntax adjustments.

b) Try to match each of the SQL commands on the left with a verb from the list on the right:

ANSWER: The following shows how these commands match with the appropriate verb.

1. CREATE   a. manipulate
2. UPDATE   b. define
3. GRANT   c. control

DML is used to *manipulate* data, with the SELECT, INSERT, UPDATE, and DELETE commands. (Note that in some of Oracle's own documentation, the SELECT command is not part of DML but is considered Data Retrieval Language.) DDL is used to *define* objects such as tables with the CREATE, ALTER, and DROP commands. DCL is used to *control* access privileges in an RDBMS, such as with the GRANT and REVOKE commands to give or remove privileges. These SQL commands are written and executed against the database using a software program. In this workbook, Oracle's SQL Developer and SQL*Plus software tools are used to communicate these commands to the RDBMS. The use of these tools and the SQL commands is covered in Chapter 2.

c) Why is it important to control access to data in a database?

ANSWER: Data can contain sensitive information to which some users should have limited access privileges. Some users may be allowed to query certain data but not change it, while others may be allowed to add data to a database but not delete it. By controlling access to data, the security of the data is assured for all users. You learn about safeguarding your data in Chapter 15.

d) How is data organized in a relational database?

ANSWER: Data is organized by placing similar pieces of information together in a table that consists of columns and rows.

For example, the data found in a library is typically organized in several ways to facilitate finding a book. Figure 1.6 shows information specific to books. The data is organized into columns and rows; the columns represent a type of data (title vs. genre), and the rows contain data. A table in a database is organized in the same way. You might call this table BOOK; it contains information related to books only. Each intersection of a column and row in a table represents a value.

TITLE	AUTHOR	ISBN#	GENRE	LOCATION_ID
Magic Gum	Harry Smith	0-11-124456-2	Computer	D11
Desk Work	Robert Jones	0-11-223754-3	Fiction	H24
Beach Life	Mark Porter	0-11-922256-8	Junvenile	J3
From Here to There	Gary Mills	0-11-423356-5	Fiction	H24

FIGURE 1.6
The BOOK table

Searching for a book by location might yield the excerpt of data shown in Figure 1.7. This set of columns and rows represents another database table called LOCATION, with information specific to locations in a library.

LOCATION_ID	FLOOR	SECTION	SHELF
D11	1	3	1
H24	2	2	3
J3	3	1	1

FIGURE 1.7
The LOCATION table

The advantage to storing information about books and their locations separately is that information is not repeated unnecessarily, and maintenance of the data is much easier.

For instance, two books in the BOOK table have the same LOCATION_ID, H24. If the floor, section, and shelf information were also stored in the BOOK table, this information would be repeated for each of the two book rows. In that situation, if the floor of LOCATION_ID H24 changed, both of the rows in the BOOK table would have to change. Instead, by storing the location information separately, the floor information has to change only once in the LOCATION table.

The two tables (BOOK and LOCATION) have a common column between them, namely LOCATION_ID. In a relational database, SQL can be used to query information from more than one table at a time, making use of the common column they contain by performing a *join*. The join allows you to query both the BOOK and LOCATION tables to return a list of book titles together with floor, section, and shelf information to help you locate the books easily.

e) Is it possible to have a table with no rows at all?

ANSWER: Yes, it is possible, although clearly it is not very useful to have a table with no data.

f) Figure 1.5 displays an EMPLOYEE table and a DEPARTMENT table. Identify the columns you consider to be the primary key and foreign key columns.

ANSWER: The primary key of the EMPLOYEE table is EMPLOYEE_ID. The primary key of the DEPARTMENT table is DEPT_NO. The DEPT_NO is also the foreign key column of the EMPLOYEE table and is common between the two tables.

In the DEPT_NO column of the EMPLOYEE table you can *only* enter values that exist in the DEPARTMENT table. The DEPARTMENT table is the parent table from which the child table, the EMPLOYEE table, gets its DEPT_NO values.

g) Would it be possible to insert into the EMPLOYEE table an employee with a DEPT_NO of 10?

ANSWER: Only valid primary key values from the DEPARTMENT table are allowed in the EMPLOYEE table's foreign key DEPT_NO column. You cannot enter a DEPT_NO of 10 in the EMPLOYEE table if such a value does not exist in the DEPARTMENT table. Establishing a foreign key relationship highlights the benefit of *referential integrity*.

If the foreign key constraint between the two tables is temporarily disabled or no foreign key constraint exists, such an "invalid" entry is possible. We will discuss more on this topic in later chapters.

Note that the DEPARTMENT table contains one row with the department number 60, which does not have any corresponding employees. The referential integrity rule allows a parent without child(ren) but does not allow a child without a parent because this would be considered an orphan row. You will learn how to establish primary key and foreign key relationships in Chapter 12.

Lab 1.1 Quiz

In order to test your progress, you should be able to answer the following questions.

1) A university's listing of students and the classes they are enrolled in is an example of a database system.

   _____ a) True
   _____ b) False

2) A table must always contain both columns and rows.

   _____ a) True
   _____ b) False

3) Referential integrity ensures that each value in a foreign key column of the child table links to a matching primary key value in the parent table.

   _____ a) True
   _____ b) False

4) A null value means that that the value is unknown.

   _____ a) True
   _____ b) False

ANSWERS APPEAR IN APPENDIX A.

LAB 1.2
Data Normalization and Table Relationships

LAB OBJECTIVES

After this lab, you will be able to:

▶ Identify Data Normalization Rules and Table Relationships
▶ Read a Database Schema Diagram
▶ Understand the Database Development Context

Although this is a book about SQL, you must know the basic concepts, terminology, and issues involved in database design to be able to understand why tables are organized in specific ways. This lab introduces you to the practical aspects of designing tables and determining their respective relationships to each other.

Data Normalization

The objective of *normalization* is to eliminate redundancy in tables, therefore avoiding any future data manipulation problems. There are a number of different rules for minimizing duplication of data, which are formulated into the various *normal forms*.

The rules verify that the columns you placed in the tables do in fact belong there. You design your tables, the appropriate columns, and the matching primary and foreign keys to comply with these rules. This process is called *normalization*. The normalization rules will be quite intuitive after you have read through the examples in this lab. Although there are many normalization rules, the *five normal forms* and the *Boyce–Codd normal form* (BCNF) are the most widely accepted. This lab discusses the first three normal forms because programmers and analysts typically don't bother normalizing beyond third normal form—although experienced database designers sometimes do.

FIRST NORMAL FORM

For a table to be in *first normal form*, all repeating groups must be removed and placed in a new table. The example in Figure 1.8 illustrates the use of repeating groups in the BOOK table. The table has multiple locations of warehouses across the country where the title is stocked. The location is listed in three columns as LOCATION_1, LOCATION_2, and LOCATION_3.

BOOK_ID	TITLE	RETAIL PRICE	LOCATION_1	LOCATION_2	LOCATION_3
1010	The Invisible Force	29.95	New York	San Francisco	
1011	Into The Sky	39.95	Chicago		
1012	Making It Possible	59.95	Miami	Austin	New York

FIGURE 1.8
Repeating group in the BOOK table

Imagine a scenario in which you have more than three locations for a book. To avoid problems, the database designer will move the location information to a separate table named BOOK_LOCATION, as illustrated in Figure 1.9. This design is more flexible and allows the storing of books at an unlimited number of locations.

BOOK

BOOK_ID	TITLE	RETAIL PRICE
1010	The Invisible Force	29.95
1011	Into The Sky	39.95
1012	Making It Possible	59.95

BOOK_LOCATION

BOOK_ID	LOCATION
1010	New York
1010	San Francisco
1011	Chicago
1012	Miami
1012	Austin
1012	New York

FIGURE 1.9
Tables in first normal form

SECOND NORMAL FORM

Second normal form states that all nonkey columns must depend on the entire primary key. It applies only to tables that have composite primary keys. Figure 1.10 shows the BOOK_AUTHOR table with both the BOOK_ID and AUTHOR_ID as the composite primary key. In this example, authors with the ID 900 and 901 coauthored the book with the ID 10002. If you add the author's phone number to the table, the second normal form is violated because the phone number is dependent only on the AUTHOR_ID, not on BOOK_ID. ROYALTY_SHARE is dependent completely on the combination of both columns because the percentage of the royalty varies from book to book and is split among authors.

BOOK_ID	AUTHOR_ID	ROYALITY_SHARE	AUTHOR_PHONE_NO
10001	900	100	212-555-1212
10002	901	75	901-555-1212
10002	900	25	212-555-1212
10003	902	100	899-555-1212

FIGURE 1.10
Violation of second normal form in the BOOK_AUTHOR table

THIRD NORMAL FORM

The *third normal form* goes a step further than the second normal form: It states that every nonkey column must be a fact about the primary key. The third normal form is quite intuitive. Figure 1.11 shows a table that violates third normal form. The PUBLISHER_PHONE_NO column is not dependent on the primary key column BOOK_ID but on the PUBLISHER_NAME column. Therefore, the PUBLISHER_PHONE_NO column should not be part of the BOOK table.

BOOK_ID	TITLE	PUBLISHER_NAME	PUBLISH_DATE	PUBLISHER_PHONE_NO
1010	The Invisible Force	Literacy Circle	12/07	801-111-1111
1011	Into The Sky	Prentice Hall	10/08	999-888-1212
1012	Making It Possible	Life Books	2/06	777-555-1212
1013	Wonders of the World	Literacy Circle	2/06	801-111-1111

FIGURE 1.11
Violation of third normal form

Instead, the publisher's phone number should be stored in a separate table called PUBLISHER. This has the advantage that when a publisher's phone number is updated, it needs to be updated in only one place rather than at all occurrences of this publisher in the BOOK table. Removing the PUBLISHER_PHONE_NO column eliminates redundancy and avoids any possibilities of data inconsistencies (see Figure 1.12).

The BOOK table can also benefit by introducing a surrogate key, such as the PUBLISHER_ID column. Such a key is not subject to changes and is easily referenced in any additional tables that may need to refer to data about the publisher.

BOYCE–CODD NORMAL FORM (BCNF), FOURTH NORMAL FORM, AND FIFTH NORMAL FORM

BCNF is an elaborate version of the third normal form and deals with deletion anomalies. The *fourth normal form* tackles potential problems when three or more columns are part of the unique identifier and their dependencies to each other. The *fifth normal form* splits the tables even further apart to eliminate all redundancy. These different normal forms are beyond the scope of this book; for more details, please consult one of the many excellent books on database design.

BOOK

BOOK_ID	TITLE	PUBLISHER_ID	PUBLISH_DATE
1010	The Invisible Force	1	12/07
1011	Into The Sky	2	10/08
1012	Making It Possible	3	2/06
1013	Wonders of the World	1	2/06

PUBLISHER

PUBLISHER_ID	PUBLISHER_NAME	PUBLISHER_PHONE_NO
1	Literacy Circle	80-111-1111
2	Prentice Hall	999-888-1212
3	LIfe Books	777-555-1212

FIGURE 1.12
Tables in third normal form

Table Relationships

When two tables have a common column or columns, the tables are said to have a *relationship* between them. The *cardinality* of a relationship is the actual number of occurrences between them. We will explore one-to-many, one-to-one, and many-to-many relationships.

ONE-TO-MANY RELATIONSHIP (1:M)

Figure 1.13 shows the CUSTOMER table and the ORDER table. The common column is CUSTOMER_ID. The link between the two tables is a *one-to-many* relationship, the most common type of relationship. This means that one individual customer can have many order rows in the ORDER table. This relationship represents the business rule that "one customer can place one or many orders (or no orders)." Reading the relationship in the other direction, an order is associated with only one customer row (or no customer rows). In other words, "each order may be placed by one and only one customer."

ONE-TO-ONE RELATIONSHIP (1:1)

One-to-one relationships exist in the database world, but they are not typical because most often data from both tables are combined into one table for simplicity. Figure 1.14 shows an example of a *one-to-one* relationship between the PRODUCT table and the PRODUCT_PRICE table. For every row in the PRODUCT table, you may find only one matching row in the PRODUCT_PRICE table. And for every row in the PRODUCT_PRICE table, there is one matching row in the PRODUCT table. If the two tables are combined, the RETAIL_PRICE and IN_STOCK_QTY columns can be included in the PRODUCT table.

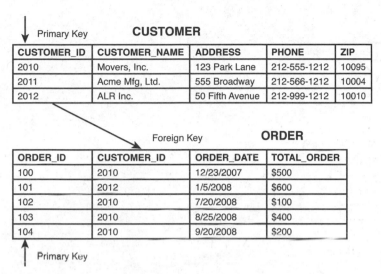

Primary Key   **CUSTOMER**

CUSTOMER_ID	CUSTOMER_NAME	ADDRESS	PHONE	ZIP
2010	Movers, Inc.	123 Park Lane	212-555-1212	10095
2011	Acme Mfg, Ltd.	555 Broadway	212-566-1212	10004
2012	ALR Inc.	50 Fifth Avenue	212-999-1212	10010

Foreign Key   **ORDER**

ORDER_ID	CUSTOMER_ID	ORDER_DATE	TOTAL_ORDER
100	2010	12/23/2007	$500
101	2012	1/5/2008	$600
102	2010	7/20/2008	$100
103	2010	8/25/2008	$400
104	2010	9/20/2008	$200

Primary Key

FIGURE 1.13
One-to-many relationship example between CUSTOMER and ORDER tables

Primary Key   **PRODUCT**

PRODUCT_ID	PRODUCT_NAME	MANUFACTURER
10001	Bolt	ACME, Inc.
10002	Screw	KR Mfg.
10003	Nail	ABC, Ltd.

Foreign and Primary Key   **PRODUCT_ PRICE**

PRODUCT_ID	RETAIL_PRICE	IN_STOCK_QTY
10001	$0.45	10,000
10002	$0.02	20,000
10003	$0.10	50,000

FIGURE 1.14
One-to-one relationship example

MANY-TO-MANY RELATIONSHIP (M:M)

The examination of Figure 1.15 reveals a *many-to-many* relationship between the BOOK and AUTHOR tables. One book can have one or more authors, and one author can write one or more books. The relational database model requires the resolution of many-to-many relationships into one-to-many relationship tables.

Primary Key   **BOOK**

BOOK_ID	TITLE	RETAIL_PRICE
10001	Call in the Dark	39.95
10002	The Spy	29.95
10003	Perspectives	59.95

Primary Key   **AUTHOR**

AUTHOR_ID	TITLE	RETAIL_PRICE
900	King	John
901	Oats	Heather
902	Turrow	Stephen

FIGURE 1.15
Many-to-many relationship example

The solution in this example is achieved by creating an *associative table* (also called an *intersection table*) via the BOOK_AUTHOR table. Figure 1.16 shows the columns of this table.

BOOK

BOOK_ID	TITLE	RETAIL_PRICE
10001	Call in the Dark	39.95
10002	The Spy	29.95
10003	Perspectives	59.95

AUTHOR

AUTHOR_ID	TITLE	FIRST_NAME
900	King	John
901	Oats	Heather
902	Turrow	Stephen

Foreign Key   Foreign Key

BOOK_ID	AUTHOR_ID	ROYALITY_SHARE
10001	900	100
10002	901	75
10002	900	25
10003	902	100

BOOK_AUTHOR

Primary Key

FIGURE 1.16
Associative BOOK_AUTHOR table that resolves the many-to-many relationship

The BOOK_AUTHOR table lists the individual author(s) for each book and shows, for a particular author, the book(s) he or she wrote. The primary key of the BOOK_AUTHOR table is the combination of both columns: the BOOK_ID column and the AUTHOR_ID column. These two columns represent the concatenated primary key that uniquely identifies a row in the table. As you may recall from Lab 1.1, multicolumn primary keys are referred to as a *composite,* or concatenated, primary key. In addition, the BOOK_AUTHOR table has AUTHOR_ID and the BOOK_ID as two individual foreign keys linking back to the AUTHOR table and the BOOK table, respectively.

The BOOK_AUTHOR table contains an additional column, the ROYALTY_SHARE column, which identifies the royalty percentage for each author for an individual book. When there are multiple authors, the percentage of the royalty is split; in the case of a sole author, the share is 100%. This column is appropriately located in the BOOK_AUTHOR table as the values are relevant for the combination of the BOOK_ID and AUTHOR_ID. These two columns uniquely identify both a book and an author and the respective percentage share of the royalty.

Database Schema Diagrams

For clarity of meaning and conceptual consistency, it is useful to show table relationships using *database schema diagrams.* There are a number of standard notations for this type of diagram. Figure 1.17 illustrates one of the ways to graphically depict the relationship between tables. The convention used in this book for a one-to-many relationship is a line with a "crow's foot" (fork) on one end indicating the "many" side of the relationship; at the other end, a "single line" depicts the "one" side of the relationship. You will see the use of the *crow's-foot notation* throughout this book. Software diagramming programs that support the graphical display of relational database models often allow you to choose your notation preference.

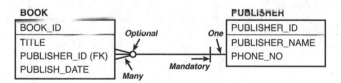

FIGURE 1.17
Crow's-foot notation

CARDINALITY AND OPTIONALITY

The cardinality expresses the ratio of a parent and child table from the perspective of the parent table. It describes how many rows you may find between the two tables for a given primary key value.

Graphical relationship lines also indicate the *optionality* of a relationship, whether a row is required or not (mandatory or optional). Specifically, optionality shows whether one row in a table can exist without a row in the related table.

Figure 1.17 illustrates a one-to-many relationship between the PUBLISHER (parent) and the BOOK (child). Examining the relationship line on the "many" end, you notice a circle identifying the *optional relationship* and a crow's foot indicating "many." The symbols indicate that a publisher *may* publish zero, one, or many books. You use the word *may* to indicate that the relationship is *optional,* and this allows a publisher to exist without a corresponding value in the BOOK table.

The relationship line also reads the other way. The solid line on the PUBLISHER end of the line indicates the "one" side, and a vertical bar intersects it. This bar identifies a *mandatory relationship*. You read this direction of the relationship as "One book *must* be published by one and only one publisher." This means a row in the BOOK table must always have the PUBLISHER_ID value filled in.

When a column is defined as NOT NULL, it must always contain a value. When a column in a row is defined as allowing NULL values, it means that a column does not need to contain a value.

The "(FK)" symbol next to the PUBLISHER_ID column on the BOOK table indicates that this is a foreign key column. In this diagram, the primary key is separated from the other columns with a line; you can see that BOOK_ID and the PUBLISHER_ID are the primary keys, or unique identifiers.

Figure 1.18 shows an optional relationship on both sides; a book may be published by zero or one publisher. Effectively, this means the value in the PUBLISHER_ID column in BOOK is optional. Reading the relationship from PUBLISHER, you can say that "one publisher may publish zero, one, or many books" (which is identical to Figure 1.17).

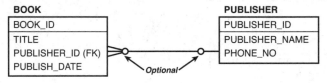

FIGURE 1.18
Optional relationship notation on both sides

Figure 1.19 shows some sample data that illustrates the optional relationships. Review the row with the BOOK_ID value of 1012; it does not contain a PUBLISHER_ID column. This means it's possible to have an entry in the BOOK table without the publisher being specified. Furthermore, the BOOK table contains multiple entries for the PUBLISHER_ID 1. This indicates that many books can be published by the same publisher.

On the PUBLISHER table, you see the PUBLISHER_ID 3, which does not exist in the BOOK table. A publisher can exist in the table without having an entry in the BOOK table.

BOOK

BOOK_ID	TITLE	PUBLISHER_ID	PUBLISH_DATE
1010	The Invisible Force	1	12/07
1011	Into The Sky	2	10/08
1012	Making It Possible		2/06
1013	Wonders of the World	1	2/06

PUBLISHER

PUBLISHER_ID	PUBLISHER_NAME	PUBLISHER_PHONE_NO
1	Literacy Circle	801-111-1111
2	Prentice Hall	999-888-1212
3	Life Books	777-555-1212

FIGURE 1.19
Sample data for BOOK and PUBLISHER, illustrating optional relationships

REAL-WORLD BUSINESS PRACTICE

You typically see only two types of relationships: first, mandatory on the "one" side and optional on the "many" end, as in Figure 1.17; and second, optional on both ends, as in Figure 1.18. Only rarely do you find other types of relationships. For example, mandatory relationships on both sides are infrequently implemented; this means that rows must be inserted in both tables simultaneously. Occasionally, you find one-to-one relationships, but most often, the columns from both tables are combined into one table. Many-to-many relationships are not allowed in the relational database; they must be resolved via an associative, or intersection, table into one-to-many relationships.

LABELING RELATIONSHIPS

To clarify and explain the nature of a relationship on a diagram, it is useful to add on the relationship line a label or name with a verb. Figure 1.20 shows an example of a labeled relationship. For the utmost clarity, a relationship should be labeled on both sides. You then read it as: "One PUBLISHER may publish zero, one, or many BOOKs; and one BOOK must be published by one and only one PUBLISHER."

Or, in the example shown in Figure 1.18, the label would need to read "One PUBLISHER may publish zero, one, or many BOOKs; and one BOOK may be published by one and only one PUBLISHER." This kind of labeling makes the relationship perfectly clear and states the relationship in terms that a business user can understand.

IDENTIFYING AND NONIDENTIFYING RELATIONSHIPS

In an *identifying relationship,* the primary key is propagated to the child entity as part of the primary key. This is in contrast to a *nonidentifying relationship,* in which the foreign key becomes one of the nonkey columns. A nonidentifying relationship may accept a null value in the foreign key column.

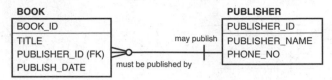

FIGURE 1.20
Labeled relationship between BOOK and PUBLISHER

If a graphical representation of a table's box has *rounded edges,* it means that the relationship is *identifying.* Effectively, one of the foreign keys became the primary key or part of the primary key. In the case of the BOOK_AUTHOR table shown in Figure 1.21, both foreign key columns constitute the primary key, and both columns may not be null because a primary key is never null.

The many-to-many relationship between the BOOK and AUTHOR tables was resolved with the associative table called BOOK_AUTHOR. The combination of the two foreign keys forms the unique primary key. This primary key also ensures that there will not be any duplicate entries. In other words, it is not possible to enter the combination of AUTHOR_ID and BOOK_ID twice.

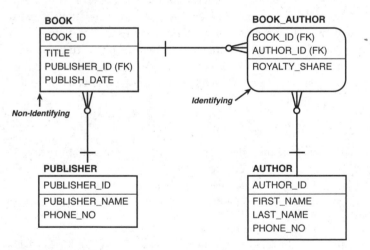

FIGURE 1.21
Identifying and nonidentifying relationships

The relationship between the PUBLISHER and BOOK tables is nonidentifying, as indicated by the sharp edges. The foreign key column PUBLISHER_ID is not part of the primary key of the BOOK table. The foreign key columns of a nonidentifying relationship may be either NULL or NOT NULL. In this instance, you can determine if a null is allowed by checking whether the relationship is optional or mandatory. Although the foreign key column allows null values in nonidentifying relationships, here the relationship depicts a single bar on the relationship line. Effectively, for every row in the BOOK table, there must be a corresponding row in the PUBLISHER table, and the PUBLISHER_ID column of the BOOK table cannot be null.

Database Development Context

Now that you are familiar with the some of the terminology and core concepts of relational databases, you are ready to learn about how all this information fits into the context of database development. From the initial idea of an application until the final system implementation, the data model is continuously refined. Figure 1.22 indicates the essential phases of the development project with respect to the database.

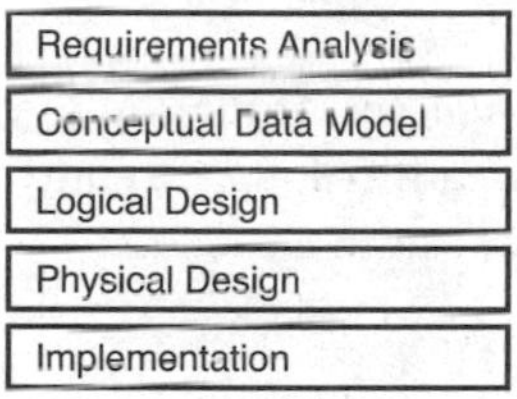

| Requirements Analysis |
| Conceptual Data Model |
| Logical Design |
| Physical Design |
| Implementation |

FIGURE 1.22
Database development and design phases

REQUIREMENTS ANALYSIS

The database development and design process starts with gathering data requirements that identify the needs and wants of the users. One of the outputs of this phase is a list of individual data elements that need to be stored in the database.

CONCEPTUAL DATA MODEL

The *conceptual data model* logically groups the major data elements from the requirements analysis into individual *entities*. An *entity* is something of significance for which you need to store data. For example, all data related to books, such as the title, publish date, and retail price, are placed in the book entity. Data elements such as the author's name and address are part of the author entity. The individual data elements are referred to as *attributes*.

You designate a *unique identifier,* or *candidate key,* that uniquely distinguishes a row in the entity. In this conceptual data model, we use the terms *entity*, *attribute*, and *candidate key* or *unique identifier* instead of *table*, *column*, and *primary key*, respectively.

Noncritical attributes are not included in the model to emphasize the business meaning of those entities, attributes, and relationships. Many-to-many relationships are acceptable and not resolved. The diagram of the conceptual model is useful to communicate the initial understanding of the requirements to business users. The conceptual model gives no consideration to the implementation platform or database software. Many projects skip the conceptual model and go directly to the logical model.

LOGICAL DATA MODEL

The purpose of the *logical data model* is to show that all the entities, their respective attributes, and the relationship between entities represent the business requirements, without considering technical issues. The focus is entirely on business problems and considers a design that accommodates growth and change. The entities and attributes require descriptive names and documentation of their meaning. Labeling and documenting the relationships between entities clarify the business rules between them.

The diagram may show the data type of an attribute in general terms, such as text, number, and date. In many logical design models, you find foreign key columns identified; in others, they are implied.

The complete model is called the *logical data model,* or *entity relationship diagram* (ERD). At the end of the analysis phase, the entities are fully normalized, the unique identifier for each entity is determined, and any many-to-many relationships are resolved into associative entities.

PHYSICAL DATA MODEL

The *physical data model*, also referred to as the *database schema diagram,* is a graphical model of the physical design implementation of the database. This physical schema diagram is what the programmers and you use to learn about the database and the relationship between the tables. In Lab 1.3 you will be introduced to the STUDENT schema diagram used throughout this book.

This physical data model is derived from the fully normalized logical model. Before the actual implementation (installation) of the physical data model in the database, multiple physical data models may exist. They represent a variety of alternative physical database designs that consider the performance implications and application constraints. One of the physical design models will be implemented in the database. The schema diagram graphically represents the chosen implemented physical data model; it is specific to a particular RDBMS product such as Oracle.

Figure 1.23 depicts the schema diagram of the book publishing database discussed in this chapter. It shows the structure of the tables with their respective columns, and it illustrates the relationships between the tables.

The physical data model has different terminology than the conceptual or logical data model. The physical data model refers to tables instead of entities; the individual pieces of data are columns instead of attributes in the logical model. This diagram graphically depicts how the physical database tables are defined, including the individual column's data type and length and whether they are mandatory (that is, require a value) or allow nulls.

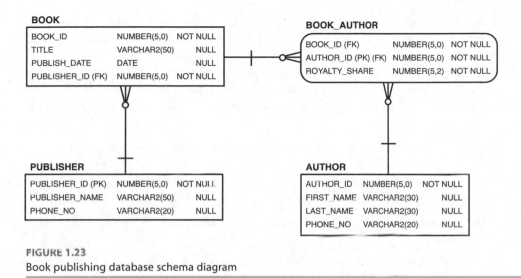

FIGURE 1.23
Book publishing database schema diagram

TRANSFER FROM LOGICAL TO PHYSICAL MODEL

The transfer from the logical to the physical models—which ultimately means the actual implementation in a database as tables, columns, primary keys, foreign keys, indexes, and so on—requires a number of steps and considerations. The entities identified in the logical data model are resolved to physical tables; the entity name is often identical to the table name. Some designers use singular names for entities and plural names for tables; others abbreviate the entity names when implementing the physical model to follow certain business naming standards. Frequently, the physical data model includes additional tables for specific technical implementation requirements and programming purposes, such as a report queue table or an error log table.

As mentioned previously, attributes become columns, with names being either identical or following business naming conventions and abbreviations. The columns are associated with the database software vendor's specific data types, which consider valid column lengths and restrictions. Individual data entry formats are determined (for example, phone numbers must be in numeric format, with dashes between). Rules for maintaining data integrity and consistency are created, and physical storage parameters for individual tables are determined. You will learn about these and many other aspects of creating these restrictions in Chapter 12. Sometimes additional columns are added that were not in the logical design, with the purpose of storing precalculated values; this is referred to as *denormalization,* which we discuss shortly.

Another activity that occurs in the physical data design phase is the design of indexes. *Indexes* are database objects that facilitate speedy access to data with the help of a specific column or combination of columns of a table. Placing indexes on tables is necessary to optimize efficient query performance. However, indexes can have the negative impact of requiring additional time for insert, update, or delete operations. Balancing the trade-offs with the advantages requires careful consideration of these factors, including knowledge in optimizing SQL statements and an understanding of the features of a particular database version. You will learn more about different types of indexes and the success factors of a well-placed index strategy in Chapter 13, "Indexes, Sequences, and Views."

Database designers must be knowledgeable and experienced in many aspects of programming, design, and database administration to fully understand how design decisions affect cost, performance, system interfaces, programming effort, and future maintenance.

 Poor physical database design is very costly and difficult to correct.

You might wonder how the graphical models you see in this book are produced. Specific software packages allow you to visually design the various models, and they allow you to display different aspects of it, such as showing only table names or showing table names, columns, and their respective data types. Many of these tools even allow you to generate the DDL SQL statements to create the tables. For a list of software tools that allow you to visually produce these diagrams, see Appendix H, "Resources."

DENORMALIZATION

Denormalization is the act of adding redundancy to the physical database design. Typically, logical models are fully normalized or at least in third normal form. When designing the physical model, database designers must weigh the benefit of eliminating all redundancy, with data split into many tables, against potentially poor performance when these many tables are joined.

Therefore, database designers, also called *database architects,* sometimes purposely add redundancy to their physical design. Only experienced database designers should denormalize. Increasing redundancy may greatly increase the overall programming effort because now many copies of the same data must be kept in sync; however, the time it takes to query data may be reduced.

In some applications, particularly data warehousing applications, where massive amounts of detailed data are stored and summarized, denormalization is required. *Data warehouse applications* are database applications that benefit users who need to analyze large data sets from various angles and use this data for reporting and decision-making purposes. Typically, the source of the data warehouse is historical transaction data, but it can also include data from various other sources for the purpose of consolidating data. For example, the purchasing department of a supermarket chain could determine how many turkeys to order for a specific store the week before Thanksgiving or use the data to determine what promotional offers have the largest sales impact on stores with certain customer demographics.

The primary purpose of a data warehouse is to query, report, and analyze data. Therefore, redundancy is encouraged and necessary for queries to perform efficiently.

▼ LAB 1.2 EXERCISES

a) Describe the nature of the relationship between the ORDER_HEADER table and the ORDER_DETAIL table in Figure 1.24.

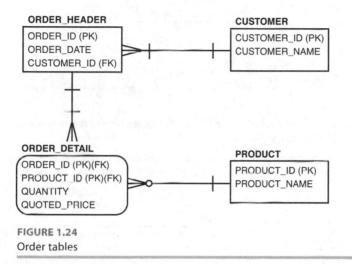

FIGURE 1.24
Order tables

b) One of the tables in Figure 1.25 is not fully normalized. Which normal form is violated? Draw a new diagram.

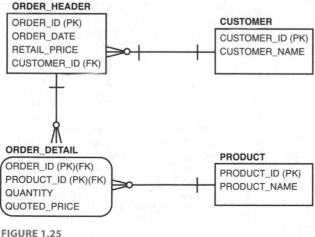

FIGURE 1.25
A table that is not fully normalized

c) How would Figure 1.25 need to be changed to add information about the sales representative who took the order?

d) How would Figure 1.26 need to be changed if an employee does not have to belong to a department?

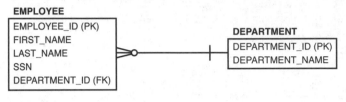

EMPLOYEE

| EMPLOYEE_ID (PK) |
| FIRST_NAME |
| LAST_NAME |
| SSN |
| DEPARTMENT_ID (FK) |

DEPARTMENT

| DEPARTMENT_ID (PK) |
| DEPARTMENT_NAME |

FIGURE 1.26
EMPLOYEE and DEPARTMENT relationship

e) Based on Figure 1.26, would the Social Security number (SSN) column be a better primary key column than the EMPLOYEE_ID column?

f) Figures 1.27 and 1.28 depict the logical and physical model of a fictional movie rental database. What differences exist between the entity relationship diagram and the physical schema diagram?

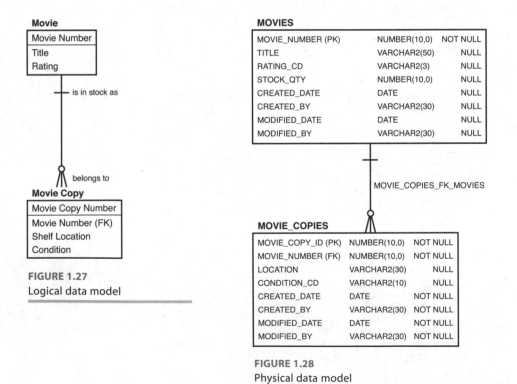

Movie

| Movie Number |
| Title |
| Rating |

is in stock as

belongs to

Movie Copy

| Movie Copy Number |
| Movie Number (FK) |
| Shelf Location |
| Condition |

FIGURE 1.27
Logical data model

MOVIES

MOVIE_NUMBER (PK)	NUMBER(10,0)	NOT NULL
TITLE	VARCHAR2(50)	NULL
RATING_CD	VARCHAR2(3)	NULL
STOCK_QTY	NUMBER(10,0)	NULL
CREATED_DATE	DATE	NULL
CREATED_BY	VARCHAR2(30)	NULL
MODIFIED_DATE	DATE	NULL
MODIFIED_BY	VARCHAR2(30)	NULL

MOVIE_COPIES_FK_MOVIES

MOVIE_COPIES

MOVIE_COPY_ID (PK)	NUMBER(10,0)	NOT NULL
MOVIE_NUMBER (FK)	NUMBER(10,0)	NOT NULL
LOCATION	VARCHAR2(30)	NULL
CONDITION_CD	VARCHAR2(10)	NULL
CREATED_DATE	DATE	NOT NULL
CREATED_BY	VARCHAR2(30)	NOT NULL
MODIFIED_DATE	DATE	NOT NULL
MODIFIED_BY	VARCHAR2(30)	NOT NULL

FIGURE 1.28
Physical data model

▼ LAB 1.2 EXERCISE ANSWERS

a) Describe the nature of the relationship between the ORDER_HEADER table and the ORDER_DETAIL table in Figure 1.24.

ANSWER: The relationship depicts a mandatory one-to-many relationship between the ORDER_HEADER and ORDER_DETAIL tables. The ORDER_HEADER table contains data found only once for each order, such as ORDER_ID, CUSTOMER_ID, and ORDER_DATE. The ORDER_DETAIL table holds information about the individual order lines of an order. One row in the ORDER_HEADER table must have one or many order details. One ORDER_DETAIL row must have one and only one corresponding row in the ORDER_HEADER table.

MANDATORY RELATIONSHIP ON BOTH ENDS

The mandatory relationship from ORDER_HEADER to ORDER_ DETAIL indicates that a row in the ORDER_HEADER table cannot exist unless a row in ORDER_DETAIL is created simultaneously. This is a "chicken and egg" problem, whereby a row in the ORDER_HEADER table cannot be created without an ORDER_DETAIL row and vice versa. In fact, it really doesn't matter as long as you create the rows within one transaction. Furthermore, you must make sure that every row in the ORDER_HEADER table has at least one row in the ORDER_DETAIL table and that each row in the ORDER_DETAIL table has exactly one corresponding row in the ORDER_HEADER table. There are various ways to physically implement this relationship.

Another example of a mandatory relationship on the figure is the relationship between ORDER_HEADER and CUSTOMER. You can see the bar on the "many side" of the relationship as an indication for the mandatory row. That means a customer must have placed an order before a row in the CUSTOMER table is saved, and an order can be placed only by a customer.

However, for most practical purposes, a mandatory relationship on both ends is rarely implemented unless there is a very specific and important requirement.

NO DUPLICATES ALLOWED

On the previous diagrams, such as Figure 1.24, you noticed that some foreign keys are part of the primary key. This is frequently the case in associative entities; in this particular example, it requires the combination of ORDER_ID and PRODUCT_ID to be unique. Ultimately, the effect is that a single order containing the same product twice is not allowed. Figure 1.29 lists sample data in the ORDER_DETAIL table for ORDER_ID 345 and PRODUCT_ID P90, which violates the primary key. Instead, you must create one order with a quantity of 10 or create a second order with a different ORDER_ID. You will learn about how Oracle responds with error messages when you attempt to violate the primary key constraint and other types of constraints in Chapter 11.

b) One of the tables in Figure 1.25 is not fully normalized. Which normal form is violated? Draw a new diagram.

ANSWER: The third normal form is violated on the ORDER_HEADER table. The RETAIL_PRICE column belongs to the PRODUCT table instead (see Figure 1.30).

ORDER_DETAIL

ORDER_ID	PRODUCT_ID	QUANTITY	QUOTED_PRICE
123	P90	5	$50
234	S999	9	$12
345	P90	7	$50
345	X85	3	$10
345	P90	3	$50

FIGURE 1.29
Sample data of the ORDER_DETAIL table

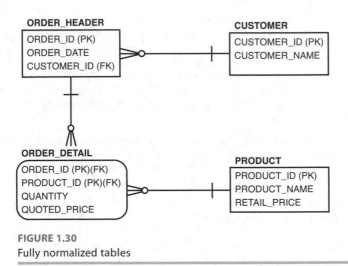

FIGURE 1.30
Fully normalized tables

Third normal form states that every nonkey column must be a fact about the primary key column, which is the ORDER_ID column in the ORDER_HEADER table. This is clearly not the case with the RETAIL_PRICE column as it is not a fact about ORDER_HEADER and does not depend on ORDER_ID; it is a fact about PRODUCT. The QUOTED_PRICE column is included in the ORDER_DETAIL table because the price may vary over time, from order to order, and from customer to customer. (If you want to track any changes in the retail price, you might want to create a separate table, called PRODUCT_PRICE_HISTORY, to keep track of the retail price per product and the effective date of each price change.) Table 1.2 provides a review of the normal forms.

TABLE 1.2   The Three Normal Forms

DESCRIPTION	RULE
First normal form (1NF)	No repeating groups are permitted.
Second normal form (2NF)	No partial key dependencies are permitted.
Third normal form (3NF)	No nonkey dependencies are permitted.

c) How would Figure 1.25 need to be changed to add information about the sales representative who took the order?

ANSWER: As you see in Figure 1.31, you need to add another table that contains the sales representative's name, SALES_REP_ID, and any other relevant information. SALESREP_ID then becomes a foreign key in the ORDER_HEADER table.

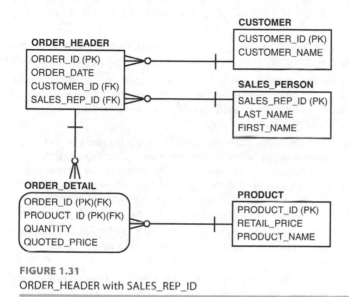

FIGURE 1.31
ORDER_HEADER with SALES_REP_ID

d) How would Figure 1.26 need to be changed if an employee does not have to belong to a department?

ANSWER: You change the relationship line on the DEPARTMENT table end to make it optional. This has the effect that the DEPARTMENT_ID column on the EMPLOYEE table can be null; that is, a value is not required (see Figure 1.32).

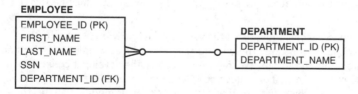

FIGURE 1.32
EMPLOYEE to DEPARTMENT with optional relationship line

e) Based on Figure 1.26 would the Social Security number (SSN) column be a better primary key column than the EMPLOYEE_ID column?

ANSWER: The requirement for a primary key is that it is unique, not subject to updates, and not null.

Although the SSN is unique, there have been incidents (though rare) of individuals with the same SSN or individuals who had to change their SSN. Even more common are data entry errors in which numbers are transposed, in which case all the tables containing the incorrect SSN would need to be changed. It is conceivable to have an employee without a SSN assigned yet, hence the column is null. There are a myriad of reasons for not using a SSN; therefore it's best to create a surrogate, or artificial, key.

f) Figures 1.27 and 1.28 depict the logical and physical model of a fictional movie rental database. What differences exist between the entity relationship diagram and the physical schema diagram?

ANSWER: You can spot a number of differences between the logical model (entity relational diagram) and the physical model (database schema diagram). While some logical and physical models are identical, these figures exhibit distinguishing differences you may find in the real world.

The entity name of the logical model is singular versus plural for the table name on the physical model. Some table names have special prefixes that denote the type of application the table belongs to. For example, if a table belongs to the purchase order system, it may be prefixed with PO_; if it belongs to the accounts payable system, the prefix is AP_; and so on. In the logical model, spaces are allowed for table and column names. Typically, in Oracle implementations, table names are defined in uppercase and use the underscore (_) character to separate words.

Although the logical model may include the data types, here the data types (for example, DATE, VARCHAR2, NUMBER) show on the physical model only. The physical model also indicates whether a column allows NULL values.

The attribute and column names differ between the two models. For example, the RATING attribute changed to RATING_CD, which indicates that the values are encoded (for example, "PG" rather than a descriptive "Parental Guidance" value). Designers create or follow established naming conventions and abbreviations for consistency. Naming conventions can help describe the type of values stored in the column.

STOCK_QTY is another example of using the abbreviation QTY to express that the column holds a quantity of copies. This column is absent from the logical model; it is a *derived column*. The quantity of movies for an individual movie title could be determined from the MOVIE_COPIES table. The database designer deliberately denormalized the table by adding this column. This simplifies any queries that determine how many copies of this particular title exist. Rather than issuing another query that counts the number of rows in MOVIE_COPIES for the specific title, this column stores the information.

Adding a derived column to a table requires that the value stay in sync with the data in the related table (MOVIE_COPIES, in this case). The synchronization can be accomplished by writing a program that is executed from the end user's screen. Alternatively, the developer could write a *trigger*, a stored database program, that executes upon a change to the table and automatically updates the STOCK_QTY value. Whenever a new row is added or data is modified on the MOVIE_COPIES table for each individual title, the quantity column can be updated. (For an example of a table trigger, refer to Chapter 12.)

The schema diagram prominently exhibits columns that did not exist in the logical data model, namely CREATED_DATE, MODIFIED_DATE, CREATED_BY, and MODIFIED_BY. Collectively, these columns are sometimes referred to as *audit columns*. They keep information about when a row was created and last changed together with the respective user who executed this action.

On the logical data model, the relationship is labeled in both directions. On the physical model, the name of the foreign key constraint between the tables is listed instead. You may find that some physical models depict no label at all. There are no set standards for how a physical or logical model must graphically look, and therefore the diagrams produced by various software vendors that offer diagramming tools not only look different but also allow a number of different display options.

Lab 1.2 Quiz

In order to test your progress, you should be able to answer the following questions.

1) An entity relationship diagram depicts entities, attributes, and tables.

_____ a) True

_____ b) False

2) The crow's foot depicts the M of a 1:M relationship.

_____ a) True

_____ b) False

3) Repeating groups are a violation of the first normal form.

_____ a) True

_____ b) False

4) The logical model is derived from the schema diagram.

_____ a) True

_____ b) False

5) The concept of denormalization deals with eliminating redundancy.

_____ a) True

_____ b) False

6) When you issue a SQL statement, you are concerned with the logical design of the database.

_____ a) True

_____ b) False

7) In a mandatory relationship, null values are not allowed in the foreign key column.

_____ a) True

_____ b) False

8) A nonidentifying relationship means that the foreign key is propagated as a nonkey attribute in the child entity or child table.

_____ a) True

_____ b) False

ANSWERS APPEAR IN APPENDIX A.

LAB 1.3
The STUDENT Schema Diagram

LAB OBJECTIVES

After this lab, you will be able to:

▶ Understand the STUDENT Schema Diagram
▶ Understand Recursive Relationships
▶ Describe Surrogate and Natural Keys
▶ Identify Table Relationships

Throughout this book, the database for a school's computer education program is used as a case study on which all exercises are based. If you have worked through the previous two labs, you know that the schema diagram is a model of data that reflects the relationships among data in a database. The name of the case study schema diagram is STUDENT. Before you begin to write SQL statements against the database, it is important to familiarize yourself with the diagram. You can find this graphical representation in Appendix D, "STUDENT Database Schema."

 You will frequently be referring to the STUDENT schema diagram shown in Appendix D. Rather than flip back and forth, you might find it more convenient to print out the schema diagram from the companion Web site to this book, located at www.oraclesqlbyexample.com.

The STUDENT Table

Examine the STUDENT schema diagram and locate the STUDENT table. This table contains data about each individual student, such as his or her name, address, employer, and the date the student registered in the program.

DATA TYPES

Next to each column name in the diagram, you find the data type of the column. Each column contains a different kind of data, which can be classified by a data type. The FIRST_NAME column is of data type VARCHAR2(25). This means that a variable length of (with a maximum of 25) alphanumeric characters (letters or numbers) may be stored in this column.

Another data type, the CHAR data type, also stores alphanumeric data but is a fixed-length data type. Unlike the VARCHAR2 data type, the CHAR data types pads any unused space in the column with blanks until it reaches the defined column length.

The STUDENT_ID column is of data type NUMBER, with a maximum number of eight integer digits and no decimal place digits; the column is the primary key, as the "(PK)" symbol indicates.

Oracle also provides a DATE data type (as seen on the CREATED_DATE and MODIFIED_DATE columns) that stores both the date and time.

You will learn more details about all the various data types in the next chapter. Next to each column, the schema diagram indicates whether a column allows NULL values. A NULL value is an unknown value. A space or value of zero is not the same as NULL. When a column in a row is defined as allowing NULL values, it means that a column does not need to contain a value. When a column is defined as NOT NULL, it must always contain a value.

You will observe that the STUDENT table does not show the city and state. This information can be looked up via the foreign key column ZIP, as indicated with the "(FK)" symbol after the column name. The ZIP column is a NOT NULL column and requires that every student row have a corresponding zip code entered.

The COURSE Table

The COURSE table lists all the available courses that a student may take. The primary key of the table is the COURSE_NO column. The DESCRIPTION column shows the course description, and the COST column lists the dollar amount charged for the enrollment in the course. The PREREQUISITE column displays the course number of a course that must be taken as a prerequisite to this course. This column is a foreign key column, and its values refer to the COURSE_NO column. Only valid COURSE_NO values may be listed in this column. The relationship line of the COURSE table to itself represents a *recursive,* or *self-referencing, relationship.*

RECURSIVE RELATIONSHIP

As the term *recursive,* or *self-referencing, relationship* implies, a column in the COURSE table refers to another column in the same table. The PREREQUISITE column refers to the COURSE_NO column, which provides the list of acceptable values (also referred to as a *domain*) for the PREREQUISITE column. Because the relationship is optional, the foreign key column PREREQUISITE column allows null. Recursive relationships are always optional relationships; otherwise, there is no starting point in the hierarchy.

Figure 1.33 lists an excerpt of data from the COURSE table. The courses with the COURSE_NO column values 10 and 20 do not have a value in the PREREQUISITE column: Those are the courses that a student must take to be able to take any subsequent courses (unless equivalent experience can be substituted). Course number 20 is a prerequisite course for course number 100, Hands-On Windows, and course number 140, Systems Analysis. You will learn more about the intricacies of recursive relationships in Chapter 16, "Regular Expressions and Hierarchical Queries."

COURSE_NO	DESCRIPTION	PREREQUISITE	...
10	Technology Concepts		...
20	Intro to Information Systems		...
100	Hands-On Windows	20	...
140	Systems Analysis	20	...
25	Intro to Programming	140	...
...	...	...	...

FIGURE 1.33
Data from the COURSE table

The SECTION Table

The SECTION table includes all the individual sections a course may have. An individual course may have zero, one, or many sections, each of which can be taught in different rooms, at different times, and by different instructors. The primary key of the table is SECTION_ID. The foreign key that links to the COURSE table is the COURSE_NO column.

NATURAL AND SURROGATE KEYS

The SECTION_NO column identifies the individual section number. For example, for the first section of a course, it contains the number 1; the second section lists the number 2, and so on. The two columns, COURSE_NO and SECTION_NO, also uniquely identify a row. This is called a *natural key*. The natural key was not chosen to be the primary key of the table. Instead, a new key column, named SECTION_ID, was created. This SECTION_ID column is called a *surrogate*, or *synthetic*, key.

This surrogate key is system generated and therefore ensures uniqueness. Database designers typically prefer surrogate keys. Imagine a scenario in which the courses of another school are merged into the database. It is conceivable that the combination of COURSE_NO and SECTION_NO are no longer unique. Users will never see or query the surrogate key because it has no business meaning. Instead, users will probably retrieve data using the COURSE_NO and SECTION_NO columns, because these columns represent meaningful data.

The column START_DATE_TIME shows the date and time the section meets for the first time. The LOCATION column lists the classroom. The CAPACITY column shows the maximum number of students that may enroll in this section.

RELATIONSHIPS TO OTHER TABLES

The INSTRUCTOR_ID column is another foreign key column in the SECTION table; it links to the INSTRUCTOR table. The relationship between the SECTION table and the INSTRUCTOR table indicates that an instructor must always be assigned to a section. The INSTRUCTOR_ID column of the SECTION table may never be null, and when you read the relationship from the opposite end, you can say that an individual instructor may teach zero, one, or multiple sections.

The relationship line leading from the COURSE table to the SECTION table means that a course may have zero, one, or multiple sections. Conversely, every individual section *must* have a corresponding row in the COURSE table.

Relationships between tables are based on *business rules*. In this case, the business rule is that a course can exist without a section, but a section cannot exist unless it is assigned to a course. As mentioned, this is indicated with the bar (|) on the other end of the relationship line. Most of the child relationships on the schema diagram are considered mandatory relationships (with two exceptions); this dictates that the foreign key columns in the child table must contain a value (that is, must be NOT NULL), and the value must correspond to a row in the parent table via its primary key value.

The INSTRUCTOR Table

The INSTRUCTOR table lists information related to an individual instructor, such as name, address, phone, and zip code. The primary key of this table is the INSTRUCTOR_ID.

The ZIP column is the foreign key column to the ZIPCODE table. The relationship between INSTRUCTOR and ZIPCODE is an optional relationship, so a null value in the ZIP column is allowed. For a given ZIP column value, there is one and only one value in the ZIPCODE table. For a given ZIP value in the ZIPCODE table, you may find zero, one, or many of the same value in the INSTRUCTOR table.

Another foreign key relationship exists to the SECTION table: An instructor may teach zero, one, or multiple sections, and an individual section can be taught by one and only one instructor.

The ZIPCODE Table

The primary key of ZIPCODE table is the ZIP column. For an individual zip code, it allows you to look up the corresponding CITY and STATE column values. This ensures that these values are not repeated in the other tables. The tables have been normalized to avoid redundancy of the data.

The data type of the ZIP column is VARCHAR2 and not NUMBER, because it allows you to enter leading zeros. Both the STUDENT table and the INSTRUCTOR table reference the ZIPCODE table. The relationship between the ZIPCODE and STUDENT tables is mandatory: For every ZIP value in the STUDENT table, there must be a corresponding value in the ZIPCODE table, and for one given zip code, there may be zero, one, or multiple students with that zip code. In contrast, the relationship between the INSTRUCTOR and ZIPCODE tables is optional; the ZIP column of the INSTRUCTOR table may be null.

WHAT ABOUT DELETE OPERATIONS?

Referential integrity does not allow deletion of a primary key value in a parent table that exists in a child as a foreign key value. This would create orphan rows in the child table. There are many ways to handle deletions, and you will learn about this topic and the effects of deletions on other tables in Chapter 11.

The ENROLLMENT Table

The ENROLLMENT table is an *intersection* table between the STUDENT and the SECTION table. It lists the students enrolled in the various sections. The primary key of the table is a composite primary key consisting of the STUDENT_ID and SECTION_ID columns. This unique combination prevents a student from registering for the same section twice.

The ENROLL_DATE column contains the date the student registered for the section. The FINAL_GRADE column lists the student's final grade. The final grade is to be computed from individual grades, such as quizzes, homework assignments, and so on. The column is a derived column because the data to compute the final grade is found in other tables. However, for simplicity, the value is stored here and not computed each time. This simplifies the querying of the final grade information.

The relationship line between the ENROLLMENT and STUDENT tables indicates that one student may be enrolled in zero, one, or many sections. For one row of the ENROLLMENT table, you can find one and only one corresponding row in the STUDENT table. The relationship between the ENROLLMENT and SECTION tables shows that a section may have zero, one, or multiple enrollments. A single row in the ENROLLMENT table always links back to one and only one row in the SECTION table.

The GRADE_TYPE Table

The GRADE_TYPE table is a lookup table for other tables as it relates to grade information. The table's primary key is the GRADE_TYPE_CODE column that lists the unique category of grade, such as MT, HW, PA, and so on. The DESCRIPTION column describes the abbreviated code. For example, for the GRADE_TYPE_CODE MT, you find the description Midterm, and for HW, you see Homework.

The GRADE Table

In this table, you find all the grades related to the section in which a student is enrolled. For example, the listed grades may include the midterm grade, individual quiz grades, final examination grade, and so on. For some grades (for example, quizzes, homework assignments), there may be multiple grades, and the sequence number is shown in the GRADE_CODE_OCCUR-RENCE column. Figure 1.34 displays an excerpt of data from the GRADE table.

The NUMERIC_GRADE column lists the actual grade received. This grade may be converted to a letter grade with the help of the GRADE_CONVERSION table discussed later.

STUDENT_ID	SECTION_ID	GRADE_TYPE_CODE	GRADE_CODE_OCCURRENCE	NUMERIC_GRADE	...
221	104	FI	1	77	...
221	104	HM	1	76	...
221	104	HM	2	76	...
221	104	HM	3	86	...
221	104	HM	4	96	...
221	104	MT	1	90	...
221	104	PA	1	83	...
221	104	QZ	1	84	...
221	104	QZ	2	83	...
...	...	...	...	...	...

FIGURE 1.34
Data from the GRADE table

The primary key columns are STUDENT_ID, SECTION_ID, GRADE_TYPE_CODE, and GRADE_CODE_OCCURRENCE. From the relationship between the ENROLLMENT and GRADE tables, you can learn that rows exist in the GRADE table only if the student is actually enrolled in the section listed in the ENROLLMENT table. In other words, it is not possible for a student to have grades for a section in which he or she is not enrolled. The foreign key columns STUDENT_ID and SECTION_ID from the ENROLLMENT table enforce this relationship.

The GRADE_TYPE_WEIGHT Table

The GRADE_TYPE_WEIGHT table aids in computation of the final grade a student receives for an individual section. This table details how the final grade for an individual section is computed. For example, the midterm may constitute 50 percent of the final grade, all the quizzes 10 percent, and the final examination 40 percent. If there are multiple grades for a given GRADE_TYPE_CODE, the lowest grade may be dropped if the column DROP_LOWEST contains the value Y.

The final grade is determined by using the individual grades of the student and section in the GRADE table in conjunction with this table. This computed final grade value is stored in the FINAL_GRADE column of the ENROLLMENT table discussed previously. (The FINAL_GRADE column is a derived column. As mentioned earlier, the values to compute this number are available in the GRADE and GRADE_TYPE_WEIGHT tables, but because the computation of this value is complex, it is stored to simplify queries.)

The primary key of the GRADE_TYPE_WEIGHT table consists of the SECTION_ID and GRADE_TYPE_CODE columns. A particular GRADE_TYPE_CODE value may exist zero, one, or multiple times in the table. For every row of the GRADE_TYPE_WEIGHT table, you find one and only one corresponding GRADE_TYPE_CODE value in the GRADE_TYPE table.

The relationship between the GRADE_TYPE_WEIGHT table and the SECTION table indicates that a section may have zero, one, or multiple rows in the GRADE_TYPE _WEIGHT table for a given SECTION_ID value. For one SECTION_ID value in the GRADE_TYPE_WEIGHT table, there must always be one and only one corresponding value in the SECTION table.

The GRADE_CONVERSION Table

The purpose of the GRADE_CONVERSION table is to convert a number grade to a letter grade. The table does not have any relationship with any other tables. The column LETTER_GRADE contains the unique letter grades, such as A+, A, A-, B, and so forth. For each of these letter grades, there is an equivalent number range. For example, for the letter B, the range is 83 through 86 and is listed in the MIN_GRADE and MAX_GRADE columns.

 You can find the individual table and column descriptions of all the tables listed in the STUDENT schema diagram in Appendix E, "Table and Column Descriptions."

▼ LAB 1.3 EXERCISES

a) What does the STUDENT schema diagram represent?

b) Does the STUDENT schema diagram tell you where a student lives? Explain.

c) What four columns are common to all tables in the STUDENT schema diagram?

d) What is the primary key of the COURSE table?

e) How many primary keys does the ENROLLMENT table have? Name the column(s).

f) How many foreign keys does the SECTION table have?

g) Will a foreign key column in a table accept any data value? Explain, using the STUDENT and ZIPCODE tables.

h) To make the relationship between the ZIPCODE and STUDENT tables optional, what would have to change in the STUDENT table?

i) From what domain of values (that is, what column in what table) does the PREREQUISITE column of the COURSE table get its values?

j) Explain the relationship(s) the ENROLLMENT table has to other table(s).

▼ LAB 1.3 EXERCISE ANSWERS

a) What does the STUDENT schema diagram represent?

ANSWER: The STUDENT schema diagram is a graphical representation of tables in a relational database.

A schema diagram is a useful tool during the software development lifecycle. English-like words should be used to name tables and columns so that anyone, whether developer or end user, can look at a schema diagram and grasp the meaning of data and the relationships. Developers study a schema diagram to understand the design of a database long before they put hands on the keyboard to develop a system, and end users can use the schema diagram to understand the relationship between the data elements.

b) Does the STUDENT schema diagram tell you where a student lives? Explain.

ANSWER: No. The STUDENT schema diagram tells you how data is organized in a relational database: the names of tables, the columns in those tables, and the relationship among them. It cannot tell you what actual data looks like. You use the SQL language to interact with a relational database to view, manipulate, and store the data in the tables.

c) What four columns are common to all tables in the STUDENT schema diagram?

ANSWER: The four columns are CREATED_BY, CREATED_DATE, MODIFIED_BY, and MODIFIED_DATE.

Database tables often contain columns similar to these four to create an audit trail. These columns are designed to identify who first created or last modified a row of a table and when the action occurred. You typically find these columns only on the physical schema diagram, not on the logical model. Some of these values in the columns can be filled in automatically by writing triggers. You will see an example of a table trigger in Chapter 12. (Triggers are described in further detail in another book in this series: *Oracle PL/SQL by Example,* 4th edition, by Benjamin Rosenzweig and Elena Silvestrova Rakhimov; Prentice Hall, 2008.)

d) What is the primary key of the COURSE table?

ANSWER: The primary key of the COURSE table is the column COURSE_NO.

You can identify the primary key because it has a PK symbol listed next to the column. In general, a primary key uniquely identifies a row in a table, and the column or columns of the primary key are defined as NOT NULL.

e) How many primary keys does the ENROLLMENT table have? Name the column(s).

ANSWER: A table can have only one primary key. The primary key of the ENROLLMENT table consists of the two columns STUDENT_ID and SECTION_ID.

As mentioned earlier, a primary key uniquely identifies a single row in a table. In the case of the ENROLLMENT table, two columns uniquely identify a row and create a composite primary key.

In the schema diagram, these two columns are also foreign keys. The STUDENT_ID column is the foreign key to the STUDENT table, and SECTION_ID is the foreign key to the SECTION table. Both foreign key relationships are identifying relationships.

f) How many foreign keys does the SECTION table have?

ANSWER: Two. The foreign keys of the SECTION table are COURSE_NO and INSTRUCTOR_ID.

g) Will a foreign key column in a table accept any data value? Explain, using the STUDENT and ZIPCODE tables.

ANSWER: No. A foreign key must use the values of the primary key it references as its domain of values.

The ZIP column is the primary key in the ZIPCODE table. The STUDENT table references this column with the foreign key ZIP column. Only values that exist in the ZIP column of the ZIPCODE table can be valid values for the ZIP column of the STUDENT table. If you attempt to create a row or change an existing row in the STUDENT table with a zip code not found in the ZIPCODE table, the foreign key constraint on the STUDENT table will reject it.

In general, a foreign key is defined as being a column, or columns, in the child table. This column refers to the primary key of another table, referred to as the parent table.

The primary key values are the domain of values for the foreign key column. A *domain* is a set of values that shows the possible values a column can have. The primary key values of the parent table are the only acceptable values that can appear in the foreign key column in the other table.

(Domains are not only used in context with primary key and foreign key relationships but can also be used for a list of values that may be stored in a table. For example, common domains include Yes/No, Gender: Male/Female/Unknown, Weekday: Sun/Mon/ Tue/Wed/Thu/Fri/Sat.)

h) To make the relationship between the ZIPCODE and STUDENT tables optional, what would have to change in the STUDENT table?

ANSWER: The foreign key column ZIP in the STUDENT table would have to be defined as allowing NULL values. It is currently defined as NOT NULL. The relationship should be indicated as optional instead of mandatory, as shown in Figure 1.35.

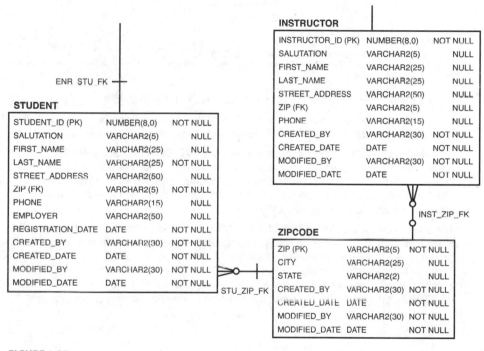

FIGURE 1.35
The relationships of the ZIPCODE table

There is such an optional relationship between the INSTRUCTOR and ZIPCODE tables. All the NOT NULL values of ZIP in the INSTRUCTOR table must be found in the ZIPCODE table.

i) From what domain of values (that is, what column in what table) does the PREREQUISITE column of the COURSE table get its values?

ANSWER: From the COURSE_NO column in the COURSE table.

In this case, the PREREQUISITE column refers to the COURSE_NO column, which provides the domain of values for the PREREQUISITE column. A prerequisite is valid only if it is also a valid course number in the COURSE table. This relationship is shown in Figure 1.36.

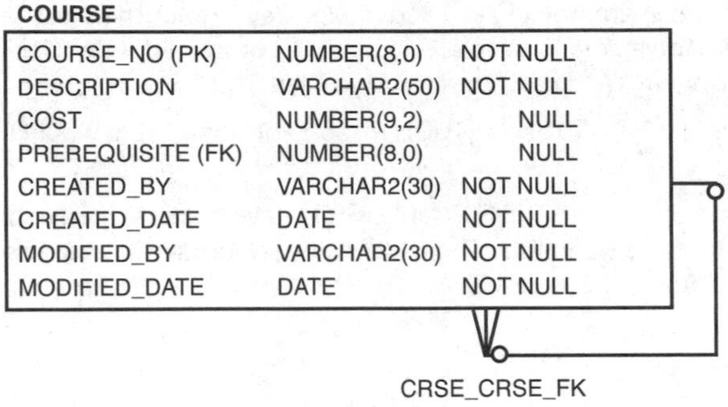

COURSE

COURSE_NO (PK)	NUMBER(8,0)	NOT NULL
DESCRIPTION	VARCHAR2(50)	NOT NULL
COST	NUMBER(9,2)	NULL
PREREQUISITE (FK)	NUMBER(8,0)	NULL
CREATED_BY	VARCHAR2(30)	NOT NULL
CREATED_DATE	DATE	NOT NULL
MODIFIED_BY	VARCHAR2(30)	NOT NULL
MODIFIED_DATE	DATE	NOT NULL

CRSE_CRSE_FK

FIGURE 1.36
The self-referencing relationship of the COURSE table

j) Explain the relationship(s) the ENROLLMENT table has to other table(s).

ANSWER: The STUDENT table and the SECTION table are the parent tables of the ENROLLMENT table. The ENROLLMENT table is one of the parent tables of the GRADE table.

As shown in Figure 1.37, the relationship between the STUDENT and SECTION tables signifies that a student may be enrolled in zero, one, or many sections. One individual student can be enrolled in one specific section only once; otherwise, the unique combination of the two columns in the ENROLLMENT table would be violated. The combination of these two foreign key columns represents the primary key of the ENROLLMENT table.

The relationship of the ENROLLMENT table as the parent of the GRADE table shows that for an individual student and her or his enrolled section, there may be zero, one, or many grades. The primary key columns of the ENROLLMENT table (STUDENT_ID and SECTION_ID) are foreign keys in the GRADE table that become part of the GRADE table's composite primary key. Therefore, only enrolled students may have rows in the GRADE, as indicated with the optional line. If a row in GRADE exists, it must be for one specific enrollment in a section, for one specific student.

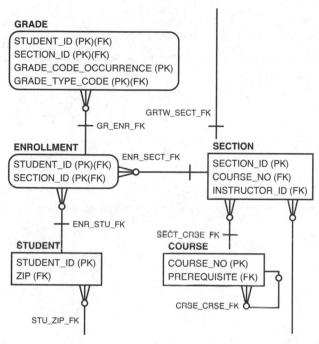

FIGURE 1.37
The relationships of the ENROLLMENT table

It is important to note that in some cases, the foreign keys become part of a table's primary key, as in the ENROLLMENT table or the GRADE table. If a composite primary key contains many columns (perhaps more than four or five), a surrogate key consisting of one column may be considered for simplicity. The decision to use a surrogate key is based on the database designer's understanding of how data is typically accessed by the application programs.

Lab 1.3 Quiz

In order to test your progress, you should be able to answer the following questions.

1) What role(s) does the STUDENT_ID column play in the GRADE table? Select all that apply.

    _____ a) Part of composite primary key

    _____ b) Primary key

    _____ c) Foreign key

2) The GRADE_TYPE table does not allow values to be NULL in any column.

    _____ a) True

    _____ b) False

3) The number of columns in a table matches the number of rows in that table.

    _____ a) True

    _____ b) False

4) The SECTION table has no foreign key columns.

    _____ a) True

    _____ b) False

5) A table can contain 10 million rows.

    _____ a) True

    _____ b) False

6) A primary key may contain NULL values.

    _____ a) True

    _____ b) False

7) A column name must be unique within a table.

    _____ a) True

    _____ b) False

8) If a table is a child table in three different one-to-many relationships, how many foreign key columns does it have?

    _____ a) One

    _____ b) Exactly three

    _____ c) Three or more

9) Referential integrity requires the relationship between foreign key and primary key to maintain values from the same domain.

    _____ a) True

    _____ b) False

10) A foreign key may be NULL.

_____ a) True

_____ b) False

11) Orphan rows are not allowed in the relational model.

_____ a) True

_____ b) False

ANSWERS APPEAR IN APPENDIX A.

▼ WORKSHOP

The projects in this section are meant to prompt you to utilize all the skills you have acquired throughout this chapter. The answers to these projects can be found at the companion Web site to this book, located at www.oraclesqlbyexample.com.

In this chapter, you learned about data, how data is organized in tables, and how the relationships among the tables are depicted in a schema diagram. Based on your newly acquired knowledge, design a schema diagram based on the fictional ACME Construction Company. Draw on your own work experience to design the following components.

1) Draw boxes for these three tables: EMPLOYEE, POSITION, and DEPARTMENT.

2) Create at least three columns for each of the tables and designate a primary key for each table.

3) Create relationships among the tables that make sense to you. At least one table should have a self-referencing relationship. Hint: Be sure to include the necessary foreign key columns.

4) Think about which columns should *not* allow NULL values.

CHAPTER 2

SQL: The Basics

CHAPTER OBJECTIVES

In this chapter, you will learn about:

- ▶ The SQL Execution Environment
- ▶ The Anatomy of a SELECT Statement
- ▶ An Introduction to SQL Developer and SQL*Plus

Now that you are familiar with the concepts of databases and schema diagrams, you are ready to start with hands-on exercises. In this chapter, you will learn the basics of the SQL language and use SQL Developer and SQL*Plus, two Oracle provided software tools that allow you to execute statements against the Oracle database.

SQL statements can range from very simple to highly complex; they can be a few words long or a few hundred words long. In this chapter, you begin by writing simple SQL statements, but you will be able to build longer, more complex SQL queries very quickly.

LAB 2.1
The SQL Execution Environment

LAB OBJECTIVES

After this lab, you will be able to:

▶ Understand Database Connectivity
▶ Execute Your First SQL Command Using SQL Developer

This lab provides you with an understanding of the basic SQL language commands. You will learn how to establish connectivity to the database server and begin executing SQL commands.

Oracle software runs on many different operating systems and hardware environments. The machine on which the Oracle database software resides is called the *Oracle database server*. A variety of tools are available to access data from the database server. In this chapter, you will be introduced to two Oracle-provided tools: SQL Developer and SQL*Plus.

The most striking difference between SQL Developer and SQL*Plus is the interface. SQL*Plus has an arcane command-line interface with old-style editing and display options.

SQL Developer is a recent addition to the Oracle tool set. It is included in the latest Oracle releases or can be downloaded free from Oracle's Web site. SQL Developer's graphical user interface greatly simplifies SQL statement execution and overall database access.

Because SQL Developer is a much easier environment to use than SQL*Plus, you start with this execution environment first to learn the basics of the SQL language.

In subsequent labs, you will explore some of the basics of SQL*Plus. While SQL*Plus seems quite outdated, you cannot ignore decades of SQL*Plus usage. It has been part of Oracle since its early beginnings and will continue to be shipped with every installation on every platform. You will find it useful to have some rudimentary knowledge of SQL*Plus. Therefore, this book describes both tools.

However, the focus of this book is learning the SQL language; the tool you use is simply the environment within which to execute the SQL language commands. Therefore, not all details of these tools are covered. Furthermore, you may also consider one of the many third-party tools available to execute your statements. No matter what tool becomes your favorite, it is beneficial to know both SQL Developer and SQL*Plus as they are found with almost every Oracle installation.

For a list of the many easy-to-use third-party tools, see Appendix H, "Resources."

Accessing the Oracle Database Server

You can access the Oracle server through various front-end tools. This lab teaches you some of the basics of SQL Developer first. This tool is Oracle's newest database query and development tool. It is also by far easier to learn and use than SQL*Plus, which is covered in Lab 2.3, "An Introduction to SQL*Plus."

The differences between SQL Developer and SQL*Plus are pointed out to you as you work through the book. You can assume, with very few exceptions, that the functionality is very similar, if not identical. You might want to use SQL Developer for execution of your SQL statements in this book because it is a more user-friendly tool than SQL*Plus for a beginning SQL user.

Getting Started with SQL Developer

Oracle SQL Developer provides a convenient way to perform essential database tasks. The tool enhances productivity and simplifies database development tasks by providing a graphical interface for executing SQL statements, browsing, and creating and updating database objects. SQL Developer connects to any Oracle database, version 9.2.0.1 and later. You can also create database connections for non-Oracle databases.

If your Oracle software installation did not come with the tool already installed, you can download the latest version of SQL Developer from Oracle's Web site. Oracle does not charge a license fee for SQL Developer. This tool is written in Java, thus providing a uniform interface across the Windows, Linux, and MAC OS X platforms. Furthermore, SQL Developer's default database connection uses a thin Java Database Connectivity (JDBC) driver, so there is no requirement for a full Oracle client software installation involving Oracle Net. This simplifies the configuration and minimizes the footprint. With a quick unzip and execution of the file, the installation is a breeze.

SQL and the Oracle Database Server

In the midst of all this software lies the SQL language. SQL commands are sent from SQL Developer, also known as the client, or *front end*, to the server, or *back end*. These commands send instructions to the server to tell the server what services to provide. The server responds by returning a result to the client, which then displays the output. Figure 2.1 shows a SQL statement that queries the DESCRIPTION column of the COURSE table. The SQL statement is sent to the Oracle server, and the result is returned to the front end, which then formats and displays the output, as appropriate.

You may run SQL Developer and your database on the same machine. Typically, this is the case when you install both the Oracle database server and SQL Developer on your individual computer.

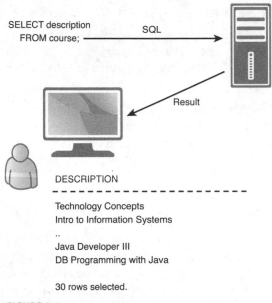

SELECT description
    FROM course;   SQL

Result

DESCRIPTION

Technology Concepts
Intro to Information Systems

..

Java Developer III
DB Programming with Java

30 rows selected.

FIGURE 2.1
SQL and the Oracle database server

The client, whether SQL Developer or SQL*Plus, sends SQL statements to the server, and the server responds with the result set. The job of the database server involves listening and managing many clients' requests, because there are often multiple client machines involved.

The means of communication is established either via the Oracle Net software, a JDBC driver, or an ODBC driver.

Creating a Database Connection for SQL Developer

Before you can send your first SQL statement to the database, you need to create a connection to the database server. A connection consists of a username, password, and connection string or hostname. This connection authenticates you to log in to the Oracle database.

When you first evoke SQL Developer, you a see screen similar to Figure 2.2. The screen is divided into several panes. The left pane, labeled Connections, allows for a list of database connections.

The name of the displayed connection is local. This database connection refers to a database installed on the same machine as SQL Developer. You can rename this connection by right-clicking the connection name, choosing Rename Connection, and providing a new name.

To create a new database connection, right-click the Connections node and choose New Connection (see Figure 2.3).

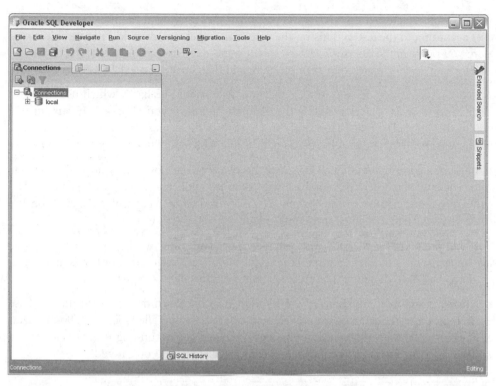

FIGURE 2.2
The Connections window in SQL Developer

FIGURE 2.3
Creating a new database connection

You can add a new connection name, such as StudentConnection, and assign a username and password. For the purposes of the examples in this book, use the username student and the password learn.

 Starting with Oracle 11g, the password is case-sensitive by default.

If you have not yet created the STUDENT schema (also referred to as the STUDENT user account) according to the instructions on the companion Web site, you will not be able to log in. Before you perform the lab exercises, you might want to finish reading this lab first, visit the Web site located at www.oraclesqlbyexample.com, and then create the STUDENT schema.

Choose as the Role option default. The Connection Type should be Basic, which uses the thin JDBC driver to connect; this is probably the simplest option. If you choose TNS, an entry is required in the TNSNAMES.ORA file, and the Oracle Net client must be installed. In Lab 2.3, we will discuss the TNSNAMES.ORA file as part of that lab's SQL*Plus connectivity topics.

Additional connection information consists of the name of the host (also called the *machine name*), the default port where the database will listen for connection requests (usually 1521), and either the Service name or the System ID (SID, to identify a particular database on the machine). Here the default name for the SID is orcl.

The Test button allows you determine whether this connection works. A "Success" status message appears above the Help button if the connection is successful. If your test is unsuccessful, you have probably chosen an incorrect hostname and/or SID.

The hostname is the machine name or the IP address of the machine on which the database resides. In Figure 2.4, the database is installed on the host machine called localhost. If your database resides on a computer different from the one on which you're running SQL Developer, the name of the machine on which the Oracle server is installed should be entered here.

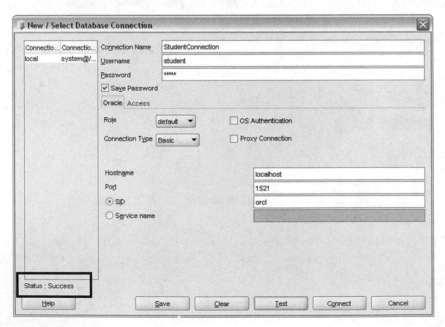

FIGURE 2.4
New / Select Database Connection dialog box

When you click the Save button, you see the connection name added to the Connections window, as shown in Figure 2.5.

FIGURE 2.5
List of connections

When you double-click the connection name, you are connected to the database, using the appropriate user account and password. If you did not check the Save Password box when you created StudentConnection, you are prompted for it each time you open the connection.

   For the majority of the exercises in this book, you will use the StudentConnection.

You can modify the connection information by right-clicking on the Student Connection node and choosing Properties from the context menu.

Exploring Database Table Objects

When you expand the StudentConnection node by clicking the plus sign, you see a list of database objects available to this user (see Figure 2.6). This pane, called the *Connections navigator,* is a tree-based object browser.

If you right-click on a node within the Connections navigator, a context-sensitive menu appears. For each object type, the menu varies, presenting you with choices to create, alter, drop, or manage the various objects. We will discuss the different object menus in detail in the chapters related to each object type.

For now, we will focus on the table objects. When you double-click an individual table node, you see various tabs displayed that provide details about the table.

COLUMNS TAB

The Columns tab displays a list of the columns, together with each column's data type. You can see whether the column allows null values, the primary key definition, and any column comments. In the Primary Key column, the value 1 indicates that this is the first column in the primary key. For the COURSE table, you can see in Figure 2.6 that the primary key consists of one column: COURSE_NO.

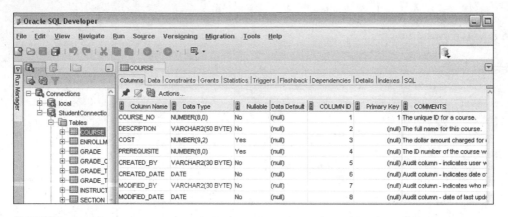

FIGURE 2.6
Column definition of the COURSE table

DATA TAB

A click on the Data tab displays the data stored in the table. This tab also contains functionality to modify the data. You will learn how to make changes to data in Chapter 11, "Insert, Update, and Delete."

CONSTRAINTS TAB

The Constraints tab is useful for determining foreign key relationships of the table with other tables and for showing the validation constraints that exists. Chapter 12, "Create, Alter, and Drop Tables" explains these topics in detail.

GRANTS TAB

The Grants tab provides details about who has access privileges to the object; this is discussed in Chapter 15, "Security."

STATISTICS TAB

The Statistics tab shows columns and table statistics, such as the number of rows, the number of distinct values for each column, and so on. The Oracle database uses these values to optimize the execution of SQL statements. Chapter 18, "SQL Optimization," expands on how these statistics affect performance.

TRIGGERS, DEPENDENCIES, INDEXES, FLASHBACK, AND SQL TABS

The Triggers, Dependencies, Indexes, and SQL tabs are discussed in Chapter 12 as well as Chapter 13, "Indexes, Sequences, and Views." You will find out what triggers are associated with a table and the event on which the trigger fires. Any indexes that are created for the tables display in the Index tab. The Dependencies tab shows any views or objects that are dependent on this table. The Flashback tab allows you to see the previous data values before a data manipulation occurred at a specific time in the past; this will be discussed in Chapter 11. The SQL Tab shows the SQL to re-create the DDL for the table and its associated objects.

DETAILS TAB

The Details tab lists various details of a table, such as the date and time the table was created, the last date and time statistics were collected, and so on. You will learn more about this in Chapter 14, "The Data Dictionary, Scripting, and Reporting."

Reviewing the various tabs for a table allows you to glance at the important characteristics of a table. To explore another table, you double-click that table's node to replace the COURSE table's information with the new table's information. If you do not want to replace the display, you can click the red Push Pin icon to freeze the display.

The SQL Developer Worksheet

Aside from clicking the Data tab, another way to display data is by using the SQL language. The command to retrieve rows is the SELECT command. You enter SQL statements into the SQL Worksheet. The easiest way to open a worksheet is by clicking the SQL Worksheet icon in the toolbar, as shown in Figure 2.7.

FIGURE 2.7
Open SQL Worksheet icon

Another way to open the worksheet is to right-click the connection name and choose Open SQL Worksheet, or you can choose Tools from the top menu bar and then SQL Worksheet.

The Connection dialog box (see Figure 2.8) allows you to select the database connection for this worksheet. The plus sign brings up the dialog box to create a new connection, and the Pencil icon facilitates editing of an existing database connection.

As you become more familiar with SQL Developer, you will find that there are many ways to perform the same action, using different menu choices. In addition to the menu on the top of the screen, there are context-sensitive menus and icons for frequently performed tasks.

When a connection is selected, the SQL Worksheet tab description shows the name of the connection on the top. You can execute SQL statements using the StudentConnection by entering a command in the SQL Worksheet.

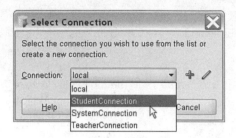

FIGURE 2.8
Select Connection dialog box

You can open multiple worksheets within SQL Developer by clicking the Open SQL Worksheet icon again. Each additional worksheet can hold different SQL statements and result sets. The worksheet tab will display the unique name of the connection on the top. For example, in Figure 2.9, a second worksheet for this connection is shown as StudentConnection~1.

The StudentConnection and StudentConnection~1 worksheets share the same database session. A *session* is an individual connection to the Oracle database server, which starts as soon as the user is logged in and authenticated. The session ends when the user disconnects or exits. Chapter 11 provides a more detailed discussion on sessions and their effect on the read consistency and locking of data during data manipulations.

Another tab, such as the TeacherConnection tab in Figure 2.9, represents another connection that may use a different database and/or login name.

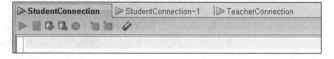

FIGURE 2.9
Multiple worksheets and their respective connections

Figure 2.10 shows the different panes within SQL Developer. You are already familiar with the Connections navigator on the left of the screen. As a separate tab next to it, you see the Reports navigator, which contains many supplied data dictionary reports, as discussed in Chapter 14.

The result of your SQL statement execution displays in the Results window, which shows the effect of the SQL statement execution. You can see a number of tabs, and SQL Developer displays most of your statement results in the Results tab. The Script Output tab shows the result of a script run (a collection of SQL statements). The Explain and the Autotrace tabs show the execution plan of a SQL statement and give an indication of how efficiently Oracle may execute your command; we discuss these tabs in Chapter 18. The DBMS Output and OWA

(Oracle Web Agent) Output tabs are relevant if you execute PL/SQL statements. (See the companion book *Oracle PL/SQL by Example,* 4th edition, by Benjamin Rosenzweig and Elena Silvestrova Rakhimov; Prentice Hall, 2008.)

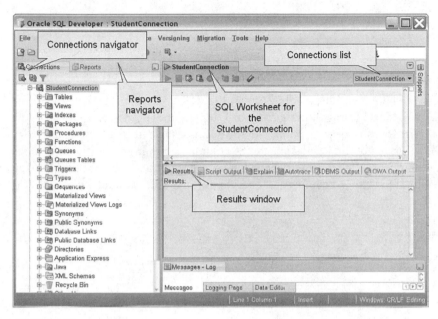

FIGURE 2.10
The various SQL Developer panes

The Connections list on the right of the SQL Worksheet allows you to switch to another connection for the current worksheet. You can execute the same statement against a different connection by choosing the connection name from the Connections list drop-down menu.

Below the Results window, you may see tabs such as Messages, Logging Page, and Data Editor. Depending on the action you are taking, you see feedback information in these tabs. You will see examples of messages in the Data Editor when you manipulate data via SQL Developer in Chapter 11.

ENTERING A SQL STATEMENT

You enter a SQL statement in the SQL Worksheet window. The following SELECT statement retrieves all the columns and rows from the COURSE table.

```
SELECT *
  FROM course
```

To execute the command, you click the green triangle. When your mouse hovers over the triangle, a ToolTip displays a description and alternative F9 function (see Figure 2.11).

FIGURE 2.11
The Execute Statement icon

THE RESULTS TAB

The Results tab (see Figure 2.12) displays the data of the COURSE table. The left side of the Results tab shows an ordered listing of numbers, which represent the order of the rows in the Results window. These row numbers are not part of the database table; they are only for display within this window. On top of the Results tab are the column names from the COURSE table. You can scroll to the right to see any additional columns and scroll down to all the rows. You can adjust the width of individual columns and drag the column order around without having to change the SQL statement.

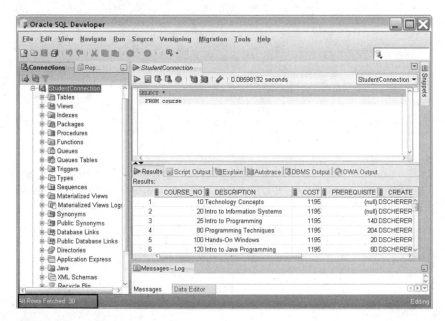

FIGURE 2.12
The SQL statement and corresponding result

On the bottom left of the screen, the status indicates how many records the statement returned to SQL Developer. If the bar is not visible, you can display it by choosing View, Status Bar.

Commonly Used Data Types

As you saw on the Data tab in SQL Developer, every column in Oracle has a data type, which determines what type of data can be stored. You need to know about the data types in order to use some of the comparison operators discussed in the next chapter.

DATE

The DATE data type stores date and time information. Depending on your setup, the default display format for a date may be DD-MON-YY. For example, July 4, 2009, displays as 04-JUL-09. There are a number of functions you can use to change the display format or to show the time. You also have menu options in SQL Developer for customizing the display. You will learn more about these topics in Chapter 5, "Date and Conversion Functions."

NUMBER

Columns with the data type NUMBER allow only numeric data; no text, hyphens, or dashes are permitted. A column defined as NUMBER(5,2) can have a maximum of three digits before the decimal point and two digits after the decimal point. The first digit (5) is called the *precision;* the second digit (2) is referred to as the *scale.* The smallest allowed number is – 999.99, and the largest is 999.99. A column definition with a zero scale, such as NUMBER(5) or NUMBER(5,0), allows integers in the range from – 99,999 to 99,999.

VARCHAR2 AND CHAR

The VARCHAR2 and CHAR data types store alphanumeric data (for example, text, numbers, special characters). VARCHAR2 is the variable-length data type and the most commonly used alphanumeric data type; its maximum size is 4,000 characters. The main difference between VARCHAR2 and CHAR is that the CHAR data type is a fixed-length data type, and any unused room is blank padded with spaces.

For example, a column defined as CHAR(10) and containing the four-character-length value JOHN in a row will have six blank characters padded at the end to make the total length 10 spaces. (If the column is stored in a VARCHAR2(10) column instead, it stores four characters only.) A CHAR column can store up to 2,000 characters.

If you want to store data containing more than 4,000 characters, you need to consider the CLOB data type, which allows you to store large amounts of textual data. It replaces the formerly used LONG data type, which is supported only for backward compatibility.

OTHER DATA TYPES

The data types BLOB and BFILE are binary data types that deal with access to multimedia content such as movies, images, or music. The main difference between these two data types is how the data is stored within the Oracle database. The BLOB data type stores the content inside the Oracle database, whereas the BFILE data type stores only a reference to the file location directory and the file name.

In order to access the binary content of the data, you need to use highly specific functions that go beyond the objectives of this book. In addition to the data types mentioned, Oracle provides data types to support specific national character sets (for example, NCLOB, NVARCHAR2), intermedia (image, audio, video) data types, and spatial (geographic) data. Oracle also gives you the ability to create your own customized object data types.

Refer to Appendix I, "Oracle Data Types," for a detailed list of the various data types. For most SQL operations, you typically use the NUMBER, VARCHAR2, and various DATE-related data types. They are the most commonly used data types, where the vast majority of data is stored.

 Now that you know how to log on to the Oracle database, this is a good time to read the readme file you downloaded from the Web site located at www.oraclesqlbyexample.com and create the STUDENT schema if you have not already done so.

▼ LAB 2.1 EXERCISES

a) How does the Oracle server communicate with the client?

b) In SQL Developer, expand the Tables node below the StudentConnection to reveal the different tables available to the STUDENT user. Double-click the INSTRUCTOR table. Then double-click the GRADE table. Is the information regarding the INSTRUCTOR table still visible?

c) What happens when you type DESCRIBE student in the SQL Worksheet pane and then click the Execute Statement icon?

▼ LAB 2.1 EXERCISE ANSWERS

a) How does the Oracle server communicate with the client?

ANSWER: SQL Developer and SQL*Plus are examples of client programs, and the Oracle database is the server. Various protocols, such as Oracle Net and JDBC, facilitate communication between the server and the client.

The client issues SQL commands, telling the server to perform specific actions. The server sends back the results of those instructions to the client software, where they are displayed.

b) In SQL Developer, expand the Tables node below StudentConnection to reveal the different tables available to the STUDENT user. Double-click the INSTRUCTOR table. Then double-click the GRADE table. Is the information regarding the INSTRUCTOR table still visible?

ANSWER: The GRADE table information replaces the INSTRUCTOR tab. A click on the Push Pin icon (see Figure 2.13) keeps the object's information displayed.

The icon next to the Push Pin is the Edit icon. Clicking the Edit icon allows you to modify the table's column definitions, add and modify constraints, and so on. You will learn about these options in Chapter 12, which explores the different choices and their effects on the entry and storage of the data.

Next to the Edit icon is the Refresh icon, which re-queries the database for the latest updates on the given object. The Actions menu provides additional options to modify the table and column properties.

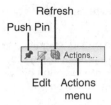

Push Pin

Refresh

Edit Actions
menu

FIGURE 2.13
The Column tab icons

c) What happens when you type DESCRIBE student in the SQL Worksheet pane and then click the Execute Statement icon?

ANSWER: The DESCRIBE command displays the structure of the STUDENT table, listing the columns, data types, and null allowed characteristics. The result of the command displays in the Scripts Output tab, not the Results tab (see Figure 2.14).

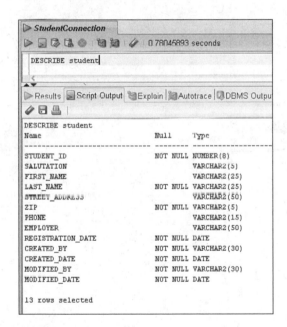

FIGURE 2.14
The DESCRIBE command

The DESCRIBE command is actually a SQL*Plus command, not a command in the SQL language. It lets you quickly show the structure of a table. SQL Developer accepts and executes many of the SQL*Plus commands.

Because this is a SQL*Plus command, the Script Output tab, not the Results tab, shows the output. The Scripts Output tab displays the result in a similar fixed-character fashion to SQL*Plus. You also get results in this tab if you click the Run Script icon (F5); this functionality tries to emulate SQL*Plus as much as possible.

Compared to the SQL*Plus DESCRIBE command, SQL Developer's Columns tab provides significantly more detailed information at once. Another way to display the Columns tab is by using the SQL Developer's Popup Describe menu option. You access the Popup Describe menu option by placing your cursor on a table in the SQL Worksheet and then right-click for the context menu (see Figure 2.15).

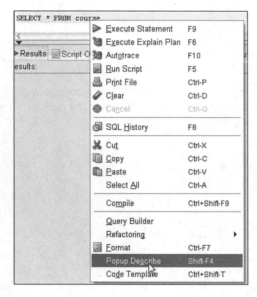

FIGURE 2.15
The Popup Describe menu option

Lab 2.1 Quiz

In order to test your progress, you should be able to answer the following questions.

1) Anyone can connect to an Oracle database, as long as he or she has the SQL Developer or SQL*Plus software.

   _____ a) True

   _____ b) False

2) When you establish a connection using SQL Developer, the hostname is the machine name or IP address where the database resides.

   _____ a) True

   _____ b) False

3) SQL*Plus is available with every version of Oracle.

   _____ a) True

   _____ b) False

4) More than one user can be connected to a database at the same time.

   _____ a) True

   _____ b) False

5) The COST column of the COURSE table is defined as NUMBER(9,2). The maximum cost of an individual course is 9,999,999.99.

   _____ a) True

   _____ b) False

6) You can store at most 4,000 characters in a VARCHAR2 column.

   _____ a) True

   _____ b) False

ANSWERS APPEAR IN APPENDIX A.

LAB 2.2
The Anatomy of a SELECT Statement

LAB OBJECTIVES

After this lab, you will be able to:

▶ Write a SQL SELECT Statement
▶ Use DISTINCT in a SQL Statement
▶ Execute Statements in SQL Developer

When you write a SQL query, it is usually to find an answer to a question such as "How many students live in New York?" or "Where, and at what time, does the UNIX class meet?" A SQL *SELECT statement,* or SQL *query,* is used to find answers to these questions. A SELECT statement can be broken down into a minimum of two parts: the *SELECT list* and the *FROM clause.* The SELECT list usually consists of the column or columns of a table or tables from which you want to display data. The FROM clause states on what table or tables this column or columns are found. Later, you will learn some of the other clauses that can be used in a SELECT statement.

How to Write a SQL Query

Before formulating the SELECT statement, you must first determine in which table the information is located. A study of the schema diagram for the STUDENT database reveals that the COURSE table provides descriptions related to courses. (You can also refer to Appendix E, "Table and Column Descriptions.")

The following SELECT statement provides a list of course descriptions. SQL does not require a new line for each clause, but using this formatting convention makes for easy readability.

```
SELECT description
  FROM course
```

The SELECT list shows the single column called DESCRIPTION, which contains this information. The DESCRIPTION column is found on the COURSE table as specified in the FROM clause. When the statement is executed, the result set is a list of all the values found in the DESCRIPTION column of the COURSE table.

```
DESCRIPTION
-------------------------
Technology Concepts
Intro to Information Systems
...
Java Developer III
DB Programming with Java
```

30 rows selected.

Many of the result sets displayed throughout this book show both the SQL statement and the resulting data in a fixed-width font. At times, you may also find screenshots of the output in SQL Developer. However, typically the result is shown in a fixed-width font for easy readability.

 The output of the command is displayed in bold font to easily distinguish between the output from the commands you enter. Not all the returned rows may be listed. A line in the output that shows ... indicates that some of the output has been omitted. Typically, you see the beginning and the ending rows of the result set and the number of rows returned.

RETRIEVING MULTIPLE COLUMNS

To retrieve a list of course descriptions and the cost of each course, include the COST column in the SELECT list.

```
SELECT description, cost
  FROM course
DESCRIPTION                        COST
------------------------------  ----
Technology Concepts             1195
Intro to Information Systems    1195
...
Java Developer III              1195
DB Programming with Java
```

30 rows selected.

When you want to display more than one column in the SELECT list, separate the columns with commas. It is good practice to include a space after the comma for readability. The order of columns in a SELECT list determines the order in which the columns are displayed in the output.

SELECTING ALL COLUMNS

You can select all columns in a table with the asterisk (*) wildcard character. This is handy because it means you don't have to type all columns in the SELECT list. The columns are displayed in the order in which they are defined in the table. This is the same order you see when you click the Columns tab in SQL Developer or issue the DESCRIBE command.

```
SELECT *
  FROM course
```

Constructing the SQL Statement in SQL Developer

You can drag tables listed in the Connections navigator into the SQL Worksheet. When you do this, you construct a SELECT statement with all columns in the table. If desired, you can then edit the statement further. Figure 2.16 shows an example.

To define the type of statement that will be generated, select Tools, Preferences, Database: Worksheet Parameter, Drag and Drop Effect.

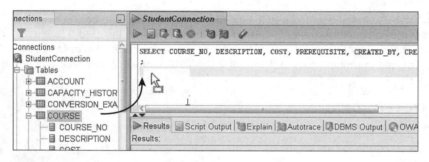

FIGURE 2.16
Result of dragging a table into the SQL Worksheet

The SQL Worksheet Icons

Figure 2.17 shows the SQL Worksheet toolbar. You are already familiar with the Execute Statement icon.

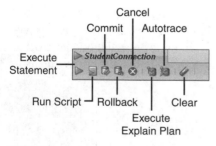

FIGURE 2.17
The SQL Worksheet icons toolbar

RUN SCRIPT

The Run Script icon allows you to execute multiple statements and emulates SQL*Plus as much as possible; the result is displayed in the Script Output tab instead of the Results tab.

COMMIT

The Commit icon looks like a database icon with the check mark. Any modifications to the data become permanent and visible to all users.

ROLLBACK

The Rollback icon looks like a database icon with an undo arrow. It undoes database changes, provided that they have not yet been committed. The COMMIT and ROLLBACK commands are discussed in Chapter 11.

CANCEL, EXECUTE EXPLAIN PLAN, AND AUTOTRACE

The Cancel icon stops a running statement that is currently executing. The Execute Explain Plan icon and the Autotrace icons are useful for optimizing SQL statements. You will learn about them in Chapter 18.

CLEAR

The eraser icon (Ctrl-D) at the end of the toolbar clears any statements in the SQL Worksheet.

Eliminating Duplicates with DISTINCT or UNIQUE

The use of the DISTINCT or UNIQUE keyword in the SELECT list eliminates duplicate data in the result set. The following SELECT statement retrieves the last name and the corresponding zip code for all rows of the INSTRUCTOR table.

```
SELECT last_name, zip
  FROM instructor
LAST_NAME                   ZIP
-------------------------   -----
Hanks                       10015
Wojick                      10025
Schorin                     10025
Pertez                      10035
Morris                      10015
Smythe                      10025
Chow                        10015
Lowry                       10025
Frantzen                    10005
Willig

10 rows selected.
```

There are 10 rows, yet only nine instructors have zip codes. Instructor Willig has a NULL value in the ZIP column. If you want to show only the distinct zip codes in the table, you write the following SELECT statement. In this example, the last row shows the NULL value.

```
SELECT DISTINCT zip
  FROM instructor
ZIP
-----
10005
10015
10025
10035


5 rows selected.
```

 By definition, a NULL is an unknown value, and a NULL does not equal another NULL. However, there are exceptions: If you write a SQL query using DISTINCT or UNIQUE, SQL considers a NULL value equal to another NULL value.

The output in SQL Developer shows the existence of the null much more obviously with a "(null)" display in the column (see Figure 2.18). Furthermore, the numbers to the left of the ZIP column display how many rows are returned.

FIGURE 2.18
Display of a null value in SQL Developer

From Chapter 1, "SQL and Data," you already know that a primary key is always unique or distinct. Therefore, the use of the DISTINCT or UNIQUE keyword in a SELECT list containing the primary key column(s) is unnecessary. The ZIP column in the INSTRUCTOR table is not the primary key and can therefore contain duplicate or null values.

Formatting a SQL Statement in SQL Developer

The SQL statements presented in this and all other books in this series follow a common format. The use of uppercase for SELECT, FROM, and other Oracle keywords is for emphasis only and distinguishes them from table and column names in SQL statements, which appear in lowercase letters. A standard format enhances the clarity and readability of your SQL statements and helps you detect errors more easily. Refer to Appendix B, "SQL Formatting Guide," for the formatting guidelines used throughout this book.

SYNTAX FORMATTING

SQL Developer provides many ways to help you achieve consistency. When you right-click within the SQL Worksheet, the menu shows a Refactoring, To Upper/Lower/Initcap menu option that lets you toggle between the different cases. The shortcut to remember is Ctrl-Quote. Another useful feature is the Format menu (Ctrl-F7); it automatically reformats your SQL statement to fit a given standard. You highlight the statement, right-click, and choose Format (see Figure 2.19) from the context menu.

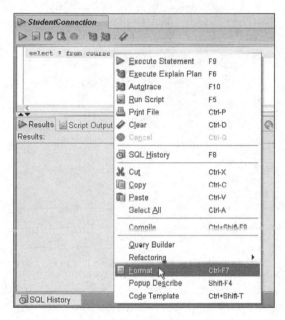

FIGURE 2.19
Format feature

Figure 2.20 shows the result of this selection. The Oracle keywords are in uppercase and right aligned, and the name of the COURSE table is in lowercase.

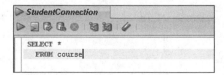

FIGURE 2.20
Format results

The Tools, Preference, SQL Formatter menu option allows you to customize the formatting to your standards (see Figure 2.21).

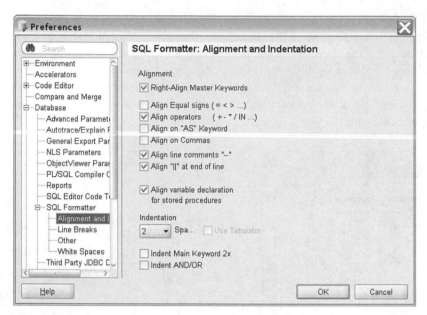

FIGURE 2.21
Preferences window

CODE COMPLETION

Another useful feature of Oracle Developer is code completion, which helps you complete your SQL statements easily. When you pause on your statement, the program prompts you for appropriate commands, column names, or table names, which you can then select from the list. Figure 2.22 shows an example. When you remove the asterisk from the statement and enter a space, you see a list of possible choices. You can then choose the DESCRIPTION column and then enter a comma to get the list of relevant columns.

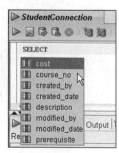

FIGURE 2.22
Code completion feature in SQL Developer

If you find the code completion feature confusing, you can turn it off by unchecking both of the Enable Auto-Popup check boxes in the Tools, Preference menu (see Figure 2.23).

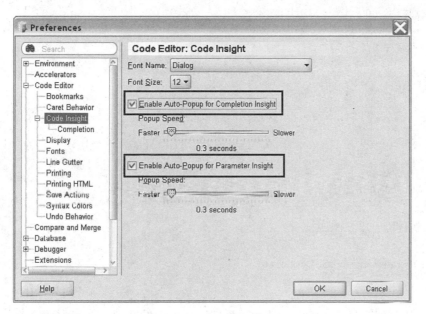

FIGURE 2.23
Code Insight preferences

SYNTAX HIGHLIGHTING

SQL Developer offers syntax highlighting, which helps distinguish the SQL language keywords with a different color. This way, you can easily identify and distinguish between the SQL language commands and any table or column names. The column and table names appear in black; SQL language commands appear in blue. This color-coding improves the readability of a statement and helps you spot syntax errors easily.

Notice that the COST column in Figure 2.24 is not colored black. Even though this is the name of the column in the table, COST also happens to be an Oracle keyword.

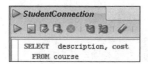

FIGURE 2.24
Syntax highlighting

Writing Multiple Statements in the SQL Worksheet

You can enter multiple statements in the SQL Worksheet and execute them individually by placing the cursor on the line of the statement (see Figure 2.25). You need to end each SQL statement with a semicolon (;) or type a forward slash (/) on a new line; otherwise, SQL Developer displays an error.

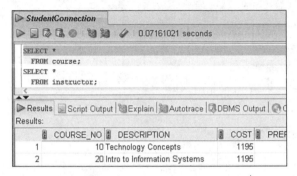

FIGURE 2.25
Executing multiple SQL statements in SQL Developer

If you want to run both statements at once, you need to run the statements as a script by clicking the Run Script icon (F5). The output is then displayed in the Script Output tab in a matter much like the SQL*Plus command-line version.

SQL Developer's Statement History

SQL Developer keeps track of your most recently executed commands in the SQL History window (see Figure 2.26) below the Results pane. If the SQL History tab is not visible, you can click View, SQL History or press F8. The SQL commands are saved even after you exit SQL Developer.

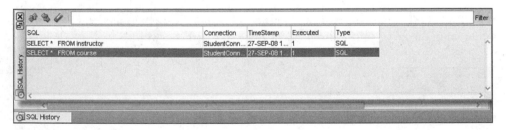

FIGURE 2.26
SQL History window

To place a command from the History window back into the SQL Worksheet, you can simply double-click the statement. If you choose the up/down arrows icon on the left, the statement is appended to any existing statements in the SQL Worksheet window. The left/right arrows icon replaces any existing SQL statement(s) in the Worksheet.

You are able to search for text within the historical SQL statements by entering the information in the box and clicking the Filter button on the right. The eraser icon clears all the statements from the SQL history. If you do not choose a statement, you can exit the SQL History window by pressing the Esc key.

▼ LAB 2.2 EXERCISES

a) Write a SELECT statement that lists the first and last names of all students.

b) Write a SELECT statement that lists all cities, states, and zip codes.

c) Why are the results of the following two SQL statements the same?

```
SELECT letter_grade
  FROM grade_conversion

SELECT UNIQUE letter_grade
  FROM grade_conversion
```

d) Explain what happens, and why, when you execute the following SQL statement.

```
SELECT DISTINCT course_no
  FROM class
```

e) Execute the following SQL statement. Then, in the Results window, right-click and choose the menu option Single Record View. Describe your observation.

```
SELECT *
  FROM student
```

▼ LAB 2.2 EXERCISE ANSWERS

a) Write a SELECT statement that lists the first and last names of all students.

ANSWER: The SELECT list contains the two columns that provide the first and last names of students; the FROM clause lists the STUDENT table where these columns are found. You can examine the rows by scrolling up and down. The rows are not returned in any particular order; you will learn about ordering the result set in Chapter 3, "The WHERE and ORDER BY Clauses."

```
SELECT first_name, last_name
  FROM student
FIRST_NAME                      LAST_NAME
------------------------------  ----------
George                          Eakheit
Leonard                         Millstein
...
```

```
Kathleen                Mastandora
Angela                  Torres
```

```
268 rows selected.
```

b) Write a SELECT statement that list all cities, states, and zip codes.

ANSWER: The SELECT list contains the three columns that provide the city, state, and zip code; the FROM clause contains the ZIPCODE table where these columns are found.

```
SELECT city, state, zip
   FROM zipcode
CITY                       ST ZIP
-------------------------- --------
Santurce                   PR 00914
North Adams                MA 01247
...
New York                   NY 10005
New York                   NY 10035
```

```
227 rows selected.
```

c) Why are the results of the following two SQL statements the same?

```
SELECT letter_grade
   FROM grade_conversion
```

```
SELECT UNIQUE letter_grade
   FROM grade_conversion
```

ANSWER: The result sets are the same because the data values in the LETTER_GRADE column of the GRADE_CONVERSION table are not repeated; the LETTER_GRADE column is the primary key of the table, so by definition its values are unique. The UNIQUE and DISTINCT keywords can be used interchangeably.

d) Explain what happens, and why, when you execute the following SQL statement.

```
SELECT DISTINCT course_no
   FROM class
```

ANSWER: Oracle returns an error because a table named CLASS does not exist.

The error message indicates the error in the query. In SQL Developer, you see a message box similar to Figure 2.27, which indicates the line and column number where the error occurs.

You can review your cursor's exact position by referring to the bottom of the screen (see Figure 2.28).

SQL is an exacting language. As you learn to write SQL, you will inevitably make mistakes. It is important to pay attention to the error messages the database returns to you so you can learn from and correct your mistakes. For example, the Oracle error message in Figure 2.27 informs you that you referenced a nonexistent table or view within the database schema. (Views are discussed in Chapter 13. You can correct your SQL statement and execute it again.

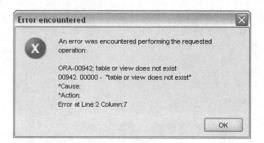

FIGURE 2.27
Error message in SQL Developer

FIGURE 2.28
Line and column indicator

e) Execute the following SQL statement. Then, in the Results window, right-click and choose the menu option Single Record View. Describe your observation.

```
SELECT *
  FROM student
```

ANSWER: The Single Record View window allows you to examine one record at a time and scroll through the records using the arrows at the top (see Figure 2.29). If there are many columns in a table, you can expand the window by dragging its sides.

FIGURE 2.29
Single Record View window

As you can see, there are many menu options available when you right-click the Results window. The Auto-fit menu options (see Figure 2.30) are very useful for formatting the Results window according to the length of the data cells or the length of the column name.

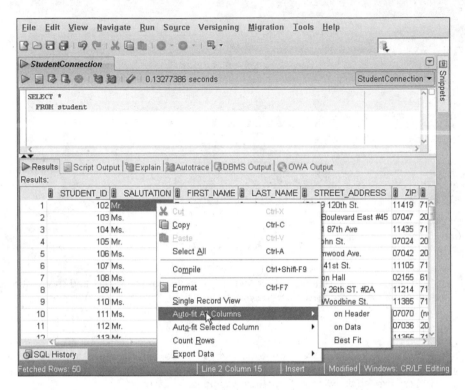

FIGURE 2.30
The Results window menu options

The Count Rows menu option returns the number of rows in the table. Not all the rows may be displayed at a given time in SQL Developer, as indicated in the Fetched Rows message on the status bar (see Figure 2.31). SQL Developer fetches additional rows, as needed, when you scroll down.

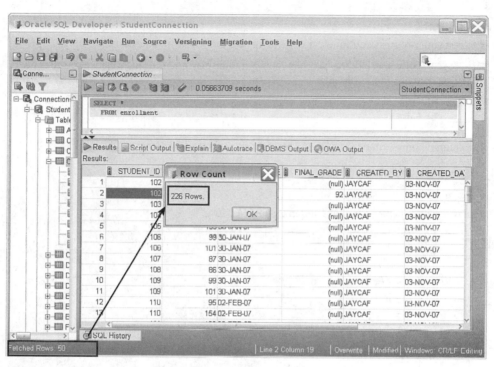

FIGURE 2.31
Row Count and Fetched Rows comparison

Lab 2.2 Quiz

In order to test your progress, you should be able to answer the following questions.

1) The SELECT clause specifies the columns you want to display, and the FROM clause specifies the table that contains these columns.

_____ a) True
_____ b) False

2) The column names listed in the SELECT list must be separated by commas.

_____ a) True
_____ b) False

3) The asterisk can be used as a wildcard in the FROM clause.

_____ a) True
_____ b) False

4) The following statement contains an error:

```
SELECT courseno
  FROM course
```

_____ a) True
_____ b) False

5) The Cancel icon stops a long-running SQL statement.

_____ a) True
_____ b) False

6) The Ctrl-Quote keystroke allows you to toggle the case of text entered in the SQL Worksheet.

_____ a) True
_____ b) False

7) Syntax highlighting in SQL Developer helps you distinguish between Oracle keywords and table/column names.

_____ a) True
_____ b) False

8) All SQL commands must be entered in uppercase only.

_____ a) True
_____ b) False

9) When you click on the Execute Statement icon, the output always displays in the Results tab.

_____ a) True
_____ b) False

ANSWERS APPEAR IN APPENDIX A.

LAB 2.3

An Introduction to SQL*Plus

LAB OBJECTIVES

After this lab, you will be able to:

▶ Understand the Essentials of SQL*Plus
▶ Execute Commands in SQL*Plus
▶ Name the Major Differences between SQL Developer and SQL*Plus

All Oracle databases include an installation of SQL*Plus by default. SQL*Plus is an Oracle software tool that allows you to execute SQL statements and SQL*Plus commands. It has been around since Oracle's early beginnings, and this command-line interface is available with every Oracle version and operating system. You can clearly see the age of SQL*Plus in its outdated interface, but this tool still serves many useful purposes.

Why Learn About SQL*Plus?

You might wonder what is the rationale of learning to use the command-line SQL*Plus when SQL Developer's graphical user interface is so much more intuitive. All the SQL statements and many SQL*Plus-specific commands work the same way in SQL Developer. Unquestionably, SQL*Plus seems quite arcane compared to SQL Developer, but knowing this old-style tool may come in handy when you're working with Oracle versions that do not support SQL Developer (such as versions prior to 9.2.0.1).

Furthermore, SQL*Plus is very suitable for executing scripts from the operating system prompt. A script is a saved file that contains one or more statements that allows you to rerun a command without retyping. This is useful when you need to rerun the same statements. You will learn about this in Chapter 14.

Starting SQL*Plus

If SQL*Plus program is installed on your Windows machine, you can access it by choosing Programs, Oracle, Application Development, SQL*Plus. This launches the program and displays the Log On dialog. Enter student as the username and learn as the password (both in lowercase) and press the Enter key. The password does not display onscreen.

Figure 2.32 illustrates a successful login with the correct username and password. Effectively, you have established a connection with the Oracle database as the user STUDENT. The client and the server can now communicate with each other.

The screen shows the version of SQL*Plus and the Oracle database. The SQL> command prompt indicates that SQL*Plus is ready to accept your commands, and you can begin to type. This is the default prompt for SQL*Plus.

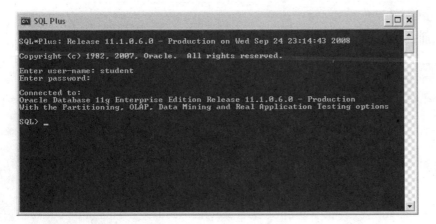

FIGURE 2.32
The SQL*Plus prompt

You can also invoke SQL*Plus by typing sqlplus at your operating system's command prompt and entering the username and password when prompted to do so. Or you can include the login username and password directly on the operating system prompt, as shown in Figure 2.33.

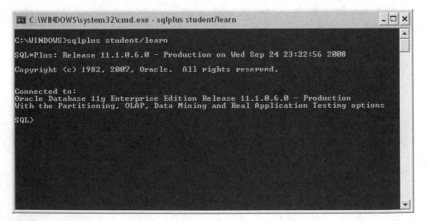

FIGURE 2.33
Invoking SQL*Plus from the Windows operating system command prompt

You can also invoke SQL*Plus without logging in to the database by using the NOLOG option (see Figure 2.34). To connect to the database, you use the CONNECT command. The DISCON-NECT (or DISC) command disconnects the session but does not exit SQL*Plus. Issuing a CONNECT command disconnects you from any previously connected session.

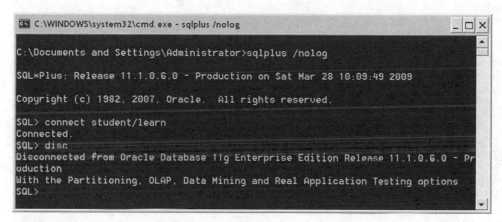

FIGURE 2.34
The NOLOG option and the CONNECT and DISCONNECT commands

Exiting SQL*Plus

To log out of SQL*Plus, either type EXIT or QUIT and press Enter. Alternatively, you can simply use your mouse to close the window. In the Windows operating system, you can also press Ctrl+C or Ctrl+Z, and in UNIX you can use Ctl+D.

Exiting ends the session, and the STUDENT user is no longer connected to the database. However, there may be other client machines connected to the Oracle database; the server software continues to run, regardless of whether a client is connected to it.

The Remote Database and SQL*Plus

Often, a database resides on a machine other than your local client machine, or you have a choice of accessing different databases. In these cases, you need to supply a *connect identifier*, which directs SQL*Plus to the appropriate database.

Furthermore, you need to have Oracle's connectivity software, called SQL Net, installed. Typically when you perform a SQL*Plus installation, the SQL Net software is automatically installed for you. This is different from SQL Developer, which works with both a JDBC connection and SQL Net.

To use SQL*Plus to connect to a remote database called ITCHY, you enter the username, followed by the @ symbol followed by the connect identifier. Figure 2.35 shows such a logon example.

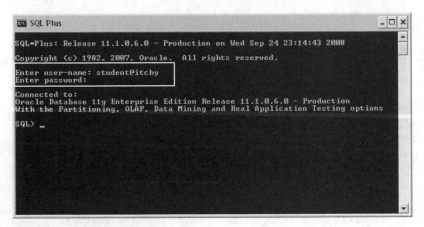

FIGURE 2.35
Using a connect identifier in SQL*Plus

The simplified syntax for the logon is as follows. The first syntax line prompts you for the password.

```
username@connect_identifier
username/password@connect_identifier
```

The connect identifier matches either an entry in a file called TNSNAMES.ORA or follows the Easy Connect syntax.

USING A TNSNAMES ENTRY

Essentially, the TNSNAMES.ORA file is a file that contains a list of databases with their respective technical connection information. It lists the database's IP address (or the machine name) and database instance name. Your database administrator can help you with the configuration and setup of this file if you have a remote database setup.

Following is an excerpt of a TNSNAMES.ORA file. The entries in your file will obviously vary. If you supply the host string ITCHY at login, SQL*Plus looks up the ITCHY entry in the TNSNAMES.ORA file. The HOST entry shows the machine name or IP address. The service name, or SID, entry identifies the name of the Oracle instance; here the instance is called ORCL. When you install Oracle with the default options, you are asked to supply an SID (system identifier). A common default name is ORCL.

The terms *SID* and *service name* are often used interchangeably, but they can be different, particularly in environments running Oracle RAC (Real Application Cluster) for fault-tolerant replication of data.

```
ITCHY =
  (DESCRIPTION =
    (ADDRESS_LIST =
      (ADDRESS =
        (PROTOCOL = TCP)
        (HOST =ibmt41)
        (PORT = 1521)
      )
    )
    (CONNECT_DATA =
      (SERVICE_NAME = ORCL)
    )
  )
SCRATCHY =
  (DESCRIPTION =
    (ADDRESS_LIST =
      (ADDRESS =
        (PROTOCOL = TCP)
        (HOST = 169.254.147.245)
        (PORT = 1521)
      )
    )
    (CONNECT_DATA =
      (SID = ORCL)
    )
  )
```

USING EASY CONNECT SYNTAX

The Easy Connect feature allows you to make a connection without the ITCHY entry being present in the TNSNAMES.ORA file. For example, you can connect to this database by supplying all the connection information.

```
student/learn@ibmt41:1521/ORCL
```

Or you can use the following.

```
student/learn@ibmt41/ORCL
```

This syntax shows the machine name called ibmt41 followed by the port number (the default port of the Oracle database is typically 1521), followed by the SID ORCL. Figure 2.36 shows how this connection is established in SQL*Plus.

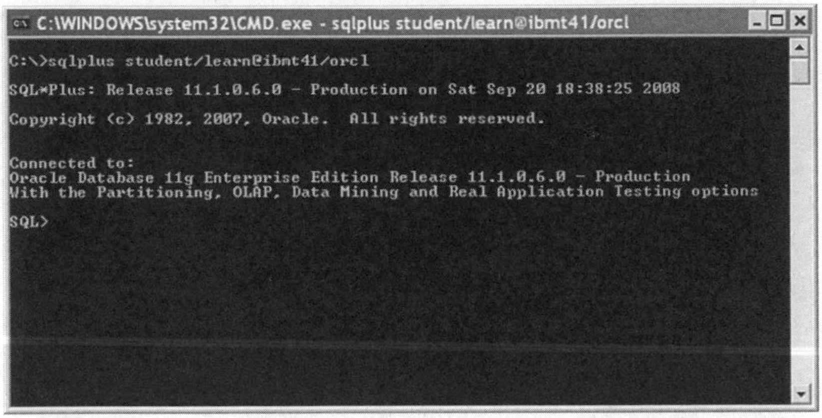

FIGURE 2.36
Connection to SQL*Plus using the Easy Connect syntax

The syntax for the connect identifier using Easy Connect follows.

```
Host[:Port]/service_name
```

The host is the machine or IP address of the database server computer. The port specifies the listening port of the database server; if it is not specified, it defaults to 1521. The service name is the name of the database instance you want to connect to on this database server.

Generally, you create a TNSNAMES entry when you use the same connection frequently; it's far quicker to enter than a long Easy Connect string. Your organization may even have a dedicated Oracle Names Server that manages the connectivity of many servers without the need to maintain a TNSNAMES entry on client machines.

Logon Problems

Although this book cannot possibly list all the errors and solutions to all logon problems, let's look at are two very common Oracle error messages you may encounter.

TNS ERROR

A TNS error is usually related to the connectivity between the server and the client, using the Oracle Net client software. The following message is displayed if the connect identifier could not be resolved. This may be due to an invalid hostname or service name. You need to check the values and retry.

```
ORA-12154: TNS: could not resolve the connect identifier specified
```

INCORRECT USERNAME OR PASSWORD

Another error occurs if you entered the wrong username or password when the Oracle server attempted to authenticate you as a valid user. You need to double-check the spelling of your username, which is student, and your password, which is learn (both in lowercase). Starting with Oracle 11g, the password is case-sensitive by default. (If you cannot log on with this ID and password, check the readme file regarding the installation of the STUDENT schema.)

```
ORA-01017: invalid username/password; logon denied
```

If you are connecting to a remote Oracle database, be sure to enter the Oracle Net connection string supplied to you by your Oracle database administrator and recorded in your TNSNAMES.ORA file.

If you want to test whether the TNSNAMES entry is resolved correctly, you can ping the database with the TNSPING command from the operating system prompt. Figure 2.37 shows the execution and result of the command to determine whether the TNSNAMES entry ITCHY is valid and whether the server's listener program is running. From the output, you can see the file location of the TNSNAMES.ORA that was used to resolve the ITCHY name. Furthermore, you can see the host or machine name value and the service or instance name. The OK message indicates that the database's listener process is ready to accept your connection request.

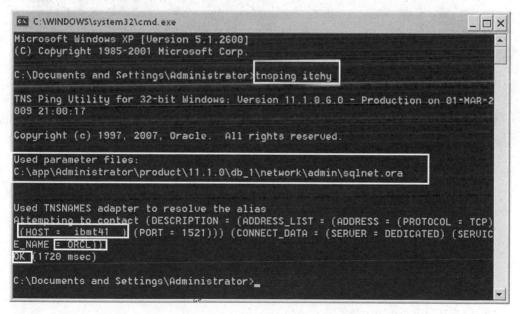

FIGURE 2.37
TNSPING command result

Executing SQL Commands Using SQL*Plus

SQL*Plus requires the use of a semicolon (;) at the end of each SQL statement to execute the statement. Alternatively, the forward slash (/) can be used on a separate line to accomplish the same thing. In the following statement, we want to show only the DESCRIPTION column of the COURSE table.

```
SQL> SELECT description
  2    FROM course;
```

Another way to do the same thing is to use the following statement.

```
SQL> SELECT description
  2    FROM course
  3  /
```

Figure 2.38 shows the result of the execution of this query in SQL*Plus. You can scroll up and down to see the results.

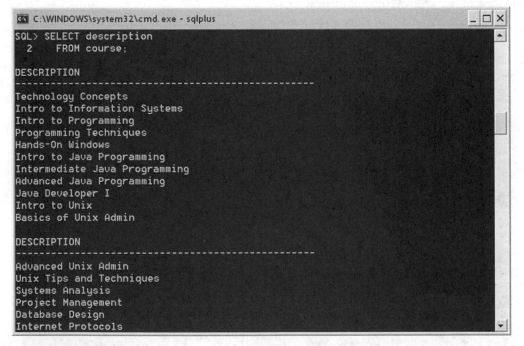

FIGURE 2.38
Executing a SELECT statement in SQL*Plus

If you want to edit the statement, you can type the EDIT or ED command at the SQL> prompt. This evokes the Notepad editor in Windows (see Figure 2.39) or the default editor currently set in SQL*Plus. When you use the EDIT command at the SQL prompt, SQL*Plus stays open in the background, and your text editor is in the foreground, automatically displaying the SQL statement in the buffer.

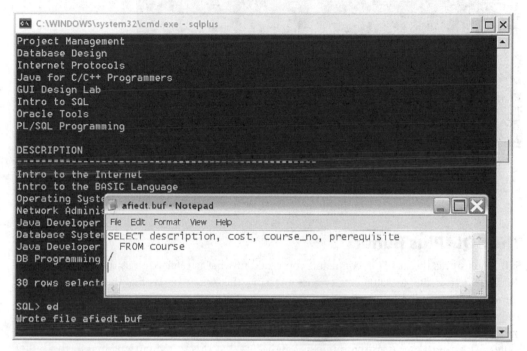

FIGURE 2.39
Using the Notepad editor to edit a SQL statement in SQL*Plus

For quick editing of statements, simply make your changes here, save the file, and exit Notepad, which brings you back to SQL*Plus. (In this example, additional columns were added to the query.)

When the changes are saved, you exit Notepad, and the revised SQL statement is placed in the buffer area of SQL*Plus. You can then execute the statement with the forward slash on a new line, as shown in Figure 2.40.

 When you invoke an editor, the SQL statement ends with a forward slash on a separate line at the end. SQL*Plus adds this character to the file so the file can be executed within SQL*Plus. Also, when you invoke the editor from SQL*Plus, you can't go back to the SQL*Plus screen until you close the editor.

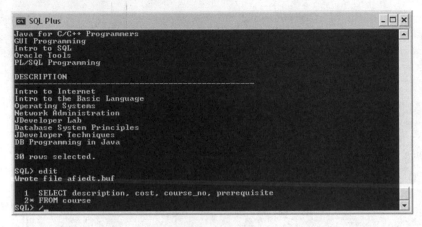

FIGURE 2.40
SQL statement that is about to be executed with the forward slash command

The SQL*Plus Buffer

SQL*Plus stores the last SQL command you typed in what is referred to as the *SQL*Plus buffer.* You can re-execute a statement by just pressing the / key or typing the SQL*Plus RUN command. The most recent statement stays in the buffer until you enter another SQL command. You can use the SQL*Plus LIST command, or simply the letter L, to list the contents of the buffer. The semicolon or the slash, either of which executes the statement, is not stored in the buffer. The asterisk next to the number 2 indicates that this is the current line in the buffer. (Aside from using Notepad or any other editor, you can also use SQL*Plus's arcane Line Editor commands; these commands are described in Appendix C, "SQL*Plus Command Reference.")

```
SQL>LIST
    1 SELECT description, cost, course_no, prerequisite
    2*  FROM course
```

 In the Windows operating system, you can use the up and down arrow keys to recall previous SQL and SQL*Plus statements.

Formatting SQL*Plus Results

The result set is difficult to read when data "wraps" itself onto the next line. The result may look similar to the screen shown in Figure 2.41. This wrapping often occurs when your SELECT statement contains multiple columns. To help you view the output more easily, SQL*Plus offers a number of formatting commands. Note that these commands are not SQL commands but commands specific only to SQL*Plus.

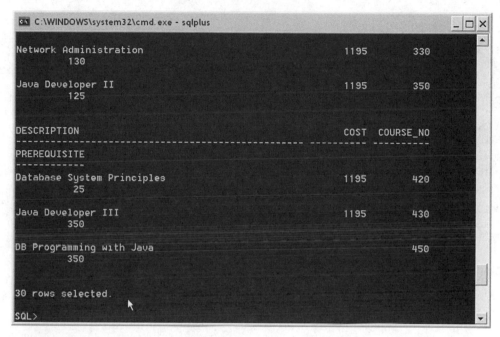

FIGURE 2.41
SQL*Plus output wrapped

FORMATTING COLUMN ATTRIBUTES

The SQL*Plus COLUMN command allows you to specify format attributes for a column.

The following statement formats the DESCRIPTION column to display a maximum of 30 characters. If the values in the columns do not fit into the space allotted, the data wraps within the column. The column headings are truncated to the specified length.

```
COL description FORMAT A30
```

When you re-execute the SQL statement, the result is more readable, as you see in the result set shown in Figure 2.42. The format for the column stays in place until you either re-specify the format for the column, specifically clear the format for the column, or exit SQL*Plus. To clear all the column formatting, execute the CLEAR COLUMNS command in SQL*Plus.

 The SQL*Plus commands such as the FORMAT command are not SQL commands and therefore do not require a semicolon or forward slash.

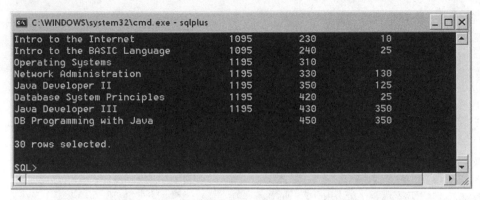

FIGURE 2.42
SQL*Plus output formatted

FORMATTING NUMBERS

If the column is a NUMBER data type column, you can change the format with a *format model* in the COLUMN command. For example, the 9 in the format model 999.99 represents the numeric digits, so the number 100 is displayed as 100.00. You can add dollar signs, leading zeros, angle brackets for negative numbers, and round values to format the display as you like.

```
COL cost FORMAT $9,999.99
        SELECT DISTINCT cost
          FROM course
               COST
          ----------
          $1,095.00
          $1,195.00
          $1,595.00


          4 rows selected.
```

One row in the COURSE table contains a null value in the COST column. As mentioned previously, DISTINCT recognizes one or more null values in a column as one distinct value when returning a result set.

If you do not allot sufficient room for numbers to fit in a column, SQL*Plus shows # symbols instead of the numbers.

```
COL cost FORMAT 999.99
            COST
          -------
          #######
          #######
          #######


          4 rows selected.
```

For more SQL*Plus COLUMN FORMAT commands, see Appendix C.

Displaying the Number of Rows Returned

SQL*Plus sometimes does not show the number of rows returned by a query but rather depends on the feedback settings for your SQL*Plus session. Typically, the feedback is set to six or more rows. In the previous example, the feedback was set to 1, which displays the feedback line even when there is only one row returned. You will find this setting useful if your result set returns less than the default six rows and if any of the rows return nulls, which display as blanks by default. Otherwise, you might think it is not a row or value. To display the exact number of rows returned until you exit SQL*Plus, enter the SET FEEDBACK SQL*Plus command.

```
SET FEEDBACK 1
```

To display your current settings, use the SHOW ALL command or simply SHOW FEEDBACK. If you want to retain certain SQL*Plus settings, you can create a login.sql file for your individual computer in a client/server setup. You can also create a glogin.sql file for all users if you want them all to have identical settings (see Appendix C, "SQL*Plus Command Reference.")

SQL*Plus Commands versus SQL Statements

A SQL*Plus command is specific to the SQL*Plus execution environment. Unlike a SQL statement, a SQL*Plus command does not require a semicolon or backslash in order to be executed. SQL*Plus commands are commonly used for formatting query and report results, setting environment variables and runtime options, describing table and object definitions, executing batch scripts, and performing database administration tasks.

SQL*Plus commands come in handy when you have to create repeatable scripts; you will learn more about some of the useful SQL*Plus commands in Chapter 14.

Saving and Running SQL Statements in SQL*Plus

You can save your SQL statements within SQL*Plus. Type the following statement.

```
SELECT *
  FROM course
```

Now edit the file in Notepad and select Save As to save it with the name C:\examples\myfile.sql. Exit Notepad and type and execute a new, different SQL statement.

```
SELECT state
  FROM zipcode
```

This new statement is now in the buffer; however, you can execute a different SQL statement, such as the one you saved in myfile.sql, with the START or @ command.

```
SQL>@c:\examples\myfile
```

The statement in the file runs, producing a result set. Because the file already contains a forward slash, the SQL statement is executed automatically. If you save myfile with an extension other than .sql, you must type the file name and extension. If you want to change myfile again, simply type the following. Notepad will open, with myfile.sql containing your SQL statement.

```
SQL>ED c:\examples\myfile
```

Discontinuation of the SQL*Plus for Windows GUI Version

So far, you have learned how to use the Windows command-line version of SQL*Plus. In prior Oracle versions, a SQL*Plus Windows GUI version for the Windows Desktop was available. The functionality of the Windows command-line version and the Windows GUI version was almost identical. Starting with Oracle 11g, Oracle no longer ships the Windows version of the product and replaced it with the SQL Developer software.

Differences Between SQL Developer and SQL*Plus

Throughout this book you will see both SQL*Plus and *SQL Developer* mentioned. For the most part, the basic functionality of the two products is identical with respect to the SQL language.

One of the most obvious differences is the visual display of the result set and the user interface. Furthermore, instead of typing and then executing commands, SQL Developer allows you to perform many operations with a few mouse clicks. Table 2.1 highlights a number of the notable differences.

While SQL Developer simplifies many tasks, it can also allow a novice user to perform some potentially damaging actions using the menus. A good understanding of the effects of the underlying SQL operations is essential for making SQL Developer a productive tool. As you learn more about the SQL language and get more experienced in SQL Developer, you will appreciate many of its advanced features.

TABLE 2.1   Key Differences Between SQL Developer and SQL*Plus

SQL DEVELOPER	SQL*PLUS
Graphical user interface.	Command-line interface
Editing in the SQL Worksheet text box.	Editing from the SQL> prompt via the command-line editor or an invoked editor.
SQL Developer automatically handles the formatting of columns to fit the width of the screen.	Columns may not fit the whole width of your screen. Use various SQL*Plus formatting commands to make them display on one line.
Allows connectivity to some non-Oracle databases.	Executes only against an Oracle database.
Works with Oracle versions 9.01 and above.	All Oracle versions are supported.

TABLE 2.1   Continued

SQL DEVELOPER	SQL*PLUS
Has an auto-completion syntax feature.	Requires knowledge of exact syntax and object names.
Many of the typical SQL actions can be performed through the GUI, without writing an explicit SQL statement.	Requires typing of the SQL command.
A null value is easily distinguishable as "(null)" in the Results tab.	There is no special display of null values unless you issue the SQL*Plus command SET NULL text.

▼ LAB 2.3 EXERCISES

a) After you have logged in to SQL*Plus with the user ID student and the password learn, what information does the SQL*Plus screen show you?

b) What do you learn when you type the command DESCRIBE instructor and press Enter?

c) Describe the result set you get when executing the following SQL statement. Format the result to make it more readable.

```
SELECT *
  FROM grade_type
```

d) Explain what happens, and why, when you execute the following SQL statement.

```
SELECT instructor_id, instructor_name
  FROM instructor
```

▼ LAB 2.3 EXERCISE ANSWERS

a) After you have logged in to SQL*Plus with the user ID student and the password learn, what information does the SQL*Plus screen show you?

ANSWER: The screen shows which version of SQL*Plus you are using, the current date and time, Oracle copyright information, and the version of the Oracle database software you are connected to. After this information is displayed, you see the SQL> command prompt. You can enter commands at this prompt.

b) What do you learn when you type the command DESCRIBE instructor and press Enter?

ANSWER: You can display the structure of your table with the SQL*Plus DESCRIBE command (see Figure 2.43). You can abbreviate the command as DESCR.

You can execute the same DESCRIBE command in SQL Developer, with the same result.

c) Describe the result set you get when executing the following SQL statement. Format the result to make it more readable.

```
SELECT *
  FROM grade_type
```

ANSWER: All columns and rows of the GRADE_TYPE table are returned in the result set. Your result may resemble the first listing of SQL output in Figure 2.44, displaying the wrapped columns. The second result shows the output nicely formatted after the SQL*Plus COLUMN commands are issued.

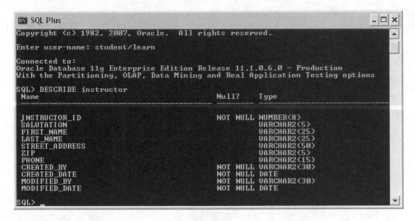

FIGURE 2.43
Executing the SQL*Plus DESCRIBE command

FIGURE 2.44
SQL*Plus output, both unformatted and formatted with SQL*Plus commands

d) Explain what happens, and why, when you execute the following SQL statement.

```
SELECT instructor_id, instructor_name
   FROM instructor
```

ANSWER: Oracle returns an error because the column INSTRUCTOR_NAME does not exist.

```
SELECT instructor_id, instructor_name
                        *
ERROR at line 1:
ORA-00904: "INSTRUCTOR_NAME": invalid identifier
```

If you use SQL*Plus, the asterisk in the error message indicates where the error occurs in the SQL statement.

The following is the correct SQL query.

```
SELECT instructor_id, last_name
   FROM instructor
```

Lab 2.3 Quiz

In order to test your progress, you should be able to answer the following questions.

1) A TNSNAMES entry is always required when you are using SQL*Plus to access an Oracle database.

_____ a) True
_____ b) False

2) SQL*Plus commands can be executed against non-Oracle databases.

_____ a) True
_____ b) False

3) SQL*Plus works with all versions of Oracle.

_____ a) True
_____ b) False

4) A SQL*Plus command must be ended with either a semicolon or a backslash.

_____ a) True
_____ b) False

ANSWERS APPEAR IN APPENDIX A.

▼ WORKSHOP

The projects in this section are meant to prompt you to utilize all the skills you have acquired throughout this chapter. The answers to these projects can be found at the companion Web site to this book, located at www.oraclesqlbyexample.com.

1) Use SQL Developer to retrieve all the STATE values from the ZIPCODE table, without repeating the values.

2) Recall one of the statements you executed in Lab 2.2, using the SQL History tab.

3) What happens if you try to log on to SQL*Plus with the uppercase version of the password learn?

4) Execute the following statements in SQL*Plus and record your observations.

```
SET NULL 'NULL'
SELECT DISTINCT cost
   FROM course
```

CHAPTER 3

The WHERE and ORDER BY Clauses

CHAPTER OBJECTIVES

In this chapter, you will learn about:

- ▶ The WHERE Clause: Comparison and Logical Operators
- ▶ The ORDER BY Clause

Now that you are familiar with the basic functionality of a SELECT statement and know your way around the execution environments, you are ready to delve into the power of the SQL language. The WHERE and ORDER BY clauses are two very commonly used clauses. The WHERE clause limits a result set, and the ORDER BY clause sorts the output. Performing the exercises in this chapter will help you master these fundamental SQL language elements.

LAB 3.1
The WHERE Clause

LAB OBJECTIVES

After this lab, you will be able to:

▶ Use Comparison and Logic Operators in a WHERE Clause
▶ Use NULL in a WHERE Clause

The *WHERE clause,* also called the *predicate,* provides the power to narrow down the scope of data retrieved. In fact, most SQL statements you write will probably contain a WHERE clause.

Comparison Operators

To filter a data set, you need to specify a WHERE clause condition, which results in true, false, or unknown. The condition consists of an *expression* that can be a column of any data type, a *string* or *text literal* (sometimes referred to as a *text constant* or *character literal*), a number, a function, a mathematical computation, or any combination of these. The comparison operators evaluate the expressions for the selection of the appropriate data.

Table 3.1 provides a list of the most common comparison operators. You will learn about additional operators, such as EXISTS, ANY, SOME, and ALL, in Chapter 8, "Subqueries," and the OVERLAPS operator in Chapter 5, "Date and Conversion Functions." All these comparison operators can be negated with the NOT logical operator.

TABLE 3.1 SQL Comparison Operators

COMPARISON OPERATOR	DEFINITION
=	Equal
!=, <>	Not equal
>, >=	Greater than, greater than or equal to
<, <=	Less than, less than or equal to
BETWEEN ... AND ...	Inclusive of two values
LIKE	Pattern matching with wildcard characters % and _
IN (...)	List of values
IS NULL	Test for null values

THE EQUALITY AND INEQUALITY OPERATORS

One of the most commonly used comparison operators is the *equality* operator, denoted by the = symbol. For example, if you are asked to provide the first name, last name, and phone number of a teacher with the last name Schorin, you write the following SQL statement.

```
SELECT first_name, last_name, phone
  FROM instructor
 WHERE last_name = 'Schorin'
FIRST_NAME LAST_NAME  PHONE
---------- ---------- ----------
Nina       Schorin    2125551212

1 row selected.
```

Here, the column LAST_NAME is the left side of the equation, and the text literal 'Schorin' is the right side. (Single quotation marks are used around the text literal 'Schorin'.) This statement retrieves only rows from the INSTRUCTOR table that satisfy this condition in the WHERE clause. In this case, only one row is retrieved.

When you review the data types of the INSTRUCTOR table, you see that the LAST_NAME column's data type is VARCHAR2. This means the data contained in this column is alphanumeric. When two values are compared to each other, they must be of the same data type; otherwise, Oracle returns an error. You will learn more about converting from one data type to another in Chapter 5.

SQL is case-insensitive when it comes to column names, table names, and keywords such as SELECT. (There are some exceptions with regard to column names and table names. For more information, see Chapter 12, "Create, Alter, and Drop Tables.") When you compare a text literal to a database column, the case of the data must match exactly. The syntax of the following statement is correct, but it does not yield any rows because the instructor's last name is obviously not in the correct case.

```
SELECT first_name, last_name, phone
  FROM instructor
 WHERE last_name = 'schorin'

no rows selected
```

Just as equality is useful, so is inequality.

```
SELECT first_name, last_name, phone
  FROM instructor
 WHERE last_name <> 'Schorin'
FIRST_NAME LAST_NAME  PHONE
---------- ---------- ----------
Fernand    Hanks      2125551212
Tom        Wojick     2125551212
```

```
...
Marilyn     Frantzen    2125551212
Irene       Willig      2125551212

9 rows selected.
```

In this example, all rows except the one with the last name 'Schorin' are retrieved. Inequality can also be expressed with the != notation.

THE GREATER THAN AND LESS THAN OPERATORS

The comparison operators >, <, >=, and <= can all be used to compare values in columns. In the following example, the >=, or *greater than or equal to,* operator is used to retrieve a list of course descriptions for which the course cost is greater than or equal to 1195.

```
SELECT description, cost
  FROM course
 WHERE cost >= 1195
DESCRIPTION                     COST
----------------------------    ----
Technology Concepts             1195
Intro to Information Systems    1195
...
Database System Principles      1195
Java Developer III              1195

26 rows selected.
```

In this example, the value 1195 is not enclosed in single quotation marks because it is a number literal.

THE BETWEEN OPERATOR

The BETWEEN operator tests for a range of values.

```
SELECT description, cost
  FROM course
 WHERE cost BETWEEN 1000 AND 1100
DESCRIPTION                       COST
--------------------------------  ----
Unix Tips and Techniques          1095
Intro to the Internet             1095
Intro to the BASIC Language       1095

3 rows selected.
```

BETWEEN is inclusive of both values defining the range; the result set includes courses that cost 1000 and 1100 and everything in between. In this example, the lower end of the range must be listed first.

BETWEEN is most useful for number and date comparisons, but it can also be used for comparing text strings in alphabetical order. Date comparisons are discussed in Chapter 5.

THE IN OPERATOR

The IN operator works with a *list of values,* separated by commas, contained within a set of parentheses. The following query looks for courses for which the cost is either 1095 or 1595.

```
SELECT description, cost
  FROM course
 WHERE cost IN (1095, 1595)
DESCRIPTION                                 COST
------------------------------------------- ----
Programming Techniques                      1595
Unix Tips and Techniques                    1095
Intro to the Internet                       1095
Intro to the BASIC Language                 1095

4 rows selected.
```

THE LIKE OPERATOR

A very useful comparison operator is LIKE, which performs pattern matching, using the percent (%) and underscore (_) characters as wildcards. The percent wildcard is used to denote multiple characters, while the underscore wildcard is used to denote a single character. The following query retrieves rows where the last name begins with the uppercase letter S and ends in anything else.

```
SELECT first_name, last_name, phone
  FROM instructor
 WHERE last_name LIKE 'S%'
FIRST_NAME LAST_NAME  PHONE
---------- ---------- ------------
Nina       Schorin    2125551212
Todd       Smythe     2125551212

2 rows selected.
```

The % character may be placed at the beginning, end, or anywhere within the literal text, but it must always be within the single quotation marks. This is also true of the underscore wildcard character, as in the following statement.

```
SELECT first_name, last_name
  FROM instructor
 WHERE last_name LIKE '_o%'
FIRST_NAME                       LAST_NAME
-------------------------------- ---------
Tom                              Wojick
Anita                            Morris
Charles                          Lowry

3 rows selected.
```

The WHERE clause returns only rows where the last name begins with any character but the second letter must be a lowercase o. The rest of the last name is irrelevant.

 The LIKE operator works well for simple pattern matching. For a more complex pattern, you might want to consider using Oracle's regular expression functionality, discussed in Chapter 16, "Regular Expressions and Hierarchical Queries."

THE NOT OPERATOR

All the previously mentioned operators can be negated with the NOT comparison operator (for example, NOT BETWEEN, NOT IN, NOT LIKE).

```
SELECT phone
  FROM instructor
 WHERE last_name NOT LIKE 'S%'
```

This query returns all the phone numbers of instructors with a last name that does not begin with the uppercase letter S. This SQL statement does not list LAST_NAME in the SELECT list. There is no rule about columns in the WHERE clause having to exist in the SELECT list.

THE IS NULL AND IS NOT NULL OPERATORS

Recall that NULL means an unknown value. The IS NULL and IS NOT NULL operators evaluate whether a data value is NULL or not. The following SQL statement returns courses that do not have a prerequisite.

```
SELECT description, prerequisite
  FROM course
 WHERE prerequisite IS NULL
DESCRIPTION                      PREREQUISITE
------------------------------   ------------
Technology Concepts
Intro to Information Systems
Java for C/C++ Programmers
Operating Systems

4 rows selected.
```

Null values represent the unknown; a null cannot be equal or unequal to any value or to another null. Therefore, you should always use the IS NULL or IS NOT NULL operator when testing for nulls. There are a few exceptions when nulls are treated differently and a null can be equal to another null. One such example is the use of DISTINCT (see Lab 2.2). You will learn about the exceptions in the treatment of nulls throughout this book.

Logical Operators

To harness the ultimate power of the WHERE clause, comparison operators can be combined with the help of the *logical operators* AND and OR. These logical operators are also referred to as *Boolean operators*. They group expressions, all within the same WHERE clause of a single SQL statement.

For example, the following SQL query combines two comparison operators with the help of the AND *Boolean* operator. The result shows rows where a course costs 1095 and the course description starts with the letter I.

```
SELECT description, cost
  FROM course
 WHERE cost = 1095
   AND description LIKE 'I%'
DESCRIPTION                               COST
----------------------------------------- ----
Intro to the Internet                     1095
Intro to the BASIC Language               1095

2 rows selected.
```

With just the = operator in the WHERE clause, the result set contains three rows. With the addition of the AND description LIKE 'I%', the result is further reduced to two rows.

PRECEDENCE OF LOGICAL OPERATORS

When AND and OR are used together in a WHERE clause, the AND operator always takes precedence over the OR operator, meaning that any AND conditions are evaluated first. If there are multiple operators of the same precedence, the left operator is executed before the right. You can manipulate the precedence in the WHERE clause with the use of parentheses. In the following SQL statement, the AND and OR logical operators are combined.

```
SELECT description, cost, prerequisite
  FROM course
 WHERE cost = 1195
   AND prerequisite = 20
   OR prerequisite = 25
DESCRIPTION                               COST PREREQUISITE
----------------------------------------- ---- ------------
Hands-On Windows                          1195           20
Systems Analysis                          1195           20
Project Management                        1195           20
GUI Design Lab                            1195           20
Intro to SQL                              1195           20
Intro to the BASIC Language               1095           25
Database System Principles                1195           25

7 rows selected.
```

The preceding SQL statement selects any record that has either a cost of 1195 and a prerequisite of 20 or just a prerequisite of 25, no matter what the cost. The sixth row, Intro to the BASIC Language, is selected because it satisfies the OR expression prerequisite = 25. The seventh row, Database System Principles, satisfies only one of the AND conditions, not both. However, the row is part of the result set because it satisfies the OR condition.

Here is the same SQL statement, but with parentheses to group the expressions in the WHERE clause.

```
SELECT description, cost, prerequisite
  FROM course
 WHERE cost = 1195
   AND (prerequisite = 20
        OR prerequisite = 25)
DESCRIPTION                            COST PREREQUISITE
------------------------------------   ---- ------------
Hands-On Windows                       1195           20
Systems Analysis                       1195           20
Project Management                     1195           20
GUI Design Lab                         1195           20
Intro to SQL                           1195           20
Database System Principles             1195           25

6 rows selected.
```

The first expression selects only courses where the cost is equal to 1195. If the prerequisite is either 25 or 20, then the second condition is also true. Both expressions need to be true for the row to be displayed. These are the basic rules of logical operators. If two conditions are combined with the AND operator, both conditions must be true; if two conditions are connected by the OR operator, only one of the conditions needs to be true for the record to be selected.

The result set returns six rows instead of seven. The order in which items in the WHERE clause are evaluated is changed by the use of parentheses and results in different output.

     To ensure that your SQL statements are clearly understood, it is always best to use parentheses.

NULLS AND LOGICAL OPERATORS

SQL uses *tri-value logic*; this means a condition can evaluate to true, false, or unknown. (This is in contrast to Boolean logic, where a condition must be either true or false.) A row is returned when the condition evaluates to true. The following query returns rows from the COURSE table, starting with the words "Intro to" as the description *and* a value equal or larger than 140 in the PREREQUISITE column.

```
SELECT description, prerequisite
  FROM course
 WHERE description LIKE 'Intro to%'
   AND prerequisite >= 140
DESCRIPTION                          PREREQUISITE
------------------------------------ ------------
Intro to Programming                          140
Intro to Unix                                 310

2 rows selected.
```

Rows with a null value in the PREREQUISITE column are not included because null is an unknown value. This null value in the column is not greater than or equal to 140. Therefore, the row Intro to Information Systems does not satisfy both conditions and is excluded from the result set. Following is the list of course descriptions with null values in the PREREQUISITE column. It shows the row Intro to Information Systems and the null value in the PREREQUISITE column.

```
SELECT description, prerequisite, cost
  FROM course
 WHERE prerequisite IS NULL
DESCRIPTION                      PREREQUISITE       COST
-------------------------------- ------------------ ----
Technology Concepts                                 1195
Intro to Information Systems                        1195
Java for C/C++ Programmers                          1195
Operating Systems                                   1195

4 rows selected.
```

The AND truth table in Table 3.2 illustrates the combination of two conditions with the AND operator. Only if *both* conditions are true is a row returned for output. In this example, with the prerequisite being null, the condition is unknown, and therefore the row is not included in the result. The comparison against a null value yields unknown unless you specifically test for it with the IS NULL or IS NOT operators.

TABLE 3.2   AND Truth Table

	TRUE	FALSE	UNKNOWN
TRUE	TRUE	FALSE	UNKNOWN
FALSE	FALSE	FALSE	FALSE
UNKNOWN	UNKNOWN	FALSE	UNKNOWN

For the OR condition, just one of the conditions needs to be true. Again, let's examine how nulls behave under this scenario, using the same query, but this time with the OR operator. The Intro to Information Systems course is now listed because it satisfies the 'Intro to%' condition only. In

addition, rows such as DB Programming with Java do not start with "Intro to" as the description
but satisfy the second condition, which is a prerequisite of greater than or equal to 140.

```
SELECT description, prerequisite
  FROM course
 WHERE description LIKE 'Intro to%'
    OR prerequisite >= 140
DESCRIPTION                          PREREQUISITE
------------------------------------ ------------
Intro to Information Systems
Intro to Programming                          140
Programming Techniques                        204
Intro to Java Programming                      80
Intro to Unix                                 310
Database Design                               420
Internet Protocols                            310
Intro to SQL                                   20
Oracle Tools                                  220
Intro to the Internet                          10
Intro to the BASIC Language                    25
Java Developer III                            350
DB Programming with Java                      350

13 rows selected
```

Table 3.3 shows the truth table for the OR operator; it highlights the fact that just one of the
conditions needs to be true for the row to be returned in the result set. It is irrelevant if the
second condition evaluates to false or unknown.

TABLE 3.3   OR Truth Table

	TRUE	FALSE	UNKNOWN
TRUE	TRUE	TRUE	TRUE
FALSE	TRUE	FALSE	UNKNOWN
UNKNOWN	TRUE	UNKNOWN	UNKNOWN

When you negate a condition with the NOT operator and the value you are comparing against
is a null value, it also results in a null (see Table 3.4). The following query demonstrates that
none of the null prerequisites are included in the result set.

TABLE 3.4   NOT Truth Table

	TRUE	FALSE	UNKNOWN
NOT	FALSE	TRUE	UNKNOWN

```
SELECT description, prerequisite
  FROM course
 WHERE NOT prerequisite >= 140
```

DESCRIPTION	PREREQUISITE
Intro to the Internet	10
Hands-On Windows	20
Systems Analysis	20
Project Management	20
GUI Design Lab	20
Intro to SQL	20
Intro to the BASIC Language	25
Database System Principles	25
Intro to Java Programming	80
PL/SQL Programming	80
Intermediate Java Programming	120
Advanced Java Programming	122
Java Developer I	122
Java Developer II	125
Basics of Unix Admin	130
Network Administration	130
Advanced Unix Admin	132
Unix Tips and Techniques	134

18 rows selected

▼ LAB 3.1 EXERCISES

a) Write a SELECT statement that lists the last names of students living in either zip code 10048, 11102, or 11209.

b) Write a SELECT statement that lists the first and last names of instructors with the letter i (either uppercase or lowercase) in their last name, living in zip code 10025.

c) Does the following statement contain an error? Explain.

```
SELECT last_name
  FROM instructor
 WHERE created_date = modified_by
```

d) What do you observe when you execute the following SQL statement?

```
SELECT course_no, cost
  FROM course
 WHERE cost BETWEEN 1500 AND 1000
```

e) Execute the following query and determine how many rows the query returns.

```
SELECT last_name, student_id
  FROM student
 WHERE ROWNUM <= 10
```

f) Write a SELECT statement that lists descriptions of courses for which there are prerequisites and that cost less than 1100.

g) Write a SELECT statement that lists the cost of courses without a known prerequisite; do not repeat the cost.

▼ LAB 3.1 EXERCISE ANSWERS

a) Write a SELECT statement that lists the last names of students living in either zip code 10048, 11102, or 11209.

ANSWER: The SELECT statement selects a single column and uses the IN comparison operator in the WHERE clause.

```
SELECT last_name
  FROM student
 WHERE zip IN ('10048', '11102', '11209')
LAST_NAME
---------------
Masser
Allende
Winnicki
Wilson
Williams
McLean
Lefkowitz

7 rows selected.
```

The statement can also be written using the equal operator (=), in combination with the logical operator OR, and yields the same result set.

```
SELECT last_name
  FROM student
 WHERE zip = '10048'
    OR zip = '11102'
    OR zip = '11209'
```

There are times when a SELECT statement can be written more than one way. The preceding statements are logically equivalent.

b) Write a SELECT statement that lists the first and last names of instructors with the letter i (either uppercase or lowercase) in their last name, living in zip code 10025.

ANSWER: The SELECT statement selects two columns and uses the LIKE, =, and AND and OR logical operators, combined with parentheses, in the WHERE clause.

```
SELECT first_name, last_name
  FROM instructor
 WHERE (last_name LIKE '%i%' OR last_name LIKE '%I%')
   AND zip = '10025'
```

FIRST_NAME	LAST_NAME
Tom	Wojick
Nina	Schorin

2 rows selected.

The LIKE operator must be used twice in this example because there is no way of knowing whether there is an uppercase or lowercase i anywhere in the last name. You must test for both conditions, which cannot be done using a single LIKE operator. If one of the OR conditions is true, the expression is true.

If you need to search for the % symbol within a column value, you can use a SQL function or an escape character. You'll learn more about this in Chapter 4, "Character, Number, and Miscellaneous Functions."

c) Does the following statement contain an error? Explain.

```
SELECT last_name
  FROM instructor
 WHERE created_date = modified_by
```

ANSWER: Yes. The two columns in the WHERE clause are not the same data type, and the Oracle database returns an error when this statement is executed.

You get an error similar to the following when you execute the statement.

```
SQL> SELECT last_name
  2    FROM instructor
  3    WHERE created_date = modified_by
  4  /
 WHERE created_date = modified_by
                      *
ERROR at line 3:
ORA-01858: a non numeric character was found where a numeric was
➥expected
```

There are times when the data types of columns do not agree, and you need to convert from one data type to another. You will learn about these circumstances in Chapter 5. (In this exercise example, data conversion is not fruitful because the data in these two columns is of a very different nature.)

d) What do you observe when you execute the following SQL statement?

```
SELECT course_no, cost
  FROM course
 WHERE cost BETWEEN 1500 AND 1000
no rows selected
```

ANSWER: The query returns no rows. Although there are courses that cost between 1000 and 1500, the BETWEEN clause requires the lower end of the range to be listed first. If the query is rewritten as follows, it returns rows.

```
SELECT course_no, cost
  FROM course
 WHERE cost BETWEEN 1000 AND 1500
```

BETWEEN AND TEXT LITERALS

As mentioned previously, BETWEEN is most often used for numbers and dates, which you will learn about in Chapter 5. You can apply the BETWEEN functions to text columns, as shown in the next example, which utilizes the BETWEEN operator with text literals W and Z. The query lists the student's ID and last name. Any students whose last name begins with the letter Z are not included, because the STUDENT table has no student with a last name of the single letter Z. If a student's last name were spelled "waldo," this student would not be included in the result, because the WHERE clause is looking only for last names that fall between the uppercase letters W and Z.

```
SELECT student_id, last_name
  FROM student
 WHERE last_name BETWEEN 'W' AND 'Z'
STUDENT_ID LAST_NAME
---------- ---------
       142 Waldman
...
       241 Yourish

11 rows selected.
```

If you are looking for "waldo", regardless of the case, use the OR operator to include both conditions.

```
SELECT student_id, last_name
  FROM student
 WHERE last_name BETWEEN 'W' AND 'Z'
    OR last_name BETWEEN 'w' AND 'z'
```

Here is another example of how you can use the BETWEEN and the >= and <= operators with text literals.

```
SELECT description
  FROM grade_type
 WHERE description BETWEEN 'Midterm' and 'Project'
```

This would be equivalent to the following.

```
SELECT description
  FROM grade_type
 WHERE description >= 'Midterm'
   AND description <= 'Project'
DESCRIPTION
----------------
Midterm
Participation
Project

3 rows selected.
```

e) Execute the following query and determine how many rows the query returns.

```
SELECT last_name, student_id
  FROM student
 WHERE ROWNUM <= 10
```

ANSWER: The query returns 10 rows. The WHERE clause uses the pseudocolumn ROWNUM, which restricts the result to the first 10 or fewer rows it finds, and there is no particular order. A pseudocolumn is not a real column that exists on a table; you can select the column, but you cannot manipulate its value.

```
LAST_NAME                    STUDENT_ID
------------------------     ----------
Kocka                            230
Jung                             232
Mulroy                           233
Brendler                         234
Carcia                           235
Tripp                            236
Frost                            237
Snow                             238
Scrittorale                      240
Yourish                          241
```

10 rows selected.

The next statement shows the value of the ROWNUM pseudocolumn in the SELECT list. The first row displays the ROWNUM value 1, the second the ROWNUM value 2, and so on. The ROWNUM pseudocolumn is useful if you want to limit the number of rows returned by a query. You will see additional examples of this and other pseudocolumns in subsequent chapters.

```
SELECT ROWNUM, last_name, student_id
  FROM student
 WHERE ROWNUM <= 10
    ROWNUM LAST_NAME                    STUDENT_ID
    ------ ------------------------     ----------
         1 Kocka                            230
         2 Jung                             232
         3 Mulroy                           233
         4 Brendler                         234
...
         9 Scrittorale                      240
        10 Yourish                          241
```

10 rows selected.

f) Write a SELECT statement that lists descriptions of courses for which there are prerequisites and that cost less than 1100.

ANSWER: The SELECT statement uses the IS NOT NULL and less than (<) comparison operators in the WHERE clause.

```
SELECT description, cost, prerequisite
  FROM course
 WHERE prerequisite IS NOT NULL
   AND cost < 1100
```

```
DESCRIPTION                                 COST PREREQUISITE
------------------------------------------- ---- ------------
Intro to the Internet                       1095           10
Intro to the BASIC Language                 1095           25
Unix Tips and Techniques                    1095          134
```

3 rows selected.

Both conditions need to be true for the row to be returned. If one of the conditions is not met, the row simply is not selected for output.

g) Write a SELECT statement that lists the cost of courses without a known prerequisite; do not repeat the cost.

ANSWER: The SELECT statement selects a single column in combination with DISTINCT and uses the IS NULL comparison operator in the WHERE clause.

```
SELECT DISTINCT cost
  FROM course
 WHERE prerequisite IS NULL
      COST
----------
      1195
```

1 row selected.

Lab 3.1 Quiz

In order to test your progress, you should be able to answer the following questions.

1) Comparison operators always compare two values only.

  _____ a) True
  _____ b) False

2) The BETWEEN operator uses a list of values.

  _____ a) True
  _____ b) False

3) The following statement is incorrect.

```
SELECT first_name, last_name
  FROM student
 WHERE employer = NULL
```

  _____ a) True
  _____ b) False

4) The following statement is incorrect.

```
SELECT description
  FROM course
 WHERE cost NOT LIKE (1095, 1195)
```

  _____ a) True
  _____ b) False

5) The following statement is incorrect.

```
SELECT city
  FROM zipcode
 WHERE state != 'NY'
```

  _____ a) True
  _____ b) False

6) The following statement returns rows in the STUDENT table where the last name begins with the letters SM.

```
SELECT last_name, first_name
  FROM student
 WHERE last_name = 'SM%'
```

  _____ a) True
  _____ b) False

ANSWERS APPEAR IN APPENDIX A.

Lab 3.2
The ORDER BY Clause

LAB OBJECTIVES

After this lab, you will be able to:

▶ Custom Sort Query Results

▶ Use Column Aliases

▶ Understand SQL Error Messages

The SQL language's ORDER BY clause allows you to sort your query result in various ways. You learn how column aliases are useful for changing the display name of a column. As you write more SQL statements, you will inevitably make mistakes; this lab provides some suggestions to help you better understand Oracle's error messages.

Using the ORDER BY Clause

Recall from Chapter 1, "SQL and Data," that data is not stored in a table in any particular order. In all the examples used thus far, the result sets display data in the order in which they happen to be returned from the database. However, you might want to view data in a certain order, and you can use the ORDER BY clause to accomplish this by ordering the data any way you wish.

For example, the following statement retrieves a list of course numbers and descriptions for courses for which there is no prerequisite, in alphabetical order by their descriptions:

```
SELECT course_no, description
  FROM course
 WHERE prerequisite IS NULL
 ORDER BY description
COURSE_NO DESCRIPTION
--------- ---------------------------
       20 Intro to Information Systems
      146 Java for C/C++ Programmers
      310 Operating Systems
       10 Technology Concepts

4 rows selected.
```

By default, when ORDER BY is used, the result set is sorted in *ascending* order; or you can be explicit by adding the abbreviation ASC after the column. If descending order is desired, you use the abbreviation DESC after the column in the ORDER BY clause.

```
SELECT course_no, description
  FROM course
 WHERE prerequisite IS NULL
 ORDER BY description DESC
COURSE_NO DESCRIPTION
--------- ---------------------------
       10 Technology Concepts
      310 Operating Systems
      146 Java for C/C++ Programmers
       20 Intro to Information Systems

4 rows selected.
```

Instead of listing the name of the column to be ordered, you can list the sequence number of the column in the SELECT list. The next SQL statement returns the same result as the prior SQL statement but uses a different ORDER BY clause. The number 2 indicates the second column of the SELECT list.

```
SELECT course_no, description
  FROM course
 WHERE prerequisite IS NULL
 ORDER BY 2 DESC
```

A result set can be sorted by more than one column. The columns you want to sort by need only be included in the ORDER BY clause, separated by commas. The ORDER BY clause is always the last clause in a SQL statement.

DISTINCT AND ORDER BY

The ORDER BY clause often contains columns listed in the SELECT clause, but it is also possible to use ORDER BY on columns that are not selected. One exception is columns qualified using the DISTINCT keyword: If the SELECT list contains DISTINCT, the column(s) the keyword pertains to must also be listed in the ORDER BY clause.

The next example shows that the STUDENT_ID column is not a column listed in the DISTINCT SELECT list and therefore results in an Oracle error message.

```
SQL> SELECT DISTINCT first_name, last_name
  2    FROM student
  3   WHERE zip = '10025'
  4   ORDER BY student_id
  5  /
 ORDER BY student_id
         *
ERROR at line 4:
ORA-01791: not a SELECTed expression
```

NULLS FIRST AND NULLS LAST

The following statement orders the COST column by the default sort order. The row with a COST column value of NULL is the last row in the sort order.

```
SELECT DISTINCT cost
  FROM course
ORDER BY cost
      COST
----------
      1095
      1195
      1595


4 rows selected.
```

You can change the ordering of the nulls with the NULLS FIRST or NULLS LAST option in the ORDER BY clause, as shown in the next statement. Here, the requested order is to list the NULL value first, followed by the other values in the default ascending sort order.

```
SELECT DISTINCT cost
  FROM course
ORDER BY cost NULLS FIRST
      COST
----------

      1095
      1195
      1595


4 rows selected.
```

Sorting Data Using SQL Developer's GUI Functionality

Instead of using ORDER BY, you can order data by using SQL Developer. In the Results tab, double-click one of the columns in the column header to sort. The up/down arrow (see Figure 3.1) indicates whether the sort is descending or ascending.

FIGURE 3.1
Column sorted in descending order

Aside from writing SQL statements, SQL Developer contains rich functionality that allows you to retrieve, filter, and sort data without having to write a SQL statement. In Chapter 2, "SQL: The Basics," you learned about the SQL Developer Data tab, which allows you to retrieve data from a table without writing a SQL statement. You can use this tab to perform sort and filter functionality. You will see both a Filter and Sort box onscreen. When you click the Sort option, a sort dialog box similar to Figure 3.2 appears. Here, you can choose multiple sort columns along with a variety of sort choices.

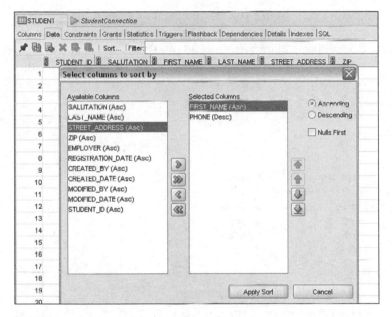

FIGURE 3.2
The Data tab sort options

The other option on the Data tab is the Filter box. Here you can enter WHERE clause conditions and then press the Enter key to retrieve only the chosen data. Figure 3.3 shows the Filter box with criteria that consists of the ZIP and SALUTATION columns of the STUDENT table.

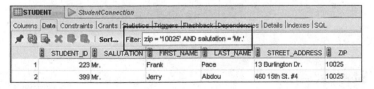

FIGURE 3.3
The Data tab's Filter criteria box

Although SQL Developer allows you to perform basic tasks with a few mouse clicks, the tool does not eliminate the need to understand the SQL language, nor does it perform advanced SQL functionality. You should consider SQL Developer a useful productivity tool to make you a more efficient and intelligent user of the SQL language. The focus of this book is on the Oracle SQL language, and SQL Developer can help you with this learning experience.

Column Alias

A column alias can be used in the SELECT list to give a column or an expression an alias; it can make the result much easier to read. In the next example, different forms of a column alias are used to take the place of the column name in the result set. An alias may contain one or more words or be spelled in exact case when enclosed in double quotation marks. The optional keyword AS can precede the alias name.

```
SELECT first_name first,
       first_name "First Name",
       first_name AS "First"
  FROM student
 WHERE zip = '10025'
FIRST             First Name        First
---------------   ---------------   ---------------
Nicole            Nicole            Nicole
Jerry             Jerry             Jerry
Frank             Frank             Frank

3 rows selected.
```

You can use the column alias to order by a specific column.

```
SELECT first_name first, first_name "First Name",
       first_name AS "First"
  FROM student
 WHERE zip = '10025'
 ORDER BY "First Name"
FIRST             First Name        First
---------------   ---------------   ---------------
Frank             Frank             Frank
Jerry             Jerry             Jerry
Nicole            Nicole            Nicole

3 rows selected.
```

Comments in SQL Statements

Placing comments or remarks in a SQL statement is very useful for documenting purpose, thoughts, and ideas. Comments are very handy when you've developed multiple statements that are saved into a file (called a *script*).

You must identify a comment as such; otherwise, you will receive an error when you run the command. There are two different types of comments: single-line comments denoted with double dashes and multiline comments spanning one or multiple lines. A multiline comment starts with the opening comment /* and ends with the closing comment */.

Following are examples of comments.

```
/* Multi-line comment
SELECT *
  FROM student;
*/

-- This is a single-line comment!
SELECT DISTINCT state
  FROM zipcode;

SELECT instructor_id, -- Comment within a SQL statement!
       zip /* Another comment example */
  FROM instructor;
```

Saving Your SQL Statements

You might want to save some statements for later use. Clicking the Save icon or choosing File, Save from the menu brings up the Save dialog box. By default, the file extension is .sql. After you save, the StudentConnection tab is renamed to the file name. For example, Figure 3.4 shows the file saved as example1.sql.

FIGURE 3.4
The file name of the saved file

You can retrieve the file by using the File, Open menu option. When you place the cursor in the statement you want to execute and click the Execute Statement button or press the F9 key, SQL Developer presents you with a Select Connection dialog box to choose the connection information.

If you are using SQL*Plus and you want to save and rerun some of your commands, see Chapter 14, "The Data Dictionary, Scripting, and Reporting."

Understanding Oracle Error Messages

As you begin to learn SQL, you will inevitably make mistakes when writing statements. Oracle returns an error number and error message to inform you of any mistake. Some error messages are easy to understand; others are not. While I cannot anticipate every possible error you may encounter, I point out common mistakes. Here are some general guidelines for dealing with Oracle errors.

READING THE ORACLE ERROR MESSAGE CAREFULLY

Oracle tells you on which line an error occurred. Figure 3.5 shows the dialog box you see after executing an erroneous SQL statement.

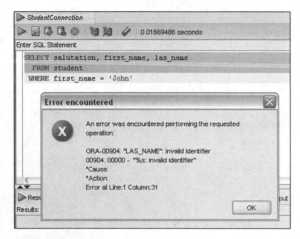

FIGURE 3.5
Error in a SQL statement

In this example, the error is very easy to spot, and the error message is self-explanatory. One of the column names is invalid; the ORA-00904 error says that it is an invalid identifier. Oracle points out the error by indicating the line and column position number; this indicates where within the line the error is located. In this case, it is the misspelled LAST_NAME column name.

RESOLVING ONE ERROR AT A TIME

Sometimes, you may have multiple errors in a single SQL statement. The Oracle *parser*, which checks the syntax of all statements, starts checking from the end of the entire statement.

The error message may leave you clueless about what could be wrong with the query. In fact, the statement in Figure 3.6 contains three errors, one in each line. Because the parser works its way backward, it complains about the first error on line 3. The position of the column name may even suggest that there is something wrong with the spelling of the FIRST_NAME column. But, in fact, it is spelled correctly; otherwise, you would see the ORA-00904 invalid identifier error listed, as in the previous example. The WHERE keyword is missing the final letter E; therefore, Oracle cannot interpret what you are attempting to do. The color coding in SQL Developer can help you spot the missing letter more easily because the word is not blue like the other keywords.

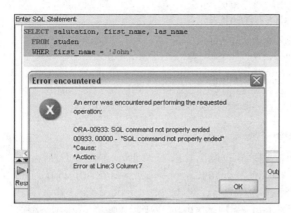

FIGURE 3.6
SQL keyword error

After you correct this error and re-execute, you see line 2 reported (see Figure 3.7), because, again, the parser works its way backward.

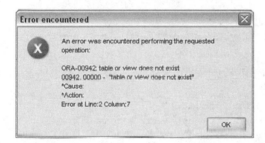

FIGURE 3.7
Table name error

Here, the table name is misspelled, and Oracle indicates that such a table does not exist.

The last error in the statement, found on line 1, is the misspelled LAST_NAME column name. The parser will report this error as the last error. You can avoid some misspelling errors when you use SQL Developer's syntax auto-completion feature, which allows you to simply pick from a list.

In any case, if you are unsure about the spelling of a column or table name, you can also review the Column tab to list the column names. You can also refer to Appendix D, "STUDENT Database Schema," for a diagram showing the table and column names.

DOUBLE-CHECKING THE SYNTAX OF YOUR STATEMENT

Simple typos, such as a stray period or comma, a missing space, or an unpaired quotation mark, can cause very strange and seemingly unrelated error messages that may have nothing to do with the problem. Therefore, it's important to carefully reread the statement or simply retype it. After you look at a statement for a long time, the error may not be apparent. Perhaps put it aside, take a break, and look at it with a fresh mind later, or ask someone for help in spotting the error.

LOOKING UP THE ORACLE ERROR NUMBER

You can look up the Oracle error number in the *Oracle Database Error Messages manual*. An error that starts with an ORA message number is a database-related error, whereas an error with a PLS prefixes indicates a PL/SQL language-specific error, and a TNS error number relates to a TNS connectivity problem between the database server and the client. When you found the error number in the manual, you will see the reason for the error and a recommended action on how to correct it. The recommended action may be general or very specific, again depending on what type of error occurred.

Often the most convenient way to look up error information is to review the online manual on the Oracle.com Web site. Also refer to Appendix G, "Navigating the Oracle Documentation," and Appendix H, "Resources." These appendixes provide tips on how to find the needed information.

In some operating systems, such as UNIX, Linux, and VMS, you can also use the Oracle program oerr to look up the error message from the operating system prompt. This does not work in the Windows environment. For example, to look up the ORA-00939 error, you type the following at the UNIX operating system prompt (indicated with the $ sign).

```
$ oerr ora 00939
00939, 00000, " too many arguments for function"
// *Cause: The function was referenced with too many arguments.
// *Action: Check the function syntax and specify only the
//          required number of arguments.
$
```

▼ LAB 3.2 EXERCISES

a) Write a SELECT statement that lists each city and zip code in New York or Connecticut. Sort the results in ascending order by zip code.

b) Write a SELECT statement that lists course descriptions and their prerequisite course numbers, sorted in ascending order by description. Do not list courses that do not have a prerequisite.

c) Show the salutation, first name, and last name of students with the last name Grant. Order the results by salutation in descending order and by first name in ascending order.

d) Execute the following query. What do you observe about the last row returned by the query?

```
SELECT student_id, last_name
  FROM student
 ORDER BY last_name
```

▼ **LAB 3.2 EXERCISE ANSWERS**

a) Write a SELECT statement that lists each city and zip code in New York or Connecticut. Sort the results in ascending order by zip code.

ANSWER: The SELECT statement selects two columns, uses the equal operator and OR logical operator to combine expressions in the WHERE clause, and uses ORDER BY and a single column to sort the results in ascending order.

```
SELECT city, zip
  FROM zipcode
 WHERE state = 'NY'
    OR state = 'CT'
 ORDER BY zip
```

CITY	ZIP
Ansonia	06401
Middlefield	06455
...	
Hicksville	11802
Endicott	13760

142 rows selected.

Alternatively, the WHERE clause can be written as follows.

```
WHERE state IN ('NY', 'CT')
```

b) Write a SELECT statement that lists course descriptions and their prerequisite course numbers, sorted in ascending order by description. Do not list courses that do not have a prerequisite.

ANSWER: The following query shows the use of the IS NOT NULL comparison operator in the WHERE clause. The result is sorted by the DESCRIPTION column in ascending order.

```
SELECT description, prerequisite
  FROM course
 WHERE prerequisite IS NOT NULL
 ORDER BY description
```

DESCRIPTION	PREREQUISITE
Advanced Java Programming	122
Advanced Unix Admin	132
...	
Systems Analysis	20
Unix Tips and Techniques	134

26 rows selected.

Alternatively, the ORDER BY clause can be written as follows.

```
ORDER BY 1
```

You can even use the column alias.

```
SELECT description "Descr", prerequisite
  FROM course
 WHERE prerequisite IS NOT NULL
 ORDER BY "Descr"
```

In most of the previous examples, the SELECT list is taking up one line only. Spreading it over several lines sometimes makes it easier to read, and this is perfectly acceptable formatting. Separating columns in the SELECT list on separate lines and indenting them makes for better readability of your statement. The following SELECT statement has multiple columns in the SELECT list.

```
SELECT description, prerequisite,
       cost, modified_date
  FROM course
 WHERE prerequisite IS NOT NULL
 ORDER BY description
DESCRIPTION                   PREREQUISITE COST MODIFIED_
----------------------------- ------------ ---- ---------
Advanced Java Programming              122 1195 05-APR-07
...
Unix Tips and Techniques               134 1095 05-APR-07

26 rows selected.
```

The result displays the column MODIFIED_DATE with an abbreviated column heading name. This is typical of the output in SQL*Plus. Because a fixed-width font is more readable than a screenshot, this book has adopted the SQL*Plus output format for many of the statements.

c) Show the salutation, first name, and last name of students with the last name Grant. Order the result by salutation in descending order and by first name in ascending order.

ANSWER: The ORDER BY clause contains two columns: SALUTATION and FIRST_NAME. The salutation is sorted first in descending order. Within each salutation, the first name is sorted in ascending order.

```
SELECT salutation, first_name, last_name
  FROM student
 WHERE last_name = 'Grant'
 ORDER BY salutation DESC, first_name ASC
SALUT FIRST_NAME        LAST_NAME
----- ----------------- ---------
Ms.   Eilene            Grant
Ms.   Verona            Grant
Mr.   Omaira            Grant
Mr.   Scott             Grant

4 rows selected.
```

Again, you can instead write the query with an ORDER BY clause.

```
ORDER BY 1 DESC, 2 ASC
```

Or you can use the default order for the second column, which is ASC and can be omitted.

```
ORDER BY 1 DESC, 2
```

If you give your column a column alias, you can also use the column alias in the ORDER BY clause.

```
SELECT salutation "Sal", first_name "First Name",
       last_name "Last Name"
  FROM student
 WHERE last_name = 'Grant'
 ORDER BY "Sal" DESC, "First Name" ASC
```

```
Sal     First Name        Last Name
-----   ----------------  ---------
Ms.     Eilene            Grant
Ms.     Verona            Grant
Mr.     Omaira            Grant
Mr.     Scott             Grant

4 rows selected.
```

d) Execute the following query. What do you observe about the last row returned by the query?

```
SELECT student_id, last_name
  FROM student
 ORDER BY last_name
```

ANSWER: The student with the STUDENT_ID of 206 has the last name entered in lowercase. When ordering the result set, the lowercase letters are listed after the uppercase letters.

```
STUDENT_ID LAST_NAME
---------- ----------
       119 Abdou
       399 Abdou
...
       184 Zuckerberg
       206 annunziato

268 rows selected.
```

Lab 3.2 Quiz

In order to test your progress, you should be able to answer the following questions.

1) The following is the correct order of all clauses in this SELECT statement.

```
SELECT ...
  FROM ...
ORDER BY ...
WHERE ...
```

   _____ a) True
   _____ b) False

2) You must explicitly indicate whether an ORDER BY is ascending.

   _____ a) True
   _____ b) False

3) The following statement is correct.

```
SELECT *
  FROM instructor
ORDER BY phone
```

   _____ a) True
   _____ b) False

4) The following statement is incorrect.

```
SELECT description "Description",
       prerequisite AS prereqs,
       course_no "Course#"
  FROM course
ORDER BY 3, 2
```

   _____ a) True
   _____ b) False

5) You can order by a column you have not selected.

   _____ a) True
   _____ b) False

ANSWERS APPEAR IN APPENDIX A.

▼ WORKSHOP

The projects in this section are meant to prompt you to utilize all the skills you have acquired throughout this chapter. The answers to these projects can be found at the companion Web site to this book, located at www.oraclesqlbyexample.com.

1) Create a SQL statement that retrieves data from the COURSE table for courses that cost 1195 and whose descriptions start with Intro, sorted by their prerequisites.

2) Create another SQL statement that retrieves data from the STUDENT table for students whose last names begin with A, B, or C and who work for Competrol Real Estate, sorted by their last names.

3) Write a SQL statement that retrieves all the descriptions from the GRADE_TYPE table, for rows that were modified by the user MCAFFREY.

4) Save all three SQL statements in a file called Workshop_Ch3.sql.

CHAPTER 4

Character, Number, and Miscellaneous Functions

CHAPTER OBJECTIVES

In this chapter, you will learn about:

▶ Character Functions
▶ Number Functions
▶ Miscellaneous Single-Row Functions

Functions are a very useful and powerful part of the SQL language. They can transform data in a way that is different from the way it is stored in a database. A function is a type of formula whose result is one of two things: either a *transformation,* such as a change in the name of a student to uppercase letters, or *information,* such as the length of a word in a column. Most functions share similar characteristics, including a name, and typically at least one input parameter, also called an *argument,* inside a pair of matching parentheses.

```
function_name(input_parameter)
```

Each function in this chapter and the next chapter is performed on a single row. This chapter discusses the character, number, and miscellaneous functions. Chapter 5, "Date and Conversion Functions," reviews the date-related functions together with data type conversion functions. Single-row functions are in contrast to aggregate functions, which are performed against multiple rows. You will learn about aggregate functions in Chapter 6, "Aggregate Functions, GROUP BY, and HAVING Clauses."

Data Types

Each value in Oracle has a data type associated with it. A data type determines the value's attributes and acceptable values. For example, you cannot enter a text value into a NUMBER data type column or enter an invalid date, such as 32-DEC-2008, into a DATE data type column. In most SQL operations, you use the NUMBER, VARCHAR2, and DATE data types. These are the commonly used data types where the vast majority of data is stored. This chapter concentrates on functions related to character and numeric data.

Reading Syntax Diagrams

In this chapter and the following chapters, you will learn about many essential SQL functions and commands. The syntax of the individual commands or functions is listed together with many examples of usage. Table 4.1 lists the symbols that describe the syntax usage.

TABLE 4.1   Syntax Symbols

SYMBOL	USAGE
[ ]	Square brackets enclose syntax options.
{ }	Braces enclose items of which only one is required.
|	A vertical bar denotes options.
…	Three dots indicate that the preceding expression can be repeated.
Delimiters	Delimiters other than brackets, braces, bars, or the three dots must be entered exactly as shown in the syntax. Examples of such delimiters are commas, parentheses, and so on.
CAPS	Words in all capital letters indicate the Oracle keywords that identify the individual elements of the SQL command or the name of the SQL function. The case of the keyword or command does not matter but for readability is in uppercase letters.
UNDERLINE	Default values are underlined.

LAB 4.1
Character Functions

LAB OBJECTIVES

After this lab, you will be able to:

▶ Use a Character Function in a SQL Statement

▶ Concatenate Strings

All character functions require alphanumeric input parameters. The input can be a *text literal* or *character literal,* sometimes referred to as a *string,* or *text, constant,* or a column of data type VARCHAR2, CHAR, or CLOB. Text literals are always surrounded by single quotation marks. This lab discusses the most frequently used character functions.

The LOWER Function

The LOWER function transforms data into lowercase. The following query shows how both a column and a text constant serve as individual parameters for the LOWER function.

```
SELECT state, LOWER(state), LOWER('State')
  FROM zipcode
ST LO LOWER
-- -- -----
PR pr state
MA ma state
...
NY ny state
NY ny state

227 rows selected.
```

The first column in the SELECT list displays the STATE column in the ZIPCODE table, without any transformation. The second column uses the LOWER function to display the values of the STATE column in lowercase letters. The third column of the SELECT list transforms the text constant 'State' into lowercase letters. Text constants used in a SELECT statement are repeated for every row of resulting output.

The UPPER and INITCAP Functions

The UPPER function is the exact opposite of the LOWER function: It transforms data into uppercase. The INITCAP function capitalizes the first letter of a word and lowercases the rest of the word.

```
SELECT UPPER(city) as "Upper Case City",   state,
       INITCAP(state)
  FROM zipcode
 WHERE zip = '10035'
Upper Case City          ST IN
------------------------ -- --
NEW YORK                 NY Ny

1 row selected.
```

The syntax of the UPPER, LOWER, and INITCAP function is listed here.

```
UPPER(char)
LOWER(char)
INITCAP(char)
```

The LPAD and RPAD Functions

The LPAD and RPAD functions also transform data: They *left pad* and *right pad* strings, respectively. When you pad a string, you add to it. These functions can add characters, symbols, or even spaces to your result set. Unlike the LOWER, UPPER, or INITCAP functions, these functions take more than one parameter as their input.

This SELECT statement displays cities right padded with asterisks and states left padded with dashes.

```
SELECT RPAD(city, 20, '*') "City Name",
       LPAD(state, 10, '-') "State Name"
  FROM zipcode
City Name            State Name
-------------------- ----------
Santurce***********  -------PR
North Adams********* -------MA
...
New York***********  -------NY
New York***********  -------NY

227 rows selected.
```

The CITY column is right padded with the asterisk (*) character, up to a length of 20 characters. The STATE column is left padded with (-), up to a total length of 10 characters. Both the LPAD and RPAD functions use three parameters, separated by commas. The first input parameter accepts either a text literal or a column of data type VARCHAR2, CHAR, or CLOB. The second argument specifies the total length to which the string should be padded. The third optional argument indicates the character(s) the string should be padded with. If this parameter is not specified, the string is padded with spaces by default.

The syntax for the LPAD and RPAD functions is as follows.

```
LPAD(char1, n [, char2])
RPAD(char1, n [, char2])
```

Shown as *char1*, is the string to perform the function on, *n* represents the length the string should be padded to, and *char2* is the optional parameter (denoted by the brackets) used to specify which character(s) to pad the string with. The next SELECT statement shows an example of the LPAD function with the third optional argument missing, thus left padding the column with spaces.

```
SELECT LPAD(city, 20) AS "City Name"
   FROM zipcode
City Name
--------------------
           Santurce
        North Adams
   ...
           New York
           New York

227 rows selected.
```

The DUAL Table

DUAL is a table unique to Oracle. It contains a single row and a single column called DUMMY (see Figure 4.1) and holds no significant data of its own. It can be used in conjunction with functions to select values that do not exist in tables, such as text literals or today's date.

A single row is always returned in the result set. Some of the subsequent SQL examples are not concerned with specific rows but instead use literals to demonstrate the purpose of a function.

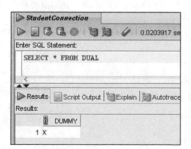

FIGURE 4.1
Selecting from the DUAL table

You might wonder why the DUAL table does not appear in the list of tables below StudentConnection. This table does not belong to the STUDENT schema. It belongs to the user SYS, which is the owner of all Oracle system tables. This table, like many other Oracle system tables, is accessible to all the users via a public synonym. We will further discuss synonyms and these special SYS tables in Chapter 15, "Security."

If you want to see more about the DUAL table's definition, right-click the table and choose the Popup Describe option or in SQL*Plus, use the DESCRIBE command to display the structure of the table.

The LTRIM, RTRIM, and TRIM Functions

LTRIM and RTRIM are the opposite of LPAD and RPAD because they *trim,* or remove, unwanted characters, symbols, or spaces in strings. In this example, you see the use of the DUAL table to trim the zero (0) from the left, the right, and both sides. If both the left and right sides of the string are trimmed, you need to nest the function. The result of one function provides the input for the other function.

```
SELECT LTRIM('0001234500', '0') left,
       RTRIM('0001234500', '0') right,
       LTRIM(RTRIM('0001234500', '0'), '0') both
  FROM dual
LEFT     RIGHT     BOTH
-------- --------- -----
1234500  00012345  12345

1 row selected.
```

Here is the syntax for the LTRIM and RTRIM functions. The optional parameter *char2* is used to specify which character(s) to trim from the string. If *char2* is not specified, the string is trimmed of spaces.

```
LTRIM(char1 [, char2])
RTRIM(char1 [, char2])
```

The TRIM function removes leading characters, trailing characters, or both, effectively doing the job of LTRIM and RTRIM in one function. If you want the function to act like LTRIM, specify LEADING as the first parameter; for RTRIM, use the TRAILING option; for both, either specify the BOTH keyword or omit it altogether.

The syntax for TRIM is as follows. The parameter named *char1* indicates the *single* character to be removed; char2 is the string to be trimmed. If you don't specify *char1*, blank spaces are assumed.

```
TRIM([LEADING|TRAILING|BOTH] char1 FROM char2)
```

The next example shows the use of LEADING, TRAILING, and BOTH (if neither LEADING nor TRAILING is specified); the result is identical to the result of the previous query.

```
SELECT TRIM(LEADING '0' FROM '0001234500') leading,
       TRIM(TRAILING '0' FROM '0001234500') trailing,
       TRIM('0' FROM '0001234500') both
  FROM dual
LEADING TRAILING BOTH
------- -------- -----
1234500 00012345 12345

1 row selected.
```

To trim blank spaces only, you can use the following syntax.

```
TRIM(char2)
```

Here is an example of a string with blank characters. Only leading and trailing blanks are trimmed, and blank spaces in the middle of the string are ignored.

```
SELECT TRIM('   00012345  00  ') AS "Blank Trim"
  FROM dual
Blank Trim
------------
00012345  00

1 row selected.
```

The SUBSTR Function

SUBSTR transforms a string, returning a *substring* or *subset* of a string, based on its input parameters. The following query displays student last names, the *first* five characters of those last names in the second column, and the *remaining* characters of those last names in the third column.

```
SELECT last_name,
       SUBSTR(last_name, 1, 5),
       SUBSTR(last_name, 6)
  FROM student
LAST_NAME                    SUBST SUBSTR(LAST_NAME,6)
-------------------------- ----- -------------------------
Eakheit                      Eakhe it
Millstein                    Mills tein
...
Mastandora                   Masta ndora
Torres                       Torre s

268 rows selected.
```

The SUBSTR function's first input parameter is a string; the second is the starting position of the subset; the third is optional, indicating the length of the subset. If the third parameter is not used, the default is to display the remainder of the string. Here is the syntax for SUBSTR.

```
SUBSTR(char1, starting_position [, substring_length])
```

If starting_position is a negative number, Oracle starts counting from the end of the string; you will see some examples of this in this chapter as part of the exercises.

The INSTR Function

INSTR, meaning *in string,* looks for the occurrence of a string inside another string, returning the starting position of the search string within the target string. Unlike the other string functions, INSTR does not return another string; rather, it returns a number. The following query displays course descriptions and the position in which the first occurrence of the string 'er', if any, in the DESCRIPTION column appears.

```
SELECT description, INSTR(description, 'er')
  FROM course
DESCRIPTION                   INSTR(DESCRIPTION,'ER')
------------------------      ------------------------
Technology Concepts                                 0
...
Java Developer III                                 13
Operating Systems                                   3
DB Programming with Java                            0

30 rows selected.
```

As you can see in the second-to-last row of the result set, the string 'er' starts in the third position of Operating Systems. The last row, DB Programming with Java, does not contain an 'er' string, and the result is therefore 0. The syntax for INSTR is as follows.

```
INSTR(char1, char2 [,starting_position [, occurrence]])
```

INSTR can take two optional input parameters. The third parameter allows you to specify the start position for the search. The fourth parameter specifies which occurrence of the string to look for. When these optional parameters are not used, the default value is 1.

The LENGTH Function

The LENGTH function determines the length of a string, expressed as a number. The following SQL statement selects a text literal from the DUAL table in conjunction with the LENGTH function.

```
SELECT LENGTH('Hello there')
  FROM dual
LENGTH('HELLOTHERE')
--------------------
                  11

1 row selected.
```

Functions in WHERE and ORDER BY Clauses

The use of functions is not restricted to the SELECT list; they are also used in other SQL clauses. In a WHERE clause, a function restricts the output to rows that only evaluate to the result of the function. In an ORDER BY clause, rows are sorted based on the result of a function. The next query uses the SUBSTR function in the WHERE clause to search for student last names that begin with the string 'Mo'. The arguments are the LAST_NAME column of the STUDENT table, starting with the first character of the column, for a length of two characters.

```
SELECT first_name, last_name
  FROM student
 WHERE SUBSTR(last_name, 1, 2) = 'Mo'
FIRST_NAME               LAST_NAME
------------------------ ---------
Edgar                    Moffat
Angel                    Moskowitz
Vinnie                   Moon
Bernadette               Montanez

4 rows selected.
```

Alternatively, you can achieve the same result by replacing the SUBSTR function with the following WHERE clause.

```
WHERE last_name LIKE 'Mo%'
```

The following SQL statement selects student first and last names, where the value in the FIRST_NAME column contains a period, and also orders the result set based on the length of students' last names.

```
SELECT first_name, last_name
  FROM student
 WHERE INSTR(first_name, '.') > 0
 ORDER BY LENGTH(last_name)
FIRST_NAME               LAST_NAME
------------------------ ---------
Suzanne M.               Abid
D.                       Orent
...
V.                       Saliternan
Z.A.                     Scrittorale

21 rows selected.
```

Nested Functions

As you saw earlier, in the example of LPAD and RPAD, functions can be nested within each other. Nested functions are evaluated starting from the inner function and working outward.

The following example shows the city column formatted in uppercase and right padded with periods.

```
SELECT RPAD(UPPER(city), 20,'.')
  FROM zipcode
 WHERE state = 'CT'
RPAD(UPPER(CITY),20,
--------------------
ANSONIA.............
MIDDLEFIELD.........
...
STAMFORD............
STAMFORD............

19 rows selected.
```

Here is a more complicated but useful example. You may have noticed that middle initials in the STUDENT table are entered in the same column as the first name. To separate the middle initial from the first name, nest the SUBSTR and INSTR functions. First, determine the position of the middle initial's period in the FIRST_NAME column with the INSTR function. From this position, deduct the number 1. This brings you to the position before the period, where the middle initial starts, which is where you want the SUBSTR function to start. The WHERE clause selects only rows where the third or any subsequent character of the first name contains a period.

```
SELECT first_name,
       SUBSTR(first_name, INSTR(first_name, '.')-1) mi,
       SUBSTR(first_name, 1, INSTR(first_name, '.')-2) first
  FROM student
 WHERE INSTR(first_name, '.') >= 3
FIRST_NAME                   MI   FIRST
------------------------     ---- ------
Austin V.                    V.   Austin
John T.                      T.   John
...
Suzanne M.                   M.   Suzanne
Rafael A.                    A.   Rafael

7 rows selected.
```

For example, in the row for Austin V., the position of the period is 9, but you need to start at 8 to include the middle initial letter. The last column of the result lists the first name without the middle initial. This is accomplished by starting with the first character of the string and ending the string before the position where the middle initial starts. The key is to determine the ending position of the string with the INSTR function and count back two characters.

When using nested functions, a common pitfall is to misplace matching parentheses or forget the second half of the pair altogether. Start by writing a nested function from the inside out. Count the number of left parentheses and make sure it matches the number of right parentheses.

Concatenation

Concatenation connects strings *together* to become one. Strings can be concatenated to produce a single column in the result set. There are two methods of concatenation in Oracle: One is with the CONCAT function, the other is the concatenation operator (||), which is two *vertical bars* or *pipe symbols*. The syntax of the CONCAT function is as follows.

```
CONCAT(char1, char2)
```

When you want to concatenate cities and states together using the CONCAT function, you can use the function as follows.

```
SELECT CONCAT(city, state)
   FROM zipcode
CONCAT(CITY,STATE)
------------------
SanturcePR
North AdamsMA
...
New YorkNY
New YorkNY

227 rows selected.
```

The result set is difficult to read without spaces between cities and states. The CONCAT function takes only two parameters. By using the || operator, you can easily concatenate several strings.

```
SELECT city||state||zip
   FROM zipcode
CITY||STATE||ZIP
------------------
SanturcePR00914
North AdamsMA01247
...
New YorkNY10005
New YorkNY10035

227 rows selected.
```

For a result set that is easier to read, concatenate the strings with spaces and separate the CITY and STATE columns with a comma.

```
SELECT city||', '||state||' '||zip
   FROM zipcode
```

```
CITY||','||STATE||' '||ZIP
--------------------------
Santurce, PR   00914
North Adams, MA   01247
...
New York, NY   10005
New York, NY   10035

227 rows selected.
```

The REPLACE Function

The REPLACE function *replaces* one string with another string. In the following example, when the string 'hand' is found within the string 'My hand is asleep', it is replaced by the string 'foot'.

```
SELECT REPLACE('My hand is asleep', 'hand', 'foot')
   FROM dual
REPLACE('MYHANDISA
------------------
My foot is asleep

1 row selected.
```

The following is the syntax for the REPLACE function.

```
REPLACE(char, if, then)
```

The second parameter looks to see if a string exists within the first parameter. If so, it displays the third parameter. If the second parameter is not found, then the original string is displayed.

```
SELECT REPLACE('My hand is asleep', 'x', 'foot')
   FROM dual
REPLACE('MYHANDISA
------------------
My hand is asleep

1 row selected.
```

The TRANSLATE Function

Unlike REPLACE, which replaces an entire string, the TRANSLATE function provides a one-for-one character substitution. For instance, it allows you to determine whether all the phone numbers in the STUDENT table follow the same format. In the next query, TRANSLATE substitutes the # character for every character from 0 to 9. Then the values are checked against the '###-###-####' format.

```
SELECT phone
  FROM student
 WHERE TRANSLATE(
```

```
        phone, '0123456789',
                '#########') <> '###-###-####'
```

no rows selected

If any phone number is entered in an invalid format, such as 'abc-ddd-efgh' or '555-1212', the query returns the row(s) with the incorrect phone format. The following is the syntax for the TRANSLATE function.

```
TRANSLATE(char, if, then)
```

The SOUNDEX Function

The SOUNDEX function allows you to compare differently spelled words that phonetically sound alike. The next query uses the SOUNDEX function to display students whose last name sounds like Martin.

```
SELECT student_id, last_name
  FROM student
 WHERE SOUNDEX(last_name) = SOUNDEX('MARTIN')
STUDENT_ID LAST_NAME
---------- ---------
       110 Martin
       324 Marten
       393 Martin

3 rows selected.
```

Which Character Function Should You Use?

It's easy to confuse character functions. When deciding which one to use, ask yourself exactly what is needed in your result set. Are you looking for the position of a string in a string? Do you need to produce a subset of a string? Do you need to know how long a string is? Or do you need to replace a string with something else? Table 4.2 lists the character functions discussed in this lab.

TABLE 4.2   Character Functions

FUNCTION	PURPOSE
LOWER(*char*)	Converts to lowercase
UPPER(*char*)	Converts to uppercase
INITCAP(*char*)	Capitalizes the first letter
LPAD(*char1*, n [, *char2*])	Left pads
RPAD(*char1*, n [, *char2*])	Right pads
LTRIM(*char1* [, *char2*])	Left trims
RTRIM(*char1* [, *char2*])	Right trims

TABLE 4.2   Continued

FUNCTION	PURPOSE
TRIM([LEADING| TRAILING|BOTH] char1 FROM char2)	Trims leading, trailing or both sides
SUBSTR(char1, starting_position [, substring_length])	Cuts out a piece of a string
INSTR(char1, char2 [, starting_position [, occurrence]])	Determines the starting location of a string
LENGTH(char)	Returns the length of a string
CONCAT(char1, char2)	Concatenates two strings
REPLACE(char, if, then)	Replaces a string with another string
SOUNDEX(char)	Returns phonetic representation
TRANSLATE(char, if, then)	Substitutes individual character

SQL Developer Snippets

SQL Developer introduced a feature called *snippets,* which are SQL functions or syntax examples. You can even create your own snippets of frequently used statements. Snippets are helpful in both SQL statements and PL/SQL programming. You find the Snippets window tab located on the right side of the Enter SQL Statement box (see Figure 4.2). You can also invoke it by choosing View, Snippets.

Figure 4.2 shows an example of the LOWER function snippet within a SQL statement. To insert a snippet, drag it into the Enter SQL Statement box. Now you can replace in the desired column or literal shown as the char parameter and complete the rest of the SQL statement. Hovering over the function reveals a brief description of the function.

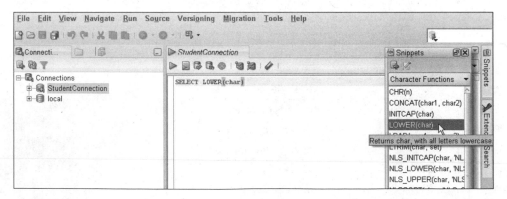

FIGURE 4.2
Inserting a snippet

Snippets are useful for storing frequently used SQL statements.

Searching, Replacing, and Validating Text

In addition to the LIKE operator and the character functions SUBSTR and INSTR, Oracle offers additional search capabilities that come in the form of Oracle Text and regular expressions.

Oracle Text expands the text search capabilities with word and theme searching, using the operators CONTAINS, CATSEARCH, and MATCHES. The database returns ranked results, based on the requested search. You can specify combinations of words with the AND and OR operators, and you can use wildcards. You can search for documents that contain words that share the same stem, words that are located close to each other, or words that revolve around the same theme. The *Oracle Text Reference* manual and the *Oracle Text Application Developer's Guide* contain more information on this functionality.

Regular expression functions are part Oracle's SQL language. A *regular expression* is a notation for describing a pattern. Regular expressions significantly expand the functionality of the LIKE operator and the INSTR, SUBSTR, and REPLACE functions to search, replace, and validate patterns. You will learn more about the sophisticated capabilities of regular expressions within the context of the Oracle database in Chapter 16, "Regular Expressions and Hierarchical Queries."

▼ LAB 4.1 EXERCISES

a) Execute the following SQL statement. Based on the result, what is the purpose of the INITCAP function?

```
SELECT description "Description",
       INITCAP(description) "Initcap Description"
  FROM course
 WHERE description LIKE '%SQL%'
```

b) What question does the following SQL statement answer?

```
SELECT last_name
  FROM instructor
 WHERE LENGTH(last_name) >= 6
```

c) Describe the result of the following SQL statement. Pay particular attention to the negative number parameter.

```
SELECT SUBSTR('12345', 3),
       SUBSTR('12345', 3, 2),
       SUBSTR('12345', -4, 3)
  FROM dual
```

d) Based on the result of the following SQL statement, describe the purpose of the LTRIM and RTRIM functions.

```
SELECT zip, LTRIM(zip, '0'), RTRIM(ZIP, '4')
  FROM zipcode
 ORDER BY zip
```

e) What do you observe when you execute the next statement? How should the statement be changed to achieve the desired result?

```
SELECT TRIM('01' FROM '01230145601')
  FROM dual
```

f) What is the result of the following statement?

```
SELECT TRANSLATE('555-1212', '0123456789',
                              '##########')
  FROM dual
```

g) Write a SQL statement to retrieve students who have a last name with the lowercase letter o occurring three or more times.

h) The following statement determines how many times the string 'ed' occurs in the phrase 'Fred fed Ted bread, and Ted fed Fred bread'. Explain how this is accomplished.

```
SELECT (
   LENGTH('Fred fed Ted bread, and Ted fed Fred bread.') -
   LENGTH(REPLACE(
          'Fred fed Ted bread, and Ted fed Fred bread.', 'ed', NULL))
             ) /2 AS occurr
  FROM dual
    OCCURR
----------
         6

1 row selected.
```

i) Write a SELECT statement that returns each instructor's last name, followed by a comma and a space, followed by the instructor's first name, all in a single column in the result set.

j) Using functions in the SELECT list and WHERE and ORDER BY clauses, write a SELECT statement that returns course numbers and course descriptions from the COURSE table and looks like the following result set. Use the SQL Developer Run Script icon to display the result in fixed-width format.

```
Description
-------------------------------------
204.......Intro to SQL
130.......Intro to Unix
25........Intro to Programming
230.......Intro to the Internet
120.......Intro to Java Programming
240.......Intro to the BASIC Language
20........Intro to Information Systems

7 rows selected.
```

▼ LAB 4.1 EXERCISE ANSWERS

a) Execute the following SQL statement. Based on the result, what is the purpose of the INITCAP function?

```
SELECT description "Description",
       INITCAP(description) "Initcap Description"
  FROM course
 WHERE description LIKE '%SQL%'
```

ANSWER: The INITCAP function capitalizes the first letter of a word and forces the remaining characters to be lowercase.

The result set contains two rows, one displaying a course description as it appears in the database and one displaying each word with only the first letter capitalized. Words are delimited by nonalphanumeric characters or spaces.

```
Description                  Initcap Description
-----------------------      --------------------
Intro to SQL                 Intro To Sql
PL/SQL Programming           Pl/Sql Programming

2 rows selected.
```

b) What question does the following SQL statement answer?

```
SELECT last_name
  FROM instructor
 WHERE LENGTH(last_name) >= 6
```

ANSWER: The question answered by the query could be phrased like this: "Which instructors have last names equal to six characters or more?"

```
LAST NAME
----------------
Wojick
Schorin
...
Frantzen
Willig

7 rows selected.
```

The LENGTH function returns the length of a string, expressed as a number. The LENGTH function takes only a single input parameter, as in the following syntax.

```
LENGTH(char)
```

c) Describe the result of the following SQL statement. Pay particular attention to the negative number parameter.

```
SELECT SUBSTR('12345', 3),
       SUBSTR('12345', 3, 2),
       SUBSTR('12345', -4, 3)
  FROM dual
```

ANSWER: The first column takes the characters starting from the third position until the end, resulting in the string '345'. The second SUBSTR function also starts at the third position but ends after two characters and therefore returns '34'. The third column has a negative number as the first parameter. It counts from the end of the string to the left four characters; thus the substring starts at position 2 and for a length of three characters, resulting in '234'.

```
SUB SU SUB
--- -- ---
345 34 234
```

```
1 row selected.
```

d) Based on the result of the following SQL statement, describe the purpose of the LTRIM and RTRIM functions.

```
SELECT zip, LTRIM(zip, '0'), RTRIM(ZIP, '4')
  FROM zipcode
 ORDER BY zip
```

ANSWER: The LTRIM and RTRIM functions left trim and right trim strings, based on the function's parameters. With the three columns in the result set side by side, you see the differences: The first column shows the ZIP column without modification, the second with ZIP left-trimmed of its 0s, and the third with ZIP right-trimmed of its 4s.

```
ZIP    LTRIM RTRIM
-----  ----- -----
00914  914   0091
01247  1247  01247
...
43224  43224 4322
48104  48104 4810
```

```
227 rows selected.
```

e) What do you observe when you execute the next statement? How should the statement be changed to achieve the desired result?

```
SELECT TRIM('01' FROM '01230145601')
  FROM dual
```

ANSWER: The query results in an error (see Figure 4.3), indicating that only one character can be trimmed at a time. This query attempts to trim two characters, which are 0 and 1. Nest the LTRIM and RTRIM functions to achieve the desired result.

```
SELECT TRIM('01' FROM '01230145601')
  FROM dual
```

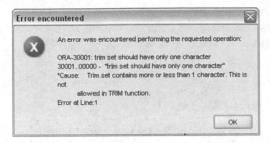

FIGURE 4.3
Error message on an invalid TRIM parameter

To trim multiple characters, use the LTRIM and RTRIM functions instead of TRIM. If you try the REPLACE function, it replaces all occurrences of the '01' string, not just the first and last.

```
SELECT LTRIM('01230145601', '01') left,
       RTRIM('01230145601', '01') right,
       RTRIM(LTRIM('01230145601', '01'), '01') both,
       REPLACE('01230145601', '01') replace
  FROM dual

LEFT        RIGHT      BOTH     REPLA
--------    --------   -------  -----
230145601   012301456  2301456  23456

1 row selected.
```

f) What is the result of the following statement?

```
SELECT TRANSLATE('555-1212', '0123456789',
                             '##########')
  FROM dual
```

ANSWER: It returns the result ###-####. The TRANSLATE function is a character substitution function. The listed SQL statement uses each of the characters in the string '555-1212' to look up the corresponding character and then returns this character. One of the uses for this function is to determine whether data is entered in the correct format.

```
TRANSLAT
--------
###-####

1 row selected.
```

USING TRANSLATE FOR PATTERN SEARCHING

The TRANSLATE function also comes in handy when you need to perform a pattern search using the LIKE operator and you are looking for the actual wildcard characters % or _. Assume that you need to query the STUDENT table, and you want to find any students whose employer spells his or her name similar to the pattern B_B. The underscore has to be taken as a literal underscore, not as a wildcard. Qualifying employer names are Bayer B_Biller and ABCB_Bellman. Unfortunately, no such employer names exist in the STUDENT database, but there are occasions when data entry errors occur and you need to figure out which are the offending rows. The following query checks whether an employer with the pattern B_B exists in the table.

```
SELECT student_id, employer
  FROM student
 WHERE TRANSLATE(employer, '_', '+') LIKE '%B+B%'
```

As you can see, the TRANSLATE function performs this trick. Here the underscore is replaced with the plus sign and then the LIKE function is applied with the replaced plus sign in the character literal.

USING INSTR FOR PATTERN SEARCHING

Another way to solve the problem in the preceding section would be to use the previously discussed INSTR function, which returns the starting position of the string.

```
SELECT student_id, employer
  FROM student
 WHERE INSTR(employer, 'B_B') > 0
```

THE ESCAPE CHARACTER AND THE LIKE OPERATOR

Yet another way to solve the problem is with the escape character functionality in conjunction with the LIKE operator. In the next example, the backslash (\) sign is selected as the escape character to indicate that the underscore character following the character is to be interpreted as a literal underscore and not as the wildcard underscore.

```
SELECT student_id, employer
  FROM student
 WHERE employer LIKE '%B\_B%' ESCAPE '\'
```

The regular expressions functionality allows sophisticated pattern searches with the REGEXP_LIKE operator. You will learn more about these capabilities in Chapter 16.

g) Write a SQL statement to retrieve students who have a last name with the lowercase letter o occurring three or more times.

ANSWER: The INSTR function determines the third or more occurrence of the lowercase letter o in the LAST_NAME column of the STUDENT table.

The INSTR function has two required parameters; the rest are optional and default to 1. The first parameter is the string or column where the function needs to be applied and where you are looking to find the desired values. The second parameter identifies the search string; here you are looking for the letter o. The third parameter determines at which starting position the search must occur. The last parameter specifies which occurrence of the string is requested.

If the INSTR function finds the desired result, it returns the starting position of the searched value. The WHERE clause condition looks for those rows where the result of the INSTR function is greater than 0.

```
SELECT student_id, last_name
  FROM student
 WHERE INSTR(last_name, 'o', 1, 3) > 0
```

```
STUDENT_ID LAST_NAME
---------- ---------
       280 Engongoro
       251 Frangopoulos
       254 Chamnonkool
```

3 rows selected.

h) The following statement determines how many times the string 'ed' occurs in the phrase 'Fred fed Ted bread, and Ted fed Fred bread'. Explain how this is accomplished.

```
SELECT (
  LENGTH('Fred fed Ted bread, and Ted fed Fred bread') -
  LENGTH(REPLACE(
          'Fred fed Ted bread, and Ted fed Fred bread', 'ed', NULL))
            ) /2 AS occurr
FROM dual
   OCCURR
----------
        6
```

1 row selected.

ANSWER: The nesting of the REPLACE and LENGTH functions determines that there are six occurrences of the string 'ed' in the phrase.

To understand the statement, it's best to break down the individual components of the statement: The first function determines the length of this tongue twister. The next component nests the LENGTH and REPLACE functions. The REPLACE function replaces every occurrence of 'ed' with a null. Effectively, the result string looks as follows.

```
SELECT REPLACE
  ('Fred fed Ted bread, and Ted fed Fred bread',
   'ed', NULL)
   FROM dual
REPLACE('FREDFEDTEDBREAD,ANDTE
-------------------------------
Fr f T bread, and T f Fr bread
```

1 row selected.

Then the LENGTH function determines the length of the reduced string. If you deduct the total length of the entire string from the length of the reduced string and divide the result by 2 (the number of letters in the string 'ed'), you determine the total number of occurrences.

 Starting with Oracle 11g, you can now use the REGEXP_COUNT function to perform the same functionality described in Exercise h. This function is discussed in Chapter 16 as part of the Regular Expression functionality.

i) Write a SELECT statement that returns each instructor's last name, followed by a comma and a space, followed by the instructor's first name, all in a single column in the result set.

ANSWER: The instructor's last name, a comma and a space, and the instructor's first name are all concatenated using the || symbol.

```
SELECT last_name||', '||first_name
   FROM instructor
LAST_NAME||','||FIRST_NAME
-------------------------
Hanks, Fernand
Wojick, Tom
...
Frantzen, Marilyn
Willig, Irene


10 rows selected.
```

j) Using functions in the SELECT list and WHERE and ORDER BY clauses, write a SELECT statement that returns course numbers and course descriptions from the COURSE table and looks like the following result set. Use the SQL Developer Run Script icon to display the result in fixed-width format.

```
Description
------------------------------------
204.......Intro to SQL
130.......Intro to Unix
25........Intro to Programming
230.......Intro to the Internet
120.......Intro to Java Programming
240.......Intro to the BASIC Language
20........Intro to Information Systems


7 rows selected.
```

ANSWER: The RPAD function right pads the COURSE_NO column with periods, up to 10 characters long; it is then concatenated with the DESCRIPTION column. The INSTR function is used in the WHERE clause to filter on descriptions, with the string 'Intro'. The LENGTH function in the ORDER BY clause sorts the result set by ascending (shortest to longest) description length.

```
SELECT RPAD(course_no, 10, '.')||description
       AS "Description"
  FROM course
 WHERE INSTR(description, 'Intro') = 1
 ORDER BY LENGTH(description)
```

The same result can be obtained without the use of the INSTR function, as in the following WHERE clause.

```
WHERE description LIKE 'Intro%'
```

Figure 4.4 shows the statement executed within SQL Developer, using the Run Script icon, and the resulting output is shown in fixed-width format in the Script Output tab.

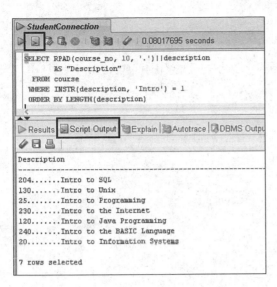

FIGURE 4.4
Script Output tab result when using SQL Developer's Run Script icon

Lab 4.1 Quiz

In order to test your progress, you should be able to answer the following questions.

1) A function that operates on a single value can have only one input parameter.

_____ a) True
_____ b) False

2) The DUAL table can be used for testing functions.

_____ a) True
_____ b) False

3) The same function can be used twice in a SELECT statement.

_____ a) True
_____ b) False

4) The following SELECT statement contains an error.

```
SELECT UPPER(description)
  FROM LOWER(course)
```

_____ a) True
_____ b) False

5) The RTRIM function is useful for eliminating extra spaces in a string.

_____ a) True
_____ b) False

6) Which one of the following string functions tells you how many characters are in a string?

_____ a) INSTR
_____ b) SUBSTR
_____ c) LENGTH
_____ d) REPLACE

7) Which result will the following query return? Note there are extra spaces between Mary and Jones.

```
SELECT TRIM('    Mary                Jones    ')
  FROM dual
```

_____ a) Mary Jones
_____ b) Mary   Jones
_____ c) MaryJones
_____ d) The query returns an error.

8) The functions INSTR, SUBSTR, and TRIM are all single-row functions.

_____ a) True
_____ b) False

9) Which character function returns a specified portion of a character string?

_____ a) INSTR
_____ b) LENGTH
_____ c) SUBSTR
_____ d) INSTRING

10) Character functions never return results in the data type NUMBER.

_____ a) True
_____ b) False

ANSWERS APPEAR IN APPENDIX A.

LAB 4.2
Number Functions

LAB OBJECTIVES

After this lab, you will be able to:

▶ Use Number Functions
▶ Perform Mathematical Computations

Number functions are valuable tools for operations such as rounding numbers or computing the absolute value of a number. There are several single-row number functions in Oracle; the most useful ones are discussed here.

The ABS Function

The ABS function computes the *absolute value* of a number, measuring its magnitude.

```
SELECT 'The absolute value of -29 is '||ABS(-29)
   FROM dual
'THEABSOLUTEVALUEOF-29IS'||ABS(
------------------------------
The absolute value of -29 is 29

1 row selected.
```

ABS takes only a single input parameter, and its syntax is as follows.

```
ABS(value)
```

The SIGN Function

The SIGN function tells you the *sign* of a value, returning a number 1 for a positive number, −1 for a negative number, or 0 for zero. The following example compares SIGN with the ABS function.

```
SELECT -14, SIGN(-14), SIGN(14), SIGN(0), ABS(-14)
   FROM dual
      -14 SIGN(-14) SIGN(14)     SIGN(0) ABS(-14)
--------- --------- ----------- -------- --------
      -14        -1           1        0       14

1 row selected.
```

SIGN also takes only a single input parameter, and its syntax is as follows.

```
SIGN(value)
```

 Most single-row functions return NULL when a NULL is the input parameter.

ROUND and TRUNC Functions

ROUND and TRUNC are two useful functions that *round* and *truncate* (or cut off) values, respectively, based on a given number of digits of precision. The next SELECT statement illustrates the use of ROUND and TRUNC, which both take two input parameters. Observe the differences in the result.

```
SELECT 222.34501,
       ROUND(222.34501, 2),
       TRUNC(222.34501, 2)
  FROM dual
222.34501 ROUND(222.34501,2) TRUNC(222.34501,2)
--------- ------------------ ------------------
222.34501             222.35             222.34

1 row selected.
```

Here, ROUND (222.34501, 2) rounds the number 222.34501 to two digits to the right of the decimal, rounding the result up to 222.35, following the normal convention for rounding. In contrast, TRUNC cuts off all digits beyond two digits to the right of the decimal, resulting in 222.34. ROUND and TRUNC can be used to affect the left side of the decimal as well by passing a negative number as a parameter.

```
SELECT 222.34501,
       ROUND(222.34501, -2),
       TRUNC(222.34501, -2)
  FROM dual
222.34501 ROUND(222.34501,-2) TRUNC(222.34501,-2)
--------- ------------------- -------------------
222.34501                 200                 200

1 row selected.
```

The following is the syntax for ROUND and TRUNC.

```
ROUND(value [, precision])
TRUNC(value [, precision])
```

Numbers with decimal places may be rounded to whole numbers by omitting the second parameter, or specifying a precision of 0.

```
SELECT 2.617, ROUND(2.617), TRUNC(2.617)
  FROM dual
2.617 ROUND(2.617) TRUNC(2.617)
----- ------------ ------------
2.617            3            2

1 row selected.
```

You can use the TRUNC and ROUND functions not only on values of the NUMBER data type but also on the DATE data type, discussed in Chapter 5.

The FLOOR and CEIL Functions

The CEIL function returns the smallest integer greater than or equal to a value; the FLOOR function returns the largest integer equal to or less than a value. These functions perform much like the ROUND and TRUNC functions, without the optional precision parameter.

```
SELECT FLOOR(22.5), CEIL(22.5), TRUNC(22.5), ROUND(22.5)
  FROM dual
FLOOR(22.5) CEIL(22.5) TRUNC(22.5) ROUND(22.5)
----------- ---------- ----------- -----------
         22         23          22          23

1 row selected.
```

The syntax for the FLOOR and CEIL functions is as follows.

```
FLOOR(value)
CEIL(value)
```

The MOD Function

MOD is a function that returns the *modulus,* or the remainder of a value divided by another value. It takes two input parameters, as in the following SELECT statement.

```
SELECT MOD(23, 8)
  FROM dual
MOD(23,8)
----------
        7

1 row selected.
```

The MOD function divides 23 by 8 and returns a remainder of 7. The following is the syntax for MOD.

```
MOD(value, divisor)
```

The MOD function is particularly useful if you want to determine whether a value is odd or even. If you divide by 2 and the remainder is a zero, this indicates that the value is even; if the remainder is 1, it means that the value is odd.

Floating-Point Numbers

Oracle's floating-point numbers support the IEEE standard for binary floating-point arithmetic, just like Java and XML. Computations on floating-point values can sometimes be on the order of 5 to 10 times faster than NUMBER because the floating-point data types use the native instruction set supplied by the hardware vendor. Compared to the NUMBER data type, the floating-point data types use up less space for values stored with significant precision.

Oracle offers the BINARY_FLOAT and BINARY_DOUBLE data types. A floating-point number consists of three components: a *sign*, the signed *exponent*, and a *significand*. The BINARY_DOUBLE data type supports a wider range of values than does BINARY_FLOAT. The special operators IS [NOT] NAN and IS [NOT] INFINITE check for is "not a number" (NAN) and infinity, respectively.

If an operation involves a mix of different numeric data types, the operation is performed in the data type with the highest precedence. The order of precedence is BINARY_DOUBLE, BINARY_FLOAT, and then NUMBER. For example, if the operation includes a NUMBER and a BINARY_DOUBLE, the value of the NUMBER data type is implicitly converted to the BINARY_DOUBLE data type. Oracle offers various functions that allow conversions to and from different data types; they are discussed in Lab 5.5.

The ROUND function takes on a slightly different behavior if the data type of the input parameter is not NUMBER but is either BINARY_FLOAT or BINARY_ DOUBLE. In this case, the ROUND function rounds toward the nearest even value.

```
SELECT ROUND(3.5), ROUND(3.5f), ROUND(4.5), ROUND(4.5f)
  FROM dual
ROUND(3.5) ROUND(3.5F) ROUND(4.5) ROUND(4.5F)
---------- ----------- ---------- -----------
        4    4.0E+000          5    4.0E+000

1 row selected.
```

The REMAINDER Function

The REMAINDER function calculates the remainder, according to the IEEE specification. The syntax is as follows.

```
REMAINDER(value, divisor)
```

The difference between REMAINDER and the MOD function is that MOD uses FLOOR in its computations, whereas REMAINDER uses ROUND. The next example shows that the results between the MOD and REMAINDER functions can be different.

```
SELECT MOD(23,8), REMAINDER(23,8)
  FROM DUAL
 MOD(23,8) REMAINDER(23,8)
---------- ---------------
         7              -1

1 row selected.
```

Effectively, the computation of the MOD function is (23-(8*FLOOR(23/8))), and the computation of REMAINDER is (23-(8*ROUND(23/8))), as illustrated by the next statement.

```
SELECT (23-(8*FLOOR(23/8))) AS mod,
       (23-(8*ROUND(23/8))) AS remainder
  FROM DUAL
        MOD REMAINDER
---------- ---------
         7        -1

1 row selected.
```

Which Number Function Should You Use?

Table 4.3 lists the functions discussed in this lab. Sometimes, you may nest these functions within other functions. As you progress through the following chapters, you will see the usefulness of some of these functions in writing sophisticated SQL statements.

TABLE 4.3   Number Functions

FUNCTION	PURPOSE
ABS(value)	Returns the absolute value
SIGN(value)	Returns the sign of a value, such as 1, –1, and 0
MOD(value, divisor)	Returns the modulus
REMAINDER (value, divisor)	Returns the remainder, according to the IEEE specification
ROUND(value [, precision])	Rounds the value
TRUNC(value [, precision])	Truncates the value
FLOOR(value)	Returns the largest integer
CEIL(value)	Returns the smallest integer

In Chapter 17, "Exploring Data Warehousing Features," you will learn about additional number functions that help you solve analytical and statistical problems. For example, these functions can help you determine rankings, such as the grades of the top 20 students, or compute the median cost of all courses.

Arithmetic Operators

The four mathematical operators (addition, subtraction, multiplication, and division) can be used in a SQL statement and can be combined.

In the following example, each of the four operators is used with course costs. One of the distinct course costs is null; here the computation with a null value yields another null.

```
SELECT DISTINCT cost, cost + 10,
       cost - 10, cost * 10, cost / 10
  FROM course
    COST     COST+10    COST-10    COST*10 COST/10
---------- --------- --------- --------- -------
    1095      1105       1085      10950   109.5
    1195      1205       1185      11950   119.5
    1595      1605       1585      15950   159.5


4 rows selected.
```

Parentheses are used to group computations, indicating precedence of the operators. The following SELECT statement returns distinct course costs increased by 10%. The computation within the parentheses is evaluated first, followed by the addition of the value in the COST column, resulting in a single number. NULL values can be replaced with a default value. You will learn about this topic in Lab 4.3.

```
SELECT DISTINCT cost + (cost * .10)
  FROM course
COST+(COST*.10)
---------------
       1204.5
       1314.5
       1754.5


4 rows selected.
```

▼ LAB 4.2 EXERCISES

a) Describe the effect of the negative precision as a parameter of the ROUND function in the following SQL statement.

```
SELECT 10.245, ROUND(10.245, 1), ROUND(10.245, -1)
  FROM dual
```

b) Write a SELECT statement that displays distinct course costs. In a separate column, show the COST increased by 75% and round the decimals to the nearest dollar.

c) Write a SELECT statement that displays distinct numeric grades from the GRADE table and half those values expressed as a whole number in a separate column.

▼ LAB 4.2 EXERCISE **ANSWERS**

a) Describe the effect of the negative precision as a parameter of the ROUND function in the following SQL statement.

```
SELECT 10.245, ROUND(10.245, 1), ROUND(10.245, -1)
  FROM dual
```

ANSWER: A negative precision rounds digits to the left of the decimal point.

```
  10.245 ROUND(10.245,1) ROUND(10.245,-1)
--------- --------------- ----------------
  10.245            10.2               10
```

1 row selected.

For example, to round to the nearest hundreds, you can use the precision parameter -2, to round to the nearest thousands, use the precision parameter -3, and so on. The next example illustrates the result of these negative parameters.

```
SELECT ROUND(120.09, -2), ROUND(1444.44, -3)
  FROM dual
ROUND(120.09,-2) ROUND(1444.44,-3)
---------------- -----------------
             100              1000
```

1 row selected.

b) Write a SELECT statement that displays distinct course costs. In a separate column, show the COST increased by 75% and round the decimals to the nearest dollar.

ANSWER: The SELECT statement uses multiplication and the ROUND function.

```
SELECT DISTINCT cost, cost*1.75, ROUND(cost*1.75)
  FROM course
     COST COST*1.75 ROUND(COST*1.75)
--------- --------- ----------------
     1095   1916.25             1916
     1195   2091.25             2091
     1595   2791.25             2791
```

4 rows selected.

c) Write a SELECT statement that displays distinct numeric grades from the GRADE table and half those values expressed as a whole number in a separate column.

ANSWER: The SELECT statement uses division to derive the value that is half the original value. The resulting value becomes the input parameter for the ROUND function. The displayed output shows a whole number because the ROUND function does not have any precision parameter specified.

```
SELECT DISTINCT numeric_grade, ROUND(numeric_grade / 2)
  FROM grade
NUMERIC_GRADE ROUND(NUMERIC_GRADE/2)
------------- ---------------------
           70                    35
           71                    36
...
           98                    49
           99                    50
```

30 rows selected.

Here, a mathematical computation is combined with a function. Be sure to place computations correctly, either inside or outside the parentheses of a function, depending on the desired result. In this case, if the /2 were on the outside of the ROUND function, a very different result would occur—not the correct answer to the problem posed.

Lab 4.2 Quiz

In order to test your progress, you should be able to answer the following questions.

1) Number functions can be nested.

_____ **a)** True

_____ **b)** False

2) The ROUND function can take only the NUMBER data type as a parameter.

_____ **a)** True

_____ **b)** False

3) The following SELECT statement is incorrect.

```
SELECT capacity - capacity
  FROM section
```

_____ **a)** True

_____ **b)** False

4) What does the following function return?

```
SELECT LENGTH(NULL)
  FROM dual
```

_____ **a)** 4

_____ **b)** 0

_____ **c)** Null

ANSWERS APPEAR IN APPENDIX A.

LAB 4.3
Miscellaneous Single-Row Functions

LAB OBJECTIVES

After this lab, you will be able to:

▸ Apply Substitution Functions and Other Miscellaneous Functions

▸ Utilize the Power of DECODE Function and the CASE Expression

In this lab, you will learn about substitution functions to replace nulls with default values. Another important topic is the DECODE function and the CASE expression. They are destined to become your favorites because they allow you to perform powerful *if-then-else* comparisons.

The NVL Function

The NVL function replaces a NULL value with a default value. NULLs represent a special challenge when used in calculations. A computation with an unknown value yields another unknown value, as shown in the following example.

```
SELECT 60+60+NULL
   FROM dual
60+60+NULL
---------------

1 row selected.
```

To avoid this problem, you can use the NVL function to substitute the NULL for another value.

```
NVL(input_expression, substitution_expression)
```

The NVL function requires two parameters: an input expression (for example, a column, literal, or computation) and a substitution expression. If the input expression does *not* contain a NULL value, the input parameter is returned. If the input parameter does contain a NULL value, the substitution parameter is returned.

In the following example, the substitution value is the number literal 1000. The NULL is substituted with 1000, resulting in the output 1120.

```
SELECT 60+60+NVL(NULL, 1000)
  FROM dual
60+60+NVL(NULL,1000)
--------------------
                1120

1 row selected.
```

When you substitute a value, the data type of the substituted value must agree with the data type of the input parameter. The next example uses the NVL function to substitute any NULL values with 'Not Applicable' in the PREREQUISITE column. An error is encountered when the statement is executed because the data types of the two parameters are different. The substitution parameter is a text literal, and the column PREREQUISITE is defined as a NUMBER data type. The error shown in Figure 4.5 indicates that Oracle cannot convert the text literal 'Not Applicable' into a NUMBER.

```
SELECT course_no, description,
       NVL(prerequisite, 'Not Applicable') prereq
  FROM course
 WHERE course_no IN (20, 100)
```

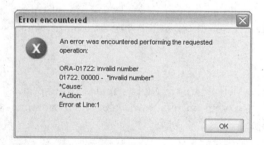

FIGURE 4.5
Error message on an invalid number

To overcome this problem, you can transform the output of the PREREQUISITE column into a VARCHAR2 data type, using the TO_CHAR data type conversion function. This function takes a NUMBER or DATE data type and converts it into a string.

```
SELECT course_no, description,
       NVL(TO_CHAR(prerequisite), 'Not Applicable') prereq
  FROM course
 WHERE course_no IN (20, 100)
COURSE_NO DESCRIPTION                         PREREQ
--------- --------------------------------- --------------
      100 Hands-On Windows                    20
       20 Intro to Information Systems Not Applicable

2 rows selected.
```

The COALESCE Function

The COALESCE function is similar to the NVL function, but with an additional twist. Instead of specifying one substitution expression for a null value, you can optionally evaluate multiple substitution columns or substitution expressions. The syntax is as follows.

```
COALESCE(input_expression, substitution_expression_1,
[, substitution_expression_n])
```

The next SQL query shows a case of two substitution expressions. A table called GRADE_SUMMARY, which is not part of the STUDENT schema, illustrates the idea.

The structure of the GRADE_SUMMARY TABLE is as follows.

```
DESCRIBE grade_summary
Name                                 Null?    Type
-------------------------------------------- ---------
STUDENT_ID                                    NUMBER(8)
MIDTERM_GRADE                                 NUMBER(3)
FINALEXAM_GRADE                               NUMBER(3)
QUIZ_GRADE                                    NUMBER(3)
```

In the following example, the resulting output in the Coalesce column shows that if the midterm grade is null, the final exam grade is substituted. If the final exam grade is also null, then the grade for the quiz is substituted. This is the case with student 678, where both the MIDTERM_GRADE and the FINALEXAM_GRADE column values are null, and therefore the value in the QUIZ_GRADE column is substituted. For student 999, all the column values are null; therefore the COALESCE function returns a null value.

```
SELECT student_id, midterm_grade, finalexam_grade, quiz_grade,
       COALESCE(midterm_grade, finalexam_grade, quiz_grade) "Coalesce"
  FROM grade_summary
```

STUDENT_ID	MIDTERM_GRADE	FINALEXAM_GRADE	QUIZ_GRADE	Coalesce
123	90	50	100	90
456	80	95		80
678			98	98
789		78	85	78
999				

```
5 rows selected.
```

The GRADE_SUMMARY table is a denormalized table, which you typically do not design in such a fashion unless you have a very good reason to denormalize. But the purpose here is to illustrate the functionality of COALESCE. If you wish, you can create this table by downloading an additional script from the companion Web site, located at www.oraclesqlbyexample.com.

The following is an example using the COALESCE function with just one substitution expression, which is equivalent to the NVL function discussed previously. The TO_CHAR function is necessary because the data types of the expressions do not agree. In this case, the PREREQUISITE column is of data type NUMBER. The 'Not Applicable' string is a character constant. You can use the TO_CHAR conversion function to make the two data types equivalent. The TO_CHAR function and conversion functions in general are covered in greater detail in Chapter 5.

```
SELECT course_no, description,
       COALESCE(TO_CHAR(prerequisite), 'Not Applicable') prereq
  FROM course
 WHERE course_no IN (20, 100)
COURSE_NO DESCRIPTION                         PREREQ
--------- ----------------------------------- ---------------
      100 Hands-On Windows                     20
       20 Intro to Information Systems Not Applicable

2 rows selected.
```

The NVL2 Function

The NVL2 function is yet another extension of the NVL function. It checks for both not null and null values and has three parameters versus NVL's two parameters. The syntax for the function is as follows:

```
NVL2(input_expr, not_null_substitution_expr, null_substitution_expr)
```

If the input expression is not null, the second parameter of the function, not_null_substitution_expr, is returned. If the input expression is null, then the last parameter, null_substitution_expr, is returned instead. This query shows how the NVL2 function works. The distinct course costs are displayed; if the value in the COST column is not null, the literal exists is displayed; otherwise the result displays the word none.

```
SELECT DISTINCT cost,
       NVL2(cost, 'exists', 'none') "NVL2"
  FROM course
      COST NVL2
---------- ------
      1095 exists
      1195 exists
      1595 exists
           none

4 rows selected.
```

The LNNVL Function

The LNNVL function can be used only in the WHERE clause of a SELECT statement. It returns either true or false. It returns true and therefore a result if the condition is either false or unknown. The LNNVL function returns the next two rows because the rows do *not* meet the condition COST < 1500. The result displays the courses in the COURSE table where the COST column value is null or greater than 1500.

```
SELECT course_no, cost
  FROM course
 WHERE LNNVL(cost < 1500)
COURSE_NO  COST
---------- ---------
       80      1595
      450

2 rows selected.
```

The syntax for the LNNVL function is as follows.

```
LNNVL(condition)
```

The NULLIF Function

The NULLIF function is unique in that it generates null values. The function compares two expressions; if the values are equal, the function returns a null; otherwise, the function returns the first expression. The following SQL statement returns null for the NULLIF function if the values in the columns CREATED_DATE and MODIFIED_DATE are equal. This is the case for the row with STUDENT_ ID of 150. Both date columns are exactly the same; therefore, the result of the NULLIF function is null. For the row with STUDENT_ID of 340, the columns contain different values; therefore, the first substitution expression is displayed. In this example, you see the use of the TO_CHAR function together with a DATE data type as the input parameter. This allows the display of dates as formatted character strings. This functionality is explained in greater detail in Chapter 5.

```
SELECT student_id,
       TO_CHAR(created_date, 'DD-MON-YY HH24:MI:SS') "Created",
       TO_CHAR(modified_date, 'DD-MON-YY HH24:MI:SS') "Modified",
       NULLIF(created_date, modified_date) "Null if equal"
  FROM student
 WHERE student_id IN (150, 340)
STUDENT_ID Created              Modified             Null if e
---------- -------------------- -------------------- ---------
       150 30-JAN-07 00:00:00   30-JAN-07 00:00:00
       340 19-FEB-07 00:00:00   22-FEB-07 00:00:00   19-FEB-07

2 rows selected.
```

The syntax for the NULLIF function is as follows.

```
NULLIF(expression1, equal_expression2)
```

The NANVL Function

The NANVL function is used only for the BINARY_FLOAT and BINARY_DOUBLE floating-point data types. The function returns a substitution value in case the input value is NAN ("not a number"). In the following query output, the last row contains such a value. In this instance, the NANVL function's second parameter substitutes the value zero.

 The FLOAT_TEST table is part of an additional script that contains sample tables, and it is available for download from the companion Web site, located at www.oraclesqlbyexample.com.

```
SELECT test_col, NANVL(test_col, 0)
  FROM float_test
TEST_COL    NANVL(TEST_COL,0)
---------- -----------------
      2.5                2.5
      NaN                  0

2 rows selected.
```

The NANVL function's input and substitution values are numeric, and the syntax is as follows.

```
NANVL(input_value, substitution_value)
```

The DECODE Function

The DECODE function substitutes values based on a condition, using *if-then-else* logic. If a value is equal to another value, the substitution value is returned. If the value compared is not equal to any of the listed expressions, an optional default value can be returned. The syntax code for the DECODE function is as follows.

```
DECODE (if_expr, equals_search,
        then_result [,else_default])
```

The search and result values can be repeated.

In the following query, the text literals 'New York' and 'New Jersey' are returned when the state is equal to 'NY' or 'NJ', respectively. If the value in the STATE column is other than 'NY' or 'NJ', a null value is displayed. The second DECODE function shows the use of the *else* condition. In the case of 'CT', the function returns the value 'Other'.

```
SELECT DISTINCT state,
       DECODE(state, 'NY', 'New York',
                     'NJ', 'New Jersey') no_default,
       DECODE(state, 'NY', 'New York',
                     'NJ', 'New Jersey',
                           'OTHER') with_default
  FROM zipcode
 WHERE state IN ('NY','NJ','CT')
ST NO_DEFAULT WITH_DEFAULT
-- ---------- ------------
CT            OTHER
NJ New Jersey New Jersey
NY New York   New York

3 rows selected.
```

THE DECODE FUNCTION AND NULLS

If you want to specifically test for the null value, you can use the keyword NULL. The following SQL statement shows, for instructors with a null value in the ZIP column, the text NO zipcode! Although one null does not equal another null, for the purpose of the DECODE function, null values are treated as equals.

```
SELECT instructor_id, zip,
       DECODE(zip, NULL, 'NO zipcode!', zip) "Decode Use"
  FROM instructor
 WHERE instructor_id IN (102, 110)
INSTRUCTOR_ID ZIP   Decode Use
------------- ----- -----------
          110       NO zipcode!
          102 10025 10025

2 rows selected.
```

THE DECODE FUNCTION AND COMPARISONS

The DECODE function does not allow greater than or less than comparisons; however, combining the DECODE function with the SIGN function overcomes this shortcoming.

The following SELECT statement combines the DECODE and SIGN functions to display the course cost as 500 for courses that cost less than 1195. If the course cost is greater than or equal to 1195, the actual cost is displayed. The calculation of the value in the COST column minus 1195 results in a negative number, a positive number, a zero, or null. The SIGN function determines the sign of the calculation and returns, respectively, −1, +1, 0, or null. The DECODE function checks whether the result equals −1. If it does, this indicates that the cost is less than 1195, and the DECODE function returns 500; otherwise, the regular cost is shown.

```
SELECT course_no, cost,
       DECODE(SIGN(cost-1195),-1, 500, cost) newcost
  FROM course
 WHERE course_no IN (80, 20, 135, 450)
 ORDER BY 2
```

COURSE_NO	COST	NEWCOST
135	1095	500
20	1195	1195
80	1595	1595
450		

4 rows selected.

The Searched CASE Expression

A searched CASE expression is extremely powerful and can be utilized in many ways. You will see examples in the SELECT list, the WHERE clause, the ORDER BY clause, as a parameter of a function, and anywhere else an expression is allowed. Using a CASE expression is, in many cases, easier to understand, less restrictive, and more versatile than applying the DECODE function. For example, the following query accomplishes the same result as the previous query.

```
SELECT course_no, cost,
       CASE WHEN cost <1195 THEN 500
            ELSE cost
       END "Test CASE"
  FROM course
 WHERE course_no IN (80, 20, 135, 450)
 ORDER BY 2
```

COURSE_NO	COST	Test CASE
135	1095	500
20	1195	1195
80	1595	1595
450		

4 rows selected.

Each CASE expression starts with the keyword CASE and ends with the keyword END; the ELSE clause is optional. A condition is tested with the WHEN keyword; if the condition is true, the THEN clause is executed. The result of the query shows 500 in the column labeled Test CASE when the value in the COST column is less than 1195; otherwise, it just displays the value of the COST column. Following is the syntax of the searched CASE expression.

```
CASE {WHEN condition THEN return_expr
   [WHEN condition THEN return_expr]... }
   [ELSE else_expr]
END
```

The next example expands the WHEN condition of the CASE expression, with multiple conditions being tested. The first condition checks whether the value in the COST column is less than 1100; when true, the result evaluates to 1000. If the value in the COST column is equal to or greater than 1100, but less than 1500, the value in the COST column is multiplied by 1.1, increasing the cost by 10%. If the value in the COST column is null, then the value zero is the result. If none of the conditions are true, the ELSE clause is returned.

```
SELECT course_no, cost,
       CASE WHEN cost <1100 THEN 1000
            WHEN cost >=1100 AND cost <1500 THEN cost*1.1
            WHEN cost IS NULL THEN 0
            ELSE cost
       END "Test CASE"
  FROM course
 WHERE course_no IN (80, 20, 135, 450)
 ORDER BY 2

COURSE_NO        COST   Test CASE
---------------  -----  ---------
      135        1095        1000
       20        1195      1314.5
       80        1595        1595
      450                       0

4 rows selected.
```

 The CASE expression lets you evaluate if-then-else conditions more simply than the DECODE function.

NESTING CASE EXPRESSIONS

A CASE expression can be nested further with additional CASE expressions, as shown in the next example. An additional row with the COURSE_NO 230 is included in this query to demonstrate the result of the nested expression. This nested expression is evaluated only if COST is less than 1100. If this expression is true, the value of the PREREQUISITE column is checked; if it is either 10 or 50, the cost is cut in half. If the PREREQUISITE column does not have the value 10 or 50, just the value in the COST is displayed.

```
SELECT course_no, cost, prerequisite,
       CASE WHEN cost <1100 THEN
                CASE WHEN prerequisite IN (10, 50) THEN cost/2
                     ELSE cost
                END
            WHEN cost >=1100 AND cost <1500 THEN cost*1.1
            WHEN cost IS NULL THEN 0
            ELSE cost
       END "Test CASE"
  FROM course
```

```
WHERE course_no IN (80, 20, 135, 450, 230)
ORDER BY 2
  COURSE_NO      COST PREREQUISITE  Test CASE
--------------- ---- ------------- ---------
        230     1095           10     547.5
        135     1095          134      1095
         20     1195                 1314.5
         80     1595          204      1595
        450                   350         0
```

5 rows selected.

CASE EXPRESSION IN THE WHERE CLAUSE

Case expressions are allowed anywhere expressions are allowed; the following example shows a CASE expression in the WHERE clause. It multiplies the CAPACITY column by the result of the CASE expression that returns either 2, 1.5, or null, depending on the starting letter of the value in the LOCATION column. Only if the result of the CASE expression is greater than 30 is the row chosen for output.

```
SELECT DISTINCT capacity, location
  FROM section
WHERE capacity*CASE
         WHEN SUBSTR(location, 1,1)='L' THEN 2
         WHEN SUBSTR(location, 1,1)='M' THEN 1.5
         ELSE NULL
       END  > 30
CAPACITY  LOCATION
--------- --------
       25 L210
...
       25 M500
```

8 rows selected.

DATA TYPE INCONSISTENCIES

You may come across the error message shown in Figure 4.6 when executing the CASE expression or the DECODE function. It indicates that the return data type of the first condition does not agree with the data type of the subsequent conditions. The first CASE condition returns a NUMBER data type, and the second condition returns the character string 'Room too small'.

```
SELECT section_id, capacity,
       CASE WHEN capacity >=15 THEN capacity
            WHEN capacity < 15 THEN 'Room too small'
       END AS "Capacity"
  FROM section
 WHERE section_id IN (101, 146, 147)
```

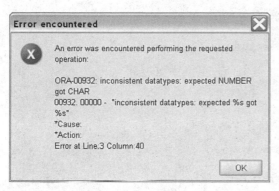

FIGURE 4.6
Error message on inconsistent data types

You match the two data types with a conversion function. The next example shows the use of the TO_CHAR conversion function to convert the values of the CAPACITY column to a character data type.

```
SELECT section_id, capacity,
       CASE WHEN capacity >=15 THEN TO_CHAR(capacity)
            WHEN capacity < 15 THEN 'Room too small'
       END AS "Capacity"
  FROM section
 WHERE section_id IN (101, 146, 147)
SECTION_ID   CAPACITY Capacity
------------ -------- --------------
       147         15 15
       146         25 25
       101         10 Room too small

3 rows selected.
```

Simple CASE Expression

If your conditions are testing for equality only, you can use a simple CASE expression, which has the following syntax.

```
CASE {expr WHEN comparison_expr THEN return_expr
          [WHEN comparison_expr THEN return_expr]...}
          [ELSE else_expr]
END
```

The next query example checks the value in the COST column to see if it equals the different amounts, and, if true, the appropriate THEN expression is executed.

```
SELECT course_no, cost,
       CASE cost WHEN 1095 THEN cost/2
                 WHEN 1195 THEN cost*1.1
                 WHEN 1595 THEN cost
                 ELSE cost*0.5
       END "Simple CASE"
  FROM course
 WHERE course_no IN (80, 20, 135, 450)
 ORDER BY 2
 COURSE_NO     COST Simple CASE
---------------- ---- -----------
       135     1095       547.5
        20     1195      1314.5
        80     1595        1595
       450


4 rows selected.
```

 Rather than hard-coding literals in CASE expressions, you can use subqueries to read dynamic values from tables instead. You will learn more about this in Chapter 8, "Subqueries."

Which Functions and CASE Expressions Should You Use?

Table 4.4 lists the miscellaneous functions and CASE expressions discussed in this lab.

TABLE 4.4   Miscellaneous Functions and CASE Expressions

FUNCTION/EXPRESSION	PURPOSE
NVL(input_expression, substitution_expression)	Null value replacement.
COALESCE(input_expression, substitution_expression_1, [, substitution_expression_n])	Null value replacement with multiple substitution expressions.
NVL2(input_expr, not_null_substitution_expr, null_substitution_expr)	Null and not null substitution replacement.
LNNVL(condition)	Returns true if the condition is false or unknown. Returns false if the condition is true.
NULLIF(expression1, equal_expression2)	Returns null if the value of two expressions are identical; otherwise, returns first expression.

TABLE 4.4   Continued

FUNCTION/EXPRESSION	PURPOSE
NANVL(input_value, substitution_value)	Returns a substitution value in the case of NAN (not a number) value.
DECODE (if_expr, equals_search, then_result [,else_default])	Substitution function based on if-then-else logic.
CASE {WHEN cond THEN return_ expr [WHEN cond THEN return_ expr]...} [ELSE else_expr] END	Searched CASE expression. It allows for testing of null values and other comparisons.
CASE {expr WHEN expr THEN return_expr [WHEN expr THEN return_expr]...} [ELSE else_expr] END	The simple CASE expression tests for equality only. No greater than, less than, or IS NULL comparisons are allowed.

▼ LAB 4.3 EXERCISES

a) List the last names, first names, and phone numbers of students who do not have phone numbers. Display 212-555-1212 for the phone number.

b) For course numbers 430 and greater, show the course cost. Add another column, reflecting a discount of 10% off the cost, and substitute any NULL values in the COST column with the number 1000. The result should look similar to the output shown in Figure 4.7.

	COURSE_NO	COST	NEW
1	430	1195	1075.5
2	450	(null)	900

Results:

FIGURE 4.7
Output reflecting the course cost with a 10% discount

c) Write the query to accomplish the following output, using the NVL2 function in the column Get this result.

```
ID  NAME            PHONE         Get this result
--- --------------  ------------- ------------------
112 Thomas Thomas   201-555-5555  Phone# exists.
111 Peggy Noviello                No phone# exists.

2 rows selected.
```

d) Rewrite the query from Exercise c, using the DECODE function instead.

e) For course numbers 20, 120, 122, and 132, display the description, course number, and prerequisite course number. If the prerequisite is course number 120, display 200; if the prerequisite is 130, display N/A. For courses with no prerequisites, display None. Otherwise, list the current prerequisite. The result should look as follows.

```
COURSE_NO DESCRIPTION                        ORIGINAL NEW
--------- ------------------------------     -------- ----
      132 Basics of Unix Admin                    130 N/A
      122 Intermediate Java Programming           120 200
      120 Intro to Java Programming                80 80
       20 Intro to Information Systems                 None

4 rows selected.
```

f) Display the student IDs, zip codes, and phone numbers for students with student IDs 145, 150, or 325. For students living in the 212 area code and in zip code 10048, display North Campus. List students living in the 212 area code but in a different zip code as West Campus. Display students outside the 212 area code as Off Campus. The result should look like the following output. Hint: The solution to this query requires nested DECODE functions or nested CASE expressions.

```
STUDENT_ID ZIP    PHONE            LOC
---------- -----  ---------------  ------------
       145 10048  212-555-5555     North Campus
       150 11787  718-555-5555     Off Campus
       325 10954  212-555-5555     West Campus

3 rows selected.
```

g) Display all the distinct salutations used in the INSTRUCTOR table. Order them alphabetically, except for female salutations, which should be listed first. Hint: Use the DECODE function or CASE expression in the ORDER BY clause.

▼ LAB 4.3 EXERCISE ANSWERS

a) List the last names, first names, and phone numbers of students who do not have phone numbers. Display 212-555-1212 for the phone number.

ANSWER: There are various solutions to obtain the desired result. First, you can determine the rows with a NULL phone number, using the IS NULL operator. Then you apply the NVL function to the column with the substitution string '212-555-1212'. The second solution uses the NVL function in both the SELECT and WHERE clauses. Another way to achieve the result is to use the COALESCE function.

```
SELECT first_name||' '|| last_name name,
       phone oldphone,
       NVL(phone, '212-555-1212') newphone
  FROM student
 WHERE phone IS NULL
```

```
NAME                              OLDPHONE         NEWPHONE
------------------------- --------------- ------------
Peggy Noviello                                     212-555-1212

1 row selected.
```

You can also retrieve the same rows by applying the NVL function in the WHERE clause.

```
SELECT first_name||' '|| last_name name,
       phone oldphone,
       NVL(phone, '212-555-1212') newphone
  FROM student
 WHERE NVL(phone, 'NONE') = 'NONE'
```

```
NAME                              OLDPHONE         NEWPHONE
------------------------- --------------- ------------
Peggy Noviello                                     212-555-1212

1 row selected.
```

The next query applies the COALESCE function to achieve the same result.

```
SELECT first_name||' '|| last_name name,
       phone oldphone,
       COALESCE(phone, '212-555-1212') newphone
  FROM student
 WHERE COALESCE(phone, 'NONE') ='NONE'
```

b) For course numbers 430 and greater, show the course cost. Add another column, reflecting a discount of 10% off the cost, and substitute any NULL values in the COST column with the number 1000. The result should look similar to the output shown in Figure 4.8.

	COURSE_NO	COST	NEW
1	430	1195	1075.5
2	450	(null)	900

FIGURE 4.8
Output reflecting the course cost with a 10% discount

ANSWER: Substitute 1000 for the null value, using the NVL function before applying the discount calculation. Otherwise, the calculation yields a NULL.

```
SELECT course_no, cost,
       NVL(cost,1000)*0.9 new
  FROM course
 WHERE course_no >= 430
```

You can use the COALESCE function instead.

```
SELECT course_no, cost,
       COALESCE(cost,1000)*0.9 new
  FROM course
 WHERE course_no >= 430
```

c) Write the query to accomplish the following output, using the NVL2 function in the column Get this result.

```
ID  NAME               PHONE          Get this result
--- --------------     ------------   ------------------
112 Thomas Thomas      201-555-5555   Phone# exists.
111 Peggy Noviello                    No phone# exists.

2 rows selected.
```

ANSWER: If the input parameter is not null, the NVL2 function's second parameter is returned. If the input parameter is null, then the third parameter is used.

```
SELECT student_id id, first_name||' '|| last_name name,
       phone,
       NVL2(phone, 'Phone# exists.', 'No phone# exists.')
       "Get this result"
  FROM student
 WHERE student_id IN (111, 112)
 ORDER BY 1 DESC
```

d) Rewrite the query from Exercise c, using the DECODE function instead.

ANSWER: The DECODE function can easily be substituted for the NVL2 function or the NVL function, because you can test for a NULL value. In this result, the DECODE function checks whether the value is null. If this is true, the 'No phone# exists.' literal is displayed; otherwise, it shows 'Phone# exists.'

```
SELECT student_id, first_name||' '|| last_name name,
       phone,
       DECODE(phone, NULL, 'No phone# exists.', 'Phone# exists.')
       "Get this result"
  FROM student
 WHERE student_id IN (111, 112)
 ORDER BY 1 DESC
```

e) For course numbers 20, 120, 122, and 132, display the description, course number, and prerequisite course number. If the prerequisite is course number 120, display 200; if the prerequisite is 130, display N/A. For courses with no prerequisites, display None. Otherwise, list the current prerequisite. The result should look as follows.

```
COURSE_NO DESCRIPTION                       ORIGINAL NEW
--------- ----------------------------      -------- ----
      132 Basics of Unix Admin                   130 N/A
      122 Intermediate Java Programming          120 200
      120 Intro to Java Programming               80 80
       20 Intro to Information Systems               None

4 rows selected.
```

ANSWER: The solution can be achieved with either the CASE expression or the DECODE function.

SOLUTION USING THE CASE EXPRESSION

The following solution query checks for nulls with the IS NULL condition. The ELSE clause requires you to convert the NUMBER data type into a VARCHAR2, using the TO_CHAR function; otherwise, you receive error ORA-00932 ("inconsistent data types"), indicating that the output data types do not match. Oracle expects the data type to be consistent, with the same data type as the first result expression, which is a string, as indicated by the single quotes around 200.

```
SELECT course_no, description, prerequisite "Original",
       CASE WHEN prerequisite = 120 THEN '200'
            WHEN prerequisite = 130 THEN 'N/A'
            WHEN prerequisite IS NULL THEN 'None'
            ELSE TO_CHAR(prerequisite)
       END "NEW"
  FROM course
 WHERE course_no IN (20, 120, 122, 132)
 ORDER BY course_no DESC
```

If you attempt to use the simple CASE expression to solve the query, the test for the null value cannot be accomplished because the simple CASE expression only allows testing for equality (=). The IS NULL operator is not permitted and returns the error ORA-00936 ("missing expression") (see Figure 4.9).

```
SELECT course_no, description, prerequisite "Original",
       CASE prerequisite WHEN 120 THEN '200'
                         WHEN 130 THEN 'N/A'
                         WHEN IS NULL THEN 'None'
                         ELSE TO_CHAR(prerequisite)
       END "NEW"
  FROM course
 WHERE course_no IN (20, 120, 122, 132)
```

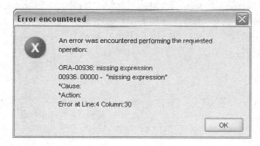

FIGURE 4.9
An ORA-00936 error

SOLUTION USING THE DECODE FUNCTION

The following solution is best approached in several steps. The PREREQUISITE column is of data type NUMBER. If you replace it in the DECODE function with another NUMBER for prerequisite 120, Oracle expects to continue to convert to the same data type for all subsequent replacements. As the other replacements ('N/A' and 'None') are text literals, you need to enclose the number 200 in single quotation marks to predetermine the data type for all subsequent substitutions as a VARCHAR2.

For any records that have a null prerequisite, None is displayed. Although one null does not equal another null, for the purpose of the DECODE function, null values are treated as equals.

```
SELECT course_no, description, prerequisite "ORIGINAL",
       DECODE(prerequisite, 120, '200',
                            130, 'N/A',
                            NULL, 'None',
                            TO_CHAR(prerequisite)) "NEW"
  FROM course
 WHERE course_no IN (20, 120, 122, 132)
 ORDER BY course_no DESC
```

Explicit data type conversion with the TO_CHAR function on PREREQUISITE is good practice, although if you omit it, Oracle implicitly converts the value to a VARCHAR2 data type. The automatic data type conversion works in this example because the data type is predetermined by the data type of the first substitution value.

f) Display the student IDs, zip codes, and phone numbers for students with student IDs 145, 150, or 325. For students living in the 212 area code and in zip code 10048, display North Campus. List students living in the 212 area code but in a different zip code as West Campus. Display students outside the 212 area code as Off Campus. The result should look like the following output. Hint: The solution to this query requires nested DECODE functions or nested CASE expressions.

```
STUDENT_ID ZIP   PHONE            LOC
---------- ----- ---------------- ------------
       145 10048 212-555-5555     North Campus
       150 11787 718-555-5555     Off Campus
       325 10954 212-555-5555     West Campus
```

3 rows selected.

ANSWER: The CASE expressions can be nested within each other to allow for the required logic. A more complicated way to obtain the desired result is by using nested DECODE statements; the output from one DECODE is an input parameter in a second DECODE function.

Following is the solution using the CASE expression.

```
SELECT student_id, zip, phone,
       CASE WHEN SUBSTR(phone, 1, 3) = '212' THEN
                 CASE WHEN zip = '10048' THEN 'North Campus'
                      ELSE 'West Campus'
                 END
            ELSE 'Off Campus'
       END loc
  FROM student
 WHERE student_id IN (150, 145, 325)
```

The next solution uses the DECODE function.

```
SELECT student_id, zip, phone,
       DECODE(SUBSTR(phone, 1, 3), '212',
                 DECODE(zip, '10048', 'North Campus',
                                      'West Campus'),
```

```
                   'Off Campus') loc
      FROM student
     WHERE student_id IN (150, 145, 325)
```

g) Display all the distinct salutations used in the INSTRUCTOR table. Order them alphabetically, except for female salutations, which should be listed first. Hint: Use the DECODE function or CASE expression in the ORDER BY clause.

ANSWER: The DECODE function or the CASE expression is used in the ORDER BY clause to substitute a number for all female salutations, thereby listing them first when executing the ORDER BY clause.

```
SELECT DISTINCT salutation
   FROM instructor
  ORDER BY DECODE(salutation, 'Ms', '1',
                              'Mrs', '1',
                              'Miss', '1',
                               salutation)
```

```
SALUT
-----
Ms
Dr
Hon
Mr
Rev

5 rows selected.
```

The following shows the CASE expression.

```
 SELECT DISTINCT salutation
    FROM instructor
   ORDER BY CASE salutation WHEN 'Ms' THEN '1'
                            WHEN 'Mrs' THEN '1'
                            WHEN 'Miss' THEN '1'
                            ELSE salutation
          END
```

The ASCII equivalent number of 1 is less than the ASCII equivalent of Dr, or any other salutation. Therefore, Ms is listed first in the sort order. (ASCII, which stands for American Standard Code for Information Interchange, deals with common formats.)

To display the decimal representation of the first character of a string, use the ASCII function. The following query is an example of how you can determine the ASCII numbers of various values.

```
SELECT ASCII('1') "1", ASCII('0') "ZERO", ASCII('D') "D",
       ASCII('a') "a", ASCII('A') "A"
   FROM dual
              1        ZERO          D          a  A
-------------- ----------- --------- --------- --
             49          48         68         97 65

1 row selected.
```

Lab 4.3 Quiz

In order to test your progress, you should be able to answer the following questions.

1) A calculation with a null always yields another null.

    _____ a) True
    _____ b) False

2) The following query is valid.

```
SELECT NVL(cost, 'None')
  FROM course
```

    _____ a) True
    _____ b) False

3) The NVL2 function updates the data in the database.

    _____ a) True
    _____ b) False

4) The DECODE function lets you perform if-then-else functionality within the SQL language.

    _____ a) True
    _____ b) False

5) The DECODE function cannot be used in the WHERE clause of a SQL statement.

    _____ a) True
    _____ b) False

6) CASE expressions can be used in the ORDER BY clause of a SELECT statement.

    _____ a) True
    _____ b) False

7) The functions discussed in this lab can be used on the VARCHAR2 data type only.

    _____ a) True
    _____ b) False

ANSWERS APPEAR IN APPENDIX A.

▼ WORKSHOP

The projects in this section are meant to prompt you to utilize all the skills you have acquired throughout this chapter. The answers to these projects can be found at the companion Web site to this book, located at www.oraclesqlbyexample.com.

1) Write the SELECT statement that returns the following output.

```
ONE_LINE
----------------------------------------------
Instructor: R. Chow...... Phone: 212-555-1212
Instructor: M. Frantzen.. Phone: 212-555-1212
Instructor: F. Hanks..... Phone: 212-555-1212
Instructor: C. Lowry..... Phone: 212-555-1212
Instructor: A. Morris.... Phone: 212-555-1212
Instructor: G. Pertez.... Phone: 212-555-1212
Instructor: N. Schorin... Phone: 212-555-1212
Instructor: T. Smythe.... Phone: 212-555-1212
Instructor: I. Willig.... Phone: 212-555-1212
Instructor: T. Wojick.... Phone: 212-555-1212
```

2) Rewrite the following query to replace all occurrences of the string 'Unix' with 'Linux'.

```
SELECT 'I develop software on the Unix platform'
  FROM dual
```

3) Determine which student does not have the first letter of her or his last name capitalized. Show the STUDENT_ID and LAST_NAME columns.

4) Check whether any of the phone numbers in the INSTRUCTOR table have been entered in the (###)###-#### format.

5) Explain the functionality of the following query.

```
SELECT section_id, capacity,
       CASE WHEN MOD(capacity, 2) <> 0 THEN 'Odd capacity'
            ELSE 'Even capacity'
       END "Odd or Even"
  FROM section
 WHERE section_id IN (101, 146, 147)
```

CHAPTER 5

Date and Conversion Functions

CHAPTER OBJECTIVES

In this chapter, you will learn about:

- ▶ Applying Oracle's Date Format Models
- ▶ Performing Date and Time Math
- ▶ Understanding Timestamp and Time Zones Data Types
- ▶ Performing Calculations with the Interval Data Types
- ▶ Converting from One Data Type to Another

In this chapter, you will gain an understanding of Oracle's two date-related categories of data types: the datetime data types and the interval data types.

The datetime data types keep track of both date and time; they consist of the individual data types DATE, TIMESTAMP, TIMESTAMP WITH TIME ZONE, and TIMESTAMP WITH LOCAL TIME ZONE. In the first two labs, you will learn about the most popular data type—the DATE data type. Lab 5.3 introduces you to the other three data types, which contain fractional seconds and time zone values. Table 5.1 shows an overview of the datetime data types.

TABLE 5.1   Overview of Datetime Data Types

DATA TYPE	FRACTIONAL SECONDS	TIME ZONE	LAB
DATE	No	No	5.1, 5.2
TIMESTAMP	Yes	No	5.3
TIMESTAMP WITH TIME ZONE	Yes	Yes	5.3
TIMESTAMP WITH LOCAL TIME ZONE	Yes	Yes	5.3

The interval data types, which are the topic of Lab 5.4, express differences between dates and times. The Oracle-supported interval data types are INTERVAL YEAR TO MONTH and INTERVAL DAY TO SECOND (see Table 5.2).

TABLE 5.2   Overview of Interval Data Types

DATA TYPE	SUPPORTED TIME DIFFERENCES
INTERVAL YEAR TO MONTH	Years and months
INTERVAL DAY TO SECOND	Days, hours, minutes, and seconds

In Lab 5.5, you will become familiar with using data type conversion functions—an important skill for dealing with data.

SQL novices often find date and conversion functions challenging, but the many examples in this chapter's labs will help you master these functions and avoid the common pitfalls.

LAB 5.1
Applying Oracle's Date Format Models

LAB OBJECTIVES

After this lab, you will be able to:

- ▶ Compare a Text Literal to a DATE Column
- ▶ Apply Various Format Models

When working with an Oracle database, you will inevitably need to query columns that contain dates. Oracle's DATE data type consists of a *date and time* that are stored in an internal format that keeps track of the century, year, month, day, hour, minute, and second.

Changing the Date Display Format

When you query a DATE data type column, Oracle displays it in the default format determined by the database NLS_DATE_FORMAT parameter. The most frequent setup values you will see are DD-MON-YYYY and DD-MON-RR. The RR represents a two-digit year based on the century: if the two-digit year is between 50 and 99, then it's the previous century; if the two-digit year is between 00 and 49, it's the current century.

```
SELECT last_name, registration_date
  FROM student
 WHERE student_id IN (123, 161, 190)
LAST_NAME  REGISTRAT
---------  ---------
Affinito   03-FEB-07
Grant      02-FEB-07
Radicola   27-JAN-07

3 rows selected.
```

To change the display format of the column REGISTRATION_DATE, you use the TO_CHAR function together with a format model, also referred to as a *format mask*. The result shows the registration date in both the default date format and the MM/DD/YYYY format.

```
SELECT last_name, registration_date,
       TO_CHAR(registration_date, 'MM/DD/YYYY')
       AS "Formatted"
  FROM student
 WHERE student_id IN (123, 161, 190)
LAST_NAME        REGISTRAT Formatted
---------        --------- ----------
Affinito         03-FEB-07 02/03/2007
Grant            02-FEB-07 02/02/2007
Radicola         27-JAN-07 01/27/2007

3 rows selected.
```

The TO_CHAR conversion function changes the DATE data type into text and applies a format mask. As you see from the syntax listed in Table 5.3, the function takes a DATE data type as the first parameter; the second optional parameter is for the format mask. Table 5.4 lists commonly used elements of date format masks.

TABLE 5.3   Date-Related Conversion Functions

FUNCTION	PURPOSE	RETURN DATA TYPE
TO_CHAR(date [,format_mask])	Converts datetime data types into VARCHAR2 to use a different display format than the default date format. (The TO_CHAR function can be used with other data types besides DATE; see Lab 5.5.)	VARCHAR2
TO_DATE(char [,format_mask])	Converts a text literal to a DATE data type. As with all other date-related conversion functions, the format_mask is optional if the literal is in the default format; otherwise, a format mask must be specified.	DATE

TABLE 5.4   Commonly Used Elements of the DATE Format Mask

FORMAT	DESCRIPTION
YYYY	Four-digit year.
YEAR	Year, spelled out.
RR	Two-digit year, based on century. If two-digit year is between 50 and 99, then it's the previous century; if the year is between 00 and 49, it's the current century.
MM	Two-digit month.
MON	Three-letter abbreviation of the month, in uppercase letters.

TABLE 5.4   Continued

FORMAT	DESCRIPTION
MONTH	Month, spelled out, in uppercase letters and padded with blanks.
Month	Month, spelled with, first letter uppercase and padded with blanks to a length of nine characters.
DD	Numeric day (1–31).
DAY	Day of the week, spelled out, in uppercase letters and padded with blanks to a length of nine characters.
DY	Three-letter abbreviation of the day of the week, in uppercase letters.
D	Day of the week number (1–7), where Sunday is day 1, Monday is day 2, and so forth.
DDD	Day of the year (1–366).
DL	Day long format; the equivalent format mask is fmDay, Month DD, YYYY.
HH or HH12	Hours (0–12).
HH24	Hours in military format (0–23).
MI	Minutes (0–59).
SS	Seconds (0–59).
SSSSS	Seconds past midnight (0–86399).
AM or PM	Meridian indicator.
TS	Short time format; the equivalent format mask is HH:MI:SS AM.
WW	Week of the year (1–53).
W	Week of the month (1–5).
Q	Quarter of the year.

The TO_DATE function does just the opposite of the TO_CHAR function: It converts a text literal into a DATE data type.

The next SQL statement shows the same student record, with the date and time formatted in various ways. The first format model is Dy, which shows the abbreviated day of the week in mixed format. The next format model is DY, and it returns the uppercase version. The fourth column has the month spelled out, but notice the extra spaces after the month. Oracle pads the month with up to nine spaces, which may be useful when you choose to align the month columns. If you want to eliminate the extra spaces, use the fill mask fm. You will see some examples of this format mask shortly. The last column shows only the time.

```
SELECT last_name,
       TO_CHAR(registration_date, 'Dy') AS "1.Day",
       TO_CHAR(registration_date, 'DY') AS "2.Day",
       TO_CHAR(registration_date, 'Month DD, YYYY')
          AS "Look at the Month",
       TO_CHAR(registration_date, 'HH:MI PM') AS "Time"
```

```
   FROM student
  WHERE student_id IN (123, 161, 190)
 LAST_NAME 1.Da 2.Da Look at the Month  Time
 --------- ---- ---- ------------------ --------
 Affinito  Sat  SAT  February  03, 2007 12:00 PM
 Grant     Fri  FRI  February  02, 2007 12:00 PM
 Radicola  Sat  SAT  January   27, 2007 12:00 PM

 3 rows selected.
```

Here is a more elaborate example, which uses the *fm* mask to eliminate the extra spaces between the month and the date in the second column of the following result set. In addition, this format mask uses the *th* suffix on the day (dd) mask, to include the st, nd, rd, and th in lowercase after each number. The third and last column spells out the date using the *sp* format parameter, with the first letter capitalized by using the Dd format. Also, you can add a text literal, as in this case with the "of" text.

```
SELECT last_name,
       TO_CHAR(registration_date, 'fmMonth ddth, YYYY')
       "Eliminating Spaces",
       TO_CHAR(registration_date, 'Ddspth "of" fmMonth')
       "Spelled out"
  FROM student
 WHERE student_id IN (123, 161, 190)
 LAST_NAME  Eliminating Spaces   Spelled out
 ---------  ------------------   ------------------------
 Affinito   February 3rd, 2007   Third of February
 Grant      February 2nd, 2007   Second of February
 Radicola   January 27th, 2007   Twenty-Seventh of January

 3 rows selected.
```

Table 5.5 shows additional examples of how the format models can be used.

TABLE 5.5   Date Format Model Examples

FORMAT MASK	EXAMPLE
DD-Mon-YYYY HH24:MI:SS	12-Apr-2009 17:00:00 (The case matters!)
MM/DD/YYYY HH:MI PM	04/12/2009 5:00 PM
Month	April
fmMonth DDth, YYYY	April 12th, 2009
Day	Sunday
DY	SUN

TABLE 5.5   Continued

FORMAT MASK	EXAMPLE
Qth YYYY	2nd 2009 (This shows the 2nd quarter of 2009.)
Ddspth	Twelfth (Spells out the date.)
DD-MON-RR	12-APR-09 (You'll learn ore on the RR format later in this lab.)

Performing a Date Search

You'll find that you often need to query data based on certain date criteria. For example, if you need to look for all students with a registration date of January 22, 2007, you write a SQL statement similar to the following.

```
SELECT last_name, registration_date
  FROM student
 WHERE registration_date = TO_DATE('22-JAN-2007', 'DD-MON-YYYY')
LAST_NAME                       REGISTRAT
------------------------------  ---------
Crocitto                        22-JAN-07
Landry                          22-JAN-07
...
Sethi                           22-JAN-07
Walter                          22-JAN-07

8 rows selected.
```

In the WHERE clause, the text literal '22-JAN-2007' is converted to a DATE data type using the TO_DATE function and the format model. The TO_DATE function helps Oracle understand the text literal, based on the supplied format mask. The text literal is converted to the DATE data type, which is then compared to the REGISTRATION_DATE column, also of data type DATE. Now you are comparing identical data types.

The format mask needs to agree with your text literal; otherwise, Oracle will not be able to interpret the text literal correctly and will return the following error message.

```
SELECT last_name, registration_date
  FROM student
 WHERE registration_date = TO_DATE('22/01/2007', 'DD-MON-YYYY')
WHERE registration_date = TO_DATE('22/01/2007', 'DD-MON-YYYY')
                                    *
ERROR at line 3:
ORA-01843: not a valid month
```

Implicit Conversion and Default Date Format

Without a format mask, Oracle can implicitly perform a conversion of the text literal to the DATE data type when the text literal is in the default date format. This default format is determined by the NLS_DATE_FORMAT, an Oracle instance parameter. The next SQL statement shows an example of this.

```
SELECT last_name, registration_date
  FROM student
 WHERE registration_date = '22-JAN-07'
LAST_NAME                   REGISTRAT
------------------------    ---------
Crocitto                    22-JAN-07
Landry                      22-JAN-07
...
Sethi                       22-JAN-07
Walter                      22-JAN-07

8 rows selected.
```

The same result can also be achieved with the following WHERE clause. In this example, it allows either a four-digit or two-digit input of the year. For a two-digit year, Oracle determines the century for you.

```
WHERE registration_date = '22-JAN-2007'
```

The NLS_DATE_FORMAT value is defined as Oracle database's initialization parameter, but you can also modify the behavior by changing the Windows registry, or within a tool such as SQL Developer, by selecting Tools, Preferences, Database, NLS Parameters and using the options there (see Figure 5.1). You can also issue the ALTER SESSION command to temporarily set the value.

```
ALTER SESSION SET NLS_DATE_FORMAT = 'DD-MON-RRRR'
```

It is always best to explicitly use the TO_DATE function along with the appropriate format mask when converting a text literal. This makes your statement explicit and independent of any settings. You will see the advantages of doing so as you go through some of the exercises in this chapter.

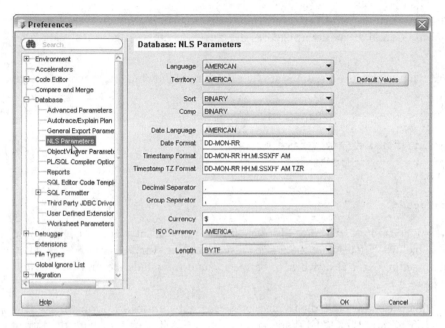

FIGURE 5.1
SQL Developer's display for NLS parameters

The RR Date Format Mask and the Previous Century

Although the year 2000 is long behind us, you still have to deal with dates in the twentieth century. For example, the next statement retrieves all rows in the GRADE_TYPE table that were created on December 31, 1998. Notice that the century is missing in the WHERE clause.

```
SELECT grade_type_code, description, created_date
  FROM grade_type
 WHERE created_date = '31-DEC-98'
GR DESCRIPTION          CREATED_D
-- -------------------- ---------
FI Final                31-DEC-98
HM Homework             31-DEC-98
MT Midterm              31-DEC-98
PA Participation        31-DEC-98
PJ Project              31-DEC-98
QZ Quiz                 31-DEC-98

6 rows selected.
```

The query will return rows only if your Oracle installation includes the DD-MON-RR or DD-MON-RRRR format mask. This special RR format mask interprets the two-digit year from

50 until 99 as the prior century, which currently is for years from 1950 through 1999. Two-digit year numbers from 00 until 49 are interpreted as the current century—that is, as years 2000 through 2049.

You can also see what your session settings are by issuing the following query, which returns session attributes.

```
SELECT SYS_CONTEXT ('USERENV', 'NLS_DATE_FORMAT')
  FROM dual
SYS_CONTEXT('USERENV','NLS_DATE_FORMAT')
----------------------------------------
DD-MON-RR

1 row selected.
```

If your default format mask is set to DD-MON-YY instead, Oracle interprets '31-DEC-98' as '31-DEC-2098', which is obviously not the desired result. Because databases can have different date configuration settings, it is always best to be specific and to include the four-digit year in your WHERE clause.

The next query illustrates how a two-digit year gets interpreted with the RR format mask. The text literals '17-OCT-67' and '17-OCT-17' are converted to a DATE data type with the format mask DD-MON-RR. Then the TO_CHAR function converts the DATE data type back to text, but this time with a four-digit year. Effectively, the two-digit year 67 is interpreted as 1967, and the two-digit year literal 17 is interpreted as 2017.

```
SELECT TO_CHAR(TO_DATE('17-OCT-67','DD-MON-RR'),'YYYY') "1900",
       TO_CHAR(TO_DATE('17-OCT-17','DD-MON-RR'),'YYYY') "2000"
  FROM dual
1900 2000
---- ----
1967 2017

1 row selected.
```

The Time Component

As previously mentioned, the Oracle DATE data type includes the time. You can query records for a specific time or ignore the time altogether. The next SQL statement displays the time as part of the result set. If no time component was included when the data was entered, Oracle assumes that the time is midnight, which is 12:00:00 AM, or 00:00:00 military time (HH24 time format mask). The WHERE clause retrieves only rows where the column has a value of January 22, 2007, midnight; other records with a different time are not returned, if any exist.

```
SELECT last_name,
       TO_CHAR(registration_date, 'DD-MON-YYYY HH24:MI:SS')
  FROM student
 WHERE registration_date = TO_DATE('22-JAN-2007', 'DD-MON-YYYY')
```

```
LAST_NAME                          TO_CHAR(REGISTRATION
------------------------           --------------------
Crocitto                           22-JAN-2007 00:00:00
Landry                             22-JAN-2007 00:00:00
...
Sethi                              22-JAN-2007 00:00:00
Walter                             22-JAN-2007 00:00:00

8 rows selected.
```

Time and the TRUNC Function

You already learned about the TRUNC function in connection with the NUMBER data type in Chapter 4, "Character, Number, and Miscellaneous Functions." The TRUNC function can also take a DATE data type as an input parameter, which interprets the time as midnight (that is, 12.00.00 AM). The next example shows the TRUNC function applied to the ENROLL_DATE column. It has the effect of including the records no matter what the time, as long as the date is February 7, 2007.

```
SELECT student_id, TO_CHAR(enroll_date, 'DD-MON-YYYY HH24:MI:SS')
  FROM enrollment
 WHERE TRUNC(enroll_date) = TO_DATE('07-FEB-2007', 'DD-MON-YYYY')
STUDENT_ID TO_CHAR(ENROLL_DATE,
---------- --------------------
       140 07-FEB-2007 10:19:00
       141 07-FEB-2007 10:19:00
...
       158 07-FEB-2007 10:19:00
       159 07-FEB-2007 10:19:00

20 rows selected.
```

The ANSI DATE and ANSI TIMESTAMP Formats

Instead of using Oracle's date literals, you can specify a date in the ANSI format listed in the next example. This format contains no time portion and must be listed exactly in the format YYYY-MM-DD, with the DATE keyword prefix.

```
SELECT student_id, TO_CHAR(enroll_date, 'DD-MON-YYYY HH24:MI:SS')
  FROM enrollment
 WHERE enroll_date >= DATE '2007-02-07'
   AND enroll_date <  DATE '2007-02-08'
```

If you want to include the time portion, use the ANSI TIMESTAMP keyword. The literal must be in the ANSI TIMESTAMP format, which is defined as YYYY-MM-DD HH24:MI:SS.

```
SELECT student_id, TO_CHAR(enroll_date, 'DD-MON-YYYY HH24:MI:SS')
  FROM enrollment
WHERE enroll_date >= TIMESTAMP '2007-02-07 00:00:00'
   AND enroll_date <  TIMESTAMP '2007-02-08 00:00:00'
```

▼ LAB 5.1 EXERCISES

a) Display the course number, section ID, and starting date and time for sections taught on May 4, 2007.

b) Show the student records that were modified on or before January 22, 2007. Display the date a record was modified and each student's first and last name, concatenated in one column.

c) Display the course number, section ID, and starting date and time for sections that start on Sundays.

d) List the section ID and starting date and time for all sections that begin and end in July 2007.

e) Determine the day of the week for December 31, 1899.

f) Execute the following statement. Write the questions to obtain the desired result. Pay particular attention to the ORDER BY clause.

```
SELECT 'Section '||section_id||' begins on '||
       TO_CHAR(start_date_time, 'fmDay')||'.' AS "Start"
  FROM section
 WHERE section_id IN (146, 127, 121, 155, 110, 85, 148)
 ORDER BY TO_CHAR(start_date_time, 'D')
```

▼ LAB 5.1 EXERCISE ANSWERS

a) Display the course number, section ID, and starting date and time for sections taught on May 4, 2007.

ANSWER: To display a DATE column in a nondefault format, use the TO_CHAR function. To compare a text literal to a DATE column, use the TO_DATE function. It is best to always use the four-digit year and the format mask when using the TO_DATE function. This is good practice because it means your queries are not subject to ambiguities if the default date format is different.

```
SELECT course_no, section_id,
       TO_CHAR(start_date_time, 'DD-MON-YYYY HH24:MI')
  FROM section
 WHERE start_date_time >= TO_DATE('04-MAY-2007', 'DD-MON-YYYY')
   AND start_date_time < TO_DATE('05-MAY-2007', 'DD-MON-YYYY')
COURSE_NO SECTION_ID TO_CHAR(START_DAT
--------- ---------- -----------------
       25         88 04-MAY-2007 09:30
      100        144 04-MAY-2007 09:30
      120        149 04-MAY-2007 09:30
      122        155 04-MAY-2007 09:30

4 rows selected.
```

The returned result set displays the starting date and time, using the TO_CHAR function and the specified format mask in the SELECT list. In the WHERE clause, the text literals '04-MAY-2007' and '05-MAY-2007' are transformed into the DATE data type with the TO_DATE function. Because no format mask for the time is specified, Oracle assumes that the time is midnight, which is 12:00:00 AM, or 00:00:00 military time (HH24 time format mask). The WHERE clause retrieves only rows where the START_DATE_TIME column has values on or after '04-MAY-2007 12:00:00 AM' and before '05-MAY-2007 12:00:00 AM'.

You can also include the time in your WHERE clause, as in the following example. It is irrelevant whether you choose AM or PM in the display 'DD-MON-YYYY HH:MI:SS AM' format mask for the display of the result, but obviously not in the WHERE clause with the actual date string listed as '04-MAY-2007 12:00:00 AM' and '04-MAY-2007 11:59:59 PM'.

```
SELECT course_no, section_id,
       TO_CHAR(start_date_time, 'DD-MON-YYYY HH24:MI')
  FROM section
 WHERE start_date_time >= TO_DATE('04-MAY-2007 12:00:00 AM',
                                  'DD-MON-YYYY HH:MI:SS AM')
   AND start_date_time <= TO_DATE('04-MAY-2007 11:59:59 PM',
                                  'DD-MON-YYYY HH:MI:SS AM')
```

The next SQL query returns the same result when the following WHERE clause is used instead. Here, note that Oracle has to perform the implicit conversion of the text literal into a DATE data type.

```
WHERE start_date_time >= '04-MAY-2007'
  AND start_date_time <  '05-MAY-2007'
```

The next WHERE clause returns the same result again, but Oracle has to perform the implicit conversion and choose the correct century.

```
WHERE start_date_time >= '04-MAY-07'
  AND start_date_time <  '05-MAY-07'
```

You can use the TRUNC function to ignore the timestamp.

```
SELECT course_no, section_id,
       TO_CHAR(start_date_time, 'DD-MON-YYYY HH24:MI')
  FROM section
 WHERE TRUNC(start_date_time) = TO_DATE('04-MAY-2007',
                                        'DD-MON-YYYY')
```

The next WHERE clause is another valid alternative; however, the previous WHERE clause is preferable because it explicitly specifies the TO_DATE data type conversion, together with the format mask, and includes the four-digit year.

```
WHERE TRUNC(start_date_time) = '04-MAY-07'
```

When you modify a database column with a function in the WHERE clause, such as the TRUNC function on the database column START_DATE_TIME, you cannot take advantage of an index if one exists on the column, unless it is a function-based index. Indexes speed up the retrieval of the data; you will learn more about the performance advantages of indexes in Chapter 13, "Indexes, Sequences, and Views."

The next statement does not return the desired rows. Only rows that have a START_DATE_TIME of midnight on May 4, 2007, qualify, and because there are no such rows, none are selected for output.

```
SELECT course_no, section_id,
       TO_CHAR(start_date_time, 'DD-MON-YYYY HH24:MI')
  FROM section
 WHERE start_date_time = '04-MAY-07'
```

no rows selected

The ANSI format is listed in the next example. The ANSI DATE format must be specified exactly in the format YYYY-MM-DD, with the DATE keyword prefix; note that it does not have a time component.

```
SELECT course_no, section_id,
       TO_CHAR(start_date_time, 'DD-MON-YYYY HH24:MI')
  FROM section
 WHERE start_date_time >= DATE '2007-05-04'
   AND start_date_time <  DATE '2007-05-05'
```

Alternatively, you can apply the TRUNC function on the START_DATE_TIME column, but be aware of the possible performance impact mentioned previously.

```
SELECT course_no, section_id,
       TO_CHAR(start_date_time, 'DD-MON-YYYY HH24:MI')
  FROM section
 WHERE TRUNC(start_date_time) = DATE '2007-05-04'
```

If you want to include the time, use the ANSI TIMESTAMP keyword. The literal must be exactly in the ANSI TIMESTAMP format, defined as YYYY-MM-DD HH24:MI:SS.

```
SELECT course_no, section_id,
       TO_CHAR(start_date_time, 'DD-MON-YYYY HH24:MI')
  FROM section
 WHERE start_date_time >= TIMESTAMP '2007-05-04 00:00:00'
   AND start_date_time <  TIMESTAMP '2007-05-05 00:00:00'
```

Error When Entering the Wrong Format

Any attempt to change the predetermined format or the use of the wrong keyword results in an error, as you see in the next example. For this query to work, the TIMESTAMP keyword must be used instead of the DATE keyword, because the literal is in the ANSI TIMESTAMP format.

```
SELECT course_no, section_id,
       TO_CHAR(start_date_time, 'DD-MON-YYYY HH24:MI')
  FROM section
 WHERE start_date_time >= DATE '2007-05-04 00:00:00'
   AND start_date_time <  DATE '2007-05-05 00:00:00'
WHERE start_date_time >= DATE '2007-05-04 00:00:00'
                              *
ERROR at line 4:
ORA-01861: literal does not match format string
```

b) Show the student records that were modified on or before January 22, 2007. Display the date a record was modified and each student's first and last name, concatenated in one column.

ANSWER: The query compares the MODIFIED_DATE column to the text literal. The text literal may be in either the Oracle default format or, better yet, formatted with the TO_DATE function and the appropriate four-digit year format model.

```
SELECT first_name||' '||last_name fullname,
       TO_CHAR(modified_date, 'DD-MON-YYYY HH:MI P.M.')
       "Modified Date and Time"
  FROM student
 WHERE modified_date < TO_DATE('01/23/2007','MM/DD/YYYY')
```

```
FULLNAME                    Modified Date and Time
------------------------    ----------------------
Fred Crocitto               22-JAN-2007 12:00 A.M.
J. Landry                   22-JAN-2007 12:00 A.M.
...
Judy Sethi                  22-JAN-2007 12:00 A.M.
Larry Walter                22-JAN-2007 12:00 A.M.

8 rows selected.
```

As previously mentioned, it is best practice to explicitly use the TO_DATE function to convert the text literal into a DATE data type. It does not really matter which format mask you use (in this case, MM/DD/YYYY was used in the WHERE clause), as long as the date literal agrees with the format mask. This allows Oracle to interpret the passed date correctly. Be sure to include the century to avoid ambiguities.

Another possible solution is the following WHERE clause, which uses the TRUNC function:

```
WHERE TRUNC(modified_date) <= TO_DATE('01/22/2007','MM/DD/YYYY')
```

c) Display the course number, section ID, and starting date and time for sections that start on Sundays.

ANSWER: The SQL statement shows all the sections that start on Sunday by using the DY format mask, which displays the abbreviated day of the week, in uppercase letters.

```
SELECT course_no, section_id,
       TO_CHAR(start_date_time, 'DY DD-MON-YYYY HH:MI am')
  FROM section
 WHERE TO_CHAR(start_date_time, 'DY') = 'SUN'
```

```
COURSE_NO SECTION_ID TO_CHAR(START_DATE_TIME,'DYDD-MON
---------- ---------- --------------------------------
        25         86 SUN 10-JUN-2007 09:30 am
       220         98 SUN 15-APR-2007 11:30 am
...
       100        143 SUN 03-JUN-2007 09:30 am
       122        152 SUN 29-APR-2007 09:30 am

13 rows selected.
```

THE FILL MODE

Some of the format masks are tricky. For example, if you choose the 'Day' format mask, you must specify the correct case and add the extra blanks to fill it up to a total length of nine characters. The following query returns no rows.

```
SELECT course_no, section_id,
       TO_CHAR(start_date_time, 'Day DD-Mon-YYYY HH:MI am')
  FROM section
 WHERE TO_CHAR(start_date_time, 'Day') = 'Sunday'
```

no rows selected

You can use the *fill mode (fm)* with the format mask to suppress the extra blanks.

```
SELECT course_no, section_id,
       TO_CHAR(start_date_time, 'Day DD-Mon-YYYY HH:MI am')
  FROM section
 WHERE TO_CHAR(start_date_time, 'fmDay') = 'Sunday'
COURSE_NO SECTION_ID TO_CHAR(START_DATE_TIME,'DAYDD-MON-YYYY')
---------- ---------- ----------------------------------------
       25         86 Sunday    10-Jun-2007 09:30 am
      220         98 Sunday    15-Apr-2007 11:30 am
...
      100        143 Sunday    03-Jun-2007 09:30 am
      122        152 Sunday    29-Apr-2007 09:30 am
```

13 rows selected.

d) List the section ID and starting date and time for all sections that begin and end in July 2007.

ANSWER: In SQL, there are often different solutions that deliver the same result set. Examine the various correct solutions and avoid the pitfalls.

SOLUTION 1

This first solution takes the time into consideration. It retrieves rows that start on July 1, 2007, at midnight or thereafter (>=); the AND condition identifies the rows that have a START_DATE_TIME prior to August 1, 2007.

```
SELECT section_id,
       TO_CHAR(start_date_time, 'DD-MON-YYYY HH24:MI:SS')
  FROM section
 WHERE start_date_time >= TO_DATE('07/01/2007', 'MM/DD/YYYY')
   AND start_date_time <  TO_DATE('08/01/2007', 'MM/DD/YYYY')
SECTION_ID TO_CHAR(START_DATE_T
---------- --------------------
        81 24-JUL-2007 09:30:00
        85 14-JUL-2007 10:30:00
...
       147 24-JUL-2007 09:30:00
       153 24-JUL-2007 09:30:00
```

14 rows selected.

The following query will *not* yield the correct result if you have a section that starts on July 31, 2007, any time after midnight. The TO_DATE function converts the string to a DATE data type and sets the timestamp to 12:00:00 A.M. Therefore, a section starting on July 31, 2007, at 18:00 is not considered part of the range.

```
SELECT section_id,
       TO_CHAR(start_date_time, 'DD-MON-YYYY HH24:MI:SS')
  FROM section
 WHERE start_date_time BETWEEN
       TO_DATE('07/01/2007', 'MM/DD/YYYY')
   AND TO_DATE('07/31/2007', 'MM/DD/YYYY')
```

SOLUTION 2

This solution includes the 24-hour time format mask.

```
SELECT section_id,
       TO_CHAR(start_date_time, 'DD-MON-YYYY HH24:MI:SS')
  FROM section
 WHERE start_date_time BETWEEN
       TO_DATE('07/01/2007', 'MM/DD/YYYY')
   AND TO_DATE('07/31/2007 23:59:59', 'MM/DD/YYYY HH24:MI:SS')
```

This WHERE clause can also be used to obtain the desired output: The query completely ignores the time on the column START_DATE_TIME.

```
WHERE TRUNC(start_date_time) BETWEEN
      TO_DATE('07/01/2007', 'MM/DD/YYYY')
  AND TO_DATE('07/31/2007', 'MM/DD/YYYY')
```

The following WHERE clause also returns the correct result if your NLS_DATE_FORMAT parameter is set to DD-MON-RR. It is best not to rely on Oracle's implicit conversion but to specify the conversion function together with the four-digit year.

```
WHERE TRUNC(start_date_time) BETWEEN '1-JUL-07' AND '31-JUL-07'
```

 When you compare dates, be sure to think about the time.

APPLYING THE WRONG DATA TYPE CONVERSION FUNCTION

Another common source of errors when using dates is applying the wrong data type conversion function, as illustrated in the following example.

```
SELECT section_id,
       TO_CHAR(start_date_time, 'DD-MON-YYYY HH24:MI:SS')
  FROM section
 WHERE TO_CHAR(start_date_time, 'DD-MON-YYYY HH24:MI:SS')
       >= '01-JUL-2007 00:00:00'
   AND TO_CHAR(start_date_time, 'DD-MON-YYYY HH24:MI:SS')
       <= '31-JUL-2007 23:59:59'
```

```
SECTION_ID TO_CHAR(START_DATE_T
---------- --------------------
        79 14-APR-2007 09:30:00
        80 24-APR-2007 09:30:00
...
       155 04-MAY-2007 09:30:00
       156 15-MAY-2007 09:30:00
```

78 rows selected.

The column START_DATE_TIME is converted to a character column in the WHERE clause and then compared to the text literal. The problem is that the dates are no longer compared. Instead, the character representation of the text literal and the character representation of the contents in column START_DATE_TIME in the format 'DD-MON-YYYY HH24:MI:SS' are compared.

A column value, such as '14-APR-2007 09:30:00' is inclusive of the text literals '01-JUL-2007 00:00:00' and '31-JUL-2007 23:59:59' because the first digit of the column value 1 falls within the range of the characters 0 and 3. Therefore, the condition is true, but we know that April 14, 2007, is not in this date range.

Let's briefly discuss character comparison semantics. The next hypothetical examples further illustrate the effects of character comparisons. The query checks whether the text literal '9' is between the text literals '01' and '31', evaluated by the first digit, 0 and 3, and it returns no row, which indicates that '9' does not fall in this range.

```
SELECT *
  FROM dual
 WHERE '9' BETWEEN '01' AND '31'
```

no rows selected

With this knowledge, you can try the text literals. As you can see, the comparison of text literals used in the query with the wrong data type makes this condition true—but not if you compared the DATE data type values, because April 14, 2007, does not fall in the month of July 2007.

```
SELECT *
  FROM dual
 WHERE '14-APR-2007 09:30:00' BETWEEN '01-JUL-2007 00:00:00'
                                  AND '31-JUL-2007 23:59:59'
D
-
X
```

1 row selected.

Be sure to choose the correct data type conversion function in your WHERE clause.

Remember to make sure your data type conversion does not cause incorrect results!

TO_CHAR FUNCTION VERSUS TO_DATE FUNCTION

The TO_DATE function converts text to the DATE data type, typically used in the WHERE clause of a SELECT statement. The TO_CHAR function converts a DATE data type to text, typically used in the SELECT clause to format the results. You can also use TO_CHAR to query for specifics in a format mask. For example, to find which sections meet on Sunday, you use the TO_CHAR function in the WHERE clause, as shown in the answer to Exercise c and listed here once again.

```
SELECT course_no, section_id,
       TO_CHAR(start_date_time, 'Day DD-Mon-YYYY HH:MI am')
  FROM section
 WHERE TO_CHAR(start_date_time, 'fmDay') = 'Sunday'
```

e) Determine the day of the week for December 31, 1899.

ANSWER: The day of the week is Sunday.

You need to nest conversion functions by using the TO_DATE function to convert the text literal to a DATE data type and then use the TO_CHAR function to display the day of the week.

First, you translate the text literal '31-DEC-1899', using the format mask 'DD-MON-YYYY' into the Oracle DATE data type. Then apply the TO_CHAR formatting function to convert the date into any format you want—in this case, to show the day of the week.

```
SELECT TO_CHAR(TO_DATE('31-DEC-1899', 'DD-MON-YYYY'),'Dy')
  FROM dual

TO_
--
Sun

1 row selected.
```

f) Execute the following statement. Write the question to obtain the desired result. Pay particular attention to the ORDER BY clause.

```
SELECT 'Section '||section_id||' begins on '||
       TO_CHAR(start_date_time, 'fmDay')||'.' AS "Start"
  FROM section
 WHERE section_id IN (146, 127, 121, 155, 110, 85, 148)
 ORDER BY TO_CHAR(start_date_time, 'D')
```

ANSWER: Your answer may be phrased similar to the following: "Display the day of the week when the sections 146, 127, 121, 155, 110, 85, and 148 start. Order the result by the day of the week starting with Sunday."

The result of the query will look similar to the following output. The statement uses the D format mask to order by the day of the week. This format assigns the number 1 for Sunday, 2 for Monday, and so on.

```
Start
---------------------------------
Section 110 begins on Sunday.
Section 121 begins on Monday.
Section 127 begins on Tuesday.
```

```
Section 146 begins on Wednesday.
Section 148 begins on Thursday.
Section 155 begins on Friday.
Section 85 begins on Saturday.

7 rows selected.
```

Lab 5.1 Quiz

In order to test your progress, you should be able to answer the following questions.

1) The TRUNC function on a date without a format model truncates the timestamp to 12:00:00 A.M.

_____ a) True
_____ b) False

2) Converting a text literal to a DATE format requires the use of the TO_CHAR function.

_____ a) True
_____ b) False

3) Which of the following is the display that results from the format mask 'Dy' for Monday?

_____ a) MON
_____ b) Monday
_____ c) MONDAY
_____ d) Mon

4) Which format mask displays December 31st, 1999?

_____ a) DD-MON-YYYY
_____ b) MONTH DDth, YYYY
_____ c) fmMONTH DD, YYYY
_____ d) Month fmDD, YYYY
_____ e) fmMonth ddth, yyyy

5) The SQL query displays the distinct hours and minutes from the SECTION table's START_DATE_TIME column.

```
SELECT DISTINCT TO_CHAR(start_date_time, 'HH24:MM')
   FROM section
```

_____ a) True
_____ b) False

ANSWERS APPEAR IN APPENDIX A.

LAB 5.2
Performing Date and Time Math

LAB OBJECTIVES

After this lab, you will be able to:

▶ Understand the SYSDATE Function
▶ Perform Date Arithmetic

You will frequently need to determine the differences between two date values or calculate dates in the future or in the past. Oracle provides functionality to help you accomplish these tasks.

The SYSDATE Function

The SYSDATE function returns the computer operating system's current date and time and does not take any parameters. If you connect to the database server via a client machine, it returns the date and time of the machine hosting the database, not the date and time of your client machine. For example, if your client workstation is located in New York, your local time zone is *Eastern Standard Time* (EST); if you connect to a server in California, you receive the server's *Pacific Standard Time* (PST) date and time. To include the time in the result, you use the TO_CHAR function together with the appropriate format mask.

```
SELECT SYSDATE, TO_CHAR(SYSDATE, 'DD-MON-YYYY HH24:MI')
   FROM dual
SYSDATE     TO_CHAR(SYSDATE,'
---------   -----------------
26-OCT-08 26-OCT-2008 19:49

1 row selected.
```

Using the SYSDATE function, you can determine the number of days until the year 2015. The following query subtracts today's date from January 1, 2015.

```
SELECT TO_DATE('01-JAN-2015','DD-MON-YYYY')-TRUNC(SYSDATE) int,
       TO_DATE('01-JAN-2015','DD-MON-YYYY')-SYSDATE dec
   FROM dual
        INT        DEC
   ----------  ----------
        2256 2256.17430

1 row selected.
```

To perform any date calculation, the column or text literal must be converted to the Oracle DATE data type. For the first column, the text literal '01-JAN-2015' is converted into a DATE data type, using the TO_DATE function and the corresponding format mask. Because a time is not specified, the text literal '01-JAN-2015' is set to 00:00:00 military time (the equivalent of 12:00:00 A.M.). From this date, the operating system's date (the result of the SYSDATE function) is subtracted. SYSDATE is nested inside the TRUNC function, which truncates the timestamp to 00:00:00. As a result, the column shows 2256 days.

The second column of the returned result performs the identical operation; however, this expression does not use the TRUNC function on the SYSDATE function, and therefore the time is factored into the calculation. The difference is now expressed in days, with the time in decimal format. To display the decimal in hours or minutes, you can use the NUMTODSINTERVAL function, discussed in Lab 5.4.

Performing Arithmetic on Dates

In the following example, three hours are added to the current date and time. To determine tomorrow's date and time, simply add the number 1 to the SYSDATE function.

```
SELECT TO_CHAR(SYSDATE, 'MM/DD HH24:MI:SS') now,
       TO_CHAR(SYSDATE+3/24, 'MM/DD HH24:MI:SS')
       AS now_plus_3hrs,
       TO_CHAR(SYSDATE+1, 'MM/DD HH24:MI:SS') tomorrow,
       TO_CHAR(SYSDATE+1.5, 'MM/DD HH24:MI:SS') AS
       "36Hrs from now"
  FROM dual
    NOW             NOW_PLUS_3HRS   TOMORROW        36Hrs from now
    --------------- --------------- --------------- ---------------
    10/26 10:34:17  10/26 13:34:17  10/27 10:34:17  10/27 22:34:17

1 row selected.
```

The fraction 3/24 represents three hours; you can also express minutes as a fraction of 1440 (60 minutes × 24 hours = 1440, which is the total number of minutes in a day). For example, 15 minutes is 15/1440, or 1/96, or any equivalent fraction or decimal number.

Oracle has a number of functions to perform specific date calculations. To determine the date of the first Sunday of the year 2000, use the NEXT_DAY function, as in the following SELECT statement.

```
SELECT TO_CHAR(TO_DATE('12/31/1999','MM/DD/YYYY'),
              'MM/DD/YYYY DY') "New Year's Eve",
       TO_CHAR(NEXT_DAY(TO_DATE('12/31/1999',
                        'MM/DD/YYYY'),
              'SUNDAY'),'MM/DD/YYYY DY')
       "First Sunday"
  FROM dual
```

```
New Year's Eve First Sunday
-------------- --------------
12/31/1999 FRI 01/02/2000 SUN
```

```
1 row selected.
```

The text string '12/31/1999' is first converted to a date. To determine the date of the next Sunday, the NEXT_DAY function is applied. Finally, format the output with a TO_CHAR format mask to display the result in the 'MM/DD/YYYY DY' format.

The ROUND Function

The ROUND function allows you to round days, months, or years. The following SQL statement lists the current date and time in the first column, using the TO_CHAR function and a format mask. The next column shows the current date and time, rounded to the next day. If the timestamp is at or past 12:00 noon and no format mask is supplied, the ROUND function rounds to the next day. The last column displays the date rounded to the nearest month, using the MM format mask.

```
SELECT TO_CHAR(SYSDATE,'DD-MON-YYYY HH24:MI') now,
       TO_CHAR(ROUND(SYSDATE),'DD-MON-YYYY HH24:MI') day,
       TO_CHAR(ROUND(SYSDATE,'MM'),'DD-MON-YYYY HH24:MI')
        mon
  FROM dual
NOW               DAY               MON
----------------- ----------------- -----------------
26-OCT-2008 10:33 26-OCT-2008 00:00 01-NOV-2008 00:00
```

```
1 row selected.
```

The EXTRACT Function

The EXTRACT function extracts the year, month, or day from a column of the DATE data type column. The next example shows rows with April values in the START_DATE_TIME column and how the various elements of the DATE data type can be extracted. Valid keyword choices are YEAR, MONTH, and DAY. You cannot extract hours, minutes, or seconds from the DATE data type. These options are available only on the other datetime-related data types you will learn about in Lab 5.3.

```
SELECT TO_CHAR(start_date_time, 'DD-MON-YYYY') "Start Date",
       EXTRACT(MONTH FROM start_date_time) "Month",
       EXTRACT(YEAR FROM start_date_time) "Year",
       EXTRACT(DAY FROM start_date_time) "Day"
  FROM section
 WHERE EXTRACT(MONTH FROM start_date_time) = 4
 ORDER BY start_date_time
```

```
Start Date      Month      Year       Day
--------------  ---------- ---------- ---
08-APR-2007                4          2007  8
09-APR-2007                4          2007  9
09-APR-2007                4          2007  9
...
29-APR-2007                4          2007  29
```

21 rows selected.

The following example of the EXTRACT function passes a text literal as the parameter, which is in ANSI DATE format.

```
SELECT EXTRACT(YEAR FROM DATE '2010-03-11') year,
       EXTRACT(MONTH FROM DATE '2010-03-11') month,
       EXTRACT(DAY FROM DATE '2010-03-11') day
  FROM dual
      YEAR     MONTH       DAY
--------- --------- ---------
      2010         3        11
```

1 row selected.

Table 5.6 summarizes some of the most frequently used DATE calculation functions and describes their purposes and respective syntax.

TABLE 5.6   Commonly Used Oracle Datetime-Related Calculation Functions

FUNCTION	PURPOSE	RETURN DATA TYPE
ADD_MONTHS(date, Integer)	Adds or subtracts the number of months from a certain date.	DATE
MONTHS_BETWEEN (date2, date1)	Determines the number of months between two dates.	NUMBER
LAST_DAY(date)	Returns the last date of the month.	DATE
NEXT_DAY(date, day_of_the_week)	Returns the first day of the week that is later than the date parameter passed.	DATE
TRUNC(date)	Ignores the hours, minutes, and seconds on the DATE data type.	DATE
ROUND(date [,format_mask])	Rounds to various DATE components, depending on the optional supplied format mask.	DATE
NEW_TIME(date, current_time_zone, new_time_zone)	Returns the date and time in another time zone; for example, EST (Eastern Standard Time), PST (Pacific Standard Time), PDT (Pacific Daylight Time).	DATE
	Oracle's time zone data types, discussed in Lab 5.3, handle conversions and computations related to various time zones with much more ease than NEW_TIME.	

Snippets

As mentioned in Chapter 4, you can use the Snippets window (see Figure 5.2) in SQL Developer to drag the function into the SQL Developer window and replace the placeholder with the appropriate expression. There is another set of snippets for date formatting masks and date/time functions.

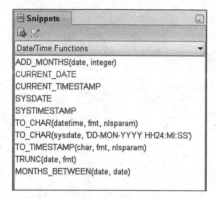

FIGURE 5.2
The Snippets window for date/time functions

The Snippets window lists commonly used functions, expressions, and code fragments. It does not provide a complete list of all available functions and syntax options in Oracle SQL. You can customize the snippets and add frequently used code fragments or functions.

▼ LAB 5.2 EXERCISES

a) Determine the number of days between February 13, 1964, and the last day of the February 1964.

b) Compute the number of months between September 29, 1999, and August 17, 2007.

c) Add three days to the current date and time.

▼ LAB 5.2 EXERCISE ANSWERS

a) Determine the number of days between February 13, 1964, and the last day of February 1964.

ANSWER: First convert the text literal '13-FEB-1964' to a DATE data type and then use the LAST_DAY function. The date returned is February 29, 1964, because 1964 was a leap year. The difference between the two dates is 16 days.

```
SELECT LAST_DAY(TO_DATE('13-FEB-1964','DD-MON-YYYY')) lastday,
       LAST_DAY(TO_DATE('13-FEB-1964','DD-MON-YYYY'))
       - TO_DATE('13-FEB-1964','DD-MON-YYYY') days
  FROM dual
```

```
LASTDAY        DAYS
---------  ---------
29-FEB-64      16
```

`1 row selected.`

The LAST_DAY function takes a single parameter and accepts only parameters of the DATE data type. Either your column must be a DATE data type column or you must convert it with the TO_DATE function.

b) Compute the number of months between September 29, 1999, and August 17, 2007.

ANSWER: The simplest solution is to use the MONTHS_BETWEEN function to determine the result.

```
SELECT MONTHS_BETWEEN(TO_DATE('17-AUG-2007','DD-MON-YYYY'),
            TO_DATE('29-SEP-1999','DD-MON-YYYY')) months
  FROM dual
        MONTHS
  --------------
    94.6129032
```

`1 row selected.`

The MONTHS_BETWEEN function takes two dates as its parameters and returns a numeric value.

c) Add three days to the current date and time.

ANSWER: The answer will vary, depending on when you execute this query. To add days to the current date and time, you add the number of days to the SYSDATE function.

```
SELECT TO_CHAR(SYSDATE, 'DD-MON-YYYY HH24:MI:SS') "Current",
            TO_CHAR(SYSDATE+3, 'DD-MON-YYYY HH24:MI:SS') "Answer"
  FROM dual
  Current                 Answer
  -------------------- --------------------
  26-OCT-2008 23:12:02 29-OCT-2008 23:12:02
```

`1 row selected.`

If you have to add hours, you can express the hour as a fraction of the day. For example, five hours is SYSDATE+5/24. To find out yesterday's date, you can subtract 1 day; thus, the SELECT clause will read SYSDATE-1. You will see additional examples of computing differences between dates in Lab 5.4, which discusses the interval data types.

Lab 5.2 Quiz

In order to test your progress, you should be able to answer the following questions.

1) You can use the ADD_MONTHS function to subtract months from a given date.

_____ a) True
_____ b) False

2) Which one of the following solutions adds 15 minutes to a given date?

_____ a) `SELECT SYSDATE+1/96 FROM dual`
_____ b) `SELECT SYSDATE+1/128 FROM dual`
_____ c) `SELECT TO_DATE(SYSDATE+1/128) FROM dual`
_____ d) `SELECT TO_CHAR(SYSDATE+1/128, 'DD-MON-YYYY 24HH:MI') FROM dual`

3) Choose the date that is calculated by the following query.

```
SELECT TO_CHAR(NEXT_DAY(TO_DATE('02-JAN-2000 SUN',
            'DD-MON-YYYY DY'), 'SUN'),
            'fmDay Month DD, YYYY')
  FROM dual
```

_____ a) Sunday January 2, 2000
_____ b) Monday January 3, 2000
_____ c) Sunday January 9, 2000
_____ d) None of the above dates
_____ e) Invalid query

4) The next query gives you which of the following results?

```
SELECT ROUND(TO_DATE('2000/1/31 11:59', 'YYYY/MM/DD HH24:MI'))
  FROM dual
```

_____ a) Returns an Oracle error message
_____ b) 30-JAN-00
_____ c) 31-JAN-00
_____ d) 01-FEB-00

ANSWERS APPEAR IN APPENDIX A.

LAB 5.3

Understanding the TIMESTAMP and TIME ZONE Data Types

LAB OBJECTIVES

After this lab, you will be able to:

▶ Use Oracle's TIMESTAMP Data Type
▶ Use TIME ZONE Data Types

Oracle offers datetime-related data types, which include fractional seconds and time zones. These three data types are TIMESTAMP, TIMESTAMP WITH TIME ZONE, and TIMESTAMP WITH LOCAL TIME ZONE.

The TIMESTAMP Data Type

The TIMESTAMP data type allows you to store optional fractional seconds with a precision of up to nine digits; the default is six digits.

An example of a text literal can look like this: '14 FEB 09 08.29.01.000123 AM'. This represents the format mask 'DD-MON-RR HH.MI.SS.FF AM'. The fractional seconds are expressed with the FF format mask. To change the default precision of the fractional seconds, you add a number from 1 to 9 after the FF mask. For example, FF4 displays the fractional seconds with a four-digit precision.

Instead of using the Oracle format model, you can represent the literal with the ANSI TIMESTAMP format as follows: TIMESTAMP '2009-02-14 08:29:01.000123'. Again, 000123 is the fractional seconds, showing a six-digit precision.

The TIMESTAMP WITH TIME ZONE Data Type

Besides the date, time, and fractional seconds, the TIMESTAMP WITH TIME ZONE data type includes the *time zone displacement value*. The time zone displacement, also called *time zone offset value,* is expressed as the difference (in hours and minutes) between your local time and *Greenwich Mean Time* (GMT), now called *Coordinated Universal Time* (UTC). The time zone along the Prime Meridian in Greenwich, England, is commonly known as GMT, against which all other time zones are compared. At noon Greenwich time, it is midnight at the International Date Line in the Pacific.

The time zone displacement value is shown as a positive or negative number (for example, -5:00), indicating the hours and minutes before or after UTC. Alternatively, the time zone can be expressed as a time zone region name, such as America/New_York instead of -5:00. The TIMESTAMP WITH TIME ZONE data type is useful when storing date and time information across geographic regions. Oracle stores all values of this data type in UTC.

The time zone region of the database is determined at the time of database creation. To find out the time zone value of your database, use the DBTIMEZONE function. The query may return a time zone displacement value such as -05:00, indicating that the time zone is 5 hours before UTC.

Instead of returning the offset number for the time zone displacement, you may see a region name instead. The time zone region equivalent for EST (Eastern Standard Time) and EDT (Eastern Daylight Time) is America/New_York and is listed in the V$TIMEZONE_NAMES data dictionary view, where you can find the list of valid time zone regions.

The data dictionary is a set of tables that provides information about the database. Data dictionary views are discussed in Chapter 14, "The Data Dictionary, Scripting, and Reporting." The server's time zone is determined when the database is created. It can be modified with an ALTER DATABASE statement. For more information on the CREATE and ALTER DATABASE statements, see the *Oracle Administrator's Guide* documentation.

The TIMESTAMP WITH LOCAL TIME ZONE Data Type

The TIMESTAMP WITH LOCAL TIME ZONE stores the date and time values of the database's own local time zone. When the user retrieves the data, the returned values are automatically converted to represent each individual user's time zone. In addition, the database does not store the time zone displacement value as part of the data type.

When performing arithmetic on this data type, Oracle automatically converts all values to UTC before doing the calculation and then converts the value back to the local time. This is in contrast to the TIMESTAMP WITH TIME ZONE data type, where the values are always stored in UTC, and a conversion is unnecessary.

Oracle provides automatic support for daylight saving time and for boundary cases when the time switches.

Common Format Masks

Table 5.7 shows the datetime-related data types and their individual components, together with commonly used format masks and examples of literals. Throughout this lab, you will use these data types in different exercises.

TABLE 5.7   Overview of Oracle Datetime-Related Data Types

DATA TYPE	COMPONENTS	COMMON FORMAT MASKS

DATE	Century, Year, Month, Day, Hour, Minute, Second	Oracle Format Masks:
		`'DD-MON-RR'  and  'DD-MON-YYYY'`
		`'14-FEB-09'  and  '14-FEB-2009'`

		ANSI Formats:
		`DATE 'YYYY-MM-DD'`
		`DATE '2009-02-14'`
		`TIMESTAMP 'YYYY-MM-DD HH24:MI:SS'`
		`TIMESTAMP '2009-02-14 16:21:04'`

TIMESTAMP	Same as DATE with additional fractional seconds	Oracle Formats:
		`'DD-MON-RR HH.MI.SS.FF AM'`
		`'14-FEB-09 04.21.04.000001 PM'`
		`'DD-MON-YYYY HH.MI.SS.FF AM'`
		`'14-FEB-2009 04.21.04.000001 PM'`

		ANSI Formats:
		`TIMESTAMP 'YYYY-MM-DD HH24:MI:SS.FF'`
		`TIMESTAMP '2009-02-14 16:21:04.000001'`

TIMESTAMP WITH TIME ZONE	Same as TIMESTAMP plus Time Zone Hour and Time Zone Minute (TZH:TZM) or Time Zone Region Name (TZR)	Oracle Formats with time offset values in hours and minutes:
		`'DD-MON-RR HH.MI.SS.FF AM TZH:TZM'`
		`'14-FEB-09 04.21.04.000001 PM -05:00'`
		`'DD-MON-YYYY HH.MI.SS.FF AM TZH:TZM'`
		`'14-FEB-2009 04.21.04.000001 PM -05:00'`
		
		Oracle Formats with time zone region:
		`'DD-MON-RR HH.MI.SS.FF AM TZR'`
		`'14-FEB-09 04.21.04.000001 PM America/`
		`New_York'`
		`'DD-MON-YYYY HH.MI.SS.FF AM TZR'`
		`'14-FEB-2009 04.21.04.000001 PM America/`
		`New_York'`

		ANSI Formats with offset value:
		`TIMESTAMP 'YYYY-MM-DD HH24:MI:SS.FF TZH:TZM'`
		`TIMESTAMP '2009-02-14 16:21:04.000001 -5:00'`

TABLE 5.7   Continued

DATA TYPE	COMPONENTS	COMMON FORMAT MASKS

		ANSI Formats with time zone region:
		`TIMESTAMP 'YYYY-MM-DD HH:MI:SS.FF TZR'`
		`TIMESTAMP '2009-02-14 16:21:04.000001`
		`America/New_York'`

TIMESTAMP WITH LOCAL TIME ZONE	Same compo-nents as the TIMESTAMP data type	See TIMESTAMP

Table 5.8 lists the valid range of values for the individual components of the datetime-related data types.

TABLE 5.8   Valid Value Ranges for Date and Time Components

DATE COMPONENT	VALID VALUES
YEAR	−4712 – 9999 (excluding year 0)
MONTH	01 – 12
DAY	01 – 31
HOUR	00 – 23
MINUTE	00 – 59
SECOND	00 – 59 (optional precision up to nine digits on TIMESTAMP, TIMESTAMP WITH TIME ZONE, and TIMESTAMP WITH LOCAL TIME ZONE data types)
TIMEZONE_HOUR	−12 – +13
TIMEZONE_MINUTE	00 – 59

Datetime Functions

Table 5.9 lists the datetime functions, which you use to determine the current date and time.

TABLE 5.9   Session and Server Datetime Functions

FUNCTION	PURPOSE	RETURN DATA TYPE
SYSDATE	Returns the database server operating system's current date and time.	DATE
CURRENT_DATE	Returns the date and time of the local *session* time zone, in the DATE data type. (The local session time can be different than the server's date and time, if the client session is in a different time zone.)	DATE

TABLE 5.9   Continued

FUNCTION	PURPOSE	RETURN DATA TYPE
CURRENT_TIMESTAMP [(optional_precision)]	Returns the individual's *session* date and time in the data type TIMESTAMP WITH TIME ZONE value.	TIMESTAMP WITH TIME ZONE
SYSTIMESTAMP	Returns the date, time, and fractional seconds and time zone of the server. This is similar to the SYSDATE function but includes the fractional seconds and time zone.	TIMESTAMP WITH TIME ZONE
LOCALTIMESTAMP [(optional_precision)]	Returns in the TIMESTAMP format the current date and time in the local *session* time.	TIMESTAMP
SESSIONTIMEZONE	Returns the time zone offset value of the *session* time zone or the time zone region name, depending on the setup of the database.	VARCHAR2
DBTIMEZONE	Returns the time zone offset value of the database *server* time zone or time zone region name, depending on the setup of the database.	VARCHAR2

THE LOCALTIMESTAMP FUNCTION

The next SQL statement shows the use of the LOCALTIMESTAMP function, which returns the current date and time, including the fractional sections in Oracle's TIMESTAMP format. This function considers the local user's *session* time; that is, if the database server is in San Francisco and the user is in New York, the time displayed is the user's local New York time.

```
SELECT LOCALTIMESTAMP
  FROM dual
LOCALTIMESTAMP
---------------------------
26-FEB-09 04.21.04.000001 PM

1 row selected.
```

THE SYSTIMESTAMP FUNCTION

Unlike the SYSDATE function, the SYSTIMESTAMP function includes fractional seconds with up to nine digits of precision. Like the SYSDATE function, it uses the *database's* time zone, not that of the client machine executing the function. The time zone displacement, or offset, in the following SQL statement is -05.00, indicating that the time is 5 hours before the UTC, which in this example represents EST. The offset is expressed in the format mask [+|-] TZH:TZM and includes either positive or negative time zone hour and time zone minute offset numbers.

```
SELECT SYSTIMESTAMP
  FROM dual
SYSTIMESTAMP
-----------------------------------
26-FEB-09 04.21.04.000001 PM -05:00

1 row selected.
```

THE CURRENT_TIMESTAMP FUNCTION

The CURRENT_TIMESTAMP function returns the current *session's* time in the data type TIMESTAMP WITH TIME ZONE value. It differs from the LOCALTIMESTAMP function in that the data type is not TIMESTAMP but TIMESTAMP WITH TIME ZONE and therefore includes the time zone displacement value (or the actual name of the time zone, depending on the client session settings).

```
SELECT CURRENT_TIMESTAMP, LOCALTIMESTAMP
  FROM dual
CURRENT_TIMESTAMP                       LOCALTIMESTAMP
-----------------------------------     ----------------------------
26-FEB-09 07.59.49.000000 PM -05:00 26-FEB-09 07.59.49.000000 PM

1 row selected.
```

THE CURRENT_DATE FUNCTION

The CURRENT_DATE function returns the date and time in the *session's* time zone. The returned values can be different than the values returned by the SYSDATE function. For example, if you execute a query on your machine located on the East Coast against a database server located on the West Coast, the SYSDATE function returns the date and time of the server in the Pacific time zone, and the CURRENT_DATE function returns your local East Coast date and time. The return data type of the CURRENT_DATE function is a DATE data type.

```
SELECT TO_CHAR(CURRENT_DATE, 'DD-MON-YYYY HH:MI:SS PM')
  FROM dual
TO_CHAR(CURRENT_DATE,'D
-----------------------
01-FEB-2009 02:37:11 AM

1 row selected.
```

You might wonder how the CURRENT_DATE function compares to the previously mentioned LOCALTIMESTAMP function. The difference is in the return data type of the function. CURRENT_DATE returns a DATE data type, and LOCALTIMESTAMP returns the TIMESTAMP data type, which includes the fractional seconds.

THE SESSIONTIMEZONE FUNCTION

Because an individual user may be in a different time zone than the database server, you can execute different functions, depending on what you want to accomplish. The SESSIONTIME ZONE function returns the session's time zone displacement value; the DBTIMEZONE function returns the server's time zone displacement value.

The next statement shows the execution of the SESSIONTIMEZONE function. It includes the time zone displacement value, indicating the difference in hours and minutes between UTC and your local time. (Depending on the client environment setup, you may see the time zone name instead.) The user's local time zone is determined by either the most recent ALTER SESSION statement setting indicating the local time zone or by your operating system's time zone. If none of them are valid, the default is UTC.

```
SELECT SESSIONTIMEZONE
  FROM dual
SESSIONTIMEZONE
---------------
-05:00

1 row selected.
```

CHANGING THE LOCAL TIME ZONE

You can experiment with changing the time zone of your local machine and the effect on the discussed functions. For example, on the Windows operating system, you can change the time zone in the Control Panel by choosing the Date and Time Properties (see Figure 5.3). If you change your default time zone to another time zone with a different time zone displacement value, the results of the SESSIONTIMEZONE function are different.

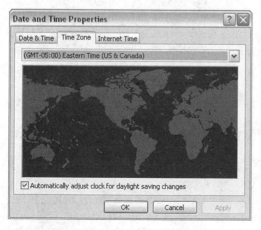

FIGURE 5.3
Changing the time zone on the Windows operating system

Make sure to exit SQL Developer or log out of the current SQL*Plus session before you do this, so the effects of the time zone change are visible.

OVERRIDING THE INDIVIDUAL SESSION TIME ZONE

You can change the time zone for an individual session by using the ALTER SESSION command. The setting remains until you exit the session. The following three statements illustrate different ways you can change the time zone offset value. The first changes the value to a time zone region name, the second makes it equivalent to the database server's time zone, and the last resets it to the session's local time zone.

```
ALTER SESSION SET TIME_ZONE = 'America/New_York'
ALTER SESSION SET TIME_ZONE = dbtimezone
ALTER SESSION SET TIME_ZONE = local
```

THE DBTIMEZONE FUNCTION

The DBTIMEZONE function displays the database server's time zone displacement value; if none has been set, it displays UTC (+00:00) as the default value.

```
SELECT DBTIMEZONE
  FROM dual
DBTIME
------
-05:00

1 row selected.
```

Extract Functions

Different functions allow you to pull out various components of the datetime data types, such as YEAR, MONTH, and so on (see Table 5.10). Similar results can also be accomplished with the TO_CHAR function and the format masks discussed in Lab 5.2.

THE SYS_EXTRACT_UTC FUNCTION

The purpose of the SYS_EXTRACT_UTC function is to extract the UTC from a passed date and time value. The next example shows two equivalent date and time values when translated to UTC. Both are ANSI literals of the data type TIMESTAMP WITH TIME ZONE.

```
TIMESTAMP '2009-02-11 7:00:00 -8:00'
TIMESTAMP '2009-02-11 10:00:00 -5:00'
```

The first timestamp shows February 11, 2009, at 7:00 A.M. PST, which is 8 hours before UTC. This value is identical to the next timestamp; it shows the same date with 10:00 A.M. EST local time, which is 5 hours before UTC. The 7:00 A.M. time on the West Coast is identical to 10:00 A.M. on the East Coast as there is a three-hour time difference. When calculating the time in UTC, you see that the two timestamps are identical in UTC. In fact, Oracle calculates the

TIMESTAMP WITH TIME ZONE data type always in UTC and then displays the local time with the time zone displacement.

```
SELECT SYS_EXTRACT_UTC(TIMESTAMP '2009-02-11 7:00:00 -8:00')
       "West coast to UTC",
       SYS_EXTRACT_UTC(TIMESTAMP '2009-02-11 10:00:00 -5:00')
       "East coast to UTC"
FROM dual
West coast to UTC                  East coast to UTC
--------------------------------   --------------------------------
11-FEB-09 03.00.00.000000000 PM    11-FEB-09 03.00.00.000000000 PM

1 row selected.
```

TABLE 5.10   Extract Functions

FUNCTION	PURPOSE	RETURN DATA TYPE
EXTRACT(YEAR FROM date)	Extracts year from a DATE data type. Valid keyword choices are YEAR, MONTH, and DAY to extract the year, month, and day, respectively.	NUMBER
EXTRACT(YEAR FROM timestamp)	Extracts the year from a TIMESTAMP data type. Valid keyword choices are YEAR, MONTH, DAY, HOUR, MINUTE, and SECOND to extract the year, month, day, hour, minute, and seconds, including fractional seconds, respectively.	NUMBER
EXTRACT(YEAR FROM timestamp_with_time_zone)	Valid keywords are YEAR, MONTH, DAY, HOUR, MINUTE, SECOND, TIMEZONE_HOUR, TIMEZONE_MINUTE, TIMEZONE_REGION, TIMEZONE_ABBR. The values are returned in UTC.	NUMBER for TIMEZONE_REGION (If TIMEZONE_ABBR is passed, the EXTRACT function returns VARCHAR2.)
SYS_EXTRACT_UTC (timestamp_with_time zone)	Returns the date and time in UTC	TIMESTAMP WITH TIME ZONE
TZ_OFFSET(time_zone)	Returns the time difference between UTC and passed time zone value	VARCHAR2

THE EXTRACT FUNCTION AND THE TIMESTAMP DATA TYPE

The following SQL statement extracts the various components of the TIMESTAMP data type, including the seconds. You cannot extract the fractional seconds only; they are included as part of the SECOND keyword specification. The passed TIMESTAMP literal is in the ANSI TIMESTAMP default format.

```
SELECT EXTRACT(HOUR FROM TIMESTAMP '2009-02-11 15:48:01.123') hour,
       EXTRACT(MINUTE FROM TIMESTAMP '2009-02-11 15:48:01.123') minute,
       EXTRACT(SECOND FROM TIMESTAMP '2009-02-11 15:48:01.123') second,
       EXTRACT(YEAR FROM TIMESTAMP '2009-02-11 15:48:01.123') year,
       EXTRACT(MONTH FROM TIMESTAMP '2009-02-11 15:48:01.123') month,
       EXTRACT(DAY FROM TIMESTAMP '2009-02-11 15:48:01.123') day
  FROM dual
```

HOUR	MINUTE	SECOND	YEAR	MONTH	DAY
15	48	1.123	2009	2	11

1 row selected.

THE EXTRACT FUNCTION AND THE TIMESTAMP WITH TIME ZONE DATA TYPE

Following are examples of the EXTRACT function that illustrate how to pull out the various components of the TIMESTAMP WITH TIME ZONE data type. Note here that when using EXTRACT on this data type, all date and time values are returned in UTC, not the time displayed by default in the column.

The next example shows just a few of the components. When examining the result, you see that the column labeled HOUR displays the time as 21, which is 9 P.M., but the actual local time is stored as 4 P.M. in the column COL_TIMESTAMP_W_TZ. This is a clear indication that the EXTRACT function uses UTC.

```
SELECT col_timestamp_w_tz,
       EXTRACT(YEAR FROM col_timestamp_w_tz) year,
       EXTRACT(MONTH FROM col_timestamp_w_tz) month,
       EXTRACT(DAY FROM col_timestamp_w_tz) day,
       EXTRACT(HOUR FROM col_timestamp_w_tz) hour,
       EXTRACT(MINUTE FROM col_timestamp_w_tz) min,
       EXTRACT(SECOND FROM col_timestamp_w_tz) sec
  FROM date_example
```

COL_TIMESTAMP_W_TZ	YEAR	MONTH	DAY	HOUR	MIN	SEC
24-FEB-09 04.25.32.000000 PM -05:00	2009	2	24	21	25	32

1 row selected.

The keywords TIMEZONE_HOUR and TIMEZONE_MINUTE allow you to display the time zone displacement value expressed in hours and minutes. The TIMEZONE_REGION and TIMEZONE_ABBR keywords indicate the time zone region information spelled out or in abbreviated format. If a region has not been set up for your database or results in ambiguity, you see the value UNKNOWN, as in this example.

```
SELECT col_timestamp_w_tz,
       EXTRACT(TIMEZONE_HOUR FROM col_timestamp_w_tz) tz_hour,
       EXTRACT(TIMEZONE_MINUTE FROM col_timestamp_w_tz) tz_min,
       EXTRACT(TIMEZONE_REGION FROM col_timestamp_w_tz) tz_region,
       EXTRACT(TIMEZONE_ABBR FROM col_timestamp_w_tz) tz_abbr
  FROM date_example
COL_TIMESTAMP_W_TZ                          TZ_HOUR TZ_MIN TZ_REGION TZ_ABBR
-----------------------------------         ------- ------ --------- -------
24-FEB-09 04.25.32.000000 PM -05:00             -5      0 UNKNOWN   UNK

1 row selected.
```

THE DATE_EXAMPLE TABLE

In the two previous SQL statements, you may have noticed the use of a table called DATE_
EXAMPLE to illustrate the different date variants. This table is not part of the STUDENT schema
but can be created based on the additional script, available for download from the companion
Web site, located at www.oraclesqlbyexample.com. Listed here are the columns of the
DATE_EXAMPLE table and their respective data types.

```
SQL> DESCRIBE date_example
Name                          Null?     Type
------------------------     --------   -----------------------------
COL_DATE                                DATE
COL_TIMESTAMP                           TIMESTAMP(6)
COL_TIMESTAMP_W_TZ                      TIMESTAMP(6) WITH TIME ZONE
COL_TIMESTAMP_W_LOCAL_TZ                TIMESTAMP(6) WITH LOCAL TIME
```

The first column, named COL_DATE, is of the familiar DATE data type. The second column,
called COL_TIMESTAMP, includes fractional seconds, with a six-digit default precision. The
third column, called COL_TIMESTAMP_W_TZ, additionally contains the time zone offset.
Finally, the fourth column is defined as the TIMESTAMP WITH LOCAL TIME ZONE data type.

Conversion Functions

To query against a datetime column using a text literal, you need to list the literal with the
appropriate format mask (refer to Table 5.7 for frequently used format masks). Table 5.11 lists
the various functions to convert to the desired data type. In the previous labs, you became
familiar with the TO_CHAR and the TO_DATE functions. TO_TIMESTAMP and
TO_TIMESTAMP_TZ work in a similar way. The TO_CHAR and TO_DATE functions are listed
for completeness.

TABLE 5.11   Datetime-Related Conversion Functions

FUNCTION	PURPOSE	RETURN DATA TYPE
TO_TIMESTAMP(char [,format_mask])	Converts text to the TIMESTAMP data type, based on format_mask. (This works similarly to the TO_DATE function.)	TIMESTAMP
TO_TIMESTAMP_TZ(char [,format_mask])	Converts text or a database column of VARCHAR2 or CHAR data type to a TIMESTAMP WITH TIME ZONE data type, based on a format_mask.	TIMESTAMP WITH TIME ZONE
TO_DATE(char [,format_mask])	Converts text to a DATE data type. As with all other datetime-related conversion functions, format_mask is optional if the value conforms to the NLS DATE_FORMAT; otherwise, format_mask must be specified.	DATE
TO_CHAR(date [,format_mask])	Converts all datetime-related data types into VARCHAR2 to display it in a different format than the default date format. (The TO_CHAR function can be used with other data types; see Lab 5.5.)	VARCHAR2
FROM_TZ(timestamp, hour_min_offset)	Converts a TIMESTAMP value into a TIMESTAMP WITH TIME ZONE data type. An example of the hour_min_offset value (time zone displacement value) is '-5:00', or it can be a time zone region name, such as 'America/New_York'.	TIMESTAMP WITH TIME
CAST	Converts TIMESTAMP, TIMESTAMP WITH TIME ZONE, and TIMESTAMP WITH LOCAL TIME ZONE (see Lab 5.5 regarding the CAST function).	Various

The next statement queries the DATE_EXAMPLE table and converts the text literal into a TIMESTAMP WITH TIME ZONE data type to be able to compare the value against the column COL_TIMESTAMP_W_TZ of the same data type.

```
SELECT col_timestamp_w_tz
  FROM date_example
 WHERE col_timestamp_w_tz = TO_TIMESTAMP_TZ
             ('24-FEB-09 04.25.32.000000 PM -05:00',
              'DD-MON-RR HH.MI.SS.FF AM TZH:TZM')
COL_TIMESTAMP_W_TZ
---------------------------------
24-FEB-09 04.25.32.000000 PM -05:00

1 row selected.
```

Datetime Expression

A datetime expression can be a column of data type TIMESTAMP WITH TIME ZONE, TIMESTAMP WITH LOCAL TIME ZONE, or TIMESTAMP or an expression that results in any of the three data types.

The expression can be shown in various time zones with the keywords AT TIME ZONE. The next example illustrates the value 24-FEB-07 04.25.32.000000 P.M. −05:00 in the COL_TIMESTAMP_W_TZ column, displayed in the Los Angeles local time instead. The expression uses the time zone region name 'America/Los_Angeles' after the keywords AT TIME ZONE.

```
SELECT col_timestamp_w_tz AT TIME ZONE 'America/Los_Angeles'
  FROM date_example
COL_TIMESTAMP_W_TZATTIMEZONE'AMERICA/LOS_ANGELES
-------------------------------------------------
24-FEB-09 01.25.32.000000 PM AMERICA/LOS_ANGELES

1 row selected.
```

The syntax of the datetime expression is as follows.

```
datetime_value_expr AT {
  LOCAL |
  TIME ZONE{'[+|-]hh:mm' |
            DBTIMEZONE |
            SESSIONTIMEZONE |
            'time_zone_name'}}
```

Besides showing the time in the local time zone, you can also choose a specific time zone displacement in the TZH:TZM format. Other syntax alternatives are DBTIMEZONE, which returns the value in the database server's time zone, and SESSIONTIMEZONE, which shows the session's time zone and the time zone name for a time zone region name.

The next example displays the same column expressed in the database server's time zone with the DBTIMEZONE keyword.

```
SELECT col_timestamp_w_tz AT TIME ZONE DBTIMEZONE
  FROM date_example
COL_TIMESTAMP_W_TZATTIMEZONEDBTIMEZONE
---------------------------------------
24-FEB-09 04.25.32.000000 PM -05:00

1 row selected.
```

Compared to the NEW_TIME function mentioned in Lab 5.2, the datetime expression is more versatile because it allows a greater number of time zone values.

▼ LAB 5.3 EXERCISES

a) Describe the default display formats of the result returned by the following SQL query.

```
SELECT col_date, col_timestamp, col_timestamp_w_tz
   FROM date_example
COL_DATE  COL_TIMESTAMP                   COL_TIMESTAMP_W_TZ
--------- -------------------------  ------------------
24-FEB-09 24-FEB-09 04.25.32.000000 PM 24-FEB-09 04.25.32.000000 PM -
➥05:00

1 row selected.
```

b) Explain the result of the following SELECT statement. Are there alternate ways to rewrite the query's WHERE clause?

```
SELECT col_timestamp
   FROM date_example
 WHERE col_timestamp = '24-FEB-09 04.25.32.000000 PM'
COL_TIMESTAMP
---------------------------
24-FEB-09 04.25.32.000000 PM

1 row selected.
```

c) What function can you utilize to display the seconds component of a TIMESTAMP data type column?

d) What do you observe about the text literal of the following query's WHERE clause?

```
SELECT col_timestamp_w_tz
   FROM date_example
 WHERE col_timestamp_w_tz = '24-FEB-09 04.25.32.000000 PM -05:00'
COL_TIMESTAMP_W_TZ
-----------------------------------
24-FEB-09 04.25.32.000000 PM -05:00

1 row selected.
```

e) The following SQL statements are issued against the database server. Explain the results.

```
SELECT SESSIONTIMEZONE
   FROM dual
SESSIONTIMEZONE
---------------
-05:00

1 row selected.

SELECT col_timestamp_w_tz, col_timestamp_w_local_tz
   FROM date_example
```

```
COL_TIMESTAMP_W_TZ                     COL_TIMESTAMP_W_LOCAL_TZ
------------------------------------   ----------------------------
24-FEB-09 04.25.32.000000 PM -05:00    24-FEB-09 04.25.32.000000 PM

1 row selected.

ALTER SESSION SET TIME_ZONE = '-8:00'
```
Session altered.

```
SELECT col_timestamp_w_tz, col_timestamp_w_local_tz
  FROM date_example
COL_TIMESTAMP_W_TZ                     COL_TIMESTAMP_W_LOCAL_TZ
------------------------------------   ----------------------------
24-FEB-09 04.25.32.000000 PM -05:00    24-FEB-09 01.25.32.000000 PM

1 row selected.

ALTER SESSION SET TIME_ZONE = '-5:00'
```
Session altered.

▼ LAB 5.3 EXERCISE ANSWERS

a) Describe the default display formats of the result returned by the following SQL query.

```
SELECT col_date, col_timestamp, col_timestamp_w_tz
  FROM date_example
COL_DATE   COL_TIMESTAMP                  COL_TIMESTAMP_W_TZ
---------  -----------------------------  -------------------------------
24-FEB-09  24-FEB-09 04.25.32.000000 PM   24-FEB-09 04.25.32.000000 PM -
➥05:00

1 row selected.
```

ANSWER: This query returns the values of three columns: COL_DATE, COL_TIMESTAMP, and COL_TIMESTAMP_W_TZ.

You are already familiar with the DD-MON-RR DATE default format listed in the right column. The display format for the Oracle TIMESTAMP data type is DD-MON-RR HH.MI.SS.FF AM, as shown in the second column. The third column, named COL_TIMESTAMP_W_TZ, also shows the time zone displacement value, in the format +/- TZH:TZM. (All the default display formats can be changed with the NLS_TIMESTAMP_FORMAT and NLS_TIMESTAMP_TZ_FORMAT parameters in the Oracle database initialization file. You can also modify within SQL Developer or using an ALTER SESSION statement. An ALTER SESSION statement changes certain values for the user's current session. These temporary settings remain until the user disconnects the session—that is, exits the program that created the session.)

b) Explain the result of the following SELECT statement. Are there alternate ways to rewrite the query's WHERE clause?

```
SELECT col_timestamp
  FROM date_example
 WHERE col_timestamp = '24-FEB-09 04.25.32.000000 PM'
COL_TIMESTAMP
---------------------------
24-FEB-09 04.25.32.000000 PM

1 row selected.
```

ANSWER: The query shows the use of the TIMESTAMP data type. There are alternative ways to achieve the same result. As you learned previously, with the DATE data type, it is always preferable to explicitly perform the data type conversion instead of use the default text literal. The following query uses the TO_TIMESTAMP function to convert the text literal into an Oracle TIMESTAMP data type, and it uses the matching format masks. The FF format mask represents the fractional seconds; the AM format mask indicates the time listed in the AM/PM format, not the 24-hour military time format.

```
SELECT col_timestamp
  FROM date_example
 WHERE col_timestamp =
       TO_TIMESTAMP('24-FEB-2009 04:25:32.000000 PM',
                    'DD-MON-YYYY HH:MI:SS.FF AM')
```

If you exclude the fractional seconds together with the FF format mask, the fractional seconds are implied to be zero, as you can see in the next example.

```
SELECT col_timestamp
  FROM date_example
 WHERE col_timestamp =
       TO_TIMESTAMP('24-FEB-2009 04:25:32 PM',
                    'DD-MON-YYYY HH:MI:SS AM')
```

The following query, using the ANSI TIMESTAMP format, also returns the correct result.

```
SELECT col_timestamp
  FROM date_example
 WHERE col_timestamp = TIMESTAMP '2009-02-24 16:25:32.000000'
```

CONVERSION BETWEEN ORACLE DATE DATA TYPES

You might wonder whether you can apply any of the previously used TO_DATE format models to query the COL_TIMESTAMP column. The next SQL statement converts the text literal to a DATE data type with the TO_DATE function. The DATE data type is implicitly converted to the TIMESTAMP data type. Because the fractional seconds in this example are equal to 000000, the result is considered equivalent, and the row is returned.

```
SELECT col_timestamp
  FROM date_example
 WHERE col_timestamp = TO_DATE('24-FEB-2009 04:25:32 PM',
                               'DD-MON-YYYY HH:MI:SS AM')
```

The following SQL statement shows what happens when you apply a TO_TIMESTAMP function to a DATE data type column. The TO_TIMESTAMP function sets the time portion of the DATE column to midnight.

```
SELECT TO_TIMESTAMP(col_date) "TO_TIMESTAMP",
       TO_CHAR(col_date, 'DD-MON-YYYY HH24:MI')
       AS "DISPLAY DATE"
  FROM date_example
TO_TIMESTAMP              DISPLAY DATE
-----------------------  -----------------
24-FEB-09 12.00.00 AM    24-FEB-2009 16:25

1 row selected.
```

c) What function can you utilize to display the seconds component of a TIMESTAMP data type column?

ANSWER: You can use either the TO_CHAR function or the EXTRACT function to display components such as the year, month, date, hour, minute, and seconds from the TIMESTAMP data type columns.

The next SQL statement shows how they are used and their respective differences.

```
SELECT col_timestamp,
       TO_CHAR(col_timestamp, 'SS') AS "CHAR Seconds",
       EXTRACT(SECOND FROM col_timestamp) AS "EXTRACT Seconds"
  FROM date_example
COL_TIMESTAMP                   CHAR Seconds EXTRACT Seconds
------------------------------  ------------ ---------------
24-FEB-09 04.25.32.000000 PM 32                           32

1 row selected.
```

The first column displays the column's value, in the default TIMESTAMP format; the second column utilizes the TO_CHAR function to display the seconds. If you want to include the fractional seconds, you need to add the FF format mask, which is omitted in this example. The third column shows the use of the EXTRACT function to return the seconds. You might notice the difference in the alignment of the result between the second and third columns. The TO_CHAR function returns the seconds as a string; the EXTRACT function returns the seconds as a NUMBER data type. The fractional seconds are always included when you use the SECOND keyword with this data type, but because they are zero, they are not shown in the result.

d) What do you observe about the text literal of the following query's WHERE clause?

```
SELECT col_timestamp_w_tz
  FROM date_example
 WHERE col_timestamp_w_tz = '24-FEB-09 04.25.32.000000 PM -05:00'
COL_TIMESTAMP_W_TZ
-----------------------------------
24-FEB-09 04.25.32.000000 PM -05:00

1 row selected.
```

ANSWER: This SQL statement queries the column called COL_TIMESTAMP_W_TZ, using a TIMESTAMP WITH TIMEZONE display format literal.

You may use other formats in the WHERE clause to accomplish the same query result. For example, you can use the TO_TIMESTAMP_TZ function to explicitly convert the text literal already in default format to a TIMESTAMP WITH TIME ZONE data type.

```
SELECT col_timestamp_w_tz
  FROM date_example
 WHERE col_timestamp_w_tz =
       TO_TIMESTAMP_TZ('24-FEB-09 04.25.32.000000 PM -05:00')
```

If you choose a text literal in a different format, you must supply the format mask, as illustrated in the next example. The TZH and TZM indicate the time zone displacement values in hours and minutes from UTC. In this example, the fractional seconds (FF) are not included because they are zero.

```
SELECT col_timestamp_w_tz
  FROM date_example
 WHERE col_timestamp_w_tz =
       TO_TIMESTAMP_TZ('24-FEB-2009 16:25:32 -05:00',
                       'DD-MON-YYYY HH24:MI:SS TZH:TZM')
```

The next WHERE clause uses the region name instead of the time zone offset number value. Region names are expressed in the TZR format mask.

```
SELECT col_timestamp_w_tz
  FROM date_example
 WHERE col_timestamp_w_tz =
       TO_TIMESTAMP_TZ('24-FEB-2009 16:25:32 EST',
                       'DD-MON-YYYY HH24:MI:SS TZR')
```

You can retrieve valid time zone region names from the data dictionary view V$TIMEZONE_NAMES.

```
SELECT *
  FROM v$timezone_names
TZNAME                          TZABBREV
-------------------------       --------
Africa/Cairo                    LMT
...
America/Los_Angeles             PST
...
America/Chicago                 CST
...
America/Denver                  MST
...
America/New_York                EST
...

1458 rows selected.
```

Alternatively, if you want to express the WHERE clause in PST, you can use the America/Los_Angeles region name and change the actual hour literal from 16 to 13 to result in the same UTC.

```
WHERE col_timestamp_w_tz = TO_TIMESTAMP_TZ(
    '24-FEB-2009 13:25:32 PST',
    'DD-MON-YYYY HH24:MI:SS TZR')
```

THE TZ_OFFSET FUNCTION

You can find out the time differences between the UTC and the individual time zones with the TZ_OFFSET function. Following is a query that illustrates the appropriate offset values. Note that the query result is different when daylight saving time is in effect.

```
SELECT TZ_OFFSET('Europe/London') "London",
       TZ_OFFSET('America/New_York') "NY",
       TZ_OFFSET('America/Chicago') "Chicago",
       TZ_OFFSET('America/Denver') "Denver",
       TZ_OFFSET('America/Los_Angeles') "LA"
  FROM dual

London   NY       Chicago  Denver   LA
-------  -------  -------  -------  ------
+01:00   -05:00   -06:00   -07:00   -08:00

1 row selected.
```

A COMMON TIME FORMAT MASK ERROR

Here's one common mistake you can avoid in conjunction with the datetime-related data types. In the next query, the HH24 mask is used simultaneously with the A.M./P.M. format mask. The Oracle error indicates that you must choose either HH24 or use the HH (or HH12) together with the A.M./P.M.. mask to adjust the time to either 24-hour or 12-hour format.

```
SQL> SELECT col_timestamp_w_tz
  2      FROM date_example
  3    WHERE col_timestamp_w_tz =
  4         TO_TIMESTAMP_TZ('24-FEB-2009 16:25:32 PM -05:00',
  5                      'DD-MON-YYYY HH24:MI:SS PM TZH:TZM')
  6  /
                    'DD-MON-YYYY HH24:MI:SS PM TZH:TZM')
                    *
ERROR at line 5:
ORA-01818: 'HH24' precludes use of meridian indicator
```

e) The following SQL statements are issued against the database server. Explain the results.

```
SELECT SESSIONTIMEZONE
  FROM dual

SESSIONTIMEZONE
---------------
-05:00

1 row selected.
```

```
SELECT col_timestamp_w_tz, col_timestamp_w_local_tz
  FROM date_example
COL_TIMESTAMP_W_TZ                    COL_TIMESTAMP_W_LOCAL_TZ
------------------------------------- ----------------------------
24-FEB-09 04.25.32.000000 PM -05:00 24-FEB-09 04.25.32.000000 PM


1 row selected.


ALTER SESSION SET TIME_ZONE = '-8:00'
Session altered.


SELECT col_timestamp_w_tz, col_timestamp_w_local_tz
  FROM date_example
COL_TIMESTAMP_W_TZ                    COL_TIMESTAMP_W_LOCAL_TZ
------------------------------------- ----------------------------
24-FEB-09 04.25.32.000000 PM -05:00 24-FEB-09 01.25.32.000000 PM


1 row selected.


ALTER SESSION SET TIME_ZONE = '-5:00'
Session altered.
```

ANSWER: The following query determines the session's current time zone offset value, which is −5 hours before UTC. (When daylight saving time is in effect, the time zone offset value changes.)

```
SELECT SESSIONTIMEZONE
  FROM dual
SESSIONTIMEZONE
---------------
-05:00


1 row selected.
```

The next query returns the currently stored values in the columns of the data types TIMESTAMP WITH TIME ZONE and TIMESTAMP WITH LOCAL TIME ZONE. The dates and timestamps are identical in both columns. They represent the same date and time.

```
SELECT col_timestamp_w_tz, col_timestamp_w_local_tz
  FROM date_example
COL_TIMESTAMP_W_TZ                    COL_TIMESTAMP_W_LOCAL_TZ
------------------------------------- ----------------------------
24-FEB-09 04.25.32.000000 PM -05:00 24-FEB-09 04.25.32.000000 PM


1 row selected.
```

Now the session's time zone is changed to be equivalent to the West Coast time zone, which is 8 hours before UTC. This statement helps simulate a user's query result on the West Coast.

```
ALTER SESSION SET TIME_ZONE = '-8:00'
Session altered.
```

The individual database user's local session time zone can be changed for the duration of the session with the ALTER SESSION command. Alternatively, this could also be achieved by changing the user's operating system time zone value, but the ALTER SESSION commands will always override the operating system settings.

The query is reissued, and when you compare the two column values, the second column with the data type TIMESTAMP WITH LOCAL TIME ZONE shows a different value. The local timestamp is adjusted to the local West Coast time.

```
SELECT col_timestamp_w_tz, col_timestamp_w_local_tz
  FROM date_example
COL_TIMESTAMP_W_TZ                     COL_TIMESTAMP_W_LOCAL_TZ
------------------------------------   ---------------------------
24-FEB-09 04.25.32.000000 PM -05:00 24-FEB-09 01.25.32.000000 PM

1 row selected.
```

The next statement resets the time zone to its initial time zone offset value, -5:00, as determined by the SESSIONTIMEZONE function issued previously.

```
ALTER SESSION SET TIME_ZONE = '-5:00'
Session altered.
```

When you reissue the query against the DATE_EXAMPLE table, the local time is back to its original value.

```
SELECT col_timestamp_w_tz, col_timestamp_w_local_tz
  FROM date_example
COL_TIMESTAMP_W_TZ                     COL_TIMESTAMP_W_LOCAL_TZ
------------------------------------   ---------------------------
24-FEB-09 04.25.32.000000 PM -05:00 24-FEB-09 04.25.32.000000 PM

1 row selected.
```

When you exit the SQL Developer or SQL*Plus session, these ALTER SESSION settings are no longer in effect. The ALTER SESSION settings persist only throughout the duration of the session.

Lab 5.3 Quiz

In order to test your progress, you should be able to answer the following questions.

1) What data type will the following function return?

```
SELECT FROM_TZ(col_timestamp, '+5:00')
  FROM date_example
FROM_TZ(COL_TIMESTAMP,'+5:00')
-----------------------------------
24-FEB-09 04.25.32.000000 PM +05:00

1 row selected.
```

_____ a) DATE
_____ b) TIMESTAMP
_____ c) TIMESTAMP WITH TIME ZONE
_____ d) An Oracle error message

2) The ALTER SESSION statement can change the session's time zone.

_____ a) True
_____ b) False

3) The TIMESTAMP WITH LOCAL TIME ZONE data type displays the local date and time.

_____ a) True
_____ b) False

4) The time zone displacement value indicates the time difference from UTC.

_____ a) True
_____ b) False

5) The TIMESTAMP WITH LOCAL TIME ZONE data type allows fractional seconds.

_____ a) True
_____ b) False

6) The following query displays five fractional seconds.

```
SELECT TO_CHAR(SYSTIMESTAMP, 'HH:MI:SS.FF5')
  FROM dual
```

_____ a) True
_____ b) False

ANSWERS APPEAR IN APPENDIX A.

LAB 5.4

Performing Calculations with the Interval Data Types

LAB OBJECTIVES

After this lab, you will be able to:

▶ Understand the Functionality of the Interval Data Types
▶ Perform Date-Related Calculations Using Intervals

Oracle has two interval data types: INTERVAL YEAR TO MONTH and INTERVAL DAY TO SECOND. These data types store the difference between two date values. Table 5.12 provides an overview of the two data types and respective example literals.

TABLE 5.12   Interval Data Types

DATA TYPE	PURPOSE AND EXAMPLES OF LITERALS
INTERVAL YEAR [(year_precision)] TO MONTH	Values are expressed in years and months. The default year precision is two digits.
	Literal examples:
	INTERVAL '3-2' YEAR TO MONTH (This translates into 3 years and 2 months.)
	INTERVAL '2' YEAR (2 years)
	INTERVAL '4' MONTH (4 months)
	INTERVAL '36' MONTH (36 months, or 3 years)
INTERVAL DAY [(day_precision)] TO SECOND [(fractional_seconds_ precision)]	Values are expressed in days, hours, minutes, and seconds. The default precision for the DAY is 2; the fractional seconds precision has a six-digit default value.
	Literal examples:
	INTERVAL '30' DAY (30 days)
	INTERVAL '200' DAY (3) (This translates to 200 days; because the literal exceeds the default DAY precision of 2, you need to explicitly specify the precision.)

TABLE 5.12 Continued

DATA TYPE	PURPOSE AND EXAMPLES OF LITERALS
	INTERVAL '12:51' HOUR TO MINUTE (12 hours and 51 minutes)
	INTERVAL '15' MINUTE (15 minutes)
	INTERVAL '3 5:10:15.10' DAY TO SECOND (3 days, 5 hours, 10 minutes, 15 seconds, and 10 fractional seconds)
	Note that the components must be contiguous; for example, you cannot skip the MINUTE component between the HOUR and SECOND components.

Using Intervals

You can use intervals for calculations as shown in the next example, where an interval of one year and six months is added to a student's registration date. The interval is represented as the literal '01-06'. The TO_YMINTERVAL function converts this text literal to the INTERVAL YEAR TO MONTH data type. The result of the query displays the graduation date as one year and six months after the REGISTRATION_DATE.

```
SELECT student_id, registration_date,
       registration_date+TO_YMINTERVAL('01-06') "Grad. Date"
  FROM student
 WHERE student_id = 123
    STUDENT_ID REGISTRAT Grad. Dat
    ---------- --------- ---------
           123 27-JAN-07 27-JUL-08

1 row selected.
```

The individual components of the interval data types are listed in Table 5.13.

TABLE 5.13 Valid Value Ranges for Interval Components

INTERVAL COMPONENT	VALID VALUES
YEAR	Positive or negative integer; default precision is 2.
MONTH	00–11 (Note that the 12th month will be converted to a year.)
DAY	Positive or negative integer; default precision is 2.
HOUR	00–23
MINUTE	00–59
SECOND	00–59 (Plus optional precision up to nine-digit fractional seconds)

EXTRACT and Intervals

Just as with other datetime data types, you can use the EXTRACT function to extract specific components. This query retrieves the minutes.

```
SELECT EXTRACT(MINUTE FROM INTERVAL '12:51' HOUR TO MINUTE)
   FROM dual
EXTRACT(MINUTEFROMINTERVAL'12:51'HOURTOMINUTE)
------------------------------------------------
                                              51

1 row selected.
```

The interval data types allow a number of useful functions, as listed in Table 5.14.

Table 5.14   Useful Interval Functions

FUNCTION	PURPOSE	RETURN DATA TYPE
TO_YMINTERVAL(char)	Converts a text literal to an INTERVAL YEAR TO MONTH data type.	INTERVAL YEAR TO MONTH
TO_DSINTERVAL(char)	Converts a text literal to an INTERVAL DAY TO SECOND data type.	INTERVAL DAY TO SECOND
NUMTOYMINTERVAL (number, 'YEAR') NUMTOYMINTERVAL (number, 'MONTH')	Converts a number to an INTERVAL YEAR TO MONTH interval. You can use the 'YEAR' or 'MONTH' parameters.	INTERVAL YEAR TO MONTH
NUMTODSINTERVAL (number, 'DAY')	Converts a number to an INTERVAL DAY TO SECOND literal. Instead of the DAY parameter, you can pass HOUR, MINUTE, or SECOND instead.	INTERVAL DAY TO SECOND
EXTRACT(MINUTE FROM interval data type)	Extracts specific components (for example, YEAR, MONTH, DAY, HOUR, MINUTE, SECOND).	NUMBER

The next example expresses the time difference between the columns START_DATE_TIME and CREATED_DATE of the SECTION table. The first row of the output indicates that the difference between the two dates is the decimal result 96.3958333 days; according to the fourth column, where the NUMTODSINTERVAL function is applied, this translates into 96 days, 9 hours, 29 minutes, and 59. 999999999 seconds.

```
SELECT DISTINCT TO_CHAR(created_date, 'DD-MON-YY HH24:MI')
       "CREATED_DATE",
       TO_CHAR(start_date_time, 'DD-MON-YY HH24:MI')
       "START_DATE_TIME",
       start_date_time-created_date "Decimal",
       NUMTODSINTERVAL(start_date_time-created_date,'DAY')
       "Interval"
```

```
   FROM section
   ORDER BY 3
   CREATED_DATE      START_DATE_TIME Decimal     Interval
   --------------    --------------- ----------  ---------------------
   02-JAN-07 00:00   08-APR-07 09:30 96.3958333  96 9:29:59.999999999
   02-JAN-07 00:00   09-APR-07 09:30 97.3958333  97 9:29:59.999999999
   02-JAN-07 00:00   14-APR-07 09:30 102.395833  102 09:29:59.999999999
   ...
   02-JAN-07 00:00   24-JUL-07 09:30 203.395833  203 09:29:59.999999999

   29 rows selected.
```

Interval Expressions

As an alternative to the NUMTODSINTERVAL or the NUMTOYMINTERVAL function, you can use an *interval expression,* which can be either DAY TO SECOND or YEAR TO MONTH. The next example shows as the first column the value of data type TIMESTAMP in the COL_TIMESTAMP column of the DATE_EXAMPLE table. The second column subtracts from the SYSTIMESTAMP function the COL_TIMESTAMP column and displays the difference as an interval of DAY TO SECOND, resulting in a difference of 38 days, 20 hours, 23 minutes, 29 seconds, and 218000 fractional seconds. The value of SYSTIMESTAMP at the time of the query was 04-APR-09 01.49.01.218000000 PM -04:00. The precision of the DAY interval is set to 4 to allow for larger numbers.

```
SELECT col_timestamp,
       (SYSTIMESTAMP - col_timestamp) DAY(4) TO SECOND
       "Interval Day to Second"
   FROM date_example
```

Depending on whether you are executing the query against SQL Developer or SQL*Plus, the interval value is displayed in a slightly different format. Following is the format in SQL Developer.

```
   COL_TIMESTAMP               Interval Day to Second
   --------------------------- ----------------------
   24-FEB-09 04.25.32.000000 PM 38 20:23:29.218000

   1 row selected.
```

The SQL*Plus command-line version displays the interval prefixed with a + or - symbol, similar to the following result.

```
   COL_TIMESTAMP               Interval Day to Second
   --------------------------- ----------------------
   24-FEB-09 04.25.32.000000 PM +0038 23:29:10.390000

   1 row selected.
```

Instead of using the DAY TO SECOND interval, the next query uses a YEAR TO MONTH interval. This result displays as zero years and 1 month.

```
SELECT col_timestamp,
       (SYSTIMESTAMP - col_timestamp) YEAR TO MONTH
       "Interval Year to Month"
  FROM date_example
COL_TIMESTAMP             Interval Year to Month
--------------------     ----------------------
24-FEB-09 04.25.32 PM    0-1

1 row selected.
```

Determining Overlaps

The overlaps functionality is implemented in Oracle but not documented. The OVERLAPS operator is useful to determine whether two time periods overlap. For example, you can use this operator to determine whether a planned meeting conflicts with other scheduled meetings.

The next table, called MEETING, contains three columns: a MEETING_ID column and two columns, MEETING_START and MEETING_END, that determine the start and end dates and times of a meeting.

```
SQL> DESCRIBE meeting
Name                     Null?     Type
--------------------- --------- ----------
MEETING_ID                         NUMBER(10)
MEETING_START                      DATE
MEETING_END                        DATE
```

The table has two rows, as you see from the following SELECT statement.

```
SELECT meeting_id,              •
       TO_CHAR(meeting_start, 'DD-MON-YYYY HH:MI PM') "Start",
       TO_CHAR(meeting_end, 'DD-MON-YYYY HH:MI PM') "End"
  FROM meeting
MEETING_ID Start                 End
---------- -------------------- --------------------
        1 01-JUL-2009 09:30 AM 01-JUL-2009 10:30 AM
        2 01-JUL-2009 03:00 PM 01-JUL-2009 04:30 PM

2 rows selected.
```

If you want to find out whether a particular date and time conflict with any of the already scheduled meetings, you can issue this SQL query with the OVERLAPS operator. This operator is used just like any of the other comparison operators in the WHERE clause of a SQL statement. Here it compares the column pair MEETING_START and MEETING_END with the date and time 01-JUL-2009 3:30 PM and a two-hour interval. The row that overlaps is returned in the output.

```
SELECT meeting_id,
       TO_CHAR(meeting_start, 'dd-mon-yyyy hh:mi pm') "Start",
       TO_CHAR(meeting_end, 'dd-mon-yyyy hh:mi pm') "End"
  FROM meeting
 WHERE (meeting_start, meeting_end)
       OVERLAPS
       (to_date('01-JUL-2009 3:30 PM', 'DD-MON-YYYY HH:MI PM'),
          INTERVAL '2' HOUR)
MEETING_ID Start                 End
---------- -------------------- --------------------
         2 01-JUL-2009 03:00 PM 01-JUL-2009 04:30 PM

1 row selected.
```

Alternatively, if you want to find out which meetings do *not* conflict, you can negate the predicate with the NOT logical operator, as shown in the next example.

```
SELECT meeting_id,
       TO_CHAR(meeting_start, 'DD-MON-YYYY HH:MI PM') "Start", ·
       TO_CHAR(meeting_end, 'DD-MON-YYYY HH:MI PM') "End"
  FROM meeting
 WHERE NOT (meeting_start, meeting_end)
       OVERLAPS
       (TO_DATE('01-JUL-2009 3:30PM', 'DD-MON-YYYY HH:MI PM'),
          INTERVAL '2' HOUR)
MEETING_ID Start                 End
---------- -------------------- --------------------
         1 01-JUL-2009 09:30 AM 01-JUL-2009 10:30 AM

1 row selected.
```

The syntax for OVERLAPS is as follows.

```
event OVERLAPS event
```

In this syntax, event is either of the following.

```
(start_event_date_time, end_event_start_time)

(start_event_date_time, interval_duration)
```

While the OVERLAP operator provides useful functionality, you need to understand Oracle's interpretation of an overlap. If the start date/time of one record and the end date/time of the other record are identical, this is not considered a conflict. For example, if one meeting starts at 1:00 P.M. and ends at 3:00 P.M., it would not be considered a conflict with another meeting that starts at 3:00 P.M. and ends at 4:30 P.M. However, if the second meeting started at 2:59 P.M., it would be an overlap.

▼ LAB 5.4 EXERCISES

a) Explain the result of the following SQL statement.

```
SELECT section_id "ID",
       TO_CHAR(created_date, 'MM/DD/YY HH24:MI')
         "CREATED_DATE",
       TO_CHAR(start_date_time, 'MM/DD/YY HH24:MI')
         "START_DATE_TIME",
       NUMTODSINTERVAL(start_date_time-created_date, 'DAY')
         "Interval"
  FROM section
 WHERE NUMTODSINTERVAL(start_date_time-created_date, 'DAY')
       BETWEEN INTERVAL '100' DAY(3) AND INTERVAL '120' DAY(3)
 ORDER BY 3
  ID CREATED_DATE    START DATE_TIM Interval
 --- -------------- --------------- ------------------- ---
  79 01/02/07 00:00 04/14/07 09:30 102 09:29:59.999999999
  87 01/02/07 00:00 04/14/07 09:30 102 09:29:59.999999999
 ...
 152 01/02/07 00:00 04/29/07 09:30 117 09:29:59.999999999
 125 01/02/07 00:00 04/29/07 09:30 117 09:29:59.999999999

17 rows selected.
```

b) Explain the result of the following SQL statements. What do you observe?

```
SELECT NUMTODSINTERVAL(360, 'SECOND'),
       NUMTODSINTERVAL(360, 'MINUTE')
  FROM dual
NUMTODSINTERVAL(360,'SECOND') NUMTODSINTERVAL(360,'MINUTE')
----------------------------- -----------------------------
0 0:6:0.0                      0 6:0:0.0

1 row selected.
SELECT NUMTODSINTERVAL(360, 'HOUR'),
       NUMTODSINTERVAL(360, 'DAY')
  FROM dual
NUMTODSINTERVAL(360,'HOUR')   NUMTODSINTERVAL(360,'DAY')
----------------------------- -----------------------------
15 0:0:0.0                     360 0:0:0.0

1 row selected.
```

▼ LAB 5.4 EXERCISE ANSWERS

a) Explain the result of the following SQL statement.

```
SELECT section_id "ID",
       TO_CHAR(created_date, 'MM/DD/YY HH24:MI')
         "CREATED_DATE",
       TO_CHAR(start_date_time, 'MM/DD/YY HH24:MI')
         "START_DATE_TIME",
       NUMTODSINTERVAL(start_date_time-created_date, 'DAY')
         "Interval"
  FROM section
 WHERE NUMTODSINTERVAL(start_date_time-created_date, 'DAY')
       BETWEEN INTERVAL '100' DAY(3) AND INTERVAL '120' DAY(3)
 ORDER BY 3
  ID CREATED_DATE    START_DATE_TIM Interval
 --- --------------- -------------- ----------------------
  79 01/02/07 00:00  04/14/07 09:30 102 09:29:59.999999999
  87 01/02/07 00:00  04/14/07 09:30 102 09:29:59.999999999
 ...
 152 01/02/07 00:00  04/29/07 09:30 117 09:29:59.999999999
 125 01/02/07 00:00  04/29/07 09:30 117 09:29:59.999999999

17 rows selected.
```

ANSWER: The query shows four columns: SECTION_ID, CREATED_DATE, START_DATE_TIME (the date and time a section starts), and Interval. The Interval column expresses the difference between the START_DATE_TIME column and the CREATED_DATE column, in days, hours, minutes, and seconds, using the NUMTODSINTERVAL function. Without this function, the calculation returns the time portion as a decimal. The WHERE clause of the query retrieves rows with a time difference value between 100 and 120 days. The ORDER BY clause sorts the result by the START_DATE_TIME column values.

The WHERE clause uses both the NUMTODSINTERVAL function and the INTERVAL expression and checks whether the result falls between the INTERVAL literals 100 and 120 days. Because INTERVAL DAY has a default precision of 2, you must include the three-digit precision as DAY(3).

b) Explain the result of the following SQL statements. What do you observe?

```
SELECT NUMTODSINTERVAL(360, 'SECOND'),
       NUMTODSINTERVAL(360, 'MINUTE')
  FROM dual
NUMTODSINTERVAL(360,'SECOND') NUMTODSINTERVAL(360,'MINUTE')
----------------------------- -----------------------------
0 0:6:0.0                       0 6:0:0.0

1 row selected.

SELECT NUMTODSINTERVAL(360, 'HOUR'),
       NUMTODSINTERVAL(360, 'DAY')
  FROM dual
```

```
NUMTODSINTERVAL(360,'HOUR')    NUMTODSINTERVAL(360,'DAY')
----------------------------   ----------------------------
15 0:0:0.0                      360 0:0:0.0
```

1 row selected.

ANSWER: These SQL statements illustrate how a number literal is translated to an interval, using the NUMSTODSINTERVAL function with various parameter options.

The first SQL statement shows the number literal 360 converted into seconds in the first column. The second column translates it into minutes. From the result, 360 seconds are now 6 minutes, as indicated with the 0 0:6.0 interval. The second column shows the 360 minutes converted into 6 hours, as displayed with the interval 0 6:0:0.0.

The second statement performs the same conversion; this time, the number literal represents hours, which are translated into 15 days. The second column displays 360 days in the interval format.

If you use the SQL*Plus command-line version, your query result may display differently, and you will receive a result similar to the following.

```
NUMTODSINTERVAL(360,'SECOND')   NUMTODSINTERVAL(360,'MINUTE')
----------------------------   ----------------------------
+000000000 00:06:00.000000000   +000000000 06:00:00.000000000
```

1 row selected.

Lab 5.4 Quiz

In order to test your progress, you should be able to answer the following questions.

1) The TO_YMINTERVAL function converts a text literal to an INTERVAL DAY TO SECOND data type.

    _____ a) True

    _____ b) False

2) The NUMTODSINTERVAL function converts a number to an INTERVAL YEAR TO MONTH data type.

    _____ a) True

    _____ b) False

3) The EXTRACT function is not valid for the INTERVAL YEAR TO MONTH data type.

    _____ a) True

    _____ b) False

4) The following interval literal is invalid.

```
INTERVAL '5 10:30:10.00' DAY TO SECOND
```

    _____ a) True

    _____ b) False

ANSWERS APPEAR IN APPENDIX A.

LAB 5.5
Converting from One Data Type to Another

LAB OBJECTIVES

After this lab, you will be able to:

► Convert Between Different Data Types
► Format Data

SQL agrees with the saying "You can't compare apples to oranges." When you compare two values or columns, they must be of the same data type or of compatible data types. Sometimes Oracle can implicitly convert from one data type to another. It is preferable to explicitly specify the conversion with a function to avoid any ambiguities or errors when your SQL statement is executed.

Data Type Conversion

You have already learned about implicit conversion in the context of the datetime functions discussed in the previous labs. In the following SQL statement, the WHERE clause compares a text literal against the numeric COURSE_NO column. When Oracle compares a character data type, in this case the text literal '350', against the NUMBER data type, which is the COURSE_NO column, Oracle implicitly converts the character data to a NUMBER. This works perfectly, as you see from the query result.

```
SELECT course_no, description
  FROM course
 WHERE course_no = '350'
COURSE_NO DESCRIPTION
--------- ------------------
      350 Java Developer II

1 row selected.
```

Clearly, in this example, you have control over the literal and can simply change the text literal '350' to a NUMBER to avoid the implicit conversion. Such a change becomes more difficult or impossible when you are working in a programming language where you may not have influence over the data type of a supplied value. Inevitably, things can go wrong, as you see illustrated in the following table, called CONVERSION_EXAMPLE. (This table is not part of the STUDENT schema, but you can download it from the companion Web site.)

```
SQL> DESCRIBE conversion_example
Name                         Null?     Type
--------------------         -------   -----------
COURSE_NO                              VARCHAR2(9)
```

The following SELECT statement retrieves all the rows from the table. The COURSE_NO column in this table is of data type VARCHAR2, and therefore it accepts both numeric and alphanumeric entries. The table contains two rows: one with the value 123 and another with the value xyz.

```
SELECT *
  FROM conversion_example
COURSE_NO
---------
123
xyz

2 rows selected.
```

To illustrate the effects of the implicit data conversion, first query the row with the value 123 in the COURSE_NO column. As you can see, this statement executes flawlessly because the COURSE_NO column is a VARCHAR2 column, and the text literal 123 is enclosed in single quotes.

```
SELECT *
  FROM conversion_example
 WHERE course_no = '123'
COURSE_NO
---------
123

1 row selected.
```

The next query does not enclose the literal in single quotes; in fact, it now represents a number literal. Oracle implicitly converts the COURSE_NO column to a NUMBER data type, resulting in an ORA-01722 ("invalid number") error. This error occurs because all the values in the COURSE_NO column are now implicitly converted into the NUMBER data type. But this conversion cannot be completed because one of the rows, the row with the value xyz, obviously cannot be converted into a NUMBER. Therefore, the query does not return any rows.

```
SELECT *
  FROM conversion_example
 WHERE course_no = 123
ERROR:
ORA-01722: invalid number

no rows selected
```

To avoid this error, it is always best to explicitly specify the conversion function to make sure the data types agree. You accomplish the conversion with the TO_CHAR function, which converts the passed parameter into a character data type, as you see in the following SQL statement.

```
SELECT *
  FROM conversion_example
 WHERE course_no = TO_CHAR(123)
```

You might wonder why you would bother even adding the TO_CHAR function if you can just enclose the values in quotation marks. Clearly, the easiest solution is to simply enclose the value in single quotes, but, as previously mentioned, you may encounter cases in which you do not have control over the literal or in which you are comparing one table's column against another table's column.

The CAST Function

The CAST function converts from one data type to another. It can be applied to Oracle's most commonly used built-in data types (that is, VARCHAR2, CHAR, NUMBER, and the datetime variants) or with a user-defined data type or subquery. (The creation of user-defined data types is beyond the scope of this book. You will learn about subqueries in Chapter 8, "Subqueries.")

The syntax for the CAST function is as follows.

```
CAST(expression AS data type)
```

Following are examples of how CAST is used with Oracle's familiar data types. The SELECT statement contains CAST instead of the TO_CHAR function. When converting to a VARCHAR2 or CHAR data type, also referred to as *casting*, you need to specify the length. In this case, it is three characters long.

```
SELECT *
  FROM conversion_example
 WHERE course_no = CAST(123 AS VARCHAR2(3))
```

The next query casts the text literal '29-MAR-09' into a DATE data type in the first column and as a TIMESTAMP WITH LOCAL TIME ZONE data type in the second column.

```
SELECT CAST('29-MAR-09' AS DATE) DT,
       CAST('29-MAR-09' AS TIMESTAMP WITH LOCAL TIME ZONE) TZ
  FROM dual
DATE      TZ
--------- ---------------------------------------------
29-MAR-09 29-MAR-09 12.00.00.000000 AM

1 row selected.
```

You can use CAST not only in the SELECT list but also in the WHERE clause.

```
SELECT section_id,
       TO_CHAR(start_date_time, 'DD-MON-YYYY HH24:MI:SS')
  FROM section
 WHERE start_date_time >= CAST('01-JUL-2007' AS DATE)
   AND start_date_time <  CAST('01-AUG-2007' AS DATE)
```

The following statement casts the literal '04-JUL-2007 10:00:00 AM' into the TIMESTAMP data type, because the FROM_TZ function requires this data type as the first parameter. The FROM_TZ function (discussed in Lab 5.3) converts the TIMESTAMP value into a TIMESTAMP WITH TIME ZONE data type. The chosen time zone for date literal is the time zone region name 'America/New_York'. The AT TIME ZONE keywords of the resulting expression display the value in the local Los Angeles time.

```
SELECT FROM_TZ(CAST('04-JUL-2007 10:00:00 AM' AS TIMESTAMP),
       'America/New_York') AT TIME ZONE 'America/Los_Angeles'
       "FROM_TZ Example"
  FROM dual
FROM_TZ Example
---------------------------------------------------
04-JUL-07 07.00.00.000000 AM AMERICA/LOS_ANGELES

1 row selected.
```

The next example illustrates the use of CAST on intervals. The text literal '1-6' is converted into the INTERVAL YEAR TO MONTH data type. As always, there are multiple ways to accomplish the same functionality in the SQL language; here the TO_YMINTERVAL function performs the identical function. The NUMTOYMINTERVAL function requires a NUMBER data type as an input parameter and translates the number 1.5 into one year and six months. (Refer to Table 5.14.)

```
SELECT CAST('1-6' AS INTERVAL YEAR TO MONTH) "CAST",
       TO_YMINTERVAL('1-6') "TO_YMINTERVAL",
       NUMTOYMINTERVAL(1.5, 'YEAR') "NUMTOYMINTERVAL"
  FROM dual
CAST    TO_YMINTERVAL NUMTOYMINTERVAL
------  ------------- ---------------
1-6     1-6           1-6

1 row selected.
```

Following is an example of a SQL statement that casts the COST column of the COURSE table into a BINARY_FLOAT data type. Alternatively, you can also use the TO_BINARY_FLOAT conversion function.

```
SELECT CAST(cost AS BINARY_FLOAT) AS cast,
       TO_BINARY_FLOAT(cost) AS to_binary_float
  FROM course
 WHERE course_no < 80
```

```
     CAST TO_BINARY_FLOAT
---------- ----------------
1.195E+003       1.195E+003
1.195E+003       1.195E+003
1.195E+003       1.195E+003

3 rows selected.
```

CAST Versus Oracle's Conversion Functions

You might wonder why you should use CAST instead of any of the other Oracle conversion functions. The CAST function is ANSI SQL 1999 compliant, so there is no need to learn multiple Oracle-specific functions. However, some of Oracle's built-in data types, such as the various LOB types, LONG RAW, and LONG, cannot be converted from one data type to another using CAST. Instead, you must use Oracle's individual conversion functions. One disadvantage of the CAST function is casting into VARCHAR2 and CHAR data types because they need to be constrained to a determined length. The TO_DATE function and TO_CHAR functions are overall very versatile as they allow you a large variety of different format model choices. So you may choose the functions that fit your specific requirements.

Table 5.15 provides an overview of Oracle conversion functions. This lab concentrates on the TO_NUMBER, TO_CHAR, and CAST functions. In previous labs, you learned about the TO_DATE and TO_CHAR conversion functions, as well as conversion functions related to datetime and interval data types (refer to Table 5.11 and Table 5.14).

TABLE 5.15   Frequently Used Data Type Conversion Functions

FUNCTION	PURPOSE
TO_NUMBER(char [, format_mask])	Converts a VARCHAR2 or CHAR to a NUMBER.
TO_BINARY_FLOAT(expression [,format_mask])	Converts a character or numeric value to BINARY_FLOAT.
TO_BINARY_DOUBLE(expression [,format_mask])	Converts a character or numeric value to BINARY_DOUBLE.
TO_CHAR(datetime [, format_mask])	Converts a datetime value to a VARCHAR2.
TO_CHAR(number [, format_mask])	Converts a NUMBER to a VARCHAR2.
TO_CLOB(char)	Converts a VARCHAR2 or CHAR to a CLOB.
TO_DATE(char [, format_mask])	Converts a VARCHAR2 or CHAR to a DATE. For timestamp and time zones, see Lab 5.3.
CAST(expression AS data type)	Converts from one data type to another. Can be used for Oracle's most commonly used data types and for user-defined data types.

Formatting Data

The TO_CHAR conversion function is useful not only for data conversions between different data types but also for formatting data. The next SQL statement shows how a format mask can be applied with this function. To display a formatted result for the COST column, for instance, you can apply the format mask '999,999'. The values in the COST column are then formatted with a comma separating the thousands.

```
SELECT course_no, cost,
       TO_CHAR(cost, '999,999') formatted
  FROM course
 WHERE course_no < 25
COURSE_NO      COST FORMATTED
--------- --------- ---------
       10      1195     1,195
       20      1195     1,195

2 rows selected.
```

The conversion function used in the SELECT statement does not modify the values stored in the database but rather performs a "temporary" conversion for the purpose of executing the statement. In Chapter 2, "SQL: The Basics," you learned about the SQL*Plus COLUMN FORMAT command, which achieves the same result. However, if you execute the SQL statement from a program other than SQL*Plus, the COLUMN command is not available, and you must use the TO_CHAR function to format the result.

The following statement shows both the effects of the SQL*Plus COLUMN FORMAT command and the TO_CHAR function. The column labeled "SQL*PLUS" is formatted with the COL "SQL*PLUS" FORMAT 999,999 command, the last column, labeled "CHAR," is formatted with the TO_CHAR function.

```
COL "SQL*PLUS" FORMAT 999,999
SELECT course_no, cost "SQL*PLUS",
       TO_CHAR(cost, '999,999') "CHAR"
  FROM course
 WHERE course_no < 25
COURSE_NO SQL*PLUS CHAR
--------- -------- --------
       10    1,195    1,195
       20    1,195    1,195

2 rows selected.
```

Table 5.16 provides an overview of the most popular NUMBER format models in conjunction with the TO_CHAR function.

Rounding can be accomplished not only with the ROUND function but also with a format model.

TABLE 5.16   Common NUMBER Format Models

FORMAT MASK	EXAMPLE VALUE	APPLIED TO_CHAR FUNCTION	RESULT
999,990.99	.45	TO_CHAR(.45, '999,990.99')	0.45 (Note the leading zero)
$99,999.99	1234	TO_CHAR(1234,'$99,999.99')	$1,234.00
0999	123	TO_CHAR(123, '0999')	0123
L9999.99	1234.99	TO_CHAR(1234.99, 'L9999.99')	$1234.99 (local currency)
L99G999D99	1234.56	TO_CHAR(1234.56, 'L99G999D99')	$1,234.56 (local values for currency, group, and decimal separators)
999PR	-123	TO_CHAR(-123,'999PR')	<123>
999MI	-123	TO_CHAR(-123, '999MI')	123-
999s	-123	TO_CHAR(-123, '999s')	123-
s999	-123	TO_CHAR(-123, 's999')	-123
999	123.59	TO_CHAR(123.59, '999')	124 (Note the rounding)

▼ LAB 5.5 EXERCISES

Use the following SQL statement as the source query for Exercises a through c.

```
SELECT zip, city
FROM zipcode
WHERE zip = 10025
```

a) Rewrite the query, using the TO_CHAR function in the WHERE clause.

b) Rewrite the query, using the TO_NUMBER function in the WHERE clause.

c) Rewrite the query, using CAST in the WHERE clause.

d) Write the SQL statement that displays the following result. Note that the last column in the result shows the formatted COST column with a leading dollar sign and a comma to separate the thousands. Include the cents in the result as well.

```
COURSE_NO    COST FORMATTED
---------- ---------- ---------
       330    1195 $1,195.00


1 row selected.
```

e) List the COURSE_NO and COST columns for courses that cost more than 1500. The third, fourth, and fifth columns show the cost increased by 15 percent. Display the increased cost columns, one with a leading dollar sign, and separate the thousands, and in another column show the same formatting but rounded to the nearest dollar. The result should look similar to the following output.

COURSE_NO	OLDCOST	NEWCOST	FORMATTED	ROUNDED
80	1595	1834.25	$1,834.25	$1,834.00

1 row selected

f) Based on Exercise e, write the query to achieve this result. Use the fm format mask to eliminate the extra spaces.

```
Increase
------------------------------------------------------------
The price for course# 80 has been increased to $1,834.25.
```

1 row selected.

▼ LAB 5.5 EXERCISE ANSWERS

Use the following SQL statement as the source query for Exercises a through c.

Type and execute the following query for the following exercises.

```
SELECT zip, city
   FROM zipcode
  WHERE zip = 10025
```

a) Rewrite the query, using the TO_CHAR function in the WHERE clause.

ANSWER: The TO_CHAR function converts the number literal to a VARCHAR2 data type, which makes it equal to the VARCHAR2 data type of the ZIP column.

```
SELECT zip, city
   FROM zipcode
  WHERE zip = TO_CHAR(10025)
ZIP    CITY
-----  --------
10025 New York
```

1 row selected.

b) Rewrite the query, using the TO_NUMBER function in the WHERE clause.

ANSWER: The VARCHAR2 data type of the ZIP column is converted to a NUMBER data type by applying the TO_NUMBER function. Oracle then compares it to the number literal 10025.

```
SELECT zip, city
   FROM zipcode
  WHERE TO_NUMBER(zip) = 10025
ZIP    CITY
-----  --------
10025 New York
```

1 row selected.

When you compare the results of the SQL statements from Answers a and b, they are identical. Answer b is less desirable because a function is applied to a database column in the WHERE clause. This disables the use of any indexes that may exist on the ZIP column and may require Oracle to read every row in the table instead of looking up the value in the index. Applying functions to database columns in the SELECT clause does not affect performance.

It is best to explicitly specify the data type conversion functions and not rely on implicit conversions: Your statements are easier to understand, and the behavior is predictable. Oracle's algorithms for implicit conversion may be subject to change across versions and products, and implicit conversion can have a negative impact on performance if the queried column is indexed. You will learn about indexes in Chapter 13 and about performance considerations in Chapter 18, "SQL Optimization."

c) Rewrite the query, using CAST in the WHERE clause.

ANSWER: You can write the query in one of the following ways.

```
SELECT zip, city
  FROM zipcode
 WHERE CAST(zip AS NUMBER) = 10025


SELECT zip, city
  FROM zipcode
 WHERE zip = CAST(10025 AS VARCHAR2(5))
```

If you specify a too-short length for the VARCHAR2 data type, you receive an error similar to the following.

```
SELECT zip, city
  FROM zipcode
 WHERE zip = CAST(10025 AS VARCHAR2(3))
WHERE zip = CAST(10025 AS VARCHAR2(3))
                 *
ERROR at line 3:
ORA-25137: Data value out of range
```

In the next SQL query result, observe the way SQL*Plus displays the result of a NUMBER column versus the result in a character type column. In the output, you see as the first column the ZIP column in data type VARCHAR2. It is left aligned, just like the VARCHAR2 column CITY. In general, both in SQL*Plus and the SQL Developer Results window, values of the NUMBER data type are always right aligned; character values are always left aligned. However, in SQL Developer's Script Output tab, all columns are left aligned.

```
SELECT zip, TO_NUMBER(zip) "TO_NUMBER",
       CAST(zip AS NUMBER) "CAST", city
  FROM zipcode
 WHERE zip = '10025'
ZIP      TO_NUMBER     CAST CITY
-------  ---------  ------- ----------
10025        10025    10025 New York

1 row selected.
```

d) Write the SQL statement that displays the following result. Note that the last column in the result shows the formatted COST column with a leading dollar sign and a comma to separate the thousands. Include the cents in the result as well.

```
COURSE_NO      COST FORMATTED
---------  --------- ---------
      330       1195 $1,195.00
```

```
1 row selected.
```

ANSWER: The TO_CHAR function, together with the format mask in the SELECT clause of the statement, achieves the desired formatting.

```
SELECT course_no, cost,
       TO_CHAR(cost, '$999,999.99') Formatted
  FROM course
 WHERE course_no = 330
```

e) List the COURSE_NO and COST columns for courses that cost more than 1500. The third, fourth, and fifth columns show the cost increased by 15 percent. Display the increased cost columns, one with a leading dollar sign, and separate the thousands, and in another column show the same formatting but rounded to the nearest dollar. The result should look similar to the following output.

```
COURSE_NO     OLDCOST  NEWCOST FORMATTED   ROUNDED
---------- ----------- -------- ---------- ----------
        80        1595  1834.25 $1,834.25  $1,834.00
```

```
1 row selected
```

ANSWER: An increase of 15 percent requires a multiplication of the column COST by 1.15. You can round to the nearest dollar by using the ROUND function.

```
SELECT course_no, cost oldcost,
       cost*1.15 newcost,
       TO_CHAR(cost*1.15, '$999,999.99') formatted,
       TO_CHAR(ROUND(cost*1.15), '$999,999.99') rounded
  FROM course
 WHERE cost > 1500
```

Alternatively, the identical result is achieved with the format mask '$999,999', which omits the digits after the decimal point and rounds the cents, as shown in the next statement.

```
SELECT course_no, TO_CHAR(ROUND(cost*1.15), '$999,999.99') rounded,
       TO_CHAR(cost*1.15, '$999,999') "No Cents"
  FROM course
 WHERE cost > 1500
```

```
COURSE_NO ROUNDED          No Cents
---------- ------------ ---------
        80 $1,834.00      $1,834
```

```
1 row selected.
```

f) Based on the Exercise e, write the query to achieve this result. Use the fm format mask to eliminate the extra spaces.

```
Increase
-------------------------------------------------------------
The price for course# 80 has been increased to $1,834.25.

1 row selected.
```

ANSWER: The following query achieves the desired result set. The fm format mask eliminates the blank padding.

```
SELECT 'The price for course# '||course_no||' has been increased to
➥'||
        TO_CHAR(cost*1.15, 'fm$999,999.99')||'.'
        "Increase"
  FROM course
 WHERE cost > 1500
```

Lab 5.5 Quiz

In order to test your progress, you should be able to answer the following questions.

1) Which SQL statement results in an error? Select all that apply.

_____ a) SELECT TO_CHAR('123') FROM dual

_____ b) SELECT TO_CHAR(123) FROM dual

_____ c) SELECT TO_NUMBER('001.99999') FROM dual

_____ d) SELECT TO_NUMBER('A123') FROM dual

_____ e) SELECT TO_CHAR('A123') FROM dual

_____ f) SELECT TO_NUMBER(' 000123 ') FROM dual

2) Which of the following NUMBER format masks are valid? Select all that apply.

_____ a) SELECT TO_CHAR(1.99,'9,9999.9X') FROM dual

_____ b) SELECT TO_CHAR(1.99,'A99.99) FROM dual

_____ c) SELECT TO_CHAR(1.99,'$000.99') FROM dual

_____ d) SELECT TO_CHAR(1.99,'999.99') FROM dual

_____ e) SELECT TO_CHAR(1.99,'.99') FROM dual

3) Explicit data type conversion is preferable to Oracle's implicit conversion.

_____ a) True

_____ b) False

4) The TO_CHAR, TO_NUMBER, and TO_DATE conversion functions are single-row functions.

_____ a) True

_____ b) False

5) How can you correct the following SQL error message?

```
SQL> SELECT *
  2     FROM conversion_example
  3   WHERE course_no = CAST(123 AS VARCHAR2)
  4  /
WHERE course_no = CAST(123 AS VARCHAR2)
                                       *
ERROR at line 3:
ORA-00906: missing left parenthesis
```

_____a) Change the data type to CHAR.

_____b) Add a column length definition.

_____c) Choose a different aggregate function.

_____d) This query does not make sense.

ANSWERS APPEAR IN APPENDIX A.

▼ WORKSHOP

The projects in this section are meant to prompt you to utilize all the skills you have acquired throughout this chapter. The answers to these projects can be found at the companion Web site to this book, located at www.oraclesqlbyexample.com.

1) Display all the sections where classes start at 10:30 A.M.

2) Write a query that accomplishes the following result. The output shows you all the days of the week where sections 99, 89, and 105 start. Note the order of the days.

```
DAY    SECTION_ID
----   ----------
Mon            99
Tue            89
Wed           105

3 rows selected.
```

3) Select the distinct course costs for all the courses. If a course cost is unknown, substitute a zero. Format the output with a leading $ sign and separate the thousands with a comma. Display two digits after the decimal point. The query's output should look like the following result.

```
COST
-----------
     $0.00
 $1,095.00
 $1,195.00
 $1,595.00

4 rows selected.
```

4) List all rows of the GRADE_TYPE table that were created in the year 1998.

5) What, if anything, is wrong with the following SQL statement?

```
SELECT zip + 100
  FROM zipcode
```

6) For the students enrolled on January 30, 2007, display the columns STUDENT_ID and ENROLL_DATE.

CHAPTER 6

Aggregate Functions, GROUP BY, and HAVING Clauses

CHAPTER OBJECTIVES

In this chapter, you will learn about:

- ▶ Aggregate Functions
- ▶ The GROUP BY and HAVING Clauses

In the last two chapters, you learned about character functions, number functions, date functions, and miscellaneous functions—all single-row functions. In this chapter, you will learn about aggregate functions, which work on groups of rows. The most commonly used aggregate functions are discussed. Aggregate functions allow you to generate summary data for a group of rows to obtain totals, averages, counts, minimum values, and maximum values. In Chapter 17, "Exploring Data Warehousing Features," you will learn about advanced SQL aggregation topics involving the ROLLUP and CUBE operators.

LAB 6.1
Aggregate Functions

LAB OBJECTIVES

After this lab, you will be able to:

▶ Use Aggregate Functions in a SQL Statement
▶ Understand the Effect of Nulls on Aggregate Functions

Aggregate functions do just as you would expect: They *aggregate,* or group together, data to produce a single result. Questions such as "How many students are registered?" and "What is the average cost of a course?" can be answered by using aggregate functions. You count the individual students to answer the first question, and you calculate the average cost of all courses to answer the second. In each case, the result is a single answer, based on several rows of data.

The COUNT Function

One of the most common aggregate functions is the COUNT function, which lets you count values in a table. The function takes a single parameter, which can be a column in a table of any data type and can even be the asterisk (*) wildcard. The following SELECT statement returns the number of rows in the ENROLLMENT table:

```
SELECT COUNT(*)
  FROM enrollment
COUNT(*)
---------
      226

1 row selected.
```

COUNT AND NULLS

The COUNT function is useful for determining whether a table has data. If the result returns the number 0 when you use COUNT(*), it means there are no rows in the table, even though the table exists.

Following is an example of the COUNT function used with a database column as a parameter. The difference is that COUNT(*) counts rows that contain null values, whereas COUNT with a column excludes rows that contain nulls.

```
SELECT COUNT(final_grade), COUNT(section_id), COUNT(*)
   FROM enrollment
COUNT(FINAL_GRADE) COUNT(SECTION_ID)  COUNT(*)
------------------ ----------------- ---------
                 1               226       226
```

1 row selected.

The FINAL_GRADE column in the ENROLLMENT table allows null values, and there is only one row with a value in the FINAL_GRADE column. Therefore, the result of the function is 1. COUNT(section_id) returns the same number as COUNT(*) because the SECTION_ID column contains no nulls.

COUNT AND DISTINCT

DISTINCT is often used in conjunction with aggregate functions to determine the number of distinct values. There are 226 rows in the ENROLLMENT table but 64 distinct section IDs. Several students are enrolled in the same section; therefore, individual section IDs usually exist more than once in the ENROLLMENT table.

```
SELECT COUNT(DISTINCT section_id), COUNT(section_id)
   FROM enrollment
COUNT(DISTINCTSECTION_ID) COUNT(SECTION_ID)
------------------------- -----------------
                       64               226
```

1 row selected.

 You can use the UNIQUE keyword in place of DISTINCT.

The SUM Function

The SUM function adds values together for a group of rows. The following example adds up all the values in the CAPACITY column of the SECTION table. The result is the total capacity of all sections. If any value in the CAPACITY column contains a null, these values are ignored.

```
SELECT SUM(capacity)
   FROM section
SUM(CAPACITY)
-------------
         1652
```

1 row selected.

The AVG Function

The AVG function returns the average of a group of rows. The following example computes the average capacity of each section. Any nulls in the capacity column are ignored. To substitute a zero for a null, use the NVL or COALESCE function, as discussed in Chapter 4, "Character, Number, and Miscellaneous Functions."

```
SELECT AVG(capacity), AVG(NVL(capacity,0))
  FROM section
AVG(CAPACITY) AVG(NVL(CAPACITY,0))
------------- --------------------
    21.179487             21.179487

1 row selected.
```

In this example, there are no sections with null values in the CAPACITY column; therefore, the results of the two functions are identical.

The MIN and MAX Functions

The MIN and MAX functions are opposites of each other, providing the minimum and maximum values, respectively, in a group of rows. The result shows the lowest value in the CAPACITY column in the SECTION table; this value is 10, and the highest value is 25.

```
SELECT MIN(capacity), MAX(capacity)
  FROM section
MIN(CAPACITY) MAX(CAPACITY)
------------- -------------
           10            25

1 row selected.
```

MIN and MAX with Different Data Types

The previous example operates on the CAPACITY column, which is of the NUMBER data type. The MIN and MAX functions can take other data types as parameters. The next example shows the use of these functions with the DATE data type and displays the first and last registration dates in the STUDENT table.

```
SELECT MIN(registration_date) "First",
       MAX(registration_date) "Last"
  FROM student
First     Last
--------- ---------
22-JAN-07 23-FEB-07

1 row selected.
```

A less frequently used data type for the MIN and MAX functions is the VARCHAR2 data type. The following query shows the minimum or maximum value of the DESCRIPTION column and returns the first and last values, in an alphabetized list of values.

```
SELECT MIN (description) AS MIN, MAX (description) AS MAX
   FROM course
MIN                              MAX
--------------------------       ------------------------
Advanced Java Programming   Unix Tips and Techniques

1 row selected.
```

The capital letter A is equal to the ASCII value 65, B is 66, and so on. Lowercase letters, numbers, and characters all have their own ASCII values. Therefore, MIN and MAX can be used to evaluate a character's respective first and last letters, in alphabetical order.

Aggregate Functions and Nulls

Except for the COUNT(*) function, all the aggregate functions you have learned about so far ignore null values. You use the NVL or COALESCE function to substitute for any null values. An aggregate function always returns a row. Even if the query returns no rows, the result is simply one row with a null value; the COUNT function always returns either a zero or a number.

Aggregate Functions and CASE

Placing a CASE expression within an aggregate function can be useful if you want to manipulate or select specific values before applying the aggregate function. For example, the following SQL statement shows the computation of the average course cost. If the value in the PREREQUISITE column is null, the value in the COST column is multiplied by 1.1; if the value is equal to 20, it is multiplied by 1.2; in all other cases, the value retrieved in the COST column remains unchanged.

```
SELECT AVG(CASE WHEN prerequisite IS NULL THEN cost*1.1
                 WHEN prerequisite = 20 THEN cost*1.2
                 ELSE cost
             END) AS avg
   FROM course
         AVG
----------
1256.13793

1 row selected.
```

Aggregate Function Syntax

Table 6.1 lists the most commonly used aggregate functions and their corresponding syntax. As you may notice, you can use the DISTINCT keyword with all these functions to evaluate only the distinct (or unique) values. The ALL keyword is the default option and evaluates all rows. The DISTINCT keyword is really useful only for the AVG, SUM, and COUNT functions. In place of DISTINCT, you can substitute the UNIQUE keyword.

TABLE 6.1   Commonly Used Aggregate Functions

FUNCTION	PURPOSE
COUNT({* | [DISTINCT|ALL] expression)	Counts the number of rows. The wildcard (*) option includes duplicates and null values.
SUM([DISTINCT|ALL] value)	Computes the total of a value; ignores nulls.
AVG([DISTINCT|ALL] value)	Finds the average value; ignores nulls.
MIN(expression)	Determines the minimum value of an expression; ignores nulls.
MAX(expression)	Determines the maximum value of an expression; ignores nulls.

▼ LAB 6.1 EXERCISES

a) Write a SELECT statement that determines how many courses do not have a prerequisite.

b) Write a SELECT statement that determines the total number of students enrolled. Count each student only once, no matter how many courses the student is enrolled in.

c) Determine the average cost for all courses. If the course cost contains a null value, substitute the value 0.

d) Write a SELECT statement that determines the date of the most recent enrollment.

▼ LAB 6.1 EXERCISE ANSWERS

a) Write a SELECT statement that determines how many courses do not have a prerequisite.

ANSWER: The COUNT function is used to count the number of rows in the COURSE table where the values in the PREREQUISITE column are null.

```
SELECT COUNT(*)
  FROM course
 WHERE prerequisite IS NULL
 COUNT(*)
---------
        4

1 row selected.
```

b) Write a SELECT statement that determines the total number of students enrolled. Count each student only once, no matter how many courses the student is enrolled in.

ANSWER: Use DISTINCT in conjunction with the COUNT function to count distinct students, regardless of how many times they appear in the ENROLLMENT table.

```
SELECT COUNT(DISTINCT student_id)
  FROM enrollment
COUNT(DISTINCTSTUDENT_ID)
-------------------------
                      165

1 row selected.
```

c) Determine the average cost for all courses. If the course cost contains a null value, substitute the value 0.

ANSWER: Both the NVL function and the COALESCE function substitute any null value with a zero. The NVL or COALESCE function must be nested inside the AVG function.

```
SELECT AVG(NVL(cost, 0))
  FROM course
AVG(NVL(COST,0))
----------------
          1158.5

1 row selected.
```

The following is another possibility.

```
SELECT AVG(COALESCE(cost, 0))
  FROM course
```

If you do not substitute the nulls for the zero value, the average course cost returns a different, more accurate, result.

```
SELECT AVG(cost)
  FROM course
AVG(COST)
---------
1198.4483

1 row selected.
```

d) Write a SELECT statement that determines the date of the most recent enrollment.

ANSWER: The MAX function determines the most recent value in the ENROLL_DATE column of the ENROLLMENT table.

```
SELECT MAX(enroll_date)
  FROM enrollment
MAX(ENROL
---------
21-FEB-07

1 row selected.
```

Lab 6.1 Quiz

In order to test your progress, you should be able to answer the following questions.

1) How many of these functions are aggregate functions? AVG, COUNT, SUM, ROUND.

   _____ a) One

   _____ b) Two

   _____ c) Three

   _____ d) Four

2) Which problem does the following SQL statement solve?

```
SELECT NVL(MAX(modified_date),
           TO_DATE('12-MAR-2012', 'DD-MON-YYYY'))
  FROM enrollment
```

   _____ a) Display the date when a STUDENT table was last modified.

   _____ b) Display the date when a STUDENT record was last modified. Replace any null value
              with the date March 12, 2012.

   _____ c) Show the date when a record in the ENROLLMENT table was last modified. If the
              result returns a null value, display March 12, 2012.

   _____ d) For all the ENROLLMENT records, show the date 12-Mar-2012.

3) An aggregate function can be applied on a single row.

   _____ a) True

   _____ b) False

4) The following SQL statement contains an error.

```
SELECT AVG(*)
  FROM course
```

   _____ a) True

   _____ b) False

5) The following SQL statement determines the average of all capacities in the SECTION table.

```
SELECT AVG(UNIQUE capacity)
  FROM section
```

   _____ a) True

   _____ b) False

6) The following SQL statement contains an error.

```
SELECT SUM(capacity*1.5)
  FROM section
```

   _____ a) True

   _____ b) False

ANSWERS APPEAR IN APPENDIX A.

LAB 6.2
The GROUP BY and HAVING Clauses

LAB OBJECTIVES

After this lab, you will be able to:

▶ Use the GROUP BY Clause
▶ Apply the HAVING Clause

The GROUP BY and HAVING clauses allow you to categorize and aggregate data further. This lab analyzes the data in the STUDENT schema tables, using various aggregation functions.

The GROUP BY Clause

The GROUP BY clause determines how rows are grouped. The aggregate function together with the GROUP BY clause shows the aggregate value for each group. For example, for all the different locations, you can determine the number of rows or the average, minimum, maximum, or total capacity.

To understand the result of the GROUP BY clause without an aggregate function, compare it to that of the DISTINCT clause.

The following two queries return the same result, which is a distinct list of the values in the LOCATION column.

```
SELECT DISTINCT location
  FROM section

SELECT location
  FROM section
 GROUP BY location
LOCATION
--------
H310
L206
...
M311
M500

12 rows selected.
```

If you want to expand on this example and now include how many times each respective location value is listed in the SECTION table, you add the COUNT(*) function in the query.

```
SELECT location, COUNT(*)
  FROM section
 GROUP BY location
LOCATION    COUNT(*)
--------    ----------
H310               1
L206               1
L210              10
L211               3
L214              15
...
M500               1

12 rows selected.
```

Essentially, the GROUP BY clause and the aggregate function work hand-in-hand. Based on the distinct values, as listed in the GROUP BY clause, the aggregate function returns the result.

You can change the SQL query to determine other values for the distinct LOCATION column. For example, the following statement includes the aggregate functions SUM, MIN, and MAX in the SELECT list. For each distinct location, you see the total capacities with the SUM function, which adds up all the values in the CAPACITY column. The MIN and MAX functions return the minimum and maximum capacities for each respective location.

```
SELECT location, COUNT(*), SUM(capacity) AS sum,
       MIN(capacity) AS min, MAX(capacity) AS max
  FROM section
 GROUP BY location
LOCATION COUNT(*)    SUM    MIN    MAX
-------- --------  ------ ------ ------
H310           1      15     15     15
L206           1      15     15     15
L210          10     200     15     25
L211           3      55     15     25
L214          15     275     15     25
...
M500           1      25     25     25

12 rows selected.
```

You can validate the result of the query by looking at one of the rows. For example, the row with the LOCATION value L211 has three rows, according to the COUNT function. The total of all the values in the CAPACITY column is 55 (25 + 15 + 15). The minimum value of the CAPACITY column is 15, and the maximum value is 25.

```
SELECT location, capacity, section_id
  FROM section
 WHERE location = 'L211'
LOCATION   CAPACITY SECTION_ID
--------   -------- ----------
L211            25        119
L211            15        133
L211            15        153

3 rows selected.
```

GROUPING BY MULTIPLE COLUMNS

The following query applies the aggregate functions to the distinct values of the LOCATION and the INSTRUCTOR_ID columns; therefore, the statement returns more rows than the previous GROUP BY query.

```
SELECT location, instructor_id,
       COUNT(*), SUM(capacity) AS sum,
       MIN(capacity) AS min, MAX(capacity) AS max
  FROM section
 GROUP BY location, instructor_id
 ORDER BY 1
LOCATION INSTRUCTOR_ID COUNT(*)    SUM    MIN    MAX
-------- ------------- --------  ------ ------ ------
H310              103         1      15     15     15
L206              108         1      15     15     15
L210              101         1      15     15     15
L210              103         2      40     15     25
L210              104         1      25     25     25
L210              105         2      40     15     25
L210              106         1      25     25     25
L210              108         3      55     15     25
L214              102         4      70     15     25
...
M500              102         1      25     25     25

39 rows selected.
```

When you examine the output, you notice that there are six rows for the L210 location. For this location, each row has a different INSTRUCTOR_ID value. On each of these six distinct LOCATION and INSTRUCTOR_ID combinations, the aggregate functions are applied. For example, the first row has only one row with this LOCATION and INSTRUCTOR_ID combination, and the second row has two rows, as you see from the number in the COUNT(*) column. Once again, you can validate the result by issuing an individual query against the SECTION table.

```
SELECT location, instructor_id, capacity, section_id
  FROM section
 WHERE location = 'L210'
 ORDER BY 1, 2
LOCATION INSTRUCTOR_ID   CAPACITY SECTION_ID
-------- ------------- ---------- ----------
L210               101         15        117
L210               103         15         81
L210               103         25        150
L210               104         25         96
L210               105         25         91
L210               105         15        129
L210               106         25         84
L210               108         15         86
L210               108         15        155
L210               108         25        124

10 rows selected.
```

ORACLE ERROR ORA-00979

Every column you list in the SELECT list, except the aggregate function column itself, must be repeated in the GROUP BY clause. Following is the error Oracle returns when you violate this rule.

```
SQL> SELECT location, instructor_id,
  2          COUNT(*), SUM(capacity) AS sum,
  3          MIN(capacity) AS min, MAX(capacity) AS max
  4     FROM section
  5    GROUP BY location
  6  /
SELECT location, instructor_id,
                 *
ERROR at line 1:
ORA-00979: not a GROUP BY expression
```

The error message indicates that Oracle does not know how to process this query. The query lists the LOCATION and INSTRUCTOR_ID columns in the SELECT list but only the LOCATION column in the GROUP BY clause. Essentially, Oracle is confused about the SQL statement. The GROUP BY clause lists only the LOCATION column, which determines the distinct values. But the statement fails to specify what to do with the INSTRUCTOR_ID column.

SORTING DATA

The GROUP BY clause groups the rows, but it does not necessarily sort the results in any particular order. To change the order, use the ORDER BY clause, which follows the GROUP BY clause. The columns used in the ORDER BY clause must appear in the SELECT list, which is unlike the normal use of ORDER BY. In the following example, the result is sorted in descending order by the total capacity. You can use the column alias in the ORDER BY clause.

```
SELECT location "Location", instructor_id,
       COUNT(location) "Total Locations",
       SUM(capacity) "Total Capacity"
  FROM section
 GROUP BY location, instructor_id
 ORDER BY "Total Capacity" DESC
```

The HAVING Clause

The purpose of the HAVING clause is to eliminate groups, just as the WHERE clause is used to eliminate rows. Expanding on the previous SQL statement, the following query showing the applied HAVING clause restricts the result set to locations with a total capacity value of more than 50 students.

```
SELECT location "Location", instructor_id,
       COUNT(location) "Total Locations",
       SUM(capacity) "Total Capacity"
  FROM section
 GROUP BY location, instructor_id
HAVING SUM(capacity) > 50j277
 ORDER BY "Total Capacity" DESC
```

Location	INSTRUCTOR_ID	Total Locations	Total Capacity
L509	106	5	115
L509	101	4	85
L507	101	3	75
L507	107	3	75
L509	105	3	75
...			
L214	106	3	55

14 rows selected.

THE WHERE AND HAVING CLAUSES

As previously mentioned, the HAVING clause eliminates groups that do not satisfy its condition. This is in contrast to the WHERE clause, which eliminates rows even before the aggregate functions and the GROUP BY and HAVING clauses are applied.

```
SELECT location "Location", instructor_id,
       COUNT(location) "Total Locations",
       SUM(capacity) "Total Capacity"
  FROM section
 WHERE section_no IN (2, 3)
 GROUP BY location, instructor_id
HAVING SUM(capacity) > 50
```

Location	INSTRUCTOR_ID	Total Locations	Total Capacity
L214	104	3	55

1 row selected.

The WHERE clause is executed by the database first, narrowing the result set to rows in the SECTION table where SECTION_NO equals either 2 or 3 (that is, the second or third section of a course). The next step is to group the results by the columns listed in the GROUP BY clause and to apply the aggregate functions. Finally, the HAVING condition is tested against the groups. Only rows with a total capacity of greater than 50 are returned in the result.

MULTIPLE CONDITIONS IN THE HAVING CLAUSE

The HAVING clause can use multiple operators to further eliminate any groups, as in the following example. Either the columns used in the HAVING clause must be found in the GROUP BY clause or they must be aggregate functions. In the following example, the aggregate COUNT function is not mentioned in the SELECT list, yet the HAVING clause refers to it. The second condition of the HAVING clause chooses only location groups with a starting value of L5. In this particular example, it is preferable to move this condition to the WHERE clause because doing so eliminates the rows even before the groups are formed, and the statement will therefore execute faster.

```
SELECT location "Location",
       SUM(capacity) "Total Capacity"
  FROM section
 WHERE section_no = 3
 GROUP BY location
HAVING (COUNT(location) > 3
        AND location LIKE 'L5%')

Location    Total Capacity
----------  --------------
L507                   100
L509                   175

2 rows selected.
```

CONSTANTS AND FUNCTIONS WITHOUT PARAMETERS

Any constant, such as a text or number literal or a function that does not take any parameters, such as the SYSDATE function, may be listed in the SELECT list without being repeated in the GROUP BY clause. This does not cause the ORA-00979 error message. The following query shows the text literal 'Hello', the number literal 1, and the SYSDATE function in the SELECT list of the query. These expressions do not need to be repeated in the GROUP BY clause.

```
SELECT 'Hello', 1, SYSDATE, course_no "Course #",
       COUNT(*)
  FROM section
 GROUP BY course_no
HAVING COUNT(*) = 5
```

```
'HELLO        1 SYSDATE      Course #   COUNT(*)
-----  ---------  ---------  ---------  ---------
Hello         1 08-APR-09        100          5
Hello         1 08-APR-09        122          5
Hello         1 08-APR-09        125          5

3 rows selected.
```

THE ORDER OF THE CLAUSES

The HAVING clause can appear before the GROUP BY clause, as shown in the following example, but this is rarely seen in practice.

```
SELECT course_no "Course #",
       AVG(capacity) "Avg. Capacity",
       ROUND(AVG(capacity)) "Rounded Avg. Capacity"
  FROM section
HAVING COUNT(*) = 2
 GROUP BY course_no
```

Nesting Aggregate Functions

Aggregate functions can be nested, as in the following example. The query returns the largest number of students that enrolled in an individual section. The COUNT function determines a count for all the sections, based on the GROUP BY clause, which lists SECTION_ID. When the MAX function is applied against this result, it returns 12 as the largest of the values. In other words, 12 students is the largest number of students enrolled in an individual section.

```
SELECT MAX(COUNT(*))
  FROM enrollment
 GROUP BY section_id
MAX(COUNT(*))
-------------
           12

1 row selected.
```

Taking Aggregate Functions and Groups to the Next Level

Each of the SQL statements described so far in this chapter has focused on a single table. You will learn how to avoid potential pitfalls when joining tables and applying aggregate functions in Chapter 8, "Subqueries."

In Chapter 17, you will learn about many additional aggregate and analytical functions, such as RANK, that allow you to analyze data even further. Some of this functionality helps you avoid the ORA-00979 error through the use of a special analytical clause. Chapter 17 also introduces the ROLLUP and CUBE operators so that you can perform multilevel aggregations.

▼ LAB 6.2 EXERCISES

a) Show a list of prerequisites and count how many times each appears in the COURSE table. Order the result by the PREREQUISITE column.

b) Write a SELECT statement that shows student IDs and the number of courses each student is enrolled in. Show only those enrolled in more than two classes.

c) Write a SELECT statement that displays the average room capacity for each course. Display the average, expressed to the nearest whole number, in another column. Use a column alias for each column selected.

d) Write the same SELECT statement as in Exercise c, except consider only courses with exactly two sections. Hint: Think about the relationship between the COURSE and SECTION tables—specifically, how many times a course can be represented in the SECTION table.

▼ LAB 6.2 EXERCISE ANSWERS

a) Show a list of prerequisites and count how many times each appears in the COURSE table. Order the result by the PREREQUISITE column.

ANSWER: The COUNT function and GROUP BY clause are used to count distinct prerequisites. The last row of the result set shows the number of prerequisites with a null value.

```
SELECT prerequisite, COUNT(*)
  FROM course
 GROUP BY prerequisite
 ORDER BY prerequisite
PREREQUISITE   COUNT(*)
------------   ---------
         10           1
         20           5
...
        350           2
        420           1
                      4
```

```
17 rows selected.
```

NULLS AND THE GROUP BY CLAUSE

If there are null values in a column, and you group on the column, all the null values are considered equal. This is different from the typical handling of nulls, where one null is not equal to another. The aforementioned query and result show that there are four null prerequisites. The nulls always appear last in the default ascending sort order.

You can change the default ordering of the nulls with the NULLS FIRST option in the ORDER BY clause, as shown in the following statement. When you look at the result set, you see that the nulls are now first, followed by the default ascending sort order.

```
SELECT prerequisite, COUNT(*)
  FROM course
 GROUP BY prerequisite
 ORDER BY prerequisite NULLS FIRST
PREREQUISITE   COUNT(*)
------------   ---------
                      4
          10          1
...
         350          2
         420          1
```

17 rows selected.

b) Write a SELECT statement that shows student IDs and the number of courses each student is enrolled in. Show only those enrolled in more than two classes.

ANSWER: To obtain the distinct students, use the STUDENT_ID column in the GROUP BY clause. For each of the groups, use the COUNT function to count records for each student. Use the HAVING clause to include only those students enrolled in more than two sections.

```
SELECT student_id, COUNT(*)
  FROM enrollment
 GROUP BY student_id
HAVING COUNT(*) > 2
STUDENT_ID  COUNT(*)
----------  ---------
       124         4
       184         3
...
       238         3
       250         3
```

7 rows selected.

c) Write a SELECT statement that displays the average room capacity for each course. Display the average, expressed to the nearest whole number, in another column. Use a column alias for each column selected.

ANSWER: The SELECT statement uses the AVG function and the ROUND function. The GROUP BY clause ensures that the average capacity is displayed for each course.

```
SELECT course_no "Course #",
       AVG(capacity) "Avg. Capacity",
       ROUND(AVG(capacity)) "Rounded Avg. Capacity"
  FROM section
 GROUP BY course_no
Course # Avg Capacity Rounded Avg Capacity
-------- ------------ --------------------
      10           15                   15
      20           20                   20
      25    22.777778                   23
...
```

350	21.666667	22
420	25	25
450	25	25

28 rows selected.

The SQL statement uses nested functions. Nested functions always work from the inside out, so the AVG(capacity) function is evaluated first, and its result is the parameter for the ROUND function. ROUND's optional precision parameter is not used, so the result of AVG(capacity) rounds to a precision of zero, or no decimal places.

COLUMN ALIASES IN THE GROUP BY CLAUSE

Sometimes you might copy the columns from a SELECT list—with the exception of the aggregate function, of course—down to the GROUP BY clause. After all, cutting and pasting saves a lot of typing. You might then end up with an error such as the following one. The ORA-00933 error message ("SQL command not properly ended") may leave you clueless as to how to solve the problem.

```
SELECT course_no "Course #",
       AVG(capacity) "Avg. Capacity",
       ROUND(AVG(capacity)) "Rounded Avg. Capacity"
  FROM section
 GROUP BY course_no "Course #"
 /
GROUP BY course_no "Course #"
                       *
ERROR at line 5:
ORA-00933: SQL command not properly ended
```

To resolve the error, you must exclude the column aliase **"Course #"** in the GROUP BY clause.

 Column aliases are not allowed in the GROUP BY clause.

d) Write the same SELECT statement as in Exercise c, except consider only courses with exactly two sections. Hint: Think about the relationship between the COURSE and SECTION tables—specifically, how many times a course can be represented in the SECTION table.

ANSWER: The HAVING clause is added to limit the result set to courses that appear exactly twice.

```
SELECT course_no "Course #",
       AVG(capacity) "Avg. Capacity",
       ROUND(AVG(capacity)) "Rounded Avg. Capacity"
  FROM section
 GROUP BY course_no
HAVING COUNT(*) = 2
```

```
Course # Avg. Capacity Rounded Avg. Capacity
--------- -------------- ----------------------
      132            25                      25
      145            25                      25
      146            20                      20
      230          13.5                      14
      240          12.5                      13
```

5 rows selected.

The COUNT(*) function in the HAVING clause does not appear as part of the SELECT list. You can include in the HAVING clause any aggregate function, even if this aggregate function is not mentioned in the SELECT list.

Lab 6.2 Quiz

In order to test your progress, you should be able to answer the following questions.

1) Which column(s) must be included in the GROUP BY clause of the following SELECT statement?

```
SELECT NVL(MAX(final_grade),0), section_id,
       MAX(created_date)
  FROM enrollment
GROUP BY _____
```

_____ a) final_grade

_____ b) section_id

_____ c) created_date

_____ d) All three

_____ e) None of the above

2) You can combine DISTINCT and a GROUP BY clause in the same SELECT statement.

_____ a) True

_____ b) False

3) There is an error in the following SELECT statement.

```
SELECT COUNT(student_id)
  FROM enrollment
WHERE COUNT(student_id) > 1
```

_____ a) True

_____ b) False

4) How many rows in the following SELECT statement will return a null prerequisite?

```
SELECT prerequisite, COUNT(*)
  FROM course
WHERE prerequisite IS NULL
GROUP BY prerequisite
```

_____ a) None

_____ b) One

_____ c) Multiple

5) Where is the error in the following SELECT statement?

```
SELECT COUNT(*)
  FROM section
GROUP BY course_no
```

_____ a) There is no error.

_____ b) Line 1.

_____ c) Line 2.

_____ d) Line 3.

ANSWERS APPEAR IN APPENDIX A.

▼ WORKSHOP

The projects in this section are meant to prompt you to utilize all the skills you have acquired throughout this chapter. The answers to these projects can be found at the companion Web site to this book, located at www.oraclesqlbyexample.com.

1) List the order in which the WHERE, GROUP BY, and HAVING clauses are executed by the database in the following SQL statement.

```
SELECT section_id, COUNT(*), final_grade
  FROM enrollment
 WHERE TRUNC(enroll_date) >
       TO_DATE('2/16/2007', 'MM/DD/YYYY')
 GROUP BY section_id, final_grade
HAVING COUNT(*) > 5
```

2) Display a count of all the different course costs in the COURSE table.

3) Determine the number of students living in zip code 10025.

4) Show all the different companies for which students work. Display only companies in which more than four students are employed.

5) List how many sections each instructor teaches.

6) What problem does the following statement solve?

```
SELECT COUNT(*), start_date_time, location
  FROM section
 GROUP BY start_date_time, location
HAVING COUNT(*) > 1
```

7) Determine the highest grade achieved for the midterm within each section.

8) A table called CUSTOMER_ORDER contains 5,993 rows, with a total order amount of $10,993,333.98, based on the orders from 4,500 customers. Given this scenario, how many rows does the following query return?

```
SELECT SUM(order_amount) AS "Order Total"
  FROM customer_order
```

CHAPTER 7

Equijoins

CHAPTER OBJECTIVES

In this chapter, you will learn about:

- ▶ The Two-Table Join
- ▶ Joining Three or More Tables

So far, you have written SQL statements against a single table. In this chapter, you will learn about joining tables, one of the most important aspects of the SQL language. The *equijoin*, *which* is by far the most common form of join, allows you to connect two or more tables. Equijoins are based on equality of values in one or more columns. You will learn about other types of joins in Chapter 10, "Complex Joins."

Lab 7.1
The Two-Table Join

LAB OBJECTIVES

After this lab, you will be able to:

- ▶ Write Simple Join Constructs
- ▶ Narrow Down Your Result Set
- ▶ Understand the Cartesian Product

In this lab, you will join information from two tables into one meaningful result. Suppose you want to list the course number, course description, section number, location, and instructor ID for each section. This data is found in two separate tables: The course number and description are in the COURSE table; the SECTION table contains the course number, section number, location, and instructor ID. One approach is to query the individual tables and record the results on paper, then match every course number in the COURSE table with the corresponding course number in the SECTION table. The other approach is to formulate a SQL statement that accomplishes the join for you.

Figure 7.1 shows part of the COURSE table. Missing columns and rows are indicated with an ellipsis (…). The primary key of the COURSE table is COURSE_NO.

COURSE_NO	DESCRIPTION			MODIFIED_DATE
10	Technology Concepts	… … … …	…	05-APR-07
20	Intro to Information Systems	… … … …	…	05-APR-07
25	Intro to Programming	… … … …	…	05-APR-07
80	Programming Techniques	… … … …	…	05-APR-07
100	Hands-On Windows	… … … …	…	05-APR-07
120	Intro to Java Programming	… … … …	…	05-APR-07
122	Intermediate Java Programming	… … … …	…	05-APR-07
124	Advanced Java Programming	… … … …	…	05-APR-07
125	Java Developer I	… … … …	…	05-APR-07
130	Intro to Unix	… … … …	…	05-APR-07
132	Basics of Unix Admin			05-APR-07

FIGURE 7.1
Excerpt of the COURSE table

Figure 7.2 shows part of the SECTION table. The COURSE_NO column is the foreign key to the COURSE table.

SECTION_ID	COURSE_NO	SECTION_NO	LOCATION	
80	10	2	L214	... ...
81	20	2	L210	... ...
82	20	4	L214	... ...
83	20	7	L509	... ...
84	20	8	L210	... ...
85	25	1	M311	... ...
86	25	2	L210	... ...
87	25	3	L507	... ...
88	25	4	L214	... ...
89	25	5	L509	... ...
90	25	6	L509	... ...
91	25	7	L210	... ...
92	25	8	L509	... ...
93	25	9	L507	... ...
141	100	1	L214	... ...
142	100	2	L500	... ...

FIGURE 7.2
Excerpt of the SECTION table

Examine the result set listed in Figure 7.3. For example, for course number 10, one section exists in the SECTION table. The result of the match is one row. Course number 20, Intro to Information Systems, has multiple rows in the section table because there are multiple classes/sections for the same course. Course number 80, Programming Techniques, is missing from the result. This course number has no matching entry in the SECTION table, and therefore this row is not in the result.

COURSE_NO	SECTION_NO	DESCRIPTION	LOCATION	INSTRUCTOR_ID
10	2	Technology Concepts	L214	102
20	2	Intro to Information Systems	L210	103
20	4	Intro to Information Systems	L214	104
20	7	Intro to Information Systems	L509	105
20	8	Intro to Information Systems	L210	106
25	1	Intro to Programming	M311	107
25	2	Intro to Programming	L210	108
25	3	Intro to Programming	L507	101
25	4	Intro to Programming	L214	102
25	5	Intro to Programming	L509	103
25	6	Intro to Programming	L509	104
25	7	Intro to Programming	L210	105
25	8	Intro to Programming	L509	106
25	9	Intro to Programming	L507	107
100	1	Hands-On Windows	L214	102
100	2	Hands-On Windows	L500	103
100	3	Hands-On Windows	L509	104

FIGURE 7.3
Result of the join between the COURSE and SECTION tables

Steps to Formulate the SQL Statement

Before you write the SQL join statement, first choose the columns you want to include in the result. Next, determine the tables to which the columns belong. Then identify the common columns between the tables. Finally, determine whether there is a one-to-one or a one-to-many relationship among the column values. Joins are typically used to join between the primary key and the foreign key. In the previous example, the COURSE_NO column in the COURSE table is the primary key, and the column COURSE_NO in the SECTION table is the foreign key. This represents a one-to-many relationship between the tables. (Joining tables related through a many-to-many relationship yields a *Cartesian product*. You'll learn more about the Cartesian product later in this chapter.)

Following is the SQL statement that achieves the result shown in Figure 7.3. It looks much like the SELECT statements you have written previously, but two tables, separated by commas, are listed in the FROM clause.

```
SELECT course.course_no, section_no, description,
       location, instructor_id
  FROM course, section
 WHERE course.course_no = section.course_no
```

The WHERE clause formulates the *join criteria,* also called the *join condition,* between the two tables using the common COURSE_NO column. Because this is an equijoin, the values in the common columns must equal each other for a row to be displayed in the result set. Each COURSE_NO value from the COURSE table must match a COURSE_NO value from the SECTION table. To differentiate between columns of the same name, *qualify* the columns by prefixing the column with the table name and a period. Otherwise, Oracle returns the error ORA-00918: column ambiguously defined.

Instead of displaying the COURSE_NO column from the COURSE table in the SELECT list, you can use the COURSE_NO column from the SECTION table. Because it is an equijoin, it returns the same result.

 The order in which the tables are listed in the FROM has no effect on the query result. But the join order can become important when optimizing SQL statement, and you will learn about this in Chapter 18, "SQL Optimization."

Table Aliases

Instead of using the table name as a prefix to differentiate between the columns, you can use a *table alias,* which qualifies the table using a short abbreviation.

```
SELECT c.course_no, s.section_no, c.description,
       s.location, s.instructor_id
  FROM course c, section s
 WHERE c.course_no = s.course_no
```

The table alias names are arbitrary. However, you cannot use any Oracle *reserved words*. (Reserved words have a special meaning in SQL or in the Oracle database and are typically associated with a SQL command. For example, SELECT and WHERE are reserved words.) It is best to keep the name short and simple, as in this example, where the COURSE table has the alias c, and the SECTION table has the alias s.

 To easily identify the source table of a column and to improve the readability of a join statement, it is best to qualify all column names with the table alias. Furthermore, this avoids any future ambiguities that may arise if a new column with the same name is added later. Without a qualified table alias, a subsequently issued SQL statement referencing both tables results in the Oracle error ORA-00918: column ambiguously defined.

When you define a table alias in SQL Developer, any subsequent reference of the alias brings up a list of columns for the table, helping you remember the column names and avoid column misspellings (see Figure 7.4). Refer to Chapter 2, "SQL: The Basics," for more information regarding the code completion feature.

FIGURE 7.4
Column list of the COURSE table

Narrowing Down Your Result Set

The previous SQL statement lists all the rows in the SECTION and COURSE tables with matching COURSE_NO values. If you want to narrow down the criteria to specific rows, you can expand the WHERE clause to include additional conditions. The next statement chooses only those courses and their respective sections where the DESCRIPTION column starts with the text Intro to.

```
SELECT c.course_no, s.section_no, c.description,
       s.location, s.instructor_id
  FROM course c, section s
 WHERE c.course_no = s.course_no
   AND c.description LIKE 'Intro to%'
```

Nulls and Joins

In an equijoin, a null value in the common column has the effect of not including the row in the result. Look at the foreign key column ZIP on the INSTRUCTOR table, which allows nulls.

First, query for records with a null value.

```
SELECT instructor_id, zip, last_name, first_name
  FROM instructor
 WHERE zip IS NULL
INSTRUCTOR_ID ZIP   LAST_NAME  FIRST_NAME
------------- ----- ---------- ----------
          110       Willig     Irene

1 row selected.
```

Next, formulate the join to the ZIPCODE table via the ZIP column. Observe that instructor Irene Willig does not appear in the result.

```
SELECT i.instructor_id, i.zip, i.last_name, i.first_name
  FROM instructor i, zipcode z
 WHERE i.zip = z.zip
INSTRUCTOR_ID ZIP   LAST_NAME  FIRST_NAME
------------- ----- ---------- ----------
          101 10015 Hanks      Fernand
          105 10015 Morris     Anita
          109 10015 Chow       Rick
          102 10025 Wojick     Tom
          103 10025 Schorin    Nina
          106 10025 Smythe     Todd
          108 10025 Lowry      Charles
          107 10005 Frantzen   Marilyn
          104 10035 Pertez     Gary

9 rows selected.
```

A null value is not equal to any other value, including another null value. In this case, the zip code of Irene Willig's record is null; therefore, this row is not included in the result. In Chapter 10, you will learn how to include null values by formulating an *outer join* condition.

ANSI Join Syntax

Starting with Oracle 9i, Oracle implemented a number of additions to SQL to conform to many aspects of the ANSI SQL/92 and SQL:1999 standards. The advantage of the ANSI join syntax over the traditional comma-separated tables FROM clause is that SQL queries can run unmodified against other non-Oracle, ANSI-compliant databases.

INNER JOINS

The term *inner join* is used to express a join that satisfies the join condition. Typically, the join condition is based on equality, thus creating an equijoin. (The inner join is in contrast to the outer join. Besides the matched rows, the outer join also includes the unmatched rows from two tables.)

The ANSI syntax has a number of differences from the previously discussed join syntax. For example, the JOIN keyword replaces the comma between the tables and identifies the tables to be joined.

The keyword INNER is optional and typically omitted. To express a join condition, you can specify either the USING condition or the ON condition.

THE USING CONDITION

The USING condition, also referred as the USING clause, identifies the common column between the tables. Here the common column is the COURSE_NO column, which has the same name and compatible data type in both tables. An equijoin is always assumed with the USING clause.

```
SELECT course_no, s.section_no, c.description,
       s.location, s.instructor_id
  FROM course c JOIN section s
 USING (course_no)
```

Alternatively, you can include the optional INNER keyword, but as mentioned, this keyword is usually omitted.

```
SELECT course_no, s.section_no, c.description,
       s.location, s.instructor_id
  FROM course c INNER JOIN section s
 USING (course_no)
```

The following query does not execute because you cannot use a table alias name with this syntax. The USING syntax implies that the column names are identical. The Oracle error identifies the C.COURSE_NO column as the column in the USING clause that has the problem.

```
SQL> SELECT course_no, s.section_no, c.description,
  2         s.location, s.instructor_id
  3    FROM course c JOIN section s
  4   USING (c.course_no)
  5  /
 USING (c.course_no)
            *
ERROR at line 4:
ORA-01748: only simple column names allowed here
```

The next query shows the COURSE_NO column in the SELECT list prefixed with the alias name, thus resulting in an error as well. This alias must also be eliminated to successfully run the query.

```
SQL>  SELECT c.course_no, s.section_no, c.description,
   2          s.location, s.instructor_id
   3    FROM course c JOIN section s
   4* USING (course_no)
SQL> /
SELECT c.course_no, s.section_no, c.description,
         *
ERROR at line 1:
ORA-25154: column part of USING clause cannot have qualifier
```

The next example illustrates the error you receive when you omit the parentheses around the column COURSE_NO in the USING clause.

```
SQL> SELECT c.course_no, s.section_no, c.description,
   2          s.location, s.instructor_id
   3    FROM course c JOIN section s
   4    USING course_no
   5  /
  USING course_no
         *
ERROR at line 4:
ORA-00906: missing left parenthesis
```

THE ON CONDITION

In case the column names on the tables are different, you use the ON condition, also referred to as the ON clause. The next query is identical in functionality to the previous query, but it is now expressed with the ON condition, and the column name is qualified with the alias both in the SELECT list and in the ON condition. This syntax allows for conditions other than equality and different column names; you will see many such examples in Chapter 10.

```
SELECT c.course_no, s.section_no, c.description,
       s.location, s.instructor_id
  FROM course c JOIN section s
    ON (c.course_no = s.course_no)
```

The pair of parentheses around the ON condition is optional. When comparing this syntax to the traditional join syntax, there are not many differences other than the ON clause and the JOIN keyword.

ADDITIONAL WHERE CLAUSE CONDITIONS

The ON and USING conditions let you specify the join condition separately from any other WHERE condition. One of the advantages of the ANSI join syntax is that it separates the join condition from the filtering WHERE clause condition.

```
SELECT c.course_no, s.section_no, c.description,
       s.location, s.instructor_id
  FROM course c JOIN section s
    ON (c.course_no = s.course_no)
  WHERE description LIKE 'B%'
```

NATURAL JOINS

A natural join joins tables based on the columns with the same name and data type. Here there is no need to prefix the column name with the table alias, and the join is indicated with the keywords NATURAL JOIN. There is not even a mention of which column(s) to join. This syntax figures out the common columns between the tables. Any use of the ON clause or the USING clause is not allowed with the NATURAL JOIN keywords, and the common columns cannot list a table alias.

```
SELECT course_no, s.section_no, c.description,
       s.location, s.instructor_id
  FROM course c NATURAL JOIN section s

no rows selected
```

You might be surprised that the query does not return any result. However, the COURSE_NO column is not the only column with a common name. The columns CREATED_BY, CREATED_DATE, MODIFIED_BY, and MODIFIED_DATE are also common to both tables. These columns record the name of the last user updating a row and the original user creating the row, including the respective date and time. The SQL statement does not return any results because there are no rows that have identical values for all five common columns.

 Using the natural join within a program is somewhat risky. There is always a chance for adding to the table columns that happen to have the same column name, and then you may not get the desired result. Therefore, the natural join works best for ad hoc queries but not for repeated use within programs.

The Cartesian Product

The Cartesian product is rarely useful in the real world. It usually indicates either that the WHERE clause has no joining columns or that multiple rows from one table match multiple rows in another table; in other words, it indicates a many-to-many relationship.

To illustrate the multiplication effect of a Cartesian product, the following query joins the INSTRUCTOR table with the SECTION table. The INSTRUCTOR table contains 10 rows; the SECTION table has 78 rows. The multiplication of all the possible combinations results in 780 rows.

```
SELECT COUNT(*)
  FROM section, instructor
 COUNT(*)
---------
      780

1 row selected.
```

Following is a partial listing of the rows, showing all the different combinations of values between the two tables.

```
SELECT s.instructor_id s_instructor_id,
       i.instructor_id i_instructor_id
  FROM section s, instructor i
S_INSTRUCTOR_ID I_INSTRUCTOR_ID
--------------- ---------------
            101             101
            101             101
            101             101
            101             101
            101             101
            101             101
            101             101
            101             101
            101             101
            101             102
            101             102
            101             102
...
            108             110
            101             110
```

780 rows selected.

In SQL*Plus, if you want to stop and examine the rows one screen at a time, you can use the SQL*Plus SET PAUSE ON command. Appendix C, "SQL*Plus Command Reference," provides more details about the various SQL*Plus commands.

THE ANSI STANDARD CROSS-JOIN

To formulate a Cartesian product using the ANSI JOIN syntax, you use the keyword CROSS JOIN in place of the comma between the two tables. Because of the nature of a cross-join as a combination of all possible values, the SQL statement does not have join criteria. The result is obviously identical to that of the Cartesian product.

```
SELECT COUNT(*)
  FROM section CROSS JOIN instructor
```

▼ LAB 7.1 EXERCISES

a) For all students, display last name, city, state, and zip code. Show the result ordered by zip code.

b) Select the first and last names of all enrolled students and order by last name in ascending order.

c) Execute the following SQL statement. Explain your observations about the WHERE clause and the resulting output.

```
SELECT c.course_no, c.description, s.section_no
  FROM course c, section s
 WHERE c.course_no = s.course_no
   AND c.prerequisite IS NULL
 ORDER BY c.course_no, s.section_no
```

d) Select the student ID, course number, enrollment date, and section ID for students who enrolled in course number 20 on January 30, 2007.

e) Select the students and instructors who live in the same zip code by joining on the common ZIP column. Order the result by the STUDENT_ID and INSTRUCTOR_ID columns. What do you observe?

▼ LAB 7.1 EXERCISE ANSWERS

a) For all students, display last name, city, state, and zip code. Show the result ordered by zip code.

ANSWER: The common column between the ZIPCODE table and the STUDENT table is the ZIP column. The ZIP column in both tables is defined as NOT NULL. For each row in the ZIPCODE table there may be zero, one, or multiple students living in one particular zip code. For each student's zip code there must be one matching row in the ZIPCODE table. Only records that satisfy the equality condition of the join are returned.

```
SELECT s.last_name, s.zip, z.state, z.city
  FROM student s, zipcode z
 WHERE s.zip = z.zip
 ORDER BY s.zip
```

```
LAST_NAME                        ZIP    ST CITY
-------------------------        -----  -- ----------
Norman                           01247  MA North Adams
Kocka                            02124  MA Dorchester
...
Gilloon                          43224  OH Columbus
Snow                             48104  MI Ann Arbor
```

268 rows selected.

Because the ZIP column has the same name in both tables, you must qualify the column when you use the traditional join syntax. For simplicity, it is best to use an alias instead of the full table name because it saves you a lot of typing and improves readability. The ORDER BY clause lists the S.ZIP column, as does the SELECT clause. Choosing the Z.ZIP column instead of S.ZIP in the SELECT list or ORDER BY clause displays the same rows because the values in the two columns have to be equal to be included in the result.

You can also write the query with the ANSI join syntax instead and use the ON condition or the USING condition. If you use the ON condition, you must prefix the common columns with either their full table name or their table alias, if one is specified.

```
SELECT s.last_name, s.zip, z.state, z.city
  FROM student s JOIN zipcode z
    ON (s.zip = z.zip)
 ORDER BY s.zip
```

If you choose the USING condition instead, do not alias the common column because doing so will cause an error.

```
SELECT s.last_name, zip, z.state, z.city
  FROM student s JOIN zipcode z
 USING (zip)
 ORDER BY zip
```

b) Select the first and last names of all enrolled students and order by last name in ascending order.

ANSWER: You need to join the ENROLLMENT and STUDENT tables. Only students who are enrolled have one or multiple rows in the ENROLLMENT table.

```
SELECT s.first_name, s.last_name, s.student_id
  FROM student s, enrollment e
 WHERE s.student_id = e.student_id
 ORDER BY s.last_name
FIRST_NAME LAST_NAME  STUDENT_ID
---------- ---------- ----------
Mardig     Abdou             119
Suzanne M. Abid              257
...
Salewa     Zuckerberg        184
Salewa     Zuckerberg        184
Salewa     Zuckerberg        184
Freedon    annunziato        206

226 rows selected.
```

Student Salewa Zuckerberg with STUDENT_ID 184 is returned three times. This is because Salewa Zuckerberg is enrolled in three sections. When the SECTION_ID column is included in the SELECT list, this fact becomes evident in the result set.

However, if you are not interested in the SECTION_ID and you want to list the names without the duplication, use DISTINCT in the SELECT statement.

```
SELECT DISTINCT s.first_name, s.last_name, s.student_id
  FROM student s, enrollment e
 WHERE s.student_id = e.student_id
 ORDER BY s.last_name
```

The STUDENT_ID column is required in the SELECT clause because there may be students with the same first and last names but who are, in fact, different individuals. The STUDENT_ID column differentiates between these students; after all, it's the primary key that is unique to each individual row in the STUDENT table.

The student with the last name annunziato is the last row. Because the last name is in lowercase, it has a higher sort order. (See Lab 4.3 regarding the sort order values and the ASCII function.)

If you use the ANSI syntax, your SQL statement may look similar to the following statement.

```
SELECT s.first_name, s.last_name, s.student_id
  FROM student s JOIN enrollment e
    ON (s.student_id = e.student_id)
 ORDER BY s.last_name
```

Or you may write the statement with the USING clause. In this particular query, all aliases are omitted, which has the disadvantage that you cannot easily recognize the source table for each column.

```
SELECT first_name, last_name, student_id
  FROM student JOIN enrollment
 USING (student_id)
 ORDER BY last_name
```

c) Execute the following SQL statement. Explain your observations about the WHERE clause and the resulting output.

```
SELECT c.course_no, c.description, s.section_no
  FROM course c, section s
 WHERE c.course_no = s.course_no
   AND c.prerequisite IS NULL
 ORDER BY c.course_no, section_no
```

ANSWER: This query includes both a join condition and a condition that restricts the rows to courses that have no prerequisite. The result is ordered by the course number and the section number.

COURSE_NO	DESCRIPTION	SECTION_NO
10	Technology Concepts	2
20	Intro to Information Systems	2
...		
146	Java for C/C++ Programmers	2
310	Operating Systems	1

```
8 rows selected.
```

The COURSE and SECTION tables are joined to obtain the SECTION_NO column. The join requires the equality of values for the COURSE_NO columns in both tables. The courses without a prerequisite are determined with the IS NULL operator.

If the query is written with the ANSI join syntax and the ON clause, you see one advantage of the ANSI join syntax over the traditional join syntax: The ANSI join distinguishes the join condition from the filtering criteria.

```
SELECT c.course_no, c.description, s.section no
  FROM course c JOIN section s
    ON (c.course_no = s.course_no)
 WHERE c.prerequisite IS NULL
 ORDER BY c.course_no, section_no
```

d) Select the student ID, course number, enrollment date, and section ID for students who enrolled in course number 20 on January 30, 2007.

ANSWER: The SECTION and ENROLLMENT tables are joined through their common column: SECTION_ID. This column is the primary key in the SECTION table and the foreign key column in the ENROLLMENT table. The rows are restricted to those records that have a course number of 20 and an enrollment date of January 30, 2007, by including this condition in the WHERE clause.

```
SELECT e.student_id, s.course_no,
       TO_CHAR(e.enroll_date,'MM/DD/YYYY HH:MI PM'),
       e.section_id
  FROM enrollment e JOIN section s
    ON (e.section_id = s.section_id)
 WHERE s.course_no = 20
   AND e.enroll_date >= TO_DATE('01/30/2007','MM/DD/YYYY')
   AND e.enroll_date < TO_DATE('01/31/2007','MM/DD/YYYY')
STUDENT_ID COURSE_NO TO_CHAR(ENROLL_DATE SECTION_ID
---------- --------- ------------------- ----------
       103        20 01/30/2007 10:18 AM         81
       104        20 01/30/2007 10:18 AM         81
```

2 rows selected.

Alternatively, you can use the USING clause or the more traditional join syntax, listed here.

```
SELECT e.student_id, s.course_no,
       TO_CHAR(e.enroll_date,'MM/DD/YYYY HH:MI PM'),
       e.section_id
  FROM enrollment e, section s
 WHERE e.section_id = s.section_id
   AND s.course_no = 20
   AND e.enroll_date >= TO_DATE('01/30/2007','MM/DD/YYYY')
   AND e.enroll_date < TO_DATE('01/31/2007','MM/DD/YYYY')
```

The WHERE clause considers the date and time values of the ENROLL_DATE column. There are alternative WHERE clause solutions, such as applying the TRUNC function on the ENROLL_DATE column. Refer to Chapter 5, "Date and Conversion Functions," for many examples of querying and displaying DATE data type columns.

e) Select the students and instructors who live in the same zip code by joining on the common ZIP column. Order the result by the STUDENT_ID and INSTRUCTOR_ID columns. What do you observe?

ANSWER: When you join the STUDENT and INSTRUCTOR tables, there is a many-to-many relationship, which causes a Cartesian product as a result.

```
SELECT s.student_id, i.instructor_id,
       s.zip, i.zip
  FROM student s, instructor i
 WHERE s.zip = i.zip
 ORDER BY s.student_id, i.instructor_id
STUDENT_ID INSTRUCTOR_ID ZIP   ZIP
---------- ------------- ----- -----
       163           102 10025 10025
       163           103 10025 10025
       163           106 10025 10025
       163           108 10025 10025
       223           102 10025 10025
       223           103 10025 10025
       223           106 10025 10025
       223           108 10025 10025
       399           102 10025 10025
       399           103 10025 10025
```

```
399                106 10025 10025
399                108 10025 10025
```

12 rows selected.

Initially, this query and its corresponding result may not strike you as a Cartesian product because the WHERE clause contains a join criteria. However, the relationship between the STUDENT table and the INSTRUCTOR table does not follow the primary key/foreign key path, and therefore a Cartesian product is possible. A look at the schema diagram reveals that no primary key/foreign key relationship exists between the two tables. To further illustrate the many-to-many relationship between the ZIP columns, select the students and instructors living in zip code 10025 in separate SQL statements.

```
SELECT student_id, zip
  FROM student
 WHERE zip = '10025'
STUDENT_ID ZIP
----------- -----
        223 10025
        163 10025
        399 10025
```

3 rows selected.

```
SELECT instructor_id, zip
  FROM instructor
 WHERE zip = '10025'
INSTRUCTOR_ID ZIP
------------- -----
          102 10025
          103 10025
          106 10025
          108 10025
```

4 rows selected.

These results validate the solution's output: the Cartesian product shows the three student rows multiplied by the four instructors, which results in 12 possible combinations. You can rewrite the query to include the DISTINCT keyword to select only the distinct student IDs. You can also write the query with a subquery construct, which avoids the Cartesian product. You will learn about this in Chapter 8, "Subqueries."

JOINING ALONG THE PRIMARY/FOREIGN KEY PATH

You can join along the primary/foreign key path by joining the STUDENT table to the ENROLLMENT table, then to the SECTION table, and finally to the INSTRUCTOR table. This involves a multitable join, discussed in Lab 7.2. However, the result is different from the Cartesian product result because it shows only instructors who teach a section in which the student is enrolled. In other words, an instructor living in zip code 10025 is included in the result only if the instructor teaches that student also living in the same zip code. This is in contrast to the Cartesian product example, which shows all the instructors and students living in the same zip code, whether the instructor teaches this student or not. You will explore the differences between these two examples once more in the Workshop section at the end of the chapter.

Lab 7.1 Quiz

In order to test your progress, you should be able to answer the following questions.

1) Find the error(s) in the following SQL statement.

```
1 SELECT stud.last_name, stud.first_name,
2        stud.zip, zip.zip, zip.state, zip.city,
3        TO_CHAR(stud.student_id)
4   FROM student stud, zipcode zip
5  WHERE stud.student_id = 102
6    AND zip.zip = '11419'
7    AND zip.zip = s.zip
```

_____ **a)** No error.

_____ **b)** This is not an equijoin.

_____ **c)** Lines 1, 2, and 3.

_____ **d)** Line 4.

_____ **e)** Lines 5 and 6.

_____ **f)** Line 7.

2) Find the error(s) in the following SQL statement.

```
1 SELECT s.*, zipcode.zip,
2        DECODE(s.last_name, 'Smith', szip,
3               UPPER(s.last_name))
4   FROM student s, zipcode
5  WHERE stud.zip = zipcode.zip
6    AND s.last_name LIKE 'Smi%'
```

_____ **a)** Lines 1 and 2

_____ **b)** Lines 1 and 4

_____ **c)** Line 3

_____ **d)** Lines 2 and 5

_____ **e)** Line 4

3) A table alias is the name of a duplicate table stored in memory.

_____ **a)** True

_____ **b)** False

4) To equijoin a table with another table involves matching the common column values.

_____ **a)** True

_____ **b)** False

5) Find the error(s) in the following SQL statement.

```
1 SELECT TO_CHAR(w.modified_date, 'dd-mon-yyyy'),
2        t.grade_type_code, description,
3        TO_NUMBER(TO_CHAR(number_per_section))
4   FROM grade_type t, grade_type_weight w
```

```
5  WHERE t.grade_type_code = w.grade_type_code_cd
6    AND ((t.grade_type_code = 'MT'
7       OR t.grade_type_code = 'HM'))
8    AND w.modified_date >=
9       TO_DATE('01-JAN-2007', 'DD-MON-YYYY')
```

_____ a) Lines 1 and 8

_____ b) Line 4

_____ c) Line 5

_____ d) Lines 6 and 7

_____ e) Lines 5, 6, and 7

6) Given two tables, T1 and T2, and their rows, as shown, which result will be returned by the following query?

```
SELECT t1.val, t2.val, t1.name, t2.location
  FROM t1, t2
 WHERE t1.val = t2.val
```

```
Table T1                Table T2
VAL NAME                VAL LOCATION
--- ----------------    --- ---------
A   Jones               A   San Diego
B   Smith               B   New York
C   Zeta                B   New York
    Miller                  Phoenix
```

_____ a)

```
V V NAME          LOCATION
- - ----------    ---------
A A Jones         San Diego
B B Smith         New York
B B Smith         New York
    Miller        Phoenix
```

_____ b)

```
V V NAME          LOCATION
- - ----------    ---------
A A Jones         San Diego
B B Smith         New York
B B Smith         New York
```

_____ c) None of the above

7) The USING clause of the ANSI join syntax always assumes an equijoin and identical column names.

_____ a) True

_____ b) False

8) The NATURAL JOIN keywords and the USING clause of the ANSI join syntax are mutually exclusive.

_____ a) True

_____ b) False

9) The common column used in the join condition must be listed in the SELECT list.

_____ a) True

_____ b) False

ANSWERS APPEAR IN APPENDIX A.

LAB 7.2
Joining Three or More Tables

LAB OBJECTIVES

After this lab, you will be able to:

▶ Join Three or More Tables

▶ Join with Multicolumn Join Criteria

You often have to join more than two tables to determine the answer to a query. In this lab, you will practice these types of joins. In addition, you will join tables with multicolumn keys.

Joining Three or More Tables

The join example at the beginning of the chapter involves two tables: the COURSE and SECTION tables. The following SQL statement repeats that query and the result of the join (see Figure 7.5). To include the instructor's first and last names, you can expand this statement to join to a third table, the INSTRUCTOR table.

```
SELECT c.course_no, s.section_no, c.description,
       s.location, s.instructor_id
  FROM course c, section s
 WHERE c.course_no = s.course_no
```

Figure 7.6 shows a partial listing of the INSTRUCTOR table. The INSTRUCTOR_ID column is the primary key of the table and is the common column with the SECTION table. Every row in the SECTION table that has a value for the INSTRUCTOR_ID column must have one corresponding row in the INSTRUCTOR table. A particular INSTRUCTOR_ID in the INSTRUCTOR table may have zero, one, or multiple rows in the SECTION table.

To formulate the SQL statement, follow the same steps performed in Lab 7.1. First, determine the columns and tables needed for output. Then confirm whether a one-to-one or a one-to-many relationship exists between the tables to accomplish the join. The changes to the previous SQL statement are indicated here in bold.

```
SELECT c.course_no, s.section_no, c.description, s.location,
       s.instructor_id, i.last_name, i.first_name
  FROM course c, section s, instructor i
 WHERE c.course_no = s.course_no
   AND s.instructor_id = i.instructor_id
```

COURSE_NO	SECTION_NO	DESCRIPTION	LOCATION	INSTRUCTOR_ID
10	2	Technology Concepts	L214	102
20	2	Intro to Information Systems	L210	103
20	4	Intro to Information Systems	L214	104
20	7	Intro to Information Systems	L509	105
20	8	Intro to Information Systems	L210	106
25	1	Intro to Programming	M311	107
25	2	Intro to Programming	L210	108
25	3	Intro to Programming	L507	101
25	4	Intro to Programming	L214	102
25	5	Intro to Programming	L509	103
25	6	Intro to Programming	L509	104
25	7	Intro to Programming	L210	105
25	8	Intro to Programming	L509	106
25	9	Intro to Programming	L507	107
100	1	Hands-On Windows	L214	102
100	2	Hands-On Windows	L500	103
100	3	Hands-On Windows	L500	104

FIGURE 7.5
Result of join between COURSE and SECTION tables

INSTRUCTOR_ID	...	FIRST_NAME	LAST_NAME					
101 Mr		Fernand	Hanks					
102 Mr		Tom	Wojick					
103 Ms		Nina	Schorin					
104 Mr		Gary	Pertez					
105 Ms		Anita	Morris					
106 Rev		Todd	Smythe					
107 Dr		Marilyn	Frantzen					
108 Mr		Charles	Lowry					
109 Hon		Rick	Chow					
110 Ms		Irene	Willig					

FIGURE 7.6
The INSTRUCTOR table

The join yields the result shown in Figure 7.7. The three-table join result now includes the instructor's first and last names. For example, INSTRUCTOR_ID 102 is listed multiple times in the SECTION table. This instructor teaches several sections; therefore, the INSTRUCTOR_ID's corresponding first and last names are repeated in the result.

COU...	SEC...	DESCRIPTION	LOC...	INSTRUC...	LAST_NAME	FIRST_NAME
10	2	Technology Concepts	L214	102	Wojick	Tom
20	2	Intro to Information Systems	L210	103	Schorin	Nina
20	4	Intro to Information Systems	L214	104	Pertez	Gary
20	7	Intro to Information Systems	L509	105	Morris	Anita
20	8	Intro to Information Systems	L210	106	Smythe	Todd
25	1	Intro to Programming	M311	107	Frantzen	Marilyn
25	2	Intro to Programming	L210	108	Lowry	Charles
25	3	Intro to Programming	L507	101	Hanks	Fernand
25	4	Intro to Programming	L214	102	Wojick	Tom
25	5	Intro to Programming	L509	103	Schorin	Nina
25	6	Intro to Programming	L509	104	Pertez	Gary
25	7	Intro to Programming	L210	105	Morris	Anita
25	8	Intro to Programming	L509	106	Smythe	Todd
25	9	Intro to Programming	L507	107	Frantzen	Marilyn
100	1	Hands-On Windows	L214	102	Wojick	Tom
100	2	Hands-On Windows	L500	103	Schorin	Nina

FIGURE 7.7
Result of join between the COURSE, SECTION, and INSTRUCTOR tables

ANSI Join Syntax for Joining Three or More Tables

A join across three tables can be expressed with the ANSI join syntax. Create the first join between the COURSE and SECTION tables via the JOIN keyword and the ON clause. To this result, you add the next table and join condition. The set of parentheses around the ON clause is optional.

```
SELECT c.course_no, s.section_no, c.description, s.location,
       s.instructor_id, i.last_name, i.first_name
  FROM course c JOIN section s
    ON (c.course_no = s.course_no)
  JOIN instructor i
    ON (s.instructor_id = i.instructor_id)
```

Alternatively, the query can be expressed with the USING clause. The table and column aliases in the SELECT and FROM clauses are optional, but the parentheses in the USING clause are required.

```
SELECT course_no, s.section_no, c.description, s.location,
       instructor_id, i.last_name, i.first_name
  FROM course c JOIN section s
 USING (course_no)
  JOIN instructor i
 USING (instructor_id)
```

Multicolumn Joins

The basic steps of a multicolumn join do not differ from the previous examples. The only variation is to make multicolumn keys part of the join criteria.

One of the multikey column examples in the schema is the GRADE table. The primary key of the table consists of the four columns STUDENT_ID, SECTION_ID, GRADE_CODE_ OCCURRENCE, and GRADE_TYPE_CODE. The GRADE table also has two foreign keys: the GRADE_TYPE_CODE column, referencing the GRADE_TYPE_WEIGHT table, and the multi-column foreign keys STUDENT_ID and SECTION_ID, referencing the ENROLLMENT table.

To help you understand the data in the table, examine a set of sample records for a particular student. The student with ID 220 is enrolled in SECTION_ID 119 and has nine records in the GRADE table: four homework assignments (HM), two quizzes (QZ), one midterm (MT), one final examination (FI), and one participation (PA) grade.

```
SELECT student_id, section_id, grade_type_code type,
       grade_code_occurrence no,
       numeric_grade indiv_gr
  FROM grade
 WHERE student_id = 220
   AND section_id = 119
```

STUDENT_ID	SECTION_ID	TY	NO	INDIV_GR
220	119	FI	1	85
220	119	HM	1	84
220	119	HM	2	84
220	119	HM	3	74
220	119	HM	4	74
220	119	MT	1	88
220	119	PA	1	91
220	119	QZ	1	92
220	119	QZ	2	91

```
9 rows selected.
```

The next SQL query joins the GRADE table to the ENROLLMENT table, to include the values of the ENROLL_DATE column in the result set. All the changes from the previous SQL query are indicated in bold.

```
SELECT g.student_id, g.section_id,
       g.grade_type_code type,
       g.grade_code_occurrence no,
       g.numeric_grade indiv_gr,
       TO_CHAR(e.enroll_date, 'MM/DD/YY') enrolldt
  FROM grade g, enrollment e
 WHERE g.student_id = 220
   AND g.section_id = 119
   AND g.student_id = e.student_id
   AND g.section_id = e.section_id
```

```
     STUDENT_ID SECTION_ID TY         NO  INDIV_GR ENROLLDT
     ---------- ---------- --  ---------- --------- --------
            220        119 FI           1        85 02/16/07
            220        119 HM           1        84 02/16/07
            220        119 HM           2        84 02/16/07
            220        119 HM           3        74 02/16/07
            220        119 HM           4        74 02/16/07
            220        119 MT           1        88 02/16/07
            220        119 PA           1        91 02/16/07
            220        119 QZ           1        92 02/16/07
            220        119 QZ           2        91 02/16/07
```

9 rows selected.

To join between the tables ENROLLMENT and GRADE, use both the SECTION_ID and STUDENT_ID columns. These two columns represent the primary key of the ENROLLMENT table and the foreign key of the GRADE table; thus a one-to-many relationship between the tables exists.

The values for the ENROLL_DATE column are repeated, because for each individual grade you have one row showing ENROLL_DATE in the ENROLLMENT table.

EXPRESSING MULTICOLUMN JOINS USING THE ANSI JOIN SYNTAX

A join involving multiple columns on a table requires the columns to be listed in the ON or the USING clause as join criteria. The next SQL statement shows the ON clause.

```
SELECT g.student_id, g.section_id,
       g.grade_type_code type,
       g.grade_code_occurrence no,
       g.numeric_grade indiv_gr,
       TO_CHAR(e.enroll_date, 'MM/DD/YY') enrolldt
  FROM grade g JOIN enrollment e
    ON (g.student_id = e.student_id
   AND g.section_id = e.section_id)
 WHERE g.student_id = 220
   AND g.section_id - 119
```

When you write the query with the USING clause, you list the join columns separated by commas.

```
SELECT student_id, section_id,
       grade_type_code type,
       grade_code_occurrence no,
       numeric_grade indiv_gr,
       TO_CHAR(enroll_date, 'MM/DD/YY') enrolldt
  FROM grade JOIN enrollment
 USING (student_id, section_id)
 WHERE student_id = 220
   AND section_id = 119
```

Joining Across Many Tables

Joining across multiple tables involves repeating the same steps of a two-join or three-join table: You join the first two tables and then join the result to each subsequent table, using the common column(s). You repeat this until all the tables are joined.

To join *n* tables together, you need at least *n*–1 join conditions. For example, to join five tables, you need at least four join conditions. If your join deals with tables containing multicolumn keys, you will obviously need to include these multiple columns as part of the join condition.

> The Oracle optimizer determines the order in which the tables are joined based on the join condition, the indexes on the table, and the various statistics about the tables (such as the number of rows or the number of distinct values in each column). The join order can have a significant impact on the performance of multitable joins. You can learn more about this topic and how to influence the optimizer in Chapter 18.

The ANSI Join Versus the Traditional Join Syntax

You might wonder which one of the join syntax options is better. The ANSI join syntax has a number of advantages.

- It helps you easily identify the join criteria and the filtering condition.

- You avoid an accidental Cartesian product because you must explicitly specify the join criteria, and any missing join conditions become evident because an error is generated.

- The syntax is easy to read and understand.

- The USING clause requires less typing, but the data types of the columns must match.

- SQL is understood by other ANSI-compliant non-Oracle databases.

Although the traditional join syntax, with the columns separated by commas in the FROM clause and the join condition listed in the WHERE clause, may become the old way of writing SQL, you must nevertheless familiarize yourself with this syntax because millions of SQL statements already use it, and it clearly performs its intended purpose.

The ANSI join syntax has some distinct functional advantages over the traditional join syntax when it comes to outer joins, which you can learn about in Chapter 10.

Using SQL Developer's Query Builder

Instead of typing your SQL statement and figuring out the joining columns, SQL Developer performs these tasks for you with the help of the Query Builder. As Figure 7.8 shows, you invoke the Query Builder from the SQL Worksheet by right-clicking and selecting Query Builder.

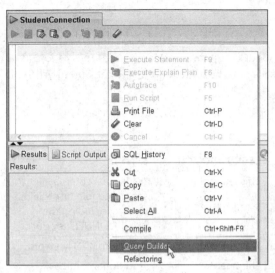

FIGURE 7.8
Query Builder

Query Builder allows you to drag the desired tables to the canvas. It builds the join criteria based on the existing primary/foreign key relationship and visually displays the relationship line between the tables (see Figure 7.9). You can check the columns you want to include in the query. To narrow down the query output, use the Create Where Clause tab at the top of the screen. SQL Developer generates a SQL statement you can view and execute.

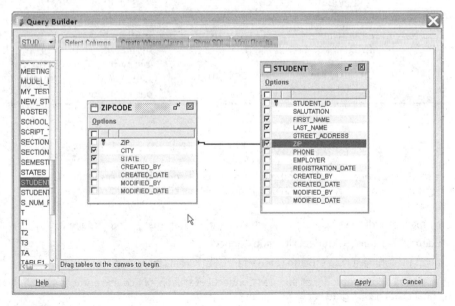

FIGURE 7.9
Query Builder canvas

Different Types of Joins

Most of the joins you will come across are based on equality, with the equijoin being the most dominant. In this chapter, you have learned about equijoins; there are other types of joins you must become familiar with, most notably the self-join, the nonequijoin, and the outer join. Table 7.1 lists the various types of joins.

TABLE 7.1 Types of Joins

JOIN TYPE	BASE OF JOIN CONDITION	LEARN ABOUT IT	SYNTAX
Equijoin or inner join	Equality	This chapter	Traditional comma-separated join or ANSI join syntax (including the optional INNER keyword).
Natural join	Equality	This chapter	NATURAL JOIN keyword.
Cross-join or Cartesian product	No join condition	This chapter	Traditional comma-separated with the missing join condition in the WHERE clause or CROSS JOIN keyword.
Self-join	Equality	Chapter 10	See equijoin or inner join.
Outer join (left, right, full)	Equality and extending the result set	Chapter 10	OUTER JOIN keywords or outer join operator (+).
Nonequijoin	Nonequality of values	Chapter 10	Traditional comma-separated join or ANSI join syntax with the ON clause. Join criteria is not based on equality.

▼ LAB 7.2 EXERCISES

a) Display the student ID, course number, and section number of enrolled students where the instructor of the section lives in zip code 10025. In addition, the course should not have any prerequisites.

b) Produce the mailing addresses for instructors who taught sections that started in June 2007.

c) List the student IDs of enrolled students living in Connecticut.

d) Show all the grades student Fred Crocitto received for SECTION_ID 86.

e) List the final examination grades for all enrolled Connecticut students of course number 420. (Note that final examination grade does not mean final grade.)

f) Display the LAST_NAME, STUDENT_ID, PERCENT_OF_FINAL_GRADE, GRADE_TYPE_CODE, and NUMERIC_GRADE columns for students who received 80 or less for their class project (GRADE_TYPE_CODE = 'PJ'). Order the result by student last name.

▼ LAB 7.2 EXERCISE **ANSWERS**

a) Display the student ID, course number, and section number of enrolled students where the instructor of the section lives in zip code 10025. In addition, the course should not have any prerequisites.

ANSWER: This query involves joining four tables. The course number is found in the SECTION and COURSE tables and the PREREQUISITE column in the COURSE table. To determine the zip code of an instructor, use the INSTRUCTOR table. To choose only enrolled students, join to the ENROLL-MENT table.

```
SELECT c.course_no, s.section_no, e.student_id
  FROM course c, section s, instructor i, enrollment e
 WHERE c.prerequisite IS NULL
   AND c.course_no = s.course_no
   AND s.instructor_id = i.instructor_id
   AND i.zip = '10025'
   AND s.section_id = e.section_id
COURSE_NO SECTION_NO STUDENT_ID
--------- ---------- ----------
       10          2        128
      146          2        117
      146          2        140
...
       20          8        158
       20          8        199

12 rows selected.
```

To obtain this result, build the four-table join as you would any other join, step by step. First, start with one of the tables, such as the COURSE table.

```
SELECT course_no
  FROM course
 WHERE prerequisite IS NULL
```

For each of these courses, find the corresponding sections when you join the COURSE table with the SECTION table. Notice the bolded additions to the SQL statement.

```
SELECT c.course_no, s.section_no
  FROM course c, section s
 WHERE c.prerequisite IS NULL
   AND c.course_no = s.course_no
```

Then include instructors who live in zip code 10025. The common column between SECTION and INSTRUCTOR is INSTRUCTOR_ID.

```
SELECT c.course_no, s.section_no
  FROM course c, section s, instructor i
 WHERE c.prerequisite IS NULL
   AND c.course_no = s.course_no
   AND s.instructor_id = i.instructor_id
   AND i.zip = '10025'
```

Finally, join the results of the ENROLLMENT table via the SECTION_ID column, which leads you to the solution shown previously.

Instead of using the traditional join syntax to obtain the result, you can use the ANSI join syntax. The query may look similar to the following statement.

```
SELECT course_no, section_no, student_id
  FROM course JOIN section
 USING (course_no)
  JOIN instructor
 USING (instructor_id)
  JOIN enrollment
 USING (section_id)
 WHERE prerequisite IS NULL
   AND zip = '10025'
```

The following is another possible alternative using the ANSI join syntax, using the ON condition instead of the USING clause.

```
SELECT c.course_no, s.section_no, e.student_id
  FROM course c JOIN section s
    ON (c.course_no = s.course_no)
  JOIN instructor i
    ON (s.instructor_id = i.instructor_id)
  JOIN enrollment e
    ON (s.section_id = e.section_id)
 WHERE c.prerequisite IS NULL
   AND i.zip = '10025'
```

b) Produce the mailing addresses for instructors who taught sections that started in June 2007.

ANSWER: This solution requires the join of three tables: You join the INSTRUCTOR, SECTION, and ZIPCODE tables to produce the mailing list.

```
SELECT i.first_name || ' ' ||i.last_name name,
       i.street_address, z.city || ', ' || z.state
       || ' ' || i.zip "City State Zip",
       TO_CHAR(s.start_date_time, 'MM/DD/YY') start_dt,
       section_id sect
  FROM instructor i, section s, zipcode z
 WHERE i.instructor_id = s.instructor_id
   AND i.zip = z.zip
   AND s.start_date_time >=
       TO_DATE('01-JUN-2007','DD-MON-YYYY')
   AND s.start_date_time <
       TO_DATE('01-JUL-2007','DD-MON-YYYY')
```

NAME	STREET_ADDRESS	City State Zip	START_DT	SECT
Fernand Hanks	100 East 87th	New York, NY 10015	06/02/07	117
Anita Morris	34 Maiden Lane	New York, NY 10015	06/11/07	83
Anita Morris	34 Maiden Lane	New York, NY 10015	06/12/07	91
Anita Morris	34 Maiden Lane	New York, NY 10015	06/02/07	113

...

```
Gary Pertez    34 Sixth Ave   New York, NY 10035 06/12/07   90
Gary Pertez    34 Sixth Ave   New York, NY 10035 06/10/07  120
Gary Pertez    34 Sixth Ave   New York, NY 10035 06/03/07  143
Gary Pertez    34 Sixth Ave   New York, NY 10035 06/12/07  151
```

17 rows selected.

One of the first steps in solving this problem is to determine what columns and tables are involved. Look at the schema diagram in Appendix D, "STUDENT Database Schema," or refer to the table and column comments listed in Appendix E, "Table and Column Descriptions."

In this example, the instructor's last name, first name, street address, and zip code are found in the INSTRUCTOR table. CITY, STATE, and ZIP are columns in the ZIPCODE table. The join also needs to include the SECTION table because the column START_DATE_TIME lists the date and time when the individual sections started. The next step is to determine the common columns. The ZIP column is the common column between the INSTRUCTOR and ZIPCODE tables. For every value in the ZIP column of the INSTRUCTOR table you have one corresponding ZIP value in the ZIPCODE table. For every value in the ZIPCODE table there may be zero, one, or multiple records in the INSTRUCTOR table. The join returns only the matching records.

The other common column is INSTRUCTOR_ID in the SECTION and INSTRUCTOR tables. Only instructors who teach have one or more rows in the SECTION table. Any section that does not have an instructor assigned is not taught.

As always, the query can be expressed with one of the ANSI join syntax variations.

```
SELECT first_name || ' ' ||last_name name,
       street_address, city || ', ' || state
       || ' ' || zip "City State Zip",
       TO_CHAR(start_date_time, 'MM/DD/YY') start_dt,
       section_id sect
  FROM instructor JOIN section s
 USING (instructor_id)
  JOIN zipcode
 USING (zip)
 WHERE start_date_time >=TO_DATE('01-JUN-2007','DD-MON-YYYY')
 AND start_date_time < TO_DATE('01-JUL-2007','DD-MON-YYYY')
```

You see that some instructors are teaching multiple sections. To see only the distinct addresses, use the DISTINCT keyword and drop the START_DATE_TIME and SECTION_ID columns from the SELECT list.

c) List the student IDs of enrolled students living in Connecticut.

ANSWER: Only students enrolled in classes are in the result; any student who does not have a row in the ENROLLMENT table is not considered enrolled. STUDENT_ID is the common column between the STUDENT and ENROLLMENT tables. The STATE column is in the ZIPCODE table. The common column between the STUDENT and ZIPCODE tables is the ZIP column.

```
SELECT student_id
  FROM student JOIN enrollment
 USING (student_id)
  JOIN zipcode
 USING (zip)
 WHERE state = 'CT'
```

```
STUDENT_ID
----------
       220
       270
       270
...
       210
       154
```

13 rows selected.

Because students can be enrolled in more than one class, add the DISTINCT keyword if you want to display each STUDENT_ID once.

Following is the SQL statement, expressed using the traditional join syntax.

```
SELECT s.student_id
  FROM student s, enrollment e, zipcode z
 WHERE s.student_id = e.student_id
   AND s.zip = z.zip
   AND z.state = 'CT'
```

d) Show all the grades student Fred Crocitto received for SECTION_ID 86.

ANSWER: The grades for each section and student are stored in the GRADE table. The primary key of the GRADE table consists of the STUDENT_ID, SECTION_ID, GRADE_TYPE_CODE, and GRADE_CODE_OCCURRENCE columns. This means a student, such as Fred Crocitto, has multiple grades for each grade type.

```
SELECT s.first_name|| ' '|| s.last_name name,
       e.section_id, g.grade_type_code,
       g.numeric_grade grade
  FROM student s JOIN enrollment e
    ON (s.student_id = e.student_id)
  JOIN grade g
    ON (e.student_id = g.student_id
   AND e.section_id = g.section_id)
 WHERE s.last_name = 'Crocitto'
   AND s.first_name ='Fred'
   AND e.section_id = 86
```

The SQL statement using the traditional join syntax may look similar to the following query.

```
SELECT s.first_name|| ' '|| s.last_name name,
       e.section_id, g.grade_type_code,
       g.numeric_grade grade
  FROM student s, enrollment e, grade g
 WHERE s.last_name = 'Crocitto'
   AND s.first_name ='Fred'
   AND e.section_id = 86
   AND s.student_id = e.student_id
   AND e.student_id = g.student_id
   AND e.section_id = g.section_id
```

```
NAME              SECTION_ID GR     GRADE
---------------   ---------- --  ---------
Fred Crocitto             86 FI         85
...
Fred Crocitto             86 QZ         90
Fred Crocitto             86 QZ         84
Fred Crocitto             86 QZ         97
Fred Crocitto             86 QZ         97
```

11 rows selected.

To build up the SQL statement step by step, you might want to start with the STUDENT table and select the record for Fred Crocitto.

```
SELECT last_name, first_name
  FROM student
 WHERE last_name = 'Crocitto'
   AND first_name = 'Fred'
```

Next, choose the section with ID 86, in which Fred is enrolled. The common column between the two tables is STUDENT_ID.

```
SELECT s.first_name||' '|| s.last_name name,
       e.section_id
  FROM student s, enrollment e
 WHERE s.last_name = 'Crocitto'
   AND s.first_name = 'Fred'
   AND e.section_id = 86
   AND s.student_id = e.student_id
```

Next, retrieve the individual grades from the GRADE table. The common columns between the GRADE table and the ENROLLMENT table are SECTION_ID and STUDENT_ID. They represent the primary key in the ENROLLMENT table and are foreign keys in the GRADE table. Both columns need to be in the WHERE clause.

If you want to expand the query, add the DESCRIPTION column of the GRADE_TYPE table for each GRADE_TYPE_CODE. The common column between the tables GRADE and GRADE_TYPE is GRADE_TYPE_CODE.

```
SELECT s.first_name||' '|| s.last_name name,
       e.section_id, g.grade_type_code grade,
       g.numeric_grade, gt.description
  FROM student s, enrollment e, grade g, grade_type gt
 WHERE s.last_name = 'Crocitto'
   AND s.first_name = 'Fred'
   AND e.section_id = 86
   AND s.student_id = e.student_id
   AND e.student_id = g.student_id
   AND e.section_id = g.section_id
   AND g.grade_type_code = gt.grade_type_code
```

If you also show the COURSE_NO column, join to the SECTION table via the ENROLLMENT table column SECTION_ID.

```
SELECT s.first_name||' '|| s.last_name name,
       e.section_id, g.grade_type_code,
       g.numeric_grade grade, gt.description,
       sec.course_no
  FROM student s, enrollment e, grade g, grade_type gt,
       section sec
 WHERE s.last_name = 'Crocitto'
   AND s.first_name = 'Fred'
   AND e.section_id = 86
   AND s.student_id = e.student_id
   AND e.student_id = g.student_id
   AND e.section_id = g.section_id
   AND g.grade_type_code = gt.grade_type_code
   AND e.section_id = sec.section_id
```

NAME	SECTION_ID	GR	GRADE	DESCRIPTION	COURSE_NO
Fred Crocitto	86	FI	85	Final	25
...					
Fred Crocitto	86	QZ	90	Quiz	25
Fred Crocitto	86	QZ	84	Quiz	25
Fred Crocitto	86	QZ	97	Quiz	25
Fred Crocitto	86	QZ	97	Quiz	25

```
11 rows selected.
```

e) List the final examination grades for all enrolled Connecticut students of course number 420.
(Note that final examination grade does not mean final grade.)

ANSWER: To find the answer, you need to join five tables. The needed joins are the ZIPCODE
table with the STUDENT table to determine the Connecticut students and the STUDENT and
ENROLLMENT tables to determine the SECTION_IDs in which the students are enrolled. From
these SECTION_IDs, you include only sections where the course number equals 420. This requires
a join of the ENROLLMENT table to the SECTION table. Finally, join the ENROLLMENT table to the
GRADE table to display the grades.

```
SELECT e.student_id, sec.course_no, g.numeric_grade
  FROM student stud, zipcode z,
       enrollment e, section sec, grade g
 WHERE stud.zip = z.zip
   AND z.state = 'CT'
   AND stud.student_id = e.student_id
   AND e.section_id = sec.section_id
   AND e.section_id = g.section_id
   AND e.student_id = g.student_id
   AND sec.course_no = 420
   AND g.grade_type_code = 'FI'
```

STUDENT_ID	COURSE_NO	NUMERIC_GRADE
196	420	84
198	420	85

```
2 rows selected.
```

You can list any of the columns you find relevant to solving the query. For this solution, the columns STUDENT_ID, COURSE_NO, and NUMERIC_GRADE were chosen.

The query can also be expressed with the ANSI join syntax, as in the following example, which shows the USING clause.

```
SELECT student_id, course_no, numeric_grade
  FROM student JOIN zipcode
 USING (zip)
    JOIN enrollment
 USING (student_id)
   JOIN section
 USING (section_id)
   JOIN grade g
 USING (section_id, student_id)
 WHERE course_no = 420
   AND grade_type_code = 'FI'
   AND state = 'CT'
```

f) Display the LAST_NAME, STUDENT_ID, PERCENT_OF_FINAL_GRADE, GRADE_TYPE_CODE, and NUMERIC_GRADE columns for students who received 80 or less for their class project (GRADE_TYPE_CODE = 'PJ'). Order the result by student last name.

ANSWER: Join the tables GRADE_TYPE_WEIGHT, GRADE, ENROLLMENT, and STUDENT.

The column PERCENT_OF_FINAL_GRADE of the GRADE_TYPE_WEIGHT table stores the weighted percentage a particular grade has on the final grade. One of the foreign keys of the GRADE table is the combination of GRADE_TYPE_CODE and SECTION_ID; these columns represent the primary key of the GRADE_TYPE_WEIGHT table.

To include the student's last name, you have two choices. Either follow the primary and foreign key relationships by joining the tables GRADE and ENROLLMENT via the STUDENT_ID and SECTION_ID columns and then join the ENROLLMENT table to the STUDENT table via the STUDENT_ID column, or skip the ENROLLMENT table and join GRADE directly to the STUDENT table via STUDENT_ID. Examine the first option of joining to the ENROLLMENT table and then joining it to the STUDENT table.

```
SELECT g.student_id, g.section_id,
       gw.percent_of_final_grade pct, g.grade_type_code,
       g.numeric_grade grade, s.last_name
  FROM grade_type_weight gw, grade g,
       enrollment e, student s
 WHERE g.grade_type_code = 'PJ'
   AND gw.grade_type_code = g.grade_type_code
   AND gw.section_id = g.section_id
   AND g.numeric_grade <= 80
   AND g.section_id = e.section_id
   AND g.student_id = e.student_id
   AND e.student_id = s.student_id
 ORDER BY s.last_name
```

```
    STUDENT_ID SECTION_ID      PCT GR     GRADE LAST_NAME
    ---------- ----------   --------- -- --------- -----------
          245         82      75 PJ          77 Dalvi
          176        115      75 PJ          76 Satterfield
          244         82      75 PJ          76 Wilson
          248        155      75 PJ          76 Zapulla

    4 rows selected.
```

SKIPPING THE PRIMARY/FOREIGN KEY PATH

The second choice is to join the STUDENT_ID from the GRADE table directly to the STUDENT_ID of the STUDENT table, thus skipping the ENROLLMENT table entirely. The following query returns the same result as the query in the preceding section.

```
SELECT g.student_id, g.section_id,
       gw.percent_of_final_grade pct, g.grade_type_code,
       g.numeric_grade grade, s.last_name
  FROM grade_type_weight gw, grade g,
       student s
 WHERE g.grade_type_code = 'PJ'
   AND gw.grade_type_code = g.grade_type_code
   AND gw.section_id = g.section_id
   AND g.numeric_grade <= 80
   AND g.student_id = s.student_id
 ORDER BY s.last_name
    STUDENT_ID SECTION_ID      PCT GR     GRADE LAST_NAME
    ---------- ----------   ------------ -- --------------------
          245         82      75 PJ          77 Dalvi
          176        115      75 PJ          76 Satterfield
          244         82      75 PJ          76 Wilson
          248        155      75 PJ          76 Zapulla

    4 rows selected.
```

This shortcut is perfectly acceptable, even if it does not follow the primary key/foreign key relationship path. In this case, you can be sure not to build a Cartesian product because you can guarantee only one STUDENT_ID in the STUDENT table for every STUDENT_ID in the GRADE table. In addition, it also eliminates a join; thus, the query executes a little faster and requires fewer resources. The effect is probably fairly negligible with this small result set.

Lab 7.2 Quiz

In order to test your progress, you should be able to answer the following questions.

1) Which SQL statement shows the sections that have instructors assigned to them?

    _____ **a)** `SELECT c.course_no, s.section_id, i.instructor_id`
        `FROM course c, section s, instructor i`
       `WHERE c.course_no = s.course_no`
        `AND i.instructor_id = s.section_id`

    _____ **b)** `SELECT c.course_no, s.section_id, i.instructor_id`
        `FROM course c, section s, instructor i`
       `WHERE c.course_no = s.course_no`
        `AND i.instructor_id = s.instructor_id`

    _____ **c)** `SELECT course_no, section_id, instructor.instructor_id`
        `FROM section, instructor`
       `WHERE instructor.instructor_id = section.section_id`

    _____ **d)** `SELECT c.section_id, i.instructor_id`
        `FROM course c, instructor i`
       `WHERE i.instructor_id = c.section_id`

    _____ **e)** `SELECT c.course_no, i.instructor_id`
        `FROM course c JOIN instructor`
       `USING (instructor_id)`

2) How do you resolve the Oracle error ORA-00918: column ambiguously defined?

    _____ **a)** Correct the join criteria and WHERE clause condition.
    _____ **b)** Choose another column.
    _____ **c)** Add the correct table alias.
    _____ **d)** Correct the spelling of the column name.

3) Joins involving multiple columns must always follow the primary key/foreign key relationship path.

    _____ **a)** True
    _____ **b)** False

4) Find the error(s) in the following SQL statement.

```
1 SELECT g.student_id, s.section_id,
2        g.numeric_grade, s.last_name
3   FROM grade g,
4        enrollment e, student s
5  WHERE g.section_id = e.section_id
6    AND g.student_id = e.student_id
7    AND s.student_id = e.student_id
8    AND s.student_id = 248
9    AND e.section_id = 155
```

_____ **a)** Line 1

_____ **b)** Line 5

_____ **c)** Line 6

_____ **d)** Lines 5 and 6

_____ **e)** Lines 1, 5, and 6

_____ **f)** No error

5) Equijoins are the most common type of joins and are always based on equality of values.

_____ **a)** True

_____ **b)** False

6) To join four tables, you must have at least three join conditions.

_____ **a)** True

_____ **b)** False

ANSWERS APPEAR IN APPENDIX A.

▼ WORKSHOP

The projects in this section are meant to prompt you to utilize all the skills you have acquired throughout this chapter. The answers to these projects can be found at the companion Web site to this book, located at www.oraclesqlbyexample.com.

1) Select the course description, section number, and location for sections meeting in location L211.

2) Show the course description, section number, and starting date and time of the courses Joseph German is taking.

3) List the instructor ID, last name of the instructor, and section ID of sections where class participation contributes to 25 percent of the total grade. Order the result by the instructor's last name.

4) Display the first and last names of students who received 99 or more points on the class project.

5) Select the grades for quizzes of students living in zip code 10956.

6) List the course number, section number, and instructor first and last names for classes with course number 350 as a prerequisite.

7) What problem do the following two SELECT statements solve? Explain the difference between the two results.

```
SELECT stud.student_id, i.instructor_id,
       stud.zip, i.zip
  FROM student stud, instructor i
 WHERE stud.zip = i.zip

SELECT stud.student_id, i.instructor_id,
       stud.zip, i.zip
  FROM student stud, enrollment e, section sec,
       instructor i
 WHERE stud.student_id = e.student_id
   AND e.section_id = sec.section_id
   AND sec.instructor_id = i.instructor_id
   AND stud.zip = i.zip
```

CHAPTER 8

Subqueries

CHAPTER OBJECTIVES

In this chapter, you will learn about:

- ▶ Simple Subqueries
- ▶ Correlated Subqueries
- ▶ Inline Views and Scalar Subquery Expressions
- ▶ ANY, SOME, and ALL Operators in Subqueries

A subquery is a SELECT statement nested in various clauses of a SQL statement. It allows you to use the output from one query as the input of another SQL statement. Subqueries make it easy to break down problems into logical and manageable pieces.

LAB 8.1
Simple Subqueries

LAB OBJECTIVES

After this lab, you will be able to:

▶ Write Subqueries in the WHERE and HAVING Clauses

▶ Write Subqueries That Return Multiple Rows

▶ Write Subqueries That Return Multiple Columns

As mentioned earlier, a subquery allows you to break down a problem into individual components and solve it by nesting the queries. Although subqueries can be nested several levels deep, nesting beyond four or five levels is impractical. Subqueries are sometimes also referred to as *sub-SELECTs* or *nested SELECTs*.

Subqueries are not used just in SELECT statements but also in other SQL statements that allow subqueries (for example, the WHERE clause of DELETE statements, the SET and WHERE clauses of UPDATE statements, or part of the SELECT clause of INSERT statements). You use these SQL statements in Chapter 11, "Insert, Update, and Delete."

In this book, a *subquery* is referred to as an *inner query*, and the surrounding statement is known as the *outer query*. In a simple subquery, the inner query is executed once, before the execution of the outer query. (This is in contrast to the correlated subquery, where the inner query executes repeatedly. You will learn to write correlated subqueries in Lab 8.2.)

Scalar Subqueries

A *scalar subquery,* also called a *single-row subquery*, returns a single column with one row. When you want to show the courses with the lowest course cost, you can write two separate queries. First, determine the lowest cost by applying the aggregate function MIN to the COST column of the COURSE table.

```
SELECT MIN(cost)
  FROM course
MIN(COST)
---------
     1095

1 row selected.
```

Then write another SELECT statement that retrieves courses equaling the cost.

```
SELECT course_no, description, cost
  FROM course
 WHERE cost = 1095
```

COURSE_NO	DESCRIPTION	COST
135	Unix Tips and Techniques	1095
230	Intro to the Internet	1095
240	Intro to the BASIC Language	1095

3 rows selected.

The subquery construct simplifies the writing of two separate queries and the recording of the intermediate result. The following SQL statement nests the subquery in the WHERE clause of the outer query. The inner query, which is the query that determines the lowest cost from the COURSE table, is executed first. The result is fed to the outer query, which retrieves all the values that qualify.

```
SELECT course_no, description, cost
  FROM course
 WHERE cost =
       (SELECT MIN(cost)
          FROM course)
```

COURSE_NO	DESCRIPTION	COST
135	Unix Tips and Techniques	1095
230	Intro to the Internet	1095
240	Intro to the BASIC Language	1095

3 rows selected.

Instead of performing equality conditions, you might need to construct >, <, >=, <=, or <> comparisons against a result. Just like the aforementioned statement, these comparisons will work only if the subquery returns a single row.

Subqueries That Return Multiple Rows

Subqueries can return one or multiple rows. If a subquery returns a single row, the =, <, >, <=, >=, or <> operator can be used for comparison with the subquery. If multiple records are returned, the IN, ANY, ALL, or SOME operator must be used; otherwise, Oracle returns an error message.

The following query displays the course number, description, and cost of courses with a cost equal to the highest cost of all the courses. The highest cost requires the use of the aggregate function MAX. As discussed in Chapter 6, "Aggregate Functions, GROUP BY, and HAVING Clauses," aggregate functions, when used alone, without the presence of any nonaggregate expressions in the SELECT list, always return one row. The subquery returns the single value

1595. All the rows of the COURSE table are compared to this value to see if any rows have the same course cost. Only one record in the COURSE table equals this cost.

```
SELECT course_no, description, cost
  FROM course
 WHERE cost =
       (SELECT MAX(cost)
          FROM course)
```

COURSE_NO	DESCRIPTION	COST
80	Programming Techniques	1595

```
1 row selected.
```

The next SQL statement is an example of a subquery that returns several rows.

```
SELECT course_no, description, cost
  FROM course
 WHERE cost =
       (SELECT cost
          FROM course
         WHERE prerequisite = 20)
ERROR at line 4:
ORA-01427: single-row subquery returns more than one row
```

Multiple rows of the subquery satisfy the criteria of a prerequisite course number equal to 20. Therefore, Oracle returns an error message. To eliminate the error, change the = operator of the outer query to the IN operator. The IN operator compares a list of values for equivalency. If any of the values in the list satisfy the condition, the record is included in the result set.

```
SELECT course_no, description, cost
  FROM course
 WHERE cost IN
       (SELECT cost
          FROM course
         WHERE prerequisite = 20)
```

COURSE_NO	DESCRIPTION	COST
10	Technology Concepts	1195
20	Intro to Information Systems	1195
...		
122	Intermediate Java Programming	1195
100	Hands-On Windows	1195

```
25 rows selected.
```

You can also negate the criteria of the subquery and include only records with values that are not in the subquery's result. You accomplish this by applying the NOT IN operator.

```
SELECT course_no, description, cost
  FROM course
 WHERE cost NOT IN
       (SELECT cost
          FROM course
         WHERE prerequisite = 20)
COURSE_NO DESCRIPTION                                     COST
--------- -------------------------------------------- ----
       80 Programming Techniques                        1595
      135 Unix Tips and Techniques                      1095
      230 Intro to the Internet                         1095
      240 Intro to the BASIC Language                   1095

4 rows selected.
```

 If the subquery returns multiple rows and you want to perform a comparison other than equality or inequality, use the ALL, ANY, and SOME operators, discussed in Lab 8.4, to perform such comparisons.

Table 8.1 provides an overview of the various comparison operators available for subqueries. If your subquery returns more than one row, you have to choose a different operator than if your subquery retrieves at most one row only.

TABLE 8.1   Comparison Operators for Subqueries

COMPARISON OPERATOR	SUBQUERY RETURNS ONE ROW	SUBQUERY RETURNS MULTIPLE ROWS
Equality	=	IN.
Inequality	<>	NOT IN.
Greater than	>	Use the ANY, ALL, and SOME operators
Less than	<	(see Lab 8.4).
Greater than or equal to	>=	
Less than or equal to	<−	

Nesting Multiple Subqueries

You can nest one subquery within another subquery. The innermost query is always evaluated first, then the next highest one, and so on. The result of each subquery is fed into the enclosing statement.

The next query determines the last and first names of students enrolled in section number 8 of course number 20.

```
SELECT last_name, first_name
  FROM student
 WHERE student_id IN
       (SELECT student_id
          FROM enrollment
         WHERE section_id IN
               (SELECT section_id
                  FROM section
                 WHERE section_no = 8
                 AND course_no = 20))
LAST_NAME                       FIRST_NAME
------------------------        ----------
Limate                          Roy
Segall                          J.

2 rows selected.
```

The innermost nested subquery, the last subquery in the example, is executed first; it determines the SECTION_ID for section number 8 and course number 20. The surrounding query uses this resulting SECTION_ID in the WHERE clause to select student IDs from the ENROLLMENT table. These STUDENT_ID rows are fed to the outermost SELECT statement, which then displays the first and last names from the STUDENT table.

Subqueries and Joins

A subquery that uses the IN or = operator can often be expressed as an equijoin if the subquery does not contain an aggregate function. The following query can be transformed into an equijoin.

```
SELECT course_no, description
  FROM course
 WHERE course_no IN
       (SELECT course_no
          FROM section
         WHERE location = 'L211')
COURSE_NO DESCRIPTION
--------- ----------------------------
      142 Project Management
      125 Java Developer I
      122 Intermediate Java Programming

3 rows selected.
```

The following is the same query now expressed as an equijoin.

```
SELECT c.course_no, c.description
  FROM course c, section s
 WHERE c.course_no = s.course_no
   AND s.location = 'L211'
```

Subqueries That Return Multiple Columns

SQL allows you to compare multiple columns in the WHERE clause to multiple columns of a subquery. The values in the columns must match both sides of the equation in the WHERE clause for the condition to be true. This means the data type must be compatible and the number and order of columns must match.

For example, for each section, determine the students with the highest grades for their project (PJ). The following query does not accomplish this goal. It returns the highest project grade for each section but does not list the individual student(s).

```
SELECT section_id, MAX(numeric_grade)
  FROM grade
 WHERE grade_type_code = 'PJ'
 GROUP BY section_id
SECTION_ID MAX(NUMERIC_GRADE)
---------- ------------------
        82                 77
        88                 99
...
       149                 83
       155                 92

8 rows selected.
```

The following query obtains the desired result by transforming the query into a subquery. The outer query displays the desired STUDENT_ID column, and the WHERE clause compares the column pairs against the column pairs in the subquery.

```
SELECT student_id, section_id, numeric_grade
  FROM grade
 WHERE grade_type_code = 'PJ'
   AND (section_id, numeric_grade) IN
       (SELECT section_id, MAX(numeric_grade)
          FROM grade
         WHERE grade_type_code = 'PJ'
         GROUP BY section_id)
STUDENT_ID SECTION_ID NUMERIC_GRADE
---------- ---------- -------------
       245         82            77
       166         88            99
...
       232        149            83
       105        155            92

8 rows selected.
```

The execution steps are just like those for the previous simple subqueries. First, the innermost query determines the highest grade for each section. Then the pairs of columns are compared. If the column pair matches, Oracle displays the record.

If you were to write the query using literals instead of a subquery, the query would look like the following. It shows column pairs whereby the values of each expression pair is surrounded by parentheses.

```
SELECT student_id, section_id, numeric_grade
  FROM grade
 WHERE grade_type_code = 'PJ'
   AND (section_id, numeric_grade) IN
        ((82, 77),
         (88, 99),
...
         (149, 83),
         (155, 92))
```

Subqueries and Nulls

One easily overlooked behavior of subqueries is the occurrence of null values. The next example illustrates this concept on the COURSE table and the PREREQUISITE column. The first query shows a subquery that returns all the COURSE_NO and PREREQUISITE column values for courses with COURSE_NO 120, 220, and 310 in the COURSE table. Course number 310 has a null value in the PREREQUISITE column, meaning that the individual course does not have any prerequisites.

```
SELECT course_no, prerequisite
  FROM course
 WHERE course_no IN (120, 220, 310)
COURSE_NO PREREQUISITE
--------- ------------
      120           80
      220           80
      310

3 rows selected.
```

If you use this result to formulate a subquery for these rows specifically and negate it with NOT, you obtain an interesting result: The outer query does not return any rows, despite the fact that there are rows with PREREQUISITE column values other than 80 and null.

```
SELECT course_no, prerequisite
  FROM course
 WHERE prerequisite NOT IN
        (SELECT prerequisite
           FROM course
          WHERE course_no IN (310, 220))

no rows selected
```

If you translate the result of the subquery into a list of values, you see the same result: No rows are returned from the query because the condition evaluates to unknown when any value in the list is a null.

```
SELECT course_no, prerequisite
  FROM course
 WHERE prerequisite NOT IN (80, NULL)
```

no rows selected

You typically come across this type of scenario only in subqueries; therefore, you must be aware of any NOT IN operator subqueries that can potentially return null values. The way to solve this null dilemma is to use the NOT EXISTS operator discussed in Lab 8.2. The next query returns the desired result.

```
SELECT course_no, prerequisite
  FROM course c
 WHERE NOT EXISTS
       (SELECT '*'
          FROM course
         WHERE course_no IN (310, 220)
           AND c.prerequisite = prerequisite)
```

The NVL and COALESCE functions are useful in dealing with null values. You can substitute a default value and apply the function to both the subquery and the WHERE clause condition.

ORDER BY Clause in Subqueries

With the exception of the inline view discussed in Lab 8.3, the ORDER BY clause is not allowed inside a subquery. If you attempt to include an ORDER BY clause, you receive an error message.

```
SELECT course_no, description, cost
  FROM course
 WHERE cost IN
       (SELECT cost
          FROM course
         WHERE prerequisite = 420
         ORDER BY cost)
         ORDER BY cost)
         *
ERROR at line 7:
ORA-00907: missing right parenthesis
```

It is not immediately apparent where the problem lies unless you already know about this rule. The message essentially indicates that an ORDER BY clause is not permitted in a subquery and that Oracle is expecting to see the right parenthesis, signifying the closing of the subquery. An ORDER BY clause is certainly valid for the outer query—just not for the nested subquery.

▼ LAB 8.1 EXERCISES

a) Write a SQL statement that displays the first and last names of the students who registered first.

b) Show the sections with the lowest course cost and a capacity equal to or lower than the average capacity. Also display the course description, section number, capacity, and cost.

c) Select the course number and total capacity for each course. Show only the courses with a total capacity less than the average capacity of all the sections.

d) Choose the most ambitious students: Display the STUDENT_ID for the students enrolled in the most sections.

e) Select the STUDENT_ID and SECTION_ID of enrolled students living in zip code 06820.

f) Display the course number and course description of the courses taught by instructor Fernand Hanks.

g) Select the last names and first names of students not enrolled in any class.

h) Determine the STUDENT_ID and last name of students with the highest FINAL_GRADE for each section. Also include the SECTION_ID and the FINAL_GRADE columns in the result.

i) Select the sections and their capacity, where the capacity equals the number of students enrolled.

▼ LAB 8.1 EXERCISE ANSWERS

a) Write a SQL statement that displays the first and last names of the students who registered first.

ANSWER: You break down the query into logical pieces by first determining the earliest registration date of all students. The aggregate function MIN obtains the result in the subquery. The earliest date is compared to the REGISTRATION_DATE column for each student, and only records that are equal to the same date and time are returned.

```
SELECT first_name, last_name
  FROM student
 WHERE registration_date =
       (SELECT MIN(registration_date)
          FROM student)
```

```
FIRST_NAME                        LAST_NAME
------------------------------    ---------
J.                                Landry
Judith                            Olvsade
...
Larry                             Walter
Catherine                         Mierzwa

8 rows selected.
```

b) Show the sections with the lowest course cost and a capacity equal to or lower than the average capacity. Also display the course description, section number, capacity, and cost.

ANSWER: First, split the problem into individual queries. Start by determining the average capacity of all sections and the lowest course cost of all courses. To compare both cost and capacity against the subqueries, add a join to the SECTION and COURSE tables.

```
SELECT c.description, s.section_no, c.cost, s.capacity
  FROM course c, section s
 WHERE c.course_no = s.course_no
   AND s.capacity <=
       (SELECT AVG(capacity)
          FROM section)
   AND c.cost =
       (SELECT MIN(cost)
          FROM course)
```

DESCRIPTION	SECTION_NO	COST	CAPACITY
Intro to the Internet	1	1095	12
Intro to the Internet	2	1095	15
...			
Unix Tips and Techniques	2	1095	15
Unix Tips and Techniques	4	1095	15

6 rows selected.

c) Select the course number and total capacity for each course. Show only the courses with a total capacity less than the average capacity of all the sections.

ANSWER: To determine the total capacity per course, use the SUM function to add the values in the SECTION table's CAPACITY column. Compare the total capacity for each course to the average capacity for all sections and return those courses that have a total capacity less than the average capacity.

```
SELECT course_no, SUM(capacity)
  FROM section
 GROUP BY course_no
HAVING SUM(capacity) <
       (SELECT AVG(capacity)
          FROM section)
```

COURSE_NO	SUM(CAPACITY)
10	15
144	15

2 rows selected.

The solution shows only courses and their respective capacities that satisfy the condition in the HAVING clause.

To determine the solution, first write the individual queries and then combine them. The following query first determines the total capacity for each course.

```
SELECT course_no, SUM(capacity)
  FROM section
 GROUP BY course_no
```

```
COURSE_NO SUM(CAPACITY)
--------- -------------
       10            15
       20            80
...
      420            25
      450            25
```

28 rows selected.

You can easily obtain the average capacity for all sections by using the AVG function.

```
SELECT AVG(capacity)
  FROM section
AVG(CAPACITY)
-------------
    21.179487
```

1 row selected.

d) Choose the most ambitious students: Display the STUDENT_ID for the students enrolled in the most sections.

ANSWER: A count of records for each student in the ENROLLMENT table shows how many sections each student is enrolled in. Determine the highest number of enrollments per student by nesting the aggregate functions MAX and COUNT.

```
SELECT student_id, COUNT(*)
  FROM enrollment
 GROUP BY student_id
HAVING COUNT(*) =
       (SELECT MAX(COUNT(*))
          FROM enrollment
         GROUP BY student_id)
STUDENT_ID  COUNT(*)
----------- --------
        124         4
        214         4
```

2 rows selected.

To reach the subquery solution, determine the number of enrollments for each student. The STUDENT_ID column is not listed in the SELECT list. Therefore, only the result of the COUNT function is shown.

```
SELECT COUNT(*)
  FROM enrollment
 GROUP BY student_id
COUNT(*)
---------
        2
        1
...
```

```
         2
         2
```

165 rows selected.

The second query combines two aggregate functions to determine the highest number of sections any student is enrolled in. This subquery is then applied in the HAVING clause of the solution.

```
SELECT MAX(COUNT(*))
  FROM enrollment
 GROUP BY student_id
MAX(COUNT(*))
-------------
            4
```

1 row selected.

e) Select the STUDENT_ID and SECTION_ID of enrolled students living in zip code 06820.

ANSWER: The IN operator is necessary because the subquery returns multiple rows.

```
SELECT student_id, section_id
  FROM enrollment
 WHERE student_id IN
       (SELECT student_id
          FROM student
         WHERE zip = '06820')
STUDENT_ID SECTION_ID
---------- ----------
       240         81
```

1 row selected.

Alternatively, you can write the query as a join and achieve the same result.

```
SELECT e.student_id, e.section_id
  FROM enrollment e, student s
 WHERE e.student_id = s.student_id
   AND s.zip = '06820'
```

f) Display the course number and course description of the courses taught by instructor Fernand Hanks.

ANSWER: To determine the courses taught by this instructor, nest multiple subqueries.

```
SELECT course_no, description
  FROM course
 WHERE course_no IN
       (SELECT course_no
          FROM section
         WHERE instructor_id IN
               (SELECT instructor_id
                  FROM instructor
```

```
                      WHERE last_name = 'Hanks'
                        AND first_name = 'Fernand'))
COURSE_NO DESCRIPTION
--------- -----------------------------
       25 Intro to Programming
      240 Intro to the BASIC Language
...
      120 Intro to Java Programming
      122 Intermediate Java Programming
```

9 rows selected.

You can also solve this problem by using an equijoin.

```
SELECT c.course_no, c.description
  FROM course c, section s, instructor i
 WHERE c.course_no = s.course_no
   AND s.instructor_id = i.instructor_id
   AND i.last_name = 'Hanks'
   AND i.first_name = 'Fernand'
```

g) Select the last names and first names of students not enrolled in any class.

ANSWER: Use the NOT IN operator to eliminate student IDs not found in the ENROLLMENT table. The result is a list of students with no rows in the ENROLLMENT table. They may be newly registered students who have not yet enrolled in any courses.

```
SELECT last_name, first_name
  FROM student
 WHERE student_id NOT IN
       (SELECT student_id
          FROM enrollment)
```

LAST_NAME	FIRST_NAME
Eakheit	George
Millstein	Leonard
...	
Larcia	Preston
Mastandora	Kathleen

103 rows selected.

You might wonder why the solution does not include the DISTINCT keyword in the subquery. This keyword is not required and does not alter the result, nor does it change the efficiency of the execution. Oracle automatically eliminates duplicates in a list of values as a result of the subquery.

h) Determine the STUDENT_ID and last name of students with the highest FINAL_GRADE for each section. Also include the SECTION_ID and the FINAL_GRADE columns in the result.

ANSWER: The solution requires pairs of columns to be compared. First, determine the subquery to show the highest grade for each section. Then match the result to the columns in the outer query.

```
SELECT s.student_id, s.last_name, e.final_grade,
       e.section_id
  FROM enrollment e, student s
 WHERE e.student_id = s.student_id
   AND (e.final_grade, e.section_id) IN
       (SELECT MAX(final_grade), section_id
          FROM enrollment
         GROUP BY section_id)
STUDENT_ID LAST_NAME   FINAL_GRADE SECTION_ID
---------- ----------  ----------- ----------
       102 Crocitto             92         89

1 row selected.
```

 There is no need to add a table alias to the subquery. Table aliases in subqueries are typically used only in correlated subqueries or in subqueries that contain joins. Correlated subqueries are discussed in Lab 8.2.

i) Select the sections and their capacity, where the capacity equals the number of students enrolled.

ANSWER: Use a subquery to determine the number of enrolled students per section. Then compare the resulting set to the column pair SECTION_ID and CAPACITY.

```
SELECT section_id, capacity
  FROM section
 WHERE (section_id, capacity) IN
       (SELECT section_id, COUNT(*)
          FROM enrollment
         GROUP BY section_id)
SECTION_ID  CAPACITY
----------  --------
        99        12

1 row selected.
```

Lab 8.1 Quiz

In order to test your progress, you should be able to answer the following questions.

1) The ORDER BY clause is not allowed in subqueries.

_____ a) True

_____ b) False

2) Subqueries are used only in SELECT statements.

_____ a) True

_____ b) False

3) The most deeply nested, noncorrelated subquery always executes first.

_____ a) True

_____ b) False

4) What operator would you choose to prevent Oracle error ORA-01427: single-row subquery returns more than one row?

_____ a) >=

_____ b) =

_____ c) IN

_____ d) <=

5) Subqueries can return multiple rows and columns.

_____ a) True

_____ b) False

ANSWERS APPEAR IN APPENDIX A.

LAB 8.2
Correlated Subqueries

LAB OBJECTIVES

After this lab, you will be able to:

▶ Write Correlated Subqueries
▶ Use the EXISTS and NOT EXISTS Operators

Correlated subqueries are probably one of the most powerful, yet initially very difficult, concepts of the SQL language. Correlated subqueries are different from the simple subqueries discussed so far. First, they allow you to reference columns from the outer query in the subquery. Second, they execute the inner query repeatedly.

Reviewing Rows with Correlated Subqueries

A correlated subquery is so named because of the reference of a column from the outer query. You use a correlated subquery when you need to review every row of the outer query against the result of the inner query. The inner query is executed repeatedly, each time specific to the correlated value of the outer query. In contrast, in previous subquery examples, the inner query is executed only once.

One example in Lab 8.1 illustrates how to determine the students with the highest grades for their project (PJ), within their respective sections. The solution is accomplished with the IN operator, which compares the column pairs. The following SELECT statement repeats the solution.

```
SELECT student_id, section_id, numeric_grade
  FROM grade
 WHERE grade_type_code = 'PJ'
   AND (section_id, numeric_grade) IN
       (SELECT section_id, MAX(numeric_grade)
          FROM grade
         WHERE grade_type_code = 'PJ'
         GROUP BY section_id)
```

Here is the query rewritten as a correlated subquery.

```
SELECT student_id, section_id, numeric_grade
  FROM grade outer
```

```
    WHERE grade_type_code = 'PJ'
      AND numeric_grade =
          (SELECT MAX(numeric_grade)
             FROM grade
            WHERE grade_type_code = outer.grade_type_code
              AND section_id = outer.section_id)
STUDENT_ID SECTION_ID NUMERIC_GRADE
---------- ---------- -------------
       245         82            77
       166         88            99
...
       232        149            83
       105        155            92

8 rows selected.
```

This query is a correlated subquery because the inner query refers to columns from the outer query. The GRADE table is the parent query, or the outer query. For simplicity, the table alias OUTER is used.

You can refer to columns of the outer query by using the alias. In this example, the values of the columns SECTION_ID and GRADE_TYPE_CODE of the outer query are compared to the values of the inner query. The inner query determines the highest project grade for the SECTION_ID and GRADE_TYPE_CODE values of the current outer row.

STEPS PERFORMED BY THE CORRELATED SUBQUERY

To select the correct records, Oracle performs the following steps.

1. Select a row from the outer query.

2. Determine the value of the correlated column(s).

3. Execute the inner query for each record of the outer query.

4. Feed the result of the inner query to the outer query and evaluate it. If it satisfies the criteria, return the row for output.

5. Select the next record of the outer query and repeat steps 2 through 4 until all the records of the outer query are evaluated.

Let's look at these steps in more detail.

STEP 1: SELECT A ROW FROM THE OUTER QUERY

Choose a record in the outer query where GRADE_TYPE_CODE equals 'PJ'. The row returned in this step will be further evaluated in the steps that follow.

```
SELECT student_id, section_id, numeric_grade
  FROM grade outer
 WHERE grade_type_code = 'PJ'
```

```
STUDENT_ID SECTION_ID NUMERIC_GRADE
---------- ---------- -------------
       105        155            92
       111        133            90
...
       245         82            77
       248        155            76
```

21 rows selected.

STEP 2: DETERMINE THE VALUE OF THE CORRELATED COLUMN(S)
Starting with the first returned row with STUDENT_ID 105, the value of the correlated column OUTER.SECTION_ID equals 155. For the column OUTER.GRADE_TYPE_CODE, the value is 'PJ'.

STEP 3: EXECUTE THE INNER QUERY
Based on the correlated column values, the inner query is executed. It shows the highest grade for the respective section ID and grade type code.

```
SELECT MAX(numeric_grade)
  FROM grade
 WHERE grade_type_code = 'PJ'
   AND section_id = 155
MAX(NUMERIC_GRADE)
------------------
                92
```

1 row selected.

STEP 4: EVALUATE THE CONDITION
Because NUMERIC_GRADE equals 92, the row for STUDENT_ID 105 evaluates to true and is included in the result.

STEP 5: REPEAT STEPS 2 THROUGH 4 FOR EACH SUBSEQUENT ROW OF THE OUTER QUERY
Evaluate the next row containing values STUDENT_ID 111 and SECTION_ID 133. The highest grade for the section and grade type code is 92, but student 111 does not have a NUMERIC_GRADE equal to this value. Therefore, the row is not returned. Each row of the outer query repeats these steps until all the rows are evaluated.

```
SELECT MAX(numeric_grade)
  FROM grade
 WHERE grade_type_code = 'PJ'
   AND section_id = 133
MAX(NUMERIC_GRADE)
------------------
                92
```

1 row selected.

Unlike the subqueries discussed in Lab 8.1, where the inner query is evaluated once, a correlated subquery executes the inner query repeatedly, once for each row in the outer query.

The EXISTS Operator

The EXISTS operator is used for correlated subqueries. It tests whether the subquery returns at least one row. The EXISTS operator returns either true or false, never unknown. Because EXISTS tests only whether a row exists, the columns shown in the SELECT list of the subquery are irrelevant. Typically, you use a single-character text literal, such as '1' or 'X', or the keyword NULL.

The following correlated subquery displays instructors where the INSTRUCTOR_ID has a matching row in the SECTION table. The result shows the INSTRUCTOR_ID, FIRST_NAME, LAST_NAME, and ZIP column values of instructors assigned to at least one section.

```
SELECT instructor_id, last_name, first_name, zip
  FROM instructor i
 WHERE EXISTS
       (SELECT 'X'
          FROM section
         WHERE i.instructor_id = instructor_id)
```

INSTRUCTOR_ID	LAST_NAME	FIRST_NAME	ZIP
101	Hanks	Fernand	10015
102	Wojick	Tom	10025
103	Schorin	Nina	10025
104	Pertez	Gary	10035
105	Morris	Anita	10015
106	Smythe	Todd	10025
108	Lowry	Charles	10025
107	Frantzen	Marilyn	10005

8 rows selected.

For every row of the INSTRUCTOR table, the outer query evaluates the inner query. It checks whether the current row's INSTRUCTOR_ID value exists for the SECTION table's INSTRUCTOR_ID column. If a row with the appropriate value is found, the condition is true, and the outer row is included in the result.

The query can also be written using the IN operator.

```
SELECT instructor_id, last_name, first_name, zip
  FROM instructor
 WHERE instructor_id IN
       (SELECT instructor_id
          FROM section)
```

Alternatively, you can write this query with an equijoin.

```
SELECT DISTINCT i.instructor_id, i.last_name,
       i.first_name, i.zip
  FROM instructor i JOIN section s
    ON i.instructor_id = s.instructor_id
```

This equijoin solution allows you to list columns found on the SECTION table, whereas the subquery solution does not. The subquery has the advantage of breaking problems into individual pieces. Not all subqueries can be transformed into joins; for example, a subquery containing an aggregate function cannot be transformed into a join.

The NOT EXISTS Operator

The NOT EXISTS operator is the opposite of the EXISTS operator; it tests whether a matching row cannot be found. The operator is the most frequently used type of correlated subquery construct. The following query displays the instructors not assigned to any section.

```
SELECT instructor_id, last_name, first_name, zip
  FROM instructor i
 WHERE NOT EXISTS
       (SELECT 'X'
          FROM section
         WHERE i.instructor_id = instructor_id)
```

INSTRUCTOR_ID	LAST_NAME	FIRST_NAME	ZIP
109	Chow	Rick	10015
110	Willig	Irene	

```
2 rows selected.
```

You cannot rewrite this particular query using an equijoin, but you can rewrite it with the NOT IN operator. However, the NOT IN operator does not always yield the same result if null values are involved, as you will see in the following example.

NOT EXISTS Versus NOT IN

Display the INSTRUCTOR_ID, FIRST_NAME, LAST_NAME, and ZIP columns from the INSTRUCTOR table where there is no corresponding zip code in the ZIPCODE table. Note that the ZIP column in the INSTRUCTOR table allows NULL values.

USING NOT EXISTS

The query with the NOT EXISTS operator retrieves instructor Irene Willig.

```
SELECT instructor_id, last_name, first_name, zip
  FROM instructor i
 WHERE NOT EXISTS
       (SELECT 'X'
```

```
        FROM zipcode
       WHERE i.zip = zip)
INSTRUCTOR_ID LAST_NAME          FIRST_NAME      ZIP
------------- ----------------   ---------------- ---
          110 Willig             Irene

1 row selected.
```

USING NOT IN

The same query rewritten with NOT IN does not return a record.

```
SELECT instructor_id, last_name, first_name, zip
  FROM instructor
 WHERE zip NOT IN
       (SELECT zip
          FROM zipcode)

no rows selected
```

As you can see, the difference between NOT EXISTS and NOT IN lies in the way NULL values are treated. Instructor Irene Willig's ZIP column contains a NULL value. The NOT EXISTS operator tests for NULL values; the NOT IN operator does not.

Avoiding Incorrect Results Through the Use of Subqueries

Many SQL statements may contain joins and aggregate functions. When you join tables together, some values may be repeated as a result of a one-to-many relationship between the joined tables. If you apply an aggregate function to the resulting repeating values, the result of the calculation may be incorrect. The following example shows a list of the total capacity for courses with enrolled students.

```
SELECT s.course_no, SUM(s.capacity)
  FROM enrollment e, section s
 WHERE e.section_id = s.section_id
 GROUP BY s.course_no
COURSE_NO SUM(S.CAPACITY)
--------- ---------------
       10              15
       20             175
...
      420              50
      450              25

25 rows selected.
```

To illustrate that the result is incorrect, look at the value for the CAPACITY column of COURSE_NO 20. The following query shows the capacity for each section, resulting in a total capacity of 80 students, rather than 175 students, as shown in the previous result.

```
SELECT section_id, capacity
  FROM section
 WHERE course_no = 20
SECTION_ID  CAPACITY
----------- --------
        81        15
        82        15
        83        25
        84        25
```

4 rows selected.

A closer look at the effect of the join without the aggregate function reveals the problem.

```
SELECT s.section_id, s.capacity, e.student_id,
       s.course_no
  FROM enrollment e, section s
 WHERE e.section_id = s.section_id
   AND s.course_no = 20
 ORDER BY section_id
SECTION_ID CAPACITY STUDENT_ID COURSE_NO
---------- -------- ---------- ---------
        81       15        103        20
        81       15        104        20
        81       15        240        20
        82       15        244        20
        82       15        245        20
        83       25        124        20
        83       25        235        20
        84       25        158        20
        84       25        199        20
```

9 rows selected.

For each enrolled student, the capacity record is repeated as the result of the join. This is correct, because for every row in the ENROLLMENT table, the corresponding SECTION_ID is looked up in the SECTION table. But when the SUM aggregate function is applied to the capacity, the capacity value of every returned record is added to the total capacity for each course. To achieve the correct result, the query needs to be written as follows.

```
SELECT course_no, SUM(capacity)
  FROM section s
 WHERE EXISTS
       (SELECT NULL
          FROM enrollment e, section sect
         WHERE e.section_id = sect.section_id
           AND sect.course_no = s.course_no)
 GROUP BY course_no
```

```
COURSE_NO  SUM(CAPACITY)
---------  -------------
       10             15
       20             80
...
      420             25
      450             25


25 rows selected.
```

The outer query checks for every row if there is a matching COURSE_NO value in the subquery. If the COURSE_NO exists, the EXISTS operator evaluates to true and will include the row of the outer query in the result. The outer query sums up the values for every row of the SECTION table. The EXISTS operator solves this particular problem, but not all queries can be solved this way; some may need to be written using inline views (see Lab 8.3).

Unnesting Queries

Sometimes Oracle implicitly transforms a subquery into a join by unnesting the query as part of its optimization strategy. For example, in the background Oracle rewrites the query if the primary and foreign keys exist on the tables and the join does not cause a Cartesian product or incorrect results because of an aggregate function in the SELECT clause.

Some subqueries cannot be unnested because they contain an aggregate function, a ROWNUM pseudocolumn (discussed in Lab 8.3), a set operator (see Chapter 9, "Set Operators"), or because it is a correlated subquery that references a query that is not in the immediate outer query block.

Subquery Performance Considerations

When you initially learn SQL, your utmost concern must be to obtain the correct result. Performance considerations should be secondary. However, as you get more experienced with the language or as you work with large data sets, you want to consider some of the effects of your constructed statements. As you have seen, sometimes you can achieve the same result with a join, a correlated subquery, or a noncorrelated subquery.

As previously mentioned, under specific circumstances, Oracle may automatically optimize your statement and implicitly transform your subquery to a join. This implicit transformation frequently results in better performance without your having to worry about applying any optimization techniques.

Performance benefits of one type of subquery over another type may be noticeable when you are working with very large volumes of data. To optimize subqueries, you must understand the key difference between correlated and noncorrelated subqueries.

A correlated subquery evaluates the inner query for every row of the outer query. Therefore, your optimization strategy should focus on eliminating as many rows as possible from the outer query. You can do this by adding additional restricting criteria in the WHERE clause of the statement. The advantage of correlated subqueries is that they can use indexes on the correlated columns, if any exist.

A noncorrelated subquery executes the inner query first and then feeds this result to the outer query. The inner query is executed once. Generally speaking, this query is best suited for situations in which the inner query does not returns a very large result set and where no indexes exist on the compared columns.

If your query involves a NOT EXISTS condition, you cannot modify it to a NOT IN condition if the subquery can return null values. In many circumstances, NOT EXISTS offers better performance because indexes are usually used.

Because the STUDENT schema contains a fairly small number of records, the difference in execution time is minimal. The illustrated various solutions throughout this book allow you to look at different ways to approach and solve problems. You might want to use those solutions as starting points for ideas and perform your own tests, based on your distinct environment, data volume, and requirements.

Good performance is subject to many variables that can have a significant impact on the execution time of your statements. In Chapter 18, "SQL Optimization," you will learn more about the topic of SQL performance optimization.

▼ LAB 8.2 EXERCISES

a) Explain what the following correlated subquery accomplishes.

```
SELECT section_id, course_no
  FROM section s
 WHERE 2 >
        (SELECT COUNT(*)
           FROM enrollment
          WHERE section_id = s.section_id)
```

SECTION_ID	COURSE_NO
79	350
80	10
...	
145	100
149	120

27 rows selected.

b) List the sections where the enrollment exceeds the capacity of a section and show the number of enrollments for the section using a correlated subquery.

c) Write a SQL statement to determine the total number of students enrolled, using the EXISTS operator. Count students enrolled in more than one course as one.

d) Show the STUDENT_ID, last name, and first name of each student enrolled in three or more classes.

e) Which courses do not have sections assigned? Use a correlated subquery in the solution.

f) Which sections have no students enrolled? Use a correlated subquery in the solution and order the result by the course number, in ascending order.

▼ LAB 8.2 EXERCISE ANSWERS

a) Explain what the following correlated subquery accomplishes.

```
SELECT section_id, course_no
  FROM section s
 WHERE 2 >
       (SELECT COUNT(*)
          FROM enrollment
         WHERE section_id = s.section_id)
```

SECTION_ID	COURSE_NO
79	350
80	10
...	
145	100
149	120

27 rows selected.

ANSWER: The correlated subquery displays the SECTION_ID and COURSE_NO of sections with fewer than two students enrolled. It includes sections that have no students enrolled.

For each row of the SECTION table, the number literal 2 is compared to the result of the COUNT(*) function of the inner subquery. For each row of the outer SECTION table with the S.SECTION_ID column being the correlated column, the inner query counts the number of rows for this individual SECTION_ID. If no enrollment is found for the particular section, the COUNT function returns a zero; the row satisfies the criteria that 2 is greater than zero and is included in the result set.

Let's look at one of the rows of the SECTION table, specifically the row with the SECTION_ID value 80. The inner query returns a count of 1.

```
SELECT COUNT(*)
  FROM enrollment
 WHERE section_id = 80
```

COUNT(*)
1

1 row selected.

When the number 1 is compared in the WHERE clause of the outer query, you see that 2 > 1 is true; therefore, this section is returned in the result.

You can write two queries to verify that the result of the correlated query is correct. First, write a query that shows sections where the enrollment is fewer than 2 students. This query returns 13 rows.

```
SELECT section_id, COUNT(*)
  FROM enrollment
 GROUP BY section_id
HAVING COUNT(*) < 2
```

SECTION_ID	COUNT(*)
80	1
96	1
...	
145	1
149	1

13 rows selected.

Then write a second query to show the sections that have no enrollments (that is, the SECTION_ID does not exist in the ENROLLMENT table). To determine these sections, you can use the NOT IN operator because the SECTION_ID in the ENROLLMENT table is defined as NOT NULL.

```
SELECT section_id
  FROM section
 WHERE section_id NOT IN
       (SELECT section_id
          FROM enrollment)
```

SECTION_ID
79
93
...
136
139

14 rows selected.

The combination of the 13 and 14 rows from the last two queries returns a total of 27.

Alternatively, you can combine the results of the two queries with the UNION operator, as discussed in Chapter 9.

b) List the sections where the enrollment exceeds the capacity of a section and show the number of enrollments for the section using a correlated subquery.

ANSWER: The correlated query solution executes the outer query's GROUP BY clause first; then, for every group, the subquery is executed to determine whether it satisfies the condition in the HAVING clause. Only sections where the number of enrolled students exceeds the capacity for the respective section are returned for output.

```
SELECT section_id, COUNT(*)
  FROM enrollment e
 GROUP BY section_id
```

```
HAVING COUNT(*) >
        (SELECT capacity
           FROM section
          WHERE e.section_id = section_id)
SECTION_ID  COUNT(*)
----------- --------
       101       12
```

1 row selected.

Alternatively, you can solve this problem by using an equijoin and an aggregate function. You evaluate the enrollment count in the HAVING clause and compare it with the capacity. The additional CAPACITY column in the output validates the correct result.

```
SELECT e.section_id, COUNT(*), s.capacity
  FROM enrollment e, section s
 WHERE e.section_id = s.section_id
 GROUP BY e.section_id, s.capacity
HAVING COUNT(*) > s.capacity
SECTION_ID  COUNT(*)  CAPACITY
----------  ----------  --------
       101        12        10
```

1 row selected.

When you join tables and apply aggregate functions, be sure the resulting rows provide the correct result of the aggregate function.

c) Write a SQL statement to determine the total number of students enrolled, using the EXISTS operator. Count students enrolled in more than one course as one.

ANSWER: For every student, the query checks whether a row exists in the ENROLLMENT table. If this is true, the record is part of the result set. After Oracle determines all the rows that satisfy the EXISTS condition, the aggregate function COUNT is applied to determine the total number of students.

```
SELECT COUNT(*)
  FROM student s
 WHERE EXISTS
        (SELECT NULL
           FROM enrollment
          WHERE student_id = s.student_id)
 COUNT(*)
---------
      165
```

1 row selected.

The same result can be obtained with the following query. Because the ENROLLMENT table may contain multiple STUDENT_IDs if the student is enrolled in several sections, you need to count the distinct occurrences of STUDENT_ID to obtain the correct result.

```
SELECT COUNT(DISTINCT student_id)
  FROM enrollment
 COUNT(DISTINCT STUDENT_ID)
--------------------------
                       165
```

1 row selected.

d) Show the STUDENT_ID, last name, and first name of each student enrolled in three or more classes.

   ANSWER: There are four possible solutions to illustrate alternate ways to obtain the same result set.

SOLUTION 1: CORRELATED SUBQUERY

For each record in the STUDENT table, the inner query is executed to determine whether the STUDENT_ID occurs three or more times in the ENROLLMENT table. The inner query's SELECT clause lists the NULL keyword, whereas in the previous examples, a text literal was selected. It is completely irrelevant what columns are selected in the subquery with the EXISTS and NOT EXISTS operators because these operators only check for the existence or nonexistence of rows.

```
SELECT first_name, last_name, student_id
  FROM student s
 WHERE EXISTS
        (SELECT NULL
           FROM enrollment
          WHERE s.student_id = student_id
          GROUP BY student_id
         HAVING COUNT(*) >= 3)
 FIRST_NAME                     LAST_NAME      STUDENT_ID
 ------------------------------ -------------- ----------
 Daniel                         Wicelinski            124
 Roger                          Snow                  238
 ...
 Salewa                         Zuckerberg            184
 Yvonne                         Williams              214
```

7 rows selected.

SOLUTION 2: EQUIJOIN

The next solution joins the STUDENT and ENROLLMENT tables. Students enrolled multiple times are grouped into one row, and the COUNT function counts the occurrences of each student's enrollment record. Only those having three or more records in the ENROLLMENT table are included.

```
SELECT first_name, last_name, s.student_id
  FROM enrollment e, student s
 WHERE e.student_id = s.student_id
 GROUP BY first_name, last_name, s.student_id
HAVING COUNT(*) >= 3
```

Although Solution 2 achieves the correct result, you need to be aware of the dangers of aggregate functions in joins.

SOLUTION 3: IN SUBQUERY

This subquery returns only STUDENT_IDs with three or more enrollments. The result is then fed to the outer query.

```
SELECT first_name, last_name, student_id
  FROM student
 WHERE student_id IN
         (SELECT student_id
            FROM enrollment
          GROUP BY student_id
          HAVING COUNT(*) >= 3)
```

SOLUTION 4: ANOTHER CORRELATED SUBQUERY

The number literal 3 is compared to the result of the correlated subquery. It counts the enrollment records for the individual students. This solution is similar to the solution in exercise a in this lab.

```
SELECT last_name, first_name, student_id
  FROM student s
 WHERE 3 <= (SELECT COUNT(*)
               FROM enrollment
              WHERE s.student_id = student_id)
```

e) Which courses do not have sections assigned? Use a correlated subquery in the solution.

ANSWER: For every course in the COURSE table, the NOT EXISTS condition probes the SECTION table to determine whether a row with the same course number *does not* exist. If the course number is not found, the WHERE clause evaluates to true, and the record is included in the result set.

```
SELECT course_no, description
  FROM course c
 WHERE NOT EXISTS
         (SELECT 'X'
            FROM section
           WHERE c.course_no = course_no)
```

```
COURSE_NO DESCRIPTION
--------- ----------------------------
       80 Programming Techniques
      430 Java Developer III

2 rows selected.
```

Note you can also write the query as follows.

```
SELECT course_no, description
  FROM course c
 WHERE NOT EXISTS
         (SELECT 'X'
            FROM section s
           WHERE c.course_no = s.course_no)
```

The SECTION table uses the table alias named s, which the S.COURSE_NO column refers to. This alias is not required; it simply clarifies the column's source table. When you use a columns without an alias, it is understood that the columns refers to the table in the current subquery. However, you must use a table alias for the C.COURSE_NO column, referencing the COURSE_NO in the outer query; otherwise, the query is not correlated.

As an alternative, you can obtain the same result by using the NOT IN operator. Because the COURSE_NO column in the SECTION table is defined as NOT NULL, the query returns the same result.

```
SELECT course_no, description
  FROM course
 WHERE course_no NOT IN
       (SELECT course_no
          FROM section)
```

f) Which sections have no students enrolled? Use a correlated subquery in the solution and order the result by the course number, in ascending order.

ANSWER: The result contains only rows where the SECTION_ID does not exist in the ENROLLMENT table. The inner query executes for each row of the outer query.

```
SELECT course_no, section_id
  FROM section s
 WHERE NOT EXISTS
       (SELECT NULL
          FROM enrollment
         WHERE s.section_id = section_id)
 ORDER BY course_no
```

COURSE_NO	SECTION_ID
25	93
124	129
...	
350	79

```
14 rows selected.
```

You can achieve the same result by using the NOT IN operator because the SECTION_ID column in the ENROLLMENT table is defined as NOT NULL.

```
SELECT course_no, section_id
  FROM section
 WHERE section_id NOT IN
       (SELECT section_id
          FROM enrollment)
 ORDER BY course_no
```

Lab 8.2 Quiz

In order to test your progress, you should be able to answer the following questions.

1) The NOT EXISTS operator tests for occurrences of nulls.

   _____ a) True
   _____ b) False

2) In a correlated subquery, the inner query is executed repeatedly.

   _____ a) True
   _____ b) False

3) The operators IN and EXISTS are somewhat equivalent.

   _____ a) True
   _____ b) False

4) What problem does the following SQL statement solve?

```
SELECT student_id, section_id
  FROM enrollment e
 WHERE NOT EXISTS
        (SELECT '1'
           FROM grade g
          WHERE e.section_id = section_id
            AND e.student_id = student_id)
```

   _____ a) Show the enrolled students and their respective sections that have grades assigned.
   _____ b) Determine the students and their sections where no grades have been assigned.
   _____ c) Determine which students are not enrolled.
   _____ d) Determine which students are not enrolled and do not have grades.
   _____ e) This is an invalid query.

5) Always evaluate the result of a join first, before applying an aggregate function.

   _____ a) True
   _____ b) False

ANSWERS APPEAR IN APPENDIX A.

LAB 8.3
Inline Views and Scalar Subquery Expressions

LAB OBJECTIVES

After this lab, you will be able to:

▶ Write Inline Views
▶ Write Scalar Subquery Expressions

Inline views and scalar subquery expressions help you simplify the writing of SQL statements. They allow you to break down complicated query requests into individual queries and then combine the results.

Inline Views

Inline views, also referred to as queries in the FROM clause, allow you to treat a query as a virtual table or view. The following is an example of an inline view.

```
SELECT e.student_id, e.section_id, s.last_name
  FROM (SELECT student_id, section_id, enroll_date
          FROM enrollment
         WHERE student_id = 123) e,
       student s
 WHERE e.student_id = s.student_id
STUDENT_ID SECTION_ID LAST_NAME
---------- ---------- ---------
       123         87 Radicola

1 row selected.
```

An inline view is written in the FROM clause of a query and enclosed in a set of parentheses; this query has the alias e. The result of this query is evaluated and executed first, and then the result is joined to the STUDENT table.

An inline view acts just like a virtual table, or, for that matter, like a view. A view is a query definition stored in the database that looks just like a table. It does not have any physical rows because a view is actually a stored query that is executed only when the view is accessed. You'll learn more about views in Chapter 13, "Indexes, Sequences, and Views."

One of the differences between a view and an inline view is that an inline view does not need to be created and stored in the data dictionary. You can create an inline view or a virtual table by placing your query in the FROM clause of a SQL statement.

Inline view queries may look complicated, but they are easy to understand. They allow you to break down complex problems into simple queries. The following query uses two inline views to return the actual number of enrollments for course number 20 and joins this result to the capacity of the course. The actual and potential revenue are then computed by multiplying the course cost by the number of enrollments and the by the respective capacity of the course.

```
SELECT enr.num_enrolled "Enrollments",
       enr.num_enrolled * c.cost "Actual Revenue",
       cap.capacity "Total Capacity",
       cap.capacity * c.cost "Potential Revenue"
  FROM (SELECT COUNT(*) num_enrolled
          FROM enrollment e, section s
         WHERE s.course_no = 20
           AND s.section_id = e.section_id) enr,
       (SELECT SUM(capacity) capacity
          FROM section
         WHERE course_no = 20) cap,
       course c
 WHERE c.course_no = 20
```

Enrollments	Actual Revenue	Total Capacity	Potential Revenue
9	10755	80	95600

1 row selected.

The easiest way to understand the query is to look at the result set for each inline view. The first query, referenced with the alias enr, returns the number of students enrolled in course number 20. It requires a join between the ENROLLMENT table and the SECTION table, because the number of students enrolled per section is in the ENROLLMENT table, and the COURSE_NO column is found in the SECTION table. The column joining the two tables is the SECTION_ID. The query returns one row and indicates that nine students are enrolled in course number 20.

```
SELECT COUNT(*) num_enrolled
  FROM enrollment e, section s
 WHERE s.course_no = 20
   AND s.section_id = e.section_id
```

NUM_ENROLLED
9

1 row selected.

The second query, with the alias cap, uses the aggregate function SUM to add all the values in the CAPACITY column for course number 20. Because the SUM function is an aggregate function, it returns one row with the total capacity of 80 for all the sections for course number 20.

```
SELECT SUM(capacity) capacity
  FROM section
 WHERE course_no = 20
CAPACITY
---------
       80
```

1 row selected.

The last table in the FROM clause of the query is the COURSE table. This table holds the course cost to compute the actual revenue and the potential revenue. The query also retrieves one row.

The results of the inline views, which are identified with the aliases enr and cap, are not joined together with the COURSE table, thus creating a Cartesian product. Because a multiplication of the number of rows from each involved inline view and table, 1*1*1, results in one row, this query returns the one row for course number 20. A join condition is not required in this case, but it can be added for clarification.

TOP-N QUERY

An example of a top-n query is a query that allows you to determine the top three students for a particular section. To accomplish this, you need to understand the use of the ROWNUM pseudocolumn.

This column returns a number indicating the order in which Oracle returns the rows from a table or set of tables. You can use ROWNUM to limit the number of rows returned, as in the following example. It returns the first five rows.

```
SELECT last_name, first_name
  FROM student
 WHERE ROWNUM <=5
LAST_NAME                       FIRST_NAME
------------------------        ----------
Cadet                           Austin V.
M. Orent                        Frank
Winnicki                        Yvonne
Madej                           Mike
Valentine                       Paula
```

5 rows selected.

A pseudocolumn is not a real column in a table; you can use SELECT on this column, but you cannot manipulate its values. You will learn more about other pseudocolumns (for example, LEVEL, NEXTVAL, CURRVAL, ROWID) throughout this book.

You can combine the ROWNUM pseudocolumn and an inline view to determine the three highest final examination grades of section 101, as illustrated in the following query.

```
SELECT ROWNUM, numeric_grade
  FROM (SELECT DISTINCT numeric_grade
          FROM grade
         WHERE section_id = 101
           AND grade_type_code = 'FI'
         ORDER BY numeric_grade DESC)
 WHERE ROWNUM <= 3
  ROWNUM NUMERIC_GRADE
--------- -------------
        1            99
        2            92
        3            91
```

3 rows selected.

The inline view selects the distinct values in the NUMERIC_GRADE column for all final examination grades where SECTION_ID equals 101. This result is ordered by the NUMERIC_GRADE, in descending order, with the highest NUMERIC_GRADE listed first. The outer query uses the ordered result of the inline view and the ROWNUM column to return only the first three. By ordering the results within the inline view, this construct provides a method to both limit and order the number of rows returned. For even more sophisticated ranking functionality and for analytical and statistical functions, see Chapter 17, "Exploring Data Warehousing Features."

PRACTICAL USES OF INLINE VIEWS

If you face a problem that is complex and challenging, using inline views may be the best way to solve the problem without violating any of the SQL syntax restrictions. Inline views allow you to break down the problem into individual queries and then combine the results through joins. If you want to write top-n queries without using any of the ranking functions (discussed in Chapter 17), you need to use an inline view.

Scalar Subquery Expressions

You have already learned about the scalar subquery, which is a query that returns a single-column, single-row value. You can use a scalar subquery expression in most syntax that calls for an expression. The next examples show you how to use this functionality in the SELECT list, in the WHERE clause, in the ORDER BY clause of a query, in a CASE expression, or as part of a function call.

SCALAR SUBQUERY EXPRESSION IN THE SELECT CLAUSE

The following query returns all the Connecticut zip codes and a count of how many students live in each zip code. The query is correlated as the scalar subquery, and it is executed for each individual zip code. For some zip codes, no students are in the STUDENT table; therefore, the subquery's COUNT function returns a zero. (The query can also be written as an outer join, as discussed in Chapter 10, "Complex Joins.")

```
SELECT city, state, zip,
       (SELECT COUNT(*)
          FROM student s
         WHERE s.zip = z.zip) AS student_count
  FROM zipcode z
 WHERE state = 'CT'
CITY                      ST ZIP   STUDENT_COUNT
-------------------       -------- -------------
Ansonia                   CT 06401             0
...
Stamford                  CT 06907             1

19 rows selected.
```

Scalar subquery expressions can become notoriously inefficient because Oracle can often execute table joins faster, particularly when scans of the entire result set are involved. Following is an example where the result of an equijoin is achieved by using a scalar subquery.

```
SELECT student_id, last_name,
       (SELECT state
          FROM zipcode z
         WHERE z.zip = s.zip) AS state
  FROM student s
 WHERE student_id BETWEEN 100 AND 120
STUDENT_ID LAST_NAME                        ST
---------- ------------------------         --
       102 Crocitto                         NY
...
       120 Alexander                        NY

17 rows selected.
```

SCALAR SUBQUERY EXPRESSION IN THE WHERE CLAUSE

The following query is an example of a scalar subquery expression in the WHERE clause of a SELECT statement. The WHERE clause limits the result set to those students who enrolled in more courses than the average student. The equivalent equijoin is probably more efficient.

```
SELECT student_id, last_name
  FROM student s
 WHERE (SELECT COUNT(*)
          FROM enrollment e
         WHERE s.student_id = e.student_id) >
              (SELECT AVG(COUNT(*))
                 FROM enrollment
                GROUP BY student_id)
 ORDER BY 1
STUDENT_ID LAST_NAME
---------- ---------
       102 Crocitto
```

```
...
      283 Perkins

52 rows selected.
```

SCALAR SUBQUERY EXPRESSION IN THE ORDER BY CLAUSE

You might wonder why you would ever need to execute a scalar subquery expression in the ORDER BY clause. The following example illustrates that you can sort by a column that does not even exist in the STUDENT table. The query lists the STUDENT_ID and LAST_NAME columns of those students with an ID between 230 and 235. The result is ordered by the number of sections a respective student is enrolled in. If you execute a separate query to verify the result, you see that student Brendler is enrolled in one section and student Jung in three sections.

```
SELECT student_id, last_name
  FROM student s
 WHERE student_id BETWEEN 230 AND 235
 ORDER BY (SELECT COUNT(*)
             FROM enrollment e
            WHERE s.student_id = e.student_id) DESC
STUDENT_ID LAST_NAME
---------- ---------
       232 Jung
...
       234 Brendler

5 rows selected.
```

SCALAR SUBQUERY EXPRESSION AND THE CASE EXPRESSION

Scalar subquery expressions are particularly handy in CASE expressions and within the DECODE function. The following example demonstrates their extraordinarily powerful functionality. The SELECT statement lists the costs of COURSE_NO 20 and 80. The column labeled Test CASE illustrates the result of the CASE expression.

Depending on the value of the COST column, a comparison against a scalar subquery expression is executed. For example, the COST column is compared to the average COST of all courses, and if the value in the COST column is less than or equal to that average, the value in the COST column is multiplied by 1.5.

The next WHEN comparison checks whether the cost is equal to the highest course cost. If so, it displays the value of the COST column for COURSE_NO 20. If the scalar subquery expression determines that the row with COURSE_NO 20 does not exist, the scalar subquery expression evaluates to NULL.

```
SELECT course_no, cost,
       CASE WHEN cost <= (SELECT AVG(cost) FROM course) THEN
                cost *1.5
```

```
                    WHEN cost =  (SELECT MAX(cost) FROM course) THEN
                                 (SELECT cost FROM course
                                     WHERE course_no = 20)
                    ELSE cost
                 END "Test CASE"
       FROM course
    WHERE course_no IN (20, 80)
    ORDER BY 2
    COURSE_NO      COST Test CASE
    -------------- ---- ---------
           20      1195    1792.5
           80      1595      1195
```

2 rows selected.

The next example shows the use of the scalar subquery expression in the condition part of the CASE expression. The cost of course number 134, which is 1195, is multiplied by 2, effectively doubling the cost. This result is then compared to see if it's less than or equal to the average cost of all courses.

```
SELECT course_no, cost,
       CASE WHEN (SELECT cost*2
                    FROM course
                   WHERE course_no = 134)
                 <= (SELECT AVG(cost) FROM course) THEN
                    cost *1.5
            WHEN cost = (SELECT MAX(cost) FROM course) THEN
                        (SELECT cost FROM course
                            WHERE course_no = 20)
            ELSE cost
         END "Test CASE"
   FROM course
  WHERE course_no IN (20, 80)
  ORDER BY 2
  COURSE_NO       COST  Test CASE
  --------------  ----- ----------
         20       1195       1195
         80       1595       1195
```

2 rows selected.

SCALAR SUBQUERY EXPRESSIONS AND FUNCTIONS

The next example shows the use of a scalar subquery expression within a function. For every retrieved row, the UPPER function is executed, which in turn retrieves the respective student's last name from the STUDENT table. A join between the STUDENT and ENROLLMENT tables to obtain the same information is typically more efficient, but the example illustrates another of the many versatile uses of scalar subquery expressions.

```
SELECT student_id, section_id,
       UPPER((SELECT last_name
                FROM student
               WHERE student_id = e.student_id))
       "Last Name in Caps"
  FROM enrollment e
 WHERE student_id BETWEEN 100 AND 110
STUDENT_ID SECTION_ID Last Name in Caps
---------- ---------- -----------------
       102         86 CROCITTO
       102         89 CROCITTO
...
       110         95 MARTIN
       110        154 MARTIN

13 rows selected.
```

ERRORS IN SCALAR SUBQUERY EXPRESSIONS

Just as you learned in Lab 8.1, the scalar subquery expression must always return one row and one column. Otherwise, Oracle returns error ORA-01427: single-row subquery returns more than one row. If you list multiple columns, you receive error ORA-00913: "too many values." If your subquery does not return any row, a null value is returned.

PERFORMANCE CONSIDERATIONS

While you have seen that scalar subquery expressions can be used anywhere expressions are allowed, their application may not be practical under all circumstances. For example, to display a value from another table, a join is frequently more efficient than a scalar subquery in the SELECT list. Because the scalar subquery expression will be evaluated for each row, you should try to eliminate as many rows as possible prior to the execution of the scalar subquery expression step. This can be achieved by adding additional restricting conditions to the WHERE clause. As you might expect, there are many ways to achieve the same result, using various SQL syntax options; this chapter illustrates some of these possibilities. Unfortunately, there is no specific set of guidelines you can follow to ensure that your SQL statement executes in a timely manner. Many variables affect performance; however, the Oracle optimizer (discussed in Chapter 18) typically does a pretty good job of efficiently processing your statement.

▼ LAB 8.3 EXERCISES

a) Write a query that displays the SECTION_ID and COURSE_NO columns, along with the number of students enrolled in sections with the IDs 93, 101, and 103. Use a scalar subquery to write the query. The result should look similar to the following output.

```
SECTION_ID COURSE_NO NUM_ENROLLED
---------- --------- ------------
        93        25            0
       103       310            4
       101       240           12
```

3 rows selected.

b) What problem does the following query solve?

```
SELECT g.student_id, section_id, g.numeric_grade,
       gr.average
  FROM grade g JOIN
       (SELECT section_id, AVG(numeric_grade) average
          FROM grade
         WHERE section_id IN (94, 106)
           AND grade_type_code = 'FI'
         GROUP BY section_id) gr
 USING (section_id)
 WHERE g.grade_type_code = 'FI'
   AND g.numeric_grade > gr.average
STUDENT_ID SECTION_ID NUMERIC_GRADE   AVERAGE
---------- ---------- ------------- ---------
       140         94            85      84.5
       200        106            92        89
       145        106            91        89
       130        106            90        89
```

4 rows selected.

c) For each course number, display the total capacity of the individual sections. Include the number of students enrolled and the percentage of the course that is filled. The result should look similar to the following output.

```
COURSE_NO TOTAL_CAPACITY TOTAL_STUDENTS Filled Percentage
--------- -------------- -------------- ------------------
      240             25             13                 52
      230             27             14              51.85
...
      450             25              1                  4
      134             65              2               3.08
```

25 rows selected.

d) Determine the top five courses with the largest numbers of enrollments.

▼ LAB 8.3 EXERCISE ANSWERS

a) Write a query that displays the SECTION_ID and COURSE_NO columns, along with the number of students enrolled in sections with the IDs 93, 101, and 103. Use a scalar subquery to write the query. The result should look similar to the following output.

```
SECTION_ID COURSE_NO NUM_ENROLLED
---------- --------- ------------
        93        25            0
       103       310            4
       101       240           12
```

3 rows selected.

ANSWER: This query uses a scalar subquery in the SELECT clause of the SQL statement. The scalar subquery is correlated and determines for each of the three SECTION_ID values the number of rows in the ENROLLMENT table.

```
SELECT section_id, course_no,
       (SELECT COUNT(*)
          FROM enrollment e
         WHERE s.section_id = e.section_id)
         AS num_enrolled
  FROM section s
 WHERE section_id IN (101, 103, 93)
```

b) What problem does the following query solve?

```
SELECT g.student_id, section_id, g.numeric_grade,
       gr.average
  FROM grade g JOIN
       (SELECT section_id, AVG(numeric_grade) average
          FROM grade
         WHERE section_id IN (94, 106)
           AND grade_type_code = 'FI'
         GROUP BY section_id) gr
 USING (section_id)
 WHERE g.grade_type_code = 'FI'
   AND g.numeric_grade > gr.average
```

```
STUDENT_ID SECTION_ID NUMERIC_GRADE   AVERAGE
---------- ---------- ------------- ---------
       140         94            85      84.5
       200        106            92        89
       145        106            91        89
       130        106            90        89
```

4 rows selected.

ANSWER: The query show for sections 94 and 106 those students with a final examination grade higher than the average for each respective section.

The inline view determines the average final examination grade for each of the sections 94 and 106. This query is executed first. The result is then joined with the GRADE table, where the

SECTION_ID column agrees. The filtering criteria is that the GRADE_TYPE_CODE column equals 'FI', which stands for final examination grade, and the last condition chooses only those rows that have a grade higher than the average for each respective section.

c) For each course number, display the total capacity of the individual sections. Include the number of students enrolled and the percentage of the course that is filled. The result should look similar to the following output.

```
COURSE_NO TOTAL_CAPACITY TOTAL_STUDENTS Filled Percentage
--------- -------------- -------------- -----------------
      240             25             13                52
      230             27             14             51.85
...
      450             25              1                 4
      134             65              2              3.08
```

25 rows selected.

ANSWER: This query uses inline views to retrieve the total capacity and number of students enrolled. The Filled Percentage column is calculated using the resulting values from the inline views and is used to order the result.

```
SELECT a.course_no, total_capacity, total_students,
       ROUND(100/total_capacity*total_students, 2)
       "Filled Percentage"
  FROM (SELECT COUNT(*) total_students, s.course_no
          FROM enrollment e, section s
         WHERE e.section_id = s.section_id
         GROUP BY s.course_no) a,
       (SELECT SUM(capacity) total_capacity, course_no
          FROM section
         GROUP BY course_no) b
 WHERE b.course_no = a.course_no
 ORDER BY "Filled Percentage" DESC
```

It helps to build the query step by step, looking at the individual queries. The first query, with the alias a, returns the total number of students enrolled in each course.

```
SELECT COUNT(*) total_students, s.course_no
  FROM enrollment e, section s
 WHERE e.section_id = s.section_id
 GROUP BY s.course_no
TOTAL_STUDENTS COURSE_NO
-------------- ---------
             1        10
             9        20
...
             2       420
             1       450
```

25 rows selected.

The second query, with the alias b, returns the total capacity for each course.

```
SELECT SUM(capacity) total_capacity, course_no
  FROM section
 GROUP BY course_no
TOTAL_CAPACITY COURSE_NO
-------------- ---------
           15        10
           80        20
...
           25       420
           25       450

28 rows selected.
```

Then you join the two queries by the common column, COURSE_NO, using the aliases a and b assigned in the inline view queries. The outer query references the columns TOTAL_STUDENTS and TOTAL_CAPACITY. The ROUND function computes the percentage, with two-digit precision after the comma. The result is sorted by this percentage, in descending order.

d) Determine the top five courses with the largest numbers of enrollments.

ANSWER: This question is solved with an inline view and the ROWNUM pseudocolumn. You will learn about more advanced ranking functionality in Chapter 17.

```
SELECT ROWNUM Ranking, course_no, num_enrolled
  FROM (SELECT COUNT(*) num_enrolled, s.course_no
          FROM enrollment e, section s
         WHERE e.section_id = s.section_id
         GROUP BY s.course_no
         ORDER BY 1 DESC)
 WHERE ROWNUM <= 5
   RANKING COURSE_NO NUM_ENROLLED
--------- --------- ------------
        1        25           45
        2       122           24
        3       120           23
        4       140           15
        5       230           14

5 rows selected.
```

Lab 8.3 Quiz

In order to test your progress, you should be able to answer the following questions.

1) The ORDER BY clause is allowed in an inline view.

    _____ a) True
    _____ b) False

2) Scalar subqueries return one or more rows.

    _____ a) True
    _____ b) False

3) Inline views are stored in the data dictionary.

    _____ a) True
    _____ b) False

4) ROWNUM is an actual column in a table.

    _____ a) True
    _____ b) False

ANSWERS APPEAR IN APPENDIX A.

LAB 8.4
ANY, SOME, and ALL Operators in Subqueries

LAB OBJECTIVES

After this lab, you will be able to:

▶ Use the ANY, SOME, and ALL Operators in Subqueries
▶ Understand the Differences between These Operators

You are already familiar with the IN operator, which compares a list of values for equality. The ANY, SOME, and ALL operators are related to the IN operator as they also compare against a list of values. In addition, these operators allow >, <, >=, and <= comparisons.

The ANY operator checks whether any value in the list makes the condition true. The ALL operator returns rows if the condition is true for all the values in the list. The SOME operator is identical to ANY, and the two can be used interchangeably. Before applying these operators to subqueries, examine their effect on a simple list of values.

The following query retrieves all the grades for SECTION_ID 84.

```
SELECT section_id, numeric_grade
  FROM grade
 WHERE section_id = 84
SECTION_ID NUMERIC_GRADE
---------- -------------
        84            88
        84            99
        84            77
        84            88

4 rows selected.
```

The familiar IN operator in the next SQL statement chooses all the grades that are equal to either 77 or 99.

```
SELECT section_id, numeric_grade
  FROM grade
 WHERE section_id = 84
   AND numeric_grade IN (77, 99)
```

```
SECTION_ID NUMERIC_GRADE
---------- -------------
        84            99
        84            77
```

2 rows selected.

If you want to perform a comparison such as less than (<) against a list of values, use either the ANY, SOME, or ALL operator.

ANY and SOME

The following SQL query looks for any rows where the value in the NUMERIC_GRADE column is less than either value in the list.

```
SELECT section_id, numeric_grade
  FROM grade
 WHERE section_id = 84
   AND numeric_grade < ANY (80, 90)
SECTION_ID NUMERIC_GRADE
---------- -------------
        84            88
        84            88
        84            77
```

3 rows selected.

The query returns the NUMERIC_GRADE values 77 and 88. For the rows with NUMERIC_GRADE 88, the condition is true because 88 is less than 90, but the condition is not true for the value 80. However, because the condition needs to be true for any of the records compared in the list, the row is included in the result.

The following query performs a greater-than comparison with the ANY operator.

```
SELECT section_id, numeric_grade
  FROM grade
 WHERE section_id = 84
   AND numeric_grade > ANY (80, 90)
SECTION_ID NUMERIC_GRADE
---------- -------------
        84            88
        84            99
        84            88
```

3 rows selected.

Because the records with NUMERIC_GRADE 88 are greater than 80, they are included. NUMERIC_GRADE 99 is greater than both 80 and 90 and is therefore also included in the result set, although just one of the conditions is sufficient to be included in the result set.

The ANY operator with the = operator is the equivalent of the IN operator. There are no rows that have a NUMERIC_GRADE of either 80 or 90.

```
SELECT section_id, numeric_grade
  FROM grade
 WHERE section_id = 84
   AND numeric_grade = ANY (80, 90)
```

no rows selected

The following query is the logical equivalent to the = ANY condition.

```
SELECT section_id, numeric_grade
  FROM grade
 WHERE section_id = 84
   AND numeric_grade IN (80, 90)
```

no rows selected

The ALL Operator

The ALL operator returns true if every value in the list satisfies the condition. In the following example, all the records in the GRADE table must be less than 80 and 90. This condition is true only for the row with the NUMERIC_GRADE value 77, which is less than both 80 and 90.

```
SELECT section_id, numeric_grade
  FROM grade
 WHERE section_id = 84
   AND numeric_grade < ALL (80, 90)
SECTION_ID NUMERIC_GRADE
---------- -------------
        84            77
```

1 row selected.

A SQL statement using <> ALL is equivalent to NOT IN.

```
SELECT section_id, numeric_grade
  FROM grade
 WHERE section_id = 84
   AND numeric_grade <> ALL (80, 90)
SECTION_ID NUMERIC_GRADE
---------- -------------
        84            88
        84            99
        84            77
        84            88
```

4 rows selected.

Whenever a subquery with the ALL operator fails to return a row, the query is automatically true. This is different from the ANY operator, which returns false.

▼ LAB 8.4 EXERCISES

a) Write a SELECT statement to display the STUDENT_ID, SECTION_ID, and grade for every student who received a final examination grade better than *all* of his or her individual homework grades.

b) Based on the result of exercise a, what do you observe about the row with STUDENT_ID 102 and SECTION_ID 89?

c) Select the STUDENT_ID, SECTION_ID, and grade of every student who received a final examination grade better than *any* of his or her individual homework grades.

d) Based on the result of exercise c, explain the result of the row with STUDENT_ID 102 and SECTION_ID 89.

▼ LAB 8.4 EXERCISE **ANSWERS**

a) Write a SELECT statement to display the STUDENT_ID, SECTION_ID, and grade for every student who received a final examination grade better than *all* of his or her individual homework grades.

ANSWER: Use a correlated subquery to compare each individual student's final examination grade with his or her homework grades for a particular section. The output includes only those records where the final examination grade is higher than all the homework grades.

```
SELECT student_id, section_id, numeric_grade
  FROM grade g
 WHERE grade_type_code = 'FI'
   AND numeric_grade > ALL
       (SELECT numeric_grade
          FROM grade
         WHERE grade_type_code = 'HM'
           AND g.section_id = section_id
           AND g.student_id = student_id)
```

STUDENT_ID	SECTION_ID	NUMERIC_GRADE
102	89	92
124	83	99
143	85	92
...		
215	156	90
283	99	85

96 rows selected.

To verify the result, use STUDENT_ID 143 and SECTION_ID 85 as an example. The highest grade for all of the homework is 91, and the lowest is 81. The grade achieved on the final examination is 92.

```
SELECT student_id, section_id, grade_type_code,
       MAX(numeric_grade) max, MIN(numeric_grade) min
  FROM grade
 WHERE student_id = 143
   AND section_id = 85
   AND grade_type_code IN ('HM', 'FI')
 GROUP BY student_id, section_id, grade_type_code
STUDENT_ID SECTION_ID GR          MAX   MIN
---------- ---------- -------- ----- -----
       143         85 FI         92    92
       143         85 HM         91    81
```

2 rows selected.

The student with ID 143 enrolled in section 85 is correctly selected for output. As shown in the result, the condition that the final examination grade be greater than all the homework grades is satisfied.

The following query verifies that the student with ID 179 enrolled in section 116 has a lower grade in the final exam than in all the homework grades. Therefore, the row is not included in the set.

```
SELECT student_id, section_id, grade_type_code,
       MAX(numeric_grade) max, MIN(numeric_grade) min
  FROM grade
 WHERE student_id = 179
   AND section_id = 116
   AND grade_type_code IN ('HM', 'FI')
 GROUP BY student_id, section_id, grade_type_code
STUDENT_ID SECTION_ID GR MAX MIN
---------- ---------- -- --- ---
       179        116 FI  90  90
       179        116 HM  99  99
```

2 rows selected.

b) Based on the result of exercise a, what do you observe about the row with STUDENT_ID 102 and SECTION_ID 89?

ANSWER: When the subquery with the ALL operator fails to return a row, the query is automatically true. Therefore, this student is also included in the result set.

The interesting aspect of the relationship between ALL and NULL is that here the student for this section has no homework grades, yet the row is returned for output.

```
SELECT student_id, section_id, grade_type_code,
       MAX(numeric_grade) max, MIN(numeric_grade) min
  FROM grade
 WHERE student_id = 102
   AND section_id = 89
   AND grade_type_code IN ('HM', 'FI')
 GROUP BY student_id, section_id, grade_type_code
```

```
STUDENT_ID SECTION_ID GR MAX MIN
---------- ---------- -- --- ---
       102         89 FI  92  92
```

1 row selected.

c) Select the STUDENT_ID, SECTION_ID, and grade of every student who received a final examination grade better than *any* of his or her individual homework grades.

ANSWER: Using the ANY operator together with the correlated subquery achieves the desired result.

```
SELECT student_id, section_id, numeric_grade
  FROM grade g
 WHERE grade_type_code = 'FI'
   AND numeric_grade > ANY
       (SELECT numeric_grade
          FROM grade
         WHERE grade_type_code = 'HM'
           AND g.section_id = section_id
           AND g.student_id = student_id)
STUDENT_ID SECTION_ID NUMERIC_GRADE
---------- ---------- -------------
       102         86            85
       103         81            91
       143         85            92
...
       283         99            85
       283        101            88
```

157 rows selected.

Examine the grades for the homework and the final examination for STUDENT_ID 102 and SECTION_ID 86. This student's final examination grade of 85 is better than the homework grade of 82. The ANY operator tests for an OR condition, so the student and section are returned because only one of the homework grades has to satisfy the condition.

```
SELECT student_id, section_id, grade_type_code,
       numeric_grade
  FROM grade
 WHERE student_id = 102
   AND section_id = 86
   AND grade_type_code IN ('HM', 'FI')
 GROUP BY student_id, section_id, grade_type_code,
       numeric_grade
STUDENT_ID SECTION_ID GR NUMERIC_GRADE
---------- ---------- -- -------------
       102         86 FI            85
       102         86 HM            82
       102         86 HM            82
       102         86 HM            90
       102         86 HM            99
```

5 rows selected.

d) Based on the result of exercise c, explain the result of the row with STUDENT_ID 102 and SECTION_ID 89.

ANSWER: This record is not returned because unlike the ALL operator, the ANY operator returns false.

The following example illustrates the effect of no records in the subquery on the ANY operator. STUDENT_ID 102 enrolled in SECTION_ID 89 has no homework grades, and, therefore, does not appear in the result set for question c.

```
SELECT student_id, section_id, grade_type_code,
       numeric_grade
  FROM grade
 WHERE student_id = 102
   AND section_id = 89
   AND grade_type_code IN ('HM', 'FI')
STUDENT_ID SECTION_ID GR NUMERIC_GRADE
---------- ---------- -- -------------
       102         89 FI            92

1 row selected.
```

Lab 8.4 Quiz

In order to test your progress, you should be able to answer the following questions.

1) Are the operators NOT IN and <> ANY equivalent, as illustrated in the following example?

```
SELECT 'TRUE'
  FROM dual
 WHERE 6 <> ANY (6, 9)
```

```
SELECT 'TRUE'
  FROM dual
 WHERE 6 NOT IN (6, 9)
```

_____ a) Yes

_____ b) No

2) The following queries are logically equivalent.

```
SELECT 'TRUE'
  FROM dual
 WHERE 6 IN (6, 9)
```

```
SELECT 'TRUE'
  FROM dual
 WHERE 6 = ANY (6,9)
```

_____ a) True

_____ b) False

3) The operators ANY and SOME are equivalent.

_____ a) True

_____ b) False

4) To perform any >=, <=, >, or < comparison with a subquery returning multiple rows, you need to use either the ANY, SOME, or ALL operator.

_____ a) True

_____ b) False

ANSWERS APPEAR IN APPENDIX A.

▼ WORKSHOP

The projects in this section are meant to prompt you to utilize all the skills you have acquired throughout this chapter. The answers to these projects can be found at the companion Web site to this book, located at www.oraclesqlbyexample.com.

1) Using a subquery construct, determine which sections the student Henry Masser is enrolled in.

2) What problem does the following SELECT statement solve?

```
SELECT zip
  FROM zipcode z
 WHERE NOT EXISTS
        (SELECT '*'
           FROM student
          WHERE z.zip = zip)
   AND NOT EXISTS
        (SELECT '*'
           FROM instructor
          WHERE z.zip = zip)
```

3) Display the course number and description of courses with no enrollment. Also include courses that have no section assigned.

4) Can the ANY and ALL operators be used on the DATE data type? Write a simple query to prove your answer.

5) If you have a choice to write either a correlated subquery or a simple noncorrelated subquery, which one would you choose? Why?

6) Determine the top three zip codes where most of the students live.

CHAPTER 9

Set Operators

CHAPTER OBJECTIVES

In this chapter, you will learn about:

- ▶ The Power of UNION and UNION ALL
- ▶ The MINUS and INTERSECT Set Operators

Set operators combine two or more sets of data to produce a single result set. Oracle has four set operators: UNION, UNION ALL, MINUS, and INTERSECT. The UNION and UNION ALL operators combine results. The INTERSECT operator determines common rows. The MINUS operator shows differences between sets of rows.

The sets of data in a set operation are SELECT statements and when writing any set operation, there are two rules to remember.

- ▶ Each of the SELECT lists must contain the same number of columns.
- ▶ The matching columns in each of the SELECT lists must be the same data type. (Oracle considers CHAR and VARCHAR2 to be data type compatible.)

In this chapter, you will use set operators to retrieve data from many tables throughout the STUDENT schema.

LAB 9.1
The Power of UNION and UNION ALL

LAB OBJECTIVES

After this lab, you will be able to:

▶ Use the UNION Set Operator
▶ Use the UNION ALL Set Operator

The UNION operator is probably the most commonly used set operator. It combines two or more sets of data to produce a single set of data. Think of the UNION operator as two overlapping circles, as illustrated in Figure 9.1. The union of the two circles is everything from both circles. There are duplicates where they overlap, and there may even be duplicates within each set, but the final result shows these values only once. The UNION ALL operator includes these duplicates.

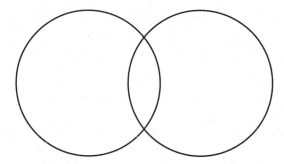

FIGURE 9.1
UNION and UNION ALL set operators

The UNION Operator

Imagine that you need to create a phone list of all instructors and students. The following set operation uses the UNION operator to combine instructor and student names and phone numbers from the INSTRUCTOR and STUDENT tables into a single result set.

```
SELECT first_name, last_name, phone
  FROM instructor
 UNION
SELECT first_name, last_name, phone
  FROM student
FIRST_NAME LAST_NAME          PHONE
---------- ----------------   ------------

A.         Tucker             203-555-5555
Adele      Rothstein          718-555-5555


...

Z.A.       Scrittorale        203-555-5555
Zalman     Draquez            718-555-5555

276 rows selected.
```

The same three columns are selected from each table, effectively stacking the columns one on top of the other in the result set. The results are automatically sorted by the order in which the columns appear in the SELECT list.

The result returns 276 rows, even though there are 268 student rows and 10 instructor rows. What happened to the other 2 rows? The following query shows duplicate rows in the STUDENT table.

```
SELECT first_name, last_name, phone, COUNT(*)
  FROM student
 GROUP BY first_name, last_name, phone
HAVING COUNT(*) > 1
FIRST_NAME LAST_NAME          PHONE              COUNT(*)
---------- ----------------   ------------       ------------

Kevin      Porch              201-555-5555              2
Thomas     Edwards            201-555-5555              2

2 rows selected.
```

Because the UNION operator shows only distinct rows, the duplicate student row appears just once in the result of the UNION set operation. To list all the instructors and students, including duplicates, you can take either of two approaches. One approach is to add the ID of the INSTRUCTOR and STUDENT tables to the set operation, plus a text literal such as 'instructor' or 'student'. The other approach is to use the UNION ALL operator.

The UNION ALL Operator

UNION ALL includes any duplicates when sets of data are added. Think again of the two overlapping circles shown in Figure 9.1. UNION ALL not only adds the two sets of data but includes the overlapping duplicates as well. Duplicates that may exist within each set are also included.

```
SELECT first_name, last_name, phone
  FROM instructor
```

```
 UNION ALL
 SELECT first_name, last_name, phone
   FROM student
 FIRST_NAME LAST_NAME         PHONE
 ---------- ---------------- ------------
 Fernand    Hanks             2125551212
 Tom        Wojick            2125551212
 ...
 Kathleen   Mastandora        718-555-5555
 Angela     Torres            718-555-5555

 278 rows selected.
```

UNION ALL results in 278 rows, which includes the duplicates in the STUDENT table. Also, the result set is no longer sorted; UNION ALL does not perform a sort. Therefore, a query containing the UNION operator is more time-consuming to execute than a query with the UNION ALL operator. Unless you have a reason to show only distinct rows, use UNION ALL instead of UNION because it will yield better performance.

ORDER BY and Set Operations

Just like the result of any SELECT statement, the result of a set operation can be sorted using the ORDER BY clause. Instead of naming the column by which you want to sort the result, refer to its position in the SELECT list instead. Consider what happens if you add the instructor and student IDs to the previous example by using UNION and order the results by the LAST_NAME column.

```
 SELECT instructor_id id, first_name, last_name, phone
   FROM instructor
 UNION
 SELECT student_id, first_name, last_name, phone
   FROM student
 ORDER BY 3
         ID FIRST_NAME LAST_NAME         PHONE
 --------- ---------- ---------------- ------------
        119 Mardig     Abdou             718-555-5555
        399 Jerry      Abdou             718-555-5555
 ...
        184 Salewa     Zuckerberg        718-555-5555
        206 Freedon    annunziato        718-555-5555

 278 rows selected.
```

The ORDER BY clause can also refer to a column alias, such as the ID used for the first column. However, referring to the column position in the ORDER BY clause is ANSI standard and is also independent of the column names in either SELECT statement.

With the addition of the instructor and student IDs, the unique combination of those IDs with first name, last name, and phone number now produces all 278 rows between the INSTRUCTOR and STUDENT tables.

The first columns in each of the individual SELECT statements, INSTRUCTOR_ID and STUDENT_ID, have different names but are of the same data type. Use an alias to give the column in the result set a meaningful name for both instructor and student IDs.

> SQL always takes its cue from the topmost SELECT statement when naming columns in the result set. When you want the result set to display a specific column name that is not dependent on the names of columns listed in the topmost statement, you must use a column alias.

▼ LAB 9.1 EXERCISES

a) Explain the result of the following set operation and explain why it works.

```
SELECT first_name, last_name,
       'Instructor' "Type"
  FROM instructor
 UNION ALL
SELECT first_name, last_name,
       'Student'
  FROM student
```

b) Write a set operation, using the UNION set operator, to list all the zip codes in the INSTRUCTOR and STUDENT tables.

c) What problem does the following set operation solve?

```
SELECT created_by
  FROM enrollment
 UNION
SELECT created_by
  FROM grade
 UNION
SELECT created_by
  FROM grade_type
 UNION
SELECT created_by
  FROM grade_conversion
CREATED_BY
----------
ARISCHER
BMOTIVAL
BROSENZW
CBRENNAN
DSCHERER
```

JAYCAF
MCAFFREY

7 rows selected.

d) Explain why the result of the following set operation returns an error.

```
SELECT course_no, description
  FROM course
 WHERE prerequisite IS NOT NULL
 ORDER BY 1
 UNION
SELECT course_no, description
  FROM course
 WHERE prerequisite IS NULL
```

e) What is wrong with the following set operation, and what do you have to change to make it work correctly?

```
SELECT instructor_id, last_name
  FROM instructor
 UNION
SELECT last_name, student_id
  FROM student
```

▼ LAB 9.1 EXERCISE ANSWERS

a) Explain the result of the following set operation and explain why it works.

```
SELECT first_name, last_name,
       'Instructor' "Type"
  FROM instructor
 UNION ALL
SELECT first_name, last_name,
       'Student'
  FROM student
```

ANSWER: The result set displays the first and last names of instructors and students. The third column identifies what type of person each is. 'Instructor' and 'Student' are both text literals and are in the same position in each SELECT list. Therefore, the two SELECT statements are row compatible.

FIRST_NAME	LAST_NAME	Type
A.	Tucker	Student
Adele	Rothstein	Student
...		
Z.A.	Scrittorale	Student
Zalman	Draquez	Student

278 rows selected.

As your SELECT statements and set operations become more complex, it can be difficult to identify the data in your result sets accurately. This technique of identifying each row in the result set coming from one or the other set of data may be very useful.

b) Write a set operation, using the UNION set operator, to list all the zip codes in the INSTRUCTOR and STUDENT tables.

ANSWER: The query combines two SELECT statements, using the UNION set operator, for a result set displaying zip codes from both tables, eliminating any duplicates.

```
SELECT zip
  FROM instructor
 UNION
SELECT zip
  FROM student
ZIP
-----
01247
02124
...
43224
48104

149 rows selected.
```

c) What problem does the following set operation solve?

```
SELECT created_by
  FROM enrollment
 UNION
SELECT created_by
  FROM grade
 UNION
SELECT created_by
  FROM grade_type
 UNION
SELECT created_by
  FROM grade conversion
CREATED_BY
----------
ARISCHER
BMOTIVAL
BROSENZW
CBRENNAN
DSCHERER
JAYCAF
MCAFFREY

7 rows selected.
```

ANSWER: The query displays a list of users who created rows in the ENROLLMENT, GRADE, GRADE_TYPE, and GRADE_CONVERSION tables. It shows each user name only once.

As mentioned in the beginning of this lab, set operators can be used with two or more sets of data. This exercise combines the data from four separate tables into a single result set, eliminating duplicates where they occur.

CONTROLLING THE SORT ORDER

Sometimes you want to choose a specific sort order. This can be accomplished with a literal by which you can order the result.

```
SELECT created_by, 'GRADE' AS SOURCE, 1 AS SORT_ORDER
  FROM grade
 UNION
SELECT created_by, 'GRADE_TYPE', 2
  FROM grade_type
 UNION
SELECT created_by, 'GRADE_CONVERSION', 3
  FROM grade_conversion
 UNION
SELECT created_by, 'ENROLLMENT', 4
  FROM enrollment
 ORDER BY 3
```

CREATED_BY	SOURCE	SORT_ORDER
ARISCHER	GRADE	1
BROSENZW	GRADE	1
CBRENNAN	GRADE	1
MCAFFREY	GRADE_TYPE	2
BMOTIVAL	GRADE_CONVERSION	3
DSCHERER	ENROLLMENT	4
JAYCAF	ENROLLMENT	4

```
7 rows selected.
```

d) Explain why the result of the following set operation returns an error.

```
SELECT course_no, description
  FROM course
 WHERE prerequisite IS NOT NULL
 ORDER BY 1
 UNION
SELECT course_no, description
  FROM course
 WHERE prerequisite IS NULL
```

ANSWER: Oracle returns the following error message because the ORDER BY clause must be used at the end of a set operation.

```
ORA-00933: SQL command not properly ended
```

SQL expects the ORDER BY clause to be the very last command in a SQL statement, including set operations. An ORDER BY clause logically has no purpose in the topmost statement; it is applied only to the single set of data in the result set, which is a combination of all data from all SELECT statements in a set operation.

e) What is wrong with the following set operation, and what do you have to change to make it work correctly?

```
SELECT instructor_id, last_name
  FROM instructor
 UNION
SELECT last_name, student_id
  FROM student
```

ANSWER: Oracle returns the error ORA-01790: expression must have same data type as corresponding expression. The data types of columns must be the same for columns in the same position in each SELECT list of a set operation. Either the order of the columns in the first or the second statement must be switched for the statement to work correctly.

Sometimes, the data types of columns do not match because of the way the columns were created, in which case you can use the data conversion functions to change from one data type to another.

DATA TYPE CONVERSIONS AND NULLS

You want to combine distinct result sets together by using the UNION ALL operator and place a null value for those columns where you want to omit the value. The following query uses the CAST function and the TO_DATE function to make sure the null columns are set to the same data type, and it avoids implicit data type conversion.

```
SELECT DISTINCT salutation, CAST(NULL AS NUMBER),
       state, z.created_date
  FROM instructor i, zipcode z
 WHERE i.zip = z.zip
UNION ALL
SELECT salutation, COUNT(*),
       state, TO_DATE(NULL)
  FROM student s, zipcode z
 WHERE s.zip = z.zip
 GROUP BY salutation, state
SALUT CAST(NULLASNUMBER) ST CREATED_D
----- ------------------ -- ---------
DR                       NY 03-AUG-03
HON                      NY 03-AUG-03
...
MS.                  69  NY
MS.                   1  WV
REV                   1  NJ

19 rows selected.
```

Lab 9.1 Quiz

In order to test your progress, you should be able to answer the following questions.

1) It is redundant to use DISTINCT in a UNION set operation.

   _____ a) True

   _____ b) False

2) Each of the SELECT statements in a set operation must have an ORDER BY clause when you want the results to be ordered.

   _____ a) True

   _____ b) False

3) A UNION set operation always returns the same result set as an equijoin.

   _____ a) True

   _____ b) False

4) You cannot use UNION to combine data from two tables that do not have a primary key/foreign key relationship.

   _____ a) True

   _____ b) False

5) There must be the same number of columns in each SELECT statement of a set operation.

   _____ a) True

   _____ b) False

ANSWERS APPEAR IN APPENDIX A.

LAB 9.2

The MINUS and INTERSECT Set Operators

LAB OBJECTIVES

After this lab, you will be able to:

▶ Use the MINUS Set Operator
▶ Use the INTERSECT Set Operator

The MINUS set operator subtracts one set of data from another, identifying what data exists in one table but not the other. The INTERSECT set operator is the intersection of sets of data, identifying data common to all of them.

The MINUS Operator

The MINUS operator returns the difference between two sets. Effectively, you use it to subtract one set from another set. The gray area of the circle in Figure 9.2 shows the difference between the sets and indicates the data that is in one circle but not in another.

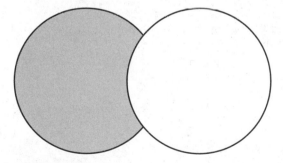

FIGURE 9.2
The MINUS set operators

The following set operation lists instructors not currently teaching any classes (sections).

```
SELECT instructor_id
  FROM instructor
 MINUS
SELECT instructor_id
  FROM section
INSTRUCTOR_ID
-------------
          109
          110
```

2 rows selected.

The first SELECT statement returns the complete list of instructors.

```
SELECT instructor_id
  FROM instructor
INSTRUCTOR_ID
-------------
          101
          102
          103
          104
          105
          106
          109
          108
          107
          110
```

10 rows selected.

The second SELECT statement returns a distinct list of instructors currently teaching.

```
SELECT DISTINCT instructor_id
  FROM section
INSTRUCTOR_ID
-------------
          101
          102
          103
          104
          105
          106
          107
          108
```

8 rows selected.

Subtracting the second result set from the first result set leaves a list of instructors not currently teaching, which are the INSTRUCTOR_ID values 109 and 110. Just like the UNION set operator, MINUS eliminates duplicates when evaluating sets of data. DISTINCT is used in the preceding second SELECT statement when it is written separately.

The following set operation implies distinct values in both SELECT statements.

```
SELECT created_by
  FROM enrollment
 MINUS
SELECT created_by
  FROM course
CREATED_BY
---------------
JAYCAF

1 row selected.
```

Written separately, the two SELECT statements use DISTINCT.

```
SELECT DISTINCT created_by
  FROM enrollment
CREATED_BY
---------------
DSCHERER
JAYCAF

2 rows selected.

SELECT DISTINCT created_by
  FROM course
CREATED_BY
---------------
DSCHERER

1 row selected.
```

The second SELECT statement results in the distinct value DSCHERER. This is subtracted from the result of the first statement, which consists of the distinct values JAYCAF and DSCHERER. This results in the value JAYCAF because JAYCAF is not found in the COURSE table, only in the ENROLLMENT table. This type of statement, whereby you retrieve data that exists in one table but not in another, is sometimes referred to as an *antijoin*.

 Be careful when positioning the SELECT statements in a MINUS set operation because their order makes a big difference. Be sure to place the set you want to subtract from first.

The INTERSECT Operator

The INTERSECT operator determines the common values between two sets. Figure 9.3 illustrates the two overlapping circles, and the gray color indicates the area where the two circles intersect.

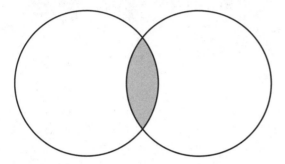

FIGURE 9.3
The INTERSECT set operator

When you use INTERSECT instead of MINUS in the previous statement, the result is quite different.

```
SELECT created_by
  FROM enrollment
INTERSECT
SELECT created_by
  FROM course
CREATED_BY
---------------
DSCHERER

1 row selected.
```

The result set contains DSCHERER, which is the distinct value where the two sets overlap or intersect. Unlike with MINUS, the order of the SELECT statements in an INTERSECT set operation does not matter.

USING INTERSECT INSTEAD OF EQUIJOINS

The equijoin discussed in Chapter 7, "Equijoins," produces a result set that is the intersection of two or more tables—the same result as with INTERSECT.

The following is an equijoin that returns a list of course numbers for courses with corresponding sections.

```
SELECT DISTINCT c.course_no
  FROM course c, section s
 WHERE c.course_no = s.course_no
```

```
COURSE_NO
---------
       10
       20
...
      420
      450
```

28 rows selected.

This INTERSECT set operation returns the same result.

```
SELECT course_no
  FROM course
INTERSECT
SELECT course_no
  FROM section
COURSE_NO
---------
       10
       20
...
      420
      450
```

28 rows selected.

The drawback to using INTERSECT instead of an equijoin is that INTERSECT operates on all columns in each SELECT list of the set operation. Therefore, you cannot include columns that exist in one table and not the other.

Execution Order of Set Operations

The execution order for all set operations is from top to bottom. You can see the effect in the following query, which involves three tables: T1, T2, and T3. The query combines the values of table T1 and T2, and the subsequent MINUS operation compares this result to the values of T3. (These three tables are not found in the STUDENT schema unless you installed the additional tables from the companion Web site.)

```
SELECT col1
  FROM t1
UNION ALL
SELECT col2
  FROM t2
MINUS
SELECT col3
  FROM t3
      COL1
----------
```

```
           1
           4
```

2 rows selected.

You use parentheses to indicate a change in the execution order, as in the following example. The query in parentheses is executed first; it determines the differences between T2 and T3 and then uses the UNION ALL operator to combine the result with T1. The output is quite different from the previous result.

```
SELECT col1
   FROM t1
UNION ALL
(SELECT col2
   FROM t2
MINUS
SELECT col3
   FROM t3)
      COL1
----------
         1
         2
         3
         4
```

4 rows selected.

Comparing Two Tables

Set operators are very useful if you need to determine the differences between two tables. For example, say that you want to compare test and production database tables or check data generated by a program to a previous state of the table. The following statement involves two tables: OLD_TABLE contains the original state of the table, and NEW_TABLE shows the data after the execution of various data manipulation statements. The queries inside the parentheses are executed first, and then the UNION ALL operation is performed. The SQL statement returns the differences between the two tables.

```
(SELECT *
   FROM old_table
 MINUS
 SELECT *
   FROM new_table)
UNION ALL
(SELECT *
   FROM new_table
 MINUS
 SELECT *
   FROM old_table)
```

Ideally, your tables have a primary key or unique key to uniquely identify the rows. If that's not the case, duplicate rows in the table may be possible. You might want to include the COUNT(*) function along with all the columns and a GROUP BY clause.

Another way to find differences is to use Oracle's Flashback query, which allows you to list the changes performed between specific time intervals. You will learn more about this feature in Chapter 11, "Insert, Update, and Delete."

▼ LAB 9.2 EXERCISES

a) Explain the result of the following set operation.

```
SELECT course_no, description
  FROM course
 MINUS
SELECT s.course_no, c.description
  FROM section s, course c
 WHERE s.course_no = c.course_no
```

b) Use the MINUS set operator to create a list of courses and sections with no students enrolled. Add to the result set a column with the title Status and display the text No Enrollments in each row. Order the results by the COURSE_NO and SECTION_NO columns.

c) Use the appropriate set operator to list all zip codes that are in both the STUDENT and INSTRUCTOR tables.

d) Use the INTERSECT set operator to list student IDs for students who are enrolled.

▼ LAB 9.2 EXERCISE ANSWERS

a) Explain the result of the following set operation.

```
SELECT course_no, description
  FROM course
 MINUS
SELECT s.course_no, c.description
  FROM section s, course c
 WHERE s.course_no = c.course_no
```

ANSWER: The set operation subtracts all courses having sections from all courses, resulting in the two courses without matching sections.

```
COURSE_NO DESCRIPTION
--------- ----------------------------------
       80 Programming Techniques
      430 Java Developer III

2 rows selected.
```

Another way to formulate the query is to write a subquery using the NOT IN operator or the NOT EXISTS operator.

```
SELECT course_no, description
  FROM course c
 WHERE NOT EXISTS
       (SELECT '*'
          FROM section
         WHERE c.course_no = course_no)
```

In Chapter 10, "Complex Joins," you will learn about using an outer join as another way to achieve a similar result.

b) Use the MINUS set operator to create a list of courses and sections with no students enrolled. Add to the result set a column with the title Status and display the text No Enrollments in each row. Order the results by the COURSE_NO and SECTION_NO columns.

ANSWER: The first SELECT statement is the set of all courses with sections. The second SELECT statement subtracts the set of courses and sections having enrollments, leaving the courses and sections without enrollments.

```
SELECT course_no, section_no, 'No Enrollments' "Status"
  FROM section
 MINUS
SELECT course_no, section_no, 'No Enrollments'
  FROM section s
 WHERE EXISTS (SELECT section_id
                 FROM enrollment e
                WHERE e.section_id = s.section_id)
 ORDER BY 1, 2
COURSE_NO SECTION_NO Status
--------- ---------- --------------
       25          9 No Enrollments
      124          4 No Enrollments
...
      220          1 No Enrollments
      350          3 No Enrollments

14 rows selected.
```

This statement makes use of the literal 'No Enrollments' in the SELECT statement. Even though it is not a column in either table, as long as it is in the first statement, there is a column for it in the result set. And, as long as it is in the second statement, it matches the first and, therefore, allows the MINUS to work correctly, subtracting one set from a similar set.

c) Use the appropriate set operator to list all zip codes that are in both the STUDENT and INSTRUCTOR tables.

ANSWER: INTERSECT is used to find the intersection of distinct zip codes in the INSTRUCTOR and STUDENT tables.

```
SELECT zip
  FROM instructor
INTERSECT
SELECT zip
  FROM student
```

```
ZIP
-----
10025
```

`1 row selected.`

Be careful when deciding to use INTERSECT versus UNION. The key phrase in this exercise is "zip codes that are in both." INTERSECT achieves the intersection of both tables alone, whereas UNION returns all zip codes from both tables combined.

d) Use the INTERSECT set operator to list student IDs for students who are enrolled.

ANSWER: The intersection of student IDs in the STUDENT and ENROLLMENT tables yields all students who are enrolled.

```
SELECT student_id
  FROM student
INTERSECT
SELECT student_id
  FROM enrollment
STUDENT_ID
----------
       102
       103
...
       282
       283

165 rows selected.
```

Lab 9.2 Quiz

In order to test your progress, you should be able to answer the following questions.

1) The following two SELECT statements are equivalent and return the same rows.

```
SELECT student_id              SELECT student_id
  FROM enrollment                FROM student
MINUS                          MINUS
SELECT student_id              SELECT student_id
  FROM student                   FROM enrollment
```

   _____ a) True
   _____ b) False

2) The SELECT statements in an INTERSECT set operation can contain a correlated subquery.

   _____ a) True
   _____ b) False

3) The following SQL statement executes without an error.

```
SELECT TO_CHAR(1)
  FROM dual
MINUS
SELECT TO_NUMBER('1')
  FROM dual
```

   _____ a) True
   _____ b) False

4) It is redundant to use DISTINCT in either a MINUS or INTERSECT set operation.

   _____ a) True
   _____ b) False

ANSWERS APPEAR IN APPENDIX A.

▼ WORKSHOP

The projects in this section are meant to prompt you to utilize all the skills you have acquired throughout this chapter. The answers to these projects can be found at the companion Web site to this book, located at www.oraclesqlbyexample.com.

1) List all the zip codes in the ZIPCODE table that are not used in the STUDENT or INSTRUCTOR tables. Write two different solutions, using set operators for both.

2) Write a SQL statement, using a set operator, to show which students enrolled in a section on the same day they registered.

3) Find the students who are not enrolled in any classes. Write three solutions: a set operation, a subquery, and a correlated subquery.

4) Show the students who have received grades for their classes. Write four solutions: a set operation, a subquery, a correlated subquery, and a join.

CHAPTER 10

Complex Joins

CHAPTER OBJECTIVES

In this chapter, you will learn about:

▶ Outer Joins
▶ Self-Joins

Outer joins and self-joins are extensions of the equijoins you learned about in Chapter 7, "Equijoins." An outer join includes the result rows returned by an equijoin, plus extra rows where no matches are found. The self-join, as implied by the name, joins a table to itself. This type of join is useful for tables with a self-referencing relationship or when you want to determine data inconsistencies. Self-joins are useful for analyzing and exploring the relationships within your data.

LAB 10.1
Outer Joins

LAB OBJECTIVES

After this lab, you will be able to:

▶ Write Outer Joins with Two Tables
▶ Write Outer Joins with Three Tables

An outer join is similar to an equijoin because it returns all the records an equijoin returns. But it also returns records that are in one of the tables with no matching records in another table. The following example shows an equijoin and its result. The SQL statement returns all the rows where a match for the COURSE_NO column is found in both the COURSE and SECTION tables.

```
SELECT course_no, description,
       section_id
  FROM course JOIN section
 USING (course_no)
 ORDER BY course_no
```

COURSE_NO	DESCRIPTION	SECTION_ID	COURSE_NO
10	Technology Concepts	80	10
20	Intro to Information Systems	81	20
...			
420	Database System Principles	108	420
450	DB Programming with Java	109	450

78 rows selected.

Some courses are not included in the result because there are no matching course numbers in the SECTION table. To determine which courses are not assigned to any sections, write a NOT EXISTS subquery, a NOT IN subquery, or use the MINUS operator.

```
SELECT course_no, description
  FROM course c
 WHERE NOT EXISTS
       (SELECT 'X'
          FROM section
         WHERE c.course_no = course_no)
```

```
COURSE_NO DESCRIPTION
--------- ----------------------------------
       80 Programming Techniques
      430 Java Developer III

  2 rows selected.
```

The previous equijoin does not return the two courses because there are no matches for course numbers 80 and 430 in the SECTION table. To include these courses in the result, you need to perform an outer join.

The ANSI Outer Join

An outer join is typically formed with one of three different syntax options: Either you can use the ANSI join syntax, Oracle's outer join operator denoted with the (+), or you can express the query as a UNION. In this lab you will learn how to write the queries in various ways.

Typically, it is best to use the ANSI outer join syntax, as it greatly increases the SQL functionality and flexibility. It can also be easily understood by any non-Oracle databases and is not subject to the many limitations the Oracle-specific outer join operator imposes. If your SQL needs to run against Oracle versions prior to 9i, you have no choice but to use Oracle's outer join operator or a UNION ALL set operator.

The following query shows the use of the ANSI outer join syntax. The keywords LEFT OUTER are added to the JOIN keyword, indicating that the rows in the table to the left side of the JOIN keyword are to be listed. This left table is the COURSE table, and all rows are shown, including any rows where there is no matching COURSE_NO value in the SECTION table.

```
  SELECT c.course_no, c.description,
         s.section_id, s.course_no
    FROM course c LEFT OUTER JOIN section s
      ON c.course_no = s.course_no
  ORDER BY c.course_no
COURSE_NO DESCRIPTION                        SECTION_ID COURSE_NO
--------- ---------------------------------- ---------- ---------
       10 Technology Concepts                        80        10
       20 Intro to Information Systems               81        20
...
       80 Programming Techniques
...
      430 Java Developer III
      450 DB Programming with Java                  109       450

  80 rows selected.
```

Look closely at the result for course numbers 80 and 430. These courses have no sections assigned. For example, COURSE_NO 430 of the COURSE table (c.course_no) shows the COURSE_NO value, but COURSE_NO from the SECTION table (s.course_no) displays a null.

The outer join displays null values for the columns s.course_no and s.section_id where no match exists.

If you want to include all the rows in the SECTION table, you can use the RIGHT OUTER JOIN syntax. This does not really make any sense when reviewing the schema diagram: Every row in the SECTION table must have a corresponding row in the COURSE table. Orphan rows, which are rows that exist in the SECTION table but not in the COURSE table, are not allowed.

However, if you switch the order of the tables to list the SECTION table first, you can write a RIGHT OUTER JOIN. This is essentially the same as the previous LEFT OUTER JOIN. The only differences are the order of the tables in the FROM clause and the RIGHT keyword. Based on the order of the tables in the FROM clause, you must choose either the RIGHT or the LEFT keyword to include all the rows of the outer joined table.

```
SELECT c.course_no, c.description,
       s.section_id, s.course_no
  FROM section s RIGHT OUTER JOIN course c
    ON c.course_no = s.course_no
 ORDER BY c.course_no
```

You can also write the outer join with another ANSI join syntax, such as the USING clause.

```
SELECT course_no, description,
       section_id
  FROM section RIGHT OUTER JOIN course
 USING (course_no)
 ORDER BY course_no
COURSE_NO DESCRIPTION                   SECTION_ID
--------- --------------------------- ----------
       10 Technology Concepts                 80
       20 Intro to Information Systems        81
...
       80 Programming Techniques
...
      430 Java Developer III
      450 DB Programming with Java           109

80 rows selected.
```

The query and the returned result do not include both COURSE_NO columns because you are not allowed to alias the joined column when writing the query with the USING clause. The column now also contains a non-null value, unlike the previous result, where the corresponding COURSE_NO column from the SECTION table showed a null. For the SECTION_ID column, you continue to see a null value because there is obviously no matching value in the SECTION table.

The Oracle Outer Join Operator (+)

The second way to express an outer join is with Oracle's outer join operator (+). The next query looks very much like the equijoin you are already familiar with, except for the (+) next to the SECTION table's COURSE_NO column in the WHERE clause. Oracle uses the outer join operator (+) to indicate that nulls are shown for non-matching rows. As in the previous result set, for those rows of the COURSE table where a match does not exist in the SECTION table (course numbers 80 and 430), there are null values displayed in the SECTION table columns.

You place the outer join operator on the table for which you want to return null column values when a match is not found. In this case, all the rows from the COURSE table are desired, and for every row in the COURSE table for which a match cannot be found in the SECTION table, a null is shown. Therefore, the (+) operator is placed on the COURSE_NO column of the SECTION table.

```
SELECT c.course_no, c.description,
       s.section_id, s.course_no
  FROM course c, section s
 WHERE c.course_no = s.course_no(+)
 ORDER BY c.course_no
```

If the order of the tables in the FROM clause changes, the (+) operator still needs to remain on the S.COURSE_NO column.

The Outer Join and the UNION ALL Operator

Instead of using the (+) operator or the ANSI join syntax, you can achieve the same result with two SQL statements: an equijoin and a correlated subquery, with the results combined using the UNION ALL operator.

```
SELECT c1.course_no, c1.description,
       s.section_id, s.course_no
  FROM course c1, section s
 WHERE c1.course_no = s.course_no
UNION ALL
SELECT c2.course_no, c2.description,
       TO_NUMBER(NULL), TO_NUMBER(NULL)
  FROM course c2
 WHERE NOT EXISTS
       (SELECT 'X'
          FROM section
         WHERE c2.course_no = course_no)
```

In this example, the UNION ALL operator is used to combine the result of the equijoin (all courses with sections) with the result of the correlated subquery (courses with no match in the SECTION table). Duplicate rows are not returned between the two SELECT statements; each SELECT statement returns a different set. Therefore, it is more efficient to use UNION ALL rather than the UNION operator because UNION ALL avoids the sort required by the UNION operator to eliminate the duplicates.

The TO_NUMBER data type conversion is performed to match the data types of the columns in each of the SELECT statements in the set operation. Alternatively, you can substitute CAST (NULL AS NUMBER) for the TO_NUMBER(NULL) function.

> The outer join (+) syntax and the UNION ALL syntax options are the only way to express outer joins in Oracle versions prior to Oracle9*i*. If you have a choice, use the ANSI join syntax instead; it is easy and, overall, more flexible and functional.

The Full Outer Join

A full outer join includes rows from both tables. Oracle does not support a full outer join with the (+) outer join operator. To accomplish a full outer join, you need to use either the ANSI full outer join syntax or the UNION operator.

ANSI FULL OUTER JOIN

To fully illustrate the effects of an outer join, the following are tables named T1 and T2 and the data in them. Table T1 has one numeric column named COL1, and table T2 also consists of a numeric column called COL2. (These tables are not found in the STUDENT schema unless you installed the additional tables from the companion Web site.)

```
SELECT col1
  FROM t1
     COL1
---------
        1
        2
        3

3 rows selected.


SELECT col2
  FROM t2
     COL2
---------
        2
        3
        4

3 rows selected.
```

To understand the result of a full outer join on tables T1 and T2, first write an outer join on table T1 with the following SELECT statement, which is a left outer join. The result includes all the rows from table T1.

```
SELECT col1, col2
  FROM t1 LEFT OUTER JOIN t2
    ON t1.col1 = t2.col2
    COL1 COL2
--------- ----
        1
        2    2
        3    3
```

3 rows selected.

The next SELECT statement returns all the rows from T2, whether a match is found or not. This outer join is a right outer join. All the rows on the right table are returned, including non-matching rows.

```
SELECT col1, col2
  FROM t1 RIGHT OUTER JOIN t2
    ON t1.col1 = t2.col2
    COL1 COL2
--------- ----
        2    2
        3    3
             4
```

3 rows selected.

The full outer join includes all the rows from both tables, whether a match is found or not.

```
SELECT col1, col2
  FROM t1 FULL OUTER JOIN t2
    ON t1.col1 - t2.col2
    COL1 COL2
--------- ----
        1
        2    2
        3    3
             4
```

4 rows selected.

FULL OUTER JOIN USING THE UNION OPERATOR

You can express the full outer join from the preceding section by using the Oracle outer join operator and combining the two SELECT statements with the UNION operator. The UNION operator eliminates the duplicate rows from the two statements. If you want to include duplicates, use UNION ALL.

```
SELECT col1, col2
  FROM t1, t2
 WHERE t1.col1 = t2.col2(+)
```

```
UNION
SELECT col1, col2
  FROM t1, t2
 WHERE t1.col1(+) = t2.col2
```

The first SELECT statement performs an outer join on table T1; the second SELECT statement performs an outer join on table T2. The results of the queries are combined, and duplicates are eliminated with the UNION operator.

▼ LAB 10.1 EXERCISES

a) Explain why Oracle returns an error message when you execute the following SELECT statement.

```
SELECT c.course_no, s.course_no, s.section_id,
       c.description, s.start_date_time
  FROM course c, section s
 WHERE c.course_no(+) = s.course_no(+)
```

b) Show the description of all courses with the prerequisite course number 350. Include in the result the location where the sections meet. Return course rows even if no corresponding row in the SECTION table is found.

c) Rewrite the following SQL statement using an outer join.

```
SELECT course_no, description
  FROM course c
 WHERE NOT EXISTS
       (SELECT 'X'
          FROM section
         WHERE c.course_no = course_no)
```

```
COURSE_NO DESCRIPTION
--------- --------------------------------
       80 Programming Techniques
      430 Java Developer III

2 rows selected.
```

d) Show all the city, state, and zip code values for Connecticut. Display a count of how many students live in each zip code. Order the result alphabetically by city. The result should look similar to the following output. Note that the column STUDENT_COUNT displays a zero when no student lives in a particular zip code.

```
CITY                      ST ZIP   STUDENT_COUNT
------------------------- -- ----- -------------
Ansonia                   CT 06401             0
Bridgeport                CT 06605             1
...
Wilton                    CT 06897             0
Woodbury                  CT 06798             1

19 rows selected.
```

e) Display the course number, description, cost, class location, and instructor's last name for all the courses. Also include courses where no sections or instructors have been assigned.

f) For students with the student ID 102 and 301, determine the sections they are enrolled in. Also show the numeric grades and grade types they received, regardless of whether they are enrolled or received any grades.

▼ LAB 10.1 EXERCISE ANSWERS

a) Explain why Oracle returns an error message when you execute the following SELECT statement.

```
SELECT c.course_no, s.course_no, s.section_id,
       c.description, s.start_date_time
  FROM course c, section s
 WHERE c.course_no(+) = s.course_no(+)
```

ANSWER: The outer join symbol can be used only on one side of the equation, not both.

```
ERROR at line 4:
ORA-01468: a predicate may reference only one outer-joined table
```

This SQL statement attempts to include rows from the COURSE table for which no match exists in the SECTION table and include rows from the SECTION table where no match is found in the COURSE table. This is referred to as a full outer join; you want to include the rows from both tables, including rows for which a match cannot be found in either table.

If you want to write such an outer join, use the ANSI join syntax Instead.

```
SELECT c.course_no, s.course_no, s.section_id,
       c.description, s.start_date_time
  FROM course c FULL OUTER JOIN section s
    ON c.course_no = s.course_no
```

When you look at the relationship between the SECTION and COURSE tables, you notice a section cannot exist unless a corresponding course exists. Therefore, finding any sections for which no course exists is impossible unless the foreign key constraint is disabled or dropped. (To learn how to determine whether the foreign key is disabled or enabled, see Chapter 12, "Create, Alter, and Drop Tables.")

b) Show the description of all courses with the prerequisite course number 350. Include in the result the location where the sections meet. Return course rows even if no corresponding row in the SECTION table is found.

ANSWER: To show all the courses with this prerequisite, you need to write an outer join. For any records where no match in the SECTION table is found, null values are displayed for the respective SECTION table columns.

There are only two courses with a PREREQUISITE value of 350: courses 430 and 450.

```
SELECT course_no, description
  FROM course
 WHERE prerequisite = 350
```

```
COURSE_NO DESCRIPTION
---------- ------------------------
       430 Java Developer III
       450 DB Programming with Java
```

2 rows selected.

Only course number 450 has a matching course number in the SECTION table. Course number 430, Java Developer III, does not exist in the SECTION table.

```
SELECT section_id, course_no
  FROM section
 WHERE course_no IN (430, 450)
SECTION_ID  COURSE_NO
----------- ---------
        109       450
```

1 row selected.

The solution can be written as follows.

```
SELECT c.course_no cno, s.course_no sno,
       c.description,
       c.prerequisite prereq,
       s.location loc, s.section_id
  FROM course c LEFT OUTER JOIN section s
    ON c.course_no = s.course_no
 WHERE c.prerequisite = 350
CNO SNO DESCRIPTION                    PREREQ LOC  SECTION_ID
--- --- ------------------------ ------ ---- ----------
430     Java Developer III             350
450 450 DB Programming with Java       350 L507        109
```

2 rows selected.

Alternatively, it can be written as follows.

```
SELECT c.course_no cno, s.course_no sno,
       c.description,
       c.prerequisite prereq,
       s.location loc, s.section_id
  FROM course c, section s
 WHERE c.course_no = s.course_no(+)
   AND c.prerequisite = 350
```

As you see from the result, the columns of the SECTION table, such as S.LOCATION (with LOC as the column alias), S.COURSE_NO (with SNO as the column alias), and S.SECTION_ID show null values for the unmatched row.

The solution can also be expressed with the USING clause as shown in the next statement. The COURSE_NO is listed here only once because the USING clause does not you to reference the COURSE_NO column on both tables.

```
SELECT course_no cno,
       description,
       prerequisite prereq,
       location loc, section_id
  FROM course LEFT OUTER JOIN section
 USING (course_no)
 WHERE prerequisite = 350
```

ORACLE OUTER JOIN OPERATOR RESTRICTIONS

Oracle imposes a number of restrictions and caveats on using the (+) outer join operator. For example, the outer join operator restricts the use of an outer joined column involving a subquery. You also cannot use the OR logical operator and IN comparison. If you incorrectly place the necessary (+) symbols on the correct WHERE clause conditions and join criteria, you form an equijoin rather than an outer join. This occurs without warning, as you will see in the following examples.

WHERE CONDITIONS AND THE ORACLE OUTER JOIN OPERATOR

There are some things you need to watch out for when you use Oracle's proprietary outer join operator, particularly when it comes to conditions in WHERE clauses. The previously listed outer join is repeated here for your reference. The condition in the WHERE clause is applied to the prerequisite column. This column is in the COURSE table, the outer joined table that includes all rows, including non-matching rows.

```
SELECT c.course_no cno, s.course_no sno,
       c.description,
       c.prerequisite prereq,
       s.location loc, s.section_id
  FROM course c, section s
 WHERE c.course_no = s.course_no(+)
   AND c.prerequisite = 350
```

The next SQL statement modifies the WHERE condition and adds a condition specific to the SECTION table. The query retrieves classes that meet only in S.LOCATION L507. Observe the output of the query and compare it to the previous result.

```
SELECT c.course_no cno, s.course_no sno,
       c.description,
       c.prerequisite prereq,
       s.location loc, s.section_id
  FROM course c, section s
 WHERE c.course_no = s.course_no(+)
   AND c.prerequisite = 350
   AND s.location = 'L507'
```

CNO	SNO	DESCRIPTION	PREREQ	LOC	SECTION_ID
450	450	DB Programming with Java	350	L507	109

```
1 row selected.
```

You might wonder what happened to course number 430. The course is no longer included in the result, even though the outer join operator is applied to return all the rows, whether a match is found in the SECTION table or not.

When a WHERE clause contains a condition that compares a column from the outer joined table to a literal, such as the text literal 'L507', you also need to include the outer join operator on the column. Otherwise, Oracle returns only the results of the equijoin rather than displaying nulls for the columns. The following query adds the outer join symbol to the LOCATION column.

```
SELECT c.course_no cno, s.course_no sno,
       c.description,
       c.prerequisite prereq,
       s.location loc, s.section_id
  FROM course c, section s
 WHERE c.course_no = s.course_no(+)
   AND c.prerequisite = 350
   AND s.location(+) = 'L507'
```

CNO	SNO	DESCRIPTION	PREREQ	LOC	SECTION_ID
430		Java Developer III	350		
450	450	DB Programming with Java	350	L507	109

2 rows selected.

These two records satisfy the condition of the prerequisite. The outer join operator applied to the S.LOCATION column includes records where either (a) the location equals L507, (b) the location is null, or (c) the location is different from L507. You will see an example shortly of why the location can be different.

When you apply the outer join operator to a column on the outer joined table, you need to understand that the conditions are processed in a particular order. First, the records on the table where you want to include all the rows are processed. This is the condition C.PREREQUISITE = 350. Next, the matching records in the SECTION table are identified. If a match is not found, the records with the prerequisite 350 are still returned. The next condition, LOCATION(+) = 'L507', shows rows in the SECTION table that satisfy this condition; otherwise, a null is displayed.

What happens when you choose a different location, such as L210? Neither course meets in this location.

```
SELECT c.course_no cno, s.course_no sno,
       SUBSTR(c.description, 1,20),
       c.prerequisite prereq,
       s.location loc, s.section_id
  FROM course c, section s
 WHERE c.course_no = s.course_no(+)
   AND c.prerequisite = 350
   AND s.location(+) = 'L210'
```

CNO	SNO	DESCRIPTION	PREREQ	LOC	SECTION_ID
430		Java Developer III	350		
450		DB Programming with Java	350		

2 rows selected.

Here, you see both courses with this prerequisite. This contrasts with the earlier output because now both the LOCATION and SECTION_ID columns display nulls. When the WHERE clause is evaluated, the PREREQUISITE condition is evaluated first, and then matches are found in the SECTION table with the condition s.location(+) = 'L210'. Because none of the sections matches this LOCATION condition for this course number, nulls are shown for SECTION_ID and LOCATION.

WHERE CONDITIONS AND ANSI OUTER JOINS

When you compare the previous, proprietary Oracle syntax to the ANSI outer join syntax, you see that there are some differences. Following is the query of the first outer join with the condition location = 'L507'. The ANSI join returns the result of the equijoin, which is one row. This is not the desired result.

```
   SELECT c.course_no cno, s.course_no sno,
          c.description,
          c.prerequisite prereq,
          s.location loc, s.section_id
     FROM course c LEFT OUTER JOIN section s
       ON c.course_no = s.course_no
    WHERE c.prerequisite = 350
      AND location = 'L507'
   CNO SNO DESCRIPTION                PREREQ LOC  SECTION_ID
   --- --- ------------------------   ------ ---- ----------
   450 450 DB Programming with Java      350 L507        109

   1 row selected.
```

Instead, the query needs to be changed with the use of parentheses to obtain the correct result. The order of execution matters, and the order is determined by the parentheses. The join on the COURSE_NO column together with the condition location = 'L507' is enclosed by parentheses; the join and LOCATION condition are then executed first. This intermediate result includes all matching rows between the COURSE and SECTION tables based on the COURSE_NO column and those rows from the SECTION table where the LOCATION column has the value L507.

```
   SELECT c.course_no cno, s.course_no sno,
          c.description,
          c.prerequisite prereq,
          s.location loc, s.section_id
     FROM course c LEFT OUTER JOIN section s
       ON (c.course_no = s.course_no
      AND location = 'L507')
    WHERE c.prerequisite = 350
```

Here is an intermediate result listing of the join condition without the WHERE clause condition applied.

```
       ON (c.course_no = s.course_no
      AND location = 'L507')
   CNO SNO DESCRIPTION                PREREQ LOC  SECTION_ID
   --- --- ------------------------   ------ ---- ----------
   100 100 Hands-On Windows               20 L507        144
   450 450 DB Programming with Java      350 L507        109
   ...
   350     Java Developer II             125
```

```
430        Java Developer III              350
220        PL/SQL Programming               80
230        Intro to the Internet            10
```

33 rows selected.

Based on this intermediate result set, the WHERE clause is applied; only rows with a prerequisite value of 350 are chosen for output, and just two rows qualify for the final result. This works because the LOCATION column condition is part of the outer join criteria on the table for which nulls are to be displayed.

USING INLINE VIEWS AND OUTER JOINS

You can use inline views to control the execution order. You can get the same result as in the preceding section by using the following query, which chooses all the rows from the COURSE table with a value of 350 in the PREREQUISITE column. This result set is then left outer joined with the inline view of the SECTION table, which retrieves only sections with the location column value 'L507'.

```
SELECT c.course_no cno, s.course_no sno,
       c.description,
       c.prerequisite prereq,
       s.location loc, s.section_id
  FROM (SELECT *
          FROM course
         WHERE prerequisite = 350) c LEFT OUTER JOIN
       (SELECT * FROM section
         WHERE location = 'L507') s
    ON (c.course_no = s.course_no)
```

WHERE clauses and outer joins may give you unexpected results unless you carefully craft your conditions. Inline views and the ANSI join syntax are best for complicated conditions because they give you control over the execution order of the conditions and subsequent joins. ANSI joins are preferable over Oracle's proprietary outer join operator because the ANSI join syntax is less restrictive and easier to read, and it allows your SQL statements to be portable to non-Oracle databases.

c) Rewrite the following SQL statement using an outer join.

```
SELECT course_no, description
  FROM course c
 WHERE NOT EXISTS
       (SELECT 'X'
          FROM section
         WHERE c.course_no = course_no)
COURSE_NO DESCRIPTION
--------- -----------------------------------
       80 Programming Techniques
      430 Java Developer III

2 rows selected.
```

ANSWER: You can rewrite a NOT EXISTS condition as an outer join condition by querying the SECTION table for nulls.

You can write your query in many different ways. The following example shows the use of the (+) outer join operator.

```
SELECT c.course_no, c.description
  FROM course c, section s
 WHERE c.course_no = s.course_no(+)
   AND s.course_no IS NULL
```

Or you can write it with the ANSI outer join syntax and the USING clause.

```
SELECT course_no, description
  FROM course LEFT OUTER JOIN section
 USING (course_no)
 WHERE section_id IS NULL
```

d) Show all the city, state, and zip code values for Connecticut. Display a count of how many students live in each zip code. Order the result alphabetically by city. The result should look similar to the following output. The column STUDENT_COUNT displays a zero when no student lives in a particular zip code.

```
CITY                        ST ZIP    STUDENT_COUNT
------------------------     -- -----  -------------
Ansonia                     CT 06401             0
Bridgeport                  CT 06605             1
...
Wilton                      CT 06897             0
Woodbury                    CT 06798             1

19 rows selected.
```

ANSWER: The query that achieves the correct solution requires the use of an outer join on the ZIPCODE table and the use of the aggregate function COUNT. When using an aggregate function together with outer joins, you must be careful to apply the aggregate function to the correct column.

```
SELECT city, state, z.zip,
       COUNT(s.zip) AS student_count
  FROM zipcode z LEFT OUTER JOIN student s
    ON (z.zip = s.zip)
 WHERE state = 'CT'
 GROUP BY city, state, z.zip
```

In this query, the parameter in the COUNT function is the S.ZIP column instead of Z.ZIP. The COUNT function requires the STUDENT table's ZIP column as a parameter to ensure that if the zip code is not found in the STUDENT table, the COUNT function will return a zero.

To illustrate this important issue, the following query shows the result of both the Z.ZIP and S.ZIP columns in the SELECT list and as a parameter in the COUNT function. The SZIP column in the result is null, and the column WRONG_VALUE has a count of one even though this zip code does not exist in the STUDENT table. The COUNT function for this column is counting the occurrence of the zip code in the ZIPCODE table, not the desired STUDENT table's zip code.

```
SELECT city, state, z.zip AS zzip, s.zip AS szip,
       COUNT(s.zip) AS student_count,
       COUNT(z.zip) AS wrong_value
  FROM zipcode z LEFT OUTER JOIN student s
    ON (z.zip = s.zip)
 WHERE state = 'CT'
 GROUP BY city, state, z.zip, s.zip
CITY               ST ZZIP  SZIP  STUDENT_COUNT WRONG_VALUE
------------------ -- ----- ----- ------------- -----------
Ansonia            CT 06401                   0           1
...
Woodbury           CT 06798 06798             1           1

19 rows selected.
```

ALTERNATIVE SOLUTION WITH A SCALAR SUBQUERY

A scalar subquery, discussed in Chapter 8, "Subqueries," can provide some simplicity and less chance for errors. The query is correlated as the scalar subquery is executed for each individual zip code. However, scalar subqueries can be notoriously inefficient because Oracle can often execute table joins more quickly, particularly when scans of the entire result set are involved.

```
SELECT city, state, zip,
       (SELECT COUNT(*)
  FROM student s
       WHERE s.zip = z.zip) AS student_count
  FROM zipcode z
 WHERE state = 'CT'
CITY               ST ZIP   STUDENT_COUNT
------------------ -- ----- -------------
Ansonia            CT 06401             0
...
Stamford           CT 06907             1

19 rows selected.
```

e) Display the course number, description, cost, class location, and instructor's last name for all the courses. Also include courses where no sections or instructors have been assigned.

ANSWER: This outer join involves three tables: COURSE, SECTION, and INSTRUCTOR. You want to include all the courses from the COURSE table, whether a section exists for it or not. Also, if no instructor is assigned to a section or no match is found, the rows of the SECTION table should still be included.

```
SELECT course_no cou, description, cost,
       location, last_name
  FROM course LEFT OUTER JOIN section
 USING (course_no)
  LEFT OUTER JOIN instructor
 USING (instructor_id)
 ORDER BY course_no
```

```
COU DESCRIPTION                      COST LOCA LAST_NAME
---- ----------------------------- ---- ---- ---------
  10 Technology Concepts            1195 L214 Wojick
  20 Intro to Information Systems   1195 L210 Schorin
  20 Intro to Information Systems   1195 L214 Pertez
  20 Intro to Information Systems   1195 L509 Morris
  20 Intro to Information Systems   1195 L210 Smythe
...
 430 Java Developer III             1195
 450 DB Programming with Java            L507 Hanks

80 rows selected.
```

When you review the result, recall from the previous examples that course number 430 does not have a section assigned. Therefore, the column LOCATION displays a null value. Also, the instructor's last name shows a null value because there cannot be an instructor assigned if a row in the SECTION table does not exist.

Alternatively, you can use the Oracle outer join operator. In this case, the SQL statement looks similar to the following.

```
SELECT c.course_no cou, c.description, c.cost,
       s.location, i.last_name
  FROM course c, section s, instructor i
 WHERE c.course_no = s.course_no(+)
   AND s.instructor_id = i.instructor_id(+)
 ORDER BY c.course_no
```

The SELECT statement requires the outer join operator to be placed on the COURSE_NO column of the SECTION table. This indicates that you want to see all the courses, whether there are corresponding sections or not. The outer join operator is also applied to the INSTRUCTOR_ID column of the INSTRUCTOR table. This directs Oracle to include rows from the SECTION table even if it doesn't find a matching record in the INSTRUCTOR table.

f) For students with the student ID 102 and 301, determine the sections they are enrolled in. Also show the numeric grades and grade types they received, regardless of whether they are enrolled or received any grades.

ANSWER: You can write outer joins that include rows from all three tables: STUDENT, ENROLLMENT, and GRADE.

```
SELECT student_id, section_id, grade_type_code,
       numeric_grade
  FROM student LEFT OUTER JOIN enrollment
 USING (student_id)
  LEFT OUTER JOIN grade
 USING (student_id, section_id)
 WHERE student_id IN (102, 301)
```

Or you can write them as follows.

```
SELECT s.student_id, en.section_id, grade_type_code,
       numeric_grade
  FROM student s LEFT OUTER JOIN enrollment en
```

```
      ON (s.student_id = en.student_id)
   LEFT OUTER JOIN grade g
      ON (s.student_id = g.student_id
   AND en.section_id = g.section_id)
 WHERE s.student_id IN (102, 301)
STUDENT_ID SECTION_ID GR NUMERIC_GRADE
---------- ---------- -- -------------
       102         86 FI            85
       102         86 HM            90
       102         86 HM            99
       102         86 HM            82
       102         86 HM            82
       102         86 MT            90
       102         86 PA            85
       102         86 QZ            90
       102         86 QZ            84
       102         86 QZ            97
       102         86 QZ            97
       102         89 FI            92
       102         89 MT            91
       301
```

14 rows selected.

The student with ID 102 is enrolled and received grades. His rows are returned as part of an equi-join. However, student 301 is not enrolled in any section and does not have any grades.

You can also write the query using the traditional join syntax and the Oracle (+) outer join operator.

```
SELECT s.student_id, e.section_id, g.grade_type_code,
       g.numeric_grade
  FROM student s, enrollment e, grade g
 WHERE s.student_id IN (102, 301)
   AND s.student_id = e.student_id(+)
   AND e.student_id = g.student_id(+)
   AND e.section_id = g.section_id(+)
```

Because the outer join operator is applied to both the ENROLLMENT and the GRADE tables, STUDENT_ID 301 is included in the result. The condition s.student_id IN (102, 301) does not require an outer join operator because it is based on the STUDENT table, and this is the table from which you want all the rows that satisfy this condition.

Lab 10.1 Quiz

In order to test your progress, you should be able to answer the following questions.

1) A WHERE clause containing an outer join (+) operator cannot contain another condition with the OR operator, as in the following example.

```
SELECT *
  FROM course c, section s
 WHERE c.course_no = s.course_no(+)
    OR c.course_no = 100
```

_____ a) True
_____ b) False

2) A column with the outer join (+) operator cannot use the IN operator, as in the following example.

```
SELECT *
  FROM course c, section s
 WHERE c.course_no = s.course_no(+)
   AND c.course_no(+) IN (100, 200)
```

_____ a) True
_____ b) False

3) An outer join between two tables returns all rows that satisfy the equijoin condition plus records from the outer joined tables for which no matches are found.

_____ a) True
_____ b) False

4) Which of the WHERE clauses results in the following error message?

```
ORA-01468: a predicate may reference only one outer joined table
```

```
SELECT c.course_no, s.course_no,
       SUBSTR(c.description, 1,20), s.start_date_time
  FROM course c, section s
```

_____ a) WHERE course_no – course_no
_____ b) WHERE c.course_no(+) = s.course_no
_____ c) WHERE c.course_no = s.course_no(+)
_____ d) WHERE c.course_no(+) = s.course_no(+)

ANSWERS APPEAR IN APPENDIX A.

LAB 10.2
Self-Joins

LAB OBJECTIVES

After this lab, you will be able to:

- ▶ Write Self-Joins
- ▶ Detect Data Inconsistencies

An equijoin always joins one or multiple tables. A self-join joins a table to itself by pretending there are different tables involved. This is accomplished by using table aliases. One table has one alias, and the same table also has another alias. For the purpose of executing the query, Oracle treats them as two different tables.

Constructing a Self-Join

Self-joins are quite useful for performing comparisons and checking for inconsistencies in data. Sometimes a self-join is needed to report on recursive relationships. Chapter 16, "Regular Expressions and Hierarchical Queries," provides detailed examples of reporting on recursive relationships using the CONNECT BY operator.

One example that lends itself very well to illustrating the functionality of self-joins is the COURSE table. The PREREQUISITE column is a foreign key to the primary key column COURSE_NO of the COURSE table, reflecting a recursive relationship between the two columns. PREREQUISITE is valid only if it is also a valid COURSE_NO; otherwise, the data manipulation operation on the table is rejected.

Many queries executed on the COURSE table so far in this book typically show only the prerequisite number, as in the following example.

```
SELECT course_no, description, prerequisite
  FROM course
```

If you also want to show the description of the prerequisite, you need to write a self-join. This is accomplished by pretending to have two separate tables via table aliases, such as C1 and C2. You join the PREREQUISITE column of table C1 with the COURSE_NO column of table C2, If matching records are found, the description of the prerequisite is displayed.

```
SELECT c1.course_no,
       c1.description course_descr,
```

```
        c1.prerequisite as prereq,
        c2.description pre_req_descr
   FROM course c1 JOIN course c2
     ON (c1.prerequisite = c2.course_no)
   ORDER BY 3, 1
   COURSE_NO COURSE_DESCR                 PREREQ PRE_REQ_DESCR
   --------- ----------------------       ------ --------------------------
         230 Intro to the Internet           10 Technology Concepts
         100 Hands-On Windows                20 Intro to Information Systems
   ...
         450 DB Programming with Java       350 Java Developer II
         144 Database Design               420 Database System Principles
   26 rows selected.
```

Examine the first row of the result, COURSE_NO 230, with the prerequisite course number of 10. The course description for course number 10 is Technology Concepts. This join works just like the equijoins you learned about in Chapter 7. If a prerequisite is NULL or a match is not found, the self-join, just like an equijoin, does not return the record.

The self-join acts like other joins with primary key and foreign key columns. However, here the relationship is to the table itself. The PREREQUISITE column is a foreign key to the primary key COURSE_NO. The PREREQUISITE values come from the child table, and the COURSE_NO values come from the parent table. Every COURSE_NO may have zero or one PREREQUISITE.

 To qualify as a prerequisite, the PREREQUISITE course number must be listed in the PREREQUISITE column for at least one course.

The USING clause cannot be applied to the self-join because this clause requires identical column names on both tables. This is obviously a problem because the join needs to be executed on the columns PREREQUISITE and COURSE_NO.

The query can also be expressed in the traditional join format with the following SQL statement.

```
   SELECT c1.course_no,
          c1.description course_descr,
          c1.prerequisite,
          c2.description pre_req_descr
     FROM course c1, course c2
    WHERE c1.prerequisite = c2.course_no
    ORDER BY 3, 1
```

The Nonequijoin

Occasionally, you need to construct joins that are not based on equality of values. The following query illustrates such an example, using the BETWEEN operator, where you have values that fall into a range. The result shows a list of grades for student ID 107, including the respective letter grades.

```
SELECT grade_type_code, numeric_grade, letter_grade
  FROM grade g JOIN grade_conversion c
    ON (g.numeric_grade BETWEEN c.min_grade AND c.max_grade)
 WHERE g.student_id = 107
 ORDER BY 1, 2 DESC
    GR NUMERIC_GRADE LE
    -- ------------- --
    FI            76 C
    HM            96 A
    HM            96 A
    ...
    HM            73 C
    MT            91 A-
```

12 rows selected.

The BETWEEN operator checks for each value in the NUMERIC_GRADE column to see if the individual grade is between the values found in the columns MIN_GRADE and MAX_GRADE of the GRADE_CONVERSION table. If a match is found, the corresponding letter grade is returned. For example, the first row of the result shows the value 76 in the NUMERIC_GRADE column for a final examination. The appropriate letter grade for the value 76 is C.

You can also express the query with the traditional join syntax instead.

```
SELECT grade_type_code, numeric_grade, letter_grade,
       min_grade, max_grade
  FROM grade g, grade_conversion c
 WHERE g.numeric_grade BETWEEN c.min_grade AND c.max_grade
   AND g.student_id = 107
 ORDER BY 1, 2 DESC
```

▼ LAB 10.2 EXERCISES

a) For SECTION_ID 86, determine which students received a lower grade on their final than on their midterm. In your result, list the STUDENT_ID and the grade for the midterm and final.

b) What problem does the following query solve?

```
SELECT DISTINCT a.student_id, a.first_name, a.salutation
  FROM student a, student b
 WHERE a.salutation <> b.salutation
   AND b.first_name = a.first_name
   AND a.student_id <> b.student_id
 ORDER BY a.first_name
```

c) Display the student ID, last name, and street address of students living at the same address and zip code.

d) Write a query that shows the course number, course description, prerequisite, and description of the prerequisite. Include courses without any prerequisites. (This requires a self-join and an outer join.)

▼ LAB 10.2 EXERCISE ANSWERS

a) For SECTION_ID 86, determine which students received a lower grade on their final than on their midterm. In your result, list the STUDENT_ID and the grade for the midterm and final.

ANSWER: Using a self-join, you can compare the grade for the midterm with the grade for the final and determine whether the final is lower than the midterm grade.

```
SELECT fi.student_id, mt.numeric_grade "Midterm Grade",
       fi.numeric_grade "Final Grade"
  FROM grade fi JOIN grade mt
    ON (fi.section_id = mt.section_id
   AND fi.student_id = mt.student_id)
 WHERE fi.grade_type_code = 'FI'
   AND fi.section_id = 86
   AND mt.grade_type_code = 'MT'
   AND fi.numeric_grade < mt.numeric_grade
STUDENT_ID Midterm Grade Final Grade
---------- ------------- -----------
       102            90          85
       108            91          76
       211            92          77

3 rows selected.
```

Three students have a lower grade in the final than the grade they achieved in the midterm. Using a self-join allows you to easily determine the correct result. Imagine that you are actually joining to a different table, even though it is really the same table. Visualize one table as the midterm table and the other as the final table, and the formulation of your SQL statement falls into place.

Start with the table representing the final grade for SECTION_ID 86. Then compare the result with the table representing the midterm grade (grade_type_code = 'MT'). Also join STUDENT_ID and SECTION_ID to make sure you match the same individuals and sections. Finally, compare the numeric grades between the midterm and final.

Using the traditional join syntax, you can also write the query as follows.

```
SELECT fi.student_id, mt.numeric_grade "Midterm Grade",
       fi.numeric_grade "Final Grade"
  FROM grade fi, grade mt
 WHERE fi.grade_type_code = 'FI'
   AND fi.section_id = 86
   AND mt.grade_type_code = 'MT'
   AND fi.section_id = mt.section_id
   AND fi.student_id = mt.student_id
   AND fi.numeric_grade < mt.numeric_grade
```

Alternatively, you can obtain a somewhat similar solution by using the ANY operator and a correlated subquery (see Chapter 8).

```
SELECT student_id, section_id, numeric_grade
  FROM grade g
 WHERE grade_type_code = 'FI'
   AND section_id = 86
```

```
AND numeric_grade < ANY
    (SELECT numeric_grade
       FROM grade
      WHERE grade_type_code = 'MT'
        AND g.section_id = section_id
        AND g.student_id = student_id)
```

b) What problem does the following query solve?

```
SELECT DISTINCT a.student_id, a.first_name, a.salutation
  FROM student a, student b
 WHERE a.salutation <> b.salutation
   AND a.first_name = b.first_name
   AND a.student_id <> b.student_id
 ORDER BY a.first_name
```

ANSWER: The query determines the students who might have inconsistent salutations for their respective first names.

This self-join is used to check for errors and inconsistency of data. A number of students have different salutations for the same first name. According to the query result, Kevin is both a female and male name. The same holds true for Daniel, Roger, and some other students as well.

```
STUDENT_ID FIRST_NAME                              SALUT
---------- ------------------------------------    -----
       124 Daniel                                  Mr.
       242 Daniel                                  Mr.
       315 Daniel                                  Ms.
...
       272 Kevin                                   Ms.
       341 Kevin                                   Mr.
       368 Kevin                                   Mr.
       238 Roger                                   Mr.
       383 Roger                                   Ms.

17 rows selected.
```

The query self-joins by the first name and shows only those having a different salutation for the same name. Because there are multiple names for each table alias, this results in a Cartesian product. Eliminate any records where the student_ids are identical with the condition a.student_id <> b.student_id. Further eliminate duplicate rows by using DISTINCT.

c) Display the student ID, last name, and street address of students living at the same address and zip code.

ANSWER: You can use a self-join to compare the street address and the zip code.

```
SELECT DISTINCT a.student_id, a.last_name,
       a.street_address
  FROM student a, student b
 WHERE a.street_address = b.street_address
   AND a.zip = b.zip
   AND a.student_id <> b.student_id
 ORDER BY a.street_address
```

```
STUDENT_ID LAST_NAME              STREET_ADDRESS
---------- --------------------   --------------------
       390 Greenberg              105-34 65th Ave.  #6B
       392 Saliternan             105-34 65th Ave.  #6B
       234 Brendler               111 Village Hill Dr.
       380 Krot                   111 Village Hill Dr.
...
       217 Citron                 PO Box 1091
       182 Delbrun                PO Box 1091
```

22 rows selected.

The condition a.student_id <> b.student_id eliminates the student itself from the result.

Alternatively, your ANSI join solution may be similar to the following SELECT statement.

```
SELECT DISTINCT a.student_id, a.last_name,
       a.street_address
  FROM student a JOIN student b
    ON (a.street_address = b.street_address
   AND a.zip = b.zip
   AND a.student_id <> b.student_id)
 ORDER BY a.street_address
```

Or, your join and WHERE clause may look like the following, which provides the same result. The ON clause and the WHERE condition all need to be true and are connected by the logical AND.

```
    ON (a.street_address = b.street_address
   AND a.zip = b.zip)
 WHERE a.student_id <> b.student_id
 ORDER BY a.street_address
```

You can also expand the query to include the city and state information for the particular zip code by joining to a third table, the ZIPCODE table.

```
SELECT DISTINCT b.student_id id, b.last_name,
       b.street_address ||' '|| city || ', '
       || state address
  FROM student a, student b, zipcode z
 WHERE a.street_address = b.street_address
   AND a.zip = b.zip
   AND a.student_id <> b.student_id
   AND z.zip = b.zip
 ORDER BY address
```
```
  ID LAST_NAME    ADDRESS
---- ------------ -------------------------------------
 390 Greenberg    105-34 65th Ave.  #6B Forest Hills, NY
 392 Saliternan   105-34 65th Ave.  #6B Forest Hills, NY
...
 217 Citron       PO Box 1091 Ft. Lee, NJ
 182 Delbrun      PO Box 1091 Ft. Lee, NJ
```

22 rows selected.

As always, you can use many alternatives to achieve the same result; for example, you can also write a subquery like the following.

```
SELECT DISTINCT student_id id, last_name,
       street_address ||' '|| city || ', '
       || state address
  FROM student s, zipcode z
 WHERE s.zip = z.zip
   AND (street_address, s.zip) IN
       (SELECT street_address, zip
          FROM student
         GROUP BY street_address, zip
         HAVING COUNT(*) > 1)
 ORDER BY address
```

d) Write a query that shows the course number, course description, prerequisite, and description of the prerequisite. Include courses without any prerequisites. (This requires a self-join and an outer join.)

ANSWER: The SELECT statement joins the courses and their corresponding prerequisites. It also includes courses that do not have any prerequisites, using an outer join, and displays a NULL for the prerequisite description column labeled PRE_REQ_DESCR.

```
SELECT c1.course_no,
       SUBSTR(c1.description, 1,15) course_descr,
       C1.prerequisite,
       SUBSTR(c2.description,1,15) pre_req_descr
  FROM course c1 LEFT OUTER JOIN course c2
    ON c1.prerequisite = c2.course_no
 ORDER BY 1
```

COURSE_NO	COURSE_DESCR	PREREQUISITE	PRE_REQ_DESCR
10	Technology Conc		
20	Intro to Inform		
25	Intro to Progra	140	Systems Analysi
...			
145	Internet Protoc	310	Operating Syste
146	Java for C/C++		
147	GUI Design Lab	20	Intro to Inform
...			
430	Java Developer	350	Java Developer
450	DB Programming	350	Java Developer

30 rows selected.

Using the traditional syntax, you can write the query as follows.

```
SELECT c1.course_no,
       SUBSTR(c1.description, 1,15) course_descr,
       C1.prerequisite,
       SUBSTR(c2.description,1,15) pre_req_descr
```

```
   FROM course c1, course c2
  WHERE c1.prerequisite = c2.course_no(+)
  ORDER BY 1
```

Or, you can write the query with a UNION ALL.

```
SELECT c1.course_no, c1.description course_descr,
       c1.prerequisite, c2.description pre_req_descr
  FROM course c1 JOIN course c2
    ON (c1.prerequisite = c2.course_no)
 UNION ALL
SELECT course_no, description, prerequisite, NULL
  FROM course
 WHERE prerequisite IS NULL
```

Lab 10.2 Quiz

In order to test your progress, you should be able to answer the following questions.

1) A self-join requires you to always join the foreign key with the primary key in the same table.

_____ a) True
_____ b) False

2) Self-joins work only when you have a recursive relationship in your table.

_____ a) True
_____ b) False

3) You cannot use subqueries or ORDER BY clauses with self-joins.

_____ a) True
_____ b) False

4) You need to use a table alias to be able to write a self-join.

_____ a) True
_____ b) False

ANSWERS APPEAR IN APPENDIX A.

▼ WORKSHOP

The projects in this section are meant to prompt you to utilize all the skills you have acquired throughout this chapter. The answers to these projects can be found at the companion Web site to this book, located at www.oraclesqlbyexample.com.

1) Write a query that shows all the instructors who live in the same zip code.

2) Are any of the rooms overbooked? Determine whether any sections meet at the same date, time, and location.

3) Determine whether there is any scheduling conflict for instructors: Are any instructors scheduled to teach one or more sections at the same date and time? Order the result by the INSTRUCTOR_ID and the starting date and time of the sections.

4) Show the course number, description, course cost, and section ID for courses that cost 1195 or more. Include courses that have no corresponding section.

5) Write a query that lists the section numbers and students IDs of students enrolled in classes held in location L210. Include sections for which no students are enrolled.

CHAPTER 11

Insert, Update, and Delete

CHAPTER OBJECTIVES

In this chapter, you will learn about:

- ▶ Creating Data and Transaction Control
- ▶ Updating and Deleting Data
- ▶ The SQL Developer Data Tab

In Chapters 1 through 10, you learned what data is and how to query and present data. In this chapter, you will learn how to modify the data in tables with the INSERT, UPDATE, DELETE, and MERGE statements, which are known as Data Manipulation Language (DML).

These statements enable you to create, change, or delete data from tables. In Lab 11.1 you will learn about creating data in tables with the different INSERT command options and how to make these changes permanent. Lab 11.2 illustrates how to delete data and shows various ways to change existing data in the tables. Furthermore, you will learn about Oracle's locking and read-consistency features. Lab 11.3 shows how you can use SQL Developer's Data tab to manipulate data using the graphical user interface (GUI) screen functionality, which is useful when you need to modify a small number of records.

LAB 11.1
Creating Data and Transaction Control

LAB OBJECTIVES

After this lab, you will be able to:

▶ Insert Data
▶ Rollback and Commit Transactions

When you create new data in a table, you need to not only understand the syntax options but also know about referential integrity, column defaults, and data types. You can insert into a table one row at a time or write an INSERT statement that creates data in multiple tables. A major key to understanding SQL is the concept of transaction control, which ensures data consistency.

Inserting an Individual Row

The INSERT statement creates new data in a table. It can insert into a table a single row or multiple rows (based on a subquery).

The following INSERT statement inserts one individual row into the ZIPCODE table.

```
INSERT INTO zipcode
VALUES
   ('11111', 'Westerly', 'MA',
    USER, TO_DATE('18-JAN-2010', 'DD-MON-YYYY'),
    USER, SYSDATE)
```

When the statement is executed, Oracle responds with the following message.

1 row created.

The INSERT INTO keywords always precede the name of the table into which you want to insert data. The VALUES keyword precedes a set of parentheses that enclose the values you want to insert. For each of the seven columns of the ZIPCODE table there are seven corresponding values with matching data types in the INSERT statement separated by commas. The values in the list are in the same order as the columns when you use the DESCRIBE command on the ZIPCODE table. It is good practice to include a column list, though, in case of future table changes. Following is the INSERT statement with the column list.

```
INSERT INTO zipcode
  (zip, city, state,
   created_by, created_date,
   modified_by, modified_date)
VALUES
  ('11111', 'Westerly', 'MA',
   USER, TO_DATE('18-JAN-2010', 'DD-MON-YYYY'),
   USER, SYSDATE)
```

The syntax of the single-row, single-table INSERT statement is as follows.

```
INSERT INTO tablename [(column [, column]...)]
VALUES (expression|DEFAULT [,expression|DEFAULT]...)
```

 Remember that the syntax convention is to enclose optional parts in brackets, denoted as [ ]. Keywords are in uppercase. The three dots (...) means that the expression can be repeated. The vertical bar denotes options, and the braces, { }, enclose items of which only one is required.

You notice from the INSERT statement into the ZIPCODE table that a text literal such as 'Westerly' is enclosed in single quotation marks and to insert a date requires the TO_DATE function with the format mask unless the date has the appropriate NLS_DATE_FORMAT value.

The INSERT statement uses the SYSDATE function to insert the current date and time into the MODIFIED_DATE column. Similar to the SYSDATE function, the USER function is another function that does not take a parameter. It returns the schema name of the user logged in—in this case, the value STUDENT. This value is inserted in the CREATED_BY and MODIFIED_BY columns. You see the result of the USER function in the following example.

```
SELECT USER
  FROM dual
USER
---------------
STUDENT

1 row selected.
```

Not all columns of the ZIPCODE table require values; only columns defined as NOT NULL. When you are not inserting data into all columns of a table, you must explicitly name the columns to insert data into. The following statement inserts values into just five of the seven columns in the ZIPCODE table; no data is inserted into the CITY and STATE columns.

```
INSERT INTO zipcode
  (zip, created_by, created_date,
   modified_by, modified_date)
VALUES
  ('11111', USER, SYSDATE, USER, SYSDATE)
```

Some columns may have default values defined as part of their column definition. Not listing the column in the INSERT statement automatically places the default value in the column, or you can also explicitly use the keyword DEFAULT.

Alternatively, you can write the statement to omit the columns altogether and to insert NULL values in some of the columns instead.

```
INSERT INTO zipcode
VALUES
    ('11111', NULL, NULL, USER, SYSDATE, USER, SYSDATE)
```

When an INSERT command is successful, SQL Developer responds with a message on the left of the screen (see Figure 11.1). Later in the lab, you will see how to make this change permanent in the Oracle database by issuing a COMMIT command.

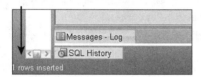

FIGURE 11.1
Message indicating a successfully issued INSERT statement

Data Types and Inserts

When inserting records, you always need to take the data type into consideration.

INSERTING DATES AND TIMES

To insert into a DATE data type column, you must specify the data in the required format for Oracle to understand and store the data. This is similar to using these literals in the WHERE clause of a SELECT statement. Following is the structure of the DATE_EXAMPLE table used in Chapter 5, "Date and Conversion Functions."

```
SQL> DESCRIBE date_example
    Name                         Null? Type
    ------------------------     ----- ----------------------------
    COL_DATE                           DATE
    COL_TIMESTAMP                      TIMESTAMP(6)
    COL_TIMESTAMP_W_TZ                 TIMESTAMP(6) WITH TIME ZONE
    COL_TIMESTAMP_W_LOCAL_TZ           TIMESTAMP(6) WITH LOCAL TIME
                                       ZONE
```

The next INSERT statement populates the table; it explicitly converts the literals, using the conversion functions, into the respective data types. The first column value is a DATE data type, and you use the TO_DATE function; the second value is a TIMESTAMP data type, and the literal is converted to this data type with the TO_TIMESTAMP function. The third column value is of data type TIMESTAMP WITH TIME ZONE and uses the corresponding TO_TIMESTAMP_TZ function to convert to the correct data type. Finally, the fourth column is the date and time in the local time zone. There is no specific conversion function for this data type; it always displays the value in the local time.

```
INSERT INTO date_example
  (col_date,
   col_timestamp,
   col_timestamp_w_tz,
   col_timestamp_w_local_tz)
VALUES
  (TO_DATE('24-FEB-2007 16:25:32',
           'DD-MON-YYYY HH24:MI:SS'),
   TO_TIMESTAMP('24-FEB-2007 16:25:32.0000000',
                'DD-MON-YYYY  HH24:MI:SS.FF'),
   TO_TIMESTAMP_TZ('24-FEB-2007 16:25:32.0000000 -5:00',
                   'DD-MON-YYYY HH24:MI:SS.FF TZH:TZM'),
   TO_TIMESTAMP('24-FEB-2007 16:25:32.0000000',
                'DD-MON-YYYY HH24:MI:SS.FF'))
```

THE NUMBER DATA TYPE AND ROUNDING OF NUMBERS

The next statement attempts to insert a value that exceeds the scale of the COST column in the COURSE table. The COST column is defined as NUMBER(9,2), and the inserted value is 50.57499.

```
INSERT INTO course
  (course_no, description, cost, prerequisite,
   created_by, created_date, modified_by, modified_date)
VALUES
  (900, 'Test Course', 50.57499, NULL,
   'Your name', SYSDATE, 'Your name', SYSDATE)
1 row created.
```

The INSERT statement proceeds successfully without any error, and the SELECT statement against the table reveals that Oracle rounds the number to 50.57.

```
SELECT cost, course_no
  FROM course
 WHERE course_no = 900
     COST COURSE_NO
--------- ---------
    50.57       900

1 row selected.
```

If the value exceeds the precision of the COST column, you get an error like the next message, where the precision is exceeded by one digit. The COST column is defined as NUMBER(9,2) with a two-digits scale, thus allowing a maximum number of seven digits to the left of the decimal point.

```
INSERT INTO course
   (course_no, description, cost, prerequisite,
    created_by, created_date, modified_by, modified_date)
VALUES
   (901, 'Test Course',12345678, NULL,
    'Your name', SYSDATE, 'Your name', SYSDATE)
   (901, 'Test Course',12345678, NULL,
                        *
ERROR at line 5:
ORA-01438: value larger than specified precision allows for this
➥column
```

USING THE BINARY_FLOAT DATA TYPE AND INSERTING A FLOATING-POINT NUMBER

The following INSERT statement adds a floating-point number of the data type BINARY_FLOAT into the FLOAT_TEST table. A literal of the BINARY_FLOAT data type is followed by either an f or F.

```
INSERT INTO float_test
   (test_col)
VALUES
   (5f)
```

To indicate a BINARY_DOUBLE in a literal, follow it with d or D. You can also use the conversion functions TO_BINARY_FLOAT and TO_BINARY_DOUBLE to ensure the correct data type conversion.

If a value needs to be expressed as infinity or as not a number (NAN), you use the special literals BINARY_FLOAT_NAN, BINARY_DOUBLE_NAN, BINARY_FLOAT_INFINITY, and BINARY_DOUBLE_INFINITY.

```
INSERT INTO float_test
   (test_col)
VALUES
   (BINARY_FLOAT_INFINITY)

SELECT *
   FROM float_test
TEST_COL
--------
5.0E+000
2.5E+000
     Nan
     Inf

4 rows selected.
```

INSERTING DATA INTO A BFILE DATA TYPE

The BFILE data type allows you to store the pointer to an external binary file, such as an image file. The actual file content is not stored within the database but in a specific file location or directory to which the pointer in the BFILE data type refers. You define this location of the files within Oracle by using the CREATE DIRECTORY command. (To issue this command successfully, you need the CREATE ANY DIRECTORY privileges. Chapter 15, "Security," discusses the granting of privileges.)

```
CREATE DIRECTORY my_docs AS 'c:\ora_docs'
```

The DOCS table has a column called DOC_FILE with the BFILE data type.

```
SQL> DESCR DOCS
Name           Null    Type
------------   ------   --------
DOC_ID                  NUMBER
DOC_FILE                BFILE
```

To insert into the table, you must use the BFILENAME function with two parameters: the directory and the file name.

```
INSERT INTO docs VALUES
(1, BFILENAME('my_docs','test.pdf'))
```

SQL*Plus shows the result as follows.

```
SELECT *
  FROM docs
DOC_ID     DOC_FILE
--------   -------------------------------------------
       1   bfilename('my_docs','test.pdf')

1 rows selected
```

If you want to store multimedia content in the Oracle database, use the BLOB data type. You need to use a programming language and specialized functionality to accomplish this.

Inserts and Scalar Subqueries

A scalar subquery, which is defined as a subquery that returns a single row and column, is allowed within the VALUES clause of an INSERT statement. The following example shows two scalar subqueries: One inserts the description of COURSE_NO 10 and concatenates it with the word Test; the second scalar subquery inserts into the COST column the highest cost of any rows in the course table.

```
INSERT INTO course
   (course_no, description, cost,
    prerequisite, created_by, created_date,
    modified_by, modified_date)
```

```
VALUES
  (1000, (SELECT description||' - Test'
             FROM course
          WHERE course_no = 10),
    (SELECT MAX(cost)
       FROM course),
    20, 'MyName', SYSDATE,
    'MyName', SYSDATE)
```

Verify the result of the INSERT statement by querying the COURSE table for the COURSE_NO equal to 1000.

```
SELECT description, cost, course_no
  FROM course
 WHERE course_no = 1000
DESCRIPTION                      COST COURSE_NO
------------------------------- ---- ---------
Technology Concepts - Test 1595      1000

1 row selected.
```

Inserting Multiple Rows

Another method for inserting data is to select data from another table via a subquery. The subquery may return one or multiple rows; thus, the INSERT statement inserts one or multiple rows at a time. Suppose there is a table called INTRO_COURSE in the STUDENT schema with columns similar to those in the COURSE table. The corresponding columns have compatible data types and column lengths; they do not have to have the same column names or column order. The following INSERT statement inserts data into the INTRO_COURSE table based on a query against the rows of the COURSE table. According to the subquery's WHERE clause, the only rows chosen are those where the course has no prerequisite.

```
INSERT INTO intro_course
  (course_no, description_tx, cost, prereq_no,
   created_by, created_date, modified_by,
   modified_date)
SELECT course_no, description, cost, prerequisite,
       created_by, created_date, 'Melanie',
       TO_DATE('01-JAN-2008', 'DD-MON-YYYY')
  FROM course
 WHERE prerequisite IS NULL
```

The following is the syntax for a multiple-row INSERT based on a subquery.

```
INSERT INTO tablename [(column [, column]...)]
subquery
```

Inserting into Multiple Tables

While most often you use a single-table, single-row INSERT command, you may occasionally need to insert rows into multiple tables simultaneously. This feature is useful when data is transferred from other system sources and the destination is a data warehouse system where the data is consolidated and denormalized for the purpose of providing end users simple query access to this data. You may also use a multitable INSERT command when you need to archive old data into separate tables.

Compared to executing multiple individual INSERT statements, using a multitable INSERT is not only faster but allows additional syntax options, providing further flexibility by enabling the conditional insert of data and perhaps eliminating the need to write specific programs. There are two different types of multitable inserts: INSERT ALL and INSERT FIRST. INSERT ALL can be divided into the unconditional INSERT and the conditional INSERT.

The next examples demonstrate multitable INSERT statements with the SECTION_HISTORY and the CAPACITY_HISTORY tables. You can add them to the STUDENT schema with the supplemental table scripts available from the companion Web site, at www.oraclesqlbyexample.com.

THE UNCONDITIONAL INSERT ALL STATEMENT

The INSERT statement chooses the sections that started more than one year ago and inserts these rows into both tables—SECTION_HISTORY and CAPACITY_HISTORY. There is no condition on the INSERT statement, other than the WHERE clause condition that determines the rows to be selected from the SECTION table.

```
INSERT ALL
  INTO section_history
    VALUES (section_id, start_date_time, course_no, section_no)
  INTO capacity_history
    VALUES (section_id, location, capacity)
SELECT section_id, start_date_time, course_no, section_no,
       location, capacity
  FROM section
 WHERE TRUNC(start_date_time) < TRUNC(SYSDATE)-365
156 rows created.
```

THE CONDITIONAL INSERT ALL STATEMENT

The following statement chooses the same sections and inserts these rows into the tables, depending on whether the individual INSERT condition is satisfied. For example, for a SECTION_ID value of 130 and a capacity of 25, the statement enters the row in both tables. If only one of the conditions is true, it inserts the row only into the table with the true condition. If both conditions are false, the selected row is not inserted into either of the tables.

```
INSERT ALL
 WHEN section_id BETWEEN 100 and 400 THEN
  INTO section_history
    VALUES (section_id, start_date_time, course_no, section_no)
 WHEN capacity >= 25 THEN
  INTO capacity_history
    VALUES (section_id, location, capacity)
SELECT section_id, start_date_time, course_no, section_no,
       location, capacity
  FROM section
 WHERE TRUNC(start_date_time) < TRUNC(SYSDATE)-365
106 rows created.
```

The following is the syntax for the conditional INSERT ALL.

```
INSERT ALL
WHEN condition THEN
insert_clause [insert_clause...]
[WHEN condition THEN
insert_clause [insert_clause...]...]
[ELSE
insert_clause [insert_clause...]]
(query)
```

The insert_clause syntax is defined as follows.

```
INTO tablename [(column [, column]...)]
[VALUES (expression|DEFAULT[,expression|DEFAULT]...)]
```

THE CONDITIONAL INSERT FIRST STATEMENT

The INSERT FIRST statement evaluates the WHEN clauses in order; if the first condition is true, the row is inserted, and subsequent conditions are no longer tested. For example, with a SECTION_ID value of 130 and a capacity of 25, the statement inserts the row in the SECTION_ HISTORY tables only because the first condition of the WHEN clause is satisfied. You can have an optional ELSE condition in case none of the conditions are true.

```
INSERT FIRST
 WHEN section_id BETWEEN 100 and 400 THEN
  INTO section_history
    VALUES (section_id, start_date_time, course_no, section_no)
 WHEN capacity >= 25 THEN
  INTO capacity_history
    VALUES (section_id, location, capacity)
SELECT section_id, start_date_time, course_no, section_no,
       location, capacity
  FROM section
 WHERE TRUNC(start_date_time) < TRUNC(SYSDATE)-365
71 rows created.
```

The syntax for the INSERT FIRST command is identical to that of the conditional INSERT ALL command except that you use the FIRST keyword instead of the ALL keyword.

PIVOTING INSERT ALL

The pivoting INSERT ALL statement is just like the unconditional INSERT ALL statement: It inserts the rows into multiple tables, and it also does not have a WHEN condition. The following is an example of pivoting a table (that is, flipping it on its side). The table used here, called GRADE_DISTRIBUTION, has a count of the different grades per each section. The first row, with SECTION_ID 400, shows 5 students with the letter grade A, 10 students with the letter grade B, 3 students with the letter grade C, and no D or F grades for any students in the section.

```
SELECT *
  FROM grade_distribution
SECTION_ID GRADE_A GRADE_B GRADE_C GRADE_D GRADE_F
---------- ------- ------- ------- ------- -------
       400       5      10       3       0       0
       401       1       3       5       1       0
       402       5      10       3       0       1

3 rows selected.
```

Suppose you want to move the data into a more normalized table format. In this case, you can use a pivoting INSERT ALL statement. The following example illustrates the insertion of the data into the table GRADE_DISTRIBUTION_NORMALIZED, which just lists the letter grade and the number of students. Here is the structure of the table.

```
SQL> DESCR grade_distribution_normalized
Name                        Null      Type
-------------------         --------  ------------
SECTION_ID                            NUMBER(9)
LETTER_GRADE                          VARCHAR2(2)
NUM_OF_STUDENTS                       NUMBER(4)
```

To insert the same data about SECTION_ID 400, five individual rows are needed. The following INSERT ALL statement transfers each individual selected row into the table, but in a normalized format whereby each grade is its own row.

```
INSERT ALL
   INTO grade_distribution_normalized
     VALUES (section_id, 'A', grade_a)
   INTO grade_distribution_normalized
     VALUES (section_id, 'B', grade_b)
   INTO grade_distribution_normalized
     VALUES (section_id, 'C', grade_c)
   INTO grade_distribution_normalized
     VALUES (section_id, 'D', grade_d)
   INTO grade_distribution_normalized
     VALUES (section_id, 'F', grade_f)
```

```
SELECT section_id, grade_a, grade_b,
       grade_c, grade_d, grade_f
  FROM grade_distribution
15 rows created.
```

When selecting from the GRADE_DISTRIBUTION_NORMALIZED table, you see the rows in a normalized format.

```
SELECT *
  FROM grade_distribution_normalized
SECTION_ID LE NUM_OF_STUDENTS
---------- -- ---------------
       400 A                5
       401 A                1
       402 A                5
       400 B               10
...
       400 F                0
       401 F                0
       402 F                1

15 rows selected.
```

Transaction Control

Just as important as manipulating data is controlling when a change becomes permanent. DML statements are controlled within the context of a transaction. A transaction is a DML statement or group of DML statements that logically belong together, also referred to as a logical unit of work. The group of statements is defined by the commands COMMIT and ROLLBACK, in conjunction with the SAVEPOINT command.

COMMIT

The COMMIT command makes a change to data permanent. Any previously uncommitted changes are now committed and cannot be undone. The effect of the COMMIT command is that it allows other sessions to see the data. The session issuing the DML command can always see the changes, but other sessions can see the changes only after you use COMMIT. Another effect of a commit is that locks for the changed rows are released, and other users can perform changes on the rows. You will learn more about locking in Lab 11.2.

Instead of typing the COMMIT command after your INSERT statement, you can click on the Commit icon in SQL Developer (see Figure 11.2).

Data Definition Language (DDL) statements, such as the CREATE TABLE command, or Data Control Language (DCL) statements, such as the GRANT command, implicitly issue a COMMIT to the database; there is no need to issue a COMMIT command. You'll learn about DDL commands in Chapter 12, "Create, Alter, and Drop Tables," and DCL commands in Chapter 15.

FIGURE 11.2
The COMMIT icon in SQL Developer

WHAT IS A SESSION?

A session is an individual connection to the Oracle database server. It starts as soon as the user is logged in and authenticated by the server with a valid login ID and password. The session ends when you explicitly disconnect, such as by using the Disconnect menu in SQL Developer (see Figure 11.3) or by exiting SQL Developer. In SQL*Plus, you log out by issuing a DISCON-NECT command, using the EXIT command, or clicking the Close Window box.

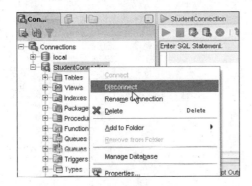

FIGURE 11.3
Disconnecting from a session in SQL Developer

An individual database user may be connected to multiple concurrent sessions simultaneously. For example, if you invoke SQL Developer or SQL*Plus multiple times, each time, you establish an individual session.

ROLLBACK

The ROLLBACK command undoes any DML statements back to the last COMMIT command issued. Any pending changes are discarded, and any locks on the affected rows are released. In SQL Developer, you can click the Rollback icon (F12) instead of issuing the ROLLBACK command (see Figure 11.4).

FIGURE 11.4
The Rollback icon in SQL Developer

AN EXAMPLE OF A TRANSACTION

The following SQL statements all constitute a single transaction. The first INSERT statement starts the transaction, and the ROLLBACK command ends it.

```
INSERT INTO zipcode
   (zip, city, state,
    created_by, created_date, modified_by, modified_date)
VALUES
   ('22222', NULL, NULL,
    USER, SYSDATE, USER, SYSDATE)
1 row created.


INSERT INTO zipcode
   (zip, city, state,
    created_by, created_date, modified_by, modified_date)
VALUES
   ('33333', NULL, NULL,
    USER, SYSDATE, USER, SYSDATE)
1 row created.


INSERT INTO zipcode
   (zip, city, state,
    created_by, created_date, modified_by, modified_date)
VALUES
   ('44444', NULL, NULL,
    USER, SYSDATE, USER, SYSDATE)
1 row created.
```

The following is a query of the ZIPCODE table for the values inserted.

```
SELECT zip, city, state
  FROM zipcode
 WHERE zip IN ('22222', '33333', '44444')
ZIP    CITY                          ST
-----  ------------------------   --
22222
33333
44444

3 rows selected.
```

Then, the following example issues the ROLLBACK command and performs the same query.

```
ROLLBACK
Rollback complete.

SELECT zip, city, state
  FROM zipcode
 WHERE zip IN ('22222', '33333', '44444')

no rows selected
```

The values inserted are no longer in the ZIPCODE table; the ROLLBACK command prevents the values inserted by all three statements from being committed to the database. If a COMMIT command is issued between the first and second statements, the value '22222' would be found in the ZIPCODE table, but not the values '33333' and '44444'.

SAVEPOINT

The SAVEPOINT command allows you to save the results of DML transactions temporarily. The ROLLBACK command can then refer to a particular SAVEPOINT and roll back the transaction up to that point; any statements issued after the SAVEPOINT are rolled back.

The following example shows the same three DML statements used previously, but with SAVEPOINT commands issued in between.

```
INSERT INTO zipcode
    (zip, city, state,
     created_by, created_date, modified_by, modified_date)
VALUES
    ('22222', NULL, NULL,
     USER, SYSDATE, USER, SYSDATE)
1 row created.

SAVEPOINT zip22222
Savepoint created.

INSERT INTO zipcode
    (zip, city, state,
     created_by, created_date, modified_by, modified_date)
VALUES
    ('33333', NULL, NULL,
     USER, SYSDATE, USER, SYSDATE)
1 row created.

SAVEPOINT zip33333
Savepoint created.

INSERT INTO zipcode
    (zip, city, state,
     created_by, created_date, modified_by, modified_date)
```

```
VALUES
  ('44444', NULL, NULL,
   USER, SYSDATE, USER, SYSDATE)
1 row created.
```

The next query checks the ZIPCODE table for the inserted values.

```
SELECT zip, city, state
  FROM zipcode
 WHERE zip IN ('22222', '33333', '44444')
ZIP   CITY                        ST
----- ------------------------- --
22222
33333
44444

3 rows selected.
```

Then, issue the command ROLLBACK TO SAVEPOINT zip33333 and perform the same query.

```
ROLLBACK TO SAVEPOINT zip33333
Rollback complete.

SELECT zip, city, state
  FROM zipcode
 WHERE zip IN ('22222', '33333', '44444')
ZIP   CITY                        ST
----- ------------------------- --
22222
33333

2 rows selected.
```

All statements issued after the zip33333 SAVEPOINT are rolled back. When you rollback to the previous SAVEPOINT, the same result occurs, and so on.

```
ROLLBACK TO SAVEPOINT zip22222
Rollback complete.

SELECT zip, city, state
  FROM zipcode
 WHERE zip IN ('22222', '33333', '44444')
ZIP   CITY                        ST
----- ------------------------- --
22222

1 row selected.
```

The three statements still constitute a single transaction; however, it is possible to mark parts of the transaction with savepoints in order to control how a statement is rolled back with the ROLLBACK TO SAVEPOINT command.

CONTROLLING TRANSACTIONS

It is important to control DML statements by using COMMIT, ROLLBACK, and SAVEPOINT. If the three previous statements logically belong together—in other words, one does not make sense without the others occurring—then another session should not see the results until all three are committed at once. Until the user performing the inserts issues a COMMIT command, no other database users or sessions are able to see the changes. A typical example of such a transaction is a transfer from a savings account to a checking account. You obviously want to avoid the scenario where transactions from one account are missing and the balances are out of sync. Unless both data manipulations are successful, the change does not become permanent and visible to other users.

Oracle places a lock on a row whenever the row is manipulated through a DML statement. This prevents other users from manipulating the row until it is either committed or rolled back. Users can continue to query the row and see the old values until the row is committed.

STATEMENT-LEVEL ROLLBACKS

If one individual statement fails in a series of DML statements, only this statement is rolled back, and Oracle issues an implicit SAVEPOINT. The other changes remain until a COMMIT or ROLLBACK occurs to end the transaction.

The following example shows two SQL statements. The first INSERT statement executes successfully, and the second fails.

```
INSERT INTO zipcode
   (zip, city, state,
    created_by, created_date, modified_by, modified_date)
VALUES
   ('99999', NULL, NULL,
    USER, SYSDATE, USER, SYSDATE)
1 row created.

INSERT INTO zipcode
   (zip, city, state,
    created_by, created_date, modified_by, modified_date)
VALUES
   (NULL, NULL, NULL,
    USER, SYSDATE, USER, SYSDATE)
INSERT INTO zipcode
*
ERROR at line 1:
ORA-01400: cannot insert NULL into ("STUDENT"."ZIPCODE"."ZIP")
```

The error message indicates the problem with the statement; it shows that a null value cannot be inserted into the ZIP column of the ZIPCODE table located in the STUDENT schema. Only the second statement is rolled back. The first statement remains intact and uncommitted, as you see when executing the next query. The entire transaction ends when a ROLLBACK or COMMIT occurs.

```
SELECT zip
  FROM zipcode
 WHERE zip = '99999'
ZIP
-----
99999

1 row selected.
```

▼ LAB 11.1 EXERCISES

a) Write and execute an INSERT statement to insert a row into the GRADE_TYPE table for a grade type of 'Extra Credit', identified by the code 'EC'. Issue a COMMIT command afterward.

b) Explain what is wrong with the following INSERT statement. Hint: It is not the value course_no_seq.NEXTVAL, which inserts a value from a sequence, thus generating a unique number.

```
INSERT INTO course
   (course_no, description, cost)
VALUES
   (course_no_seq.NEXTVAL, 'Intro to Linux', 1295)
```

c) Execute the following SQL statement. The SAMPLE clause chooses a random sample of 10 percent. Explain your observations and undo the change.

```
INSERT INTO instructor
  (instructor_id,
   salutation, first_name, last_name,
   street_address, zip, phone,
   created_by, created_date, modified_by, modified_date)
SELECT instructor_id_seq.NEXTVAL,
       salutation, first_name, last_name,
       street_address, zip, phone,
       USER, SYSDATE, USER, SYSDATE
  FROM student
SAMPLE (10)
```

d) Issue the following INSERT statements. Are the statements successful? If not, what do you observe?

```
INSERT INTO section
   (section_id, course_no, section_no,
    start_date_time,
    location, instructor_id, capacity, created_by,
    created_date, modified_by, modified_date)
VALUES
   (500, 90, 1,
    TO_DATE('03-APR-2008 15:00', 'DD-MON-YYYY HH24:MI'),
    'L500', 103, 50, 'Your name here',
    SYSDATE, 'Your name here', SYSDATE)
```

```
INSERT INTO instructor
   (last_name, salutation, instructor_id,
    created_by, created_date, modified_by, modified_date)
VALUES
   ('Spencer', 'Mister', 200,
    'Your name', SYSDATE, 'Your name', SYSDATE)
```

e) Insert the following row into the GRADE table and exit/log off SQL Developer or SQL*Plus without issuing a COMMIT statement. Log back in to the server and query the GRADE table for the inserted row. What do you observe?

```
INSERT INTO grade
   (student_id, section_id, grade_type_code,
    grade_code_occurrence, numeric_grade, created_by,
    created_date, modified_by, modified_date)
VALUES
   (124, 83, 'MT',
    1, 90, 'MyName',
    SYSDATE, 'MyName', SYSDATE)
```

▼ LAB 11.1 EXERCISE ANSWERS

a) Write and execute an INSERT statement to insert a row into the GRADE_TYPE table for a grade type of 'Extra Credit', identified by the code 'EC'. Issue a COMMIT command afterward.

ANSWER: All columns of the GRADE_TYPE table are identified as NOT NULL, so the INSERT statement needs to list all the columns and corresponding values.

```
INSERT INTO grade_type
   (grade_type_code, description,
    created_by, created_date, modified_by, modified_date)
VALUES
   ('EC', 'Extra Credit',
    USER, SYSDATE, USER, SYSDATE)
```
1 row created.

```
COMMIT
```
Commit complete.

It is not necessary to explicitly list the columns of the GRADE_TYPE table because values are supplied for all columns. However, it is good practice to name all the columns in the column list because if additional columns are added in the future or the order of columns in the table changes, the INSERT statement will fail. This is particularly important when the INSERT statement is used in a program for repeated use.

b) Explain what is wrong with the following INSERT statement. Hint: It is not the value course_no_seq.NEXTVAL, which inserts a value from a sequence, thus generating a unique number.

```
INSERT INTO course
   (course_no, description, cost)
VALUES
   (course_no_seq.NEXTVAL, 'Intro to Linux', 1295)
```

ANSWER: The INSERT statement fails because it does not insert values into the NOT NULL columns CREATED_BY, CREATED_DATE, MODIFIED_BY, and MODIFIED_ DATE in the COURSE table.

```
INSERT INTO course
              *
ERROR at line 1:
ORA-01400: cannot insert NULL into
("STUDENT"."COURSE"."CREATED_BY")
```

The Oracle error message informs you that the column CREATED_BY requires a value. The correct command includes the NOT NULL columns and is successfully executed when issued as follows:

```
INSERT INTO course
   (course_no, description, cost, created_date,
    modified_date, created_by, modified_by)
VALUES
   (course_no_seq.NEXTVAL, 'Intro to Linux', 1295, SYSDATE,
    SYSDATE, 'AliceRischert', 'AliceRischert')
1 row created.
```

If you don't want to make this change permanent in the database, issue the ROLLBACK command.

```
ROLLBACK
Rollback complete.
```

The value supplied for the COURSE_NO column, course_no_seq.NEXTVAL, is not a text literal, number, or date. It is a value generated from a sequence called COURSE_NO_SEQ. A sequence is an Oracle database object that generates sequential numbers to ensure uniqueness whenever it is used, most commonly for generating primary keys. The keyword NEXTVAL indicates to Oracle to select the next value from the sequence. You'll learn more about sequences in Chapter 13, "Indexes, Sequences, and Views."

c) Execute the following SQL statement. The SAMPLE clause chooses a random sample of 10 percent. Explain your observations and undo the change.

```
INSERT INTO instructor
  (instructor_id,
   salutation, first_name, last_name,
   street_address, zip, phone,
   created_by, created_date, modified_by, modified_date)
SELECT instructor_id_seq.NEXTVAL,
       salutation, first_name, last_name,
       street_address, zip, phone,
       USER, SYSDATE, USER, SYSDATE
  FROM student
SAMPLE (10)
```

ANSWER: This is an example of a multirow INSERT statement. The INSERT statement contains a SELECT clause that retrieves values from all columns of the STUDENT table and inserts them into the INSTRUCTOR table. While there is no WHERE clause present in this SELECT statement, it contains the SAMPLE clause, which randomly chooses 10 percent of the students as rows for the insert operation. INSTRUCTOR_ID_SEQ is the name of the sequence that generates unique numbers. The pseudocolumn NEXTVAL retrieves the next value from the sequence. In this example, these generated unique numbers get inserted into the INSTRUCTOR_ID primary key column.

Be sure to undo the change afterward by using the ROLLBACK command.

```
ROLLBACK
Rollback complete.
```

d) Issue the following INSERT statements. Are the statements successful? If not, what do you observe?

```
INSERT INTO section
   (section_id, course_no, section_no,
    start_date_time,
    location, instructor_id, capacity, created_by,
    created_date, modified_by, modified_date)
VALUES
   (500, 90, 1,
    TO_DATE('03-APR-2008 15:00', 'DD-MON-YYYY HH24:MI'),
    'L500', 103, 50, 'Your name here',
    SYSDATE, 'Your name here', SYSDATE)


INSERT INTO instructor
   (last_name, salutation, instructor_id,
    created_by, created_date, modified_by, modified_date)
VALUES
   ('Spencer', 'Mister', 200,
    'Your name', SYSDATE, 'Your name', SYSDATE)
```

ANSWER: Both of the INSERT statements fail. You see the reason why after each individual statement is issued.

```
INSERT INTO section
   (section_id, course_no, section_no,
    start_date_time,
    location, instructor_id, capacity, created_by,
    created_date, modified_by, modified_date)
VALUES
   (500, 90, 1,
    TO_DATE('03-APR-2008 15:00', 'DD-MON-YYYY HH24:MI'),
    'L500', 103, 50, 'Your name here',
    SYSDATE, 'Your name here', SYSDATE)
INSERT INTO section
*
ERROR at line 1:
ORA-02291: integrity constraint (STUDENT.SECT_CRSE_FK)
violated - parent key not found
```

This statement fails because a parent row cannot be found. The foreign key constraint SECT_CRSE_FK is violated; this means a course number with the value 90 does not exist in the COURSE table, and thus the foreign key constraint prevents the creation of an orphan row. The constraint name is determined when you create a foreign key constraint, as discussed in Chapter 12. Ideally, you want to name the constraint so that it is apparent which columns and tables are involved. If you are unsure which column and table the constraint references, you can check the Constraints tab in SQL Developer or query the data dictionary view USER_CONSTRAINTS or

ALL_CONSTRAINTS, as discussed in Chapter 14, "The Data Dictionary, Scripting, and Reporting." In this example, the constraint name is prefixed with the STUDENT schema name; this is unrelated to the STUDENT table name.

The next INSERT statement also fails because it attempts to insert a value that is larger than the defined five-character width of the SALUTATION column of the INSTRUCTOR table. The value 'Mister' is six characters long and therefore causes the following error message.

```
INSERT INTO instructor
   (last_name, salutation, instructor_id,
    created_by, created_date, modified_by, modified_date)
VALUES
   ('Spencer', 'Mister', 200,
    'Your name', SYSDATE, 'Your name', SYSDATE)
INSERT INTO instructor
            *
ERROR at line 1:
ORA-01401: inserted value too large for column
```

USING SPECIAL CHARACTERS IN SQL STATEMENTS

Some characters, such as the ampersand and the single quotation mark, have special meanings in SQL*Plus or within SQL statements.

THE AMPERSAND (&)

If you attempt to insert the following record, notice the message you receive. Oracle interprets any attempt to insert or update a column with a value containing an ampersand as a substitution variable and prompts you to enter a value. You will learn about this variable in Chapter 14. The & substitution parameter prompts for a value in Oracle's SQL*Plus and SQL Developer (see Figure 11.5).

```
INSERT INTO instructor
   (salutation, last_name, instructor_id,
    created_by, created_date, modified_by, modified_date)
VALUES
   ('Mr&Ms', 'Spencer', 300,
    'Your name', SYSDATE, 'Your name', SYSDATE)
```

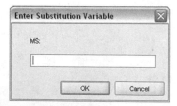

FIGURE 11.5
The Enter Substitution Variable dialog box

To temporarily turn off the substitution parameter functionality, you issue the SET DEFINE OFF command. Don't forget to reset it back to its default value with the SET DEFINE ON command.

```
SQL>set define off
  SQL>INSERT INTO instructor
     (salutation, last_name, instructor_id,
        created_by, created_date, modified_by, modified_date)
  VALUES
     ('Mr&Ms', 'Spencer', 300,
      'Your name', SYSDATE, 'Your name', SYSDATE)
  /
  1 row created.

SQL> set define on
```

Alternatively, you can break the string into pieces and place the ampersand at the end of one string and then concatenate it with the remainder of the string.

```
INSERT INTO instructor
   (salutation, last_name, instructor_id,
    created_by, created_date, modified_by, modified_date)
VALUES
   ('Mr&'||'Ms', 'Spencer', 301,
    'Your name', SYSDATE, 'Your name', SYSDATE)
```

THE SINGLE QUOTE (')

If you want to insert the instructor named O'Neil, you need to use a double set of single quotes to make Oracle understand that the single quote is to be taken as a literal quote.

```
INSERT INTO instructor
   (salutation, last_name, instructor_id,
    created_by, created_date, modified_by, modified_date)
VALUES
   ('Mr.', 'O''Neil', 305,
    'Your name', SYSDATE, 'Your name', SYSDATE)
1 row created.

SELECT last_name
  FROM instructor
 WHERE instructor_id = 305
LAST_NAME
---------------
O'Neil

1 row selected.
```

You can choose alternate quoting, as indicated with the letter q or Q. For example, the string 'O"Neil' can be written as q'!O'Neil!', where the q indicates the alternate quoting mechanism. The letter q or Q follows a single quote and the chosen quote delimiter. In this example, the ! is the delimiter. The literal ends with the chosen delimiter and a single quote. As you see, O'Neil no longer requires two single quotes. You can choose as a delimiter any character except space, tab, and return. However, if the quote delimiter is [, {, <, or (, you must choose the corresponding closing delimiter.

```
INSERT INTO instructor
  (salutation, last_name, instructor_id,
   created_by, created_date, modified_by, modified_date)
VALUES
  ('Mr.', q'<O'Neil>', 305,
   'Your name', SYSDATE, 'Your name', SYSDATE)
```

e) Insert the following row into the GRADE table and exit/log off SQL Developer or SQL*Plus without issuing a COMMIT statement. Log back in to the server and query the GRADE table for the inserted row. What do you observe?

```
INSERT INTO grade
  (student_id, section_id, grade_type_code,
   grade_code_occurrence, numeric_grade, created_by,
   created_date, modified_by, modified_date)
VALUES
  (124, 83, 'MT',
   1, 90, 'MyName',
   SYSDATE, 'MyName', SYSDATE)
```
1 row created.

ANSWER: Depending on the program and how you exit each program, the data may or may not commit implicitly.

EXITING SQL DEVELOPER WITH UNCOMMITTED CHANGES

If you completely exit SQL Developer and then invoke the program again, you will not see the inserted row. SQL Developer assumes that unless you explicitly commit the data, the change should not occur.

If you disconnect from the session by using the Disconnect menu option available in the Connections pane (see Figure 11.6), you see the dialog box shown in Figure 11.7. It warns you that you have uncommitted changes and provides you with the choice to commit, roll back, or abort/cancel the disconnect operation.

FIGURE 11.6
Disconnecting from a SQL Developer session

FIGURE 11.7
Warning upon disconnect of uncommitted changes

EXITING SQL*PLUS WITH UNCOMMITTED CHANGES

With SQL*Plus, after you log back in to the server and you query the GRADE table, the row exists, despite the missing COMMIT command. SQL*Plus implicitly issues the COMMIT when you correctly exit the program by typing the EXIT or DISCONNECT command.

```
SELECT student_id, section_id, created_by, created_date
  FROM grade
 WHERE section_id = 83
   AND student_id = 124
   AND grade_type_code = 'MT'
   AND TRUNC(created_date) = TRUNC(SYSDATE)
STUDENT_ID SECTION_ID CREATED_BY CREATED_D
---------- ---------- ---------- ---------
       124         83 MyName     08-MAY-09

1 row selected.
```

The implicit commit behavior is part of Oracle's SQL*Plus program. You should explicitly commit or roll-back your transactions. If you exit from either SQL Developer or SQL*Plus by clicking the CLOSE button in the window, the INSERT statement does not commit to the database. This is considered an abnormal exit, and modified rows are locked.

LOCKING OF ROWS THROUGH ABNORMAL TERMINATION

Rows may become locked when a session abnormally terminates, such as when a user reboots the machine without properly exiting or when the application program connected to the database raises an unhandled exception. If you do not exit your session properly, an uncommitted transaction may be pending, and the row is locked until Oracle eventually detects the dead session and rolls back the transaction. You can verify if in fact a lock is held on a particular row and table by querying the Oracle data dictionary view or using the SQL Developer Tools, Monitor Sessions menu, which is discussed in Lab 11.2. Sometimes, the database administrator (DBA) must intervene and manually release the lock if Oracle does not resolve the problem automatically.

 Clean exits and frequent commits are some good habits that you should adopt; otherwise, locks will not be released, and other users cannot make modifications to the same rows you changed.

AUTOCOMMIT

In SQL Developer and SQL*Plus, you can choose to automatically commit every statement without allowing for rollbacks. In SQL Developer, you need to select Tools, Preferences, Database, Worksheet Parameters and then check the option Autocommit in SQL Worksheet (see Figure 11.8). The settings in the Preferences dialog in SQL Developer are valid for the current and all future sessions.

For SQL*Plus, you can use the command AUTOCOMMIT during a SQL*Plus session by typing SET AUTO-COMMIT ON or set AUTOCOMMIT IMMEDIATE. This command is valid only for the duration of the SQL*Plus session. (You can create a glogin.sql file that modifies session settings whenever you log in. You'll learn more about this in Appendix C, "SQL*Plus Command Reference.")

 Clearly, the AUTOCOMMIT command and the corresponding menu option in SQL Developer are dangerous. A ROLLBACK command issued during that session has no effect because every statement has already automatically been committed.

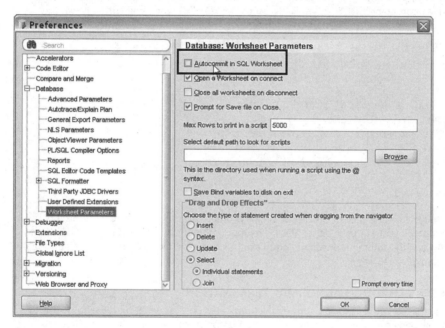

FIGURE 11.8
Worksheet Parameters screen in SQL Developer

Lab 11.1 Quiz

In order to test your progress, you should be able to answer the following questions.

1) A DML command automatically issues a COMMIT.

    _____ a) True

    _____ b) False

2) A statement-level rollback ends a transaction.

    _____ a) True

    _____ b) False

3) An INSERT statement can insert only one row at a time into a table.

    _____ a) True

    _____ b) False

4) A COMMIT or ROLLBACK command ends a transaction.

    _____ a) True

    _____ b) False

5) Uncommitted changes can be seen by all users.

    _____ a) True

    _____ b) False

6) A transaction is a logical unit of work.

    _____ a) True

    _____ b) False

ANSWERS APPEAR IN APPENDIX A.

LAB 11.2
Updating and Deleting Data

LAB OBJECTIVES

After this lab, you will be able to:

▶ Update, Delete, and Merge Data

▶ Understand the Effect of Data Manipulation on Other Users

The UPDATE, DELETE, and MERGE commands manipulate data. A database is usually shared by many users. At times, they contend for the same information simultaneously. It is helpful to understand how data manipulation affects your and other users' ability to change and query the data in a read-consistent way.

Updating Data

The UPDATE command manipulates existing data in a table. It always refers to a single table. For example, the following UPDATE statement updates the FINAL_GRADE column in the ENROLLMENT table to 90 for all students who enrolled in January 2007.

```
UPDATE enrollment
   SET final_grade = 90
 WHERE enroll_date >= TO_DATE('01/01/2007', 'MM/DD/YYYY')
   AND enroll_date < TO_DATE('02/01/2007', 'MM/DD/YYYY')
11 rows updated.
```

The keyword UPDATE always precedes the name of the table to be updated, and the SET keyword precedes the column or columns to be changed. An UPDATE statement can update all rows in a table at once or just certain rows when restricted with a WHERE clause, as in the previous example. The general syntax for the UPDATE command is as follows.

```
UPDATE tablename
SET {{(column[,column]...)=(subquery)|
       column={expression|(subquery)|DEFAULT}
     }[,{(column[,column]...)=(subquery)|
       column={expression|(subquery)|DEFAULT}
     }]...}
[WHERE condition]
```

Updating Columns to Null Values

An UPDATE statement can update columns with a NULL value. The following UPDATE statement sets the FINAL_GRADE column to NULL for all rows in the ENROLLMENT table because there is no WHERE clause.

```
UPDATE enrollment
   SET final_grade = NULL
```

 The IS NULL operator is used in a WHERE clause, not in the SET clause of an UPDATE statement.

Column Default Value

A column may have a default value defined; this value is entered when an INSERT statement did not specify an explicit value for a column. You can use the DEFAULT keyword in the UPDATE or INSERT command to explicitly set the default value defined for the column. The NUMERIC_GRADE column of the GRADE table has a default value of 0 defined. Examine the row before the change to the DEFAULT value.

```
SELECT numeric_grade
  FROM grade
 WHERE student_id = 211
   AND section_id = 141
   AND grade_type_code = 'HM'
   AND grade_code_occurrence = 1
NUMERIC_GRADE
-------------
           99

1 row selected.
```

To update the column to the default value of 0 for the first homework grade of student ID 211 in SECTION_ID 141, you issue the following UPDATE command.

```
UPDATE grade
   SET numeric_grade = DEFAULT
 WHERE student_id = 211
   AND section_id = 141
   AND grade_type_code = 'HM'
   AND grade_code_occurrence = 1
1 row updated.
```

Examine the result of the change by requerying the record. The column default value of 0 is now shown.

```
SELECT numeric_grade
  FROM grade
 WHERE student_id = 211
   AND section_id = 141
   AND grade_type_code = 'HM'
   AND grade_code_occurrence = 1
NUMERIC_GRADE
-------------
            0

1 row selected.
```

Now restore the value to the original value of 99 with the ROLLBACK command.

```
ROLLBACK
Rollback complete.
```

If you want to find out which columns have column default values, review the Data Default column on the Columns tab of the GRADE table (see Figure 11.9).

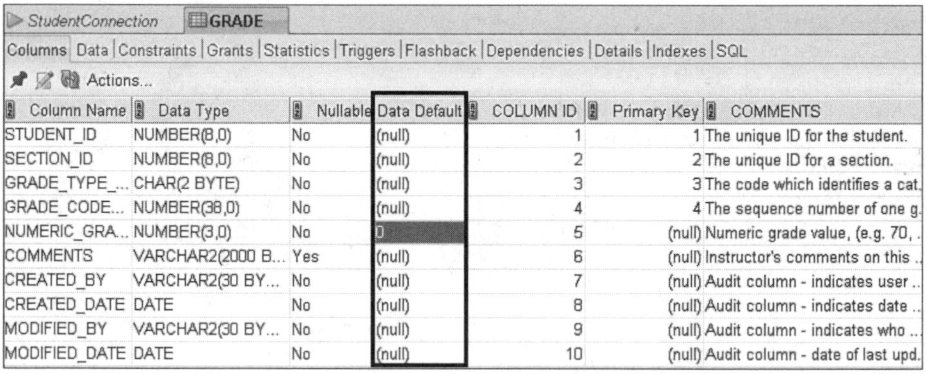

Column Name	Data Type	Nullable	Data Default	COLUMN ID	Primary Key	COMMENTS
STUDENT_ID	NUMBER(8,0)	No	(null)	1	1	The unique ID for the student.
SECTION_ID	NUMBER(8,0)	No	(null)	2	2	The unique ID for a section.
GRADE_TYPE_...	CHAR(2 BYTE)	No	(null)	3	3	The code which identifies a cat.
GRADE_CODE...	NUMBER(38,0)	No	(null)	4	4	The sequence number of one g.
NUMERIC_GRA...	NUMBER(3,0)	No	0	5	(null)	Numeric grade value, (e.g. 70, .
COMMENTS	VARCHAR2(2000 B...	Yes	(null)	6	(null)	Instructor's comments on this ..
CREATED_BY	VARCHAR2(30 BY...	No	(null)	7	(null)	Audit column - indicates user ..
CREATED_DATE	DATE	No	(null)	8	(null)	Audit column - indicates date ..
MODIFIED_BY	VARCHAR2(30 BY...	No	(null)	9	(null)	Audit column - indicates who ..
MODIFIED_DATE	DATE	No	(null)	10	(null)	Audit column - date of last upd.

FIGURE 11.9
Data Default value on the GRADE table

You can also query the data dictionary view USER_TAB_COLUMNS or ALL_TAB_COLUMNS, as discussed in detail in Chapter 14.

You will learn about the syntax for creating column defaults in Chapter 12.

Updates and the CASE Expression

CASE expressions can be used anywhere expressions are allowed. The following example shows the CASE expression in the SET clause of the UPDATE statement. The FINAL_GRADE column of the ENROLLMENT table is updated so that students enrolled in SECTION_ID 100 receive extra points for their FINAL_GRADE score.

```
UPDATE enrollment
    SET final_grade = CASE WHEN final_grade <=80 THEN
                                final_grade+5
                           WHEN final_grade > 80 THEN
                                final_grade+10
                    END
  WHERE section_id = 100
```

The CASE expression evaluates the current value of the FINAL_GRADE column. If the value is less than or equal to 80, the value of FINAL_GRADE is increased by 5 points; if the value is greater than 80, the increase is 10 points. No provision is made for null values; they remain unchanged because they do not satisfy any of the WHEN conditions. A null value is not greater than, less than, or equal to any value, and there is no ELSE clause in this statement.

Subqueries and the UPDATE Command

An update can occur based on data from other tables, using a subquery. The following example uses a subquery in the SET clause of the UPDATE command, and it updates the ZIP column of INSTRUCTOR_ID 108 to be equal to the ZIP value of the state of Florida.

```
UPDATE instructor
    SET zip = (SELECT zip
                 FROM zipcode
                WHERE state = 'FL')
  WHERE instructor_id = 108
```

In our ZIPCODE table, the state of Florida has a single value in the ZIPCODE table.

```
SELECT zip
  FROM zipcode
 WHERE state = 'FL'
ZIP
-----
33431

1 row selected.
```

The result of the update effectively changes the zip code to 33431 for INSTRUCTOR_ID 108.

```
SELECT instructor_id, zip
  FROM instructor
 WHERE instructor_id = 108
```

```
INSTRUCTOR_ID ZIP
------------- -----
          108 33431
```

1 row selected.

SUBQUERIES THAT RETURN NULL VALUES

The following UPDATE query statement attempts to update the same instructor's zip code with a value for which you will not find any zip code in the ZIPCODE table.

```
UPDATE instructor
   SET zip = (SELECT zip
                  FROM zipcode
                 WHERE state = 'CA')
 WHERE instructor_id = 108
1 row updated.
```

When you issue the query to see the effect of the update, the subquery returns a null value; it therefore updated the ZIP column to a null.

```
SELECT instructor_id, zip
  FROM instructor
 WHERE instructor_id = 108
INSTRUCTOR_ID ZIP
------------- ---
          108
```

1 row selected.

SUBQUERIES THAT RETURN MULTIPLE VALUES

The following subquery returns multiple zip codes for the state of Connecticut. The error message indicates that the subquery returns multiple rows, which is not allowed for an equal sign (=); therefore, the UPDATE statement fails.

```
UPDATE instructor
   SET zip = (SELECT zip
                  FROM zipcode
                 WHERE state = 'CT')
 WHERE instructor_id = 108
   SET zip = (SELECT zip
                 *
ERROR at line 2:
ORA-01427: single-row subquery returns more than one row
```

If you want just any one of the zip codes, no matter which one, you can use the MAX or MIN function. An aggregate function guarantees the return of a single row.

```
UPDATE instructor
   SET zip = (SELECT MAX(zip)
                FROM zipcode
               WHERE state = 'CT')
 WHERE instructor_id = 108
1 row updated.
```

UPDATES AND CORRELATED SUBQUERIES

The following statement updates the FINAL_GRADE column to 90 and the MODIFIED_DATE column to March 13, 2009, for those sections taught by the instructor Hanks.

```
UPDATE enrollment e
   SET final_grade = 90,
       modified_date = TO_DATE('13-MAR-2009', 'DD-MON-YYYY')
 WHERE EXISTS
        (SELECT '*'
           FROM section s, instructor i
          WHERE e.section_id = s.section_id
            AND s.instructor_id = i.instructor_id
            AND i.last_name = 'Hanks')
```

You can use any of the SELECT statements you have learned about to restrict the result set. In this example, a correlated subquery identifies the rows to be updated. A column from the outer table, in this case ENROLLMENT, is referenced in the subquery through the column E.SECTION_ID. Every row of the ENROLLMENT table is updated where a corresponding SECTION_ID is returned by the subquery. As in the other correlated subqueries, every row in the outer table, here the ENROLLMENT table, is examined and evaluated against the inner query. The update occurs for those rows where the condition of the correlated subquery evaluates to true.

AVOIDING A COMMON SCENARIO WITH CORRELATED SUBQUERIES

The following correlated update, which involves tables TA and TB, changes one column with a value from another table. The values from TA need to be updated to reflect changes made in TB. The query shows a list of all the rows in the TA table.

```
SELECT *
  FROM ta
       ID COL1
--------- ----
        1 a
        2 b
        3 c
        4 d

4 rows selected.
```

This is a list of all the rows in table TB. The idea of the correlated update is to update the rows of TA based on table TB by joining on the common column called ID.

```
SELECT *
  FROM tb
        ID COL2
--------- ----
        1 w
        2 x
        5 y
        6 z

4 rows selected.
```

When you execute the UPDATE statement and subsequently query table TA, the rows with IDs 3 and 4 are updated with null values. The intention is to retain the original values.

```
UPDATE ta
   SET col1 = (SELECT col2
                 FROM tb
                WHERE ta.id = tb.id)
4 rows updated.

SELECT *
  FROM ta
        ID COL1
--------- ----
        1 w
        2 x
        3
        4

4 rows selected.
```

The correlated update query does not have a WHERE clause; therefore, all the rows of table TA are evaluated. The correlated subquery returns a null value for any row that was not found in table TB. You can avoid this behavior and retain the values in COL1 by including only the rows found in table TB with an appropriate WHERE clause in the UPDATE statement.

```
ROLLBACK
Rollback complete.

UPDATE ta
   SET col1 = (SELECT col2
                 FROM tb
                WHERE ta.id = tb.id)
 WHERE id IN (SELECT id
                FROM tb)
2 rows updated.
```

A query against the TB table verifies that the desired updates are done correctly.

```
SELECT *
  FROM ta
        ID COL1
--------- ----
         1 w
         2 x
         3 c
         4 d

4 rows selected.
```

 Be sure to check your results before committing, especially when you perform complicated updates to a table.

UPDATES AND SUBQUERIES THAT RETURN MULTIPLE COLUMNS

The following example uses the tables EMPLOYEE and EMPLOYEE_CHANGE. The EMPLOYEE table contains a list of employees, with their IDs, names, salaries, and titles. The purpose of the EMPLOYEE_CHANGE table is to hold all the changes that need to be made to the EMPLOYEE table. Perhaps the names, titles, and salary information comes from various other systems and are then recorded in the EMPLOYEE_CHANGE table that is to be used for updates to the master EMPLOYEE table.

```
SELECT *
  FROM employee
EMPLOYEE_ID NAME          SALARY TITLE
----------- ------------- ------ ---------
          1 John            1000 Analyst
          2 Mary            2000 Manager
          3 Stella          5000 President
          4 Fred             500 Janitor

4 rows selected.

SELECT *
  FROM employee_change
EMPLOYEE_ID NAME          SALARY TITLE
----------- ------------- ------ ---------
          1 John            1500 Programmer
          3 Stella          6000 CEO
          4 Fred             600 Clerk
          5 Jean             800 Secretary
          6 Betsy           2000 Sales Rep

5 rows selected.
```

The next statement updates both the SALARY and TITLE columns of the EMPLOYEE table with the corresponding values from the EMPLOYEE_CHANGE table for the employee with ID 4, which is Fred the Janitor. In the subquery of this UPDATE statement, the equal sign indicates that the subquery must return a single row.

```
UPDATE employee
   SET (salary, title) = (SELECT salary, title
                            FROM employee_change
                           WHERE employee_id = 4)
   WHERE employee_id = 4
1 row updated.
```

You now see the change, and Fred now earns a different salary and has the title Clerk.

```
SELECT *
  FROM employee
EMPLOYEE_ID NAME              SALARY TITLE
----------- --------------    ------ ---------
          1 John                1000 Analyst
          2 Mary                2000 Manager
          3 Stella              5000 President
          4 Fred                 600 Clerk

4 rows selected.

ROLLBACK
Rollback complete.
```

Undo the change with the ROLLBACK command. The next example shows how to update all the rows in the EMPLOYEE table instead of just one individual employee.

```
UPDATE employee e
   SET (salary, title) =
       (SELECT salary, title
          FROM employee_change c
         WHERE e.employee_id = c.employee_id)
   WHERE employee_id IN (SELECT employee_id
                           FROM employee_change)
3 rows updated.
```

Three rows are updated—for employees John, Stella, and Fred. The records for employees Jean and Betsy are not inserted into the EMPLOYEE table because the UPDATE statement just updates existing records and does not insert any new rows.

```
SELECT *
  FROM employee
EMPLOYEE_ID NAME              SALARY TITLE
----------- --------------    ------ ---------
          1 John                1500 Programmer
          2 Mary                2000 Manager
```

```
        3 Stella              6000 CEO
        4 Fred                 600 Clerk


4 rows selected.


ROLLBACK
Rollback complete.
```

MERGE: Combining INSERTs, UPDATEs, and DELETEs

You can perform combined INSERT, UPDATE, and DELETE operations with the MERGE command, using the following syntax.

```
MERGE INTO tablename
USING {query|tablename} ON (condition)
[WHEN MATCHED THEN UPDATE set_clause
      [DELETE condition]]
[WHEN NOT MATCHED THEN INSERT values_clause]
```

The table EMPLOYEE_CHANGE contains two additional rows, Jean and Betsy, that are not found in the EMPLOYEE table. The MERGE statement allows you to update the matching rows and lets you insert the rows found in the EMPLOYEE_CHANGE table but missing from the EMPLOYEE table.

```
MERGE INTO employee e
USING (SELECT employee_id, salary, title, name
         FROM employee_change) c
   ON (e.employee_id = c.employee_id)
WHEN MATCHED THEN
   UPDATE SET e.salary = c.salary,
              e.title = c.title
WHEN NOT MATCHED THEN
   INSERT (e.employee_id, e.salary, e.title, e.name)
   VALUES (c.employee_id, c.salary, c.title, c.name)
5 rows merged.
```

When you query the EMPLOYEE table, you see the changed values and the addition of the employees Jean and Betsy. Mary did not have a record in the EMPLOYEE_CHANGE table; therefore, no modification to her record is performed.

```
SELECT *
  FROM employee
ORDER BY 1
EMPLOYEE_ID NAME              SALARY TITLE
----------- --------------- ------ ---------
          1 John              1500 Programmer
          2 Mary              2000 Manager
          3 Stella            6000 CEO
          4 Fred               600 Clerk
```

```
        5 Jean              800 Secretary
        6 Betsy            2000 Sales Rep
```

6 rows selected.

The MERGE syntax contains an optional DELETE condition to the WHEN MATCHED THEN UPDATE clause. It allows you to remove rows from the table during this operation. The only rows deleted are the ones that satisfy both the DELETE and the ON conditions. The DELETE condition evaluates the rows based on the values after the update—not the original values. The next statement adds the DELETE condition, which effectively deletes Stella from the EMPLOYEE table because her SALARY column value now equals 6000.

```
ROLLBACK
```
Rollback complete.

```
MERGE INTO employee e
  USING (SELECT employee_id, salary, title, name
           FROM employee_change) c
     ON (e.employee_id = c.employee_id)
  WHEN MATCHED THEN
    UPDATE SET e.salary = c.salary,
               e.title = c.title
    DELETE WHERE salary = 6000
  WHEN NOT MATCHED THEN
    INSERT (e.employee_id, e.salary, e.title, e.name)
    VALUES (c.employee_id, c.salary, c.title, c.name)
```
5 rows merged.

```
SELECT *
  FROM employee
ORDER BY 1
```

EMPLOYEE_ID	NAME	SALARY	TITLE
1	John	1500	Programmer
2	Mary	2000	Manager
4	Fred	600	Clerk
5	Jean	800	Secretary
6	Betsy	2000	Sales Rep

5 rows selected.

Deleting Data

You remove data from a table with the DELETE statement. It can delete all rows or just specific rows. The syntax is as follows.

```
DELETE FROM tablename
[WHERE condition]
```

The following statement deletes all rows in the GRADE table.

```
DELETE FROM grade
2004 rows deleted.
```

When a ROLLBACK command is issued, the DELETE command is undone, and the rows are back in the GRADE table.

```
ROLLBACK
Rollback complete.

SELECT COUNT(*)
  FROM grade
 COUNT(*)
---------
    2004

1 row selected.
```

Referential Integrity and the DELETE Command

A DELETE operation on a row with dependent children rows has different effects, depending on how DELETEs on the foreign key are defined. There are three different ways you can specify a foreign key constraint with respect to deletes: RESTRICT, CASCADE, or SET NULL.

If you issue a DELETE on a parent table with associated child records, and the foreign key constraint is set to ON DELETE CASCADE, the children are automatically deleted. If the foreign key constraint is set to ON DELETE SET NULL, the child rows are updated to a null value, provided that the foreign key column of the child table allows nulls. The default option for a foreign key constraint with respect to DELETEs is RESTRICT. It disallows the deletion of a parent if child rows exist. In this case, you must delete the child rows first, before you delete the parent row.

    In the STUDENT schema, all foreign key constraints are set to the default option, which restricts INSERT, UPDATE, and DELETE operations.

DELETES AND REFERENTIAL INTEGRITY IN ACTION

The default foreign key constraint does not allow you to delete any parent row, if any child records exist. In the following example, an attempt is made to delete zip code 10025. Because the ZIP column of the ZIPCODE table is referenced as a foreign key column in the STUDENT table and the table contains student rows with this zip code, you cannot delete the row. Oracle prevents you from creating orphan rows and responds with an error message.

```
DELETE FROM zipcode
 WHERE zip = '10025'
DELETE FROM zipcode
*
ERROR at line 1:
ORA-02292: integrity constraint (STUDENT.INST_ZIP_FK)
violated - child record found
```

The constraint name error message consists of not only the constraint name but also the name of the schema, which in this case is the STUDENT schema. If you installed the tables into another user account, your schema name will be different. You will learn how to create constraints and specify constraint names in Chapter 12.

A DELETE statement may delete rows in other tables. If the foreign key constraint specifies the ON DELETE CASCADE option, a deletion of a parent row automatically deletes the associated child rows. Imagine that the referential integrity constraint between the STUDENT and ENROLLMENT tables is DELETE CASCADE. A DELETE statement would delete not only the individual STUDENT row but also any associated ENROLLMENT rows.

To take the scenario a step further, suppose that the student also has records in the GRADE table. The delete will be successful only if the constraint between the ENROLLMENT table and the GRADE table is also DELETE CASCADE. Then the corresponding rows in the GRADE tables are deleted as well. If the DELETE is RESTRICT, the ORA-02292 error will appear, informing you to delete all the child records first.

As you know, the ZIPCODE table is not only referenced by the STUDENT table but also by the INSTRUCTOR table. Suppose you have the ON DELETE SET NULL constraint as the foreign key. A deletion of zip code 10025 would cause an update of the ZIP column on the INSTRUCTOR table to a null value, provided that the STUDENT table does not contain this zip code.

To find out which foreign keys have DELETE CASCADE, the SET NULL constraint, or the default RESTRICT constraint, you can query the data dictionary views USER_CONSTRAINTS or ALL_CONSTRAINTS, as discussed in Chapter 14.

In SQL Developer, you can refer to the Delete Rule column displayed in the Constraints tab of the table. Figure 11.10 shows the value NO ACTION on the foreign key constraint between the INSTRUCTOR and ZIPCODE tables, which means that any deletions from the ZIPCODE parent table are restricted and do not cause any delete or update action on any related child rows contained in the INSTRUCTOR table.

StudentConnection	▦INSTRUCTOR				
Columns	Data	Constraints	Grants	Statistics	Triggers	Flashback	Dependencies	Details	Indexes	SQL

⬆ ✎ ⓠ Actions...

▤ Constraint Name	▤ Constrai...	▤▤ Referenced Table	▤ Reference Constraint Name	▤ Delete Rule	▤▤
INST_CREATED_BY_NNULL	Check	... ... (null)	(null)	(null)	... ...
INST_CREATED_DATE_NN...	Check	... ... (null)	(null)	(null)	... ...
INST_INSTRUCTOR_ID_NN...	Check	... ... (null)	(null)	(null)	... ...
INST_MODFIED_BY_NNULL	Check	... ... (null)	(null)	(null)	... ...
INST_MODIFIED_DATE_NN...	Check	... ... (null)	(null)	(null)	... ...
INST_PK	Primary_Key	... ... (null)	(null)	(null)	... ...
INST_ZIP_FK	Foreign_Key	... ... ZIPCODE	ZIP_PK	NO ACTION	... ...

FIGURE 11.10
The Delete Rule column value of the INSTRUCTOR table

THE SCHEMA DIAGRAM

Sometimes, schema diagrams depicting the physical relationships between tables show the referential integrity rules in place. Three types of data manipulation operations are possible in SQL: INSERT, UPDATE, and DELETE. On some schema diagrams, you may also find the letters I, U, and D, which are abbreviations for INSERT, UPDATE, and DELETE, respectively. These abbreviated letters indicate the valid rules that these data manipulation operations must follow.

Figure 11.11 shows a schema diagram of the PUBLISHER table and the BOOK table. The foreign key column PUBLISHER_ID is found in the BOOK table. A one-to-many mandatory relationship exists between the PUBLISHER and BOOK tables. I:R indicates that any INSERT operation filling in values in PUBLISHER_ID of the BOOK table is RESTRICTED to values found in the PUBLISHER table. By default, most database systems require this condition when a foreign key is defined on a column.

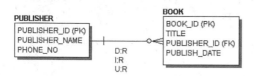

FIGURE 11.11
Relationship between PUBLISHER and BOOK tables

The U:R notation indicates that any UPDATE to the PUBLISHER_ID column of the BOOK table is RESTRICTED to values found in the PUBLISHER table. Attempting to UPDATE the column with an invalid value violates the U:R data integrity constraint and generates an error. Both the U:R and the I:R referential integrity rules are the default behaviors and are often not listed on schema diagrams.

The notation for the DELETE operation is listed as D:R, indicating that DELETE operations are restricted. Specifically, this means that you cannot delete a publisher row that is referenced in the BOOK table. If you were allowed to delete the row, you would not be able to tell the publisher of the book, and you would create an orphan row. The relationship between the two tables is mandatory, indicating that a null value for the PUBLISHER_ID is not acceptable.

If instead you see a D:C notation, it indicates DELETE CASCADE, meaning a deletion of a PUBLISHER row deletes any associated children rows in the BOOK table.

D:N indicates DELETE SET NULL. This means that upon the deletion of a PUBLISHER row, any corresponding child rows are automatically set to null in the PUBLISHER_ID column of the BOOK table, provided that nulls are allowed.

The TRUNCATE Command

The TRUNCATE command deletes all rows from a table, just like the DELETE command. However, the TRUNCATE command does not allow a WHERE clause and automatically issues a COMMIT. All rows are deleted, and you cannot roll back the change.

```
TRUNCATE TABLE class
Table truncated.
```

The TRUNCATE statement works more quickly than the DELETE statement to remove all rows from a table because the database does not have to store the undo information in case a ROLLBACK command is issued.

If you attempt to use TRUNCATE on a table that is referenced by another table as a foreign key, Oracle issues an error message, indicating that this action is not allowed because it doesn't let you create orphan rows. You must disable the foreign key constraint before you can succeed. Enabling and disabling constraints is discussed in Chapter 12.

```
TRUNCATE TABLE student
TRUNCATE TABLE student
            *
ERROR at line 1:
ORA-02266: unique/primary keys in table referenced by
enabled foreign keys
```

Triggers and DML Commands

Oracle enables you to attach triggers to tables that fire on DELETE, INSERT, and UPDATE commands. A table's triggers do not execute when the table is truncated. Triggers are written in the PL/SQL language and can perform sophisticated actions (for example, recording changes to another table for auditing purpose or updating summary values on derived columns).

Locking

In a real-world database system, many users access data concurrently. Occasionally, users collide because they want to manipulate the same piece of information. Locking ensures data consistency.

When you issue an INSERT, UPDATE, DELETE, or MERGE statement, Oracle automatically locks the modified rows. The lock prevents other sessions from making changes to these rows. The lock is released when the session initiating the change commits or rolls back. Other users or sessions can then modify the rows.

Queries do not place locks on rows. Data can always be queried, despite being locked; however, other sessions can see the committed data only. After the successful commit of a transaction, the new change is visible to all sessions, and the lock is released.

If a row is locked by a session, another session cannot acquire the lock and modify the row. The session attempting to acquire the locked row waits until the lock is released. The session might appear frozen while it waits. Users often think that perhaps their connection to the server dropped or that the DML operation is extremely slow. Users might terminate their session or reboot the machine, only to find out that if they retry the same action, the session continues to behave identically. Oracle waits until the lock is released by the other session before it proceeds with the new change.

When you anticipate multiple users contending for the same row(s) simultaneously, you should commit your data frequently.

THE LOST UPDATE PROBLEM

The WHERE clause of the next UPDATE statement not only lists the primary key column (the COURSE_NO column) but also includes the old COST column value.

```
UPDATE course
   SET cost = 800
 WHERE course_no = 25
   AND cost = 1195
```

Although this is may seem unnecessary, it can be helpful in case another user made changes to the values in the meantime. Then the UPDATE statement is not successful and returns 0 rows updated. This indicates that the row containing the old value is no longer found. Many end-user application programs append the values displayed on a user's screen to the WHERE clause of an UPDATE statement. If the UPDATE returns with the 0 rows updated message, the program can alert the user that changes have been made and request the user to requery the data. This prevents the user from unknowingly overwriting data that changed since he or she last retrieved the data.

You might wonder why Oracle doesn't automatically lock the data to prevent such a situation or place locks on queries. Oracle releases the lock after the user issues a COMMIT or ROLLBACK. A SELECT does not cause any locks; the other user may have queried the data, updated the data, and issued a COMMIT immediately afterward. Therefore, any subsequent updates do not interfere with another user's UPDATE statement because the lock is already released.

While Oracle automatically takes care of locking, you can explicitly acquire a lock by using the SELECT FOR UPDATE or the LOCK TABLE statement. This will override the default locking mechanism; however, this functionality is infrequently used in the real world. Oracle's implicit and automatic locking mechanism works very well for the vast majority of scenarios, and by adding the "old" values to the WHERE clause, you avoid overwriting any unwanted changes.

LOCKING OF ROWS BY DDL OPERATIONS

Locks are not just acquired on individual rows but also on the entire table when a DDL operation such as an ALTER TABLE or a CREATE INDEX command is issued. A DML operation cannot update the table while the DDL operation is in progress (for example, you cannot update rows while a table is being altered), and the same holds true for the reverse: A DDL command on a table cannot be executed if users are holding locks on the table (with some exceptions, such as the creation of online indexes, as discussed in Chapter 13).

Read Consistency of Data

Whenever a user changes data with a DML operation, Oracle keeps track of the old values on a rollback segment. If the user rolls back the transaction with the ROLLBACK command, Oracle reads the old values from the rollback segment and returns the data to the previous state.

THE ROLLBACK SEGMENT AND UNDO TABLESPACE

The UNDO tablespace contains the rollback segments that keep track of changes not yet committed. It allows users to issue the ROLLBACK command to restore the data to its original state. Uncommitted data is not permanent and therefore not ready for other users to see yet. Before any data is changed on the actual table, the change is written to the rollback segments first.

Figure 11.12 illustrates the visibility and timing of any changes made to the COST column of the COURSE table for two individual sessions. For example, Session #2 updates the COST column value for COURSE_NO 20 to 2000 but does not commit the change. Session #1 still sees the old values, which are retrieved from the rollback segments. Session #1, or any other session for that matter, does not see the modified data until the user performing the change makes it permanent by issuing a COMMIT. Furthermore, until a COMMIT or a ROLLBACK is issued by Session #2, the row is locked and cannot be manipulated by another session.

Time	Session #1	Session #2
T1	SELECT cost FROM course WHERE course_no = 20 **COST** ---------- 1195 1 row selected.	
T2		UPDATE course SET cost = 2000 WHERE course_no = 20 1 row updated.
T3	SELECT cost FROM course WHERE course_no = 20 **COST** ---------- 1195 1 row selected.	
T4		SELECT cost FROM course WHERE course_no = 20 **COST** ---------- 2000 1 row selected.
T5		COMMIT Commit completed.
T6	SELECT cost FROM course WHERE course_no = 20 **COST** ---------- 2000 1 row selected.	

FIGURE 11.12
The effect of the COMMIT command

THE SYSTEM CHANGE NUMBERS (SCN) AND MULTI-VERSIONING

When long running queries and DML operations occur simultaneously, Oracle automatically handles this with the use of the System Change Number (SCN), a unique number that tracks the order in which events occur. This feature enables queries to return a read-consistent result. For example, say that a query starts at 10:00 A.M. and ends at 10:05 A.M., and during this time it computes the sum of all salaries for all employees. At 10:03 A.M., the salary of one employee is updated, and a COMMIT is issued. What result does the query return? Because the query began before the UPDATE was issued, the result will return a read-consistent result, based on the point in time when the query started, which is 10:00 A.M. When a query reads the newly changed salary row, it recognizes that the SCN of the UPDATE is issued after the start of the query, and it looks for the old salary value on the rollback segment.

If you have very long-running queries, you might get an ORA-1555 ("snapshot too old") error message; this indicates that Oracle had to overwrite the rollback information you are attempting to access and therefore cannot return a read-consistent result. Rollback data can be overwritten by other transactions when the previous transaction is committed or rolled back. When this rollback data is no longer available, the long-running query is looking for undo information that no longer exists, so you get this error message. To eliminate this error, you can attempt to reissue the query, or, if there is a lot of activity on the system, you might need to increase the UNDO_RETENTION setting of the UNDO tablespace.

For more information on read consistency, database recovery, and the management of the rollback/UNDO tablespace, refer to the *Oracle Database Administrator's Guide*.

Flashback Queries

Oracle's flashback query feature allows you to look at values of a query at a specific time in the past, such as before specific DML statements occurred. This can be useful in case a user accidentally performs an unintended but committed DML change. Another possible application of the feature is to compare the current data against the previous day's data to see the changes. When using the flashback query, you can either specify an explicit time expression (such as an interval or a specific timestamp value) or indicate an individual SCN.

Data for flashback queries is kept only for a certain time period that is dependent on the undo management implemented by the DBA. You must familiarize yourself with the limitations of this feature. For example, issuing certain DDL commands, such as altering a table by dropping or modifying columns, invalidates the undo data for the individual table.

 Not every user can perform flashbacks; the DBA has to provide a user with the either the FLASHBACK object privilege on the specific table or the FLASHBACK ANY TABLE system privilege. For the STUDENT user to be able to run these queries, you need to request these privileges; they are not part of the default privileges assigned to the account.

Following is an example that illustrates the use of the flashback query feature. The SELECT statement returns the current value of the table before any changes occur. You see the cost of course number 10 displayed as 1195. The subsequent UPDATE statement changes the cost to 9999 and makes the change permanent with the COMMIT command.

```
SELECT course_no, cost
  FROM course
 WHERE course_no = 10
COURSE_NO        COST
---------------- ----
              10 1195

1 row selected.
```

```
UPDATE course
   SET cost = 9999
 WHERE course_no = 10
1 row updated.
```

```
COMMIT
Commit complete.
```

STATEMENT-LEVEL FLASHBACK

The statement-level flashback ability allows the AS OF clause in the SELECT statement followed either by a TIMESTAMP value or a particular SCN. The next statement shows use of the TIME-STAMP clause to retrieve the value for the COST column for course number 10 as of February 3, 2009, at 4:30 P.M.

```
SELECT course_no, cost
   FROM course AS OF TIMESTAMP
   TO_TIMESTAMP('03-Feb-2009 04:30:00 PM',
                'DD-MON-YYYY HH:MI:SS AM')
 WHERE course_no = 10
COURSE_NO        COST
---------------- ----
           10 1195
```

```
1 row selected.
```

If flashback data is not available anymore, Oracle informs you with an ORA-08180: no snapshot found based on specified time error message. The syntax for the flashback query clause is as follows.

```
AS OF SCN|TIMESTAMP expr
```

If you want to run the flashback versions query using a specific SCN number, you can obtain the number with the next SQL statement. This may be useful for querying the number before the start of a batch job, and if anything goes wrong, you can query the changes easily. (The DBA has to grant you the EXECUTE privilege on the DBMS_FLASHBACK package to be able to run this query.)

```
SELECT DBMS_FLASHBACK.GET_SYSTEM_CHANGE_NUMBER
   FROM dual
GET_SYSTEM_CHANGE_NUMBER
------------------------
                 4423510
```

```
1 row selected.
```

The following statement retrieves the rows that were inserted or updated in the COURSE table within the last 30 minutes. If you want to find out what data was updated and deleted, reverse the two SELECT statements. If you prefer to see a detailed log of the changes, use the VERSIONS BETWEEN parameter, discussed next.

```
SELECT *
  FROM course
MINUS
SELECT *
  FROM course AS OF TIMESTAMP
       SYSTIMESTAMP - INTERVAL '30' MINUTE
```

RETRIEVING FLASHBACK HISTORY WITH THE VERSIONS BETWEEN PARAMETER

The VERSIONS BETWEEN parameter allows you to retrieve the history of changes during a particular time period. For example, if the column value changes again—say the COST column is updated to 5555—you see each individual change.

```
UPDATE course
   SET cost = 5555
 WHERE course_no = 10
1 row updated.

COMMIT
Commit complete.
```

The query determines the changes that occurred on the row within the last 10 minutes.

```
SELECT course_no, cost, VERSIONS_XID,
       VERSIONS_OPERATION
  FROM course
       VERSIONS BETWEEN TIMESTAMP
       SYSTIMESTAMP - INTERVAL '10' MINUTE
   AND SYSTIMESTAMP - INTERVAL '1' SECOND
 WHERE course_no = 10

 COURSE_NO  COST VERSIONS_XID      VERSIONS_OPERATION
---------- ----- ---------------- -------------------
        10  5555 0001001A000028B4 U
        10  9999 00030028000028B7 U
        10  1195

3 rows selected.
```

The columns VERSIONS_XID and VERSIONS_OPERATION in the SELECT list are pseudo-columns that store the transaction reference information regarding the change and the type of change. The VERSIONS_OPERATION pseudocolumn indicates the type of data manipulation that took place (for example, INSERT, UPDATE, DELETE). The VERSIONS_XID column allows you to trace back the various modification details in the data dictionary view FLASHBACK_TRANSACTION_QUERY. (You will see an example of this shortly. Also refer to Chapter 14 for more information about data dictionary views.) You can also see the timestamp of the changes. Table 11.1 lists other pseudocolumns that contain more details about DML changes.

TABLE 11.1   VERSIONS Query Pseudocolumns

PSEUDOCOLUMN	DESCRIPTION
VERSIONS_STARTTIME	The timestamp of the first version of the row.
VERSIONS_ENDTIME	The timestamp of the last version of the row.
VERSIONS_OPERATION	The type of operation the row was subject to. Values are I (for INSERT), U (for UPDATE), and D (for DELETE).
VERSIONS_STARTSCN	The SCN for the first version of the row.
VERSIONS_ENDSCN	The SCN for the last version of the row.
VERSIONS_XID	The transaction ID generated by the change.

The syntax of this flashback query is as follows. Instead of the TIMESTAMP expression, you can choose a specific SCN.

```
VERSIONS BETWEEN {SCN|TIMESTAMP} {expr|MINVALUE} AND {expr|MAXVALUE}
```

FLASHBACK_TRANSACTION_QUERY

The FLASHBACK_TRANSACTION_QUERY data dictionary contains not only details about the transaction, such as who performed the change and when, but also the SQL statement to undo the operation. The following SQL*Plus DESCRIBE command shows the available columns. The data dictionary references the XID column, which corresponds to the previously listed VERSIONS_XID pseudocolumn.

```
SQL> DESCRIBE flashback_transaction_query
 Name                        Null?     Type
 --------------------------- --------- -------------
 XID                                   RAW(8)
 START_SCN                             NUMBER
 START_TIMESTAMP                       DATE
 COMMIT_SCN                            NUMBER
 COMMIT_TIMESTAMP                      DATE
 LOGON_USER                            VARCHAR2(30)
 UNDO_CHANGE#                          NUMBER
 OPERATION                             VARCHAR2(32)
 TABLE_NAME                            VARCHAR2(256)
 TABLE_OWNER                           VARCHAR2(32)
 ROW_ID                                VARCHAR2(19)
 UNDO_SQL                              VARCHAR2(4000)
```

The following statement lists one of the undo SQL statements for the table COURSE, which is owned by the STUDENT user. The UNDO statement lists the ROWID pseudocolumn, showing a unique way to identify a row within a table. You'll learn more about the ROWID pseudocolumn in Chapter 13.

```
SELECT undo_sql
  FROM flashback_transaction_query
 WHERE table_name = 'COURSE'
```

```
        AND table_owner = 'STUDENT'
UNDO_SQL
------------------------------------------------
update "STUDENT"."COURSE" set "COST" = '1195'
 where ROWID = 'AAAKgzAAAAAAAAAAAA';
...
```

Another noteworthy observation you might make is the double quotation marks around the schema, table, and column names. Oracle object names can be case-sensitive; using double quotes ensures the correct spelling of the object. Chapter 12 discusses the case-sensitivity of column and table names in more detail.

FLASHBACK TABLE AND FLASHBACK DATABASE COMMANDS

Oracle has implemented two more flashback-related commands. FLASHBACK TABLE and FLASHBACK DATABASE allow you to revert an individual table and an entire database, respectively.

 Keep in mind that while the flashback choices provide a fallback option for application or user error, flashback data is retained only up to a specific period in time.

The following statement illustrates a FLASHBACK TABLE statement that restores the COURSE table to its state 5 minutes ago.

```
FLASHBACK TABLE course
   TO TIMESTAMP(SYSTIMESTAMP - INTERVAL '5' MINUTE)
Flashback complete.
```

To flashback a table or an entire database, you need special permissions, as discussed in Chapter 15. Furthermore, the FLASHBACK TABLE command does not work after you perform table structure changes (for example, adding, dropping, or modifying table columns). Another requirement for the FLASHBACK TABLE command is that the table must have the ROW MOVEMENT option enabled. (This is done when a table is initially created or with the ALTER TABLE table_name ENABLE ROW MOVEMENT syntax.)

The syntax of the FLASHBACK TABLE command is as follows. The BEFORE DROP option is discussed in Chapter 12 because it allows you to restore a dropped table.

```
FLASHBACK TABLE tablename [,tablename...] TO
{{SCN|TIMESTAMP} expr [ENABLE|DISABLE TRIGGERS]|
BEFORE DROP [RENAME TO newtablename]}
```

 Although there are many options for correcting unintentional errors, you must nevertheless have proper measures in place to protect your data against any accidents or failures so you can recover at any time. The DBA is responsible for establishing, administering, and periodically testing the appropriate data safeguards and procedures.

SQL DEVELOPER AND FLASHBACK

SQL Developer includes a Flashback tab, which allows you to see the original and modified data for each row. Figure 11.13 shows the two rows; for each respective row in the table, you can see the values of the data in the Data tab below. The highlighted row shows the Original operation, and the row below shows the same course number with an updated COST column.

Next to the Data subtab is the Undo SQL tab. If you have the appropriate privileges, you can look at the Undo SQL to see the syntax required to reverse the change.

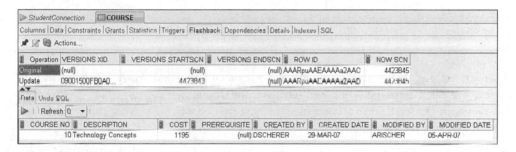

FIGURE 11.13
Flashback tab in SQL Developer

Connection Sharing in SQL Developer

In SQL Developer, a *session* is an individual database connection. For example, if you open two SQL Worksheets and the Data tab, using the Connections navigator, this is considered one session, not three separate sessions. Any changes are visible within the same session, also, there are no locking conflicts if the same row is modified. If you want to create a separate, independent session in SQL Developer, you can press Ctrl+Shift+N.

Figure 11.14 displays the Sessions screen (which you open by selecting Tools, Monitor Sessions) in SQL Developer. The Sessions tab shows the listing of current sessions against the database instance. For each connected session, you see a row listing the username, machine name, operating system user account, and tool used to connect to the database instance.

The screenshot shows you that there are three users connected in the database instance: SYSTEM, SCOTT, and STUDENT. Both the SCOTT and STUDENT sessions are initiated by the same machine and by SQL Developer. The SYSTEM session was started using SQL*Plus (see the Module column).

There are several tabs at the top of the screen. The first three tabs all share the StudentConnection, which was the STUDENT user name. These tabs collectively represent a single session. For example, StudentConnection~2 is another open Worksheet that shares the same connection. Also, the Session tab is opened with the StudentConnection (see the current connection information on the right of the screen).

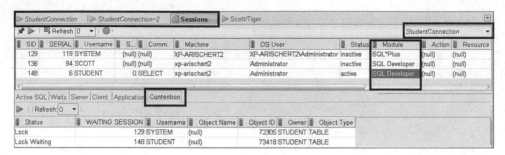

FIGURE 11.14
List of sessions

If you click on any of the rows shown in the Sessions tab, subtabs change for the individual session you select. One of the very useful subtabs is the Contention subtab, which shows which users are holding locks. If you are concerned that you may be waiting for data that another user is locking, you can review this subtab.

In this case, the SYSTEM user performed an update to all the rows of the STUDENT table without committing the change, and the STUDENT user performed the same update from his user account. Now the STUDENT user is waiting for the SYSTEM user to perform a COMMIT or ROLLBACK operation to be able to proceed with the command.

Because the SYSTEM user is one of the most privileged users in the database, this account has the right to update tables in the STUDENT schema. To simulate the lock example, the following update was issued by SYSTEM.

```
UPDATE student.student
   SET zip = 10025
```

The STUDENT table is referenced by the owner of the table (student.student). Then the STUDENT user issues a subsequent update, attempting to change all the zip codes to 10026. Because the SYSTEM user issued the command against the rows first, this user holds the locks to all the modified rows, the STUDENT user has to wait for the needed locks to be released. Then the STUDENT user can perform the respective update command. The Contention sub tab shows that the STUDENT user is waiting for the locks to be released.

You can also simulate a lock contention even within the same STUDENT account. For example, within SQL Developer you can create an unshared Worksheet by pressing Ctrl+Shift+N. This creates a separate session.

Performance Considerations When Writing DML Statements

Much like the index in a book, Oracle allows the creation of indexes on tables, which can help speed up retrieval of rows. While the discussion of indexes takes place in Chapter 13, at this point, you should be aware of the effect indexes have on the performance of your data manipulation statement.

Indexes can slow down data manipulation because they may require maintenance of the values within the indexes. For example, if an UPDATE operation affects an indexed column, the value in the index needs to be updated. A DELETE statement requires the entries in the index to be marked for deletion. An INSERT command creates index entries for all supplied column values where an index exists.

However, indexes can be beneficial for UPDATE or DELETE statements if the statement updates a small portion of the table and if it contains a WHERE clause that refers to an indexed column. Rather than look through the entire table for the desired information, Oracle finds it quickly and performs the desired operation.

One of the reasons a database designer should consider using an index on the foreign key is if updates or deletions for the primary key on the parent table occur. If an index on the foreign key is present, referential integrity is maintained by temporarily locking the index of the child table rather than the entire child table. This greatly improves performance of these types of commands.

▼ LAB 11.2 EXERCISES

a) Using an UPDATE statement, change the location to B111 for all sections where the location is currently L210.

b) Update the MODIFIED_BY column with the user login name and update the MODIFIED_DATE column with a date of March 31, 2009, using the TO_DATE function for all the rows updated in exercise a.

c) Update instructor Irene Willig's zip code to 90210. What do you observe?

d) What does the following query accomplish?

```
UPDATE enrollment e
   SET final_grade = (SELECT AVG(numeric_grade)
                        FROM grade g
                       WHERE e.student_id = g.student_id
                         AND e.section_id = g.section_id),
       modified_date = SYSDATE,
       modified_by = 'Your name here'
 WHERE student_id IN (SELECT student_id
                        FROM student
                       WHERE last_name like 'S%')
```

e) Update the first name from Rick to Nick for the instructor with the ID 104.

f) Write and execute an UPDATE statement to update the phone numbers of instructors from 2125551212 to 212-555-1212 and the MODIFIED_BY and MODIFIED_DATE columns with the user logged in and today's date, respectively. Write a SELECT statement to prove the update worked correctly. Do not issue a COMMIT command.

g) If you use SQL Developer: Create another session, independent of the current StudentConnection session, using Ctrl+Shift+N. If you use SQL*Plus: Invoke another SQL*Plus connection with student/learn.

Execute the same SELECT statement you wrote in exercise f to prove that your update worked correctly. Compare the result with the result in exercise f.

h) What is the result of the following statement?

```
MERGE INTO enrollment e
USING (SELECT AVG(numeric_grade) final_grade,
              section_id, student_id
         FROM grade
        GROUP BY section_id, student_id) g
   ON (g.section_id = e.section_id
   AND g.student_id = e.student_id)
 WHEN MATCHED THEN
    UPDATE SET e.final_grade = g.final_grade
 WHEN NOT MATCHED THEN
    INSERT (e.student_id, e.section_id, e.enroll_date,
            e.final_grade, e.created_by, e.created_date,
            e.modified_date, e.modified_by)
    VALUES (g.section_id, g.student_id, SYSDATE,
            g.final_grade, 'MERGE', SYSDATE,
            SYSDATE, 'MERGE')
```

i) Delete all rows from the GRADE_CONVERSION table. Then select all the data from the table, issue a ROLLBACK command, and explain the outcome.

j) If TRUNCATE is used in exercise i instead of DELETE, how would this change the outcome? Caution: Do not actually execute the TRUNCATE statement unless you are prepared to reload the data.

k) Delete the row inserted in exercise a in Lab 11.1 from the GRADE_TYPE table.

l) What is the effect of the following statement?

```
DELETE FROM enrollment
 WHERE student_id NOT IN
         (SELECT student_id
            FROM student s, zipcode z
           WHERE s.zip = z.zip
             AND z.city = 'Brooklyn'
             AND z.state = 'NY')
```

▼ LAB 11.2 EXERCISE ANSWERS

a) Using an UPDATE statement, change the location to B111 for all sections where the location is currently L210.

ANSWER: The UPDATE statement updates the LOCATION column in 10 rows of the SECTION table.

```
UPDATE section
   SET location = 'B111'
 WHERE location = 'L210'
10 rows updated.
```

Without a WHERE clause, all rows in the SECTION table are updated, not just 10 rows. For example, if you want to make sure all students have their last names begin with a capital letter, issue the following UPDATE statement.

```
UPDATE student
   SET last_name = INITCAP(last_name)
```

UPDATES TO MULTIPLE TABLES

Typically, the UPDATE statement affects a single table. However, if the table has a trigger associated with it, it may fire if the certain conditions specified in the trigger are true. The code in the trigger may cause insertions, updates, or deletions to other tables. Triggers can also add or modify values to rows you are changing. You can query the data dictionary view USER_TRIGGERS to see if any triggers are associated with your tables or review the Triggers tab for a table in SQL Developer.

b) Update the MODIFIED_BY column with the user login name and update the MODIFIED_DATE column with a date of March 31, 2009, using the TO_DATE function for all the rows updated in exercise a.

ANSWER: The MODIFIED_BY column is updated with the USER function to reflect an update by the user logged in, namely STUDENT, and the MODIFIED_DATE column is updated using the TO_DATE function. The update is based on the previously updated location.

```
UPDATE section
   SET modified_by = USER,
       modified_date = TO_DATE('31-MAR-2009', 'DD-MON-YYYY')
 WHERE location = 'B111'
10 rows updated.
```

Instead of writing them as individual UPDATE statements, exercises a and b can be combined in a single UPDATE statement, with the columns separated by commas.

```
UPDATE section
   SET location = 'B111',
       modified_by = USER,
       modified_date = TO_DATE('31-MAR-2009', 'DD-MON-YYYY')
 WHERE location = 'L210'
```

c) Update Instructor Irene Willig's zip code to 90210. What do you observe?

ANSWER: The attempt to change the zip code to a value that does not exist in the ZIPCODE table results in a referential integrity constraint error.

```
UPDATE instructor
   SET zip = '90210'
 WHERE last_name = 'Willig'
   AND first_name = 'Irene'
UPDATE instructor
*
ERROR at line 1:
ORA-02291: integrity constraint (STUDENT.INST_ZIP_FK)
violated - parent key not found
```

Oracle does not allow any invalid values in a column if the foreign key constraint exists and is enabled.

A query checking for this zip code in the ZIPCODE table retrieves no rows.

```
SELECT zip
  FROM zipcode
 WHERE zip = '90210'

no rows selected
```

UNIQUELY IDENTIFYING RECORDS

The WHERE clause in the previous UPDATE statement lists the first and last name of the instructor, and it happens to be unique and sufficient to identify the individual. Imagine a scenario in which you have instructors with the identical name, but who are in fact different individuals. When you perform manipulation of data, it is best to include the primary key value, such as the INSTRUCTOR_ID, to ensure that the correct row is changed.

d) What does the following query accomplish?

```
UPDATE enrollment e
   SET final_grade = (SELECT AVG(numeric_grade)
                        FROM grade g
                       WHERE e.student_id = g.student_id
                         AND e.section_id = g.section_id),
       modified_date = SYSDATE,
       modified_by = 'Your name here'
 WHERE student_id IN (SELECT student_id
                        FROM student
                       WHERE last_name like 'S%')
```

ANSWER: This query updates the FINAL_GRADE, MODIFIED_DATE, and MODIFIED_BY columns of the ENROLLMENT table for students with last names starting with the letter S. The computed average grade is based on the individual grades received by the student for the respective section.

The example illustrates a correlated UPDATE statement. The outer query identifies the students with last names of beginning with S. For each individual outer row, the inner correlated subquery executes and computes the average of the individual grades from the GRADE table. The result is then updated in the FINAL_GRADE column of the ENROLLMENT table.

e) Update the first name from Rick to Nick for the instructor with the ID 104.

ANSWER: The primary key column INSTRUCTOR_ID identifies the instructor uniquely and is therefore used in the WHERE clause. In addition, it helps to include the old value of the FIRST_NAME column in the WHERE clause, in case any previous changes to the column have been made.

```
UPDATE instructor
   SET first_name = 'Nick'
 WHERE instructor_id = 109
   AND first_name = 'Rick'
1 row updated.
```

f) Write and execute an UPDATE statement to update the phone numbers of instructors from 2125551212 to 212-555-1212 and the MODIFIED_BY and MODIFIED_DATE columns with the user logged in and today's date, respectively. Write a SELECT statement to prove the update worked correctly. Do not issue a COMMIT command.

ANSWER: A single UPDATE statement updates 3 columns in 10 rows simultaneously in the INSTRUCTOR table. The MODIFIED_BY column is updated with the USER function, and the MODIFIED_DATE column is updated with the SYSDATE function, entering today's date and time into the column.

```
UPDATE instructor
   SET phone = '212-555-1212',
       modified_by = USER,
```

```
        modified_date = SYSDATE
  WHERE phone = '2125551212'
```
10 rows updated.

```
SELECT instructor_id, phone, modified_by, modified_date
  FROM instructor
INSTRUCTOR_ID PHONE          MODIFIED_BY MODIFIED_
------------- -----------    ----------- ---------
          101 212-555-1212   STUDENT     09-MAY-09
          102 212-555-1212   STUDENT     09-MAY-09
...
          109 212-555-5555   STUDENT     09-MAY-09
          110 212-555-5555   STUDENT     09-MAY-09
```

10 rows selected.

g) If you use SQL Developer: Create another session, independent of the current StudentConnection session, using Ctrl+Shift+N. If you use SQL*Plus: Invoke another SQL*Plus connection with student/learn.

Execute the same SELECT statement you wrote in exercise f to prove that your update worked correctly. Compare the result with the result in exercise f.

ANSWER: You will observe when you execute the SQL statement from exercise f that this new session does not reflect the changes performed in the other session. Any other database user or session cannot see the updated values in the INSTRUCTOR table until a COMMIT command is issued in the original session.

```
SELECT instructor_id, phone, modified_by, modified_date
  FROM instructor
INSTRUCTOR_ID PHONE          MODIFIED_BY MODIFIED_
------------- -----------    ----------- ---------
          101 2125551212     ESILVEST    02-JAN-07
          102 2125551212     ESILVEST    02-JAN-07
...
          109 2125555555     ESILVEST    02-JAN-07
          110 2125555555     ARISCHER    11-MAR-07
```

10 rows selected.

When you are ready to move on to the next exercise, issue the ROLLBACK command in the first session to undo your changes and release the locks.

h) What is the result of the following statement?

```
MERGE INTO enrollment e
USING (SELECT AVG(numeric_grade) final_grade,
              section_id, student_id
         FROM grade
        GROUP BY section_id, student_id) g
   ON (g.section_id = e.section_id
   AND g.student_id = e.student_id)
 WHEN MATCHED THEN
   UPDATE SET e.final_grade = g.final_grade
```

```
WHEN NOT MATCHED THEN
   INSERT (e.student_id, e.section_id, e.enroll_date,
           e.final_grade, e.created_by, e.created_date,
           e.modified_date, e.modified_by)
   VALUES (g.section_id, g.student_id, SYSDATE,
           g.final_grade, 'MERGE', SYSDATE,
           SYSDATE, 'MERGE')
```

ANSWER: The MERGE statement updates the column FINAL_GRADE to the average grade per student and section, based on the GRADE table. If the section and student are not found in the ENROLLMENT table, the MERGE command inserts the row.

Actually, the INSERT part of the MERGE statement will probably never be executed because a row in the GRADE table cannot exist unless an ENROLLMENT row exists. The foreign key relationship between the two tables enforces this. In this instance, the following correlated subquery UPDATE achieves the same result as the MERGE statement.

```
UPDATE enrollment e
   SET final_grade = (SELECT AVG(numeric_grade)
                        FROM grade g
                       WHERE g.section_id = e.section_id
                         AND g.student_id = e.student_id)
```

i) Delete all rows from the GRADE_CONVERSION table. Then select all the data from the table, issue a ROLLBACK command, and explain the outcome.

ANSWER: A DELETE statement deletes all rows in the GRADE_CONVERSION table. A subsequently issued SELECT statement shows no rows in the table. Issuing a ROLLBACK undoes the delete. You can verify this by issuing another SELECT statement against the table.

```
DELETE FROM grade_conversion
15 rows deleted.

SELECT *
  FROM grade_conversion
no rows selected

ROLLBACK
Rollback complete.
```

j) If TRUNCATE is used in exercise i instead of DELETE, how would this change the outcome? Caution: Do not actually execute the TRUNCATE statement unless you are prepared to reload the data.

ANSWER: When TRUNCATE is used, the data cannot be rolled back; the ROLLBACK statement has no effect. A subsequent SELECT statement reflects no rows in the GRADE_CONVERSION table.

```
TRUNCATE TABLE grade_conversion
Table truncated.

ROLLBACK
Rollback complete.

SELECT COUNT(*)
  FROM grade_conversion
```

```
COUNT(*)
---------
        0
```

1 row selected.

 When the ROLLBACK command is issued, Oracle returns the "Rollback complete" message. This is misleading, because in this case a rollback did not occur; the data is permanently deleted. Be sure to use caution when using the TRUNCATE TABLE command.

k) Delete the row inserted in exercise a in Lab 11.1 from the GRADE_TYPE table.

ANSWER: A DELETE statement is written for the row where the grade type code is 'EC'.

```
DELETE FROM grade_type
 WHERE grade_type_code = 'EC'
```
1 row deleted.

l) What is the effect of the following statement?

```
DELETE FROM enrollment
 WHERE student_id NOT IN
       (SELECT student_id
          FROM student s, zipcode z
         WHERE s.zip = z.zip
           AND z.city = 'Brooklyn'
           AND z.state = 'NY')
```

ANSWER: The statement deletes enrollment rows for all students except those who live in Brooklyn, NY.

The DELETE statement narrows down the records in the WHERE clause by using a NOT IN subquery to find students who do not live in Brooklyn, NY. Alternatively, the DELETE statement can be rewritten as a correlated subquery, using the NOT EXISTS operator, which under certain circumstances can execute faster.

```
DELETE FROM enrollment e
 WHERE NOT EXISTS
       (SELECT 'x'
          FROM student s, zipcode z
         WHERE s.zip = z.zip
           AND s.student_id = e.student_id
           AND z.city = 'Brooklyn'
           AND z.state = 'NY')
```

Because the STUDENT_ID in the STUDENT table is defined as NOT NULL, the NOT IN and NOT EXISTS statements are equivalent. For more information on the differences between NOT IN and NOT EXISTS, see Chapter 8, "Subqueries," and Chapter 18, "SQL Optimization."

The DELETE command is not successful because GRADE records exist for these students.

Lab 11.2 Quiz

In order to test your progress, you should be able to answer the following questions.

1) It is possible to restore rows that have been deleted using the DELETE command.

_____ a) True

_____ b) False

2) There is no syntax error in the following UPDATE statement.

```
UPDATE grade_type
   SET description = 'Exams'
 WHERE grade_type_code IN ('FI', 'MT')
```

_____ a) True

_____ b) False

3) The SELECT command always places locks on retrieved rows.

_____ a) True

_____ b) False

4) Oracle achieves read consistency by reading uncommitted data.

_____ a) True

_____ b) False

5) Oracle releases the lock of a row after the session issues a COMMIT or ROLLBACK command.

_____ a) True

_____ b) False

ANSWERS APPEAR IN APPENDIX A.

LAB 11.3
The SQL Developer Data Tab

LAB OBJECTIVES

After this lab, you will be able to:

▶ Manipulate Data Using SQL Developer

▶ Export Data to Different File Formats

▶ Import Data from Different Data Sources

SQL Developer's GUI allows you to insert and manipulate existing data directly with the Data tab. This is a quick, simple, and convenient way to make changes. While the Data tab is a very powerful feature in SQL Developer, it does not eliminate the need to know DML SQL command syntax altogether.

Display the Data tab by selecting the table in the Connection navigator. You see a number of icons on the top, some of which you have already learned about. Table 11.2 provides a brief description of the icons.

TABLE 11.2 Data Tab Icons

ICON/MENU	DESCRIPTION
Freeze View (pin)	Keeps the tab displayed even if you click on another object in the Connection navigation.
Refresh (circulating arrows)	Updates the data grid with the latest changes.
Insert row (plus sign)	Inserts a new row for new data entry.
Delete row (minus sign)	Deletes the selected row.
Commit (checkmark)	Issues the COMMIT command.
Rollback (undo arrow)	Issues the ROLLBACK command.
Filter	Narrows down the data displayed; similar to a WHERE clause.
Actions	Actions you can perform within the Data tab (for example, export). Some of these are discussed in Chapter 12.

You have two additional menu choices: the Actions menu and the context-sensitive menu available within the data grid, and we will discuss the relevant choices as you work through this lab.

Inserting Data Using the SQL Developer Interface

Instead of writing and issuing a SQL INSERT command, you can add data with SQL Developer's user interface. It allows you to enter data quickly rather than write lengthy SQL statements. You access the Data tab by double-clicking the COURSE table on the Connections navigator. Click the Insert Row icon (see Figure 11.15) to show a new empty row with a plus sign in front of the row number. To enter the data, simply type the data into the appropriate columns.

FIGURE 11.15
The Data tab in SQL Developer

If you double-click the cell, you see an ellipsis (...) button, with a box next to it that looks like a drop-down box. When you double-click it, a dialog box appears. If the column is of DATE data type, the dialog box shows today's date and time (see Figure 11.16). You can simply accept it or change the date. SQL Developer enforces a valid date entry.

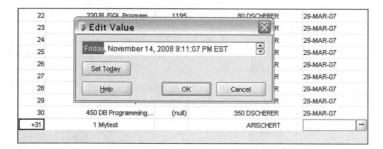

FIGURE 11.16
Inserting data using the SQL Developer Data tab

A right-click within the data grid reveals a number of context-sensitive menu choices (see Figure 11.17 and Table 11.3). Some of these choices have been described in Chapter 2, "SQL: The Basics," and you will have already found them useful for displaying the data in the manner you like.

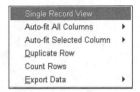

FIGURE 11.17
Context menu on the Data grid

You can copy and paste data from existing rows to create the new row; be sure to modify the primary key, otherwise your insert will not be successful. Or if you right-click the Data tab grid, you can choose to duplicate an existing row with the Duplicate Row menu option (see Figure 11.7).

TABLE 11.3   Data Grid Context Menu Choices

MENU CHOICE	DESCRIPTION
Single Record View	Edit and display one record at a time.
Auto-fit All Columns	Adjust the column width according to the submenu choices, which are either by header, by data, or by best fit.
Auto-fit Selected Columns	Adjust selected columns according to the same submenu choices.
Duplicate Row	Copy the row; useful if you need to create another row with similar values.
Count Rows	Count the number of rows in the data grid.
Export	Export data into a variety of formats.

Updating Records

Using the Data tab, you can perform updates directly in the data grid. This works well when you need to make simple data modifications affecting one or a few rows. The Filter box permits you to narrow down the records you want to update. The filter functionality performs much like a WHERE clause, without the WHERE keyword.

Figure 11.18 shows the filter used to narrow down the result set to courses with the word Java in the DESCRIPTION column of the COURSE table. Notice that a change to the COST column was performed for course number 146. As a result, the row number on the left of the grid is flagged with a change asterisks (*) after the change.

 Using the Data tab is a great way to perform an update quickly, but it does not eliminate the need to learn about the SQL UPDATE command altogether. If you want to modify large numbers of records with complex conditions, using the SQL UPDATE command is the best way to perform changes.

	StudentConnection	COURSE				
Columns	Data	Constraints	Grants	Statistics	Triggers	Flashback De

Sort... | Filter: DESCRIPTION LIKE '%Java%'

	COURSE...	DESCRIPTION	CO...	PRER
1	120	Intro to Java Programming	1195	
2	122	Intermediate Java Progra...	1195	
3	124	Advanced Java Programmi...	1195	
4	125	Java Developer I	1195	
*5	146	Java for C/C++ Programm...	1500	
6	350	Java Developer II	1195	
7	430	Java Developer III	1195	
8	450	DB Programming with Java	(null)	

FIGURE 11.18
Updated record in SQL Developer grid, as indicated by the asterisk

On the bottom of the SQL Developer screen is the Data Editor - Log tab. This tab records all changes that occur in the Data tab and translates them into SQL commands. When you review the statement in Figure 11.19, you find that the COURSE table is prefixed with the STUDENT schema name; this ensures that the correct table owned by the correct user account is updated. While the connection you are using may be called the StudentConnection, the login name and owner of the COURSE table is the STUDENT user.

The WHERE clause uses the ROWID pseudocolumn to uniquely identify which record is updated. (ROWID is discussed in greater detail in Chapter 13.) Another new column is the ORA_ROWSCN pseudocolumn, and its values represent the SCN for the given row. This pseudocolumn is not shown on the Data tab grid, but it is included in the update to ensure that the row has not changed since it was retrieved.

You cannot use the statements to collect and perform changes to another database instance because the ROWID and ORA_ROWSCN numbers will be different.

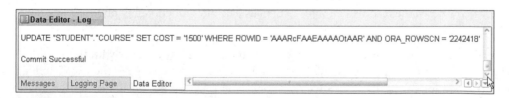

Data Editor - Log		
UPDATE "STUDENT"."COURSE" SET COST = '1500' WHERE ROWID = 'AAARcFAAEAAAAOtAAR' AND ORA_ROWSCN = '2242418'		
Commit Successful		
Messages	Logging Page	Data Editor

FIGURE 11.19
The Data Editor - Log results

After you modify any data in the grid and click the Commit icon, the log lets you know whether the transaction was successful. If an error occurs, you see an Oracle error message. Figure 11.20

shows an attempt to enter an invalid number into the COST column of the COURSE table. Oracle rolls back the change, as indicated with the ORA-01722 error message.

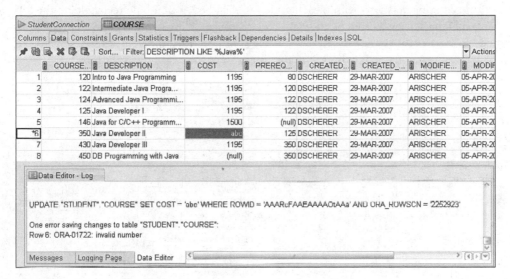

FIGURE 11.20
Error in the Data Editor - Log

Deleting Records

To remove records from a table, click the Delete icon on the Data tab; the record will be marked for deletion, as indicated by the negative number (see Figure 11.21). The change is made permanent when you click the Commit icon or rolled back when you click the Rollback icon.

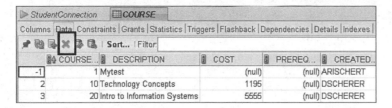

FIGURE 11.21
Deleted row in SQL Developer's Data tab

Splitting the Display Vertically and Horizontally

In the Data tab, you can split the display vertically and horizontally to scroll independently. You can perform filtering and sorts within each grid. The split box, a thin blue rectangle on the top and bottom of the screen, located on the right of the scrollbar, allows you to perform this action. Figure 11.22 shows the data of the COURSE table split into three different display screens. To remove the split, drag the screen back into the direction of the respective split box.

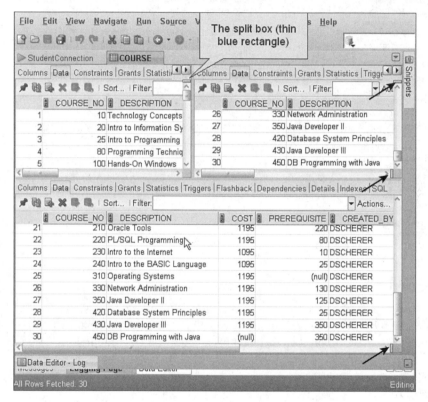

FIGURE 11.22
The Data tab, split horizontally and vertically

Exporting Data

On the Data tab's grid or within a SQL query's Results window, when you right-click, you get a context menu, and one of the options is Export. Alternatively, you can get to the Export Data menu choice by clicking the Actions menu item. As you can see, there are many different ways to perform the same task in SQL Developer.

The Export Data option allows you to export data in a variety of formats, including Excel and HTML (see Figure 11.23). Another great option is the generation of INSERT SQL statements; you can create SQL scripts that you can then use to re-create the data. The CSV option creates a comma-separated value (CSV) file, a common data format that is useful for transfer between different databases. The loader choice creates a SQL*Loader file along with the data; you can use this file to transfer data into another Oracle database.

As part of each export, you can restrict the columns and the rows you want to export. You can narrow the export criteria by using the Columns and Where tabs that are shown after you choose the Export menu option.

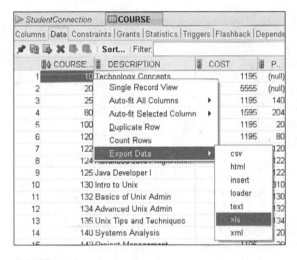

FIGURE 11.23
Export Data menu option

In the Tools menu, you can also find the Database Export menu option. It allows you to selectively generate the DDL and DML not just for one table at a time but for multiple users, tables, or objects types.

If you need to move larger volumes of data, particularly between two Oracle database instances, you might want to consider using the COPY command (select Tools, Database Copy). Unlike the previously mentioned options, which create files containing the data, this command immediately copies the appropriate information to the Oracle target database.

Outside the SQL Developer tool, Oracle provides a database utility called Data Pump that allows you to export individual tables, individual users, or the entire database, in binary format. DBAs typically use this utility for data transfer between Oracle databases or as a backup choice.

Importing Data

SQL Developer allows import of data. You can choose either Excel or CSV files and import into an existing table or create a new table. If you want to import to a nonexistent table, you right-click the Tables node below the respective connection (see Figure 11.24). To import into an existing table, right-click on the specific table to see the Import Data menu option.

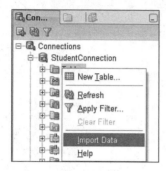

FIGURE 11.24
Import Data menu option

After you specify a file location and name, the Data Import Wizard appears. This wizard guides you through a series of steps to ensure that the data is correctly transferred into an Oracle table. In the example shown in Figure 11.25, an Excel spreadsheet was chosen to be imported. The first step in the wizard is to provide a preview of the data. You choose the Excel Worksheet tab name and identify whether the first row is the header row or data.

The second step is to choose the columns you want to import. The third step is to map the chosen source columns to the appropriate columns in the Oracle target table (see Figure 11.26). If you are choosing to import into a new table, enter a target table name and modify the suggested target column names and data types.

The last step is to verify the import parameters. If an error occurs, you must go back to the previous steps and correct the issue reported. When all is ready, you can either import the data into the table or click the box labeled Send to Worksheet, which opens a SQL Developer Worksheet window that contains the appropriate SQL INSERT statements.

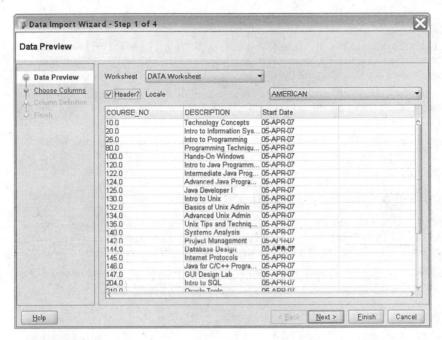

FIGURE 11.25
Import Wizard

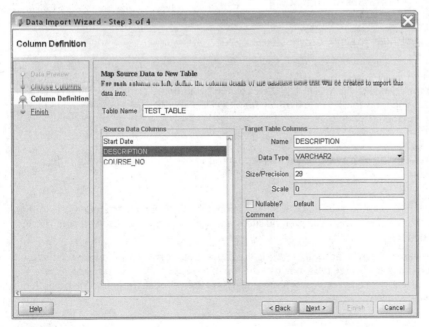

FIGURE 11.26
Map the source to the target columns

▼ LAB 11.3 EXERCISES

a) In the ZIPCODE table, change the city name for zip code 07024 from Ft. Lee to Fort Lee, using the Data tab. Update the MODIFIED_BY column with your name and the MODIFIED_DATE column with the current date and time. Commit the change. Describe the steps you performed.

b) Export the columns COURSE_NO and DESCRIPTION from the COURSE table to an Excel file format. Choose only those records where the prerequisite is not null. What do you observe about the SQL tab contained in the Excel file?

c) Export the data of the MEETING table in the INSERT format. Then execute the resulting INSERT statements.

▼ LAB 11.3 EXERCISE ANSWERS

a) In the ZIPCODE table, change the city name for zip code 07024 from Ft. Lee to Fort Lee, using the Data tab. Update the MODIFIED_BY column with your name and the MODIFIED_DATE column with the current date and time. Commit the change. Describe the steps you performed.

ANSWER: Using the Data tab, you can narrow down the result set with the filter. Figure 11.27 shows the chosen criteria. After you change the city name, you see the asterisk (*).

FIGURE 11.27
The changes performed in the Data tab

You perform the change to the MODIFIED_DATE column by double-clicking the column's cell and clicking the Set Today button. Enter your name for MODIFIED_BY. Click the Commit icon to make the change permanent.

 You can refresh the display when you make changes to the Data tab by clicking the Refresh icon.

b) Export the columns COURSE_NO and DESCRIPTION from the COURSE table to an Excel file format. Choose only those records where the prerequisite is not null. What do you observe about the SQL tab contained in the Excel file?

ANSWER: The export can be accomplished via the Export Data menu. To narrow down the result set, use the Columns and Where tabs shown at the top of the Export Data window (see Figure 11.28). Alternatively, you can execute a SQL statement and then choose the Export menu option from the Results window.

FIGURE 11.20
Export Data options

The data is shown the Export Worksheet tab in the Excel spreadsheet. The Excel file also contains a SQL tab (see Figure 11.29), which shows the SQL used to select the data in the exported file.

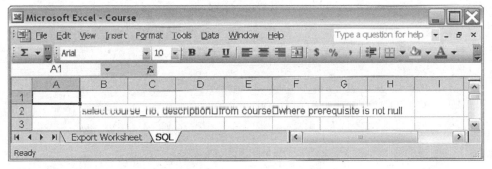

FIGURE 11.29
SQL tab within an Excel spreadsheet, showing the SQL that was used to export the data

c) Export the data of the MEETING table in the INSERT format. Then execute the resulting INSERT statements.

ANSWER: When exporting data, you can either save the data to a file or to the Clipboard. Because the table you're working with here contains only two rows, you can save it to the Clipboard and then paste the records into a SQL Worksheet window. Or, if you save it to a file, you can open the script file within SQL Developer; it will be placed in its own SQL Worksheet window.

To execute the two SQL INSERT statements, click the Run Script icon or press F5; the result of the script is displayed in the Script Output window (see Figure 11.30). You can roll back the changes afterward.

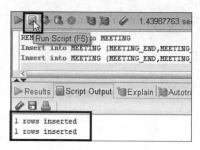

FIGURE 11.30
Result of insert script execution

Lab 11.3 Quiz

In order to test your progress, you should be able to answer the following questions.

1) The Data tab allows you to perform all the major DML commands, using SQL Developer's user interface.

    _____ a) True
    _____ b) False

2) To extract data containing multiple Oracle user accounts, you can use SQL Developer's Tools, Database Export menu.

    _____ a) True
    _____ b) False

3) The Auto-fit All Columns on Header menu option in the data grid adjusts the width of the column headers.

    _____ a) True
    _____ b) False

4) The filter box in the Data tab requires the entry of the WHERE keyword.

    _____ a) True
    _____ b) False

5) SQL Developer's Export Data option allows you to selectively export certain rows and columns.

    _____ a) True
    _____ b) False

ANSWERS APPEAR IN APPENDIX A.

▼ WORKSHOP

The projects in this section are meant to prompt you to utilize all the skills you have acquired throughout this chapter. The answers to these projects can be found at the companion Web site to this book, located at www.oraclesqlbyexample.com.

1) Write and execute two INSERT commands to create rows in the ZIPCODE table for the following two cities: Newton, MA 02199 and Cleveland, OH 43011. After your INSERT statements are successful, make the changes permanent.

2) Make yourself a student by writing and executing an INSERT statement to insert a row into the STUDENT table with data about you. Use one of the zip codes you inserted in exercise 1. Insert values into the columns STUDENT_ID (use the value 900), FIRST_NAME, LAST_NAME, ZIP, REGISTRATION_DATE (use a date that is five days after today), CREATED_BY, CREATED_DATE, MODIFIED_BY, and MODIFIED_DATE. Issue a COMMIT command when you're done.

3) Write an UPDATE statement to update the data about you in the STUDENT table. Update the columns SALUTATION, STREET_ADDRESS, PHONE, and EMPLOYER. Be sure to also update the MODIFIED_DATE column and make the changes permanent.

4) Delete the row you created in the STUDENT table and the two rows you created in the ZIPCODE table. Be sure to issue a COMMIT command afterward. You can perform this action by using a SQL command or SQL Developer's Data tab.

5) Delete the zip code 10954 from the ZIPCODE table by using SQL Developer. Commit your change after you delete the row. Describe the results of your actions.

If you performed the exercises in this chapter, you will have changed data in most of the tables of the STUDENT schema. If you go back to the previous chapters and reexecute those queries, you might find that the results are different than they were before.

Therefore, if you want to reload the tables and data, you can run the rebuildStudent.sql script. Refer to the readme file you downloaded from the companion Web site for more information on how to perform this step.

CHAPTER 12

Create, Alter, and Drop Tables

CHAPTER OBJECTIVES

In this chapter, you will learn about:

- ▸ Creating and Dropping Tables
- ▸ Altering Tables and Manipulating Constraints

This chapter introduces you to the Data Definition Language (DDL) commands associated with tables, the type of database object most frequently used. Table 12.1 provides an overview of other commonly used object types discussed in this and the following chapters.

TABLE 12.1 Commonly Used Database Object Types

DATABASE OBJECT	PURPOSE	FIND MORE INFORMATION
Table	Stores data	This chapter
View	Used for security and to hide complexity	Chapter 13, "Indexes, Sequences, and Views"
Index	Improves data access speed	Chapter 13
Sequence	Generates unique key values	Chapter 13
Synonym	Provides an alternative name for a database object	Chapter 15, "Security"
Directory	Points to a directory location outside the Oracle database	This chapter and Chapter 11, "Insert, Update, and Delete"

TABLE 12.1 Continued

STORED DATABASE OBJECTS CREATED USING PL/SQL	
Trigger	Individual PL/SQL program that executes on DML operations
Function	Program that returns a single value
Procedure	Program may return zero, one, or many values
Package	Collection of procedures, functions, or other PL/SQL constructs bundled together

The DDL commands allow you to create, modify, and remove database objects. This chapter discusses the options available with respect to tables, which allow you to manipulate column definitions and constraints. Because database constraints enforce business rules and data integrity, understanding constraints such as the primary key, foreign key, check, and unique constraints is essential to learning about a relational database.

 Keep in mind that a DDL statement automatically issues an implicit COMMIT.

LAB 12.1
Creating and Dropping Tables

LAB OBJECTIVES

After this lab, you will be able to:

▸ Create and Drop Tables
▸ Create Constraints

For your overall comprehension of the SQL language, it is very helpful to learn about the DDL involved in the creation of a physical table and its associated constraints. This lab provides an overview of naming conventions, syntax, and constraint considerations. While this chapter concentrates primarily on the SQL command and syntax options, you will see later in the lab that if you use SQL Developer, you do not need to remember the precise syntax of all the SQL commands. You can select commands using a simple menu click instead. However, you must know that choosing a menu option does not eliminate the need to understand SQL and the effects of the executed actions. Furthermore, not all the various command syntax options are available in SQL Developer.

Creating Tables

You create tables by using the CREATE TABLE command, in either of two ways. The first method is to specify the columns and their data types explicitly; the second method is to create a table based on an existing table.

The following statement creates a table called TOY that consists of four columns. A NOT NULL constraint is specified for the DESCRIPTION column. The newly created table contains no data.

```
CREATE TABLE toy
   (toy_id              NUMBER(10),
    description         VARCHAR2(15) NOT NULL,
    last_purchase_date  DATE,
    remaining_quantity  NUMBER(6))
```

When defining a table and columns, you need to know about the naming restrictions and conventions.

TABLE NAMES

A table name must be unique within a database schema; no other database object, such as another table, view, or synonym, can have the same name. Every database object name must be no longer than 30 characters; cannot include spaces or hyphens, but can have underscores; and must begin with a letter. A table name should describe the nature of the data contained in the table; for consistency, choose either singular or plural names for all your tables.

COLUMN NAMES

A column name must be unique within a table and should not exceed 30 characters. It should be descriptive of the values stored in the column. You can document the meaning of individual columns or tables in more detail with the COMMENT command, discussed later in this chapter.

A column is defined not only by a name but also by data type and length, where appropriate. When creating multiple columns, use a comma to separate the column definitions.

By default, table and column names are stored in the Oracle database in all uppercase. It is possible to create table names and column names with mixed case, special characters, and spaces if you use double quotes around the table and column names, but doing so defies the conventions used by most Oracle database installations.

Many corporations have created their own standard column and naming conventions. Compliance with naming standards simplifies the task of identifying database objects for developers. Furthermore, it shortens the learning curve for individuals involved in the maintenance and support of a system.

 Be consistent with your table and column names in terms of abbreviations and the use of either singular or plural names.

To simplify the understanding of relationships among the tables, use the identical column name for both the primary and foreign key columns whenever possible. For example, the STUDENT_ID foreign key column in the ENROLLMENT table references the primary key column of the same name in the STUDENT table.

TABLE CREATION SYNTAX

Following is the simplified syntax of a CREATE TABLE statement. (There are many more syntax options; only the most frequently used syntax choices are listed here.)

```
CREATE [GLOBAL TEMPORARY] TABLE tablename
   (columnname data_type [DEFAULT expr]|
   [GENERATED ALWAYS AS (expr) VIRTUAL]
   [column_constraint_clause]
      [, columnname data_type [DEFAULT expr]|
       [GENERATED ALWAYS AS (expr) VIRTUAL]
         [column_constraint_clause]...]
    [table_constraint_clause]
```

```
    )
[physical_storage_clause]
[ENABLE|DISABLE ROW MOVEMENT]
[temporary_table_clause]
[AS query]
```

The CREATE TABLE syntax shows that you must list the individual column name and the respective data type; the default expression, virtual column expression, and a column constraint clause are optional. The column constraint clause has a number of individual syntax options that allow you to restrict the values in an individual column. Because a table actually doesn't contain just one column, the syntax shows that the various syntax portions, consisting of column name, data type, default expression, virtual column expression, and column constraint clause, may be repeated for each subsequent column.

Besides an individual column constraint, a table may have table constraints that restrict one or multiple columns. Tables require physical storage, with individual storage parameters defined in the storage clause. As previously mentioned, you can create a table based on another table; you do this by using the AS QUERY clause. You can create a temporary table with the GLOBAL TEMPORARY keywords and the use of temporary_table_clause.

As you work your way through this lab, you will learn about all the different clauses and gain an understanding about the core functionality of the CREATE TABLE command.

Commonly Used Oracle Data Types

Based on the nature of the type of data you want to store, you choose the appropriate data type. This section reviews Oracle's most commonly used data types. You can find more details in Appendix I, "Oracle Data Types."

CHARACTER DATA

Character data is stored in columns of data type VARCHAR2, CHAR, CLOB, or LONG. When creating or altering a table, the VARCHAR2 and CHAR data types require a column length. The maximum length of a VARCHAR2 column is 4,000 bytes or 4,000 characters, depending on the syntax. (Only for multilingual databases is it important to distinguish between bytes and characters because a single character can take more than one byte. The Oracle default column definition is bytes.)

A fixed-length CHAR column has a maximum length of 2,000. A name such as Smith stored in the LAST_NAME column defined as VARCHAR2(25) stores only 6 characters versus 25 characters in fixed-length CHAR(25)-defined column because the CHAR adds trailing spaces.

The CLOB data type stores up to 4 GB of data, and a table may have multiple CLOB columns. You might still see the use of the LONG data type. It stores up to 2 GB of data in a single column; only one LONG column per table is allowed, and you cannot use character functions on a LONG column. Oracle recommends the use of the CLOB data type instead of the LONG data type because the LONG data type is used only for backward compatibility.

NUMERIC DATA

The format of the NUMBER data type is $NUMBER(p,s)$, where p is the *precision* (or total number of digits) and s is the *scale* (the number of digits to the right of the decimal point). The NUMBER data type can store up to 38 decimal digits of precision. The definition of NUMBER(5,2) on a column allows you to store values between –999.99 and 999.99. A number such as 1,000 is rejected, and a value such as 80.999 is rounded up to 81.00. Use the NUMBER data type for data on which you need to calculate, not for phone numbers or zip codes. For example, in the STUDENT schema, the ZIP column of the ZIPCODE table is stored as a VARCHAR2 rather than a NUMBER data type because it requires leading zeros.

The BINARY_FLOAT and BINARY_DOUBLE data types store floating-point numbers in 32-bit and 64-bit format. These data types are particularly useful if you require complex and/or fast arithmetic computations. Floating-point numbers do not have a scale because the number of digits to the right of the decimal point is not restricted. Floating-point numbers can have a decimal anywhere from the first to the last digit, or they can have none at all.

DATE AND TIME DATA

The DATE data type stores the century, year, month, day, hour, minute, and second. It has its own internal format, which can be displayed using different format masks. You can store dates from January 1, 4712 B.C. to December 31, 9999 A.D. The TIMESTAMP data type includes additional fractional seconds, and the TIMESTAMP WITH TIME ZONE data type enables you to keep track of time across geographic regions. The TIMESTAMP WITH LOCAL TIME ZONE is concerned with the date and time in the local region only. INTERVAL YEAR TO MONTH and INTERVAL DAY TO SECOND handle differences between dates and times.

BINARY DATA AND LARGE OBJECT DATA TYPES

Oracle allows you to save binary data such as images, audio, and video in data types called BLOB, RAW, LONG RAW, and BFILE. A BFILE data type points to a binary operating system file.

Integrity Constraints

When creating tables, you typically create them with integrity constraints. These constraints enforce the business rules of a system. For instance, "The salary of an employee may not be a negative number" may be enforced with a check constraint on the salary column, or "An employee must have a unique Social Security number" can be enforced with a NOT NULL constraint and a unique constraint. Constraints ensure data integrity and data consistency among all applications, no matter which program. They ease the burden of programming the business rules in individual applications because the database enforces the constraint.

The following CREATE TABLE statement creates a table called TAB1 with several types of constraints.

```
CREATE TABLE tab1
  (col1  NUMBER(10)   PRIMARY KEY,
   col2  NUMBER(4)    NOT NULL,
```

```
col3   VARCHAR2(5)   REFERENCES zipcode(zip)
          ON DELETE CASCADE,
col4   DATE          DEFAULT SYSDATE,
col5   VARCHAR2(20)  UNIQUE,
col6   NUMBER        CHECK(col6 < 100))
```

THE PRIMARY KEY CONSTRAINT

The first column of the table, COL1, has a PRIMARY KEY constraint, also referred to as an *entity integrity constraint*. The primary key ensures that all values in this column are NOT NULL and are unique. This is enforced through a unique index automatically created by Oracle, unless an index already exists. (Indexes are discussed in Chapter 13.) When the table TAB1 is created, Oracle automatically generates a name for this constraint, which looks something like this: SYS_C0030291. This constraint name is not terribly meaningful because it does not identify the table for which the constraint was created or the constraint type. You'll learn how to name constraints shortly.

Every table usually has one primary key, consisting of one or more columns. The combination of all values in a multicolumn primary key, also called a concatenated primary key, must also be unique. Primary keys should be static, which means no updates are usually performed. The primary key values are typically created by a number-generating sequence. This type of key is also referred to as an *artificial,* or *surrogate,* key and has the advantage that these values are completely meaningless and therefore not subject to updates. For primary keys, the NUMBER data type is a better choice than the VARCHAR2 data type because it is not prone to punctuation, case-sensitivity, and spelling mistakes, which make it more difficult to distinguish whether two records are identical. A table without a primary key should have at least a unique constraint.

UNIQUE CONSTRAINTS

To enforce unique values on an individual or a group of columns, you create a unique constraint for a table. In this example, column COL5 has a UNIQUE constraint. Before determining the primary key, there are often alternate keys that are candidates for the primary key.

Phone numbers and Social Security numbers are examples of alternate keys with unique constraints. However, these keys are often not chosen as primary keys because they may allow null values, or the values may be subject to updates. These types of business keys are very useful for end users querying the data, and often uniqueness is enforced through the unique constraint.

The most distinguishing characteristic between a primary key constraint and a unique constraint is that a unique constraint allows null values.

FOREIGN KEY CONSTRAINTS

A foreign key constraint, also referred to as a *referential integrity constraint,* ensures that the values in the foreign key correspond to values of a primary key. The column COL3 contains a FOREIGN KEY constraint. The keyword REFERENCES, followed by the ZIPCODE table and the ZIP column in the ZIPCODE table in parentheses, indicate that COL3 is a foreign key to the ZIP column of the ZIPCODE table. The FOREIGN KEY constraint indicates the domain of values for COL3; in other words, the only valid values for the COL3 column are zip codes found in the ZIP column of the ZIPCODE table and null values. Following is an excerpt from the previous CREATE TABLE statement, which shows the relevant foreign key constraint syntax.

```
CREATE TABLE tab1
...
    col3  VARCHAR2(5) REFERENCES zipcode(zip)
          ON DELETE CASCADE,
...
```

Alternatively, the foreign key can be created with this syntax; it does not mention the ZIP column. It is simply assumed that it is the primary key of the referenced table.

```
    col3  VARCHAR2(5) REFERENCES zipcode
          ON DELETE CASCADE,
```

When you're defining a FOREIGN KEY constraint on a table, the column name does not have to be identical to the column name it references. For example, COL3 is the foreign key name, and ZIP is the referencing column name, but the data type and length must agree. Foreign keys almost always reference primary keys, but they may reference unique constraints. Foreign keys should usually be indexed; you will learn more about their purpose and syntax in Chapter 13.

DELETES AND THE FOREIGN KEY

By default the foreign key constraint is of type DELETE RESTRICT; in effect, parent rows cannot be deleted if child rows exist. An ON DELETE CASCADE clause indicates that when a parent row is deleted, the corresponding row or rows in this child table will be deleted as well. In the previous SQL statement, DELETE CASCADE is explicitly specified, so if a row in the ZIPCODE table is deleted, any rows with the same zip code are deleted from the TAB1 table.

Another possible clause for defining the delete behavior of the foreign key is the clause ON DELETE SET NULL. A delete of a zip code will update the corresponding child rows in TAB1 to null, provided that the COL3 column allows null values.

RECURSIVE RELATIONSHIPS

A *recursive relationship* is also known as a self-referencing relationship; the PREREQUISITE and COURSE_NO columns of the COURSE table provide an example where a foreign key references the primary key constraint of the same table. A recursive relationship is enforced just like any other foreign key; you will see an example how to create such a relationship later in this chapter.

CHECK CONSTRAINTS

Check constraints enforce logical expressions on columns, which must evaluate to true for every row in the table. The COL6 column has a CHECK constraint that constrains the column to values less than 100. A null value is allowed, as the column does not have a NOT NULL constraint.

```
CREATE TABLE tab1
...
    col6   NUMBER CHECK(col6 < 100))
...
```

The following is another example of a check constraint; this constraint on a column called STATE restricts the values to the states listed in the IN clause.

```
state VARCHAR2(20) CHECK(state IN
    ('NY','NJ','CT','FL','CA'))
```

NOT NULL CHECK CONSTRAINTS

The column COL2 contains a check constraint you are already familiar with: NOT NULL. Any insertions or changes to data that change the values in this column to NULL are rejected.

```
CREATE TABLE tab1
...
    col2   NUMBER(4) NOT NULL,
...
```

A check constraint can also be written as follows, but the previous form is simpler.

```
col2   NUMBER(4) CHECK (col2 IS NOT NULL),
```

You define the NOT NULL constraints for columns that must always contain a value. For example, the LAST_NAME column of the INSTRUCTOR table is defined as a NOT NULL column, and therefore you cannot create or update a row in the INSTRUCTOR table unless a value exists in the column.

THE DEFAULT COLUMN OPTION

The column COL4 specifies a DEFAULT option, which is not a constraint. When a row is inserted into TAB1 and no value is supplied for COL4, SYSDATE is inserted by default.

```
CREATE TABLE tab1
...
    col4   DATE DEFAULT SYSDATE,
...
```

In an INSERT statement, the keyword DEFAULT explicitly specifies the default value. If a column is not listed in the INSERT statement and a default column value defined, then the default value is automatically inserted in the table. In an UPDATE statement the DEFAULT keyword resets a column value to the default value. Refer to Lab 12.2 for more examples.

A default value can be created for any column except the column or columns of the primary key. Often you choose a default value that represents a typical value. You can combine a default value with a NOT NULL constraint to avoid null values in columns. For example, if the typical COST of a course is 1095, you might want to create such a default value for this column. Another effect of default values and the NOT NULL constraint is that if you want to retrieve costs that are less than 1595 or null, you don't have to write the following query.

```
SELECT *
  FROM course
 WHERE NVL(cost,0) < 1595
```

Instead, you simplify the query to the following statement. In the exercises in Lab 12.2, you'll learn more about the factors to take into consideration when defining columns as null versus not null.

```
 WHERE cost < 1595
```

Naming Constraints

Applying names to all constraints is a good habit to adopt; it simplifies identifying constraint errors and avoids confusion and further research. Following is an example of how to name constraints in a CREATE TABLE statement.

```
CREATE TABLE tab1
  (col1   NUMBER(10),
   col2   NUMBER(4) CONSTRAINT tab1_col2_nn NOT NULL,
   col3   VARCHAR2(5),
   col4   DATE DEFAULT SYSDATE,
   col5   VARCHAR2(20),
   col6   NUMBER,
   CONSTRAINT tab1_pk PRIMARY KEY(col1),
   CONSTRAINT tab1_zipcode_fk FOREIGN KEY(col3)
     REFERENCES zipcode(zip),
   CONSTRAINT tab1_col5_col6_uk UNIQUE(col5, col6),
   CONSTRAINT tab1_col6_ck CHECK(col6 < 100),
   CONSTRAINT tab1_col2_col6_ck CHECK(col2 > 100 AND col6 >20))
```

Table created.

Some of the constraint names are next to each column; these are *column-level constraints*. The constraint names at the end of the statement are *table-level constraints*. Constraint names cannot exceed 30 characters and must be ·unique within the user's schema. In this example, the constraint names consist of the name of the table and column (or an abbreviated version) and a two-letter abbreviation that identifies the type of constraint.

Ideally, you follow a standard naming convention, determined by your organization. In this book, the convention for naming primary key constraints is to use the name of the table plus the _PK suffix. The foreign key constraint contains the abbreviated name of the child table, then the parent table and the _FK suffix. The unique constraint lists the table name and the columns plus the _UK suffix. Often you must abbreviate table and column names; otherwise, you exceed the 30-character constraint name limit. The CHECK constraint called TAB1_COL6_CK, contains the table name and column name plus the _CK suffix.

All the examples listed here show the constraints added at the time of table creation. In Lab 12.2 you will see how to add constraints after the table exists.

It is best to name constraints explicitly, for clarity and to manipulate them more easily, as shown in Lab 12.2. Also, when a SQL statement, such as an INSERT, an UPDATE, or a DELETE statement, violates a constraint, Oracle returns an error message with the name of the constraint, making it easy to identify and understand the source of the error.

Table-Level and Column-Level Constraints

Constraints are defined on two possible levels—either on the column level or on the table level. A column-level constraint refers to a single column and is defined together with the column. A table-level constraint references one or multiple columns and is defined separately, after the definition of all the columns. Column-level constraints are also referred to as *inline constraints*, and table-level constraints are called *out-of-line constraints*.

All constraints except for the NOT NULL constraint can be defined at the table level. You must use a table-level constraint if you are constraining more than one column.

The general syntax for the column constraint clause is listed as follows: It shows the NOT NULL, PRIMARY, FOREIGN, UNIQUE, and CHECK constraint options.

```
CONSTRAINT constraintname]
[NULL|NOT NULL] |
[REFERENCES tablename [(columname)]
   [ON DELETE {CASCADE|ON DELETE SET NULL}] |
[[UNIQUE|PRIMARY KEY]
   [USING INDEX
    [(CREATE INDEX indexname
       ON tablename (columnname[,columname...])]
          [storage_clause])]] |
[CHECK (check_condition)]
[ENABLE|DISABLE]
[VALIDATE|NOVALIDATE]
[NOT DEFERRABLE|DEFERRABLE]
[INITIALLY IMMEDIATE|INITIALLY DEFERRED]
```

The constraint name is optional and must be preceded with the keyword CONSTRAINT. Unless you specify otherwise, your column allows nulls; the underline indicates that this is the default. The foreign key constraint is defined with the REFERENCES keyword; it has two choices with regard to DELETEs, as indicated with the vertical bar, or pipe symbol (|). One is the ON DELETE CASCADE keyword, the other is ON DELETE SET NULL. If you don't list either of these two choices, the deletion of rows is restricted—that is, your deletion is successful only if no child rows exist.

Because unique and primary key constraints automatically create a unique index, you can use an optional index clause to explicitly create an index with predefined storage parameters. This allows you to define the index on a different tablespace (which is often on a different physical device) for better performance.

The next constraint option is the check constraint syntax. You see that check_condition is within a set of parentheses. All constraints can be either disabled or enabled (the default). The VALIDATE and NOVALIDATE options indicate whether the constraint is enforced for existing and new data or only for subsequently created data.

The DEFERRABLE clauses enforce the timing when the constraint is checked. The default is to check the constraint when the data manipulation occurs. If a constraint is set as DEFERRABLE, the constraint is not checked immediately but only when the transaction is committed.

The table-level constraint is listed after the column definitions. The syntax is as follows.

```
[CONSTRAINT constraintname]
  [UNIQUE (columnname[,columnname...])]|
  PRIMARY KEY (columnname[,columname...])]
    [USING INDEX
    [CREATE INDEX indexname ON tablename (columnname[,columname...])]
      [storage_clause]] |
  [FOREIGN KEY (columnname[,columnname...])]
    REFERENCES tablename [(columnname[,columnname...])]
      [ON DELETE {CASCADE|ON DELETE SET NULL}] |
  [CHECK (check_condition)]
  [ENABLE|DISABLE]
  [VALIDATE|NOVALIDATE]
  [NOT DEFERRABLE|DEFERRABLE]
  [INITIALLY IMMEDIATE|INITIALLY DEFERRED]
```

Enforcing Business Rules with Constraints

Constraints enforce rules and procedures based on rules established within an organization. For example, a rule that a student must have a last name is enforced through a NOT NULL constraint. Another rule may state that students must live in a valid zip code, and this rule can be imposed with a referential integrity constraint referencing the ZIPCODE table and a NOT NULL constraint on the ZIP column of the STUDENT table. You can apply a check constraint to make sure course costs fall within a certain range. The data type of a column determines what kind of data is allowed for entry and perhaps the maximum length. A unique constraint prevents duplicate entry of Social Security numbers into an EMPLOYEE table. A data consistency rule may state that for any deletion of a student record, all corresponding enrollment and grade records are deleted; you do this with a referential integrity foreign key constraint and the ON DELETE CASCADE keyword.

Other business rules may not be as easily enforceable with any of Oracle's declarative constraints. For instance, your rule might state that a student cannot enroll after a class has already started. To enforce this rule, you have to ensure that the value in the ENROLL_DATE column of the ENROLLMENT table contains a value less than or equal to the value in the START_DATE_TIME column of the SECTION table for the student's enrolled section. Database triggers enforce such rules and fire on the INSERT, UPDATE, or DELETE operation of a specific table and check other tables to see if the values satisfy the business rule criteria. If they do not, the operation will fail, and the statement will be rejected.

DATABASE TRIGGERS

Database triggers are PL/SQL programs associated with a table, view, system, or database event. The following trigger is used to audit data modification. The trigger fires before the UPDATE of each row on the STUDENT table, and it automatically updates the MODIFIED_DATE column with the SYSDATE function, filling in the current date and time whenever any update in the table takes place.

```
CREATE OR REPLACE TRIGGER student_trg_bur BEFORE UPDATE ON STUDENT
FOR EACH ROW
BEGIN
  :new.modified_date:=SYSDATE;
END;
/
```

This database trigger is written in Oracle's PL/SQL language and you will learn more about PL/SQL and triggers in general in *Oracle PL/SQL by Example*, 4th edition, by Benjamin Rosenzweig and Elena Silvestrova Rakhimov (Prentice Hall, 2008).

Without going into great depth about the language, you can see that the trigger has the name STUDENT_TRG_BUR, and it fires before the update of an individual row in the STUDENT table. The BEFORE keyword indicates that the trigger can access the new value before it is applied and can change the value with the :NEW.column name correlation value. The value in the MODIFIED_DATE column is changed upon the UPDATE of the affected rows to the current date and time, as indicated by the SYSDATE function.

Triggers are useful for filling in primary key values from sequences, and Chapter 13 provides an example of this. Triggers can also enforce referential integrity constraints rather than apply a foreign key constraint. However, it is preferable to use Oracle's built-in declarative constraints, such as a foreign key constraint, to enforce these rules. Constraints are easier to maintain, and using them is simpler and faster than duplicating identical functionality in a trigger.

WHERE TO ENFORCE BUSINESS RULES

You can enforce business rules either on the client side through the front-end program or on the database server. Alternatively, the business logic can also reside on a third tier, perhaps an application server. At times you might see that some rules are enforced in multiple places. The decision often depends on a number of factors: Rules imposed across all applications are often done on the database server, because it enforces rules consistently without the need to change and code the logic in many programs.

On the other hand, certain data validation needs to be performed in the front-end program. For example, if a business rule states that a salary must be larger than zero and not null, you may perform this validation within the data entry screen. If the rule is violated, the user receives a friendly error message to correct the data entry. Otherwise, it is annoying to the user to enter the data, only to find out the database rejected the entry. If the salary can be updated by programs other than the front-end screen, you might consider enforcing the rules on both the client front-end program and the server. Be sure to keep the rules consistent throughout.

There are many options to keep in mind regarding the placement of business rules when you are designing applications and database systems, including considerations about user-friendliness, data integrity, consistency, future maintenance, and elimination of duplicate efforts on both the front end and the back end.

Comprehensive data validation is one of the keys to any successful database operation, and finding the right balance requires a thorough understanding of many aspects of a system. Ignorance of data validation leads to invalid data, data inconsistencies, formatting problems, programming and processing errors, and misinterpretation of data.

The Virtual Column Option

Oracle 11g added the ability to define virtual columns on a table. A virtual column can be derived from the other columns of the table, be the result of a function, or be a constant expression. There is no physical data stored in the column, and therefore no DML operations are permitted against the column.

A virtual column is helpful because it can simplify queries, and you can create indexes on it. The following example shows the creation of the CAMPUS column on the NEW_SECTION table.

```
CREATE TABLE new_section
( section_id   NUMBER(8) NOT NULL,
  course_no    NUMBER(8) NOT NULL,
  section_no   NUMBER(3) NOT NULL,
  start_date_time DATE,
  location          VARCHAR2(50),
  campus            VARCHAR2(20)
    GENERATED ALWAYS AS
    (CASE WHEN SUBSTR(location,1,1)= 'L'
       THEN 'UPTOWN'
       ELSE 'DOWNTOWN' END) VIRTUAL)
```

Depending on the location of the section, the values in the virtual column show the appropriate CAMPUS, based on the evaluation of the LOCATION expression.

```
SELECT section_id, location, campus
  FROM new_section
WHERE section_id in (82, 85)
SECTION_ID   LOCATION CAMPUS
------------ -------- --------
82           L214     UPTOWN
85           M311     DOWNTOWN

2 rows selected
```

Any DML that attempts to alter the virtual column's value is not permitted.

```
UPDATE new_section
   SET campus = 'UPTOWN'
UPDATE section
       *
ERROR at line 1:
ORA-54017: UPDATE operation disallowed on virtual columns
```

Creating Tables Based on Other Tables

One method of creating a table is to base it on another table or tables, using a query construct. You can choose to include the data or not. The following example creates a table called JAN_07_ENROLLMENT, based on the January 2007 enrollment rows in the ENROLLMENT table.

```
CREATE TABLE jan_07_enrollment AS
SELECT *
  FROM enrollment
 WHERE enroll_date >= TO_DATE('01/01/2007',
       'MM/DD/YYYY')
   AND enroll_date <  TO_DATE('02/01/2007',
       'MM/DD/YYYY')
Table created.
```

The database feedback message "Table created" confirms that the JAN_07_ENROLLMENT table is successfully created. You can see the columns and their data types by using the SQL*Plus DESCRIBE command.

```
SQL> DESCRIBE jan_07_enrollment
Name                     Null?    Type
------------------------ -------- --------------
STUDENT_ID               NOT NULL NUMBER(8)
SECTION_ID               NOT NULL NUMBER(8)
ENROLL_DATE              NOT NULL DATE
FINAL_GRADE                       NUMBER(3)
CREATED_BY               NOT NULL VARCHAR2(30)
CREATED_DATE             NOT NULL DATE
MODIFIED_BY              NOT NULL VARCHAR2(30)
MODIFIED_DATE            NOT NULL DATE
```

The new table has the same columns, data types, and lengths as the ENROLLMENT table on which it is based. A SELECT statement on the new table confirms that the inserted data is equal to the condition listed in the WHERE clause.

```
SELECT student_id, section_id, enroll_date
  FROM jan_07_enrollment
```

```
STUDENT_ID SECTION_ID ENROLL_DA
---------- ---------- ----------
       102         89 30-JAN-07
       102         86 30-JAN-07
...
       109        101 30-JAN-07
       109         99 30-JAN-07
```

11 rows selected.

You can use the same syntax to create a table without data. Instead of the WHERE clause restricting specific rows from the ENROLLMENT table, here no rows are returned. The ROWNUM pseudocolumn indicates the order in which Oracle selects rows from a table or set of tables. The first selected row has ROWNUM 1, the second has ROWNUM 2, and so on. Because the query asks for less than one row, the statement subsequently creates an empty table.

```
CREATE TABLE jan_07_enrollment AS
SELECT *
  FROM enrollment
 WHERE rownum < 1
```

Alternatively, you can also write the statement with a query that never evaluates to true, such as in the next example.

```
CREATE TABLE jan_07_enrollment AS
SELECT *
  FROM enrollment
 WHERE 1 = 2
```

 Tables created with this syntax construct do not inherit the primary key, foreign keys, constraints, indexes, column default values, or any other objects associated with the base table except the NOT NULL constraints, which receive a system-generated name that starts with SYS_.

If a SELECT statement in a CREATE TABLE statement joins two tables or more, it is best not to use the asterisk wildcard in the SELECT list. The tables being joined may contain columns with the same name, and you get an error message when Oracle attempts to create two columns with the same name in one table.

Renaming Tables

You can rename tables by using the RENAME command. The syntax of the command is as follows.

```
RENAME oldname TO newname
```

You can use the RENAME command to rename not just tables but also views and synonyms; these object types are discussed in the following chapters.

The following statement renames the JAN_07_ENROLLMENT table JAN_07.

```
RENAME jan_07_enrollment TO jan_07
Table renamed.
```

Alternatively, you can execute the ALTER TABLE command, which is discussed in Lab 12.2, or use SQL Developer's Rename menu option.

```
ALTER TABLE jan_07_enrollment RENAME TO jan_07
```

Constraint names and dependent database objects, such as indexes and triggers, are not renamed when the table name is changed. Any privileges on the table that have been granted to other users remain intact. Dependent objects such as views become invalid and need to be recompiled.

Dropping Tables

You can drop tables when they are no longer needed by using the DROP TABLE command, whose syntax is a follows.

```
DROP TABLE tablename [CASCADE CONSTRAINTS] [PURGE]
```

When you drop a table, the table and its data are removed, along with any indexes, triggers, and constraints.

```
DROP TABLE jan_07
Table dropped.
```

Starting with Oracle 10g, the table is moved into a recycle bin from which it can be recovered; this is also referred to as *flashback drop*. Prior Oracle versions permanently removed the table and reclaimed the space from the database. If you do not want to place the table in the recycle bin, use the PURGE syntax option.

Other tables may be dependent on the dropped table as a domain for a foreign key reference. For example, if you drop the ZIPCODE table, an Oracle error message occurs because there are other tables with a foreign key referencing the ZIP column of the ZIPCODE table. One solution is to disable or drop the individual foreign key constraints with individual ALTER TABLE commands on these dependent tables, which you will learn about in Lab 12.2. Another is to let Oracle drop the foreign key constraints with the CASCADE CONSTRAINTS option.

 Do not actually execute the following statement unless you are prepared to reload the data from the ZIPCODE table and add the foreign key constraints on the STUDENT and INSTRUCTOR tables.

```
DROP TABLE zipcode CASCADE CONSTRAINTS
```

When you use the DROP TABLE command, database objects that depend on the table, such as a view referencing the table, synonyms, or PL/SQL packages, procedures, and functions, become invalid. To find out which objects reference a table, query the data dictionary view ALL_DEPENDENCIES or USER_DEPENDENCIES or click on SQL Developer's Dependencies tab for a given object. If any rights on the table were granted to other users (for example privileges to SELECT, INSERT, UPDATE, or DELETE), they are removed. If you re-create the table with the same name and want other users to continue having these privileges, you need to reissue the privileges (see Chapter 15).

Restoring a Dropped Table

You learned about some of the capabilities of the FLASHBACK TABLE command in Chapter 11. The FLASHBACK TABLE command allows you to restore a dropped table from the recycle bin. The syntax of the FLASHBACK TABLE command is repeated here.

```
FLASHBACK TABLE table name [, tablename...] TO
{{SCN|TIMESTAMP} expr [ENABLE|DISABLE TRIGGERS]|
  BEFORE DROP [RENAME TO newtablename]}
```

The following statements show how the table JAN_07 is dropped and subsequently restored.

```
DROP TABLE jan_07
Table dropped.
```

Data associated with the dropped table is stored in the recycle bin. You can query the USER_RECYCLEBIN data dictionary table or its synonym RECYCLEBIN.

```
SELECT object_name, original_name, type
  FROM user_recyclebin
```

OBJECT_NAME	ORIGINAL_NAME	TYPE
RB$$43144$TABLE$0	JAN_07	TABLE

```
1 row selected.
```

The following command restores the dropped table. You can refer to the table by either the original name or the system-generated recycle bin name.

```
FLASHBACK TABLE jan_07 TO BEFORE DROP
Flashback complete.
```

If any triggers, constraints, or indexes are associated with the table, they are restored as well, except for bitmap join indexes and referential integrity constraints to other tables. All these objects have their recycle bin names, not the original name. Before you issue the FLASHBACK TABLE command, make a note of the names so you can rename them to their original names.

PURGING THE RECYCLE BIN

You can use the PURGE command to purge an individual table or index, or the entire recycle bin. The syntax is as follows.

```
PURGE {{TABLE|INDEX} recyclebin_objectname|
    RECYCLEBIN|DBA_RECYCLEBIN|
    TABLESPACE tablespacename [USER user]}
```

The following command reclaims all the space in the user's recycle bin.

```
PURGE RECYCLEBIN
```
Recyclebin purged.

A database administrator (DBA) has the additional option of reclaiming all objects from the systemwide DBA_RECYCLEBIN or can use the TABLESPACE clause of the PURGE command to reclaim space in a specific tablespace for a specific user account. You will learn more about tablespaces shortly.

THE RECYCLE BIN AND SQL DEVELOPER

You can view the recycle bin from SQL Developer (see Figure 12.1). Clicking on one of the objects in the recycle bin provides you with the details similar to the USER_RECYCLEBIN data dictionary table. When you right-click the table, you get two menu options: You can either purge the table or flash back to the state before the drop.

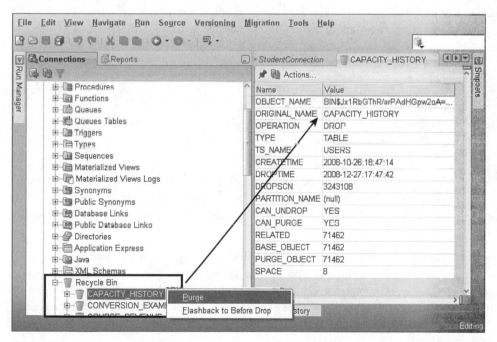

FIGURE 12.1
Recycle bin in SQL Developer

TRUNCATE TABLE Versus DROP TABLE

The TRUNCATE TABLE command, discussed in Chapter 11, removes all data from the table; however, the structure of the table remains intact, as do any triggers and grants. Like the DROP TABLE command, it does not generate any rollback information and does not fire any triggers, should they exist on the table. The TRUNCATE statement is a DDL command and implicitly issues a COMMIT. By default, the TRUNCATE TABLE command deallocates all of the table's storage except for the initial extent(s); you can retain all the existing storage extents with the REUSE STORAGE clause.

```
TRUNCATE TABLE grade REUSE STORAGE
```

The Storage Clause

A CREATE TABLE statement may have an optional storage clause that specifies space definition attributes. Each table allocates an initial extent that defines how much diskspace is reserved for the table at the time of creation. After the table runs out of the initial extent, Oracle automatically allocates additional space, based on the storage parameters of the NEXT extent parameter.

The following statement creates a table called CTX_BOOKMARK with a storage clause specifying an initial size of 5 MB on the tablespace called USERS. Once the table is out of the allocated space, each subsequent extent allotted is 1 MB, as indicated with the NEXT parameter.

```
CREATE TABLE ctx_bookmark
   (bookmark_id    NUMBER,
    container_id   NUMBER,
    bookmark_tx    VARCHAR2(300) NULL,
    modified_date  DATE)
     TABLESPACE users
       STORAGE (INITIAL 5M NEXT 1M)
       PCTFREE 20
```

A tablespace consists of one or more physical data files. For performance reasons, tables and indexes are usually stored in separate tablespaces, located on different physical disk drives. To find out which tablespaces are available to you, query the data dictionary view USER_TABLESPACES.

If no specific storage parameters are defined, the default storage parameters of the tablespace apply. Statements with a missing tablespace name create the data on the default tablespace assigned when the user was created and listed in the USER_USERS data dictionary view. If a user account does not have any rights to create any table objects, or no rights on certain tablespaces, these rights must be granted to the user first. You will learn more about granting access to tablespaces in Chapter 15.

ESTIMATING THE TABLE SIZE

Estimating the size of a table is useful to reduce the amount of wasted space. When you create a table, you can pre-allocate space with the INITIAL syntax parameter and plan for any subsequent expansion with the NEXT parameter option.

While determining how much space will actually be consumed by the table is an inexact science; you can estimate how much initial space to allocate. You determine a rough size by entering sample data in the table and then computing the statistics (discussed in Chapter 18, "SQL Optimization"). This way you can update the data dictionary information with statistics about the table, including the average row length in bytes (the AVG_ROW_LEN column in the USER_TABLES data dictionary view).

You multiply the average row length figure by the number of rows you expect in the table plus about 10 to 15 percent for overhead. Increase the number by how much free space you want to leave in each data block for updates that increase the size of the rows; you determine this figure as a percentage with the PCTFREE ("percent free") parameter in the storage clause.

```
avg_row_len in bytes * number of rows * (1 + PCTFREE/100) * 1.15
```

Next, you see the most frequently used options of the storage clause. The PCTUSED parameter determines when a block becomes available again for insertions after its used space falls below the PCTUSED integer.

```
[TABLESPACE tablespacename]
[PCTFREE integer]
[PCTUSED integer]
[COMPRESS|NOCOMPRESS]
[STORAGE
   ([INITIAL integer [K|M]]
    [NEXT integer [K|M]])]
```

To determine the total allocated space of an existing table, you query the BYTES column in the data dictionary view USER_SEGMENTS or DBA_SEGMENTS.

 The SQL command syntax in this book highlights the most relevant syntax options. Oracle's SQL commands often include a myriad of different options, some of which are rarely used and therefore not included here. If you need to look up the complete syntax in the Oracle documentation, refer to Appendix G, "Navigating the Oracle Documentation."

PARTITIONING TABLES

Partitioning a table essentially means splitting a table into smaller pieces. The individual partitions often are stored in different tablespaces. Very large tables become more manageable for database administration tasks when they are stored on different partitions. Partitioning can also improve performance because input/output (I/O) can be balanced. Partitioning can be accomplished in many different ways, and Oracle offers a variety of syntax options. For example, you can place sales data by year in individual partitions. There is no need to change any SQL statements for DML operations because the partitioning is completely transparent. If you want to access an individual partition specifically with a DML statement, Oracle provides syntax to do so. You most often use partitioning if the tables are very large, such as tables in the gigabyte range and tables containing hundreds of millions of rows.

DATA COMPRESSION

Oracle enables you to use data compression to save storage space; this can be desirable for large database tables in data warehouses where very few updates and deletes take place.

Oracle's Other Table Types

The vast majority of data is stored in an "ordinary" Oracle table. The following paragraphs list other table types (temporary tables, index-organized tables, and external tables) for completeness only; a detailed discussion of these table types goes beyond the scope of this book.

 Oracle allows object-oriented capabilities with tables; in practice, however, object-oriented database table features are only slowly gaining acceptance.

TEMPORARY TABLES

When a query becomes too complicated, you can resolve it by writing part of the data to a temporary table before continuing with the main query. Oracle allows two types of temporary tables: session-specific and transaction-specific. The data in a temporary table is visible to multiple sessions or transactions, but only with respect to the data created by each session or transaction. When the session or transaction is complete, the data is deleted.

A temporary table is session-specific when created with the ON COMMIT PRESERVE ROWS keywords and transaction specific when created with the ON COMMIT DELETE ROWS keywords.

The following statement creates a session-specific temporary table that will retain its value until the session ends, not when a transaction ends because of an issued COMMIT or ROLLBACK command.

```
CREATE GLOBAL TEMPORARY TABLE s_num_rows
  (student_id             NUMBER,
   last_name              VARCHAR2(25),
   num_classes_enrolled NUMBER)
  ON COMMIT PRESERVE ROWS
```

You enter values into the table with an INSERT statement.

```
INSERT INTO s_num_rows
VALUES (123, 'Hesse', 5)
```

The next temporary table is transaction-specific, as you can tell from the ON COMMIT DELETE ROWS keywords. You use the SELECT command to populate rows to this table.

```
CREATE GLOBAL TEMPORARY TABLE t_grade
   ON COMMIT DELETE ROWS AS
   SELECT student_id, AVG(numeric_grade) AS avg_grade
     FROM grade
    WHERE student_id IN (SELECT student_id
                           FROM enrollment
                          WHERE final_grade IS NOT NULL)
      GROUP BY student_id
```

Temporary tables behave much like regular tables, whereby you can add indexes, triggers, and some types of constraints. However, certain restrictions apply. For example, no referential integrity constraints are allowed.

```
SQL> DESCRIBE t_grade
Name                           Null?     Type
-------------------------      --------  ---------
STUDENT_ID                     NOT NULL  NUMBER(8)
AVG_GRADE                                NUMBER
```

When are temporary tables useful? Use temporary tables in cases where doing so simplifies the query logic and the query is infrequently executed. Keep in mind that this may not be the most efficient way to execute the query, but as with all other queries, testing against a representative data set will determine whether a temporary table solves your complicated query dilemma.

 Data in temporary tables is not stored permanently; it persists only during a session or transaction; however, the structure of the temporary table exists until it is explicitly dropped with a DROP TABLE command.

INDEX-ORGANIZED TABLES

When the primary key of a table comprises most or all of the columns in a table, you might want to consider storing the data in an index-organized table. An index-organized table is useful for frequently used lookup tables that hold currencies, state abbreviations, or stock prices with their respective dates. This type of table quickly executes queries that are looking for the primary key value. Queries do not require the lookup of a value in the index first and then the corresponding retrieval of the row in the table because all the data is stored only in the index. You cannot disable or drop the primary key of an index-organized table.

```
CREATE TABLE states
   (state_code     VARCHAR2(2),
    state_tx       VARCHAR2(200),
    CONSTRAINT state_pk PRIMARY KEY (state_code))
    ORGANIZATION INDEX
```

EXTERNAL TABLES

With the help of external tables, Oracle allows read access to data stored outside the database, such as legacy systems. SELECT statements are issued against external tables, much as with any other table. You cannot insert into or update and delete from an external table, nor can you build an index on an external table.

To define an external table, you describe the individual columns with Oracle data types and how to map to these columns. A data access driver and external table layer perform the necessary transformation. Because external data remains stored outside the database, no backup or recovery capabilities within Oracle are performed. External tables are useful for loading data into the database, but their setup requires the help of a DBA, and some knowledge of Oracle's SQL*Loader bulk-load utility is useful.

The following is a simple example of a flat ASCII sample file that is located on one of the directories of the Oracle database server. The file may have data such as the following, where the values are separated by commas.

```
102,Crocitto,Fred
103,Landry,J.
104,Enison,Laetia
105,Moskowitz,Angel
106,Olvsade,Judith
107,Mierzwa,Catherine
108,Sethi,Judy
109,Walter,Larry
```

You need to create an ORACLE DIRECTORY entry so the database knows where to find the file on an accessible directory and drive. If you use the Windows operating system, you may choose to specify a directory such as C:\GUEST as the directory (or wherever your file is located).

```
CREATE DIRECTORY dir_guest AS 'C:\GUEST'
Directory created.
```

You must make sure the Oracle database has operating system read and write access to the operating system directory; otherwise, Oracle cannot load the data. To create an ORACLE DIRECTORY entry within the Oracle database, you must have the DBA privilege or the CREATE ANY DIRECTORY system privilege. Log on as a user with DBA rights or the SYSTEM account then issue the following command.

```
GRANT CREATE ANY DIRECTORY TO student
```

You create the external table based on the contents of the flat file by using the CREATE TABLE command. The table is named STUDENT_EXTERNAL, and it has three columns: STUDENT_ID, LAST_NAME, and FIRST_NAME. The keywords ORGANIZATION EXTERNAL identify that this table is located outside the Oracle database. TYPE indicates the driver used to read the data. DEFAULT DIRECTORY identifies the directory where the file is located. The structure of the flat file is defined by the individual field names that are to be read, as well as how these individual fields are separated from each other. In this example, commas separate the fields. In addition, the LOCATION keyword indicates the name of the file. This temp.lst file must be located in the directory defined as DIR_GUEST, which maps to the server's C:\GUEST directory.

```
CREATE TABLE student_external
   (student_id NUMBER(3),
    last_name VARCHAR2(25),
    first_name VARCHAR2(25))
  ORGANIZATION EXTERNAL
  (TYPE oracle_loader
   DEFAULT DIRECTORY dir_guest
   ACCESS PARAMETERS
  (FIELDS TERMINATED BY ','
   (student_id, last_name, first_name))
   LOCATION ('temp.lst'))
```

Table created.

There are different types of files; this example shows a comma-separated value (CSV) file. Some files enclose the text fields in double quotation marks; others have fixed lengths, where the starting and ending positions of each column is predetermined.

After you successfully create the table and place the temp.lst file in the appropriate directory, you can retrieve data from the table.

```
SELECT *
  FROM student_external
STUDENT_ID LAST_NAME                          FIRST_NAME
---------- ------------------------- --------------------
       102 Crocitto                  Fred
       103 Landry                    J.
       104 Enison                    Laetia
       105 Moskowitz                 Angel
       106 Olvsade                   Judith
       107 Mierzwa                   Catherine
       108 Sethi                     Judy
       109 Walter                    Larry

8 rows selected.
```

 Although you have learned about the different Oracle table types, most times you will deal with ordinary Oracle tables, and the aforementioned table types currently represent the exception to the norm.

Using the SQL Developer Graphical User Interface (GUI)

The SQL Developer GUI allows you to perform many DDL operations without having to remember the syntax. The result of menu actions can generate the desired SQL language commands.

SQL DEVELOPER'S TABLE-RELATED MENU OPTIONS

The table-related menu in SQL Developer's Connections pane has many choices. Figure 12.2 shows the different menu options available when you right-click an individual table. Some of the menu options are described in this chapter; others are discussed in the chapters that follow. Table 12.2 provides an overview of the functionality and purpose of each menu option.

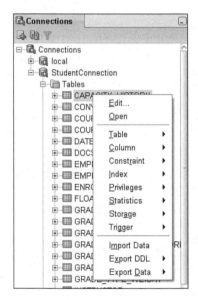

FIGURE 12.2
Table-related menu choices

TABLE 12.2   Overview of SQL Developer Table-Related Menu Choices

MENU CHOICE	DESCRIPTION
Edit	Allows you to modify any of the properties related to the table, its columns, constraints, indexes, or storage parameters and more (see Lab 12.2).
Open	Has the same effect as double-clicking the table's node. Displays the various tabs related to showing columns, data, constraints, grants, triggers, flashback data, and so on.
Table	Displays table submenu functions, such as Rename, Copy, Drop, and Truncate. It allows the addition of table comments and counting of the number of rows.

TABLE 12.2   Continued

MENU CHOICE	DESCRIPTION
Column	Allows the addition, renaming, and dropping of columns, as well as the addition of column comments (see Lab 12.2).
Constraint	Performs adding, dropping, renaming, disabling, and enabling of constraints (see Lab 12.2).
Index	Provides functionality to add, drop, and rebuild indexes (see Chapter 13).
Privileges	Grants privileges to and revokes privileges from other users (see Chapter 15).
Statistics	Gathers statistics (see Chapter 18) and validates object (see Chapter 13)
Storage	Is useful for mainly DBAs for managing the storage spaces of objects, including moves between tablespaces and compressing of segments.
Trigger	Allows the creation, dropping, enabling, and disabling of triggers; includes an option to create a trigger to populate the primary key from a sequence.
Import Data	Imports data from an XLS (Microsoft Excel) or CSV (comma-separated value) file into an Oracle table.
Export DDL	Exports the table's DDL to a file, the Clipboard, or the SQL Worksheet window.
Export Data	Exports a table's data into various formats, such as XLS, CSV, SQL*Loader, and INSERT statements.

CREATING A NEW TABLE

To create a new table, you right-click the Tables node and choose New Table. The dialog box shown in Figure 12.3 appears. You can enter the table name and column names, data type, length, and not null constraint, and you can select a check box to indicate whether this column is part of the primary key. When you click the DDL tab, you can see the DDL command to perform the same functionality.

On the top right of the screen is the Advanced check box, which allows for a wide range of additional syntax options, such as the creation of check constraints, setup of foreign keys, and more.

If you want to create a table based on an existing table and/or change the new table's table or column definitions somewhat, you can extract the DDL for the existing table. This allows you to modify the DDL and create the new table. One of the ways to extract the DDL is by clicking on the SQL tab (see Figure 12.4).

The DDL shows the table name prefixed with the schema name of STUDENT. All the table and column names are in quotation marks to ensure that they are stored in exactly the same case. The last column is followed by the storage clause.

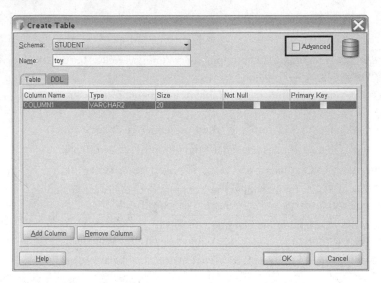

FIGURE 12.3
Create Table dialog box for SQL Developer

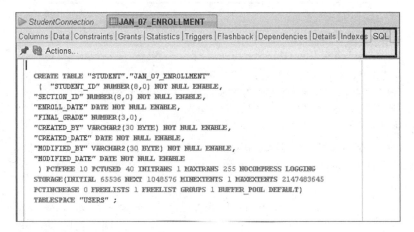

FIGURE 12.4
SQL tab showing the DDL for the table

Using SQL Developer's Extended Search Capabilities

If you want to find any table, index, or column name associated with a specific connection, you can use the Extended Search box to search for the name. The Extended Search box is shown to the right of the SQL Worksheet pane (see Figure 12.5). Alternatively, you can access it by selecting View, Extended Search.

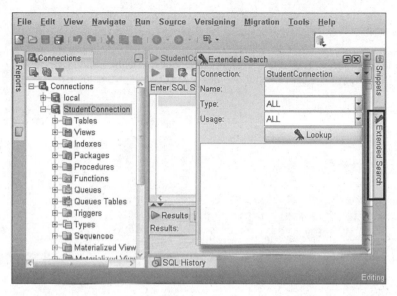

FIGURE 12.5
Extended Search box

▼ LAB 12.1 EXERCISES

a) Explain the error(s) in the following CREATE TABLE statement and rewrite the statement correctly.

```
CREATE TABLE student_candidate
   (name       VARCHAR2(25)
    address    VARCHAR2(30)
    city       VARCHAR2
    zip        NUMBER)
```

b) Write and execute a CREATE TABLE statement to create an empty table called NEW_STUDENT that contains the following columns: first name, last name, the description of the first course the student takes, and the date the student registered in the program. Determine the data type and length necessary for each column, based on the tables in the STUDENT schema.

c) Execute the following CREATE TABLE statement and explain the result.

```
CREATE TABLE school_program AS
SELECT last_name||', '||first_name name
  FROM student
UNION
SELECT last_name||', '||first_name
  FROM instructor
```

d) Rename the SCHOOL_PROGRAM table you created in exercise c to SCHOOL_PROGRAM2. Then drop both the SCHOOL_PROGRAM and SCHOOL_PROGRAM2 tables and explain your observations.

e) Execute the following SQL statements to create an empty table called COURSE2 and insert two rows into COURSE2. What do you observe about the values of the COURSE_NO column in the COURSE2 table?

```
CREATE TABLE course2 AS
SELECT *
  FROM course
 WHERE 1 = 2
Table created.


INSERT INTO course2
   (course_no, description, cost, prerequisite,
    created_by, created_date, modified_by, modified_date)
VALUES
   (999, 'Teaching SQL - Part 1', 1495, NULL,
    'AMORRISON', SYSDATE, 'AMORRISON', SYSDATE)
1 row created.


INSERT INTO course2
   (course_no, description, cost, prerequisite,
    created_by, created_date, modified_by, modified_date)
VALUES
   (999, 'Teaching SQL - Part 2', 1495, NULL,
    'AMORRISON', SYSDATE, 'AMORRISON', SYSDATE)
1 row created.
```

f) Identify the constraints in the following CREATE TABLE statement and explain their purpose.

```
CREATE TABLE extinct_animal
   (animal_id         NUMBER,
    species_id        NUMBER,
    name              VARCHAR2(30) NOT NULL,
    native_country    VARCHAR2(20)
      CONSTRAINT extinct_animal_country_fk
      REFERENCES country(country_name),
    remaining         NUMBER(2,0),
    CONSTRAINT extinct_animal_pk PRIMARY KEY(animal_id,
      species_id),
    CONSTRAINT extinct_animal_remaining_ck
      CHECK (remaining BETWEEN 0 and 10))
```

g) Rewrite and execute the following CREATE TABLE statement to give the primary key and the foreign key constraints names.

```
CREATE TABLE former_student
   (studid    NUMBER(8) PRIMARY KEY,
    first_nm  VARCHAR2(25),
    last_nm   VARCHAR2(25),
```

```
enrolled  VARCHAR2(1) DEFAULT 'N',
zip       VARCHAR2(5) REFERENCES zipcode(zip))
```

h) Rewrite the solution to exercise g to add a UNIQUE constraint on the FIRST_NM and LAST_NM columns.

i) Using the extended search capability of SQL Developer, search for the Student ID column.

▼ LAB 12.1 EXERCISE **ANSWERS**

a) Explain the error(s) in the following CREATE TABLE statement and rewrite the statement correctly.

```
CREATE TABLE student candidate
    (name      VARCHAR2(25)
    address    VARCHAR2(20)
    city       VARCHAR2
    zip        NUMBER)
```

ANSWER: The statement will not execute because there are three errors. The first error is in the table name; it contains spaces. The next error is the nonexistent length of the CITY column's VARCHAR2 definition. Finally, commas are required to separate the column definitions. Following is the corrected syntax.

```
CREATE TABLE student_candidate
    (name      VARCHAR2(25),
    address    VARCHAR2(20),
    city       VARCHAR2(15),
    zip        NUMBER)
```

If you create the table using SQL Developer, you can avoid some of the simple syntax errors (see Figure 12.6).

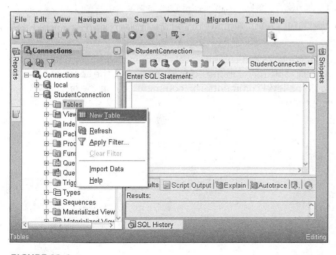

FIGURE 12.6
New Table menu

b) Write and execute a CREATE TABLE statement to create an empty table called NEW_STUDENT that contains the following columns: first name, last name, the description of the first course the student takes, and the date the student registered in the program. Determine the data type and length necessary for each column, based on the tables in the STUDENT schema.

ANSWER: The table contains the four columns FIRST_NAME, LAST_NAME, DESCRIPTION, and REGISTRATION_DATE. The first three are of data type VARCHAR2, and REGISTRATION_DATE is of data type DATE.

```
CREATE TABLE new_student
   (first_name            VARCHAR2(25),
    last_name             VARCHAR2(25),
    description           VARCHAR2(50),
    registration_date     DATE)
```

DOCUMENTING THE TABLES AND COLUMNS

When you create tables and columns, you can add comments to them to document their purposes. These comments are stored in the data dictionary for reporting and self-documentation. You can query the involved data dictionary views ALL_COL_COMMENTS and ALL_TAB_COMMENTS or view them in SQL Developer in various menus.

If you want to write SQL to create or modify the comments, the following is an example of how to create a table comment on the NEW_STUDENT table. The comment is enclosed in single quotation marks.

```
COMMENT ON TABLE new_student IS 'Table holding student information
used for exercises'
Comment created.
```

The following is an example of a column comment for the FIRST_NAME column on the NEW_STUDENT table. Two individual quotation marks are necessary to represent a single quote when issuing this statement.

```
COMMENT ON COLUMN new_student.first_name is 'The student''s first
name.'
Comment created.
```

Figure 12.7 shows where you can edit the table-level and column-level comments within in SQL Developer. This screen is accessed via the Edit Table menu in the Connections pane. The comment box on the bottom right of the screen is for column-level comments. The comment box on the left allows you to edit the comments for the respective table.

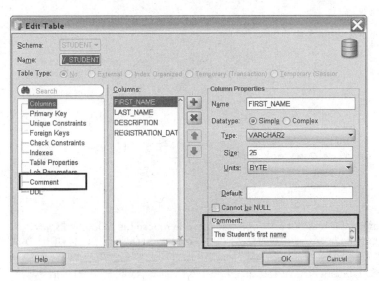

FIGURE 12.7
Entry for table and column comments

---

c) Execute the following CREATE TABLE statement and explain the result.

```
CREATE TABLE school_program AS
SELECT last_name||', '||first_name name
  FROM student
UNION
SELECT last_name||', '||first_name
  FROM instructor
```

ANSWER: The statement creates a table called SCHOOL_PROGRAM, based on a query of two other tables that combines student and instructor names. The first and last names are concatenated into one column.

```
SQL> DESC school_program
 Name                           Null?    Type
 ------------------------------ -------- ------------
 NAME                                    VARCHAR2(52)
```

The Name column in the new table is long enough to accommodate the combined length of the first and last names, plus a comma and a space.

d) Rename the SCHOOL_PROGRAM table you created in exercise c to SCHOOL_PROGRAM2. Then drop both the SCHOOL_PROGRAM and SCHOOL_PROGRAM2 tables and explain your observations.

ANSWER: Use the RENAME and DROP TABLE commands.

The DROP TABLE command fails because the SCHOOL_PROGRAM table no longer exists; it has been renamed SCHOOL_PROGRAM2.

```
RENAME school_program TO school_program2
Table renamed.

DROP TABLE school_program
DROP TABLE school_program
               *
ERROR at line 1:
ORA-00942: table or view does not exist

DROP TABLE school_program2
Table dropped.
```

Because the newly created table may not be in your Tables node, refresh the listing to display it. If you use SQL Developer's Rename menu to change the table name, you can look at the DDL tab to see the respective DDL command.

e) Execute the following SQL statements to create an empty table called COURSE2 and insert two rows into COURSE2. What do you observe about the values of the COURSE_NO column in the COURSE2 table?

```
CREATE TABLE course2 AS
SELECT *
  FROM course
 WHERE 1 = 2
Table created.

INSERT INTO course2
   (course_no, description, cost, prerequisite,
    created_by, created_date, modified_by, modified_date)
VALUES
   (999, 'Teaching SQL - Part 1', 1495, NULL,
    'AMORRISON', SYSDATE, 'AMORRISON', SYSDATE)
1 row created.

INSERT INTO course2
   (course_no, description, cost, prerequisite,
    created_by, created_date, modified_by, modified_date)
VALUES
   (999, 'Teaching SQL - Part 2', 1495, NULL,
    'AMORRISON', SYSDATE, 'AMORRISON', SYSDATE)
1 row created.
```

ANSWER: The primary key constraint is not preserved.

When a table is created from another table, constraints are not automatically preserved in the new table, except for the NOT NULL constraints. The COURSE_NO column is the primary key in the COURSE table and, therefore, prevents duplicate values. But when the COURSE2 table is created from the COURSE table, a primary key constraint is not created, so the COURSE_NO column in the COURSE2 table allows duplicate values to be inserted.

In Lab 12.2, you will learn how to add constraint to an existing table.

f) Identify the constraints in the following CREATE TABLE statement and explain their purpose.

```
CREATE TABLE extinct_animal
  (animal_id        NUMBER,
   species_id       NUMBER,
   name             VARCHAR2(30) NOT NULL,
   native_country   VARCHAR2(20)
     CONSTRAINT extinct_animal_country_fk
     REFERENCES country(country_name),
   remaining        NUMBER(2,0),
   CONSTRAINT extinct_animal_pk PRIMARY KEY(animal_id,
     species_id),
   CONSTRAINT extinct_animal_remaining_ck
     CHECK (remaining BETWEEN 0 AND 10))
```

ANSWER: The first constraint in the EXTINCT_ANIMAL table is a NOT NULL constraint on the NAME column, and because it is not named, it receives a system-generated name. The NATIVE_COUNTRY column is a constraint with a foreign key to values from the COUNTRY_NAME column in a table called COUNTRY, which must exist for the command to be successful.

The concatenated PRIMARY KEY constraint called EXTINCT_ANIMAL_PK consists of the ANIMAL_ID and SPECIES_ID columns. When a primary key on a table contains more than one column, the constraint must be written as a table-level constraint on a separate line of the CREATE TABLE statement. The CHECK constraint on the column called EXTINCT_ANIMAL_REMAINING_CK checks whether a number inserted or updated is between the values 0 and 10, inclusive.

A NOT NULL constraint on the ANIMAL_ID and SPECIES_ID columns is not required because the columns are defined as the primary key.

g) Rewrite and execute the following CREATE TABLE statement to give the primary key and the foreign key constraints names.

```
CREATE TABLE former_student
  (studid    NUMBER(0) PRIMARY KEY,
   first_nm    VARCHAR2(25),
   last_nm     VARCHAR2(25),
   enrolled  VARCHAR2(1) DEFAULT 'N',
   zip       VARCHAR2(5) REFERENCES zipcode(zip))
```

ANSWER: You can write the syntax in various forms. In addition, SQL Developer can perform the same tasks to create the table and accompanying constraints.

Following are some SQL syntax variations. The constraint definitions are moved to the end of the CREATE TABLE statement, where they are created with specific names.

```
CREATE TABLE former_student
  (studid    NUMBER(8),
   first_nm  VARCHAR2(25),
   last_nm   VARCHAR2(25),
   enrolled  VARCHAR2(1) DEFAULT 'N',
   zip       VARCHAR2(5),
   CONSTRAINT former_student_pk PRIMARY KEY(studid),
   CONSTRAINT former_student_zipcode_fk FOREIGN KEY(zip)
     REFERENCES zipcode(zip))
```

Alternatively, the following is syntax that uses the column-level constraints.

```
CREATE TABLE former_student
(studid    NUMBER(8) CONSTRAINT former_student_pk PRIMARY KEY,
 first_nm  VARCHAR2(25),
 last_nm   VARCHAR2(25),
 enrolled  VARCHAR2(1) DEFAULT 'N',
 zip       VARCHAR2(5) CONSTRAINT former_student_zipcode_fk
           REFERENCES zipcode(zip))
```

When a constraint is not named and an error occurs, you receive a system-generated constraint error. The following shows such an example.

```
INSERT INTO former_student
  (studid, first_nm, last_nm, enrolled, zip)
VALUES
  (101, 'Alex', 'Morrison', NULL, '10005')
1 row created.


INSERT INTO former_student
  (studid, first_nm, last_nm, enrolled, zip)
VALUES
  (101, 'Alex', 'Morrison', NULL, '11717')
INSERT INTO former_student
            *
ERROR at line 1:
ORA-00001: unique constraint (STUDENT.SYS_C001293) violated
```

From this error message, it is impossible to figure out which column(s) caused the error; you can only determine that the constraint is in the STUDENT schema. You need to look up the name of the constraint in the Oracle data dictionary view USER_CONSTRAINTS or ALL_CONSTRAINTS to determine the reason for the error.

The system-generated name is not informative; therefore, always name your constraints.

In SQL Developer, to create a new table and associated constraints, choose the New Table menu option. You see this menu option when you right-click on the Tables node in the Connection pane. This will bring up the Create Table screen (see Figure 12.8). Note the Advanced check box; when you click on this box, you can add the primary key with the name FORMER_STUDENT_PK and STUDENT_ID as the selected primary key column.

In the Advanced tab, you can easily add a column default value of 'N' for the ENROLLED column, as shown in Figure 12.9.

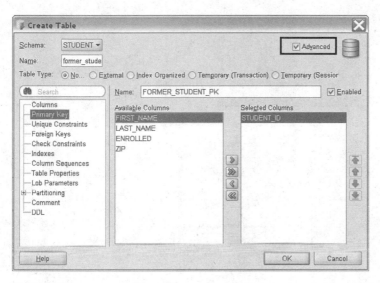

FIGURE 12.8
Adding the primary key constraint

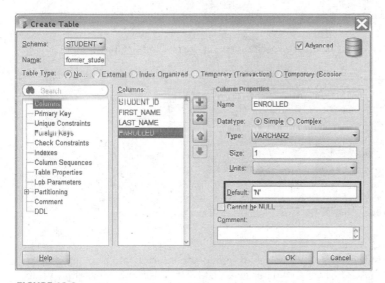

FIGURE 12.9
Adding a default value

Figure 12.10 illustrates the addition of the foreign key constraint on the ZIP column. The foreign key constraint name is suggested, and you can alter it. The foreign key column references the primary key column of the STUDENT schema's ZIPCODE table. The foreign key is a DELETE RESTRICT constraint as shown on the bottom of the screen.

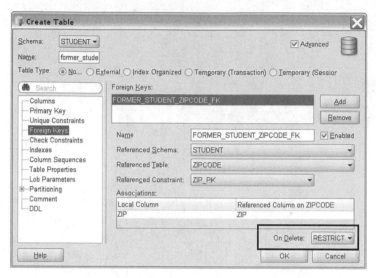

FIGURE 12.10
Adding the foreign key constraint

h) Rewrite the solution to exercise g to add a UNIQUE constraint on the FIRST_NM and LAST_NM columns.

ANSWER: You add the constraint, using a specific name, at the end of the CREATE TABLE statement.

```
CREATE TABLE former_student
   (studid    NUMBER(8),
    first_nm  VARCHAR2(25),
    last_nm   VARCHAR2(25),
    enrolled  VARCHAR2(1) DEFAULT 'N',
    zip       VARCHAR2(5),
    CONSTRAINT former_student_pk PRIMARY KEY(studid),
    CONSTRAINT former_student_zipcode_fk FOREIGN KEY(zip)
      REFERENCES zipcode(zip),
    CONSTRAINT former_student_uk UNIQUE(first_nm, last_nm))
```

 A UNIQUE constraint prevents duplicate values from being inserted into a column. It is different from a PRIMARY KEY constraint because a UNIQUE constraint allows NULL values.

Figure 12.11 shows how to add this in SQL Developer.

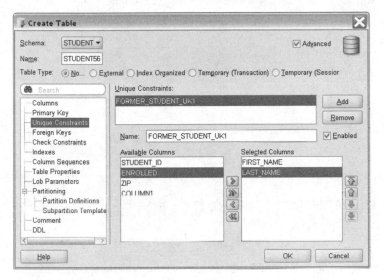

FIGURE 12.11
Adding the unique key constraint

I) Using the extended search capability of SQL Developer, search for the STUDENT_ID column.

ANSWER: Your results may look similar to Figure 12.12. When you double-click one of the result rows, you can view the respective object. Extended search allows the use of wildcard characters such as % to perform sophisticated searches.

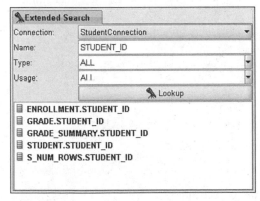

FIGURE 12.12
The Extended Search box with a result

Lab 12.1 Quiz

In order to test your progress, you should be able to answer the following questions.

1) The primary key of the following CREATE TABLE statement is a concatenated primary key.

```
CREATE TABLE class_roster
  (class_id         NUMBER(3),
   class_name       VARCHAR2(20) UNIQUE,
   first_class      DATE NOT NULL,
   num_of_students  NUMBER(3),
   CONSTRAINT class_roster_pk
     PRIMARY KEY(class_id, class_name))
```

_____ a) True

_____ b) False

2) It is possible to create one table from three different tables in a single CREATE TABLE statement.

_____ a) True

_____ b) False

3) The CASCADE CONSTRAINTS keywords in a DROP TABLE statement drop all referencing child tables.

_____ a) True

_____ b) False

4) Every column of a table can have one or more constraints.

_____ a) True

_____ b) False

5) You cannot create a table from another table if it has no rows.

_____ a) True

_____ b) False

6) A CREATE TABLE statement automatically commits all previously issued DML statements.

_____ a) True

_____ b) False

7) A foreign key must match a primary key or unique key.

_____ a) True

_____ b) False

8) Primary key values should always be subject to frequent change.

_____ a) True

_____ b) False

9) The STORAGE clause on a CREATE TABLE statement can specify how much space to allocate.

_____ a) True

_____ b) False

10) The data type definitions NUMBER(10) and NUMBER(10,0) are equivalent.

_____ a) True

_____ b) False

11) The maximum value for a column defined as NUMBER(3,2) is 999.

_____ a) True

_____ b) False

ANSWERS APPEAR IN APPENDIX A.

LAB 12.2
Altering Tables and Manipulating Constraints

LAB OBJECTIVES

After this lab, you will be able to:

▶ Alter Tables
▶ Manipulate Constraints

After a table is created, you sometimes need to change its characteristics. The ALTER TABLE command, in conjunction with the ADD, DROP, MODIFY, and RENAME clauses, allows you to do this. You can add or delete a column; change the length, data type, or default value of a column; or add, drop, enable, disable, or rename a table's integrity constraints.

Following is the general syntax for the ALTER TABLE command. You will see examples of these many options throughout this lab and in the following exercises.

```
ALTER TABLE tablename
    [ADD [(columnname data_type[DEFAULT expr]
          [column_constraint]
          [, columnname data_type[DEFAULT expr]
          [column_constraint]]...)]
          [, table_constraint [, table_constraint...]]
    [MODIFY [(columnname data_type [DEFAULT expr]
          [column_constraint]
    [MODIFY CONSTRAINT constraint_name
          [ENABLE|DISABLE] [NOVALIDATE|VALIDATE]]
    [DROP CONSTRAINT constraint_name|
          PRIMARY KEY|
          UNIQUE (columnname[,columnname...])
          [CASCADE]
    [DISABLE|ENABLE] [VALIDATE|NOVALIDATE]
      CONSTRAINT constraint_name|
        PRIMARY KEY|
        UNIQUE (columnname[,columnname]...)
        [USING INDEX indexname [storage_clause]]
        [CASCADE] [{KEEP|DROP}INDEX]]
   [NOT DEFERRABLE|DEFERRABLE]
```

```
[INITIALLY IMMEDIATE|INITIALLY DEFERRED]
    [RENAME CONSTRAINT constraint_name TO new_constraint_name
    [DROP (columnname)|DROP COLUMN (columnname[,columnname...])]
    [SET UNUSED COLUMN columnname|SET UNUSED
        (columnname[,columnname...])]
    [DROP UNUSED COLUMNS]
    [RENAME COLUMN columnname TO newcolumnname]
    [RENAME TO newtablename]
[storage_clause]
```

Adding Columns

This section takes a look at the columns of the TOY table created at the beginning of Lab 12.1. Following is the SQL*Plus DESCRIBE command to display the structure of the table.

```
SQL> DESC toy
Name                          Null?      Type
----------------------        --------   ------------
TOY_ID                                   NUMBER(10)
DESCRIPTION                   NOT NULL   VARCHAR2(15)
LAST_PURCHASE_DATE                       DATE
REMAINING_QUANTITY                       NUMBER(6)
```

The following statement alters the TOY table to add a new column called MANUFACTURER.

```
ALTER TABLE toy
    ADD (manufacturer VARCHAR2(30) NOT NULL)
Table altered.
```

The "Table altered" response indicates the successful completion of the operation. When the column is added, it is defined as VARCHAR2(30). The column also has a NOT NULL constraint. When you issue another DESCRIBE command, you see the new column.

```
SQL> DESC toy
Name                          Null?      Type
----------------------        --------   ------------
TOY_ID                                   NUMBER(10)
DESCRIPTION                   NOT NULL   VARCHAR2(15)
LAST_PURCHASE_DATE                       DATE
REMAINING_QUANTITY                       NUMBER(6)
MANUFACTURER                  NOT NULL   VARCHAR2(30)
```

Alternatively, you can add the column and name the constraint as in the following example.

```
ALTER TABLE TOY
    ADD (manufacturer VARCHAR2(30)
        CONSTRAINT toy_manufacturer_nn NOT NULL)
```

Using SQL Developer for ALTER TABLE Operations

SQL Developer allows you to perform many of the ALTER TABLE commands in this lab by using the menu options. Rather than requiring you to remember the syntax, the program generates the DDL. To modify any of the table or column characteristics, it is easiest to right-click on the table name in the Connection pane and to choose the Edit menu.

Using SQL Developer, you can add the constraint to the TOY table as shown in Figure 12.13. To obtain the appropriate ALTER TABLE statement, click on the DDL on the left side of the screen to obtain the generated DDL shown in Figure 12.14.

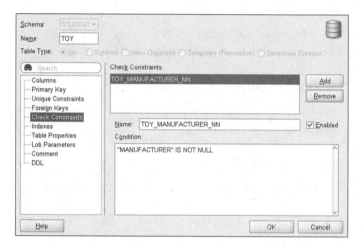

FIGURE 12.13
Adding a NOT NULL check constraint

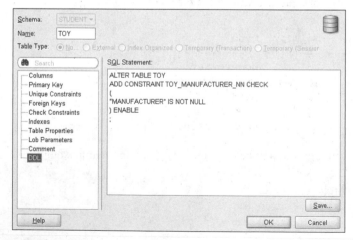

FIGURE 12.14
DDL for adding a NOT NULL check constraint

You can only add a column together with a NOT NULL constraint if the table contains no data or if you specify a default. You will see examples of this in this lab's exercises.

Dropping Columns

You can drop columns from a table by using the ALTER TABLE command and the DROP clause. The following statement drops the LAST_PURCHASE_DATE column from the TOY table.

```
ALTER TABLE toy
   DROP (last_purchase_date)
Table altered.
```

If you want to drop multiple columns, separate the columns with commas.

```
ALTER TABLE toy
   DROP (manufacturer, remaining_quantity)
Table altered.
```

Instead of dropping a column, you can mark it as unused with the SET UNUSED clause of the ALTER TABLE statement. With the current version of SQL Developer (version 1.5.3, as of this writing), the unused option is not available from a menu.

```
ALTER TABLE toy
   SET UNUSED (last_purchase_date)
Table altered.
```

Setting the column as unused is useful if you want to make the column no longer visible but do not want to physically remove it yet. When you issue a subsequent ALTER TABLE command with the DROP COLUMN clause or the ALTER TABLE command with the DROP UNUSED COLUMNS clause, Oracle physically removes the column from the database.

```
ALTER TABLE toy
   DROP UNUSED COLUMNS
Table altered.
```

Changing a column to UNUSED instead of dropping it is quicker, because it does not demand a lot of system resources. When the system is less busy, you can then physically remove the column.

Renaming Columns

You can rename an individual column with the following command.

```
ALTER TABLE toy RENAME COLUMN description TO
   description_tx
```

 Keep in mind that any dependent objects that reference this column become invalid.

Modifying Columns

You modify the data type, length, and column default of existing columns with the ALTER TABLE statement. There are a number of restrictions, as you'll see in the lab exercises.

The following statement changes the length of the DESCRIPTION column from 15 to 25 characters.

```
ALTER TABLE toy
   MODIFY (description VARCHAR2(25))
Table altered.
```

The next statement modifies the data type of the REMAINING_QUANTITY column from NUMBER to VARCHAR2 and makes the column not null simultaneously. This statement executes successfully because the table contains no data.

```
ALTER TABLE toy
   MODIFY (remaining_quantity VARCHAR2(6) NOT NULL)
Table altered.
```

You can also execute the statements individually, as in the following example.

```
ALTER TABLE toy
   MODIFY (remaining_quantity VARCHAR2(6))
Table altered.
```

```
ALTER TABLE toy
   MODIFY (remaining_quantity NOT NULL)
Table altered.
```

If you want to give the NOT NULL constraint a name, you use the following command. Instead of the system-generated SYS_ name, the constraint's name is then REMAIN_QT_NN.

```
ALTER TABLE toy
   MODIFY (remaining_quantity
   CONSTRAINT remain_qt_nn NOT NULL)
Table altered.
```

Any changes to the structure of a table will invalidate other dependent database objects, such as views, triggers, and stored PL/SQL objects. The next time they are accessed, Oracle will attempt to compile or revalidate them. You can find the list of invalid objects in the ALL_OBJECTS or ALL_OBJECTS data dictionary view. Before making any changes, you can find out which objects are dependent on the table by querying the USER_DEPENDENCIES or ALL_DEPENDENCIES data dictionary views or the SQL Developer Dependencies tab. Alternatively, you can use Extended Search to find out which objects reference the table.

Adding, Dropping, Disabling, and Enabling Constraints

Business rules are subject to occasional changes, and new constraints may be added or existing constraints modified. At times, you may temporarily disable a constraint for the purpose of loading data quickly and then re-enable the constraint afterward.

DROPPING CONSTRAINTS

When a constraint is no longer needed, you can drop it with the ALTER TABLE command and the DROP clause. The following statement drops a constraint by explicitly specifying the constraint name.

```
ALTER TABLE toy
    DROP CONSTRAINT toy_pk
Table altered.
```

Alternatively, you can drop a primary key constraint with the following statement.

```
ALTER TABLE toy
    DROP PRIMARY KEY
```

If there is a unique constraint, you either issue the command with the constraint name or use a statement similar to the following.

```
ALTER TABLE toy
    DROP UNIQUE (description)
```

SQL Developer allows you to drop constraints by using the menu below the table node; choose Constraint, Drop (see Figure 12.15).

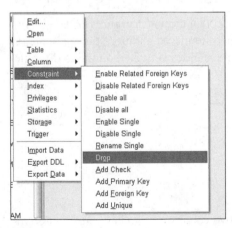

FIGURE 12.15
Dropping a constraint

ADDING CONSTRAINTS

You can add to a table any of the constraints you learned about in Lab 12.1 by using the ALTER TABLE...ADD command. When the TOY table was created, no primary key was specified. The following statement alters the TOY table to add a primary key constraint based on the TOY_ID column.

```
ALTER TABLE toy
   ADD PRIMARY KEY(toy_id)
Table altered.
```

For unique and primary key constraints, Oracle checks for the existence of an index to enforce uniqueness of the constraint. If no index exists, Oracle automatically creates the index.

The preceding statement can be rewritten with a constraint name and a storage clause for the to-be-created index, as well as the tablespace on which the index is to be stored. This statement gives you control over the storage characteristics of the index.

```
ALTER TABLE toy
   ADD CONSTRAINT toy_pk PRIMARY KEY(toy_id)
   USING INDEX TABLESPACE store_idx
   STORAGE (INITIAL 1M NEXT 500 K)
Table altered.
```

For performance reasons, you typically separate indexes and data by storing them on separate tablespaces, on different physical devices. The index is created in a tablespace called STORE_IDX. Other characteristics of a table, such as its storage parameters and size, can also be specified with the ALTER TABLE command. In the previous example, 1MB of space is allocated, regardless of whether any rows exist. After this space is used, each subsequent amount of space allocated is 500K in size.

The following statement is an example of a SQL statement that creates the concatenated primary key constraint for the GRADE table, consisting of four columns. In addition, the space allocation and tablespace for the automatically associated unique index is located on the INDX tablespace, and 100K is used for the initial extent.

```
ALTER TABLE grade
   ADD CONSTRAINT gr_pk PRIMARY KEY
   (student_id, section_id, grade_type_code,
   grade_code_occurrence)
   USING INDEX TABLESPACE indx
   STORAGE (INITIAL 100K NEXT 100K)
```

ADDING A FOREIGN KEY

The following statement illustrates the creation of the two-column foreign key constraint on the GRADE table, referencing the concatenated primary key columns of the ENROLLMENT table.

```
ALTER TABLE grade
   ADD CONSTRAINT gr_enr_fk FOREIGN KEY
   (student_id, section_id)
   REFERENCES enrollment (student_id, section_id)
```

ADDING A SELF-REFERENCING FOREIGN KEY

The COURSE table has a recursive relationship; the PREREQUISITE column refers to the COURSE_NO column. It checks whether the values in the PREREQUISITE column are in fact valid COURSE_NO values. The following SQL statement shows the foreign key constraint command used to create the self-referencing constraint on the COURSE table.

```
ALTER TABLE course
    ADD CONSTRAINT crse_crse_fk FOREIGN KEY (prerequisite)
    REFERENCES course (course_no)
```

If you are loading large amounts of data, you might want to consider temporarily disabling this constraint unless you can be sure that the sequence in which the data is inserted into the table is correct. The enabled constraint requires any courses that are prerequisites for other courses to be entered first.

ADDING A UNIQUE INDEX

The following example shows how the ALTER TABLE command on the SECTION table creates the unique index on the SECTION_NO and COURSE_NO columns. Because unique constraints automatically create an associated index, you want to place the index on a separate tablespace. Following is the syntax to place the index on the INDX tablespace, and the command also defines the initial and each subsequent extent.

```
ALTER TABLE section
    ADD CONSTRAINT sect_sect2_uk
        UNIQUE (section_no, course_no)
    USING INDEX TABLESPACE indx
    STORAGE
    (INITIAL 120K NEXT 120K)
```

ADDING A CHECK CONSTRAINT

The following statement adds a check constraint to the ZIPCODE table. It verifies that the entries in the ZIP primary key column are exactly five characters long and only numbers, not letters or special characters. The TRANSLATE function converts each entered digit into a 9 and then checks whether the format equals 99999. Any nonnumeric digits are not translated; therefore, the result of TRANSLATE is unequal to 99999, and the value is rejected.

```
ALTER TABLE zipcode
    ADD CONSTRAINT zipcode_zip_ck
    CHECK (TRANSLATE(zip, '1234567890',
                          '9999999999') = '99999')
```

Alternatively, you could come up with the following check constraint, but it has one drawback: A value such as '123.4' does not raise an error when the TO_NUMBER conversion function is applied. The LENGTH function is also fine because this is a string with a five-character length. There are many ways to handle data validity checking. You can also use a regular expression, which offers even more flexibility, as you will see shortly.

```
ALTER TABLE zipcode
  ADD CONSTRAINT zipcode_zip_ck
  CHECK (TO_NUMBER(zip)>0 AND LENGTH(zip)= 5)
```

This check constraint is applied to the SALUTATION column of the INSTRUCTOR table.

```
ALTER TABLE instructor
  ADD CONSTRAINT instructor_salutation_ck
  CHECK (salutation IN ('Dr', 'Hon', 'Mr', 'Ms', 'Rev')
        OR salutation IS NULL)
```

RENAMING CONSTRAINTS

You might want to use the RENAME CONSTRAINT command to change any system-generated constraint name to a more descriptive name. You can rename a constraint name with the following command.

```
ALTER TABLE section RENAME CONSTRAINT sect_crse_fk TO sect_fk_crse
```

In SQL Developer, you can access the Rename menu via the Actions... menu on SQL Developer's display of the table or from the Table node in the Connections pane. You see a Rename Single menu similar to Figure 12.6.

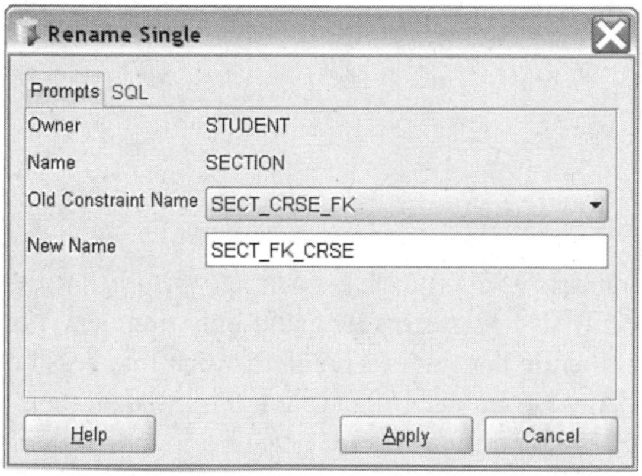

FIGURE 12.16
Renaming a constraint

DISABLING AND ENABLING CONSTRAINTS

You can enable and disable constraints as necessary by using the ALTER TABLE command. By default, when a constraint is created, it is enabled, unless you explicitly disable it. You might want to disable constraints when updating massive volumes of data or inserting large amounts of data at once to decrease overall time for these operations. After the data manipulation is performed, you re-enable the constraint.

The following statement disables an existing primary key constraint named TOY_PK on the TOY table.

```
ALTER TABLE toy
   DISABLE CONSTRAINT toy_pk
Table altered.
```

When a primary key or unique constraint is disabled, by default any associated index is dropped. When the constraint is re-enabled, a unique index is re-created.

Alternatively, you can preserve the index of a unique or primary key if you specify the KEEP INDEX clause of the ALTER TABLE statement, as shown in the following statement.

```
ALTER TABLE toy
   DISABLE CONSTRAINT toy_pk KEEP INDEX
```

When data changes are complete, you can enable the primary key with the following statement.

```
ALTER TABLE toy
   ENABLE PRIMARY KEY
Table altered.
```

Naming constraints helps when you want to disable or enable them. This statement explicitly specifies the constraint name and creates the index on a specified tablespace, with the listed storage parameters.

```
ALTER TABLE toy
   ENABLE CONSTRAINT toy_pk
   USING INDEX TABLESPACE store_idx
   STORAGE (INITIAL 1 M
            NEXT 500 K)
Table altered.
```

 To find out the name of a constraint and its status (enabled or disabled), query the data dictionary views USER_CONSTRAINTS and USER_CONS_COLUMNS or use the SQL Developer Constraints tab.

If an index does not exist for a constraint, and you don't specify the tablespace name when you enable the constraint, the index is stored on your default tablespace, with the default storage size parameters. The storage clause on constraints is relevant only with primary and unique constraints because they create indexes.

The following statement disables the foreign key constraint between the COURSE and SECTION tables.

```
ALTER TABLE section
   DISABLE CONSTRAINT sect_crse_fk
Table altered.
```

If you want to disable multiple constraints, you can issue multiple statements or issue them in one ALTER TABLE statement. The individual DISABLE clauses are not separated by commas.

```
ALTER TABLE section
  DISABLE CONSTRAINT sect_crse_fk
  DISABLE CONSTRAINT sect_inst_fk
```

THE VALIDATE AND NOVALIDATE OPTIONS

As part of the ALTER TABLE statement to enable and disable constraints, Oracle also provides VALIDATE and NOVALIDATE options. The NOVALIDATE option enforces subsequent DML on the table complying with the constraint; existing data in the table can violate the constraint.

ENABLING/DISABLING ALL CONSTRAINTS AND RELATED FOREIGN KEYS

SQL Developer has menu options to disable or enable all constraints for a given table. This is useful when you load large volumes of data and you want to disable all the constraints. You do not need to disable/enable each constraint individually. The DDL tab reveals that SQL Developer generates a PL/SQL program to loop through the data dictionary to find all the constraints and then executes the commands to enable/disable each individual constraint.

You can also disable/enable all the related foreign keys with a separate menu option. If you execute this menu option for the ZIPCODE table, the foreign keys on the STUDENT and INSTRUCTOR tables related to the ZIP column are disabled.

Determining Which Rows Violate Constraints

Unless the NOVALIDATE option is used, when a constraint is re-enabled, Oracle checks to see if all the rows satisfy the condition of the constraint. If some rows violate the constraint, the statement fails, and Oracle issues an error message. The constraint cannot be enabled unless all exceptions are fixed or the offending rows are deleted.

FOREIGN KEY CONSTRAINT VIOLATIONS

If a row with a new course number was added to the SECTION table but the COURSE table has no such COURSE_NO, the foreign key constraint cannot be enabled, as indicated by the error message.

```
ALTER TABLE section
  ENABLE CONSTRAINT sect_crse_fk
ALTER TABLE section
*
ERROR at line 1:
ORA-02298: cannot validate (STUDENT.SECT_CRSE_FK) - parent keys not
found
```

There are a variety of ways to determine which rows are the offending rows. For example, you can issue the following statement to display the rows.

```
SELECT course_no
  FROM section
 MINUS
SELECT course_no
  FROM course
```

PRIMARY KEY CONSTRAINT VIOLATIONS

To determine which rows violate the primary key constraint, you can group by the primary key column and query for duplicates with the HAVING clause, as shown in the following SQL command.

```
SELECT section_id, COUNT(*)
  FROM section
 GROUP BY section_id
HAVING COUNT(*) > 1
```

A subsequent DELETE operation of the duplicate rows might look as follows.

```
DELETE
  FROM section
 WHERE ROWID IN (SELECT MAX(ROWID)
                   FROM section
                  GROUP BY section_id
                 HAVING COUNT(*) > 1)
```

The subquery identifies the duplicate SECTION_ID column values. The SELECT of the subquery retrieves the largest value of the ROWID pseudocolumn. Each Oracle table has a pseudocolumn called ROWID, which is not visible when describing the table or with a SELECT * statement. The ROWID is unique for every row, and this subquery statement picks the largest ROWID value, using the MAX function. The rows with these duplicate SECTION_ID values is deleted. (Make sure the non-primary key column values are identical, so you don't inadvertently delete rows that you want to keep.)

MORE WAYS TO IDENTIFY CONSTRAINT VIOLATIONS

Oracle allows you to record all the rows that violate a constraint in a table called EXCEPTIONS, and you can create the table with the Oracle script utlexcpt.sql, found in the %ORACLE_HOME%\rdbms\admin directory. You can then use the following syntax to place the violating rows in the EXCEPTIONS table.

```
ALTER TABLE tablename ENABLE CONSTRAINT
    constraint_name EXCEPTIONS INTO exceptions
```

Writing Complex Check Constraints

You have seen a number of check constraint examples that validate data against simple logic. Sometimes a seemingly straightforward requirement can turn into a fairly complex check constraint. For example, imagine that you need to add validation to the PHONE column of the

STUDENT table to ensure that the entered number fits the ###-###-#### format. You can perform this validation with the TRANSLATE function (discussed in Lab 4.1), as you can see in the following statement.

```
ALTER TABLE student
  ADD CONSTRAINT student_phone_ck CHECK
      (TRANSLATE(phone,
       '012345678',
       '999999999') = '999-999-9999')
```

The TRANSLATE function determines whether any of the characters listed in the PHONE column have any of values of '0123456789'. When true, it translates them to the corresponding 9 value. Any character not listed is not translated and is retained as the original character. If the result of the TRANSLATE function equals to the pattern '999-999-9999', the value passes the check constraint.

If you want to include phone numbers without area codes or allow an optional period or space instead of the hyphen as a separation character, your check constraint quickly becomes complex, as you need to cover all the various combinations with OR conditions. You may even end up writing a trigger to make the logic more transparent.

Oracle includes regular expressions capabilities in the SQL language. A *regular expression* is pattern-matching functionality found in many programming languages. While regular expressions look fairly complex initially, you will appreciate their power and flexibility when you understand the meaning of the metacharacters that make up the regular expression. The following example duplicates the identical functionality of the TRANSLATE function to illustrate the meaning of some of the metacharacters.

```
ALTER TABLE student
  ADD CONSTRAINT student_phone_ck CHECK
      (REGEXP_LIKE(phone,
       '^[[:digit:]]{3}-[[:digit:]]{3}-[[:digit:]]{4}$'))
```

The REGEXP_LIKE operator is similar to the LIKE operator in that it checks whether a pattern is found. The first metacharacter, ^, indicates that there may not be any characters before the pattern, just like the $ at the end of the regular expression indicates that there may not be any extra characters at the end of the line. The [[:digit:]] character class and list specify that only a digit is allowed. The digit class is repeated three times, as indicated with the {3} repetition operator. This part of the regular expression represents the area code. The pattern continues with a hyphen, followed by another three digits, a hyphen, and then another four digits.

If characters other than a hyphen are valid in your phone number format, you can modify the regular expression by including those characters inside a character list enclosed by square brackets, [ ]. In this instance, spaces, periods, and dashes are allowed, or consecutive numbers without any separator. The character list now reads as [-.]?, with the ? metacharacter indicating that 0 or 1 repetition of this class list is allowed.

```
ALTER TABLE student
   ADD CONSTRAINT student_phone_ck CHECK
      (REGEXP_LIKE(phone,
      '^[[:digit:]]{3}[-. ]?[[:digit:]]{3}[-. ]?[[:digit:]]{4}$'))
```

You can take the regular expression functionality a step further and add validation for phone extension numbers, area codes beginning only with numbers 2 through 9, optional area code parentheses, and alphanumeric formats such as 800-REGEXPR. In Chapter 16, "Regular Expressions and Hierarchical Queries," you will learn more about the many other metacharacters that help you validate patterns such as zip codes, e-mail addresses, or URLs.

Restrictions on Check Constraints

Check constraints impose a few restrictions you should be aware of. A check constraint cannot refer to a column in another table, only columns within the same table are allowed. You cannot use subqueries or scalar subquery expressions. References to nondeterministic functions such as SYSDATE, USER, and CURRENT_TIMESTAMP are not allowed because they may return different results each time they are called. (You can use them for default values.) The pseudocolumns CURRVAL, NEXTVAL, LEVEL, and ROWNUM are also not permitted.

You can overcome these restrictions by writing triggers using PL/SQL. For example, you can write a trigger to reference columns in other tables to validate data, call the SYSDATE function to fill in the current date and time into the LASTMOD_DT column, or automatically create primary key column values that reference the NEXTVAL pseudocolumn of a sequence. At the beginning of this chapter, a trigger example illustrates the use of the SYSDATE function; you will see another PL/SQL trigger example referencing a sequence in Chapter 13.

Read-only Tables

For any table you own, you can modify the data or alter the object. Oracle 11g introduced the ability to make a table read-only; this prevents even the owner from performing any data manipulations or issuing any changes to the structure of the table. To make a table read-only or return it to write mode, you use the following syntax options.

```
ALTER TABLE tablename READ ONLY
ALTER TABLE tablename READ WRITE
```

 You can still drop the table from the schema. If you accidentally drop a table, and you might be able to restore it from the recycle bin.

▼ LAB 12.2 EXERCISES

a) Alter the table called NEW_STUDENT that you created in exercise b in Lab 12.1 by adding four columns. The columns should be called PHONE, NUM_COURSES with data type and length NUMBER(3), CREATED_BY, and CREATED_DATE. Determine the other column data types and lengths, based on the STUDENT table. The PHONE, NUM_COURSES, and CREATED_BY columns should allow null values, with the CREATED_BY column defaulting to the user's login name. The CREATED_DATE column should not allow null values and should default to today's date. Describe the table when you have finished.

b) Execute the following INSERT statement to insert a row into the NEW_STUDENT table. Then alter the table to change the PHONE column from NULL to NOT NULL. What do you observe?

```
INSERT INTO new_student
   (first_name, last_name, description, registration_date)
VALUES
   ('Joe', 'Fisher', 'Intro to Linux', SYSDATE)
```

c) Alter the NEW_STUDENT table to change the REGISTRATION_DATE column from the DATE data type to the VARCHAR2 data type. What do you observe?

d) Alter the NEW_STUDENT table to create a primary key consisting of the FIRST_NAME and LAST_NAME columns.

e) Alter the NEW_STUDENT table to change the length of the LAST_NAME column from 25 to 2. What do you observe?

f) Disable the primary key constraint on the NEW_STUDENT table and write an INSERT statement with the value Joe Fisher for the first and last names to prove it is successful. Then enable the constraint again and describe the result.

g) Add to the NEW_STUDENT table the column STUDY_DURATION of data type INTERVAL YEAR TO MONTH and the column ALUMNI_JOIN_DATE with the data type TIMESTAMP WITH TIME ZONE and a six-digit precision.

h) Drop the foreign key constraint FORMER_STUDENT_ZIPCODE_FK on the FORMER_STUDENT table and change it to an ON DELETE SET NULL foreign key constraint. Test the behavior by inserting a new zip code in the ZIPCODE table and creating a new student row with this new zip code and then deleting the same zip code from the ZIPCODE table. Query the FORMER_STUDENT table to see the effect.

i) Drop all the tables created throughout the labs. The table names are STUDENT_CANDIDATE, NEW_STUDENT, COURSE2, EXTINCT_ANIMAL, and FORMER_STUDENT.

▼ LAB 12.2 EXERCISE **ANSWERS**

a) Alter the table called NEW_STUDENT that you created in exercise b in Lab 12.1 by adding four columns. The columns should be called PHONE, NUM_COURSES with data type and length NUMBER(3), CREATED_BY, and CREATED_DATE. Determine the other column data types and lengths, based on the STUDENT table. The PHONE, NUM_COURSES, and CREATED_BY columns should allow null values, with the CREATED_BY column defaulting to the user's login name. The CREATED_DATE column should not allow null values and should default to today's date. Describe the table when you have finished.

ANSWER: You add the four columns by using a single ALTER TABLE command, separating the column names with commas. The CREATED_BY column has a DEFAULT clause to default the column to the value of the user's login name; the CREATED_DATE column contains a NOT NULL constraint and defaults the column to the value SYSDATE.

```
ALTER TABLE new_student
  ADD (phone VARCHAR2(15),
       num_courses NUMBER(3),
       created_by VARCHAR2(30) DEFAULT USER,
       created_date DATE DEFAULT SYSDATE NOT NULL)
Table altered.
```

```
SQL> DESC new_student
Name                            Null?     Type
------------------------------- --------- -----------
FIRST_NAME                                VARCHAR2(25)
LAST_NAME                                 VARCHAR2(25)
DESCRIPTION                               VARCHAR2(50)
REGISTRATION_DATE                         DATE
PHONE                                     VARCHAR2(15)
NUM_COURSES                               NUMBER(3)
CREATED_BY                                VARCHAR2(30)
CREATED_DATE                    NOT NULL  DATE
```

A column or columns can be added to a table, regardless of whether the table contains data. However, you cannot add columns with a NOT NULL constraint if the column contains NULL values. Therefore, you must first add the column with the NULL constraint, update the column with values, and then alter the table to modify the column to add the NOT NULL constraint. Starting with Oracle 11g, you can make use of the DEFAULT clause to avoid having to update the table, as you'll see shortly.

SETTING COLUMNS TO THE DEFAULT VALUES

How do default values behave when you insert data into a column? The CREATED_DATE column has a default value of SYSDATE. If you want this default value to appear in an INSERT statement, you can either not list the column in the INSERT statement or you can explicitly state the DEFAULT keyword.

In the next example, the CREATED_DATE column is explicitly specified, and the DEFAULT keyword is used to place the current date and time into the column. The CREATED_BY default returns the value of the USER function, which is the name of the user currently logged in. Because it's not listed in the following INSERT statement, this default value is used.

```
INSERT INTO new_student
  (first_name, last_name, description, created_date)
VALUES
  ('Julian', 'Soehner', 'Test#1', DEFAULT)

SELECT description, created_by, created_date
  FROM new_student
```

DESCRIPTION	CREATED_BY	CREATED_D
Test#1	STUDENT	18-MAY-09

1 row selected.

ROLLBACK
Rollback complete.

MODIFYING OR REMOVING COLUMN DEFAULT VALUES

A column with a DEFAULT option can be removed or changed to another default value. The following example removes the default value for the CREATED_BY column and changes the value for the CREATED_DATE column to '01-JAN-2009'.

```
ALTER TABLE new_student
    MODIFY (created_by VARCHAR2(30) DEFAULT NULL,
            created_date DATE DEFAULT TO_DATE('01-Jan-2009'))
Table altered.
```

 A DDL command such as this ALTER TABLE command cannot be rolled back, and it issues an implicit COMMIT.

The following example shows an update of a column to reset its present value to the default value using the DEFAULT keyword.

```
UPDATE new_student
    SET created_date = DEFAULT
 WHERE description = 'Test#1'
```

The result now shows the CREATED_DATE column with the value 01-Jan-2009.

```
SELECT description, created_date
  FROM new_student
```
DESCRIPTION	CREATED_D
Test#1	01-JAN-09

1 row selected.

New with Oracle 11g, you do not have to update the column first want to add a NOT NULL constraint to a table with existing data. The default value is stored in the data dictionary, and when the user selects the column, the default value is retrieved from the data dictionary.

This new feature is particularly helpful if the table has many rows; it avoids time-consuming updates and the associated the generation of large undo segments and redo logs.

Following is an example of adding a column along with the new associated column default performed against an Oracle 11g database.

```
ALTER TABLE new_student
  ADD (student_status VARCHAR2(2)
      DEFAULT 'A' NOT NULL)
```

A subsequent query against the table's newly added STUDENT_STATUS column displays the column default.

```
SELECT first_name, student_status
  FROM new_student
FIRST_NAME                STUDENT_STATUS
--------------------      --------------
Julian                    A

1 rows selected
```

b) Execute the following INSERT statement to insert a row in the NEW_STUDENT table. Then alter the table to change the PHONE column from NULL to NOT NULL. What do you observe?

```
INSERT INTO new_student
   (first_name, last_name, description, registration_date)
VALUES
   ('Joe', 'Fisher', 'Intro to Linux', SYSDATE)
```

ANSWER: The column cannot be modified to have a NOT NULL constraint because there is already a row in the table that contains a NULL value in the column.

```
ALTER TABLE new_student
  MODIFY (phone NOT NULL)
MODIFY (phone NOT NULL)
       *
ERROR at line 2:
ORA-02296: cannot enable (STUDENT.) - null values found
```

You cannot modify an existing column to NOT NULL if it contains NULL values. You must first add data to the column and then modify the column to add the constraint. If you use Oracle 11g, you can add a default value without having to update all the rows (see exercise a).

```
UPDATE new_student
   SET phone = '917-555-1212'


ALTER TABLE new_student
  MODIFY (phone NOT NULL)
Table altered.

SQL> DESC new_student
  Name                             Null?    Type
  -------------------------------- -------- ------------
  FIRST_NAME                                VARCHAR2(25)
  LAST_NAME                                 VARCHAR2(25)
  DESCRIPTION                               VARCHAR2(50)
  REGISTRATION_DATE                         DATE
```

PHONE	NOT NULL VARCHAR2(15)
NUM_COURSES	NUMBER(3)
CREATED_BY	NOT NULL VARCHAR2(30)
CREATED_DATE	NOT NULL DATE

You can also change the column back to NULL with the following statement.

```
ALTER TABLE new_student
  MODIFY (phone NULL)
```
Table altered.

```
SQL> DESC new_student
```

Name	Null?	Type
FIRST_NAME		VARCHAR2(25)
LAST_NAME		VARCHAR2(25)
DESCRIPTION		VARCHAR2(50)
REGISTRATION_DATE		DATE
PHONE		VARCHAR2(15)
NUM_COURSES		NUMBER(3)
CREATED_BY	NOT NULL	VARCHAR2(30)
CREATED_DATE	NOT NULL	DATE

DEFINING A COLUMN AS NULL VERSUS NOT NULL

Deciding whether a column should be NOT NULL or NULL leads into a discussion of nulls in general. A column that allows null values is subject to different interpretations. If you find a null value in a column, it might mean many things: Perhaps the value is simply unknown, unspecified (the user didn't choose any of the available choices), or perhaps not applicable. An encoded value can help distinguish between these differences.

Suppose you have a table that holds client demographic data including a GENDER column. There simply aren't just two genders—male and female. What if your client is not an individual, but a corporation? Do you enter a null value, and does a null value mean not applicable? What if the gender is unknown? You can come up with a lot of other scenarios for a seemingly simple GENDER column. Therefore, database designers use consistent values throughout to ensure that null values are interpreted correctly. For example, you can enter the value ? for unknown, N/A for not applicable, and OTH for other, or you can create a default value for unspecified.

Writing queries against data that contains null values poses another challenge. Unless you specifically use the IS NULL operator (or the NVL or COALESCE function) on a column, null values are ignored. You must always keep in mind the possibility of null values when dealing with data. Furthermore, if you apply a function to an indexed column or query using the IS NULL or IS NOT NULL operator, the query won't be able to take advantage of the index. Nulls can also have positive effects. An example of this is an order status flag column on an order table, indicating whether the order needs to be processed. If you enter YES, it indicates that the order is incomplete; if you enter NO, it indicates that the order is processed. If instead you allow only YES and a null value, you can actually improve the performances of queries looking for orders to be processed, because you can build an index on this status flag column, and only non-null entries are stored in the index, which is rather small because there are few entries. Values are then retrieved quickly.

c) Alter the NEW_STUDENT table to change the REGISTRATION_DATE column from the DATE data type to the VARCHAR2 data type. What do you observe?

ANSWER: A column's data type cannot be changed when there is data in the column.

```
ALTER TABLE new_student
  MODIFY (registration_date VARCHAR2(12))
MODIFY (registration_date VARCHAR2(12))
       *
ERROR at line 2:
ORA-01439: column to be modified must be empty to change datatype
```

CHANGING A COLUMN'S DATA TYPE

It is possible to change a column's data type in two circumstances. The first circumstance is when changing from one data type to a compatible data type, such as VARCHAR2 to CHAR. The following statement changes the REGISTRATION_DATE column from the DATE data type to the compatible TIMESTAMP data type. You can't change from a TIMESTAMP back to a DATE data type unless the column is null.

```
ALTER TABLE new_student
  MODIFY (registration_date TIMESTAMP(3))
Table altered.
```

The second circumstance is when the column is empty, as in the following example. This statement sets the column to NULL to facilitate the change to a completely different data type.

```
UPDATE new_student
   SET registration_date = NULL
1 row updated.

ALTER TABLE new_student
  MODIFY (registration_date VARCHAR2(12))
Table altered.
```

d) Alter the NEW_STUDENT table to create a primary key consisting of the FIRST_NAME and LAST_NAME columns.

ANSWER: The NEW_STUDENT table is altered to add a PRIMARY KEY constraint consisting of the two columns.

```
ALTER TABLE new_student
  ADD CONSTRAINT new_student_pk
    PRIMARY KEY(first_name, last_name)
Table altered.
```

The ADD PRIMARY KEY keywords are used to add the primary key constraint.

Actually, the choice of this primary key is not a very good one, aside from students having the same name, because a name entered in all uppercase is considered different from a name entered in mixed case.

e) Alter the NEW_STUDENT table to change the length of the LAST_NAME column from 25 to 2. What do you observe?

ANSWER: The length of a column cannot be decreased when the existing values in the column are larger than the new column width. Figure 12.17 shows the error message and the failed SQL statement.

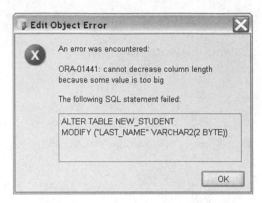

Edit Object Error

An error was encountered:

ORA-01441: cannot decrease column length
because some value is too big

The following SQL statement failed:

ALTER TABLE NEW_STUDENT
MODIFY ("LAST_NAME" VARCHAR2(2 BYTE))

OK

FIGURE 12.17
Error message after an attempt to decrease column length

For columns containing data, the length of the column can always be increased, as in the following example, but it cannot be decreased if existing data is larger than the new column width.

```
ALTER TABLE new_student
   MODIFY (last_name VARCHAR2(30))
```
Table altered.

f) Disable the primary key constraint on the NEW_STUDENT table and write an INSERT statement with the value Joe Fisher for the first and last names to prove it is successful. Then enable the constraint again and describe the result.

ANSWER: The value Joe Fisher exists twice in the FIRST_NAME and LAST_NAME columns so the primary key constraint cannot be enabled on the table.

```
ALTER TABLE new_student
   DISABLE PRIMARY KEY
```
Table altered.

```
INSERT INTO new_student
   (first_name, last_name, phone, created_by, created_date)
VALUES
   ('Joe', 'Fisher', '718-555-1212', USER, SYSDATE)
```
1 row created.

```
ALTER TABLE new_student
   ENABLE PRIMARY KEY
```
ALTER TABLE new_student
*
ERROR at line 1:
ORA-02437: cannot enable (STUDENT.NEW_STUDENT_PK) - primary **key**
violated

It is dangerous to disable a table's primary key because the integrity of the data may be violated. The only time you might want to temporarily disable constraints is when you are performing large data loads. Otherwise, if the constraints are enabled, each row must be evaluated to ensure that it does not violate any of the constraints, thus slowing down the data-loading process. After the data load or update is done, you re-enable the constraints.

Dropping all constraints may not always help speed-up all data updates, particularly if some constraints are associated with indexes that are used as part of an UPDATE's WHERE clause.

g) Add to the NEW_STUDENT table the column STUDY_DURATION of data type INTERVAL YEAR TO MONTH and the column ALUMNI_JOIN_DATE with the data type TIMESTAMP WITH TIME ZONE and a six-digit precision.

ANSWER: The ALTER TABLE statement adds both columns simultaneously. The six-digit fractional seconds are the default for the TIMESTAMP WITH TIME ZONE data type and do not need to be specified explicitly.

```
ALTER TABLE new_student
   ADD (study_duration INTERVAL YEAR TO MONTH,
        alumni_join_date TIMESTAMP (6) WITH TIME ZONE)
Table altered.
```

h) Drop the foreign key constraint FORMER_STUDENT_ZIPCODE_FK on the FORMER_STUDENT table and then change it to an ON DELETE SET NULL foreign key constraint. Test the behavior by inserting a new zip code in the ZIPCODE table and creating a new student row with this new zip code and then deleting the same zip code from the ZIPCODE table. Query the FORMER_STUDENT table to see the effect.

ANSWER: The DROP CONSTRAINT clause removes the constraint, and you can then add the foreign key with the ON DELETE SET NULL constraint instead.

```
ALTER TABLE former_student
   DROP CONSTRAINT former_student_zipcode_fk
Table altered.


ALTER TABLE former_student
   ADD CONSTRAINT former_student_zipcode_fk
      FOREIGN KEY(zip)
      REFERENCES zipcode (ZIP) ON DELETE SET NULL
Table altered.
```

The follow example inserts a new zip code with the value 90210 into the ZIPCODE table.

```
INSERT INTO zipcode
   (zip, city, state, created_by,
    created_date, modified_by, modified_date)
VALUES
   ('90210','Hollywood', 'CA', 'Alice',
    sysdate, 'Alice', sysdate);
1 row created.
```

To demonstrate the functionality, insert a zip code into the FORMER_STUDENT table.

```
INSERT INTO former_student
   (studid, first_nm, last_nm, enrolled, zip)
VALUES
   (109, 'Alice', 'Rischert', 3, '90210')
1 row created.
```

Now delete zip code 90210 from the ZIPCODE table.

```
DELETE FROM zipcode
 WHERE zip = '90210'
 1 row deleted.
```

A query against the FORMER_STUDENT table reveals the effect; the column ZIP is updated to a null value. The ZIP column must permit entry of null values.

```
SELECT studid, zip
  FROM former_student
 WHERE studid = 109
    STUDID ZIP
---------- -----
       109

1 row selected.
```

If you attempt to delete a row that exists not just in the NEW_STUDENT table but perhaps also in the STUDENT or INSTRUCTOR table, such as the value 10025, you will be prevented from using the DELETE operation because these other tables are referencing ZIPCODE with a DELETE restrict. In this case, the INSTRUCTOR table is referencing this value as well, and orphan rows are not allowed.

```
DELETE FROM zipcode
 WHERE zip = '10025'
DELETE FROM zipcode
*
ERROR at line 1:
ORA-02292: integrity constraint (STUDENT.INST_ZIP_FK)
violated - child record found
```

 If your schema name is not STUDENT, but a different account name, the constraint name error will be prefixed with the respective schema/user name.

The other foreign key alternatives to the ON DELETE SET NULL options are the two statements listed next. The first adds the DELETE RESTRICT default, and the second shows the ON DELETE CASCADE constraint alternative.

```
ALTER TABLE former_student
  ADD CONSTRAINT former_student_zipcode_fk
      FOREIGN KEY(zip)
      REFERENCES zipcode (ZIP)
```

```
ALTER TABLE former_student
  ADD CONSTRAINT former_student_zipcode_fk
      FOREIGN KEY(zip)
      REFERENCES zipcode (ZIP) ON DELETE CASCADE
```

The foreign key constraint enforces the relationship between the tables also with respect to insertions and updates. Only values found in the parent table are allowed. Null values are allowed if the foreign key column is defined as NULL.

i) Drop all the tables created throughout the labs. The table names are STUDENT_CANDIDATE, NEW_STUDENT, COURSE2, EXTINCT_ANIMAL, and FORMER_STUDENT.

   ANSWER: Use the DROP TABLE command to remove the tables from the schema.

```
DROP TABLE student_candidate
```
Table dropped.

```
DROP TABLE new_student
```
Table dropped.

```
DROP TABLE course2
```
Table dropped.

```
DROP TABLE extinct_animal
```
Table dropped.

```
DROP TABLE former_student
```
Table dropped.

Lab 12.2 Quiz

In order to test your progress, you should be able to answer the following questions.

1) The following ALTER TABLE statement contains an error.

```
ALTER TABLE new_student
  DROP CONSTRAINT PRIMARY_KEY
```

_____ a) True
_____ b) False

2) The ADD and MODIFY keywords can be used interchangeably in an ALTER TABLE statement.

_____ a) True
_____ b) False

3) You can always add a NOT NULL constraint.

_____ a) True
_____ b) False

4) A constraint must have a name in order for it to be disabled.

_____ a) True
_____ b) False

5) A column's data type can be changed only when the column contains no data.

_____ a) True
_____ b) False

6) On a read-only table, no DDL commands except for DROP TABLE and ALTER TABLE to READ WRITE are permitted.

_____ a) True
_____ b) False

ANSWERS APPEAR IN APPENDIX A.

▼ WORKSHOP

The projects in this section are meant to prompt you to utilize all the skills you have acquired throughout this chapter. The answers to these projects can be found at the companion Web site to this book, located at www.oraclesqlbyexample.com.

1) Create a table called TEMP_STUDENT with the following columns and constraints: a column STUDID for student ID that is NOT NULL and is the primary key, a column FIRST_NAME for student first name, a column LAST_NAME for student last name, a column ZIP that is a foreign key to the ZIP column in the ZIPCODE table, and a column REGISTRATION_DATE that is NOT NULL and has a CHECK constraint to restrict the registration date to dates after January 1, 2000.

2) Write an INSERT statement that violates one of the constraints for the TEMP_STUDENT table you created in exercise 1. Write another INSERT statement that succeeds when executed and commit your work.

3) Alter the TEMP_STUDENT table to add two more columns called EMPLOYER and EMPLOYER_ZIP. The EMPLOYER_ZIP column should have a foreign key constraint that references the ZIP column of the ZIPCODE table. Update the EMPLOYER column and alter the table once again to make the EMPLOYER column NOT NULL. Drop the TEMP_STUDENT table when you are done with the exercise.

CHAPTER 13

Indexes, Sequences, and Views

CHAPTER OBJECTIVES

In this chapter, you will learn about:

▶ Indexes
▶ Sequences
▶ Views

This chapter covers three different yet very important database objects: indexes, sequences, and views. Indexes are required for good performance of any database. A well-thought-out indexing strategy entails the careful placement of indexes on relevant columns. In this chapter, you will gain an understanding about the advantages and trade-offs when using indexes on tables.

Sequences generate unique values and are used mainly for creating primary key values. In this chapter, you will learn how to create and use sequences.

Views are significant in a database because they can provide row-level and column-level security to the data; they allow you to look at the data differently and/or display only specific information to the user. Views are also useful for simplifying the writing of queries for end users because they can hide the complexities of joins and conditional statements.

LAB 13.1
Indexes

LAB OBJECTIVES

After this lab, you will be able to:

▶ Create Indexes
▶ Understand the Impact of Indexes

To achieve good performance for data retrieval and data manipulation statements, you need to understand Oracle's use of indexes. Just as you use the index in the back of a book to quickly find information, Oracle uses indexes to speed up data retrieval. If the appropriate index does not exist on a table, Oracle needs to examine every row. This is called a *full table scan*.

If an index decreases query time, why not just index every column in a table? When you retrieve a large number of rows in a table, it might be more efficient to read the entire table rather than look up the values from the index. It also takes a significant amount of time and storage space to build and maintain an index. For each DML statement that changes a value in an indexed column, the index needs to be maintained.

The B-Tree Index

In this book, you will perform exercises related to Oracle's most popular index storage structure—the B-tree index. The merits and uses of another type of index, the bitmap index, are discussed briefly at the end of the lab; this type of index can be created only in Oracle's Enterprise Server Edition.

The B-tree (balanced tree) index is by far the most common type of index. It provides excellent performance in circumstances in which there are many distinct values on a column or columns. If you have several low-selectivity columns, you can also consider combining them into one *composite index*, also called a *concatenated index*. B-tree indexes are best for exact match and range searches against both small and very large tables.

Figure 13.1 shows the structure of a B-tree index. It looks like an inverted tree and consists of two types of blocks: *root/branch blocks* and *leaf blocks*. Root or branch blocks are used for storing the key together with a pointer to the child block containing the key; leaf blocks store the key values along with the ROWID, which is the physical storage location for the data in the table.

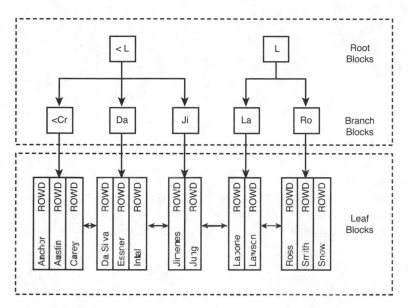

FIGURE 13.1
B-tree index

SEARCHING FOR VALUES IN A B-TREE INDEX

The first step in searching for values in a B-tree index is to start with the root block of the index. The searched value is compared with the root block keys. For example, if you are looking for a student with the last name Essner, you must go down the root block < L. This block points to the next leaf blocks, which are greater than Da and less than Ji; going down on this leaf block, you find the value Essner and the associated ROWID, the physical address of the row. A leaf block also contains links to the next and previous leaf blocks, which allow scanning the index for ranges.

THE ROWID PSEUDOCOLUMN

A pseudocolumn is not an actual column, but it acts like one. One of the pseudocolumns you have already used is ROWNUM, which restricts the number of rows a query returns. The ROWID pseudocolumn is a unique address to a particular row, and every row has a ROWID.

Indexes store the ROWID to retrieve rows quickly because the ROWID consists of several components: the data object number, the number of the data block, the number of rows within the data block, and the data file number. The data block and the data file define the physical storage characteristics of data within the individual Oracle database. This allows you to quickly access the physical row. Following is an example of a ROWID value.

```
SELECT ROWID, student_id, last_name
  FROM student
```

```
  WHERE student_id = 123
ROWID                  STUDENT_ID LAST_NAME
------------------     ---------- ---------

AAADA1AABAAARAIAAD            123 Radicola


1 row selected.
```

 A ROWID is always unique. It is the fastest way to access a row.

Rather than make Oracle search through the index, you can use the ROWID in UPDATE statements to directly access the row. For example, because the ROWID of the student named Radicola is already selected as part of the query, a subsequent update to the name of the student can find the row in the table immediately, without having to scan the entire table or use an index.

```
UPDATE student
   SET last_name = 'Radicolament'
 WHERE ROWID = 'AAADA1AABAAARAIAAD'
   AND last_name = 'Radicola'
   AND student_id = 123
```

You cannot update the ROWID, but the ROWID may change if you first delete the row and then reinsert the row because it can now be placed in another physical location. If your table moves to another database instance or another schema, the ROWID will be different.

As you learned in Chapter 11, "Insert, Update, and Delete," it is always good practice to include the old values in the WHERE clause of UPDATE to ensure that another session or user has not changed the name in the meantime.

Creating an Index

You create an index by using the following general syntax.

```
CREATE [UNIQUE|BITMAP] INDEX indexname
  ON tablename
  (column|col_expression [ASC|DESC]
   [,column|col_expression [ASC|DESC]]...)
  [PCTFREE integer]
  [TABLESPACE tablespacename|DEFAULT]
  [STORAGE ([INITIAL integer [K|M]]
            [NEXT integer [K|M)]])]
  [ONLINE]
  [VISIBLE|INVISIBLE]
  [LOGGING|NOLOGGING]
  [NOPARALLEL|PARALLEL [INTEGER]]
```

The following statement creates an index named SECT_LOCATION_I on the LOCATION column of the SECTION table.

```
CREATE INDEX sect_location_i
  ON section(location)
Index created.
```

A subsequent query to find all the classes held in LOCATION L206 can take advantage of this index. Oracle looks up the value in the index. This retrieves the row faster than reading every row, particularly if the table has many records.

```
SELECT course_no, section_no, start_date_time, location
  FROM section
 WHERE location = 'L206'
COURSE_NO SECTION_NO START_DAT LOCATION
--------- ---------- --------- --------
      120          2 24-JUL-07 L206

1 row selected.
```

Composite Indexes

Sometimes, it is useful to build indexes based on multiple columns; this type of index is called a *composite index,* or *concatenated index.* For example, you can create a composite index on two columns with a low selectivity (that is, not many distinct values). The combination of these low-selectivity values makes the composite index more selective. When you compare the query access time of a composite index to that of two individual single-column indexes, you find that the composite index offers better performance.

The following statement creates a composite index on the columns DESCRIPTION and COST. The first column of the index, also called the *leading edge* of the index, is the DESCRIPTION column; the second column of the index is the COST column.

```
CREATE INDEX course_description_cost_i
  ON course (description, cost)
```

Columns that are used together frequently in a WHERE clause and combined with the AND logical operator are often good candidates for a composite index, particularly if their combined selectivity is high. The order of the individual columns in the index can affect query perform-ance. Choose the column you use most frequently in the WHERE clause first. If both columns are accessed with equal frequency, then choose the column with the highest selectivity. In this example, the COST column has very few distinct values and is therefore considered a low-selectivity column; access against an index with a low-selectivity column as the leading edge requires more index block reads and is therefore less desirable.

There are some caveats about composite indexes you must know about when writing queries. When executed in Oracle versions prior to 9i, a query such as the following, using the COST column in the WHERE clause, cannot use the COURSE_DESCRIPTION_COST_I index because it is not the leading edge of the index.

```
SELECT course_no, description, cost
  FROM course
 WHERE cost = 1095
```

However, Oracle can use a technique called *skip scan*, which may use the index nonetheless. As you work your way through this lab, you will learn more about this feature.

To find out what columns of a table are indexed and the order of the columns in an index, you can query the data dictionary views USER_INDEXES and USER_IND_COLUMNS or review the Indexes tab in SQL Developer for the respective table.

NULLs and Indexes

NULL values are not stored in a B-tree index, unless it is a composite index where at least the first column of the index contains a value. The following query does not make use of the single-column index on the FIRST_NAME column.

```
SELECT student_id, first_name
  FROM student
 WHERE first_name IS NULL
```

Functions and Indexes

Even when you create an index on one or multiple columns of a table, Oracle may not be able to use it. In the next scenario, assume that the LAST_NAME column of the STUDENT table is indexed. The following SQL query applies the UPPER function on the LAST_NAME column. You can use this WHERE clause expression if you don't know how the last name is stored in the column—it may be stored with the first initial in uppercase, in all uppercase, or perhaps in mixed case. This query does not take advantage of the index because the column is modified by a function.

```
SELECT student_id, last_name, first_name
  FROM student
 WHERE UPPER(last_name) = 'SMITH'
```

You can avoid this behavior by creating a function-based index instead, as in the following example. This allows for case-insensitive searches on the LAST_NAME column.

```
CREATE INDEX stud_last_name_i
    ON student(UPPER(last_name))
```

Indexes and Tablespaces

To optimize performance, it is important that you separate indexes from data by placing them in separate tablespaces, residing on different physical devices. This significantly improves the performance of your queries. Use the following statement to create an index named SECT_LOCATION_I on a tablespace called INDEX_TX, with an initial size of 500K and 100K in size for each subsequent extent.

```
CREATE INDEX sect_location_i
  ON section(location)
  TABLESPACE index_tx
  STORAGE (INITIAL 500K NEXT 100K)
```

The storage clause of indexes is similar to the storage clause discussed in Chapter 12, "Create, Alter, and Drop Tables"; however, the PCTUSED parameter is not applicable for indexes. If you want to see a list of tablespaces accessible to you, query the data dictionary view USER_TABLE-SPACES.

Unique Index Versus Unique Constraint

At times you might want to enforce a unique combination of the values in a table (for example, the COURSE_NO and SECTION_NO columns of the SECTION table). You can create a unique constraint on the table that automatically creates a unique index.

```
ALTER TABLE section
  ADD CONSTRAINT sect_sect2_uk UNIQUE
  (section_no, course_no)
  USING INDEX
  TABLESPACE index_tx
  storage (initial 12K next 12K)
```

Or you can use the CREATE UNIQUE INDEX command.

```
CREATE UNIQUE INDEX section_sect_course_no_i
  ON section (section_no, course_no)
  TABLESPACE index_tx
  storage (initial 12K next 12K)
```

Oracle prefers that you use the unique constraint syntax for future compatibility.

Indexes and Constraints

When you create a primary key constraint or a unique constraint, Oracle creates the index automatically unless a suitable index already exists. In Chapter 12, you learned about various syntax options you can use.

The index NEW_TERM_PK is created as part of the CREATE TABLE statement and is associated with the primary key constraint.

```
CREATE TABLE new_term
  (term_no NUMBER(8) NOT NULL PRIMARY KEY USING INDEX
    (CREATE INDEX new_term_pk ON new_term(term_no)
      STORAGE (INITIAL 100 K NEXT 100K)),
  season_tx VARCHAR2(20),
  sequence_no NUMBER(3))
```

The advantage of using this syntax is that you can create an index in the same statement of the CREATE TABLE command, whereby you have control over the storage characteristics of the index. It doesn't require two separate statements: a CREATE TABLE statement and an ALTER TABLE statement that adds the constraint and the index plus storage clause.

If you already have an existing index and you want to associate a constraint with it, you can use a statement similar to the following. It assumes an existing index called SEMESTER_SEMESTER_ID_I, based on the SEMESTER_ID column.

```
ALTER TABLE semester
   ADD CONSTRAINT semester_pk PRIMARY KEY (semester_id)
   USING INDEX semester_semester_id_i
```

The next statement shows an example of a unique constraint that is associated with a unique index.

```
CREATE TABLE semester
  (semester_id NUMBER(8),
   semester_name VARCHAR2(8) NOT NULL,
   year_no  NUMBER(4) NOT NULL,
   CONSTRAINT semester_uk UNIQUE (semester_name, year_no)
   USING INDEX
   (CREATE UNIQUE INDEX semester_sem_yr_uk
      ON semester(semester_name, year_no)))
```

 When disabling a unique or primary key, you can keep the index if you specify the KEEP INDEX clause in an ALTER TABLE statement (see Chapter 12).

Indexes and Foreign Keys

You should almost always index foreign keys because they are frequently used in joins. In addition, if you intend to delete or update unique or primary keys on the parent table, you should index the foreign keys to improve the locking of child records. Foreign keys that are not indexed require locks to be placed on the entire child table when a parent row is deleted or the primary or unique keys of the parent table are updated. This prevents any insertions, updates, and deletions on the entire child table until the row is committed or rolled back. The advantage of an index on the foreign key column is that the locks are placed on the affected indexed child rows, thus not locking up the entire child table. This is more efficient and allows data manipulation of child rows *not* affected by the updates and deletions of the parent table.

This key issue has caused headaches for many unwitting programmers who spent days reviewing their code for performance improvements. The lack of a foreign index key frequently turns out to be the culprit for the slow performance of updates and deletions.

Dropping an Index

To drop an index, use the DROP INDEX command. You might drop an index if queries in your applications do not utilize the index. You find out which indexes are used by querying the V$OBJECT_USAGE data dictionary view.

```
DROP INDEX sect_location_i
Index dropped.
```

 When you drop a table, all associated indexes are dropped automatically.

Bitmap Indexes

Oracle supports bitmap indexes, which are typically used in a data warehouse where the primary goal is querying and analyzing data, with bulk data loads occurring at certain intervals. Bitmap indexes are not suitable for tables with heavy data manipulation activity by many users because any such changes on this type of index may significantly slow down the transactions. A bitmap index is typically used on columns with a very low selectivity—that is, columns with very few distinct values. For example, a column such as GENDER—with the four distinct values female, male, unknown, and not applicable (in case of a legal entity such as a corporation)—has a very low selectivity.

A low selectivity is expressed as the number of distinct values as a total against all the rows in the database. For example, if you had 9,000 distinct values in a table with one million rows, it would be considered a low-selectivity column. In this scenario, the number of distinct values represents less than 1 percent of the entire rows in the table, and this column may be a viable column choice for a bitmap index.

Figure 13.2 illustrates the concept of a bitmap index. The example shows a hypothetical CUSTOMER table with a bitmap index on the GENDER column. The bitmap index translates the distinct values for the GENDER column of individual customers. In this simplified example, the customers with the IDs 1 and 2 have GENDER = F, which makes the bit turned on to 1. The other values, such as GENDER = M, GENDER = N/A, and GENDER = UNKNOWN, have a 0, indicating that these values are not true for the row. The next customer, with the ID of 3, has the 1 bit turned on GENDER = M, the other values are zero.

CUSTOMER Table

ID	FIRST_NAME	LAST_NAME	GENDER
1	Mary	Jones	F
2	Carol	Smith	F
3	Fred	O1son	M
4		ABC, Inc.	N/A
...	...	...	...

Bitmapped index on GENDER column

CUSTOMER ID	1	2	3	4	...
GENDER = F	1	1	0	0	...
GENDER = M	0	0	1	0	...
GENDER = N/A	0	0	0	1	...
GENDER = Unknown	0	0	0	0	...

FIGURE 13.2
A bitmap index

The following statement creates a bitmap index on the GENDER column of a CUSTOMER table.

```
CREATE BITMAP INDEX customer_bm_gender_i
   ON customer(gender)
```

If you have multiple bitmap indexes, such as one for GENDER, MARITAL STATUS, and ZIP, and you need to retrieve rows based on certain AND and OR conditions, then bitmap indexes perform very fast. They quickly compare and merge the bit settings of these conditions and are therefore highly effective for large tables. Bitmap indexes require less storage space than traditional B-tree indexes, but they do not perform as well for less-than or greater-than comparisons. Bitmap indexes are available only with Oracle's Enterprise Edition.

Bitmap Join Indexes

The bitmap join index is another type of index that reduces the amount of data to be joined during a query. Essentially, it precomputes the join and stores the result in a bitmap; this type of index is useful in data warehousing environments. The following statement shows the creation of such an index.

```
CREATE BITMAP INDEX enroll_bmj_student_i
    ON enrollment(e.student_id)
  FROM enrollment e, student s
 WHERE e.student_id = s.student_id
Index created.
```

Guidelines for When to Index

You want to consider indexing columns frequently used in the WHERE clause of SQL statements and foreign key columns. Oracle automatically creates a unique index to enforce the primary key constraint and the unique constraint. The following are some general guidelines when an index is typically useful.

▶ Frequently accessed columns containing highly selective data for B-tree indexes.

▶ Columns frequently accessed with a small range of values for bitmap indexes.

▶ Columns that are frequently accessed and that contain many null values, but the query is looking for the NOT NULL values.

▶ Frequent queries against large tables retrieving less than 5 to 15 percent of the rows. The percentage may vary, depending on a number of factors, including the size of the table.

Building an index is often useless if:

▶ The table is small, but you should nevertheless create unique and primary constraints to enforce business rules.

▶ The query retrieves more than 5 to 15 percent of the rows.

▶ The indexed column is part of an expression. In this case, consider creating a function-based index instead.

In Chapter 18, "SQL Optimization," you'll learn to verify that SQL statements issued actually use an index.

Although adding indexes may improve performance of certain queries, you must realize that Oracle may use this new index for other queries that previously used a different index. This rarely has an adverse effect, but you must nevertheless make certain that your overall application performance does not suffer because of this change.

Keep in mind that adding indexes may increase the time required for data manipulation operations, such as INSERT, UPDATE, and DELETE. If you primarily query the table, then creating the index may offset the disadvantage of additional time required for DML statements.

Altering an Index

A number of syntax options let you change various characteristics of an index, such as renaming or rebuilding the index or altering the storage clause. The following are some of the general syntax options.

```
ALTER INDEX indexname
   [STORAGE ([NEXT integer [K|M]])]
   [REBUILD [ONLINE]
[RENAME TO newindexname]
[VISIBLE|INVISIBLE]
```

The following SQL statement shows the rebuild of an index. Periodically, you need to rebuild an index to compact the data and balance the index tree. This is particularly important after data is subject to a large number of DML changes; the rebuild operation will improve the performance of the queries. Using the index REBUILD option is faster than dropping and re-creating the index; furthermore, the index continues to be available for queries while the REBUILD operation is in progress.

```
ALTER INDEX stu_zip_fk_i REBUILD
Index altered.
```

Because a DDL command requires exclusive access to the table or index, other sessions issuing any DML commands prevent such changes. Therefore, data structure changes are usually performed during times when users are not accessing the system. However, you can create or rebuild indexes with the ONLINE option while users are performing DML commands.

```
ALTER INDEX stu_zip_fk_i REBUILD ONLINE
```

Invisible Indexes

Oracle 11g added the ability to make an index invisible. The Oracle optimizer, which evaluates the best and most efficient access path for a SQL statement, ignores the index. This feature may come in handy if you consider removing a possibly unused index without dropping it to ensure that there is not an adverse impact on your application. If it turns out that the index is required after all, it is easy to make the index visible again without having to spend time and computing resources to re-create it.

Another possible use of this feature is when you want to use the index only for certain applications that find this index useful. These applications can execute an ALTER SESSION command and make the index visible.

```
ALTER SESSION
   SET OPTIMIZER_USE_INVISIBLE_INDEXES=TRUE
```

Although the index may be invisible to users, DML operations still have to maintain the invisible index. The index still remains; however, the index is no longer used by Oracle's optimizer.

To change the visibility on an index, use the following syntax.

```
ALTER INDEX indexname INVISIBLE
ALTER INDEX indexname VISIBLE
```

You can also create an index as invisible.

```
CREATE INDEX indexname
   ON tablename(columnname) INVISIBLE
```

Loading Large Amounts of Data

When you insert or update large amounts of data, you might want to consider dropping certain indexes not used for the DML operation's WHERE clause to improve performance. After the operation is complete, you can re-create the appropriate indexes.

One fast way to re-create indexes is by using the NOLOGGING option. It avoids writing to the redo log, which keeps track of all the database changes. If you incur a fatal database error and you need to recover from the redo log, the index will not be recovered. This may be fine because an index can always be re-created.

You can also create an index by using the PARALLEL option. This allows parallel scans of the table to create the index and can make index creation much faster, provided that you have the appropriate hardware configuration, such as multiple CPUs.

Indexes and SQL Developer

SQL Developer allows you to easily determine the existing indexes and their indexed columns on a given table. When you double-click one of the tables and review the Indexes tab, you see a list similar to the one shown in Figure 13.3. This example shows a list of indexes for the ENROLLMENT table. The table displays the primary key index consisting of the two columns. The second index is on the SECTION_ID column, which is a foreign key column.

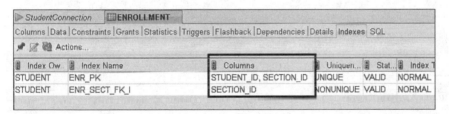

FIGURE 13.3
List of indexes for the ENROLLMENT table

Another way to access index information in SQL Developer is to use the Indexes node in the Connections pane. To create a new index you right-click on the Indexes node and select the New Index menu choice. This will bring up a screen similar to Figure 13.4. You choose the indexed columns at the bottom of the screen. The Order drop-down box on the right of the column name or expression allows for ASC or DESC ordering of the columns within the index. This can be useful when you expect to retrieve the result columns in this order.

Create Index

Schema: STUDENT

Name: INDEX1

Advanced ☐

| Definition | DDL |

Schema: STUDENT

Table: 🏢 SECTION

Type: ⦿ Normal ○ Domain

⦿ Non-unique ○ Unique ○ Bitmap

Index:

SECTION_NO

Column Name or Expression:

SECTION_NO

Order:

Help   OK   Cancel

FIGURE 13.4
Create Index screen in SQL Developer

You can find a number of different index options by using SQL Developer's menu screens when you right-click on a specific index (see Figure 13.5).

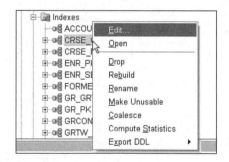

Indexes
- ACCOU | Edit...
- CRSE_ | Open
- CRSE_F |
- ENR_PI | Drop
- ENR_SI | Rebuild
- FORME | Rename
- GR_GR | Make Unusable
- GR_PK | Coalesce
- GRCON | Compute Statistics
- GRTW_ | Export DDL ▶

FIGURE 13.5
Menu options for an index

Table 13.1 highlights the functionality and purpose of each menu option.

TABLE 13.1   Overview of SQL Developer Index-Related Menu Choices

MENU CHOICE	DESCRIPTION
Edit	Allows you to modify properties related to the index, such as its columns or storage parameters. This results in a drop and re-creation of the index, as you can see when you click the DDL tab.
Open	Has the same effect as a double-click on the index name's node; this displays the column listing of the index, the data dictionary details, statistics, partition information, and the SQL DDL to re-create the index.
Drop	Drops the index.
Rebuild	Rebuilds the index. Creates a new index, based on the old index.
Rename	Renames the index.
Make Unusable	Makes the index unusable for SQL statements. To reuse the index, it must be either rebuilt or dropped and then re-created. Consider using the INVISIBLE option instead.
Coalesce	Merges index blocks to create a more compact and efficient index; useful when many deletes occurred against the table and its affected index.
Compute Statistics	Gathers the latest statistics (see Chapter 18).
Export DDL	Exports the index's DDL to a file, the Clipboard, or the SQL Worksheet window.

Indexes and Statistics

The Oracle optimizer makes a determination on how to execute your SQL statement. If an index exists, the optimizer evaluates whether the index is useful in achieving good performance. Because there are so many variables when determining how to best process a SQL statement, the Oracle optimizer relies on statistics about the tables and indexes, such as the number of rows and the number of distinct column values, among other variables.

These statistics need to be updated periodically to ensure good judgment by the optimizer. With Oracle version 10g and above, when you create an index, Oracle automatically collects the statistics. You can see the information in the Statistics tab of the given index within SQL Developer (see Figure 13.6).

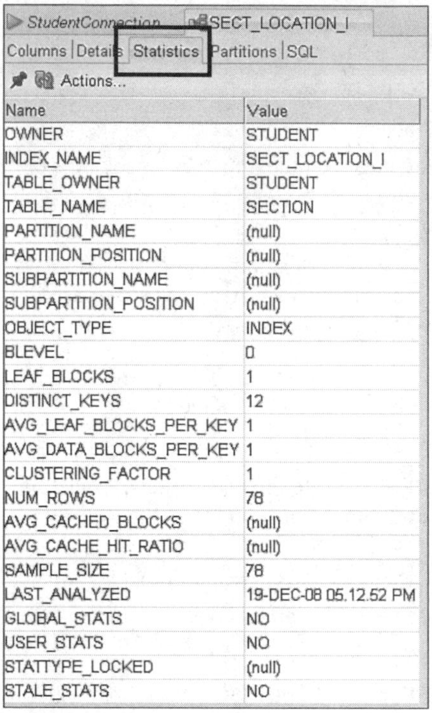

Name	Value
OWNER	STUDENT
INDEX_NAME	SECT_LOCATION_I
TABLE_OWNER	STUDENT
TABLE_NAME	SECTION
PARTITION_NAME	(null)
PARTITION_POSITION	(null)
SUBPARTITION_NAME	(null)
SUBPARTITION_POSITION	(null)
OBJECT_TYPE	INDEX
BLEVEL	0
LEAF_BLOCKS	1
DISTINCT_KEYS	12
AVG_LEAF_BLOCKS_PER_KEY	1
AVG_DATA_BLOCKS_PER_KEY	1
CLUSTERING_FACTOR	1
NUM_ROWS	78
AVG_CACHED_BLOCKS	(null)
AVG_CACHE_HIT_RATIO	(null)
SAMPLE_SIZE	78
LAST_ANALYZED	19-DEC-08 05.12.52 PM
GLOBAL_STATS	NO
USER_STATS	NO
STATTYPE_LOCKED	(null)
STALE_STATS	NO

FIGURE 13.6
The Statistics tab for the SECT_LOCATION_I index in SQL Developer

The Index Details tab is much like the Details tab for a table. On it, you find information such as the storage parameters, the date created, and the date the index was last analyzed; this tab primarily reflects data from the data dictionary view ALL_INDEXES.

The Partitions tab shows whether the index is split into multiple partitions that can be managed independently. Index and table partitioning are useful for large-scale databases.

▼ LAB 13.1 EXERCISES

a) Create an index on the PHONE column of the STUDENT table. Drop the index after you successfully create it to return the STUDENT schema to its original state.

b) Create a composite index on the FIRST_NAME and LAST_NAME columns of the STUDENT table. Drop the index when you have finished.

c) Create an index on the DESCRIPTION column of the COURSE table. Note that queries against the table often use the UPPER function. Drop the index after you successfully create it.

d) Execute the following SQL statements. Explain the reason for the error.

```
CREATE TABLE test (col1 NUMBER)
CREATE INDEX test_col1_i ON test(col1)
DROP TABLE test
DROP INDEX test_col1_i
```

e) Would a B-tree index work on a frequently accessed column with few distinct values? Explain.

f) List the advantages and disadvantages of indexes on performance.

g) Assume that an index exists on the column ENROLL_DATE in the ENROLLMENT table. Change the following query so it uses that index.

```
SELECT student_id, section_id,
       TO_CHAR(enroll_date,'DD-MON-YYYY')
  FROM enrollment
 WHERE TO_CHAR(enroll_date,'DD-MON-YYYY') = '12-MAR-2007'
```

▼ LAB 13.1 EXERCISE **ANSWERS**

a) Create an index on the PHONE column of the STUDENT table. Drop the index after you successfully create it to return the STUDENT schema to its original state.

ANSWER: To create the index on the table, issue a CREATE INDEX statement.

```
CREATE INDEX stu_phone_i
  ON student(phone)
Index created.
```

Include the name of the table and the indexed column(s) in the index name; this convention allows easier identification of indexes and their respective columns in a particular table. As always, you can use SQL Developer to review the index listings or query the data dictionary views USER_INDEXES and USER_IND_COLUMNS. Remember that no database object's name, such as an index, cannot be longer than 30 characters.

To drop the index, simply issue the DROP INDEX command.

```
DROP INDEX stu_phone_i
Index dropped.
```

b) Create a composite index on the FIRST_NAME and LAST_NAME columns of the STUDENT table. Drop the index when you have finished.

ANSWER: There are two possible solutions for creating a composite index using the FIRST_NAME and LAST_NAME columns.

A composite, or concatenated, index is an index that consists of more than one column. Depending on how you access the table, you need to order the columns in the index accordingly.

To determine the best column order in the index, determine the selectivity of each column. This means determining how many distinct values each column has. You also need to determine what types of queries to write against the table. All this information helps you choose the best column order for the index.

SOLUTION 1

The index is created in the order FIRST_NAME, LAST_NAME.

```
CREATE INDEX stu_first_last_name_i
   ON student(first_name, last_name)
```

This index is used in a SQL statement if you refer in the WHERE clause to either both columns or the FIRST_NAME column. Oracle can access the index if the WHERE clause lists the leading column of the index. The leading column, also called the leading edge, of the aforementioned index is the FIRST_NAME column. If the WHERE clause of a SQL statement lists only the LAST_NAME column, the SQL statement cannot access the index. For example, the next two WHERE clauses do not use the index.

```
WHERE last_name = 'Smith'
WHERE last_name LIKE 'Sm%'
```

SOLUTION 2

The index is created in the order LAST_NAME, FIRST_NAME. The LAST_NAME column is the leading column of the index.

```
CREATE INDEX stu_last_first_name_i
   ON student(last_name, first_name)
```

This index is used in a SQL statement if you query both columns or the LAST_NAME column. If a WHERE clause in a SQL statement lists only the FIRST_NAME column, Oracle does not use the index because it is not the leading column of the index.

COMPOSITE INDEXES VERSUS INDIVIDUAL INDEXES

An alternative to using a composite index is to create two separate indexes: one for the FIRST_NAME column and one for the LAST_NAME column.

```
CREATE INDEX stu_first_name_i
   ON student(first_name)
Index created.

CREATE INDEX stu_last_name_i
   ON student(last_name)
Index created.
```

A SQL statement with one of the columns in the WHERE clause uses the appropriate index. In a case where both columns are used in the WHERE clause, Oracle typically merges the two indexes together to retrieve the rows. Why, then, have concatenated indexes at all? A composite index outperforms individual column indexes, provided that all the columns are referenced in the WHERE clause.

SKIP SCAN

A feature called skip scan allows the skipping of the leading edge of an index. During a skip scan, the B-tree index is probed for the distinct values of the leading edge column. Ideally in such a scenario, the column has only very few distinct values. In the case of the FIRST_NAME and LAST_NAME columns, there are many different values, which means the Oracle optimizer will probably not use the skip scan feature.

A skip scan is not as fast as an index lookup because for each distinct leading edge value, the index needs to be probed. But if no leading edge index exists, the skip scan feature can allow queries to use the composite index instead of reading the entire table.

A second benefit of the skip scan feature is the reduced need for indexes; fewer indexes require less storage space and therefore result in better performance of DML statements.

 Skip scan is not supported for bitmap and function-based indexes.

The database designer, together with the application developer, decides how to structure the indexes to make them most useful, based on the SQL statements issued. Make sure to verify that Oracle actually uses the index in your statement; you can do this with the help of an explain plan, as discussed in Chapter 18.

Assume that on a given table, you create a composite index on columns A, B, and C, in this order. To make use of the index, specify in the WHERE clause either column A; columns A and B; columns A, B, and C; or columns A and C. Queries listing column C only, or B only, or B and C only do not use the index because they are not leading edge columns.

To determine the best order, again think about the types of queries issued and the selectivity of each column. The following three indexes cover all the query possibilities. This solution requires the least amount of storage and offers the best overall performance.

```
CREATE INDEX test_table_a_b_c ON test_table(a, b, c)
CREATE INDEX test_table_b_c ON test_table(b, c)
CREATE INDEX test_table_c ON test_table(c)
```

Your queries may take be able to take advantage of the skip scan feature, and you may not need to build as many indexes. You must test your statements carefully to ensure adequate performance.

c) Create an index on the DESCRIPTION column of the COURSE table. Note that queries against the table often use the UPPER function. Drop the index after you successfully create it.

ANSWER: A function-based index is created on the DESCRIPTION column.

```
CREATE INDEX crse_description_i
  ON course(UPPER(description))
```

A function-based index stores the indexed values and uses the index on the following SELECT statement, which retrieves the course number for the course called Hands-On Windows. If you don't know in what case the description was entered into the COURSE table, you might want to apply the UPPER function to the column.

```
SELECT course_no, description
  FROM course
 WHERE UPPER(description) = 'HANDS-ON WINDOWS'
```

Any query that modifies a column with a function in the WHERE clause does not make use of an index unless you create a function-based index.

An index like the following cannot be used for the previously issued SQL statement.

```
CREATE INDEX crse_description_i
  ON course(description)
```

To restore the schema to its previous state, drop the index.

```
DROP INDEX crse_description_i
```
Index dropped.

d) Execute the following SQL statements. Explain the reason for the error.

```
CREATE TABLE test (col1 NUMBER)
CREATE INDEX test_col1_i ON test(col1)
DROP TABLE test
DROP INDEX test_col1_i
```

ANSWER: Dropping a table automatically drops any associated index. There is no need to drop the index separately.

```
DROP INDEX test_col1_i
              *
ERROR at line 1:
ORA-01418: specified index does not exist
```

e) Would a B-tree index work on a frequently accessed column with few distinct values? Explain.

ANSWER: It may be advantageous to create a B-tree index even on a low-selectivity column.

Assume that you have an EMPLOYEE table with a column named GENDER that you consider indexing. Also assume that 90 percent of your employees are male and 10 percent are female. You frequently query for female employees. In this case, the index is helpful and improves the performance of your query. A query for male employees will probably perform a full table scan because this is more efficient than looking up all the values in the index; the Oracle optimizer (discussed in Chapter 18) makes the decision regarding the best access path.

f) List the advantages and disadvantages of indexes on performance.

ANSWER: Advantages: Adding an index on a table increases the performance of SQL statements using the indexed column(s) in the WHERE clause. This assumes that only a small percentage of the rows are accessed. If you access many rows in the table, accessing the entire table via a full table scan probably yields better performance. Indexes on the foreign key columns also improve locking.

Disadvantages: Adding indexes may increase the time required for insert, update, and delete operations because the index needs to be updated. Indexes also require additional disk space.

g) Assume that an index exists on the column ENROLL_DATE in the ENROLLMENT table. Change the following query so it uses that index.

```
SELECT student_id, section_id,
       TO_CHAR(enroll_date,'DD-MON-YYYY')
  FROM enrollment
 WHERE TO_CHAR(enroll_date,'DD-MON-YYYY') = '12-MAR-2007'
```

ANSWER: When you modify an indexed column with a function, such as the function TO_CHAR in the WHERE clause, the SQL statement is not able to access the index. The exception is when you create a function-based index on the column. In this case, you do not need a function-based index. The SQL statement is changed so it does not modify the indexed column with a function. Chapter 5, "Date and Conversion Functions," discusses the dangers of using TO_CHAR with a DATE column in the WHERE clause.

```
SELECT student_id, section_id,
       TO_CHAR(enroll_date,'DD-MON-YYYY')
  FROM enrollment
 WHERE enroll_date = TO_DATE('12-MAR-2007','DD-MON-YYYY')
```

Lab 13.1 Quiz

In order to test your progress, you should be able to answer the following questions.

1) For the following query, choose which index or indexes, if any, probably yield the best performance.

```
SELECT student_id, last_name, employer, phone
  FROM student
 WHERE employer = 'FGIC'
   AND phone = '201-555-5555'
```

_____ a) Index on employer

_____ b) Index on phone

_____ c) Index in the order employer, phone

_____ d) Index in the order phone, employer

_____ e) No index

2) You should always index as many columns as possible.

_____ a) True

_____ b) False

3) Frequently queried columns and foreign keys should almost always be indexed.

_____ a) True

_____ b) False

4) The ROWID is the fastest way to access a row.

_____ a) True

_____ b) False

5) The following query uses the single-column B-tree index on the ZIP column of the INSTRUCTOR table.

```
SELECT instructor_id, last_name, first_name, zip
  FROM instructor
 WHERE zip IS NULL
```

_____ a) True

_____ b) False

6) The following SQL statement benefits from an index on the column INSTRUCTOR_ID.

```
UPDATE instructor
   SET phone = '212-555-1212'
 WHERE instructor_id = 123
```

_____ a) True

_____ b) False

ANSWERS APPEAR IN APPENDIX A.

LAB 13.2
Sequences

LAB OBJECTIVES

After this lab, you will be able to:

▶ Create Sequences
▶ Use Sequences

Sequences are Oracle database objects that allow you to generate unique integers. Recall the STUDENT table with the primary key column STUDENT_ID. The value of STUDENT_ID is a *surrogate key* or an *artificial key* generated from a sequence. This key is useful to the system but usually has no meaning for the user, is not subject to changes, and is never NULL.

Assume that a student is uniquely identified by first name, last name, and address. These columns are called the **alternate key**. If you choose these columns as the primary key, imagine a scenario in which a student's name or address changes. A large number of updates are required in many tables because all the foreign key columns need to be changed; these changes involve a lot of customized programming. Instead, you can create a surrogate key column and populated it with a sequence. This surrogate key is not subject to change, and the users rarely see this column.

Sequences ensure that no user gets the same value from the sequence, thus guaranteeing unique values for primary keys. Sequences are typically incremented by 1, but other increments can be specified. You can also start sequences at a specific number.

Because you still need to enforce your users' business rules and prevent duplicate student entries, consider creating a unique constraint on the alternate key.

Creating a Sequence

The syntax for creating sequences is as follows.

```
CREATE SEQUENCE sequencename
  [INCREMENT BY integer]
  [START WITH integer]
  [CACHE integer|NOCACHE]
  [MAXVALUE integer|NOMAXVALUE]
  [MINVALUE integer|NOMINVALUE]
  [CYCLE|NOCYCLE]
  [ORDER|NOORDER]
```

To create a sequence named STUDENT_ID_SEQ_NEW, issue the CREATE SEQUENCE command.

```
CREATE SEQUENCE student_id_seq_new START WITH 1 NOCACHE
Sequence created.
```

Basing the name of the sequence on the name of the column for which you want to use it is helpful for identification, but it does not associate the sequence with a particular column or table. The START WITH clause starts the sequence with the number 1.

The NOCACHE keyword indicates that sequence numbers should not be kept in memory, so that when the system shuts down, you do not lose any cached numbers. However, losing numbers is not a reason for concern because there are many more available from the sequence. It is useful to leave the sequence numbers in the cache only if you access the sequence frequently. If you don't specify a CACHE choice, by default the first 20 numbers are cached.

The MAXVALUE and MINVALUE parameters determine the minimum and maximum range values of the sequence; the defaults are NOMAXVALUE and NOMINVALUE. The ORDER option, which is the default, ensures that the sequence numbers are generated in order of request. The CYCLE parameter recycles the numbers after it reaches the maximum or minimum value, depending on whether it's an ascending or descending sequence; it restarts at the minimum and maximum values, respectively. The default value is NOCYCLE.

Using Sequence Numbers

To increment the sequence and display the unique number, use the NEXTVAL pseudocolumn. The following SQL statement takes the next value from the sequence. Because the sequence was just created and starts with the number 1, it takes the number 1 as the first available value.

```
SELECT student_id_seq_new.NEXTVAL
   FROM dual
   NEXTVAL
---------
        1

1 row selected.
```

Typically, you use NEXTVAL in INSERT and UPDATE statements. To display the current value of the sequence after it is incremented, use the CURRVAL pseudocolumn.

Altering a Sequence

The ALTER SEQUENCE command allows you to change the properties of a sequence, such as the increment value, min and max values, and cache option. The syntax of the ALTER SEQUENCE command is as follows.

```
ALTER SEQUENCE sequencename
  [INCREMENT BY integer]
  [MAXVALUE integer|NOMAXVALUE]
  [MINVALUE integer|NOMINVALUE]
  [CACHE integer|NOCACHE]
  [CYCLE|NOCYCLE]
  [ORDER|NOORDER]
```

To restart a sequence at a lower number, you can drop and re-create the sequence. Any GRANTs to other users of the sequence must be reissued. For more on the GRANT command, see Chapter 15, "Security."

Alternatively, you can issue an ALTER SEQUENCE command to reduce MAXVALUE to a number close to the current sequence value. Also make sure the sequence is set to restart from the beginning by setting the CYCLE value and, if desired, the appropriate MINVALUE. Get NEXTVAL from the sequence to restart the sequence. Remember to reset the MAXVALUE value to a larger number when you are done.

Renaming a Sequence

As with other Oracle objects, you can rename a sequence with the RENAME command. When you rename an object, dependent objects become invalid. Therefore, review the Dependencies tab in SQL Developer or query the data dictionary view USER_DEPENDENCIES to determine the impact of your change.

```
RENAME student_id_seq_new TO student_id_seq_newname
```

Using Sequence Values

The NEXTVAL and CURRVAL pseudocolumns can be used in the following SQL constructs.

▸ VALUES clause of an INSERT statement

▸ SET clause of an UPDATE statement

▸ SELECT list (unless it is part of a subquery, view, or materialized view)

▸ SELECT list of a subquery in an INSERT statement

Sequence values are not allowed in the following statements.

▸ Subquery of a SELECT, UPDATE, or DELETE statement

▸ SELECT statement containing DISTINCT, GROUP BY, ORDER BY, UNION, UNION ALL, INTERSECT, or MINUS

▸ WHERE clause of a SELECT statement

▸ DEFAULT clause of a column in a CREATE or ALTER TABLE statement

▸ CHECK constraint condition

SQL Developer and Sequences

SQL Developer allows you to create, alter, and drop sequences using the graphical user interface. When you double-click one of the sequences, you see a screen similar to Figure 13.7.

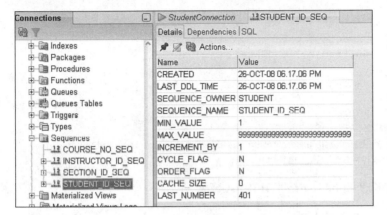

FIGURE 13.7
Details tab for the STUDENT_ID_SEQ index in SQL Developer

The Details tab shows the creation date of the sequence, along with the last number used on the sequence; most of this information is from the ALL_SEQUENCES data dictionary view.

The Dependencies tab shows whether any object refers to the sequence. An example of a reference to a sequence is a trigger that selects from this sequence.

▼ LAB 13.2 EXERCISES

a) Describe the effects of the following SQL statement on the sequence SECTION_ID_SEQ.

```
INSERT INTO section
  (section_id, course_no, section_no,
   start_date_time, location,
   instructor_id, capacity, created_by,
   created_date, modified_by, modified_date)
VALUES
  (section_id_seq.NEXTVAL, 122, 6,
   TO_DATE('15-MAY-2007', 'DD-MON-YYYY'), 'R305',
   106, 10, 'ARISCHERT',
   SYSDATE, 'ARISCHERT', SYSDATE)
```

b) Write a SQL statement that increments the sequence STUDENT_ID_SEQ_NEW with NEXTVAL and then issue a ROLLBACK command. Determine the effect on the sequence number.

c) Drop the sequence STUDENT_ID_SEQ_NEW.

▼ LAB 13.2 EXERCISE **ANSWERS**

a) Describe the effects of the following SQL statement on the sequence SECTION_ID_SEQ.

```
INSERT INTO section
   (section_id, course_no, section_no,
    start_date_time, location,
    instructor_id, capacity, created_by,
    created_date, modified_by, modified_date)
VALUES
   (section_id_seq.NEXTVAL, 122, 6,
    TO_DATE('15-MAY-2007', 'DD-MON-YYYY'), 'R305',
    106, 10, 'ARISCHERT',
    SYSDATE, 'ARISCHERT', SYSDATE)
```

ANSWER: The sequence is accessible from within an INSERT statement. The next value is incremented, and this value is inserted into the table.

AUTOMATING PRIMARY KEY CREATION WITH TRIGGERS

You can automatically increment a sequence and insert the primary key value whenever you insert a new row in a table. This can be accomplished when you write a trigger. Following is the code for a trigger associated with the SECTION table. The trigger fires upon INSERT to the SECTION table. It checks whether a value for the SECTION_ID column is supplied as part of the INSERT statement. If not, it retrieves the value from the SECTION_ID_SEQ sequence and holds the value in the correlation variable :new.SECTION_ID. This value is then inserted into the SECTION_ID column.

```
CREATE OR REPLACE TRIGGER section_trg_bir
BEFORE INSERT ON section
FOR EACH ROW
BEGIN
 IF :new.SECTION_ID IS NULL THEN
    SELECT section_id_seq.NEXTVAL
      INTO :new.SECTION_ID
      FROM DUAL;
  END IF;
END;
/
```

The next command shows the primary key column SECTION_ID not listed as part of the INSERT statement. The command is successful; it does not return an error message indicating that the primary key column SECTION_ID is missing.

```
INSERT INTO section
   (course_no, section_no, instructor_id, created_by, created_date,
    modified_by, modified_date)
VALUES
   (20, 99, 109, 'Alice', SYSDATE,
    'Alice', SYSDATE)
1 row created.
```

A subsequent SELECT statement queries the newly inserted row and displays the automatically created SECTION_ID value.

```
SELECT section_id, course_no, section_no, created_date
  FROM section
 WHERE course_no = 20
   AND section_no = 99
SECTION_ID  COURSE_NO  SECTION_NO  CREATED_D
----------  ---------  ----------  ---------
       161         20          99  12-SEP-08

1 row selected.
```

SQL Developer can create triggers to generate primary key values from sequences. When you right-click on a table's node and then select Trigger, you will see the Create (PK from Sequence) menu option (see Figure 13.8). Oracle lets you choose the sequence to generate the primary key value. The DDL tab shows the dynamically created trigger PL/SQL source code.

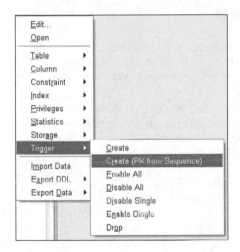

FIGURE 13.8
SQL Developer menu option for creating a primary key sequence trigger

For more information on triggers and PL/SQL, refer to *Oracle PL/SQL by Example,* 4th Edition, by Benjamin Rosenzweig and Elena Silvestrova Rakhimov (Prentice Hall, 2008) or the *Oracle Application Developer's Guide—Fundamentals Manual.*

b) Write a SQL statement that increments the sequence STUDENT_ID_SEQ_NEW with NEXTVAL and then issue a ROLLBACK command. Determine the effect on the sequence number.

ANSWER: After a sequence is incremented, the ROLLBACK command does not restore the number.

If you haven't already done so, create the sequence with the CREATE SEQUENCE student_id_seq_new command. Then retrieve the next number from the sequence.

```
SELECT student_id_seq_new.NEXTVAL
  FROM dual
  NEXTVAL
---------
        2
```

1 row selected.

```
ROLLBACK
```
Rollback complete.

```
SELECT student_id_seq_new.NEXTVAL
  FROM dual
  NEXTVAL
---------
        3
```

1 row selected.

If there are any gaps in the primary key sequence numbers, it really doesn't matter because the numbers have no meaning to the user, and there are many more numbers available from the sequence. One of the unique properties of sequences is that no two users receive the same number.

You can see information about the sequence in the USER_SEQUENCES data dictionary view. Here the LAST_NUMBER column indicates the last used number of the sequence. Alternatively, you can see this information in SQL Developer's Details tab for the sequence.

```
SELECT sequence_name, last_number, cache_size
  FROM user_sequences
 WHERE sequence_name = 'STUDENT_ID_SEQ_NEW'
SEQUENCE_NAME                     LAST_NUMBER CACHE_SIZE
------------------------------- ----------- ----------
STUDENT_ID_SEQ_NEW                        3          0
```

1 row selected.

You can obtain the current number of the sequence by using CURRVAL, provided that the sequence was incremented by the user's session.

```
SELECT student_id_seq_new.CURRVAL
  FROM dual
  CURRVAL
----------
        3
```

1 row selected.

c) Drop the sequence STUDENT_ID_SEQ_NEW.

ANSWER: As with other database objects, you use the DROP command to drop a sequence.

```
DROP SEQUENCE student_id_seq_new
```
Sequence dropped.

Lab 13.2 Quiz

In order to test your progress, you should be able to answer the following questions.

1) Sequences are useful for generating unique values.

    _____ a) True

    _____ b) False

2) A student's Social Security number is a good choice for a primary key value instead of a sequence.

    _____ a) True

    _____ b) False

3) The default increment of a sequence is 1.

    _____ a) True

    _____ b) False

4) When you drop a table, the associated sequence is also dropped.

    _____ a) True

    _____ b) False

5) The following statement creates a sequence named EMPLOYEE_ID_SEQ, which starts at the number 1000.

    ```
    CREATE SEQUENCE employee_id_seq START WITH 1000
    ```

    _____ a) True

    _____ b) False

ANSWERS APPEAR IN APPENDIX A.

LAB 13.3
Views

LAB OBJECTIVES

After this lab, you will be able to:

▶ Create, Alter, and Drop Views

▶ Understand the Data Manipulation Rules for Views

A view is a virtual table that consists of columns and rows, but it is only the SELECT statement that is stored, not a physical table with data. A view's SELECT query may reference one or multiple tables, called *base tables*. The base tables are typically actual tables or other views.

Advantages of Views

Views simplify the writing of queries. You can query a single view instead of writing a complicated SQL statement that joins many tables. The complexity of the underlying SQL statement is hidden from the user and contained only in the view.

Views are useful for security reasons because they can hide data. The data retrieved from a view can show only certain columns if you list those columns in the SELECT list of the query. You can also restrict the view to display specific rows with the WHERE clause of the query.

In a view, you can give a column a different name from the one in the base table. Views may be used to isolate an application from a change in the definition of the base tables. Rather than change the program, you can make changes to the view.

A view looks just like any other table. You can describe and query the view and also issue INSERT, UPDATE, and DELETE statements to a certain extent, as you will see when performing the exercises in this lab.

Creating a View

The simplified syntax for creating a view is as follows.

```
CREATE [OR REPLACE] [FORCE|NOFORCE] VIEW viewname
[(column_alias[, column_alias]...)]
AS query
[WITH CHECK OPTION|WITH READ ONLY [CONSTRAINT constraintname]]
```

The following statements create a view called COURSE_NO_COST and describe the new view.

```
CREATE OR REPLACE VIEW course_no_cost AS
SELECT course_no, description, prerequisite
  FROM course
View created.
```

```
SQL> DESC course_no_cost
  Name                         Null?     Type
  ---------------------------  --------  ----------------
  COURSE_NO                    NOT NULL  NUMBER(8)
  DESCRIPTION                  NOT NULL  VARCHAR2(50)
  PREREQUISITE                           NUMBER(8)
```

The COURSE_NO_COST view hides a number of columns that exist in the COURSE table. You do not see the COST column or the CREATED_DATE, CREATED_BY, MODIFIED_DATE, and MODIFIED_BY columns. The main purpose of this view is security. You can grant access just to the view COURSE_NO_COST instead of to the COURSE table itself. For more information on granting access privileges to database objects, see Chapter 15.

Using Column Aliases

The following statement demonstrates a view with column names different from the column names in the base tables. Here the view named STUD_ENROLL shows a list of the STUDENT_ID, the last name of the student in capital letters, and the number of classes the student is enrolled in. The column STUDENT_ID from the STUDENT table is renamed in the view to STUD_ID, using a column alias. When a column contains an expression such as a function, a column alias is required. The two expressions in the STUD_ENROLL view, namely the student last name in caps and the count of classes enrolled, are therefore aliased.

```
CREATE OR REPLACE VIEW stud_enroll AS
SELECT s.student_id stud_id,
       UPPER(s.last_name) last_name,
       COUNT(*) num_enrolled
  FROM student s, enrollment e
 WHERE s.student_id = e.student_id
 GROUP BY s.student_id, UPPER(s.last_name)
```

The OR REPLACE keyword is useful if the view already exists. It allows you to replace the view with a different SELECT statement without having to drop the view first. This also means you do not have to re-grant privileges to the view; the rights to the view are retained by those who have already been granted access privileges.

The following example shows an alternate SQL statement for naming columns in a view, whereby the view's columns are listed in parentheses after the view name.

```
CREATE OR REPLACE VIEW stud_enroll
       (stud_id, last_name, num_enrolled) AS
SELECT s.student_id,
       UPPER(s.last_name),
       COUNT(*)
  FROM student s, enrollment e
 WHERE s.student_id = e.student_id
 GROUP BY s.student_id, UPPER(s.last_name)
```

Altering a View

You use the ALTER VIEW command to recompile a view if it becomes invalid. This can occur after you alter one of the base tables. The syntax of the ALTER VIEW statement is as follows.

```
ALTER VIEW viewname COMPILE
```

The ALTER VIEW command allows for additional syntax options not mentioned. These options let you create primary or unique constraints on views. However, these constraints are not enforced and do not maintain data integrity, and an index is never built because they can only be created in DISABLE NOVALIDATE mode. These constraint types are primarily useful with *materialized views*, a popular data warehousing feature that allows you to physically store pre-aggregated results and/or joins for speedy access. Unlike the views discussed in this chapter, materialized views result in physical data stored in tables.

Renaming a View

The RENAME command allows you to change the name of a view.

```
RENAME stud_enroll TO stud_enroll2
```

All underlying constraints and granted privileges remain intact. However, any objects that use this view (perhaps another view or a PL/SQL procedure, package, or function) become invalid and need to be compiled.

Dropping a View

To drop a view, you use the DROP VIEW command. The following statement drops the STUD_ENROLL2 view.

```
DROP VIEW stud_enroll2
View dropped.
```

▼ LAB 13.3 EXERCISES

a) Create a view called LONG_DISTANCE_STUDENT with all the columns in the STUDENT table plus the CITY and STATE columns from the ZIPCODE table. Exclude students from New York, New Jersey, and Connecticut.

b) Create a view named CHEAP_COURSE that shows all columns of the COURSE table where the course cost is 1095 or less.

c) Issue the following INSERT statement. What do you observe when you query the CHEAP_COURSE view?

```
INSERT INTO cheap_course
   (course_no, description, cost,
    created_by, created_date, modified_by,
    modified_date)
VALUES
   (900, 'Expensive', 2000,
    'ME', SYSDATE, 'ME', SYSDATE)
```

d) Drop the views named LONG_DISTANCE_STUDENT and CHEAP_COURSE.

e) Using the following statement, create a table called TEST_TAB and build a view over it. Then, add a column to the table and describe the view. What do you observe? Drop the table and view after you complete the exercise.

```
CREATE TABLE test_tab
   (col1 NUMBER)
```

f) Create a view called BUSY_STUDENT, based on the following query. Update the number of enrollments for STUDENT_ID 124 to five through the BUSY_STUDENT view. Record your observation.

```
SELECT student_id, COUNT(*)
   FROM enrollment
 GROUP BY student_id
HAVING COUNT(*) > 2
```

g) Create a view that lists the addresses of students. Include the columns STUDENT_ID, FIRST_NAME, LAST_NAME, STREET_ADDRESS, CITY, STATE, and ZIP. Using the view, update the last name of STUDENT_ID 237 from Frost to O'Brien. Then update the state for the student from NJ to CT. What do you notice for the statements you issue?

▼ LAB 13.3 EXERCISE **ANSWERS**

a) Create a view called LONG_DISTANCE_STUDENT with all the columns in the STUDENT table plus the CITY and STATE columns from the ZIPCODE table. Exclude students from New York, New Jersey, and Connecticut.

ANSWER: To select all columns from the STUDENT table, use the wildcard symbol. For the columns CITY and STATE in the view, join to the ZIPCODE table. With this view definition, you see only records where the state is not equal to New York, Connecticut, or New Jersey.

```
CREATE OR REPLACE VIEW long_distance_student AS
SELECT s.*, z.city, z.state
   FROM student s, zipcode z
  WHERE s.zip = z.zip
```

```
    AND state NOT IN ('NJ','NY','CT')
```
View created.

You can issue a query against the view or describe the view. You can restrict the columns and/or the rows of the view.

```
SELECT state, first_name, last_name
  FROM long_distance_student
```

ST	FIRST_NAME	LAST_NAME
MA	James E.	Norman
MA	George	Kocka
...		
OH	Phil	Gilloon
MI	Roger	Snow

10 rows selected.

You might want to validate the view by querying for students living in New Jersey.

```
SELECT *
  FROM long_distance_student
 WHERE state = 'NJ'
```

no rows selected

The query finds no students living in New Jersey because the view's defining query excludes those records.

b) Create a view named CHEAP_COURSE that shows all columns of the COURSE table where the course cost is 1095 or less.

ANSWER: Creating a view as follows restricts the rows to courses with a cost of 1095 or less.

```
CREATE OR REPLACE VIEW cheap_course AS
SELECT *
  FROM course
 WHERE cost <= 1095
```

c) Issue the following INSERT statement. What do you observe when you query the CHEAP_COURSE view?

```
INSERT INTO cheap_course
  (course_no, description, cost,
   created_by, created_date, modified_by,
   modified_date)
VALUES
  (900, 'Expensive', 2000,
   'ME', SYSDATE, 'ME', SYSDATE)
```

ANSWER: You can insert records through the view, violating the view's defining query condition.

A cost of 2000 is successfully inserted into the COURSE table through the view, even though this is higher than 1095, which is the defining condition of the view.

You can query CHEAP_VIEW to see if the record is there. The course was successfully inserted in the underlying COURSE base table, but it does not satisfy the view's definition and is not displayed.

```
SELECT course_no, cost
  FROM cheap_course
COURSE_NO      COST
---------  ---------
      135      1095
      230      1095
      240      1095

3 rows selected.
```

A view's WHERE clause works for any query, but not for DML statements. The course number 900 is not visible through the CHEAP_COURSE view, but insert, update, or delete operations are permitted despite the conflicting WHERE condition. To change this security-defying behavior, create the view with the WITH CHECK OPTION constraint. But first undo the INSERT statement with the ROLLBACK command because any subsequent DDL command, such as the creation of a view, automatically commits the record.

```
ROLLBACK
Rollback complete.

CREATE OR REPLACE VIEW cheap_course AS
SELECT *
  FROM course
 WHERE cost <= 1095
WITH CHECK OPTION CONSTRAINT check_cost
View created.
```

It is a good habit to name constraints. You understand the benefit of well-named constraints when you query the Oracle data dictionary or when you violate constraints with data manipulation statements.

The following error message appears when insertions, updates, and deletions issued against a view violate the view's defining query. The previous INSERT statement would now be rejected, with the error ORA-01402 view WITH CHECK OPTION where-clause violation.

What happens if you attempt to insert a record with a value of NULL for the course cost? Again, Oracle rejects the row because the condition is not satisfied. The NULL value is not less than or equal to 1095.

VIEW CONSTRAINTS

You can enforce constraints in a variety of ways: The underlying base tables automatically ensure data integrity, or you can use the WITH CHECK OPTION. You can also avoid any data manipulation on the view by using the READ ONLY syntax option. The following statement creates a read-only view named COURSE_V.

```
CREATE OR REPLACE VIEW course_v AS
SELECT course_no, description,
       created_by, created_date,
       modified_by, modified_date
```

```
      FROM course
      WITH READ ONLY CONSTRAINT course_v_read_check
   View created.
```

d) Drop the views named LONG_DISTANCE_STUDENT and CHEAP_COURSE.

ANSWER: Just like other operations on data objects, the DROP keyword removes a database object from the database.

```
   DROP VIEW long_distance_student
   View dropped.


   DROP VIEW cheap_course
   View dropped.
```

 Remember that any DDL operation, such as the creation of a view, cannot be rolled back, and any prior DML operations, such as inserts, updates, and deletes, are automatically committed.

e) Using the following statement, create a table called TEST_TAB and build a view over it. Then add a column to the table and describe the view. What do you observe? Drop the table and view after you complete the exercise.

```
   CREATE TABLE test_tab
     (col1 NUMBER)
```

ANSWER: The view does not show the newly added column.

```
   CREATE OR REPLACE VIEW test_tab_view AS
   SELECT *
     FROM test_tab
   View created.
```

After the table creation, the view is created. Here, the name TEST_TAB_VIEW is used. Then you add an additional column to the TEST_TAB table; here it is named COL2.

```
   ALTER TABLE test_tab
     ADD (col2 NUMBER)
   Table altered.
```

A subsequently issued DESCRIBE of the view reveals an interesting fact.

```
   SQL> DESC test_tab_view
```

Name	Null?	Type
COL1		NUMBER

Where is the new column that was added? Whenever a view is created with the wildcard (*) character, Oracle stores the individual column names in the definition of the view. When you review the Details tab of the view (see Figure 13.9) in SQL Developer, you see that the view consists only of one column. This is the view's definition at the time of view creation. Note the column is also listed with enclosed quotation marks, just in case of mixed case column names.

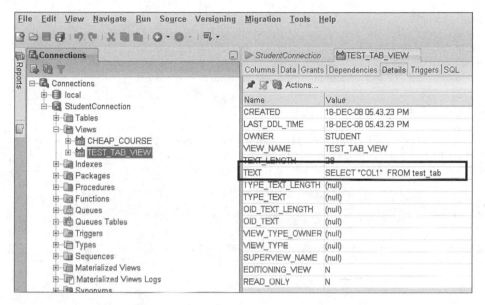

FIGURE 13.9
The TEXT box shows the view's query definition

Alternatively, you can query Oracle's data dictionary view USER_VIEWS.

```
SELECT text
  FROM user_views
 WHERE view_name = 'TEST_TAB_VIEW'
TEXT
------------------------------------------
SELECT "COL1"
  FROM test_tab


1 row selected.
```

You need to reissue the creation of the view statement for the view to include the new column.

```
CREATE OR REPLACE VIEW test_tab_view AS
SELECT *
  FROM test_tab
View created.
```

Now, when a DESCRIBE is issued on the view, the new column is included.

```
SQL> DESC test_tab_view
Name                                 Null?    Type
------------------------------------ -------- ------
COL1                                          NUMBER
COL2                                          NUMBER
```

COMPILING A VIEW

You can use the ALTER VIEW command to define, modify, or drop view constraints. Also, the command ALTER VIEW viewname COMPILE command explicitly compiles the view to make sure it is valid. A view may become invalid if the underlying table is altered or dropped. If you use Oracle 11g, the view remains valid if you modify a column in the base table that's not being used by this view.

DEPENDENCIES TAB

You can see in the Dependencies tab for a given table whether any objects access the table; this helps you assess the impact of changes. Figure 13.10 shows the dependencies of the TEST_TAB table. As you see, TEST_TAB_VIEW depends on this table, and f you click the Dependencies tab for the TEST_TAB_VIEW, you find that the TEST_TAB table is referenced in the view.

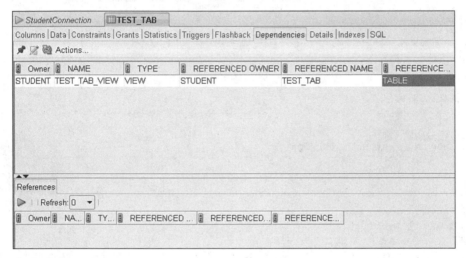

FIGURE 13.10
Dependencies tab

ACCESSING AN INVALID VIEW

When you access an invalid view, Oracle attempts to recompile it automatically. It is useful to explicitly compile to the view, as shown in the next command, to ensure that there are no problems with the view after you make database changes.

```
ALTER VIEW test_tab_view COMPILE
```
View altered.

Drop the no-longer-needed table and notice the effect on the view.

```
DROP TABLE test_tab
```
Table dropped.

```
ALTER VIEW test_tab_view COMPILE
```
Warning: View altered with compilation errors.

Following is an attempt to retrieve data from the invalid view; Oracle returns an error message to the user, indicating that the view exists. However, it is currently invalid because the underlying objects were altered or dropped. Any subsequent attempt to access the view or to compile it returns an error.

```
SELECT *
  FROM test_tab_view
ERROR at line 2:
ORA-04063: view "STUDENT.TEST_TAB_VIEW" has errors
```

Drop the view to restore the STUDENT schema to its previous state.

```
DROP VIEW test_tab_view
View dropped.
```

FORCING THE CREATION OF A VIEW

If a view's base tables do not exist or if the creator of the view doesn't have privileges to access the view, the creation of the view fails. The following example shows the creation of the view named TEST, based on a nonexistent SALES table.

```
CREATE VIEW test AS
SELECT *
  FROM sales
ERROR at line 3:
ORA-00942: table or view does not exist
```

If you want to create the view, despite its being invalid, you can create it with the FORCE option; the default in the CREATE VIEW syntax is NOFORCE. This FORCE option is useful if you need to create the view and you add the referenced table later or if you expect to obtain the necessary privileges to the referenced object shortly.

```
CREATE OR REPLACE FORCE VIEW test AS
SELECT *
  FROM sales
Warning: View created with compilation errors.
```

The view, though invalid, now exists in the database.

f) Create a view called BUSY_STUDENT, based on the following query. Update the number of enrollments for STUDENT_ID 124 to five through the BUSY_STUDENT view. Record your observation.

```
SELECT student_id, COUNT(*)
  FROM enrollment
 GROUP BY student_id
HAVING COUNT(*) > 2
```

ANSWER: The UPDATE operation fails. Data manipulation operations on a view impose a number of restrictions.

To create the view, you need to give the COUNT(*) expression a column alias; otherwise, the following error occurs.

```
ERROR at line 2:
ORA-00998: must name this expression with a column alias
```

```
CREATE OR REPLACE VIEW busy_student AS
SELECT student_id, COUNT(*) enroll_num
  FROM enrollment
 GROUP BY student_id
HAVING COUNT(*) > 2
```
View created.

You can now attempt to update the ENROLLMENT table using the view with the following UPDATE statement.

```
UPDATE busy_student
    SET enroll_num = 5
  WHERE student_id = 124
```
ORA-01732: data manipulation operation not legal on this view

DATA MANIPULATION RULES ON VIEWS

For a view to be updatable, it needs to conform to a number of rules. The view cannot contain any of the following.

- ▶ An expression (for example, TO_DATE(enroll_date))

- ▶ An aggregate function

- ▶ A set operator, such as UNION, UNION ALL, INTERSECT, or MINUS

- ▶ The DISTINCT keyword

- ▶ The GROUP BY clause

- ▶ The ORDER BY clause

Special rules apply to views that contain join conditions, as shown in exercise g.

g) Create a view that lists the addresses of students. Include the columns STUDENT_ID, FIRST_NAME, LAST_NAME, STREET_ADDRESS, CITY, STATE, and ZIP. Using the view, update the last name of STUDENT_ID 237 from Frost to O'Brien. Then update the state for the student from NJ to CT. What do you notice for the statements you issue?

ANSWER: Not all updates to views containing joins are allowed. The update of the last name is successful, but the update of the STATE column is not.

```
CREATE OR REPLACE VIEW student_address AS
SELECT student_id, first_name, last_name,
       street_address, city, state, s.zip szip,
       z.zip zzip
  FROM student s, zipcode z
 WHERE s.zip = z.zip
```
View created.

Now update the last name to O'Brien by using the following statement. To indicate a single quotation mark, prefix it with another quotation mark.

```
UPDATE student_address
   SET last_name = 'O''Brien'
 WHERE student_id = 237
```
1 row updated.

Because the test was successful, roll back the update to retain the current data in the table.

```
ROLLBACK
Rollback complete.
```

You can update the data in the underlying base table STUDENT. Now update the column STATE in the base table ZIPCODE through the STUDENT_ADDRESS view.

```
UPDATE student_address
   SET state = 'CT'
 WHERE student_id = 237
ORA-01779: cannot modify a column which maps to a nonkey-preserved
table
```

JOIN VIEWS AND DATA MANIPULATION

Understanding the concept of key-preserved tables is essential to understanding the restrictions on join views. A table is considered key preserved if every key of the table can also be a key of the result of the join. In this case, the STUDENT table is the key-preserved, or child, table.

For a join view to be updatable, the DML operation may affect only the key-preserved table (also known as the child base table), and the child's primary key must be included in the view's definition. In this case, the child table is the STUDENT table, and the primary key is the STUDENT_ID column.

If you are in doubt regarding which table is the key-preserved table, query the Oracle data dictionary table USER_UPDATABLE_COLUMNS. The result shows you which columns are updatable. Also, the STUDENT table's ZIP column is updatable, but the ZIP column from the ZIPCODE table is not. Only the STUDENT table's ZIP column (aliased as SZIP) is considered key preserved.

```
SELECT column_name, updatable
  FROM user_updatable_columns
 WHERE table_name = 'STUDENT_ADDRESS'
```

COLUMN_NAME	UPD
STUDENT_ID	YES
FIRST_NAME	YES
LAST_NAME	YES
STREET_ADDRESS	YES
CITY	NO
STATE	NO
SZIP	YES
ZZIP	NO

```
8 rows selected.
```

The data dictionary is covered in greater detail in Chapter 14, "The Data Dictionary, Scripting, and Reporting." If you need to manipulate key-preserved data through a view, you overcome this limitation by using an INSTEAD OF trigger. This trigger works only against views and allows you to manipulate data based on the code within the trigger. The INSTEAD OF trigger fires in place of your issued INSERT, UPDATE, or DELETE command against the view. For example, if you execute an INSERT command against the view, the statement may actually perform an UPDATE instead. The view's associated INSTEAD OF trigger code can perform any type of data manipulation against one or multiple tables. You create these powerful INSTEAD OF triggers by using Oracle PL/SQL, as covered in great detail in *Oracle PL/SQL by Example*, 4th Edition, by Benjamin Rosenzweig and Elena Silvestrova Rakhimov (Prentice Hall, 2008).

Lab 13.3 Quiz

In order to test your progress, you should be able to answer the following questions.

1) Views are useful for security, for simplifying the writing of queries, and for hiding data complexity.

   _____ a) True
   _____ b) False

2) Under what circumstances can views become invalid? Select all that apply.

   _____ a) The data type of a column referenced in the view changes.
   _____ b) One of the underlying base tables is dropped.
   _____ c) Views never become invalid; they automatically recompile.

3) Identify the error in the following view definition.

```
CREATE OR REPLACE VIEW my_student
      (studid, slname, szip) AS
SELECT student_id, last_name, zip
  FROM student
 WHERE student_id BETWEEN 100 AND 200
```

   _____ a) Line 1
   _____ b) Line 2
   _____ c) Line 4
   _____ d) Lines 1, 2, and 4
   _____ e) No error

4) An UPDATE to the STATE column in the ZIPCODE table is permitted using the following view.

```
CREATE OR REPLACE VIEW my_zipcode AS
SELECT zip, city, state, created_by,
       created_date, modified_by,
       TO_CHAR(modified_date, 'DD-MON-YYYY') modified_date
  FROM zipcode
```

   _____ a) True
   _____ b) False

5) Views provide security by restricting access to specific rows and/or columns of a table.

   _____ a) True
   _____ b) False

6) A column in a view may have a different name than in the base table.

   _____ a) True
   _____ b) False

ANSWERS APPEAR IN APPENDIX A.

▼ WORKSHOP

The projects in this section are meant to prompt you to utilize all the skills you have acquired through-out this chapter. The answers to these projects can be found at the companion Web site to this book, located at www.oraclesqlbyexample.com.

1) . Who can update the SALARY column through the MY_EMPLOYEE view? Hint: The USER function returns the name of the user who is currently logged in.

```
CREATE OR REPLACE VIEW my_employee AS
SELECT employee_id, employee_name, salary, manager
  FROM employee
 WHERE manager = USER
  WITH CHECK OPTION CONSTRAINT my_employee_ck_manager
```

2) Which columns in a table should you consider indexing?

3) Explain the purpose of the following Oracle SQL command.

```
ALTER INDEX crse_crse_fk_i REBUILD
```

4) Are null values stored in an index? Explain.

CHAPTER 14

The Data Dictionary, Scripting, and Reporting

CHAPTER OBJECTIVES

In this chapter, you will learn about:

▶ The Oracle Data Dictionary Views
▶ Writing SQL Scripts
▶ Creating SQL Developer Reports

The Oracle data dictionary is a set of tables and views that contains data about the database; it is also sometimes referred to as the *catalog*. Oracle uses the data dictionary internally for many purposes (for instance, to determine whether a SQL statement contains valid column and table names, to determine the privileges of an individual user, to check if a column is indexed).

Although the SQL Developer's Details tab displays a lot about an object, you will find it useful to know about and query the wealth of information available in the data dictionary views. What you learn in this chapter about data dictionary views will add significantly to your understanding of Oracle technology and the related database concepts.

In this chapter, you will also learn about SQL Developer's built-in reporting capabilities. SQL Developer provides an extensive list of useful reports and offers the capability to create your own user-defined reports.

This chapter will expand your knowledge of the SQL*Plus and SQL Developer execution environments and their respective scripting and reporting capabilities. You will discover that you can simplify the writing of SQL statements and some database administration tasks by writing SQL scripts that generate and execute other SQL statements.

LAB 14.1
The Oracle Data Dictionary Views

LAB OBJECTIVES

After this lab, you will be able to:

▶ Query the Data Dictionary

The data dictionary has two distinct sets of views: the *static* data dictionary views and the *dynamic* data dictionary views, also referred to as *dynamic performance views,* or *V$TABLES* ("V-dollar tables").

The Static Data Dictionary Views

The static data dictionary stores details about database objects, such as tables, indexes, and views. It also lists information about referential integrity constraints and indexed columns. Whenever a new object is added or an object is changed, data about the object is recorded in the data dictionary.

Most of the static dictionary views begin with the prefix USER_, ALL_, or DBA_. The USER_ views show information belonging to the user querying the data dictionary. For example, when you log in as STUDENT, the views that begin with the USER_ prefix show all the objects belonging to the STUDENT owner. The ALL_ views show the same information, any information granted to the STUDENT user by another user, and any public objects. You'll learn how to grant and receive access rights in Chapter 15, "Security." The DBA_ views show all objects in the entire database, but you need database administrator (DBA) privileges or the SELECT ANY DICTIONARY privilege to be able to query these views.

The Dynamic Data Dictionary Views

The dynamic views begin with V$ and are typically used by a DBA to monitor the system. They are called dynamic because they are continuously updated by the background processes in the Oracle instance but never by the user. Table 14.1 shows the different types of data dictionary views.

TABLE 14.1   Overview of Oracle Data Dictionary Views

PREFIX	PURPOSE
USER_	Objects that belong to the user querying
ALL_	Objects that belong to the user and objects that are accessible to the user
DBA_	All objects in the entire database, accessible only to users with DBA or SELECT ANY DICTIONARY privileges
V$	Dynamic performance views, accessible only to users with DBA privileges or the SELECT ANY DICTIONARY privileges

The Dictionary

The collection of static and dynamic data dictionary tables and views, along with a description of each, is listed in the view called DICTIONARY, also known by the synonym DICT. You can examine the columns of the DICT view by issuing the SQL*Plus DESCRIBE command.

A synonym is another name for a database object; for example, instead of using DICTIONARY, you can use the shorter synonym DICT. You'll learn about synonyms and their use in Chapter 15.

```
SQL> DESC dict
    Name                        Null?      Type
    --------------------        --------   --------------
    TABLE_NAME                             VARCHAR2(30)
    COMMENTS                              VARCHAR2(4000)
```

The column TABLE_NAME contains the name of the individual data dictionary view accessible to you, together with a brief description in the COMMENTS column.

For example, to find information about sequences in the database, you can query the DICT view. The column TABLE_NAME stores the names of the data dictionary views, in uppercase. The following query results in the selection of all data dictionary views with the letters SEQ in their name.

```
SELECT table_name, comments
  FROM dict
  WHERE table_name LIKE '%SEQ%'
TABLE_NAME        COMMENTS
---------------   -------------------------------------------------
ALL_SEQUENCES     Description of SEQUENCEs accessible to the user
DBA_SEQUENCES     Description of all SEQUENCEs in the database
USER_SEQUENCES    Description of the user's own SEQUENCEs
SEQ               Synonym for USER_SEQUENCES

4 rows selected.
```

Four different data dictionary views contain information about sequences.

 If you do not have DBA access or the SELECT ANY DICTIONARY privileges, you cannot see the DBA_SEQUENCES view.

To display the columns of the ALL_SEQUENCES data dictionary view, issue the DESCRIBE command at the SQL*Plus prompt.

```
SQL> DESC ALL_SEQUENCES
Name                                 Null?     Type
---------------------------------    --------  ----------
SEQUENCE_OWNER                       NOT NULL  VARCHAR2(30)
SEQUENCE_NAME                        NOT NULL  VARCHAR2(30)
MIN_VALUE                                      NUMBER
MAX_VALUE                                      NUMBER
INCREMENT_BY                         NOT NULL  NUMBER
CYCLE_FLAG                                     VARCHAR2(1)
ORDER_FLAG                                     VARCHAR2(1)
CACHE_SIZE                           NOT NULL  NUMBER
LAST_NUMBER                          NOT NULL  NUMBER
```

If you are unclear about the meanings of the different columns, you can query yet another view, named DICT_COLUMNS. It provides a definition for each column.

```
SELECT column_name, comments
  FROM dict_columns
 WHERE table_name = 'ALL_SEQUENCES'
COLUMN_NAME      COMMENTS
---------------  -------------------------------------
SEQUENCE_OWNER   Name of the owner of the sequence
SEQUENCE_NAME    SEQUENCE name
MIN_VALUE        Minimum value of the sequence
...
CACHE_SIZE       Number of sequence numbers to cache
LAST_NUMBER      Last sequence number written to disk

9 rows selected.
```

To find out which individual sequences are in the STUDENT schema, query the view.

```
SELECT sequence_name
  FROM seq
SEQUENCE_NAME
-------------------------------
COURSE_NO_SEQ
INSTRUCTOR_ID_SEQ
SECTION_ID_SEQ
STUDENT_ID_SEQ

4 rows selected.
```

The SQL Developer Details Tab

The information displayed in the ALL_SEQUENCES view is very similar to the information shown in the Details tab in SQL Developer (see Figure 14.1). The source of the first two values is the ALL_OBJECTS data dictionary, which records when an object was first created and the date any DDL modifications last occurred.

The Details tab provides easy and quick access to the relevant data dictionary views, without requiring you to remember the view names or write any queries. A simple mouse click on the tab displays the desired information.

StudentConnection	COURSE_NO_SEQ
Details Dependencies SQL	
Actions...	

Name	Value
CREATED	21-DEC-08
LAST_DDL_TIME	21-DEC-08
SEQUENCE_OWNER	STUDENT
SEQUENCE_NAME	COURSE_NO_SEQ
MIN_VALUE	1
MAX_VALUE	999999999999999999999999999
INCREMENT_BY	1
CYCLE_FLAG	N
ORDER_FLAG	N
CACHE_SIZE	0
LAST_NUMBER	452

Figure 14.1
SQL Developer's Details tab

 SQL Developer offers many useful data dictionary reports that provide detailed information about the database. You will learn about these reports in Lab 14.2.

▼ LAB 14.1 EXERCISES

If you have performed most of the exercises in the previous chapters, your results will differ from the results shown in the outputs of this chapter as you have added new objects and altered existing objects in the STUDENT schema. To bring the STUDENT schema back to its original state, run the rebuildStudent.sql script. This script drops the STUDENT account-related tables, re-creates the tables, and reloads the data. If you added the supplemental tables mentioned in the previous chapters, you can drop them by using the sql_book_drop_extra_tables.sql script. (These scripts are part of the downloaded scripts you used when you first created the STUDENT user.)

To run the script within SQL Developer, open the file. All buttons are grayed out. To execute the script, click the Run Script icon (or press F5) to execute the script. After you select a database connection, the result will show in the Script Output tab, on the bottom of the screen.

a) For the USER_OBJECTS view, what information is stored in the columns CREATED, LAST_DDL_TIME, and STATUS?

b) Which data dictionary view lists only tables in the STUDENT schema?

c) Query the data dictionary view USER_TAB_COLUMNS for the GRADE table and describe the information in the columns DATA_TYPE, DATA_LENGTH, NULLABLE, and DATA_DEFAULT.

d) Show a list of all indexes and their columns for the ENROLLMENT table.

e) Write a query that displays a list of all the sequences in the STUDENT schema and the current value of each.

f) Execute the following two SQL statements. The first statement creates a view, and the second queries the data dictionary view called USER_VIEWS. What information is stored in the TEXT column of USER_VIEWS? Drop the view after you answer these questions.

```
CREATE OR REPLACE VIEW my_test AS
SELECT first_name, instructor_id
   FROM instructor


SELECT view_name, text
   FROM user_views
 WHERE view_name = 'MY_TEST'
```

g) Execute the following query. What do you observe?

```
SELECT constraint_name, table_name, constraint_type
   FROM user_constraints
```

h) What columns are listed in the data dictionary view USER_CONS_COLUMNS?

i) Execute the following SQL statement. Describe the result.

```
SELECT username
   FROM all_users
```

j) Execute the following query. What do you observe about the result?

```
SELECT segment_name, segment_type, bytes/1024
   FROM user_segments
 WHERE segment_name = 'ZIPCODE'
   AND segment_type = 'TABLE'
```

▼ LAB 14.1 EXERCISE ANSWERS

a) For the USER_OBJECTS view, what information is stored in the columns CREATED, LAST_DDL_TIME, and STATUS?

ANSWER: The CREATED column shows the creation date of an object. The LAST_DDL_TIME column indicates when an object was last modified via a DDL command, such as when a column was added to a table or when a view was recompiled. The STATUS column displays whether an object is valid or invalid.

The resulting output may vary, depending on the objects in your schema.

```
SELECT object_name, created, last_ddl_time, status
   FROM user_objects
```

```
OBJECT_NAME            CREATED     LAST_DDL_ STATU
--------------------   ---------   --------- -----
COURSE                 14-AUG-08   23-OCT-08 VALID
...
ZIP_PK                 14-AUG-08   14-AUG-08 VALID

36 rows selected.
```

A view may become invalid if the underlying table is modified or dropped. Other objects, such as PL/SQL procedures, packages, or functions, may become invalid if dependent objects are modified and they subsequently need to be recompiled.

If you are unclear about the meaning of a particular column, refer to the DICT_COLUMNS view for information.

```
SELECT column_name, comments
  FROM dict_columns
 WHERE table_name = 'USER_OBJECTS'
   AND column_name IN ('STATUS', 'LAST_DDL_TIME',
                       'CREATED')
COLUMN_NAME          COMMENTS
------------------   -------------------------------------------
CREATED              Timestamp for the creation of the object
LAST_DDL_TIME        Timestamp for the last DDL change (including
                     GRANT and REVOKE) to the object
STATUS               Status of the object

3 rows selected.
```

b) Which data dictionary view lists only tables in the STUDENT schema?

ANSWER: You can find out which data dictionary table contains this information by querying the DICT view. The view is USER_TABLES.

```
SELECT table_name
  FROM user_tables
TABLE_NAME
------------------
COURSE
...
ZIPCODE

10 rows selected.
```

c) Query the data dictionary view USER_TAB_COLUMNS for the GRADE table and describe the information in the columns DATA_TYPE, DATA_LENGTH, NULLABLE, and DATA_DEFAULT.

ANSWER: The column DATA_TYPE shows the data type of the column, DATA_LENGTH displays the length of the column in bytes, and there is either a Y or an N in the column NULLABLE, indicating whether NULL values are allowed in the column. The column DATA_DEFAULT represents the default value for the column, if any.

```
SELECT table_name, column_name, data_type, data_length,
       nullable, data_default
```

```
    FROM user_tab_columns
   WHERE table_name = 'GRADE'
TABLE_NA COLUMN_NAME        DATA_TYP DATA_LENGTH N DATA_
-------- ----------------   -------- ----------- - -----
GRADE    STUDENT_ID         NUMBER            22 N
...
GRADE    NUMERIC_GRADE      NUMBER            22 N 0
...
GRADE    MODIFIED_BY        VARCHAR2          30 N
GRADE    MODIFIED_DATE      DATE               7 N

10 rows selected.
```

Note the zero value in the last column, named DATA_DEFAULT. This means the column called NUMERIC_GRADE has a column default value of zero. This value is inserted into a table's row if the NUMERIC_GRADE column is not specified during an INSERT operation. For example, the following INSERT statement does not list the NUMERIC_GRADE column and, therefore, the NUMERIC_GRADE column is zero; alternatively, you can use the DEFAULT keyword discussed in Chapter 11, "Insert, Update, and Delete."

```
INSERT INTO GRADE
   (student_id, section_id, grade_type_code,
    grade_code_occurrence,
    created_by, created_date,
    modified_by, modified_date)
VALUES
   (102, 89, 'FI',
    2,
    'ARISCHERT', SYSDATE,
    'ARISCHERT', SYSDATE)
1 row created.
```

d) Show a list of all indexes and their columns for the ENROLLMENT table.

Answer: The data dictionary view USER_IND_COLUMNS lists the desired result.

```
SELECT index_name, table_name, column_name,
       column_position
  FROM user_ind_columns
 WHERE table_name = 'ENROLLMENT'
 ORDER BY 1, 4
INDEX_NAME        TABLE_NAME COLUMN_NAM COLUMN_POSITION
---------------   ---------- ---------- ---------------
ENR_PK            ENROLLMENT STUDENT_ID               1
ENR_PK            ENROLLMENT SECTION_ID               2
ENR_SECT_FK_I     ENROLLMENT SECTION_ID               1

3 rows selected.
```

The ENROLLMENT table has two indexes: ENR_PK and ENR_SECT_FK_I. The first index, a unique index created by the primary key constraint, has the columns STUDENT_ID and SECTION_ID, in that order. COLUMN_POSITION shows the order of the columns within the index. The second index is the foreign key column SECTION_ID.

If you want to show just the listing of indexes, without the individual indexed column, you can query USER_INDEXES. This view also indicates whether an index is unique.

You can find details about function-based indexes listed in the USER_IND_EXPRESSIONS view.

e) Write a query that displays a list of all the sequences in the STUDENT schema and the current value of each.

ANSWER: The USER_SEQUENCES data dictionary view shows the sequence name and the current value of the sequence. The resulting output may vary, depending on the sequences in your schema.

```
SELECT sequence_name, last_number
  FROM user_sequences
```

SEQUENCE_NAME	LAST_NUMBER
COURSE_NO_SEQ	451
INSTRUCTOR_ID_SEQ	111
SECTION_ID_SEQ	157
STUDENT_ID_SEQ	400

```
4 rows selected.
```

f) Execute the following two SQL statements. The first statement creates a view, and the second queries the data dictionary view called USER_VIEWS. What information is stored in the TEXT column of USER_VIEWS? Drop the view after you answer these questions.

```
CREATE OR REPLACE VIEW my_test AS
SELECT first_name, instructor_id
  FROM instructor

SELECT view_name, text
  FROM user_views
 WHERE view_name = 'MY_TEST'
```

ANSWER: The TEXT column of the USER_VIEWS data dictionary view stores the view's defining SQL statement.

VIEW_NAME	TEXT
MY_TEST	SELECT first_name, instructor_id FROM instructor

```
1 row selected.
```

From Chapter 13, "Indexes, Sequences, and Views," recall the definition of a view as a stored query. The query is stored in the column named TEXT of USER_VIEWS.

OBJECT DEPENDENCIES

An object, such as a view, synonym, procedure, function, or package, may depend on other objects. For example, the view MY_TEST depends on the INSTRUCTOR table. You can find out about these dependencies in the USER_DEPENDENCIES view. The query shows that this object is a view and that it references the INSTRUCTOR table. While this is easy to determine with a simple view, some objects are more complicated, and querying this view helps identify the effect of any potential change.

```
SELECT name, type, referenced_name
  FROM user_dependencies
 WHERE name = 'MY_TEST'
NAME          TYPE          REFERENCED_NAME
----------    ------------  --------------------
MY_TEST       VIEW          INSTRUCTOR

1 row selected.
```

SQL Developer displays this information as part of the Dependencies tab, discussed in Chapter 13.

You drop the MY_TEST view by using the DROP VIEW command.

```
DROP VIEW my_test
View dropped.
```

g) Execute the following query. What do you observe?

```
SELECT constraint_name, table_name, constraint_type
  FROM user_constraints
```

ANSWER: The output shows the constraints on the various tables. The foreign key constraint is listed as constraint type R (for referential integrity constraint), the NOT NULL and CHECK constraints are shown as constraint type C, and the primary key constraints are displayed as constraint type P. The SECTION table has a unique constraint listed as constraint type U.

```
CONSTRAINT_NAME                     TABLE_NAME C
----------------------------------  ---------- -
CRSE_CRSE_FK                        COURSE     R
...
SYS_C001441                         GRADE      C
ENR_STU_FK                          ENROLLMENT R
...
SECT_SECT2_UK                       SECTION    U
...
ZIP_PK                              ZIPCODE    P
...
ZIP_MODIFIED_BY_NNULL               ZIPCODE    C

94 rows selected.
```

Any constraint that is not explicitly named receives a system-assigned name (for example, SYS_C001441).

The USER_CONSTRAINTS view contains additional useful columns, particularly for referential integrity constraints. For example, query the view for the foreign key constraint called ENR_STU_FK. The next following result shows the name of the primary key constraint in the R_CONSTRAINT_NAME column. This constraint is referenced by the foreign key.

```
SELECT r_owner, r_constraint_name, delete_rule
  FROM user_constraints
 WHERE constraint_name = 'ENR_STU_FK'
```

R_OWNER	R_CONSTRAINT_NAME	DELETE_RU
STUDENT	STU_PK	NO ACTION

```
1 row selected.
```

You can see in the result that the delete rule on the ENR_STU_FK constraint specifies NO ACTION, which means any deletion of a student row (parent record) is restricted if dependent enrollment rows (child records with the same STUDENT_ID) exist. This is in contrast to a CASCADE, which means that if a parent record is deleted, the children are automatically deleted. If the referential integrity constraint is ON DELETE SET NULL, you would see the value SET NULL in the DELETE_RULE column.

The referential integrity constraints prevent the creation of orphan rows (that is, enrollment records without corresponding students). Also, the parent table may not be dropped unless the foreign key constraint is dropped. To disable constraints, use the ALTER TABLE command. Alternatively, the parent table may be dropped using the DROP TABLE command with the CASCADE CONSTRAINTS clause, automatically dropping the foreign key constraints.

You can retrieve constraint information for an individual table by using the Constraints tab in SQL Developer (see Figure 14.2).

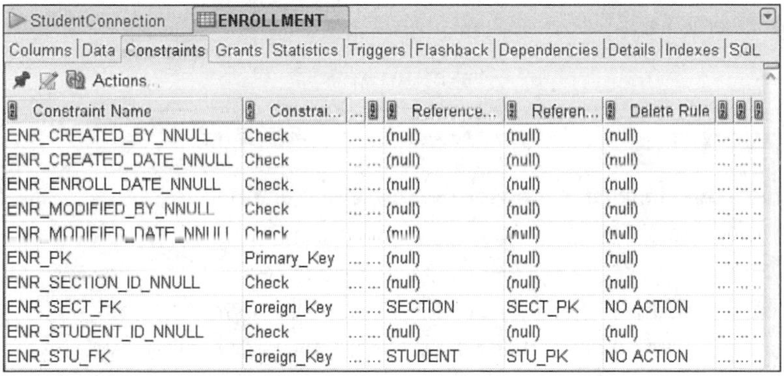

FIGURE 14.2
The Constraints tab in SQL Developer

OTHER CONSTRAINT TYPES

Table 14.2 lists the constraint types. In addition to the constraint types already mentioned in this chapter, it lists the view constraint with check option (V) and the view constraint with the read-only option (O).

TABLE 14.2   Constraint Types

CONSTRAINT TYPE	DESCRIPTION
R	Referential integrity constraint
C	Check constraint, including NOT NULL constraint
P	Primary key constraint
U	Unique constraint
V	View constraint with check option
O	View constraint with read-only option

DISTINGUISHING NOT NULL CONSTRAINTS FROM CHECK CONSTRAINTS

The NOT NULL constraint is listed as a check constraint, and you can distinguish this type from other user-defined check constraints by looking at the SEARCH_CONDITION column. The following query shows the constraints of the GRADE_TYPE table. For example, the NOT NULL constraint called GRTYP_DESCRIPTION_NNULL on the DESCRIPTION column lists the NOT NULL column, with the column name in quotes (in case of case-sensitive column names), together with the words IS NOT NULL. Compare this to the check constraint GRTYP_GRADE_TYPE_CODE_LENGTH, which checks whether the length of the GRADE_TYPE_CODE column is exactly 2.

```
SELECT constraint_name, search_condition
  FROM user_constraints
 WHERE constraint_type = 'C'
   AND table_name = 'GRADE_TYPE'
CONSTRAINT_NAME                  SEARCH_CONDITION
------------------------------   ------------------------------
GRTYP_DESCRIPTION_NNULL          "DESCRIPTION" IS NOT NULL
...
GRTYP_GRADE_TYPE_CODE_LENGTH     LENGTH(grade_type_code)=2

7 rows selected.
```

h) What columns are listed in the data dictionary view USER_CONS_COLUMNS?

ANSWER: The columns are OWNER, CONSTRAINT_NAME, TABLE_NAME, COLUMN_NAME, and POSITION.

This data dictionary view shows the columns referenced in the constraint. A query against the view illustrates this on the example of the primary key constraint ENR_PK, which consists of the two columns STUDENT_ID and SECTION_ID.

```
SELECT constraint_name, column_name, position
  FROM user_cons_columns
 WHERE constraint_name = 'ENR_PK'
CONSTRAINT_NAME       COLUMN_NAME             POSITION
--------------------  --------------------  ----------
ENR_PK                STUDENT_ID                     1
ENR_PK                SECTION_ID                     2

2 rows selected.
```

i) Execute the following SQL statement. Describe the result.

```
SELECT username
  FROM all_users
```

ANSWER: It shows a list of all the users in the database. The resulting output may vary, depending on your database.

```
USERNAME
-------------------------
SYS
SYSTEM
...
SCOTT
...
STUDENT

15 rows selected.
```

Note that in this example output, there are two users, named SYS and SYSTEM. The SYS user is the owner of the Oracle data dictionary. Never log in as this "super user" unless you are an experienced Oracle DBA or unless Oracle instructs you to do so. Otherwise, you might inadvertently perform actions that could adversely affect the database. The SYSTEM user has DBA privileges but does not own the data dictionary. You will learn more about these two user accounts in Chapter 15.

Another useful view is the USER_USERS view. Following is a query that displays information about the current user or schema. It shows your login name and the name of the default tablespace on which any tables or indexes you create are stored, unless you explicitly specify another tablespace. It also shows when your account was created.

```
SELECT username, default_tablespace, created
  FROM user_users
```

USERNAME	DEFAULT_TABLESPACE	CREATED
STUDENT	USERS	04-MAY-08

```
1 row selected.
```

j) Execute the following query. What do you observe about the result?

```
SELECT segment_name, segment_type, bytes/1024
  FROM user_segments
 WHERE segment_name = 'ZIPCODE'
   AND segment_type = 'TABLE'
```

ANSWER: The query displays the size of the ZIPCODE table.

SEGMENT_NA	SEGMENT_TYPE	BYTES/1024
ZIPCODE	TABLE	64

```
1 row selected.
```

The most common segment types are tables and indexes. The USER_SEGMENT view shows the storage, in bytes, for a particular segment. Dividing the bytes by 1024 displays the size in kilobytes (K). Your actual number of bytes may vary from the figure listed here, depending on the storage parameter chosen for the default tablespace in your individual user account.

To see a list of the different available tablespaces, you query the USER_TABLESPACES or DBA_TABLESPACES view. You get a result similar to the following.

```
SELECT tablespace_name
  FROM user_tablespaces
 ORDER BY tablespace_name
TABLESPACE_NAME
------------------------------
INDX
SYSTEM
TEMP
USERS

4 rows selected.
```

To find out how much space is available in total on each of the tablespaces, you write a SQL statement against the view USER_FREE_SPACE. The result shows you the available megabytes (MB) for each tablespace. To learn more about tablespace and space management topics, see the *Oracle Database Administrator's Guide*.

```
SELECT tablespace_name, SUM(bytes)/1024/1024
  FROM user_free_space
 GROUP BY tablespace_name
TABLESPACE_NAME                  SUM(BYTES)/1024/1024
------------------------------  --------------------
INDX                                         24.8125
SYSTEM                                     14.6796875
USERS                                        82.8125

3 rows selected.
```

Lab 14.1 Quiz

In order to test your progress, you should be able to answer the following questions.

1) The data dictionary contains data about the database.

_____ a) True
_____ b) False

2) The data dictionary view USER_OBJECTS stores information about tables, indexes, and sequences.

_____ a) True
_____ b) False

3) The dynamic data dictionary views are updated only by the Oracle database.

_____ a) True
b) False

4) The ALL_TABLES data dictionary view shows all the tables in the entire database.

_____ a) True
_____ b) False

5) The OBJ view is a public synonym for the USER_OBJECTS view.

_____ a) True
_____ b) False

ANSWERS APPEAR IN APPENDIX A.

LAB 14.2
Scripting and Reporting

LAB OBJECTIVES

After this lab, you will be able to:

▶ Write and Execute Scripts
▶ Develop Interactive SQL Statements and Reports

So far, you have written and executed many SQL statements. This lab shows you how you can collect SQL statements and SQL*Plus commands into a script file for execution. You will find it useful to write SQL statements that allow user input and execute commands that create and execute other SQL statements.

In Lab 14.1, you learned about the many available data dictionary views. This knowledge will help you understand and appreciate SQL Developer's supplied data dictionary reports and help you write your own SQL Developer reports.

This lab contains many references specific to either SQL*Plus or SQL Developer. There are sometimes different ways to obtain the solution with either of the tools. As mentioned at the beginning of the book, it is useful to know how to use both tools. SQL Developer is a very useful productivity tool, but you cannot erase decades' worth of currently used SQL*Plus scripts and functionality. Furthermore, SQL*Plus continues to be the tool of choice for executing scripts from an operating system prompt.

What Is a Script?

Before you implement database changes to the production environment, you will develop the DDL and DML and then test the changes in a development environment. Then you need to perform the same changes again in the QA environment and finally in the production environment.

A *script* is essentially a collection of statements to be executed. Typically, scripts are tested and modified multiple times due to changes, retests, preproduction dry runs, and so on. To ensure that you will not miss any of the SQL commands, it is useful to collect these statements in a script. Scripting the statements ensures that the same commands can be executed repeatedly and in the same sequence.

When you created the objects in the STUDENT schema, you executed a script containing the DDL statements to create tables, indexes, sequences, and constraints together with the DML statements to insert the data. This script also contains SELECT statements to validate the number of inserted rows.

A script is useful if you need to run a set of SQL statements at specific time periods or on an ad hoc basis. Rather than retype and remember the same statements, you can execute the script to perform the task.

A script can contains variables that allow for user input prompts or different runtime parameters.

Executing a Script in SQL Developer

To execute a script, you need to load the SQL statements into the SQL Statement box. To do so, you select File, Open menu and choose the appropriate file name. After the statements are displayed in the SQL worksheet, you click the Run Script icon (or press the F5 key) to execute the statements. Each SQL statement must end with a semicolon or a backslash on a separate line.

Figure 14.3 shows the Run Script icon on the top of the screen and the result of the script execution in the Script Output tab. The my_script.sql script shown is a simple script consisting of two SELECT statements and a CREATE TABLE statement.

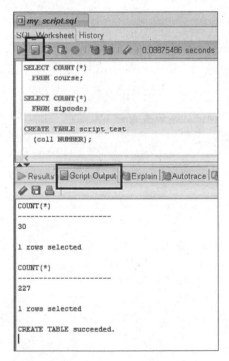

FIGURE 14.3
Run Script icon and Script Output tab

USING THE START @ COMMAND

Instead of selecting File, Open to retrieve the file and then executing the script, you can use the SQL*Plus @ or START command, as discussed in Chapter 2, "SQL: The Basics." You can use this command not only from a SQL*Plus prompt but also within SQL Developer. The @ or START command runs the script. Figure 14.4 displays the use of the command in SQL Developer, along with the result. You need to include the file extension only if it is something other than .sql.

The Run Script functionality in SQL Developer executes many of the SQL*Plus commands. If a command is not supported, SQL Developer ignores the command and displays a warning message. For a list of supported SQL*Plus commands for use in SQL Developer, refer to Appendix C, "SQL*Plus Command Reference."

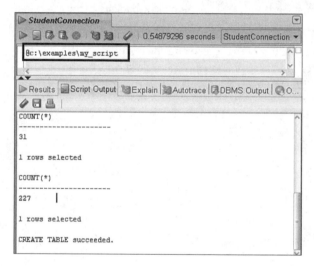

FIGURE 14.4
Using the SQL*Plus @ or START command in SQL Developer

If you don't want to enter a directory path, you can set up a default directory in SQL Developer (see Figure 14.5). Then you can run the script as @my_script, and SQL Developer will find the file in the default directory.

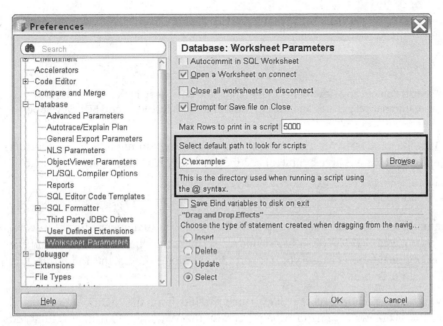

FIGURE 14.5
Default path for scripts In SQL Developer

RUNNING MULTIPLE SQL STATEMENTS

The Run Script icon is useful not only for scripts that are saved in files but also for multiple statements listed in the SQL Worksheet. When you click the Execute Statement icon (or press F9), only the statement on which the cursor resides or the highlighted text is executed. If you run the statements with the Run Scripts icon (or press F5), all statements in the SQL Worksheet are executed.

The result of the Run Script icon appears in the Script Output tab, which is not graphical but emulates SQL*Plus as much as possible.

Running a Script in SQL*Plus

You can run a script from the SQL*Plus prompt as follows.

```
SQL>@c:\examples\myfile
```

Alternatively, you can evoke the script from the operating system prompt, as shown next.

```
sqlplus student/learn @c:\examples\myfile
```

The following is the content of the myfile.sql script. It simply counts the number of courses. The file contains an EXIT command that causes SQL*Plus to return to the operating system after the script finishes executing. (In SQL Developer, the EXIT command does not end the program.)

```
SELECT COUNT(*)
  FROM course;
EXIT
```

 If your scripts contain any statements that manipulate data, keep in mind that the EXIT command automatically issues an implicit COMMIT in both SQL*Plus and SQL Developer.

If you need to run the same script or a series of scripts repeatedly, you might want to consider writing a batch file. Following is an example of a Windows batch file called daily_batch.bat.

```
REM This is the batch file for the myfile script
sqlplus student/learn @c:\examples\myfile
```

The REM command in the first line is a remark or comment statement. In the second line, SQL*Plus is invoked together with the myfile.sql script. The full path for the script file (c:\examples\) is optional here because you are already executing this in the same directory where the myfile.sql file is located.

Figure 14.6 shows the execution of the daily_batch.bat file from the Windows command prompt. (To see the Windows command prompt, choose the Windows Start menu, Run and then enter CMD.)

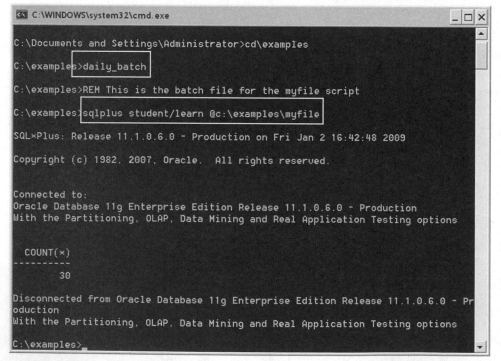

FIGURE 14.6
Run of a batch file invoking SQL*Plus

You can substitute the username, password, and connect string with operating system variables for additional flexibility. Consult your operating system manual regarding the creation of operating system variables.

Substitution Variables

If you find yourself executing a similar SQL statement over and over again, you can write your statement using substitution variables. In this case, part of the SQL statement is replaced with a variable. When the statement is executed in either SQL Developer or SQL*Plus, you supply the appropriate value for the variable. The substitution variable is prefixed with an arbitrary variable name and an ampersand (&) symbol. When you execute the statement, SQL Developer or SQL*Plus prompts you for a value, and the supplied value is assigned to the variable.

For example, the variable in the following statement is named v_course_no.

```
SELECT course_no, description
  FROM course
 WHERE course_no = &v_course_no
```

SUBSTITUTION VARIABLES IN SQL DEVELOPER

The prompt you see in SQL Developer looks similar to Figure 14.7.

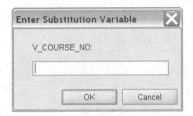

FIGURE 14.7
Substitution variable prompt in SQL Developer

If you enter the value 240 and click OK, this value will be assigned to the variable v_course_no during execution.

SUBSTITUTION VARIABLES IN SQL*PLUS

If you use the command-line version of SQL*Plus, your prompt looks as follows.

```
SQL> SELECT course_no, description
  2    FROM course
  3   WHERE course_no = &v_course_no
  4  /
Enter value for v_course_no: 240
old   3:  WHERE course_no = &v_course_no
new   3:  WHERE course_no = 240
```

```
COURSE_NO DESCRIPTION
---------- ------------------------------------
       240 Intro to the BASIC Language

1 row selected.
```

The text displayed after the substitution variable prompt shows the value before (old) and after the substitution of the value (new). The number 3 indicates that the substitution variable is found on line 3 of the SQL statement. You can change this default behavior with the SET VERIFY OFF SQL*Plus command, and SQL*Plus will no longer display the old and new values.

If you want to re-execute the statement in the buffer, use the forward slash (/), and you are prompted for a value for the v_course_no substitution variable each time.

USING SUBSTITUTION VARIABLES

You can use a substitution variable in any SQL statement executed within the SQL Developer and SQL*Plus environments. Substitution variables are not limited to the WHERE clause of a statement. You can also use them in the ORDER BY clause or the FROM clause to substitute a table name, you can use them in individual column expressions, or you can even substitute an entire WHERE clause.

SUPPRESSING THE USE OF SUBSTITUTION VARIABLES

There are times when you want the ampersand to be a literal ampersand rather than an indicator that a substitution variable follows. The following example illustrates this scenario.

```
UPDATE student
   SET employer = 'Soehner & Peter'
 WHERE student_id = 135
Enter value for peter:
```

SQL*Plus and SQL Developer think you want to use a substitution parameter rather than the literal ampersand. To remedy this, use the SET DEFINE command to turn the use of substitution parameters on or off.

```
SET DEFINE OFF
UPDATE student
   SET employer = 'Soehner & Peter'
 WHERE student_id = 135
1 row updated.
SET DEFINE ON
```

Issue a ROLLBACK command to undo the change of employer and set it back to the original value.

```
ROLLBACK
Rollback complete.
```

Running a Script with a Parameter in SQL*Plus

The s_query.sql file contains the following SQL statement. Like all other SQL statements in scripts, every statement must end with a semicolon or a forward slash on a separate line. Only SQL*Plus commands do not require a semicolon.

```
SET VERIFY OFF
SELECT last_name, student_id
  FROM student
 WHERE last_name like '&1'||'%'
   AND student_id > &2;
EXIT
```

You can pass parameters (arguments) from the operating system when running a script file in SQL*Plus. This works only if your substitution variable is a numeral from 1 through 9. The &1 parameter is substituted with the first parameter passed. If you include another parameter, such as &2, you can pass a second argument, and so on.

This functionality is most useful when executed from an operating system command prompt, as shown in Figure 14.8. Here the first parameter consists of 'Ta' followed by the number 250. Therefore, any students with a last name that begins with the letters Ta and a STUDENT_ID greater than 250 are displayed.

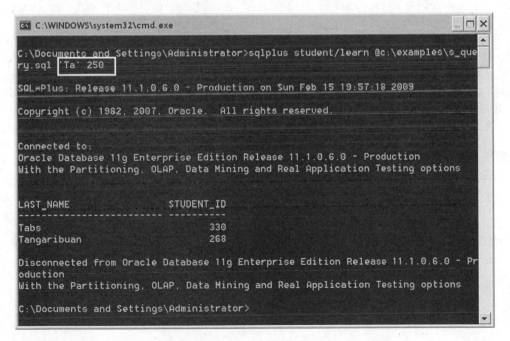

FIGURE 14.8
Running a SQL*Plus script with script arguments

Common SQL*Plus Commands

The SQL*Plus commands within a script change the settings of the SQL*Plus environment. Following are some of the commonly used SQL*Plus commands. Many of these SQL*Plus commands are listed in Appendix C, and you will see them used in the lab exercises.

SPOOL

The SPOOL command, together with a file name, spools any subsequently issued SQL*Plus or SQL command to a file. The following example creates a file named temp.lst. If a file with the same name already exists, it is overwritten without warning, unless you use the CREATE syntax option. You can also optionally append a file with the APPEND syntax option.

```
SPOOL temp.lst CREATE
```

To show the name of the file you are currently spooling to, use the SPOOL command.

```
SPOOL
currently spooling to temp.lst
```

To end the spooling and close the file, enter the following command:

```
SPOOL OFF
```

Just as with other file names, you can add a path to store the file in a directory other than your SQL*Plus default directory.

PAGESIZE

The SQL*Plus default value for PAGESIZE is 14; when you use the default, you repeat the heading every 14 lines. The PAGESIZE 0 command suppresses the column headings. If you want just the first row to have a column heading, set it to a large number, such as 50,000, the largest possible setting.

FEEDBACK

The FEEDBACK command returns the number of records returned by a query. If you are spooling to a file, you may not want to see this value. To suppress the feedback, issue either the command SET FEEDBACK 0 or SET FEEDBACK OFF.

TERMOUT

The SET TERMOUT OFF or SET TERM OFF command controls the display of output generated by the commands. The OFF setting suppresses the output from the screen only when the command is executed from a script file.

LINESIZE

The SET LINESIZE command determines the total number of characters SQL*Plus displays in one line before beginning a new line. Setting it to 80 makes it easy to read the spooled output in a text editor.

SHOW ALL

To see the current settings of all SQL*Plus settings, use the SHOW ALL command.

Generating HTML Reports in SQL*Plus

You can generate reports in SQL*Plus by using various SQL*Plus formatting commands. These reports are formatted as plain text and fixed-character-length format. For a more formatted look, SQL*Plus allows you to generate HTML pages. The file called c:\examples\s_lname_rep.sql contains the following statements.

```
SET ECHO OFF
SET TERM OFF
SET FEEDBACK OFF
SET PAGESIZE 50000
SPOOL C:\examples\s_lname_result.HTML
SET MARKUP HTML ON SPOOL ON
SELECT last_name, first_name, student_id
  FROM student
 WHERE last_name like 'R%'
 ORDER BY 1, 2;
SPOOL OFF
EXIT
```

The various SQL*Plus commands at the beginning of the script define the SQL*Plus environment settings. The SET ECHO OFF command prevents the display of each command in the script. The SET TERM OFF command prevents the display of output generated by the commands. The FEEDBACK OFF command avoids returning the number of records returned by a query.

The PAGESIZE command shows only one header at the beginning of the output. The script spools the result into the file s_lname_result.HTML in the c:\examples directory. The SET MARKUP HTML ON SPOOL ON command creates the tags for HTML format. The SQL statement shows students with a last name starting with the letter R. The SPOOL OFF command closes the file, and the EXIT command exits SQL*Plus and returns you to the operating system command prompt.

The result of this script produces an HTML file that looks similar to Figure 14.9 when opened in a Web browser.

LAST_NAME	FIRST_NAME	STUDENT_ID
Radicola	Pierre	123
Ramesh	Simon	179
Reed	James	133
Reyes	Deborah	189
Roberts	Bharat	243
Robichaud	Barbara	212
Robles	Brian	290
Rosenberg	Rawan	361
Ross	George	275
Rothstein	Adele	265
Runyan	Jeff	128

FIGURE 14.9
HTML output from a SQL*Plus report

Generating Dynamic SQL

Dynamic SQL allows you to build SQL commands at runtime. Dynamic SQL is often executed in Oracle's PL/SQL, but it can also be generated and executed in SQL*Plus, using SQL*Plus scripts. These scripts are often referred to as *SQL to generate SQL scripts* or *master/slave scripts*. By using SQL*Plus, you can automatically generate SQL statements and spool them to a file for use.

For example, say that you made some database changes to tables, causing other database objects, such as views, to become invalid. To compile the views, you can repeatedly type the ALTER VIEW command for each invalid view, or you can wait for the user to access the views and let Oracle compile them. However, it is best to compile them after the table changes to make sure there are no errors. You can do this by writing a script to generate the ALTER VIEW state-ment for each invalid view. The following SQL statement generates the required SQL.

```
SELECT 'ALTER VIEW '|| object_name || ' COMPILE;'
  FROM user_objects
 WHERE object_type = 'VIEW'
   AND status <> 'VALID'
```

If you have any invalid views, your result might look as follows.

```
'ALTERVIEW'||OBJECT_NAME||'COMPILE;'
--------------------------------------
ALTER VIEW CAPACITY_V COMPILE;
ALTER VIEW CT_STUDENT_V COMPILE;
```

```
ALTER VIEW NJ_STUDENT_V COMPILE;
ALTER VIEW NY_STUDENT_V COMPILE;

4 rows selected.
```

The text literal 'ALTER VIEW' is concatenated with the view name and then with the text literal 'COMPILE;'. You can save the result to a file by using the SPOOL command and then execute it to compile all the invalid views.

One of SQL Developer's useful features is that it contains a few scripts to accomplish some of these tasks for you. In the example of the invalid views, you can use the Compile Invalid menu option (see Figure 14.10), which you see when you right-click the Views node.

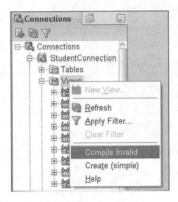

FIGURE 14.10
The Compile Invalid menu item

The resulting screen shows a small PL/SQL program that loops through the ALL_OBJECTS data dictionary view to find all the invalid objects for the current user account and the currently selected object type. It then executes for each row the required command to compile the object. To learn more about PL/SQL, see *Oracle PL/SQL by Example,* 4th Edition, by Benjamin Rosenzweig and Elena Silvestrova Rakhimov (Prentice Hall 2008).

While SQL Developer includes functionality for some of these commonly performed tasks, there will be instances when you need to write your own script to solve a particular problem or automate a task. Being able to write a dynamic script will enable you to solve a given problem in an efficient and repeatable manner.

Following is a script that shows how to disable constraints using a dynamic SQL script. There are times when you want to disable constraints temporarily, such as when you must bulk load data or update large quantities of data quickly. Afterward, you enable the constraints again. For example, the following SQL statement disables the foreign key constraint on the ZIP column of the STUDENT table.

```
ALTER TABLE student DISABLE CONSTRAINT stu_zip_fk
```

Disabling the constraint allows child values to be entered where no corresponding parent exists. This means, for example, that you can insert or update in the STUDENT table a zip code that does not have a corresponding value in the ZIPCODE table. To perform this task for all constraints in your schema, you start by writing the following statement.

```
SELECT 'ALTER TABLE ' || table_name
  FROM user_constraints
 WHERE constraint_type = 'R'
```

The statement generates a list of all the tables with foreign key constraints, together with the literal 'ALTER TABLE'. There are multiple rows with the same table name because a table may have multiple foreign keys.

```
'ALTERTABLE'||TABLE_NAME
-------------------------------------
ALTER TABLE COURSE
...
ALTER TABLE SECTION
ALTER TABLE SECTION
ALTER TABLE STUDENT


11 rows selected.
```

The following SQL statement expands the previous statement. You add the DISABLE clause to the statement by concatenating the text literal 'DISABLE CONSTRAINT' with the constraint name and then with another text literal containing the semicolon. The resulting output looks as follows.

```
SELECT 'ALTER TABLE ' || table_name ||
       ' DISABLE CONSTRAINT '|| constraint_name||';'
  FROM user_constraints
 WHERE constraint_type = 'R'
'ALTERTABLE'||TABLE_NAME||'DISABLECONSTRAINT'||CONSTRAIN
-------------------------------------------------------
ALTER TABLE COURSE DISABLE CONSTRAINT CRSE_CRSE_FK;
...
ALTER TABLE SECTION DISABLE CONSTRAINT SECT_CRSE_FK;
ALTER TABLE SECTION DISABLE CONSTRAINT SECT_INST_FK;
ALTER TABLE STUDENT DISABLE CONSTRAINT STU_ZIP_FK;


11 rows selected.
```

Now the syntax of the SQL statement works perfectly. You can save the SQL statement in a file named disable_fk.sql. Add the following SQL*Plus statements at the beginning of the file. (The double dashes indicate single-line comments.)

```
-- File Name: disable_fk.sql
-- Purpose: Disable Foreign Key constraints.
-- Created Date: Place current date here
-- Author: Put your name here
```

```
SET PAGESIZE 0
SET LINESIZE 80
SET FEEDBACK OFF
SET TERM OFF
SPOOL disable_fk.out
```

Add a semicolon at the end of the SQL statement and the following SQL*Plus commands afterward.

```
SPOOL OFF
SET PAGESIZE 20
SET LINESIZE 100
SET FEEDBACK ON
SET TERM ON
```

After editing the file, the disable_fk.sql script should look similar to the following. This script includes the CHR function with a value of 10, which automatically returns a new line in the result.

```
-- File Name: disable_fk.sql
-- Purpose: Disable Foreign Key constraints.
-- Created Date: Place current date here
-- Author: Put your name here
SET PAGESIZE 0
SET LINESIZE 80
SET FEEDBACK OFF
SET TERM OFF
SPOOL disable_fk_result.sql CREATE
SELECT 'ALTER TABLE ' || table_name || CHR(10)||
       '       DISABLE CONSTRAINT '|| constraint_name||';'
  FROM user_constraints
 WHERE constraint_type = 'R';
SPOOL OFF
SET PAGESIZE 20
SET LINESIZE 100
SET FEEDBACK ON
SET TERM ON
```

Executing the script disable_fk.sql with the @ command results in the disable_fk_result.sql file, which looks like the following.

```
ALTER TABLE COURSE
       DISABLE CONSTRAINT CRSE_CRSE_FK;
...
ALTER TABLE STUDENT
       DISABLE CONSTRAINT STU_ZIP_FK;
```

The spooled file contains a list of all SQL statements necessary to disable all the foreign constraints for the user. You can execute the commands in the file by typing @disable_fk_result.sql at the SQL*Plus prompt.

SQL Developer does not support the SPOOL command (see Appendix C for a list of supported commands). Use SQL*Plus in the lab exercises involving the generation of dynamic SQL statements and the SPOOL command.

You should document your scripts by using comments. Begin a single-line comment with two hyphens (--). Begin a multiline comment with a slash and an asterisk (/*) and end it with an asterisk and a slash (*/). In SQL*Plus scripts, you can also use the REMARK (REM) command to indicate a comment.

```
/* This is a multi-line
comment */
-- A single-line comment, it ends with a line break.
REM Another single-line comment, only used in SQL*Plus.
```

SQL Developer's Data Dictionary Reports

SQL Developer offers a number of helpful, predefined reports you can run against the data dictionary. The supplied reports cover a range of topics and illustrate a number of different presentation styles. You will find simple reports such as a list of all objects, complex reports detailing foreign keys without indexes, and graphical reports listing the occurrences of various column types.

Figure 14.11 shows the Reports navigator pane. If this tab is not visible on the left of the window, choose View, Reports. The folders in the Reports navigator pane show three sets of folders: The All Reports folder, which contains a list of Oracle-supplied reports; the Migration Reports folder, which is related to migrating third-party database to Oracle; and the User Defined Reports folder, which is where you create your own reports.

FIGURE 14.11
SQL Developer's Reports navigator pane

Table 14.3 provides a brief description of the different standard reports in the All Reports folder supplied within SQL Developer. The best reports to review are the reports listed in the All Objects, Data Dictionary, Database Administration, and Table folders.

TABLE 14.3   Overview of the SQL Developer All Reports Folder

REPORT FOLDER	DESCRIPTION
About Your Database	Lists release information and National Language Support (NLS) parameters.
All Objects	Lists all objects accessible for the chosen database connection. Also lists a helpful Dependencies report for assessing change impact.
Application Express	Contains reports useful for developers of Oracle's Application Express software.
ASH and AWR	Lists information on Active Session History (ASH) and Automated Workload Repository (AWR); useful for DBAs and installations where this Oracle add-on option is licensed.
Charts	Provides a graphical report showing distribution of objects.
Database Administration	Lists many reports intended for DBAs and developers, such as information on tables, constraints, indexes, users, and sessions.
Data Dictionary	Lists the data dictionary views and data dictionary columns.
Jobs	Lists jobs running in the database; helpful for DBAs.
PL/SQL	Lists PL/SQL objects and searches the PL/SQL source code of these objects.
Security	Displays information related to grants and privileges within the database.
Streams	Lists reports related to Oracle Steams, which manages sharing of data and events in a distributed environment.
Table	Lists information related to tables, such as columns, indexes, and constraints; contains quality assurance reports to indicate any possibly missing indexes or constraints.
XML	Lists information regarding Oracle XML objects; helpful for XML developers.

Running SQL Developer Reports

When you click on one of the reports, you need to choose the connection against which you would like to run the report. For example, if you open the Table folder, you see another subfolder related to comments. This folder contains various reports displaying information about table and column comments (see Figure 14.12).

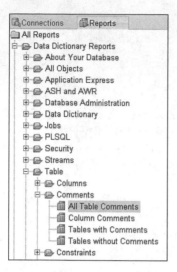

FIGURE 14.12
Various reports related to table and column comments

To run the report, double-click it. You are prompted for the connection (see Figure 14.13).

FIGURE 14.13
Select Connection box

Some of the reports have parameters, called bind variables, where you can enter values before the report is executed. These parameters narrow down the result. The All Table Comments report prompts you on a specific table name for which you would like to see the data; this report contains one bind value parameter (see Figure 14.14).

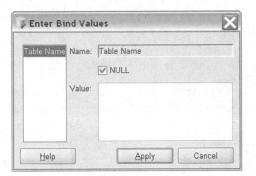

FIGURE 14.14
Bind Value dialog box

If you do not want to restrict the report for specific values, you can run the report without any bind variables by simply clicking the Apply button, which in this example will include all the tables, not just a specific table. The default value for bind variables is NULL, which indicates in SQL Developer that there is no restriction.

Bind variables are similar to the substitution variables discussed earlier. Instead of an ampersand, you see a colon before a bind variable's name.

Figure 14.15 displays an excerpt of the All Table Comments report.

Owner	Table Name	Table Type	Comments
STUDENT	ZIPCODE	TABLE	City, state and zip code information.
STUDENT	GRADE_CONVERSION	TABLE	Converts a number grade to a letter grade.
STUDENT	COURSE	TABLE	Information for a course.
STUDENT	ENROLLMENT	TABLE	Information for a student registered for a particular section (class).
STUDENT	SECTION	TABLE	Information for an individual section (class) of a particular course.
STUDENT	GRADE_TYPE_WEIGHT	TABLE	Information on how the final grade for a particular section is computed. For
STUDENT	GRADE_TYPE	TABLE	Lookup table of a grade types (code) and its description.
STUDENT	STUDENT	TABLE	Profile information for a student.
STUDENT	INSTRUCTOR	TABLE	Profile information for an instructor.
STUDENT	ZIPCODE_EXAMPLE	TABLE	Regular Expression examples
STUDENT	COURSE_REVENUE	TABLE	Revenues of courses
STUDENT	GRADE	TABLE	The individual grades a student received for a particular section(class).

FIGURE 14.15
SQL Developer's All Table Comments report

The resulting report contains icons similar to the Results pane in the SQL Worksheet. The Push Pin icon leaves the information in place instead of replacing it with the next report. The triangle allows you to rerun the report.

Next to the triangle is the SQL Worksheet icon. You can click on this icon to copy the report's underlying SQL statement into the SQL Worksheet box; this allows you to examine the report's SQL query. The Refresh drop-down choice enables you to rerun the report at specific intervals; this may be useful if your data changes frequently.

The Connection box to the right displays the StudentConnection, but you can choose another connection from the drop-down menu and run the report from a different user account. Depending on the underlying SQL statement, the results may vary from user account to user account because not every user may have the same access privileges and data.

The underlying SQL statement of the report shows that the report uses the SYS schema name. The SYS owner is the most privileged user in the Oracle database and the owner of the data dictionary. Many of the data dictionary views shown earlier are public synonyms or public views of these SYS owner dictionary tables. You will learn more about synonyms and the SYS user in Chapter 15.

Creating User-Defined SQL Developer Reports

In the folder User Defined Reports, you can create your own reports and folders. Any new report you create will be added in this folder. When you right-click the User Defined Reports folder, the menu options shows the Add Report choice.

Figure 14.16 displays the Create Report dialog box, which lists the report name and report style. This report is of Table style, which displays the data in columns and rows. This is the default report output style. You can fill in optional Description and Tooltip information. In the SQL box, you enter a query. This example shows a query against the USER_OBJECTS table that lists objects in the user's own schema. Click the Apply button to save the report.

Figure 14.17 displays the report result, ordered alphabetically by the object name. All the objects are owned by the current user. The result will vary from user to user. You will most likely see a list of tables, indexes, and sequences, but the list may include views, procedures, packages, functions, synonyms, triggers, and other object types.

When writing reports, you might want to use column aliases to improve the appearance and readability of the report. In the User Objects Report shown in Figure 14.17, two aliases were created: one for the formatted CREATED column and the other for the LAST_DDL_TIME column.

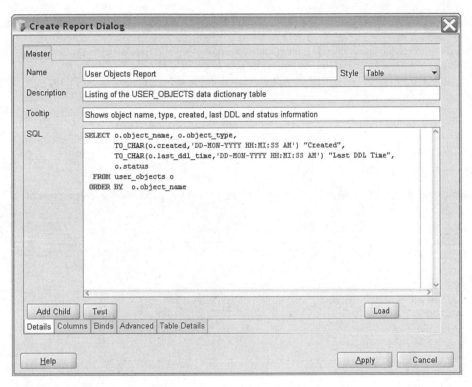

FIGURE 14.16
The Create Report Dialog screen

Object Name	Object Type	Created	Last DDL Time	Status
COURSE_REVENUE	TABLE	26-OCT-2008 06:47:14 PM	26-OCT-2008 06:47:14 PM	VALID
CRSE_CRSE_FK_I	INDEX	21-DEC-2008 04:31:48 PM	21-DEC-2008 04:31:48 PM	VALID
CRSE_PK	INDEX	21-DEC-2008 04:32:16 PM	21-DEC-2008 04:32:16 PM	VALID
DATE_EXAMPLE	TABLE	26-OCT-2008 06:47:13 PM	26-OCT-2008 06:47:13 PM	VALID
DOCS	TABLE	09-NOV-2008 12:22:05 PM	09-NOV-2008 12:22:05 PM	VALID
EMPLOYEE	TABLE	26-OCT-2008 06:47:14 PM	26-OCT-2008 06:47:14 PM	VALID
EMPLOYEE_CHANGE	TABLE	26-OCT-2008 06:47:14 PM	26-OCT-2008 06:47:14 PM	VALID
ENROLLMENT	TABLE	21-DEC-2008 04:31:47 PM	21-DEC-2008 04:32:16 PM	VALID
ENR_PK	INDEX	21-DEC-2008 04:32:16 PM	21-DEC-2008 04:32:16 PM	VALID
ENR_SECT_FK_I	INDEX	21-DEC-2008 04:31:48 PM	21-DEC-2008 04:31:48 PM	VALID

FIGURE 14.17
The report result of the user-defined User Objects report

Another way to create a new report is by copying and pasting an existing one into the User Defined Reports folder. You can also export the report in XML format and import it into other folders or distribute it to another user.

▼ LAB 14.2 EXERCISES

a) Enter all the following commands in a file named minmaxval.sql and then execute the script in SQL*Plus or SQL Developer. For the column name supply the value CAPACITY and for the table name enter the value SECTION. What do you observe in either SQL Developer or SQL*Plus?

```
ACCEPT vcol CHAR PROMPT 'Determine the minimum and maximum value of a column.
Enter the column name: '
ACCEPT vtable CHAR PROMPT 'Enter the corresponding table name: '
SET VERIFY OFF
SELECT MIN(&vcol), MAX(&vcol)
  FROM &vtable
```

b) Explain each line in the following SQL script and then, in one sentence, describe the purpose of the script.

```
01 /*
02 ----------------------------------------------------
03 File name:   rows.sql
04 Purpose:
05 Created by:  H. Ashley on January 7, 2008
06 Modified by: A. Christa on September 29, 2008
07 ----------------------------------------------------
08 */
09 SET TERM OFF
10 SET PAGESIZE 0
11 SET FEEDBACK OFF
12 SPOOL temp.lst
13 SELECT 'SELECT ' || '''' || table_name || '''' ||
14        ', COUNT(*) '||CHR(10) ||
15        ' FROM '|| LOWER(table_name) || ';'
16   FROM user_tables;
17 SPOOL OFF
18 SET FEEDBACK 1
19 SET PAGESIZE 20
20 SET TERM ON
21 @temp.lst
```

c) Explain when you would execute a script like the following.

```
--File: re_create_seq.sql
SET PAGESIZE 0
SET LINESIZE 100
SET FEEDBACK OFF
SPOOL re_create_seq.out
SELECT 'CREATE SEQUENCE '||sequence_name||
       ' START WITH '||last_number||CHR(10)||
       ' INCREMENT BY '||increment_by ||
      DECODE(cache_size, 0, ' NOCACHE',
       ' CACHE  '||cache_size)||';'
```

```
   FROM seq;
SPOOL OFF
SET PAGESIZE 20
SET LINESIZE 80
SET FEEDBACK ON
SET TERM ON
```

d) Create a user-defined report called Student Schema Indexes in SQL Developer, using the following SQL.

```
SELECT index_name,
       index_type,
       table_name,
       uniqueness
  FROM user_indexes
 ORDER BY index_name
```

▼ LAB 14.2 EXERCISE ANSWERS

a) Enter all the following commands in a file named minmaxval.sql and then execute the script in SQL*Plus or SQL Developer. For the column name supply the value CAPACITY and for the table name enter the value SECTION. What do you observe in either SQL Developer or SQL*Plus?

```
ACCEPT vcol CHAR PROMPT 'Determine the minimum and maximum value of a column.
Enter the column name: '
ACCEPT vtable CHAR PROMPT 'Enter the corresponding table name: '
SET VERIFY OFF
SELECT MIN(&vcol), MAX(&vcol)
  FROM &vtable
```

ANSWER: The PROMPT and ACCEPT commands allow for user-friendly inputs and prompts.

```
@minmaxval
Determine the minimum and maximum value of a column.
Enter the column name: CAPACITY
Enter the corresponding table name: SECTION


MIN(CAPACITY) MAX(CAPACITY)
------------- -------------
          10            25


1 row selected.
```

The ACCEPT SQL*Plus command defines a variable that can then be referenced with the ampersand symbol and permits prompting for the values. The SQL*Plus ACCEPT command allows for data type checking of the entered value.

b) Explain each line in the following SQL script and then, in one sentence, describe the purpose of the script.

```
01 /*
02 ------------------------------------------------------
03 File name:   rows.sql
```

```
04 Purpose:
05 Created by:  H. Ashley on January 7, 2008
06 Modified by: A. Christa on September 29, 2008
07 --------------------------------------------------
08 */
09 SET TERM OFF
10 SET PAGESIZE 0
11 SET FEEDBACK OFF
12 SPOOL temp.lst
13 SELECT 'SELECT ' || '''' || table_name || '''' ||
14        ', COUNT(*) '||CHR(10) ||
15        '  FROM '|| LOWER(table_name) || ';'
16   FROM user_tables;
17 SPOOL OFF
18 SET FEEDBACK 1
19 SET PAGESIZE 20
20 SET TERM ON
21 @temp.lst
```

ANSWER: The purpose of the script is to display a list of all user-accessible tables, together with a row count for each.

The script dynamically generates the following statements and spools them to the resulting temp.lst file.

```
SELECT 'course', COUNT(*)
  FROM course;
...
SELECT 'zipcode', COUNT(*)
  FROM zipcode;
```

The temp.lst file is then executed with the @temp.lst command, and a count of all rows for each table is displayed.

```
'STUDEN   COUNT(*)
-------  ---------
student        268

1 row selected.
...
'ZIPCOD   COUNT(*)
-------  ---------
zipcode        227

1 row selected.
```

Lines 1 through 8 show a multiline comment; the comment starts with /* and ends with */. In line 9, the command SET TERM OFF turns off the output to the screen. Line 10 sets the PAGESIZE to zero, line 11 avoids any FEEDBACK, and line 12 spools the result of all subsequent statements to the temp.lst file in the current directory. Line 13 shows an example of the literal SELECT, concatenated with four single quotation marks. The four single quotation marks result in a single quotation mark in the spooled file, and the table name shows between them.

USING QUOTES IN SQL

As you see in many SQL statements, single quotation marks are used to enclose a text literal.

```
SELECT last_name
   FROM student
  WHERE last_name = 'Smith'
```

If you want to query, insert, update, or delete a value containing a single quote, prefix the quote with another quote.

```
SELECT last_name
   FROM student
  WHERE last_name = 'O''Neil'
```

To replicate a single quotation mark in a dynamic SQL script, you need four quotes: two individual quotes to represent a single quotation mark and two quotes to surround this text literal.

Line 14 displays the COUNT function to count rows. The CHR(10) function issues a new line in the spooled file. The resulting concatenation is then further combined with the literal FROM in line 15, together with the table name in lowercase and a semicolon.

Line 16 shows that the query is issued against the USER_TABLES data dictionary view. Line 17 ends the spooling to the file. Lines 18, 19, and 20 reset the SQL*Plus settings to their defaults. Line 21 runs the spooled temp.lst file and automatically issues the generated SQL statements. To run this script, use SQL*Plus not SQL Developer.

c) Explain when you would execute a script like the following.

```
--File: re_create_seq.sql
SET PAGESIZE 0
SET LINESIZE 100
SET FEEDBACK OFF
SPOOL re_create_seq.out
SELECT 'CREATE SEQUENCE '||sequence_name||
       ' START WITH '||last_number||CHR(10)||
       ' INCREMENT BY '||increment_by ||
       DECODE(cache_size, 0, ' NOCACHE',
       ' CACHE'||cache_size)||';'
  FROM seq;
SPOOL OFF
SET PAGESIZE 20
SET LINESIZE 80
SET FEEDBACK ON
SET TERM ON
```

ANSWER: There are times when you need to re-create certain database objects; perhaps you need to replicate the same setup in another database or make changes to database objects without writing new scripts from scratch.

```
CREATE SEQUENCE COURSE_NO_SEQ START WITH 454
  INCREMENT BY 1 NOCACHE;
...
CREATE SEQUENCE STUDENT_ID_SEQ START WITH 401
  INCREMENT BY 1 NOCACHE;
```

d) Create a user-defined report called Student Schema Indexes in SQL Developer, using the following SQL.

```
SELECT index_name,
       index_type,
       table_name,
       uniqueness
  FROM user_indexes
 ORDER BY index_name
```

ANSWER: In the User Defined Reports folder, right-click and choose the Add Report menu option. The Create Report Dialog screen appears. Fill in the Report Name, Description, Tooltip, and SQL statement boxes (see Figure 14.18). After you enter the SQL statement, you can click the Test button to see if the report works. To save the report, click the Apply button.

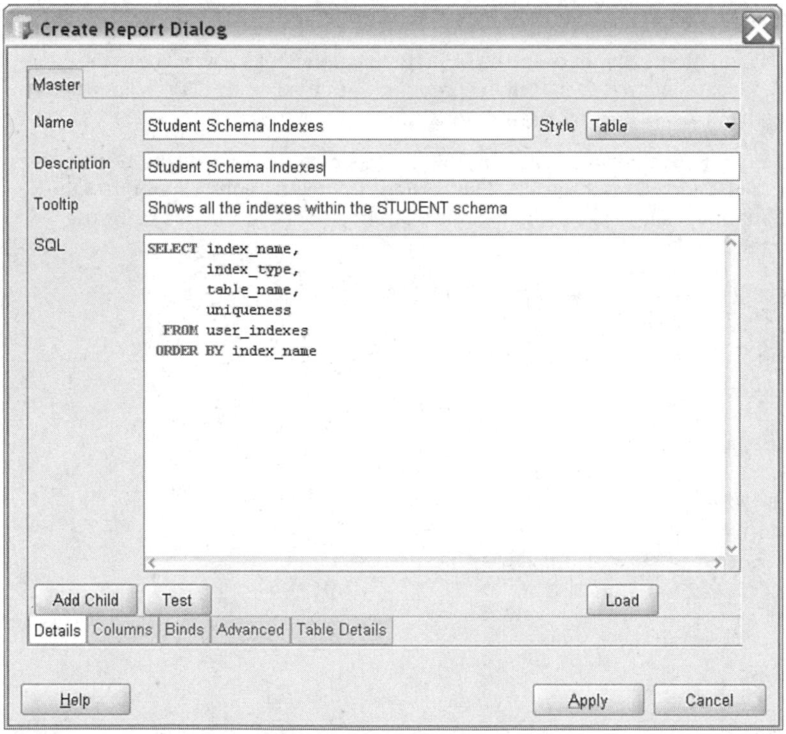

FIGURE 14.18
New report named Student Schema Indexes

Figure 14.19 shows the result of the report. It displays the index name, the type of index, the table on which the index is based, and whether the index is unique.

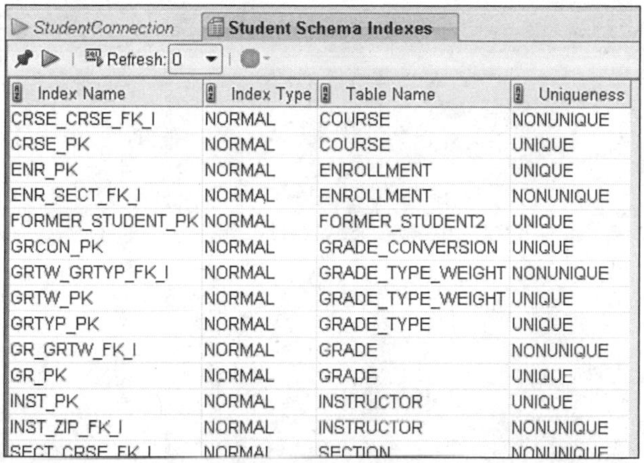

Index Name	Index Type	Table Name	Uniqueness
CRSE_CRSE_FK_I	NORMAL	COURSE	NONUNIQUE
CRSE_PK	NORMAL	COURSE	UNIQUE
ENR_PK	NORMAL	ENROLLMENT	UNIQUE
ENR_SECT_FK_I	NORMAL	ENROLLMENT	NONUNIQUE
FORMER_STUDENT_PK	NORMAL	FORMER_STUDENT2	UNIQUE
GRCON_PK	NORMAL	GRADE_CONVERSION	UNIQUE
GRTW_GRTYP_FK_I	NORMAL	GRADE_TYPE_WEIGHT	NONUNIQUE
GRTW_PK	NORMAL	GRADE_TYPE_WEIGHT	UNIQUE
GRTYP_PK	NORMAL	GRADE_TYPE	UNIQUE
GR_GRTW_FK_I	NORMAL	GRADE	NONUNIQUE
GR_PK	NORMAL	GRADE	UNIQUE
INST_PK	NORMAL	INSTRUCTOR	UNIQUE
INST_ZIP_FK_I	NORMAL	INSTRUCTOR	NONUNIQUE
SECT_CRSE_FK_I	NORMAL	SECTION	NONUNIQUE

FIGURE 14.19

Results of the Student Schema Indexes report

CREATING A MASTER/CHILD REPORT IN SQL DEVELOPER

There are many choices on the Create Report Dialog screen (refer to Figure 14.18) that allow you to modify the report's layout and formatting. A very useful feature is the ability to create a master/child report, whereby the information in the child result tab is dependent on the row of the master tab. To illustrate this capability, you will expand on the Student Schema Indexes report and add a child report to the bottom of the report. For each index in the master report, it will display the index's respective list of columns.

To modify the report, right-click the Student Schema Indexes report and choose Edit to modify the report. Click the Add Child button and enter the following SQL statement.

```
SELECT index_name, table_name,
       column_position, column_name
  FROM user_ind_columns
 WHERE index_name = :INDEX_NAME
```

The bind variable :INDEX_NAME does not prompt you for input, but it is part of the child SQL query to link the two screens together. Fill in a report name and the description (see Figure 14.20).

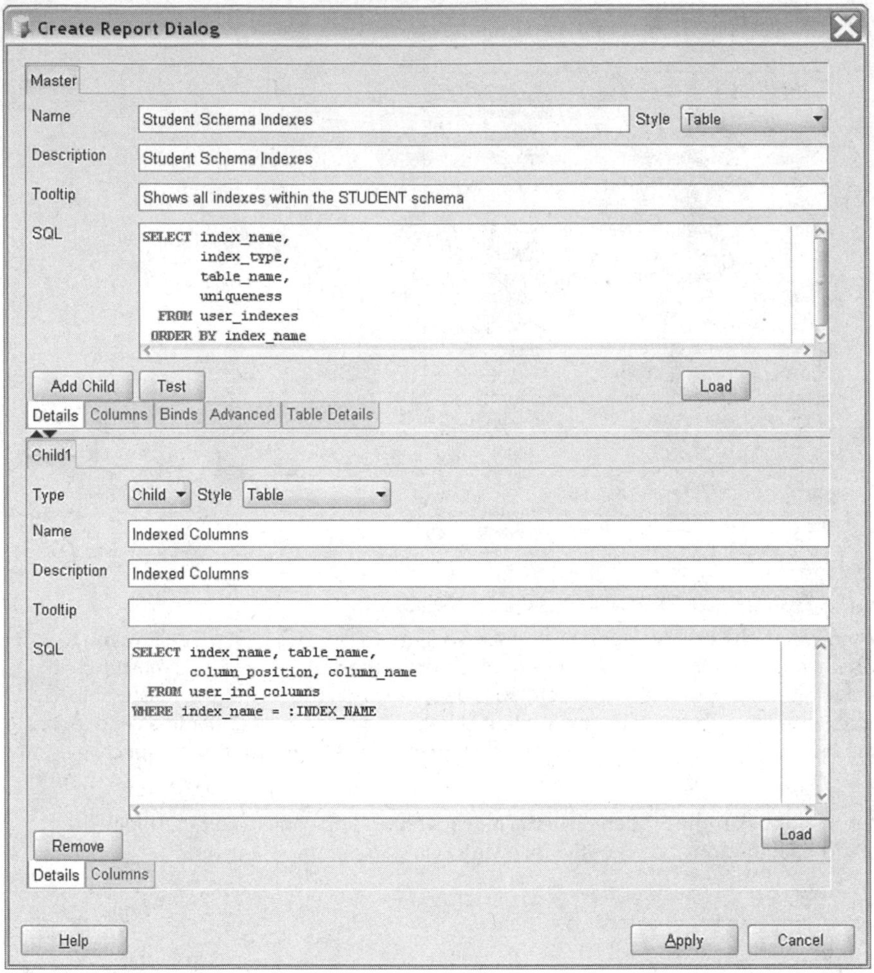

FIGURE 14.20
Entering the child report information

The last step is to create the bind variable INDEX_NAME in the Binds tab (see Figure 14.21). This establishes the link between the master report and the child report. The bind variable name in this tab and the SQL statement must agree.

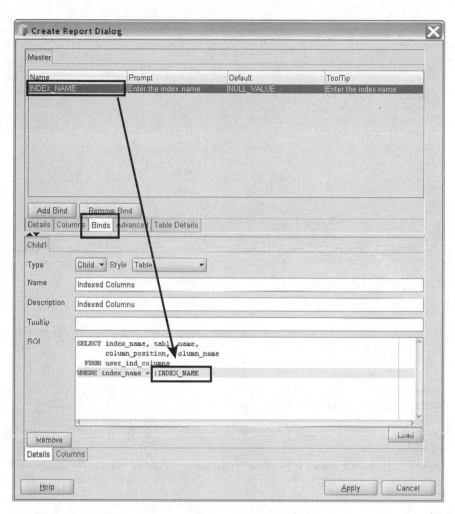

FIGURE 14.21
The Binds tab

Finally, you can run the report. When you select a row in the master, the corresponding columns that make up this index are displayed in the Indexed Columns tab. Figure 14.22 shows the GR_PK index name highlighted and the corresponding four indexed columns in the defined order.

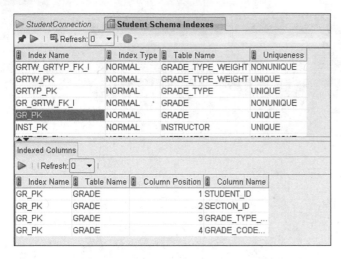

FIGURE 14.22
The master/child report for Student Schema Indexes

You can add additional child tabs to the report. These child tabs can be linked to the master report, or the reports can be independent queries.

    SQL Developer supplies many data dictionary reports, which you can review to get ideas about different presentation styles and features.

SHARING REPORTS

After you create your report, you can share the report with other users, who can then run the same report on their own, using their individual connection information and their own variables. To share the report, you need to export the report definition to an XML file on a directory where others can access this file. All users who want to run shared reports need to add a Shared Reports folder to their SQL Developer setup. You can accomplish this by selecting Tools, Preferences and then selecting Database: User Defined Extensions. In the screen that appears, add a row with the type of REPORT and add the location and name of the shared report. When you restart SQL Developer, the Reports pane will show the Shared Reports folder containing the report.

Lab 14.2 Quiz

In order to test your progress, you should be able to answer the following questions.

1) The following statements are SQL*Plus commands, not SQL commands.

```
SET FEEDBACK ON
COL student FORMAT A20
START
```

_____ a) True

_____ b) False

2) What is the result of the following SELECT statement?

```
SELECT 'HELLO ' || CHR(10) || 'THERE'
  FROM dual
```

_____ a) HELLO THERE

_____ b) HELLO

_____   THERE

_____ c) Invalid query

3) Dynamic SQL scripts are useful for generating SQL statements.

_____ a) True

_____ b) False

4) The following SELECT statement returns a single quote.

```
SELECT ''''
  FROM dual
```

_____ a) True

_____ b) False

5) Bind variables in SQL Developer allow you to prompt for user input. They can also link master/child reports.

_____ a) True

_____ b) False

ANSWERS APPEAR IN APPENDIX A.

▼ WORKSHOP

The projects in this section are meant to prompt you to utilize all the skills you have acquired throughout this chapter. The answers to these projects can be found at the companion Web site to this book, located at www.oraclesqlbyexample.com.

1) Describe the result of the following query.

```
SELECT table_name, column_name, comments
  FROM user_col_comments
```

2) Explain the differences between the views USER_USERS, ALL_USERS, and DBA_USERS.

3) What are the underlying data dictionary views for the public synonyms TABS and COLS?

4) Write a dynamic SQL script to drop all views in the STUDENT schema. If there are no views, create some to test your script.

CHAPTER 15

Security

CHAPTER OBJECTIVES

In this chapter, you will learn about:

- ▶ Users
- ▶ Privileges
- ▶ Roles
- ▶ Synonyms

Oracle protects the data in the database by implementing security via users, roles, and privileges. The SQL language commands used to accomplish these security tasks are known as Data Control Language (DCL) commands.

Oracle provides several different ways to enforce access control to ensure that only authorized users can log in and access the appropriate data. You want to avoid situations in which a user can accidentally drop an important table or side-step security rules. Every database user has certain *system privileges* that determine the type of actions the user can perform, such as create tables, drop views, or create other users.

Object privileges avoid any wrongful data modifications to individual tables or columns. The owner of database objects can assign these object privileges that control exactly who can access what objects and to what extent.

System and object privileges can be grouped together into a *role*. Part of a database administrator's (DBA's) job is to set up the correct security for database users. It is vital that the database be properly protected against any wrongful actions and unauthorized access.

LAB 15.1
Users, Privileges, Roles, and Synonyms

LAB OBJECTIVES

After this lab, you will be able to:

▶ Create Users and Grant and Revoke Privileges

▶ Create and Use Synonyms

▶ Create User-Defined Roles

Many of the commands and actions discussed throughout this lab are carried out by a DBA or an authorized user. In this lab, you will gain a better understanding of the rights required to perform the various SQL commands against the database.

What Is a Schema?

A *schema* is a collection of objects (for example, tables, views, indexes, sequences, triggers, synonyms). Each schema is owned by a single user account with the same name; in fact, the two terms *schema* and *user account* are often used interchangeably.

You can list the types of objects in the STUDENT schema by querying the USER_OBJECTS data dictionary view.

```
SELECT DISTINCT object_type
  FROM user_objects
OBJECT_TYPE
------------------
INDEX
SEQUENCE
...
VIEW

4 rows selected.
```

To see all the different types of objects available for the user accessing the database, query the ALL_OBJECTS view. The result set on your database may vary from this result, as various users may have different object types and different privileges.

```
SELECT DISTINCT object_type
  FROM all_objects
OBJECT_TYPE
------------------
...
INDEX
...
PACKAGE
PACKAGE BODY
PROCEDURE
SEQUENCE
SYNONYM
TABLE
TABLE PARTITION
TRIGGER
...

25 rows selected.
```

Special Users: SYSTEM and SYS

When an Oracle database is created, it comes with a number of default accounts. Two extremely important accounts are SYS and SYSTEM.

The SYS account is the most privileged user. It owns the data dictionary. If you drop any of the objects of the SYS schema, you endanger the critical operation of the Oracle database.

The SYSTEM account is automatically granted the DBA role for database administration tasks. This role is typically used to create regular user accounts or accounts with the DBA role. Oracle suggests that you create an administrative type of account after you create the database. You can then use this DBA account to perform daily administrative tasks, without having to use the SYS and SYSTEM accounts.

Creating Users

To log in to the Oracle database, a user must have a username, a password, and certain system privileges. A username is created with the CREATE USER command, which uses the following syntax.

```
CREATE USER user IDENTIFIED
  {BY password [REPLACE oldPassword]
    |EXTERNALLY|GLOBALLY AS 'external name'}
 [{DEFAULT TABLESPACE tablespace |
 TEMPORARY TABLESPACE {tablespace|tablespace_group}|
 QUOTA {integer[K|M] | UNLIMITED} ON tablespace
   [[QUOTA {integer[K|M] | UNLIMITED} ON tablespace]...]|
 PROFILE profile |
```

```
PASSWORD EXPIRE |
ACCOUNT {LOCK|UNLOCK}
   }]
```

To create a new user, first log in as a user with the rights to create other users (for example, an account with DBA privileges or the user SYSTEM).

 Starting with Oracle 11*g*, passwords are, by default, case-sensitive.

The following statement creates a new user called MUSIC with the password listen.

```
CREATE USER music IDENTIFIED BY listen
   DEFAULT TABLESPACE users
   TEMPORARY TABLESPACE temp
   QUOTA 15 M ON users
User created.
```

The message User created indicates the successful creation of the user. The keywords DEFAULT TABLESPACE indicate where any of the user's objects are stored. Here the tablespace is called USERS. The TEMPORARY TABLESPACE keywords allow you to determine where any sorting of data that cannot be performed in memory is temporarily stored.

In preparation for creating users in your database, you must find out what tablespaces exist in your Oracle database. Query the USER_TABLESPACES or DBA_TABLESPACES data dictionary views with the following query.

```
SELECT tablespace_name
  FROM dba_tablespaces
 ORDER BY tablespace_name
```

You can also refer to the readme.pdf file on the companion Web site, located at www.oraclesqlbyexample.com, for an example of the creation of the STUDENT user.

Assigning a default tablespace to the user does not mean that the user can actually store objects in this tablespace. The QUOTA 15 M ON users clause allows the MUSIC user to use up to 15 MB on the USERS tablespace.

If the user will create objects, it is important that you specify an appropriate default tablespace. It is never good practice to use the SYSTEM tablespace as the default tablespace because the SYSTEM tablespace should only contain the data dictionary and other internal Oracle system-related objects. If you run out of space on this SYSTEM tablespace because a user uses up a lot of space, the system comes to a complete halt.

Changing the Password and Altering the User Settings

When an individual user's account settings need to change, such as the password or the default tablespace, the user can be altered. The syntax of the ALTER USER command is as follows.

```
ALTER USER {user {IDENTIFIED
    {BY password [REPLACE oldPassword]|
     EXTERNALLY|GLOBALLY AS 'external name'}
    DEFAULT TABLESPACE tablespace |
    TEMPORARY TABLESPACE {tablespace|tablespace_group} |
    QUOTA {integer [K|M] | UNLIMITED} ON tablespace
     [[QUOTA {integer [K|M] | UNLIMITED} ON tablespace]...]|
    PROFILE profile |
    DEFAULT ROLE
     {role [,role]...|ALL[EXCEPT role [,role]...]|NONE}|
    PASSWORD EXPIRE |
    ACCOUNT {LOCK|UNLOCK}
  }}
```

The following statement changes MUSIC's password from listen to tone and changes the default tablespace from USERS to USER_DATA.

```
ALTER USER music IDENTIFIED BY tone
   DEFAULT TABLESPACE USER_DATA
User altered.
```

If you are using SQL*Plus, type the SQL*Plus PASSWORD command at the SQL> prompt and then enter the old and new passwords.

OPERATING SYSTEM AUTHENTICATION

Instead of using Oracle's logon name, a user can be authenticated through the operating system account; this is done via the IDENTIFIED BY EXTERNALLY password option. Operating system authentication is offered on some platforms (for example, UNIX, Windows), and a username and password do not need to be entered when connecting to SQL*Plus. Furthermore, the operating system controls password modifications and expirations. You can find out more about this topic in the *Oracle Platform Guide* for your operating system.

LOCKED ACCOUNTS

As part of the database installation process, Oracle creates a number of default user accounts that may be locked. You can use the ALTER USER command with the ACCOUNT UNLOCK option to unlock those accounts if your user community needs to use them.

Oracle has a large number of syntax options as part of the ALTER USER command. You will explore these different options throughout this lab.

Dropping Users

You use the following command to drop a user.

```
DROP USER music
User dropped.
```

The DROP USER command drops the user if the user does not own any objects. The syntax for the DROP USER command is a follows.

```
DROP USER user [CASCADE]
```

If you want to also drop the objects owned by the user, execute the DROP USER command with the CASCADE keyword.

```
DROP USER music CASCADE
```

 If the objects and their data need to be preserved, be sure to first back up the data by using the Oracle Data Pump utility or any other reliable method.

What Are Privileges?

A *privilege* is a right to execute a particular type of SQL statement. There are two types of privileges: system privileges and object privileges. An example of a system privilege is the right to create a table or an index. A particular object privilege allows you to access an individual object, such as the privilege to select from the INSTRUCTOR table, to delete from the ZIPCODE table, or to SELECT a number from a specific sequence.

SYSTEM PRIVILEGES

To establish a connection to the database, a user must be granted certain system privileges. These privileges are granted either individually or in the form of roles. A *role* is a collection of privileges.

Although the user MUSIC has been created, the user cannot start a session, as you see from the following error message. The user lacks the CREATE SESSION system privilege to log in to the database.

```
CONN music/tone
ERROR: ORA-01045: user MUSIC lacks CREATE SESSION
privilege; logon denied
```

Table 15.1 lists a few examples of individual system privileges that can be granted to a user. For example, if you have the CREATE TABLE privilege, you can create tables in your schema; if you have the CREATE ANY TABLE privilege, you can create tables in another user's schema. The CREATE TABLE privilege includes the CREATE INDEX privilege, but before you are allowed to create these objects, you must make sure you have either been granted a quota on the individual tablespace on which you would like to place the object or the RESOURCE role, which provides you with unlimited space on all tablespaces.

The SELECT ANY TABLE privilege gives access to all tables, but it does not permit data dictionary access; instead, an object privilege called SELECT ANY DICTIONARY provides SELECT rights on the data dictionary views.

TABLE 15.1   Examples of System Privileges

	SYSTEM PRIVILEGE NAME
Session	CREATE SESSION
	ALTER SESSION
Table	CREATE TABLE
	CREATE ANY TABLE
	ALTER ANY TABLE
	DROP ANY TABLE
	SELECT ANY TABLE
	UPDATE ANY TABLE
	DELETE ANY TABLE
	FLASHBACK ANY TABLE
Index	CREATE ANY INDEX
	ALTER ANY INDEX
	DROP ANY INDEX
Sequence	CREATE SEQUENCE
	CREATE ANY SEQUENCE
	ALTER ANY SEQUENCE
	DROP ANY SEQUENCE
View	CREATE VIEW
	CREATE ANY VIEW
	DROP ANY VIEW

OBJECT PRIVILEGES

Object privileges are granted for a particular object (for example, table, view, sequence). Table 15.2 lists examples of object privileges.

TABLE 15.2   Examples of Object Privileges

OBJECT TYPE	PRIVILEGE	PURPOSE
TABLE	SELECT	The right to query from an individual table.
	INSERT	The right to add new rows into an individual table
	UPDATE	The right to change rows in an individual table. You can optionally specify to allow UPDATE rights only on individual columns.
	DELETE	The right to remove rows from an individual table.
	REFERENCES	The right to reference a table in a foreign key constraint.

TABLE 15.2   Continued

OBJECT TYPE	PRIVILEGE	PURPOSE
	ALTER	The right to change table and column definitions.
	INDEX	The right to create indexes on the individual table.
	FLASHBACK	The right to flashback a table.
	ALL	All possible object privileges on a table.
SEQUENCE	SELECT	The right to increment values from a sequence and retrieve current values.
	ALTER	The right to change the sequence definition.
PL/SQL Stored Objects	EXECUTE	The right to execute any stored procedure, function, or package.

The GRANT Command

You give a system privilege or an object privilege to a user by using the GRANT command. You can grant privileges individually or through a role.

The syntax for granting system privileges is as follows.

```
GRANT {system_privilege|role|ALL PRIVILEGES}
   [,{system_privilege|role|ALL PRIVILEGES}]...
TO {user|role|PUBLIC}[,{user|role|PUBLIC}]...
[WITH ADMIN OPTION]
```

The following statement grants the CREATE SESSION system privilege to the MUSIC user. This allows the MUSIC user to establish a session to the database.

```
GRANT CREATE SESSION TO music
```

Object privileges grant certain privileges on specific objects, such as tables, views, or sequences. You can grant object privileges to other users when you want them to have access to objects you created. You can also grant the user access to objects you do not own if the object's owner gives you permission to extend rights to others.

The following is the general syntax for granting object privileges.

```
GRANT {object_privilege|ALL [PRIVILEGES]}
        [(column[,column]... )]
   [,{object_privilege|ALL [PRIVILEGES]}
        [(column[,column]... )]]...
ON objectname
TO {user|role|PUBLIC}[,{user|role|PUBLIC}]...
[WITH GRANT OPTION]
```

For example, the following statement connects as the STUDENT user account within SQL*Plus and grants the SELECT privilege on the COURSE table to the new user MUSIC.

```
CONN student/learn
Connected.

GRANT SELECT ON course TO music
Grant succeeded.
```

In this case, the STUDENT user is the grantor, and MUSIC is the grantee, the recipient of the privileges. Now the MUSIC user can query the COURSE table.

In addition to SELECT, other object privileges can be granted on a table, such as INSERT, UPDATE, DELETE, ALTER, INDEX, and REFERENCES (refer to Table 15.2). The ALTER privilege allows another user to change table definitions with the ALTER table command, the INDEX privilege allows the creation of indexes on the table, and the REFERENCES privilege allows the table to be referenced with a foreign key constraint. You can also grant all object privileges at once by using the GRANT ALL command.

Object privileges can be assigned to other database objects, such as sequences, packages, procedures, and functions. SELECT and ALTER privileges can be granted on sequences. Packages, procedures, and functions require the EXECUTE privilege if other users want to run these stored programs.

If an object, such as a table, is dropped and then re-created, the grants need to be reissued. This is not the case if the object is replaced with the CREATE OR REPLACE keywords available for views and stored programs.

You can grant UPDATE and REFERENCES privileges on individual columns on a table. For example, to grant update on the columns COST and DESCRIPTION of the COURSE table, execute the following command.

```
GRANT UPDATE (cost, description) ON course TO music
Grant succeeded.
```

Roles

A role is several privileges collected under one role name. Using roles aids in administration of multiple privileges to users. Oracle includes predefined roles; three popular ones that contain a number of different system privileges are CONNECT, RESOURCE, and DBA.

The CONNECT role contains the CREATE SESSION system privilege that allows a user to start a session. (In prior Oracle versions, this role could also create views, tables, and sequences, among other operations.)

The RESOURCE role allows a user to create tables and indexes on any tablespace and to create PL/SQL stored objects (for example, packages, procedures, functions).

The DBA role includes all system privileges. This role is usually granted to a user who performs database administration tasks. Table 15.3 lists the system privileges associated with each role.

TABLE 15.3   The CONNECT, RESOURCE, and DBA Roles

ROLE	PURPOSE
CONNECT	Contains CREATE SESSION system privilege.
RESOURCE	Includes these system privileges: CREATE TABLE, CREATE SEQUENCE, CREATE TRIGGER, CREATE PROCEDURE, CREATE CLUSTER, CREATE INDEXTYPE, CREATE OPERATOR, and CREATE TYPE.
DBA	Includes all system privileges and allows them to be granted WITH ADMIN OPTION. This does not include the privilege to start up and shut down the database.

You can also query the ROLE_SYS_PRIVS and DBA_SYS_PRIVS data dictionary views to list the individual system privileges for each role, which may change in future versions. For example, starting with Oracle 11g, the CREATE VIEW system privilege is no longer part of the standard RESOURCE role. If you want to grant this system privilege to a specific user, you need to grant it explicitly.

```
GRANT CREATE VIEW TO music
Grant succeeded.
```

When a user is granted a role, the user acquires all the privileges defined within the role. The following statement uses the two predefined Oracle roles CONNECT and RESOURCE to grant a number of system privileges to the new user.

```
GRANT CONNECT, RESOURCE TO music
Grant succeeded.
```

Extending Privileges to Others

To extend an object privilege to another user, you must be the owner of the object or have received the privilege to pass it on to others through WITH GRANT OPTION. You may also pass on the privilege if you have been granted the GRANT ANY OBJECT system privilege.

The following SQL statement grants all object privileges on the COURSE table to the MUSIC user. It also passes to the MUSIC user the ability to grant these privileges to yet other users, using the WITH GRANT OPTION. Here, MUSIC is the grantee but can become a grantor if the privilege is passed on to another user.

```
GRANT ALL ON course TO music WITH GRANT OPTION
Grant succeeded.
```

To allow users to pass on system privileges to other users, you must have been granted the system privilege with WITH ADMIN OPTION or have been granted the GRANT ANY PRIVILEGE system privilege. For example, after execution of the following statement, the user MUSIC can grant the CREATE SESSION system privilege to other users.

```
GRANT CREATE SESSION TO music WITH ADMIN OPTION
Grant succeeded.
```

If you want other users to pass on a role to others, you must have either created the role, have been granted the role through the WITH ADMIN OPTION, or been granted the GRANT ANY ROLE system privilege.

You can see which system privileges you received through a role by querying the Oracle data dictionary view ROLE_SYS_PRIVS. For granted system privileges, query the data dictionary views USER_SYS_PRIVS or DBA_SYS_PRIVS. Table 15.4 lists a number of data dictionary views you may find useful when trying to determine individual object privileges, system privileges, and roles.

TABLE 15.4   Useful Data Dictionary Views

DATA DICTIONARY VIEW	PURPOSE
SESSION_PRIVS	All current system privileges available to an individual user
USER_SYS_PRIVS	System privileges granted to the user
ROLE_SYS_PRIVS	System privileges received through a role
ROLE_TAB_PRIVS	Object privileges received through a role
USER_TAB_PRIVS	Object grants
USER_COL_PRIVS	Individual column grants
USER_TAB_PRIVS_RECD	Object privileges received by the user
USER_TAB_PRIVS_MADE	Object privileges made by the user

The REVOKE Command

Privileges can be taken away with the REVOKE command. Use the following syntax to revoke system privileges.

```
REVOKE {system_privilege|role|ALL PRIVILEGES}
   [,{system_privilege|role|ALL PRIVILEGES}]...
FROM {user|role|PUBLIC}[,{user|role|PUBLIC}]...
```

The next example shows how the RESOURCE role is revoked from the user MUSIC.

```
REVOKE RESOURCE FROM music
Revoke succeeded.
```

Object privileges can also be revoked as in the following statement.

```
REVOKE UPDATE ON course FROM music
Revoke succeeded.
```

The syntax for revoking object privileges is listed here.

```
REVOKE {object_privilege|ALL [PRIVILEGES]}
   [,{object_privilege|ALL [PRIVILEGES]}
ON objectname
FROM {user|role|PUBLIC}[,{user|role|PUBLIC}]...
[CASCADE CONSTRAINTS]
```

The CASCADE CONSTRAINTS clause is needed only if you revoke the REFERENCES or ALL privileges. The REFERENCES privilege allows you to create a referential integrity constraint based on another user's object. The CASCADE CONSTRAINT options drops any defined referential constraints when you revoke the REFERENCES privilege.

Object privileges granted using the WITH GRANT OPTION are revoked if the grantor's object privilege is revoked. For example, assume that USER1 is granted SELECT privilege on the COURSE table, using the WITH GRANT OPTION, and grants the same privilege to USER2. If the SELECT privilege is revoked from USER1, then the revoke cascades to USER2.

Revoking object privileges cascades the REVOKE to other users. However, revoking system privileges does not have a cascading effect.

Referring to Objects in Other Schemas

The MUSIC user has the SELECT privilege on the COURSE table issued earlier. Observe what occurs when you connect as the MUSIC user in SQL*Plus and attempt to query the table.

```
CONN music/tone
Connected.

SELECT description
  FROM course
  FROM course
       *
ERROR at line 2:
ORA-00942: table or view does not exist
```

Even though the user MUSIC is allowed to query the COURSE table, MUSIC does not own the COURSE table and must qualify the name of the schema where the object exists. Because the COURSE table exists in the STUDENT schema, you prefix the table name with the schema name.

```
SELECT description
  FROM student.course
DESCRIPTION
-----------------------------
Technology Concepts
Intro to Information Systems
```

```
...
Java Developer III
DB Programming with Java

30 rows selected.
```

The COURSE table is now qualified with the name of the user who owns the COURSE table (that is, STUDENT). When any query, *Data Manipulation Language* (DML), or *Data Definition Language* (DDL) statement is issued in Oracle, the database assumes that the object being referenced is in the user's own schema, unless it is otherwise qualified.

Private Synonyms

Instead of qualifying the name of an object with the object owner's name, you can use a synonym. A synonym is a way of aliasing an object with another name. You can create private and public synonyms. A private synonym is a synonym in a user's schema; public synonyms are visible to everyone.

The syntax for creating synonyms is as follows.

```
CREATE [OR REPLACE] [PUBLIC]
    SYNONYM [schema.]synonymname
    FOR [schema.]objectname[@dblink]
```

The next CREATE SYNONYM command creates a private synonym called COURSE in the MUSIC schema for the COURSE table located in the STUDENT schema.

```
CREATE SYNONYM course FOR student.course
Synonym created.
```

If you are not logged in as the MUSIC user but as a user who has rights to create synonyms in another user's schema, such as a DBA, you must prefix the synonym's name with the name of the schema in which the synonym should be created.

```
CREATE SYNONYM music.course FOR student.course
```

After the synonym is successfully created in the MUSIC schema, you can select from the COURSE table without prefixing the table with the schema name.

```
SELECT description
    FROM course
DESCRIPTION
-----------------------------
Technology Concepts
Intro to Information Systems
...
Java Developer III
DB Programming with Java

30 rows selected.
```

Oracle resolves the SELECT statement by looking at the synonym COURSE, which points to the COURSE table located in the STUDENT schema.

 Whenever any statement is executed, Oracle looks in the current schema for the object. If there is no object of that name in the current schema, Oracle checks for a public synonym of that name.

When you create a synonym, the validity of the underlying object is not checked; that is, you can create a synonym without the object existing. The synonym is created without error, but you get an error message if you attempt to access the synonym. The following synonym, called SYNONYM_TEST, is based on a nonexistent TEST_ME object, which could be a view, a table, another synonym, or another type of Oracle object.

```
CREATE SYNONYM synonym_test FOR test_me
Synonym created.
```

Accessing the synonym results in this message.

```
SQL>SELECT *
  2    FROM synonym_test;
   FROM synonym_test
        *
ERROR at line 2:
ORA-009800: synonym translation is no longer valid
```

Public Synonyms

All synonyms are private unless the keyword PUBLIC is specified. Public synonyms are visible to all users of the database. However, object privileges are not automatically granted to the underlying objects. You still need to issue grants to either individual users or to PUBLIC by referring to either the public synonym or the underlying object. For the user MUSIC, the following statements create a table, create a public synonym for the table, and grant the SELECT privilege on the table to the user STUDENT.

```
CREATE TABLE instrument
  (instrument_id  NUMBER(10),
   description     VARCHAR2(25))
Table created.

CREATE PUBLIC SYNONYM instrument FOR instrument
Synonym created.

GRANT SELECT ON instrument TO student
Grant succeeded.
```

Now the user STUDENT can perform queries against the public synonym or the table INSTRU-MENT located in the MUSIC schema. The user STUDENT—or, for that matter, any other user—does not need to prefix the INSTRUMENT table with the owner. However, a public synonym does not mean that users other than the user STUDENT have access to the table. If you want every user in the database system to have SELECT privileges, you can grant the SELECT privilege to PUBLIC by using the following command.

```
GRANT SELECT ON instrument TO PUBLIC
```

 The ability to create public synonyms is typically granted to users with DBA privileges. To complete the exercises in this chapter for public synonyms, have your DBA grant the user STUDENT this privilege or log in as SYSTEM and grant the system privilege CREATE PUBLIC SYNONYM with the following statement: GRANT CREATE PUBLIC SYNONYM TO **student.**

Dropping and Renaming Synonyms

You drop synonyms by using the DROP SYNONYM command. The next commands drop the COURSE synonym and the public INSTRUMENT synonym.

```
DROP SYNONYM course
Synonym dropped.

DROP PUBLIC SYNONYM instrument
Synonym dropped.
```

If a synonym already exists and you want to change its definition, you can use the CREATE OR REPLACE SYNONYM command instead of dropping and re-creating a synonym.

```
CREATE OR REPLACE PUBLIC SYNONYM instrument FOR guitar
```

The RENAME command renames a synonym.

```
RENAME instrument TO instrument2
```

Resolving Schema References

Suppose a schema contains a public synonym INSTRUMENT that refers to a table in another user's schema and a table named INSTRUMENT in your own schema. When you issue a query against INSTRUMENT, Oracle resolves the schema reference by referring to the object in your own schema first. If such an object does not exist, Oracle refers to the public synonym.

User-Defined Roles

In addition to using Oracle's predefined system privilege roles (for example, CONNECT, RESOURCE, DBA), you can create user-defined roles to customize a grouping of system and/or object privileges. There may be different types of users for a given system. Sometimes, there are users who only view data, and those users need only SELECT privileges. There are other users who maintain the data, and they typically need a combination of SELECT, INSERT, UPDATE, and DELETE privileges on certain tables and columns. Perhaps programmers need privileges to create procedures, functions, and packages.

The syntax to create a role is as follows.

```
CREATE ROLE rolename
```

The following statement creates a role named READ_DATA_ONLY for users who only need to query the data in the STUDENT schema.

```
CREATE ROLE read_data_only
Role created.
```

The role still does not have any privileges associated with it. The following SELECT statement generates other statements, granting SELECT privileges on all the STUDENT schema's tables to the new role READ_DATA_ONLY.

```
SELECT 'GRANT SELECT ON '||table_name||
       ' TO read_data_only;'
   FROM user_tables
```

When the statement is executed from a script that in turn executes each resulting statement, the individual commands issued look similar to the following. If you are unsure how dynamic SQL scripts work, refer to Chapter 14, "The Data Dictionary, Scripting, and Reporting."

```
GRANT SELECT ON COURSE TO read_data_only;
...
GRANT SELECT ON STUDENT TO read_data_only;
GRANT SELECT ON ZIPCODE TO read_data_only;
```

With these individually executed statements, the role READ_DATA_ONLY obtains a collection of privileges. The next step is to grant the READ_DATA_ONLY role to users so these users have the privileges defined by the role. The following statement grants every user in the database this role by granting the READ_DATA_ONLY role to PUBLIC.

```
GRANT read_data_only TO PUBLIC
Grant succeeded.
```

Now all users of the database have SELECT privileges on all of the STUDENT schema's tables. All privileges defined by the role can be revoked in a single statement, such as the following.

```
REVOKE read_data_only FROM PUBLIC
Revoke succeeded.
```

If you want none of the users to have the SELECT privilege to the COURSE table anymore, you can revoke this privilege from the individual role only, and all users that have been granted this role will no longer have the ability to query the table. This makes the management of privileges fairly easy. If you want to grant the READ_DATA_ONLY role only to individual users, such as the MUSIC user instead of PUBLIC, you can issue a statement such as the following.

```
GRANT read_data_only TO MUSIC
```

Roles can be granted with the WITH ADMIN option, which allows the user to pass these privileges on to others.

The data dictionary views shown in Table 15.5 list information about roles.

TABLE 15.5   Data Dictionary Views Related to Roles

DATA DICTIONARY VIEW	PURPOSE
DBA_ROLES	All roles in the database
USER_ROLE_PRIVS	Roles granted to the current user
DBA_ROLE_PRIVS	Roles granted to users and other roles
ROLE_ROLE_PRIVS	Roles granted to roles
ROLE_SYS_PRIVS	System privileges granted to roles
DBA_SYS_PRIVS	System privileges granted to roles and users
ROLE_TAB_PRIVS	Object privileges granted to roles
SESSION_ROLES	Roles a user currently has enabled

The ability to create roles may be performed only by users with DBA privileges or by individual users granted the CREATE ROLE privilege. To complete the exercises in this chapter for user-defined roles, have your DBA grant this privilege to the STUDENT user or log in as SYSTEM and grant this system privilege by executing the statement GRANT CREATE ROLE TO student.

You drop roles by using the DROP ROLE command.

```
DROP ROLE read_data_only
```
Role dropped.

Profiles

A *profile* is a name for identifying specific resource limits or password features. A user account is always associated with a profile. If at the creation of an account a profile is not specified, the default profile is used. With a profile, you can enforce features such as password expiration settings, maximum idle times (that is, the maximum time without any activity for a session), or the maximum number of concurrent sessions.

There are many different profile options; the following syntax lists the most commonly used options.

```
CREATE PROFILE profilename LIMIT
{{SESSIONS_PER_USER|
  CPU_PER_SESSION|
  CPU_PER_CALL|
  CONNECT_TIME|
  IDLE_TIME}
   {integer|UNLIMITED|DEFAULT}}|
{{FAILED_LOGIN_ATTEMPTS|
  PASSWORD_LIFE_TIME|
  PASSWORD_REUSE_TIME|
  PASSWORD_REUSE_MAX|
  PASSWORD_LOCK_TIME|
  PASSWORD_GRACE_TIME}
   {expression|UNLIMITED|DEFAULT}}
```

The next statement creates a profile named MEDIUM_SECURITY. With this profile, the password expires after 30 days. If the user logs in with the wrong password, the account is locked after three failed attempts. The password is then locked for one hour (1/24 of a day) unless the DBA unlocks it with the ALTER USER user_name ACCOUNT UNLOCK command. The maximum number of concurrent sessions a user may have is three, and the inactivity time, excluding long-running queries, is 15 minutes.

```
CREATE PROFILE medium_security
 LIMIT
  PASSWORD_LIFE_TIME 30
  FAILED_LOGIN_ATTEMPTS 3
  PASSWORD_LOCK_TIME 1/24
  SESSIONS_PER_USER 3
  IDLE_TIME 15
Profile created.
```

When the password expires after the 30 days, the user is prompted to change the password.

You assign a profile to an individual user with the ALTER USER command. The user's resource and password restrictions are then limited within the definition of the profile.

```
ALTER USER music
  PROFILE medium_security
User altered.
```

You can change profiles by using the ALTER PROFILE command, and you can remove them with the DROP PROFILE command. If you drop a profile, any assigned users associated with the profile are automatically assigned the DEFAULT profile.

You can see information about profiles in the data dictionary views DBA_PROFILES and DBA_USERS. These views are available only if you have the right to see DBA_ views.

Additional Security Measures

You can implement stored PL/SQL procedures to encapsulate the security access and business rules to certain transactions. For example, you can create a PL/SQL procedure to update individual employee salaries only during certain hours and within a certain percentage increase range. This way, instead of granting UPDATE rights on the SALARY column of the EMPLOYEE tabled, you grant the users the right to execute the procedure through which all salary updates must be performed. All the security and logic is enforced and encapsulated within the procedure.

For even finer-grained access control, Oracle provides a feature called the *Virtual Private Database* (VPD) that allows very sophisticated control over many aspects of data manipulation and data access.

Security Implementation

In live production environments, users typically don't log on as owners of the tables they access. Imagine a scenario in which an application user knows the password of the STUDENT account. If the user logs in as the owner of the objects, he or she has the ability to drop tables, update any of the data, or drop any of the indexes in the schema. Needless to say, this situation is a disaster waiting to happen.

A responsible and cautious DBA creates one user account that receives grants for the objects. For example, the DBA may create a STUDENT_USER account to which the application users have access. This account is granted SELECT, INSERT, UPDATE, and DELETE privileges on the various tables.

The DBA then creates synonyms (private or public) so the STUDENT_USER's queries do not need the owner prefix. This STUDENT_USER account cannot drop the STUDENT tables or alter them because the account is not the owner of the table, and the DBA does not grant the system privileges, such as DROP ANY TABLE or ALTER ANY TABLE.

Most individual applications have their own fine-grained security that restricts users to specific screens. There are many ways to implement security, and each individual security implementation depends on the unique requirements of an application. Oracle provides a variety of ways to control and manage the protection of data from unauthorized use.

Creating and Modifying Users and Their Privileges with SQL Developer

SQL Developer has a number of menu options to aid in administering users. While not all syntax options are available, the very commonly used functionality is addressed. Click your Connections node, right-click Other Users, and choose Create User. Figure 15.1 shows the dialog box you use to create a new user. On the User tab, you enter the username and password, and you assign the default and temporary tablespaces from the drop-down lists.

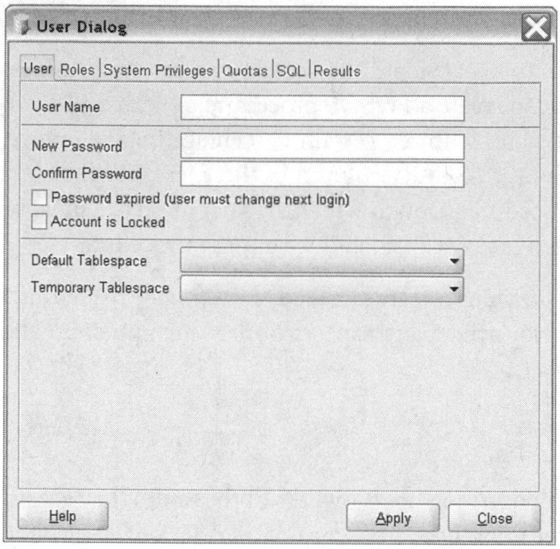

FIGURE 15.1
The User Dialog screen in SQL Developer

The Roles tab lists all the available roles, with check boxes to grant or revoke the roles to the user. Similarly, the System Privileges tab provides a list of all system privileges to choose from (see Figure 15.2). The Quotas tab allows you to define access to tablespaces and assign quotas, if any. The SQL tab generates the appropriate SQL statement, and the Results tab shows the execution result after you click the Apply button on the SQL tab.

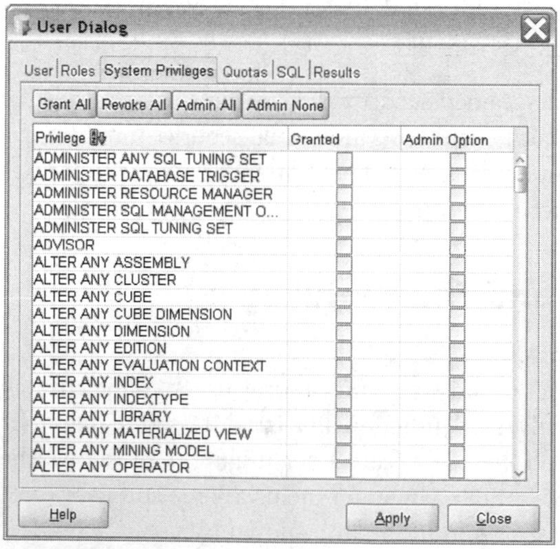

FIGURE 15.2
The System Privileges tab in SQL Developer

You may have noticed that object privileges are not part of the User Dialog screen. Instead, to grant or revoke object privileges, right-click the particular object, such as a table, and choose Privileges. If you then choose Grant, you get a screen similar to Figure 15.3. For the given object, you can choose to whom to grant the selected privileges, such as a user or a role.

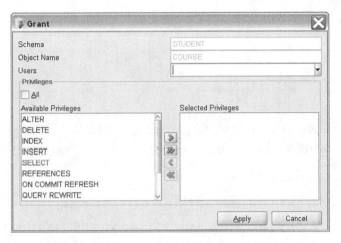

FIGURE 15.3
The Grant Object privilege screen in SQL Developer

Oracle Accounts

In the exercises so far in this book, you have been using the STUDENT account. During the lab exercises later, you will create different user accounts so that you can better understand the effects of the GRANT and REVOKE commands.

To connect to a different user account in SQL Developer, you need to create a new connection name, using the new user's name and password. In Chapter 2, "SQL: The Basics," you learned about creating a connection name in SQL Developer.

You can switch between different connections by using the SQL Worksheet icon, which invokes the dialog box shown in Figure 15.4, where you can choose a connection.

In SQL*Plus, you can start another session under a different login name by using the CONNECT command at the SQL*Plus prompt. The CONNECT command can be abbreviated to CONN, followed by the user ID, a forward slash, and the password.

```
SQL> CONN system/manager
Connected.
```

When you connect as another user while you are running a SQL*Plus session, you are no longer logged in as the previous user. If you prefer, you can just start a new SQL*Plus session to keep both sessions connected.

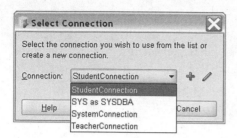

FIGURE 15.4
The Select Connection Dialog box in SQL Developer

The following is the syntax for the CONNECT command when using SQL *Plus.

```
CONN[ECT] username/password[@connect_identifier] [AS {SYSOPER|SYSDBA}]
```

The following is alternative syntax for the CONNECT command.

```
CONN[ECT] /[@connect_identifier] AS {SYSOPER|SYSDBA}
```

If you do not supply the password, you are prompted to enter it, as shown in the following example. This may be useful if you do not want to display the password on the screen.

```
SQL> CONN system
Enter password: ******
Connected.
```

The following SQL *Plus example shows how you include the host string that identifies the name of the database you want to connect if you are connecting to a database other than the default or local database. In this case, the remote database name is ITCHY, and it is referenced with the @ symbol.

```
CONN system/manager@itchy
```

 If during your SQL *Plus session you are unsure which login account you are connected to, issue the SHOW USER command or simply change your SQLPROMPT from SQL> to the current user account with the SET SQLPROMPT _USER> command. The SQLPROMPT command is discussed as part of the predefined SQL*Plus variables in Appendix C, "SQL*Plus Command Reference."

Connecting with Special Privileges: SYSOPER and SYSDBA

Oracle allows special privileged modes of connection to the database: SYSOPER and SYSDBA. The SYSOPER privilege allows startup and shutdown operations and other basic operational tasks, such as backups, but does not allow the user to look at the user data. The SYSDBA privilege allows you to perform startup and shutdown of the database and to effectively connect as the most privileged user—the SYS user account.

You connect with your user schema name and append AS SYSOPER or AS SYSDBA. For example, to connect in SQL*Plus, you can issue the following CONNECT command if the MUSIC user has been granted the SYSDBA privilege.

```
CONNECT music AS SYSDBA
```

The user MUSIC is now in a privileged mode of connection that allows the startup or shutdown of the database with the STARTUP or SHUTDOWN command.

When connected as SYSDBA or SYSOPER, you are not connected with the schema associated with your username. Rather, if you connect as SYSOPER, you connect as the owner PUBLIC, and for SYSDBA as the owner SYS, which is the most highly privileged user and owns the data dictionary.

Starting Up and Shutting Down a Database

The following statements show how to shut down a database with the SHUTDOWN command in SQL*Plus.

```
SQL> CONN system AS SYSDBA
Enter password: *****
Connected.

SQL> SHUTDOWN
Database closed.
Database dismounted.
ORACLE instance shut down.
```

To start up the database, you use the STARTUP command.

```
SQL> CONN system AS SYSDBA
Enter password: *****
Connected.

SQL> STARTUP
ORACLE instance started.

Total System Global Area   192937984 bytes
Fixed Size                    769488 bytes
Variable Size              143573552 bytes
Database Buffers            25165824 bytes
Redo Buffers                23429120 bytes
Database mounted.
Database opened.
```

In SQL Developer, you can also connect with the SYSDBA privilege. Figure 15.5 shows an example of connecting as the SYS user with the SYSDBA privilege.

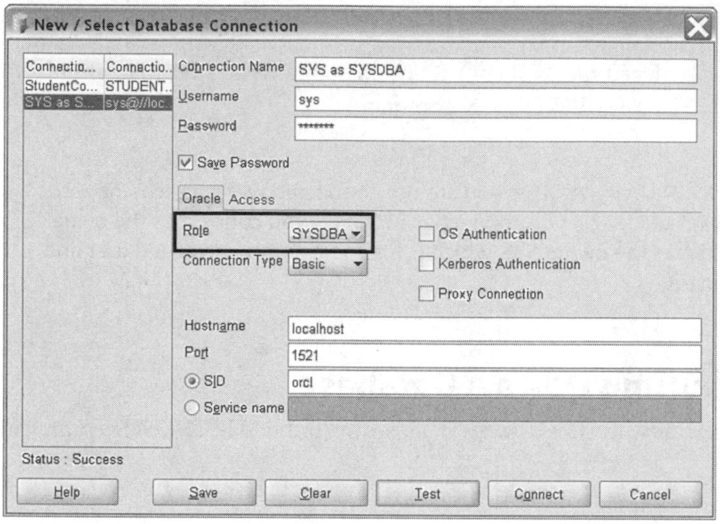

FIGURE 15.5
A SQL Developer database connection

After you have established and tested the connection successfully, you can right-click the connection and choose Manage Database. You then see a screen similar to Figure 15.6, which displays how much memory is allocated to Oracle's SGA and PGA memory areas, as well as a list of tablespaces, with the space availability. Because you are connected as SYSDBA, you see the Shutdown button to the right of the screen.

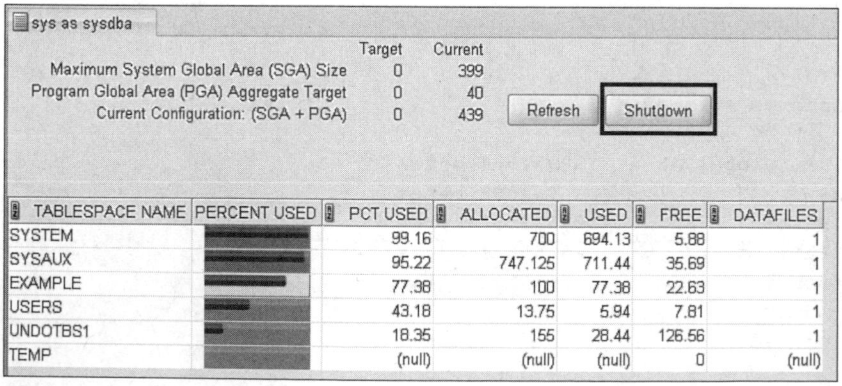

FIGURE 15.6
The Manage Database screen

▼ LAB 15.1 EXERCISES

You can perform a number of the tasks in these exercises by using SQL Developer's various menu choices. Your menu actions result in generated SQL, very much like the SQL commands listed in the exercise answers. If you choose to use SQL Developer, compare the generated SQL to the exercise answers provided here.

a) Log in as SYSTEM (or any other account that allows you to create a new user) and create a user called TEACHER with the password subject (in lowercase), with the appropriate default and temporary tablespaces for your database. Using Oracle's predefined roles, grant enough privileges to the new user that the user can create a table. Log in as the new user and create a table called ACCOUNT with these three columns: ACCOUNT_NUM as the primary key column and the columns ACCOUNT_TYPE and ACCOUNT_STATUS. Determine appropriate data types for the columns. Insert a row with the values 1001, Checking, and Active, for these columns.

b) While logged in as the new user named TEACHER created in exercise a, execute the following SELECT statements against the data dictionary views. What do these views tell you about the new user?

```
SELECT username, granted_role, admin_option
  FROM user_role_privs

SELECT *
  FROM session_privs
```

c) While logged in as the user TEACHER, grant the SELECT privilege for the ACCOUNT table to the STUDENT user and allow the STUDENT user to grant the same privilege to other users. Then log in as the STUDENT user and execute the following two statements. What do you observe?

```
SELECT *
  FROM teacher.account

INSERT INTO teacher.account
  (account_num, type, status)
VALUES
  (1002, 'Savings', 'Active')

SELECT *
  FROM teacher.account_status
```

d) Connect as SYSTEM and change the password for the user TEACHER from subject to class. Log in as TEACHER and revoke the SELECT privileges from the STUDENT user on the ACCOUNT table.

e) Execute the following query as the user TEACHER. What purpose does this data dictionary view serve?

```
SELECT username, default_tablespace, temporary_tablespace
  FROM user_users
```

f) While logged in as the user STUDENT, create a private synonym called COURSE for the COURSE table. Describe your observations.

g) Explain the result of the following SELECT statement.

```
SELECT 'CREATE PUBLIC SYNONYM '||table_name||
       ' FOR '||table_name||';'
  FROM user_tables
```

h) While logged in as the user STUDENT, create a role called STUDENT_ADMIN. Grant INSERT and UPDATE privileges on the COURSE table to the role. Then grant the role to TEACHER.

i) Execute the following SELECT statement and describe the result.

```
SELECT grantee, table_name, grantor,
       privilege, grantable
  FROM user_tab_privs_made
```

▼ LAB 15.1 EXERCISE ANSWERS

The text <default_tablespace> and <temporary_tablespace> in the following exercise answers is where the name of the appropriate tablespaces in your database should appear in your answers.

a) Log in as SYSTEM (or any other account that allows you to create a new user) and create a user called TEACHER with the password subject (in lowercase), with the appropriate default and temporary tablespaces for your database. Using Oracle's predefined roles, grant enough privileges to the new user that the user can create a table. Log in as the new user and create a table called ACCOUNT with these three columns: ACCOUNT_NUM as the primary key column and the columns ACCOUNT_TYPE and ACCOUNT_STATUS. Determine appropriate data types for the columns. Insert a row with the values 1001, Checking, and Active, for these columns.

ANSWER: In SQL*Plus, you can use the CONNECT command to connect as the SYSTEM user. In SQL Developer, you need to create a connection for the SYSTEM account if one does not already exist.

You use the CREATE USER command and the GRANT command to create the new user and grant system privileges to the user.

```
CONN system/manager
Connected.
```

```
CREATE USER teacher IDENTIFIED BY subject
  DEFAULT TABLESPACE <default_tablespace>
  TEMPORARY TABLESPACE <temporary_tablespace>
User created.
```

```
GRANT CONNECT, RESOURCE TO teacher
Grant succeeded.
```

You use the CONNECT command again to connect as the new user if you use SQL*Plus. In SQL Developer, create a new connection for the TEACHER user and connect via this new connection.

```
CONN teacher/subject
Connected.
```

The following CREATE TABLE command creates the new table within the TEACHER schema.

```
CREATE TABLE account
   (account_num   NUMBER(15),
    type          VARCHAR2(10),
    status        VARCHAR2(6),
    CONSTRAINT account_pk PRIMARY KEY(account_num))
```
Table created.

```
INSERT INTO account
   (account_num, type, status)
VALUES
   (1001, 'Checking', 'Active')
```
1 row created.

```
COMMIT
Commit complete.
```

b) While logged in as the new user named TEACHER created in exercise a, execute the following SELECT statements against the data dictionary views. What do these views tell you about the new user?

```
SELECT username, granted_role, admin_option
   FROM user_role_privs

SELECT *
   FROM session_privs
```

ANSWER: The query against the USER_ROLE_PRIVS view lists what Oracle roles the user TEACHER has been granted and whether the user has been granted the administration option on those roles. The query against the SESSION_PRIVS view shows the privileges currently available to the user TEACHER.

```
SELECT username, granted_role, admin_option
   FROM user_role_privs
```

USERNAME	GRANTED_ROLE	ADM
TEACHER	CONNECT	NO
TEACHER	RESOURCE	NO

2 rows selected.

```
SELECT *
   FROM session_privs
```
PRIVILEGE

CREATE SESSION
UNLIMITED TABLESPACE
...
CREATE SEQUENCE

10 rows selected.

If the following statement had been issued by the SYSTEM account instead, the user TEACHER would be able to grant the same system privileges to another user, becoming the grantor and enabling the TEACHER account to grant these same privileges to another user.

```
GRANT CONNECT, RESOURCE TO teacher WITH ADMIN OPTION
Grant succeeded.
```

If you subsequently re-execute the query against the USER_ROLE_PRIVS view after issuing the revised GRANT command, you would see YES in the ADMIN_OPTION column.

```
SELECT username, granted_role, admin_option
  FROM user_role_privs
```

USERNAME	GRANTED_ROLE	ADM
--------	--------------	---
TEACHER	CONNECT	YES
TEACHER	RESOURCE	YES

```
2 rows selected.
```

These privileges are sufficient to create tables, sequences, and a few other object types, but not user accounts. The ability to create users must be granted individually or via the DBA role to the TEACHER user if you choose to do so. The following grant needs to be issued by the SYSTEM user.

```
GRANT CREATE USER TO teacher
Grant succeeded.
```

If you want the teacher user to also be able to create views, you need the following system privilege grant.

```
GRANT CREATE VIEW TO teacher
Grant succeeded.
```

c) While logged in as the user TEACHER, grant the SELECT privilege for the ACCOUNT table to the STUDENT user and allow the STUDENT user to grant the same privilege to other users. Then log in as the STUDENT user and execute the following two statements. What do you observe?

```
SELECT *
  FROM teacher.account

INSERT INTO teacher.account
  (account_num, type, status)
VALUES
  (1002, 'Savings', 'Active')
```

ANSWER: The INSERT statement results in an error due to insufficient privileges.

While logged on as the TEACHER user, issue the GRANT SELECT command on the ACCOUNT table. The WITH GRANT option allows the STUDENT user to pass this privilege on to others.

```
CONN teacher/subject
Connected.

GRANT SELECT ON account TO student WITH GRANT OPTION
Grant succeeded.
```

The first statement queries the ACCOUNT table in the TEACHER schema without any problems. The SELECT privilege on the ACCOUNT table was granted. The table name must be prefixed with the schema name.

```
CONN student/learn
Connected.


SELECT *
  FROM teacher.account
ACCOUNT_NUM TYPE        STATUS
----------- ---------- ------
       1001 Checking    Active

1 row selected.
```

The second statement attempts to insert a row into the ACCOUNT table. However, the STUDENT user does not have the privilege to perform this action. No INSERT grant on the table was issued to the STUDENT user, and this leads to the insufficient privileges error.

```
INSERT INTO teacher.account
   (account_num, type, status)
VALUES
   (1002, 'Savings', 'Active')
INSERT INTO teacher.account
                     *
ERROR at line 1:
ORA-01031: insufficient privileges
```

d) Connect as SYSTEM and change the password for the user TEACHER from subject to class. Log in as TEACHER and revoke the SELECT privileges from the STUDENT user on the ACCOUNT table.

   ANSWER: You use the ALTER USER command to change the password from subject to class. The REVOKE command revokes the SELECT privilege on the ACCOUNT table from the STUDENT user.

```
CONN system/manager
Connected.


ALTER USER teacher identified by class
User altered.


CONN teacher/class
Connected.


REVOKE SELECT ON account FROM student
Revoke succeeded.
```

   If you change the password on the account and saved the password as part of the SQL Developer Connection information, you need to update the password accordingly.

e) Execute the following query as the user TEACHER. What purpose does this data dictionary view serve?

```
SELECT username, default_tablespace, temporary_tablespace
  FROM user_users
```

ANSWER: It shows the current user's default and temporary tablespace.

```
USERNAME          DEFAULT_TABLESPACE    TEMPORARY_TABLESPACE
--------------    -------------------   --------------------
TEACHER           USERS                 TEMP
```

```
1 row selected.
```

If the user has any tablespace quotas assigned, you can issue the following query to determine the quota for each tablespace. Obviously, your result may differ from the output listed here.

```
SELECT tablespace_name, bytes/1024/1024 "MB"
  FROM user_ts_quotas
TABLESPACE_NAME                       MB
-----------------------------    ----------
SYSTEM                           .95703125
USERS                            13.8125
INDX                             .125
```

```
3 rows selected.
```

You assign quotas with the ALTER USER command, as in the following statements. The first assigns 100 M of space on the USERS tablespace to the TEACHER user. Alternatively, the second statement assigns unlimited use of the tablespace USERS to the TEACHER account.

```
ALTER USER teacher QUOTA 100 M ON users
ALTER USER teacher QUOTA UNLIMITED ON users
```

A user must have a quota for the tablespace or have been granted the UNLIMITED TABLESPACE system privilege (for example, through the RESOURCE role) to be able to create indexes and tables.

f) While logged in as the user STUDENT, create a private synonym called COURSE for the COURSE table. Describe your observations.

ANSWER: Two objects with the same name cannot exist in the same schema.

```
CREATE SYNONYM course FOR course
   CREATE SYNONYM course FOR course
   *
   ERROR at line 1:
ORA-01471: cannot create a synonym with same name as object
```

It is not necessary to create private synonyms for objects you already own. It is possible to do so, but the synonym must have a different name from the underlying object. Within one schema, all object names must be unique, regardless of the type of object.

Public synonyms are not owned by the user who creates them, so there is no conflict between the public synonym name and the name of the object on which it is based.

g) Explain the result of the following SELECT statement.

```
SELECT 'CREATE PUBLIC SYNONYM '||table_name||
       ' FOR '||table_name||';'
  FROM user_tables
```

ANSWER: The SELECT statement generates other SELECT statements dynamically. Each statement generated creates a public synonym for each table owned by the current user.

When you create public synonyms for other users to see your objects, you typically do it for many objects in your schema. Using a SELECT statement to generate other statements is the fastest way to do this.

h) While logged in as the user STUDENT, create a role called STUDENT_ADMIN. Grant INSERT and UPDATE privileges on the COURSE table to the role. Then grant the role to TEACHER.

ANSWER: First, you use the CREATE ROLE command to create the role. Then you issue the GRANT command to grant INSERT and UPDATE privileges, separated by commas, to the role. Another GRANT statement grants the role to the user TEACHER.

```
CREATE ROLE student_admin
Role created.

GRANT INSERT, UPDATE ON course TO student_admin
Grant succeeded.

GRANT student_admin TO TEACHER
Grant succeeded.
```

You can use WITH ADMIN OPTION to pass on the ability to grant the privileges being granted. The following statement is the same as the previous GRANT statement except that it also gives the TEACHER user the ability to pass on the privileges that are being granted.

```
GRANT student_admin TO teacher WITH ADMIN OPTION
Grant succeeded.
```

Now the user TEACHER can pass the same set of privileges to other users.

i) Execute the following SELECT statement and describe the result.

```
SELECT grantee, table_name, grantor,
       privilege, grantable
  FROM user_tab_privs_made
```

ANSWER: The result shows the details of all grants made on tables by the STUDENT user: the recipient of the grant (the grantee); the table on which the grant was based; the grantor, or the user who granted the privilege; the privilege granted on the table; and whether the privilege can be granted to other users.

The results vary, depending on the privileges you have granted and have been granted by other users.

```
GRANTEE           TABLE_NAME GRANTOR    PRIVILEGE  GRANTABLE
----------------- ---------- ---------- ---------- ----------
STUDENT_ADMIN     COURSE     STUDENT    INSERT     NO
STUDENT_ADMIN     COURSE     STUDENT    UPDATE     NO

2 rows selected.
```

You can see that the STUDENT_ADMIN role is the grantee of INSERT and UPDATE privileges on the COURSE table, and the STUDENT user is the grantor.

You can query the DICT data dictionary view to list several other data dictionary views containing information about the roles created and privileges granted in a system or refer to Tables 15.4 and 15.5.

You can easily view any object grants issued by reviewing the Grants tab for a chosen object. Figure 15.7 shows the Grants tab in the COURSE table, with details on the grantee, whether the privilege is grantable, and so on.

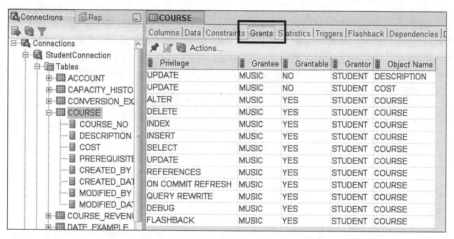

FIGURE 15.7
The Grants tab for an object in SQL Developer

Lab 15.1 Quiz

In order to test your progress, you should be able to answer the following questions.

1) A user's objects must be dropped in a separate statement before the user can be dropped.

    _____ a) True

    _____ b) False

2) The SQL*Plus CONNECT command is not the same as the CONNECT role.

    _____ a) True

    _____ b) False

3) The following statement contains an error.

```
REVOKE resource, SELECT ON course FROM music
```

    _____ a) True

    _____ b) False

4) System privileges cannot be granted through a role.

    _____ a) True

    _____ b) False

5) Dropping a role drops the underlying object on which the role's privileges are based.

    _____ a) True

    _____ b) False

6) Grants can be given to users, roles, or PUBLIC.

    _____ a) True

    _____ b) False

7) After issuing a DCL command, you must execute the COMMIT command to make a change permanent.

    _____ a) True

    _____ b) False

8) The SYSTEM Oracle account is a highly privileged account.

    _____ a) True

    _____ b) False

ANSWERS APPEAR IN APPENDIX A.

▼ WORKSHOP

The projects in this section are meant to prompt you to utilize all the skills you have acquired throughout this chapter. The answers to these projects can be found at the companion Web site to this book, located at www.oraclesqlbyexample.com.

To complete the following exercises, create a new user called SCHOOL with the password program and grant CONNECT and RESOURCE roles to this user. Then log in as the STUDENT user.

1) Create two roles: REGISTRAR and INSTRUCTOR.

2) Create a view called CURRENT_REGS that reflects all students who registered on January 25, 2007. Grant the SELECT privilege on the new view to the REGISTRAR role.

3) Create a view called ROSTER that reflects all students taught by the instructor Marilyn Frantzen. Grant the SELECT privilege on the new view to the INSTRUCTOR role.

4) Grant the REGISTRAR and INSTRUCTOR roles to the new user called SCHOOL.

5) Log in as the user SCHOOL and select from the two previously created views.

Regular Expressions and Hierarchical Queries

CHAPTER OBJECTIVES

In this chapter, you will learn about:

▶ Regular Expressions
▶ Hierarchical Queries

This lab will expand your knowledge of regular expressions so you can fully harness their potential. You will learn about the essential metacharacters and gain an understanding of how regular expressions are implemented within the context of the Oracle database.

Hierarchical queries are discussed in Lab 16.2. You will learn how to use the CONNECT BY clause and the PRIOR operator to graphically display a hierarchy and reveal the relationship of records within a table.

LAB 16.1
Regular Expressions

LAB OBJECTIVES

After this lab, you will be able to:

▶ Understand the Practical Applications for Regular Expressions
▶ Use Regular Expression Functionality within the Oracle Database

A regular expression is a notation for describing textual patterns. It consists of one or more literals and/or *metacharacters* that specify algorithms for performing complex text searches and modifications. A simple regular expression can consist only of character literals such as the regular expression 'hat'. You read it as the letter *h* followed by the letters *a* and *t*. It will match character strings such as 'hat', 'Manhattan', and 'chatter'. One of the metacharacters is the match-any character (.). For example, the regular expression 'h.t' matches strings such as 'hot', 'hat', or 'shutter'.

Data validation, identification of duplicate word occurrences, detection of extraneous white spaces, and parsing of strings are just some of the uses of regular expressions. You can take advantage of a regular expression to determine valid formats for phone numbers, zip codes, Social Security numbers, IP addresses, file and path names, and so on. Furthermore, you can locate patterns such as HTML tags, e-mail addresses, numbers, dates, or anything else that fits a pattern within any textual data and replace them with another pattern.

Regular Expressions and the Oracle Database

You find regular expressions in many programming languages, most notably in Perl and the UNIX grep, egrep, awk, and sed utilities. In addition, the power and flexibility of regular expressions are available in the Oracle database, through the use of the Oracle SQL operator REGEXP_LIKE, and the REGEXP_INSTR, REGEXP_REPLACE, and REGEXP_SUBSTR functions. The operator and functions work much like the familiar LIKE operator and the INSTR, REPLACE, and SUBSTR functions. In any SQL statement where you can use the LIKE operator or these functions, you can take advantage of regular expressions.

From Chapter 12, "Create, Alter, and Drop Tables," you may recall examples that demonstrate regular expressions in column check constraints to enforce data validation rules. You can also use regular expressions in a query to find a particular pattern, determine the starting position of a pattern, extract the substring of the pattern, or replace a pattern with another pattern.

Oracle supports POSIX ERE (Portable Operating System Interface Extended Regular Expressions)–compliant regular expressions. Learning the syntax of the regular expression language is useful because you can extend this knowledge to many other software products and languages.

Before using the regular expression functionality, you need to understand the meaning of the metacharacters. After this brief introduction, you will see how to apply the new Oracle operator and functions within the Oracle database.

The Match-Any and Anchoring Metacharacters

The period (.) matches any character (except a newline character) in a regular expression (see Table 16.1). For example, the regular expression 'x.z' matches a string containing the letter x, followed by any other single character (except newline), and followed by the letter z. The strings 'xpz', 'xxyzd', and 'xyz' contain this pattern.

TABLE 16.1   Match-Any Character

METACHARACTER	DESCRIPTION
.	Matches any single character except a newline.

If you want to exactly match a three-character string in which the line begins with x and ends with z, you must anchor the regular expression to the start and end of the regular expression pattern. The caret (^) metacharacter indicates the start of a line, and the dollar symbol ($) designates the end of the line (see Table 16.2). Therefore, the regular expression '^x.z$' matches the strings 'xaz', 'xoz', and 'xyz'. To contrast this approach with the familiar pattern matching available with the LIKE operator, you can express a pattern such as 'x_z', where the underscore (_) is the one-character wildcard.

TABLE 16.2   Anchoring Metacharacters

METACHARACTER	DESCRIPTION
^	Anchors the expression to the start of the line.
$	Anchors the expression to the end of the line.

Exploring Quantifiers

Regular expressions allow you to specify occurrences of a character with a *quantifier*, also called a *repetition operator*. If you want a match that starts with the letter x and ends with the letter z, your regular expression looks like this: '^x.*z$'. The * metacharacter repeats the preceding match-any metacharacter (.) zero, one, or more times. The equivalent pattern with the LIKE operator is 'x%z', with the percent symbol (%) indicating zero, one, or multiple occurrences of any character. Valid matches for the pattern are 'xz', 'xyyyyz', 'xyz', and 'xkkkkkz'. As you review Table 16.3, notice that these repetition choices allow more options than the LIKE wildcard characters.

TABLE 16.3   Quantifier Operators

QUANTIFIER	DESCRIPTION	EXAMPLE
*	Matches 0 or more times.	'ca*t' matches 'ct', 'cat', 'caat', 'caaat', and so on.
?	Matches 0 or 1 time.	'ca?t' matches 'ct' or 'cat'.
+	Matches 1 or more times.	'ca+t' matches 'cat', 'caat', and so on. 'ct' is not a valid match.
{m}	Matches exactly m times.	'ca{3}t' matches 'caaat'.
{m,}	Matches m or more times.	'ca{3,}t' matches 'caaat', 'caaaat', and so on.
{m, n}	Matches at least m times but no more than n times	'ca{3,5}t' matches 'caaat', 'caaaat', and 'caaaaat'.

The POSIX Character Classes

The POSIX character classes (see Table 16.4) allow you to specify what type of character you are looking for. You must specify the class name in lowercase; otherwise, the POSIX character class is invalid.

TABLE 16.4   Predefined POSIX Character Classes

CHARACTER CLASS	DESCRIPTION
[:alpha:]	Alphabetic characters
[:lower:]	Lowercase alphabetic characters
[:upper:]	Uppercase alphabetic characters
[:digit:]	Numeric digits
[:alnum:]	Alphanumeric characters
[:space:]	Space characters (nonprinting), such as carriage return, newline, vertical tab, and form feed
[:punct:]	Punctuation characters
[:cntrl:]	Control characters (nonprinting)
[:print:]	Printable characters

For example, a regular expression such as '[[:digit:]]{5}' shows the POSIX character class digit delimited by colons and square brackets. The second set of brackets (as in [[:digit:]]) encloses a character class list and is required because POSIX character classes can only be used to construct a character list. The '{5}' is a quantifier; it specifies the exact five repetitions of the digit character class.

Character Lists

In addition to the predefined POSIX character classes, you can create your own character classes or lists. The square brackets ([ ]) symbol indicates a character list where any of the characters can be matched. With the hyphen (-), you define a range between the starting and ending points. For example, the regular expression [0-5] includes characters with digits from 0 through 5. Multiple ranges such as [a-zA-Z] include the upper- and lowercase characters. Ranges must be in order; a range such as [z-a] is not valid. If you want to include all characters a through z, you might want to consider using the [:lower:] POSIX character class because the POSIX standard supports multilingual environment.

When characters are not in a range, they can be placed in any order, such as [5738]; this expression would find any string that contains a 5, 7, 3, or 8.

A hyphen placed as the first character of a list (for example, [-abc]) indicates a literal hyphen and not a range. Within a character class, most metacharacters are treated as character literals rather than as special metacharacter operators. The special cases are the hyphen, caret, and backslash. You will see some examples shortly that illustrate their use and help you understand when a metacharacter should be the literal character instead.

Negation of Character Lists

Some metacharacters have different meanings, depending on their position within the regular expression. You already learned about the ^ start-of-line metacharacter. Its second meaning is the negation metacharacter; it negates a character list if it is the first character in the character list. For example, '[^58]' matches any character except 5 or 8. The strings '0', '395', 'abc', and '5890' are valid matches because all or some characters are "not 5 or 8"; however, '58', '85', and '585' are not matches. Table 16.5 provides an overview of the character list metacharacters.

TABLE 16.5   Character List Metacharacters

METACHARACTER	DESCRIPTION
[^]	Negated. If this metacharacter is the first character in the character list, it negates the list. Otherwise, it's the literal ^. (^can also mean the beginning of a line outside the bracketed expression, as described in the section, "The Match-Any and Anchoring Metacharacters.")
[char]	Matching character list. Indicates a character list. Most metacharacters inside a character list are interpreted as literals, with the exception of ^ and -.
-	Range. Represents characters in a range. To match the literal hyphen and not a range, it must be the first character inside the character list (for example, '[-a-z]').
[::]	Character class. The predefined POSIX standard character classes include linguistic ranges for the current locale.
[.char.]	Collating sequence. Indicates a POSIX collation element, useful for foreign language support.
[=char=]	Character equivalence class. Lets you search for characters in the current locale that are equivalent. This can be useful for ignoring accents and case in foreign languages.

Perl Expressions

Oracle added Perl-influenced regular expressions, which abbreviate some of the POSIX character classes. For example, you can simplify '[[:digit:]]{5}' to '\d{5}'. The opposite of no digit in POSIX is '[^[:digit:]]', and the equivalent Perl extension is '\D'. Table 16.6 shows Oracle's Perl extensions.

TABLE 16.6   Perl Extensions

METACHARACTER	DESCRIPTION
\d	Numeric digits; same as POSIX [[:digit]].
\D	Not a digit; equivalent to POSIX [^[:digit]].
\w	A word, which includes alphanumeric values and the underscore (_). The POSIX equivalent is [[:alnum:]_].
\W	Not a word containing letters, numbers, or underscores but a special character, such as punctuation. The POSIX equivalent is [^[:alnum:]_].
\s	A white space. This is the same as POSIX [[:space:]].
\S	Not a space character; equivalent to [^[:space:]].
\A	Indicates that the following should only be considered at the beginning of a line. For example, the expression '\At' considers the first occurring letter t to be a match only if located at the beginning of a line.
\Z	This metacharacter consider the end of a string. For example, the string 'Cat Dog ' contains one space between the words 'Cat' and 'Dog' and another space after 'Dog'. The regular expression '\s\Z', successfully finds the white space at the end of the line.

The REGEXP_LIKE Operator

Now that you are familiar with the most important metacharacters, you can use the REGEXP_LIKE operator to see how the regular expression functionality is applied within the Oracle database. The following SQL query's WHERE clause shows the REGEXP_LIKE operator, which searches the ZIP column for a pattern that satisfies the regular expression [^[:digit:]]. It retrieves those rows in the ZIPCODE_EXAMPLE table for which the ZIP column values contain any character that is not a numeric digit.

```
SELECT zip
  FROM zipcode_example
 WHERE REGEXP_LIKE(zip, '[^[:digit:]]')
ZIP
-----
ab123
123xy
007ab
abcxy

4 rows selected.
```

This regular expression consists only of metacharacters—more specifically the POSIX character class digit, delimited by colons and square brackets. The second set of brackets (as in '[^[:digit:]]') encloses a character class list. As previously mentioned, this is required because you can use POSIX character classes only for constructing a character list.

 The ZIPCODE_EXAMPLE table exists in your schema only if you downloaded and installed the additional script available from the companion Web site, located at www.oraclesqlbyexample.com.

Following is the syntax of the REGEXP_LIKE operator.

```
REGEXP_LIKE(source_string, pattern
  [, match_parameter])
```

The SOURCE_STRING supports character data types. The PATTERN parameter is another name for the regular expression. The MATCH_PARAMETER allows optional parameters, such as handling the newline character, retaining multiline formatting, and providing control over case-sensitivity. You will see some examples of this parameter later in the lab.

The REGEXP_SUBSTR Function

The REGEXP_SUBSTR function returns the substring that matches the pattern, and the syntax is as follows.

```
REGEXP_SUBSTR(source_string, pattern
  [, position [, occurrence
  [, match_parameter] [,subexpr]]])
```

The POSITION parameter indicates the starting position for the search, which defaults to 1, the beginning of the string. The default value for the OCCURRENCE parameter is 1, looking for the first occurrence of the pattern.

The following query uses the new REGEXP_SUBSTR function to find and return the five-digit zip code pattern within a string. The pattern requires five consecutive digits anchored to the end of the line, as indicated with the $ metacharacter; otherwise, you get the house number 12345 instead.

```
SELECT REGEXP_SUBSTR('Joe Smith, 12345 Berry Lane, Orta, CA 91234',
       '[[:digit:]]{5}$')
       AS substr
  FROM dual
SUBST
-----
91234

1 row selected.
```

The REGEXP_INSTR Function

The REGEXP_INSTR function works somewhat like the familiar INSTR function; however, it looks for a pattern rather than a specific string.

The next example uses the function to determine the starting position of the five-digit zip code pattern within a string.

```
SELECT REGEXP_INSTR('NY 10032 USA',
       '[[:digit:]]{5}')
       AS rx_instr
  FROM dual
  RX_INSTR
----------
         4

1 row selected.
```

You can indicate the starting position of the search and which occurrence of the pattern you want to find, both of which default to 1. The default value for the RETURN_OPTION parameter is 0, and it returns the starting position of the match. Alternatively, a RETURN_OPTION parameter value of 1 indicates the starting position of the next character following the match. The syntax of the REGEXP_INSTR function is as follows.

```
REGEXP_INSTR(source_string, pattern
    [, startposition [, occurrence [, return_option
    [, match_parameter] [,subexpr]]]])
```

Subexpressions and Alternate Matches

A subexpression is a part of a regular expression and enclosed with a set of parentheses. A subexpression can be repeated a certain number of times. The regular expression 'ba(na)*split' allows 0 or more repetitions of the subexpression 'na', for matches such as 'basplit', 'banasplit', 'bananasplit', and 'banananasplit'.

Parentheses are also used for alternation, with the vertical bar | symbol separating the alternates. The regular expression 't(a|e|i)n' allows three possible choices between the letters t and n. Valid results include words such as 'tan', 'ten', 'tin', and 'Pakistan', but not 'teen', 'mountain', or 'tune'. Alternatively, a character list such as 't[aei]n' yields the identical result. Table 16.7 describes the use of these metacharacters.

TABLE 16.7   Alternate Matching and Grouping of Expressions

METACHARACTER	DESCRIPTION
|	Alternation. Separates alternates; usually used with the grouping operator ( ).
( )	Group. Group subexpressions into a unit for alternations, for quantifiers, or for backreferencing (see the section, "Backreferences," later in this chapter).

The REGEXP_REPLACE Function

You learned about the REPLACE function in Chapter 4, "Character, Number, and Miscellaneous Functions." It substitutes one string with another string. Assume that your data has extraneous spaces in the text, and you would like to replace them with a single space. If you use the REPLACE function, you have to list exactly how many spaces you want to replace. However, the number of extraneous spaces may not be the same everywhere in the text.

The following example has three spaces between 'Joe' and 'Smith'. The function's parameter specifies that two spaces are replaced with one space. In this case, the result leaves an extra space between 'Joe' and 'Smith'.

```
SELECT REPLACE('Joe   Smith','  ', ' ')
       AS replace
  FROM dual
REPLACE
----------
Joe  Smith

1 row selected.
```

The REGEXP_REPLACE function takes the substitution a step further: It replaces the matching pattern with a specified regular expression, allowing for complex search and replace operations. The following query replaces any two or more spaces, '{2,}', with a single space. The ( ) subexpression contains a single space, which can be repeated two or more times. As you see from the result, only one space exists between the 'Joe' and 'Smith'.

```
SELECT REGEXP_REPLACE('Joe   Smith',
       '( ){2,}', ' ')
       AS RX_REPLACE
  FROM dual
RX_REPLAC
----------
Joe Smith

1 row selected.
```

The syntax of the REGEXP_REPLACE function is as follows.

```
REGEXP_REPLACE(source_string, pattern
  [, replace_string [, position [,occurrence, [match_parameter]]]])
```

By default, the start position is 1, and the OCCURRENCE parameter defaults to 0, which indicates that all matches are replaced.

The REGEXP_COUNT Function

Oracle 11g introduced the REGEXP_COUNT function, which allows you to determine how many times a pattern occurs within a given string. In the following example, the REGEXP_COUNT function determines that the pattern 'el' appears four times in the sentence.

```
SELECT REGEXP_COUNT(
   'The shells she sells are surely seashells.',
   'el', 1, 'i') REGEXP_COUNT
   FROM dual
REGEXP_COUNT
---------------
4

1 rows selected
```

Exploring the Match Parameter Option

The REGEXP_LIKE operator and all regular expression functions contain an optional match parameter. It allows matching for case, ignoring newlines, and matching across multiple lines.

CASE-SENSITIVE MATCHES

The following example shows how to ignore the case. The 'i' value in the match parameter performs a case-insensitive search, and the 'c' parameter makes it case-sensitive (the default). The query searches all student rows where the first name matches the pattern 'ta', regardless of case. The result includes the name 'Tamara' in the result.

```
SELECT first_name
   FROM student
 WHERE REGEXP_LIKE(first_name, 'ta', 'i')
FIRST_NAME
-------------------------
Julita
Tamara
Benita
Rita
Sengita

5 rows selected.
```

MATCHING A PATTERN THAT CROSSES MULTIPLE LINES

Recall that the match-any character (.) matches all characters except the newline character. Sometimes you might need to search for a pattern that stretches across multiple lines. The 'n' match parameter allows you to include the newline character as part of the match-any character. The following SQL statement shows a three-line source string; the desired substring of the pattern is 'cat.*dog'.

```
SELECT REGEXP_SUBSTR('My cat could have
followed the dog almost
immediately.', 'cat.*dog', 1, 1, 'n')
   FROM dual
REGEXP_SUBSTR('MYCAT
--------------------
cat could have
followed the dog

1 row selected.
```

The displayed output shows the substring that contains this pattern. The REGEXP_SUBSTR function lists the starting position of the search as 1, followed by the first occurrence, and then the 'n' match parameter option. If the 'n' option is omitted, the substring containing the pattern is not displayed.

TREATING A STRING AS A MULTILINE SOURCE

The multiline mode, 'm', effectively retains the source string as multiple logical lines and therefore allows the matching of the start- and end-of-line metacharacters. The next example shows a three-line string and determines the position of the pattern '^cat'. As indicated with the ^ metacharacter, the desired pattern is at the start of the line. The result shows that this pattern is found at position 49 of the string.

```
SELECT REGEXP_INSTR('My cat
followed the dog who followed another
cat.',
'^cat', 1,1,1,'m') AS cat_search
   FROM dual
CAT_SEARCH
----------
        49

1 row selected.
```

COMBINING MATCH PARAMETERS

You can combine match parameters. For example, 'in' makes the result case-insensitive and includes the newline character. However, an 'ic' parameter is contradictory and will default to case-sensitive matching. Table 16.8 contains an overview of the match parameter options.

TABLE 16.8   Match Parameter Choices

PARAMETER	DESCRIPTION
i	Match case-insensitive.
c	Match case-sensitive, the default.
n	A match for any character (.) in the pattern allows your search to include the newline character.
m	The source string is retained as multiple lines, and the anchoring metacharacters (^ and $) are respected as the start and end of each line.
x	Ignores all whitespace characters.

Backreferences

A useful feature of regular expression is the ability is to store subexpressions for later reuse; this is also referred to as *backreferencing*. This functionality allows sophisticated replace capabilities, such as swapping patterns in new positions or determining repeated word or letter occurrences. The matched part of the pattern is stored in a temporary buffer that is numbered from left to right and accessed with the '\digit' notation, whereby *digit* is a number between 1 through 9 and matches the digit-th subexpression, as indicated by a set of parentheses.

The following example shows the name 'Ellen Hildi Smith' transformed to 'Smith, Ellen Hildi'.

```
SELECT REGEXP_REPLACE(
       'Ellen Hildi Smith',
       '(.*) (.*) (.*)', '\3, \1 \2')
  FROM dual
REGEXP_REPLACE('EL
------------------
Smith, Ellen Hildi

1 row selected.
```

The query lists three individual subexpressions enclosed by the parentheses. Each individual subexpression consists of a match-any metacharacter (.) followed by the * metacharacter, indicating that the match-any character must be matched 0 or more times. A space separates the subexpressions and must be matched as well. In this case, the parentheses effectively create subexpressions that capture the values and can be referenced with '\digit'. The first subexpression is assigned \1, the second \2, and so on. These stored values are then backreferenced in the function as '\3, \1 \2', which effectively transform the string to the desired order and separates the third subexpression from the first with a comma.

Backreferences are also valuable for finding duplicate words, as in the following query, which looks for one or more alphanumeric characters followed by one or more spaces, followed by the same value found in the first subexpression. The result of the REGEXP_SUBSTR function shows the duplicated word *is*.

```
SELECT REGEXP_SUBSTR(
       'There is is a speed limit!',
       '([[:alnum:]]+)([[:space:]]+)\1') AS substr
  FROM dual
SUBST
-----
is is

1 row selected.
```

Word Boundaries

At times, you might want to match entire words, not just individual characters within a word or string. This is useful if you need to enclose certain words with HTML tags or simply replace whole words. For example, the regular expression 'cat' matches 'cat', 'caterpillar', or 'location'. The following regular expression query replaces the word 'cat' in the string 'The cat sat on the roof' with the word 'mouse'. If the input string is changed, to something like 'location is everything' or 'caterpillar', the replacement does not occur.

```
SELECT REGEXP_REPLACE('The cat sat on the roof',
       '(^|[^[:alpha:]])cat($|[^[:alpha:]])', ' mouse ')
  FROM dual
REGEXP_REPLACE('THECATSAT
-----------------------------
The mouse sat on the roof

1 row selected.
```

The pattern 'cat' starts with either a beginning of-line character (^) or a non-alpha character ([^[:alpha:]]), and the two choices are separated by the alternation metacharacter (|). The non-alpha character is anything but a letter and includes punctuation, spaces, commas, and so on. Then the letters 'cat' can be followed by either the end–of-line character or another non-alpha character.

The Backslash Character

The backslash (\) has various meanings in a regular expression. You have already learned to apply it to backreference expressions; it can also be used as the escape character. For example, if you want to search for the * as a literal rather than use it as a metacharacter, you precede it with the backslash escape character. The expression then reads *, and the \ indicates that * is not the repetition operator but a literal *. Table 16.9 summarizes the escape and backreference metacharacters, and it provides some examples.

TABLE 16.9   The Escape and Backreference Metacharacters

METACHARACTER	DESCRIPTION	EXAMPLE
\char	The backslash indicates the escape character. The character following the escape character is matched as a literal rather than a metacharacter.	'abc*def' matches the string 'abc*def' because * is meant as the literal * rather than the repetition operator.
		When used within a character list, the literal \ does not need to be escaped. For example, the regular expression '[\abc]' matches the literal \. In this case, you do not need to escape the backslash.
\digit	The backslash with a digit between 1 and 9 matches the preceding digit-th parenthesized subexpression.	The regular expression '(abc)\1' checks for adjacent occurrences of the parenthesized subexpression 'abc'.

Many metacharacters do not need to be escaped when within a character list. For example, [.] indicates the literal period and does not requires a backslash escape character.

Applying Regular Expressions in Data Validation

Regular expressions are useful not only in queries but also for data validation. The following statement applies a column check constraint to the LAST_NAME column of the STUDENT table. This regular expression performs very basic validation.

```
ALTER TABLE student
  ADD CONSTRAINT stud_last_name_ck CHECK
  (REGEXP_LIKE(last_name, '^[-[:alpha:] .,()'']*$'))
```

The only allowed characters are alphabetical characters (lower- or uppercase), spaces, hyphens, periods, commas, quotation marks, and parentheses. The brackets effectively create a character list encompassing these characters and the POSIX class [:alpha:]. The characters within the character list can appear in any order within the pattern. The hyphen (-) is the first character in the list and therefore indicates the literal hyphen. Names that pass the column validation include Miller-Johnson and Smith Woldo. There are two single quotation marks in the character list; they allow the single quotation mark character to appear. For example, a name such as O'Connor is a valid pattern. The * metacharacter follows the character list, thus allowing zero-to-many repetitions. The regular expression begins and ends with the anchoring characters ^ and $ to avoid any other characters before or after the pattern.

Understanding Matching Mechanics

When you are searching for patterns within text, you may come across instances in which the pattern can be found multiple times. The following example illustrates this scenario. The letters 'is' occur multiple times in the string 'This is an isolated issue'. REGEXP_INSTR returns the first occurrence of the pattern in the first position of the string (the default), which displays the starting position of the pattern as 3 and the character following the end of the pattern as 5.

You can specify any subsequent occurrence with the appropriate occurrence parameter. If you need to find all occurrences, you might want to consider writing a small PL/SQL program to perform a loop to retrieve them.

```
SELECT REGEXP_INSTR('This is an isolated issue',
       'is', 1, 1, 0) AS start_pos,
       REGEXP_INSTR('This is an isolated issue',
       'is', 1, 1, 1) AS after_end
  FROM dual
 START_POS  AFTER_END
---------- ----------
         3          5


1 row selected.
```

The following example shows that when quantifiers are involved, Oracle's regular expressions are *greedy*. This means the regular expression engine tries to find the longest possible match. This pattern begins with an optional space, followed by the letters 'is' and then optional characters.

```
SELECT REGEXP_SUBSTR('This is an isolated issue',
       '*is.*')
  FROM dual
REGEXP_SUBSTR('THISISAN
----------------------
is is an isolated issue


1 row selected.
```

You can control the greediness of the expression with the ?' metacharacter. In Table 16.3, you learned about the various quantifier operators. Adding the ?' to the respective operator character makes a match non-greedy. The result now finds the shortest possible match.

```
SELECT REGEXP_SUBSTR('This is an isolated issue',
       '*is.*?')
  FROM dual
REGEXP_SUBSTR('THISISAN
----------------------
is


1 row selected.
```

As you have noticed by now, the same metacharacters are used for different purposes. For example, the? metacharacter can make a search non-greedy, and it can also be used as a quantifier operator. The ^ character is the start-of-line indicator, and it is also used for negating a list. Carefully read the metacharacters within the context of the regular expression to ensure your correct understanding.

Comparing Regular Expressions to Existing Functionality

Regular expressions have several advantages over the familiar LIKE operator and INSTR, SUBSTR, and REPLACE functions. These traditional SQL functions have no facility for matching patterns. Only the LIKE operator performs matching of characters, through the use of the % and _ wildcards, but LIKE does not support repetitions of expressions, complex alternations, ranges of characters, character lists, POSIX character classes, and so on. Furthermore, the new regular expression functions allow detection of duplicate word occurrences and swapping of patterns. Table 16.10 contrasts and highlights the capabilities of regular expressions versus the traditional SQL operators and functions.

TABLE 16.10   Regular Expression Pattern Matching Versus Existing Functionality

REGEXP	LIKE AND SQL FUNCTIONS
Complex pattern matching with repetitions, character classes, negation, alternations, and so on. character	Simple pattern matching for LIKE operator with % and _ indicating single or multiple characters, but does not support classes, ranges, and repetitions. The INSTR, SUBSTR, and REPLACE functions do not have any pattern-matching capabilities.
Backreference capabilities allow sophisticated replace functionality.	Very basic replace functionality.
Not supported in Oracle versions prior to 10g.	All Oracle versions.
Choices of expression patterns are easily formulated with the alternation operator.	Alternations must be formulated with OR conditions, which can easily become very complex.
Sensitive to language, territory, sort order, and character set.	No support for various locales unless specifically coded within the criteria of the query.

Regular expressions are very powerful because they help solve complex problems. Some of the functionality in regular expressions is very difficult to duplicate using traditional SQL functions. When you learn the basic building blocks of this somewhat cryptic language, you will see that regular expressions become an indispensable part of your toolkit not only in the context of SQL but also with other programming languages. While trial and error are often necessary to get your individual pattern right, the elegance and power of the regular expressions are indisputable.

Regular Expression Resources

This lab illustrates a number of regular expression patterns; you may find yourself trying to come up with your own pattern to validate an e-mail address, a URL, or a credit card number. Writing a regular expression that covers all the different pattern possibilities is not a trivial task. The Web is a good starting point for finding commonly used patterns, and it helps to review similar patterns as a starting point for your individual validation requirements.

▼ LAB 16.1 EXERCISES

a) Write a regular expression column constraint against the FIRST_NAME column of the STUDENT table to ensure that the first name starts with an uppercase character. The subsequent characters allowed are alphabetical letters, spaces, hyphens, quotation marks, and periods.

b) Describe the difference between the following two regular expressions and the corresponding result.

```
SELECT zip,
       REGEXP_INSTR(zip, '[[:digit:]]{5}') exp1,
       REGEXP_INSTR(zip, '[[:digit:]{5}]') exp2
  FROM zipcode_example
```

ZIP	EXP1	EXP2
ab123	0	3
007ab	0	1
123xy	0	1
abcxy	0	0
10025	1	1

```
5 rows selected.
```

c) The following SQL statement creates a table called DOC_LOCATION and adds a regular expression column check constraint to the FILE_NAME column. List examples of different file names that will pass the validation.

```
CREATE TABLE doc_location
   (doc_id NUMBER,
    file_name VARCHAR2(200) CONSTRAINT doc_loc_file_name_ck
    CHECK (REGEXP_LIKE(file_name,
      '^([a-zA-Z]:|[\\])[\\]([^\\]+[\\])*[^?*;"<>|\/]+\.[a-zA-Z]{1,3}$')))
```

d) Explain the regular expression metacharacters used in the following SQL statement and their effect on the resulting output.

```
SELECT REGEXP_SUBSTR('first field, second field   , third field',
       ', [^,]*,')
  FROM dual
REGEXP_SUBSTR('FIR
------------------
, second field    ,

1 row selected.
```

e) Explain what the following statement accomplishes.

```
CREATE TABLE zipcode_regexp_test
   (zip VARCHAR2(5) CONSTRAINT zipcode_example_ck
      CHECK(REGEXP_LIKE(zip,
      '[[:digit:]]{5}(-[[:digit:]]{4})?$')))
```

f) Describe the result of the following query.

```
SELECT REGEXP_INSTR('Hello', 'x?'),
       REGEXP_INSTR('Hello', 'xy?')
  FROM dual
```

g) Describe the individual components of the following regular expression check constraint.

```
ALTER TABLE instructor
   ADD CONSTRAINT inst_phone_ck CHECK
   (REGEXP_LIKE(phone,
'^(\([[:digit:]]{3}\)|[[:digit:]]{3})[- ]?[[:digit:]]{3}[- ]?[[:digit:]]{4}$'))
```

▼ LAB 16.1 EXERCISE ANSWERS

a) Write a regular expression column constraint against the FIRST_NAME column of the STUDENT table to ensure that the first name starts with an uppercase character. The subsequent characters allowed are alphabetical letters, spaces, hyphens, quotation marks, and periods.

ANSWER: The individual components of the regular expression are listed in Table 16.11.

```
ALTER TABLE student
   ADD CONSTRAINT stud_first_name_ck CHECK
   (REGEXP_LIKE(first_name, '^[[:upper:]]{1}[-[:alpha:] .'']*$'))
```

TABLE 16.11   First Name Regular Expression Example

METACHARACTER	DESCRIPTION
^	Start-of-line metacharacter; anchors the pattern to the beginning of the line and therefore does not permit leading characters before the pattern.
[	Start of class list.
[:upper:]	Uppercase alphabetic POSIX character class.
]	End of class list.
{1}	Exactly one repetition of the uppercase alphabetical character class list.
[	Start of another character list.
-	A hyphen; this does not indicate range because it is at the beginning of the character list.
[:alpha:]	POSIX alphabetical character class.
	Blank space.
.	The period, not the match-any character.

TABLE 16.11   Continued

METACHARACTER	DESCRIPTION
"	Two individual quotes, indicating a single quote.
]	End of the second character list.
*	Zero to many repetitions of the character list.
$	The end-of-line metacharacter; anchors the pattern to the end of the line and therefore does not permit any other characters following the pattern.

This solution looks for allowable characters. You can approach regular expression validation by defining which characters to exclude, with the ^negation character at the beginning of the character list, or by using the NOT REGEXP_LIKE operator. As always, there are a number of ways to solve the problem, depending on the individual requirements and circumstances. Careful testing for various ranges of values and scenarios ensures that the regular expression satisfies the desired validation rules.

b)   Describe the difference between the following two regular expressions and the corresponding result.

```
SELECT zip,
       REGEXP_INSTR(zip, '[[:digit:]]{5}') exp1,
       REGEXP_INSTR(zip, '[[:digit:]{5}]') exp2
  FROM zipcode_example
ZIP          EXP1         EXP2
------       ----------   ----------
ab123            0            3
007ab            0            1
123xy            0            1
abcxy            0            0
10025            1            1

5 rows selected.
```

ANSWER: The difference between the two regular expressions is the location of the repetition operator. The first regular expression requires exactly five occurrences of the POSIX digit class. The result shows the starting position of those rows that match the pattern. A row such as 'ab123' does not have five consecutive numbers; therefore, REGEXP_INSTR returns 0.

In the second regular expression, the position of the repetition operator '{5}' was purposely misplaced within the character list, and as a result, the regular expressions requires the occurrence of either a digit or the opening and closing braces ({ }). Therefore, the zip value 'ab123' fulfils this requirement at starting position 3.

c)   The following SQL statement creates a table called DOC_LOCATION and adds a regular expression column check constraint to the FILE_NAME column. List examples of different file names that will pass the validation.

```
CREATE TABLE doc_location
  (doc_id NUMBER,
   file_name VARCHAR2(200) CONSTRAINT doc_loc_file_name_ck
   CHECK (REGEXP_LIKE(file_name,
    '^([a-zA-Z]:|[\])[\]([^\]+[\])*[^?*;"<>|\/]+\.[a-zA-Z]{1,3}$')))
```

ANSWER: Valid file names include c:\filename.txt, c:\mydir\filename.d, c:\myfile\mydir\filename.sql, and \\myserver\mydir\filename.doc.

The regular expression checks for these valid Windows file name and directory conventions. The pattern begins with either a drive letter followed by a colon and a backslash or with a double backslash, which indicates the server name. This is possibly followed by subdirectory names. The subsequent file name ends with a one-, two-, or three-letter extension. Table 16.12 shows the individual components of the regular expression broken down by drive/machine name, directory, file name, and extension.

TABLE 16.12   File Name Validation

METACHARACTER(S)	DESCRIPTION
^	No leading characters are permitted prior to the start of the pattern.
([a-zA-Z]:|[\\])	This subexpression allows either a drive letter followed by a colon or a machine name, as indicated with the backslash. (Machine names start with two backslashes, as you'll see later.) The choices are separated by the |alternation operator. The backslash character is enclosed within the character list because it is not meant as the escape character or as a backreference. Valid patterns can start with c: or \.
[\\]	The backslash is again a literal backslash; a valid start of the pattern may now look like c:\ or \\.
([^\\]+[\\])*	The next subexpression allows 0, 1, or multiple repetitions. This subexpression builds the machine name and/or the directory name(s). It starts with one or many characters, as indicated by the + quantities, but the first character cannot be a backslash character. It is ended by a backslash. Effectively, a valid pattern so far can read as c:\, c:\mydir\, c:\mydir\mydir2\, \\myserver\, or \\myserver\mydir\.
[^?*;"<>|\\]+	This part of the regular expression validates the file name. A file name can consist of one or more characters, hence the +, but may not contain any of the characters listed in the character lists, as indicated with the ^ negation character. The start of a valid pattern may be c:\filename, c:\mydir\filename, c:\mydir\mydir2\filename, \\myserver\filename, or \\myserver\mydir\filename.
\.[a-zA-Z]{1,3}	The file name is followed by a period. Here the period must be escaped; otherwise, it indicates the match-any character. The period is followed by an alphabetical one-, two-, or three-letter extension.
$	The end-of-line metacharacter ends the regular expression and ensures that no other characters are permitted.

Compared to the other regular expressions you have seen, this regular expression is fairly long. If you try out the statement, be sure the regular expression fits on one line. Otherwise, the end-of-line character is part of the regular expression, and you will not get the desired result.

The regular expression chosen in this case permits valid Windows file names but does not include all allowable variations.

d) Explain the regular expression metacharacters used in the following SQL statement and their effect on the resulting output.

```
SELECT REGEXP_SUBSTR('first field, second field  , third field',
       ', [^,]*,')
   FROM dual
REGEXP_SUBSTR('FIR
------------------
, second field   ,

1 row selected.
```

ANSWER: The REGEXP_SUBSTR function extracts part of a string that matches the pattern ', [^,]*,'. The function looks for a comma followed by a space, then zero or more characters that are not commas, and then another comma.

As you see from this example, you can use regular expressions to extract values from a comma-separated string. The occurrence parameter of the function lets you pick the appropriate values. The pattern must be modified if you look for the first or last value in the string.

e) Explain what the following statement accomplishes.

```
CREATE TABLE zipcode_regexp_test
   (zip VARCHAR2(5) CONSTRAINT zipcode_example_ck
     CHECK(REGEXP_LIKE(zip,
      '[[:digit:]]{5}(-[[:digit:]]{4})?$')))
```

ANSWER: The statement creates a table named ZIPCODE_REGEXP_TEST with a column called ZIP. The constraint checks whether the entered value in the ZIP column is either in a 5-digit zip code or the 5-digit + 4 zip code format.

In this example, the parenthesized subexpression (-[[:digit:]]{4}) is repeated zero or one times, as indicated by the ? repetition operator. The various components of this regular expression example are explained in Table 16.13.

TABLE 16.13   Explanation of 5-digit + 4 Zip Code Expression

METACHARACTER(S)	DESCRIPTION
^	Start-of-line anchoring metacharacter.
[	Start of character list.
[:digit:]	POSIX numeric digit class.
]	End of character list.
{5}	Repeat exactly five occurrences of the character list.
(	Start of subexpression.
-	A literal hyphen, because it is not a range metacharacter inside a character list.
[	Start of character list.
[:digit:]	POSIX [:digit:] class.
]	End of character list.
{4}	Repeat exactly four occurrences of the character list.

TABLE 16.13 Continued

METACHARACTER(S)	DESCRIPTION
)	Closing parenthesis, to end the subexpression.
?	The ? quantifier matches the grouped subexpression 0 or 1 time thus making the 4-digit code optional.
$	Anchoring metacharacter, to indicate the end of the line.

f) Describe the result of the following query.

```
SELECT REGEXP_INSTR('Hello', 'x?'),
       REGEXP_INSTR('Hello', 'xy?')
  FROM dual
```

Answer: The REGEXP_INSTR function returns a starting position of 1, even though the pattern 'x?' cannot be found anywhere in the string 'Hello'. The second function call looks for the pattern 'xy?', and the function returns a 0 because the required letter x followed by an optional letter y doesn't exist in the source string.

```
SELECT REGEXP_INSTR('Hello', 'x?'),
       REGEXP_INSTR('Hello', 'xy?')
  FROM dual
REGEXP_INSTR('HELLO','X?') REGEXP_INSTR('HELLO','XY?')
-------------------------- --------------------------
                         1                          0

1 row selected.
```

The first function returns the result 1, which indicates that the pattern exists at the first position of the source string. However, 'x?' is optional, so it can match an empty string, and it does so in the example.

Passing the RETURN_OPTION parameter value 0 (beginning of the string) and 1 (the character after the end of the string) returns again the same result, indicating that it matches an empty string.

```
SELECT REGEXP_INSTR('Hello', 'x?',1,1,0)
       AS start_pos,
       REGEXP_INSTR('Hello', 'x?',1,1,1)
       AS after_end
  FROM dual
 START_POS  AFTER_END
---------- ----------
         1          1

1 row selected.
```

The next query matches an empty string, much like the previous 'x?' pattern, because the set of parentheses around the enclosed 'xy' makes both letters optional.

```
SELECT REGEXP_INSTR('Hello', '(xy)?', 1, 1, 0)
       AS start_pos,
       REGEXP_INSTR('Hello', '(xy)?', 1, 1, 1)
```

```
        AS after_end
  FROM dual
START_POS   AFTER_END
----------  ----------
        1           1
```

1 row selected.

g) Describe the individual components of the following regular expression check constraint.

```
ALTER TABLE instructor
    ADD CONSTRAINT inst_phone_ck CHECK
    (REGEXP_LIKE(phone,
'^(\([[:digit:]]{3}\)|[[:digit:]]{3})[- ]?[[:digit:]]{3}[- ]?[[:digit:]]{4}$'))
```

ANSWER: The check constraint validates the entries in the PHONE column of the INSTRUCTOR table. The phone number must follow a specific pattern, such as a ###-#######, ### #######, (###) ###-####, and so on. The individual components are listed in Table 16.14.

TABLE 16.14 A Simple Phone Number Regular Expression Example

METACHARACTER(S)	DESCRIPTION
^	Start-of-line metacharacter, which doesn't permit leading characters before the regular expression.
(	Start of subexpression, which allows two choices for area code validation: Either a three-digit number enclosed by parentheses or a three-digit number without parentheses.
\(	The backslash escape character, which indicates that the following open parenthesis character represents a literal rather than a metacharacter.
[[:digit:]]{3}	An expression indicating that the following numbers of the area code can be any three digits.
\)	Escape character, which indicates that the following character is not a metacharacter; in this case it is the closing parentheses for the area code.
|	The alternation metacharacter, which specifies the end of the first choice, which is the area code enclosed by parentheses, and the start of the next area code choice, which does not require that the area code be enclosed by parentheses.
[[:digit:]]{3}	Three required digits.
)	End of the subexpression alternation.
[-]?	An optional character consisting either of a hyphen or a space following the area code.
[[:digit:]]{3}	The first three digits of the phone number following the area code.
[-]?	The first three digits of the phone number are separated by either an optional hyphen or space.
[[:digit:]]{4}	The last four digits of the phone number.
$	End-of-line metacharacter, which ends the regular expression and ensures that no other characters are permitted.

You can expand this phone number example to include different formatting separators, such as optional extension formats or even the entry of letters, such as 800-DON-OTCAL. Perhaps you want to validate that the first digit of an area code or a phone number may not begin with a 0 or 1. As you can see, validating a seemingly simple phone number can involve complex alternations, logic, and an arsenal of metacharacters. If you want to include foreign phone numbers in your validation, then the regular expression becomes even more involved.

You might consider simplifying the validation altogether by allowing only 10 numbers in the phone column. The appropriate display of the data to the desired format can then be accomplished through a view or a SELECT statement.

Another way to approach phone number validation is to separate the entire phone number into different components, such as the area code, the exchange, and the remaining four digits.

Lab 16.1 Quiz

In order to test your progress, you should be able to answer the following questions.

1) The following query is valid.

```
SELECT REGEXP_LIKE('10025', '[[:digit:]]')
   FROM dual
```

_____ a) True
_____ b) False

2) Choose all the valid values for the regular expressions 'hat{4,1}'.

_____ a) hat
_____ b) haaat
_____ c) hatttt
_____ d) hathathat
_____ e) It is an invalid regular expression.

3) Based on the following query, which value will be shown in the resulting output?

```
SELECT REGEXP_REPLACE('ABC10025', '[^[:digit:]]{1,5}$', '@')
    FROM dual
```

_____ a) @@@@@
_____ b) ABC10025
_____ c) @@@10025
_____ d) ABC@@@@@
_____ e) @10025
_____ f) It is an invalid regular expression.

4) The following two regular expressions are equivalent.

```
([[:space:]]|[[:punct:]])+
```

```
[[:space:][:punct:]]+
```

_____ a) True
_____ b) False

5) The following query is invalid.

```
SELECT REGEXP_SUBSTR('ABC10025', '[[:ALPHA:]]')
   FROM dual
```

_____ a) True
_____ b) False

6) Based on the following regular expression, the value 'CD' will be returned.
```
SELECT REGEXP_SUBSTR('abCDefgH', '[[:upper:]]+')
  FROM dual
```

_____ a) True
_____ b) False

7) The following two regular expressions are equivalent.
```
^[[:digit:]]{5}$
```
```
^[0-9]{5}$
```

_____ a) True
_____ b) False

ANSWERS APPEAR IN APPENDIX A.

LAB 16.2
Hierarchical Queries

LAB OBJECTIVES

After this lab, you will be able to:

▶ Restrict the Result Set in Hierarchical Queries

▶ Move Up and Down the Hierarchy Tree

A *recursive relationship*, also called a *self-referencing relationship*, exists on the COURSE table in the STUDENT schema (see Figure 16.1). This recursive relationship is between the columns COURSE_NO and PREREQUISITE. It is just like any other parent–child table relationship, except the relationship is with itself.

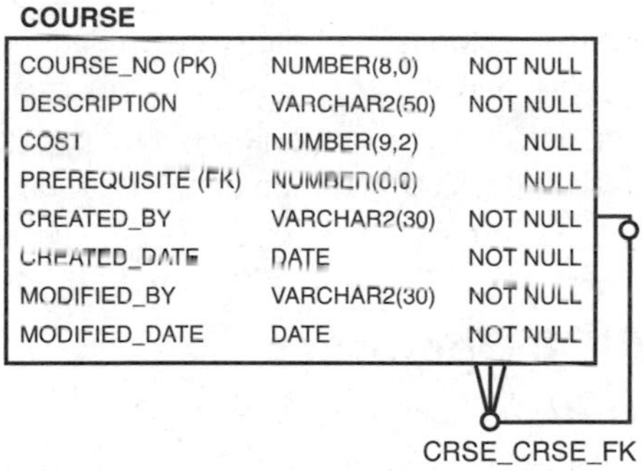

COURSE

COURSE_NO (PK)	NUMBER(8,0)	NOT NULL
DESCRIPTION	VARCHAR2(50)	NOT NULL
COST	NUMBER(9,2)	NULL
PREREQUISITE (FK)	NUMBER(0,0)	NULL
CREATED_BY	VARCHAR2(30)	NOT NULL
CREATED_DATE	DATE	NOT NULL
MODIFIED_BY	VARCHAR2(30)	NOT NULL
MODIFIED_DATE	DATE	NOT NULL

CRSE_CRSE_FK

FIGURE 16.1
The self-referencing relationship of the COURSE table

The PREREQUISITE column is a foreign key that references its own table's primary key. Only valid course numbers can be entered as prerequisites. Any attempt to insert or update the PREREQUISITE column to a value for which no COURSE_NO exists is rejected. A course can have zero or one prerequisite. For a course to be considered a prerequisite, it must appear at least once in the PREREQUISITE column.

This relationship between the parent and child can be depicted in a query result as a hierarchy or tree, using Oracle's CONNECT BY clause and the PRIOR operator. The following result visually displays the relationship of the courses that have the course number 310, Operating Systems, as their prerequisite.

```
310  Operating Systems
  130  Intro to Unix
    132  Basics of Unix Admin
      134  Advanced Unix Admin
        135  Unix Tips and Techniques
    330  Network Administration
  145  Internet Protocols
```

Reading from the outside in, the student first needs to take Operating Systems and then decide on either Intro to Unix or Internet Protocols. If the student completes the Intro to Unix course, he or she may choose between the Basics of Unix Admin class and the Network Administration class. If the student completes the Basics of Unix Admin, he or she may enroll in Advanced Unix Admin. After completion of this course, the student may enroll in Unix Tips and Techniques.

You can also travel the hierarchy in the reverse direction. If a student wants to take course number 134, Advanced Unix Administration, you can determine the required prerequisite courses until you reach the first course required.

In the business world, you may often encounter hierarchical relationships, such as the relationship between a manager and employees. Every employee may have at most one manager (parent), and to be a manager (parent), one must manage one or multiple employees (children). The root of the tree is the company's president; the president does not have a parent and, therefore, shows a NULL value in the parent column.

The CONNECT BY Clause and the PRIOR Operator

To accomplish the hierarchical display, you need to construct a query with the CONNECT BY clause and the PRIOR operator. You identify the relationship between the parent and the child by placing the PRIOR operator before the parent column. To find the children of a parent, Oracle evaluates the expression qualified by the PRIOR operator for the parent row. Rows for which the condition is true are the children of the parent. With the following CONNECT BY clause, you can see the order of courses and the sequence in which they need to be taken.

```
CONNECT BY PRIOR course_no = prerequisite
```

The COURSE_NO column is the parent, and the PREREQUISITE column is the child. The PRIOR operator is placed in front of the parent column COURSE_NO. Depending on which column you prefix with the PRIOR operator, you can change the direction of the hierarchy.

The CONNECT BY condition can contain additional conditions to filter the rows and eliminate branches from the hierarchy tree.

The START WITH Clause

The START WITH clause determines the root rows of the hierarchy. The records for which the START WITH clause is true are first selected. All children are retrieved from these records going forward. Without this clause, Oracle uses all rows in the table as root rows.

The following query selects the parent course number 310, its child rows, and, for each child, its respective descendents. The LPAD function, together with the LEVEL pseudocolumn, accomplishes the indentation.

```
SELECT LPAD(' ', 3*(LEVEL-1)) ||course_no
       || ' ' ||description
  FROM course
 START WITH course_no = 310
CONNECT BY PRIOR course_no = prerequisite
LPAD('',3*(LEVEL-1))||COURSE_NO||''||DESCRIPTION
------------------------------------------------
310  Operating Systems
   130  Intro to Unix
      132  Basics of Unix Admin
         134  Advanced Unix Admin
            135  Unix Tips and Techniques
      330  Network Administration
   145  Internet Protocols

7 rows selected.
```

Following is the syntax of the CONNECT BY clause.

```
[START WITH condition]
CONNECT BY [NOCYCLE] condition
```

The optional NOCYCLE parameter allows the query to continue even if a loop exists in the hierarchy. You will see some examples of loops later, in the exercises for this lab.

Understanding LEVEL and LPAD

The pseudocolumn LEVEL returns the number 1 for the root of the hierarchy, 2 for the child, 3 for the grandchild, and so on. The LPAD function allows you to visualize the hierarchy by indenting it with spaces. The length of the padded characters is calculated with the LEVEL function.

In Chapter 10, "Complex Joins," you learned about self-joins. You might wonder how they compare to hierarchical queries. The fundamental difference is that the CONNECT BY clause allows you to visually display the hierarchy and the relationships to other rows.

Hierarchy Path

You can show the path of a value from the root to the last node of the branch for any of the rows by using the SYS_CONNECT_BY_PATH function. The following query example displays the hierarchy path, and the course numbers are separated by forward slashes.

```
SELECT LPAD(' ', 1*(LEVEL-1))
       ||SYS_CONNECT_BY_PATH(course_no, '/') AS "Path" ,
       description
  FROM course
 START WITH course_no = 310
CONNECT BY PRIOR course_no = prerequisite
Path                            DESCRIPTION
------------------------------  ------------------------
/310                            Operating Systems
 /310/130                       Intro to Unix
  /310/130/132                  Basics of Unix Admin
   /310/130/132/134             Advanced Unix Admin
    /310/130/132/134/135        Unix Tips and Techniques
  /310/130/330                  Network Administration
 /310/145                       Internet Protocols

7 rows selected.
```

The SYS_CONNECT_BY_PATH function, which is valid only for a hierarchical query, has the following syntax.

```
SYS_CONNECT_BY_PATH (column, char)
```

Pruning the Hierarchy Tree

A hierarchy can be described as a tree; if you want to remove specific rows from the result, you can use either the WHERE clause to eliminate individual rows or the CONNECT BY clause to eliminate branches.

Figure 16.2 graphically depicts the effect of the WHERE clause on the rest of the hierarchy. The WHERE clause effectively eliminates individual rows from the hierarchy.

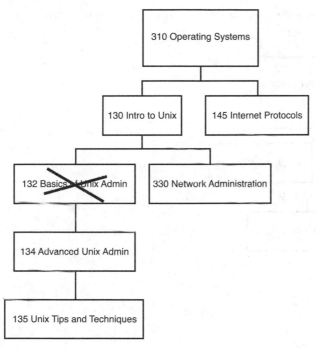

FIGURE 16.2
Using the WHERE clause to eliminate rows

Only the rows that satisfy the condition of the WHERE clause are included in the result. The following SQL statement shows the WHERE clause that eliminates the specific row. Notice that the child rows of the eliminated course are listed.

```
SELECT LPAD(' ', 3*(LEVEL-1)) ||course_no
       || ' ' ||description AS hierarchy
  FROM course
 WHERE course_no <> 132
 START WITH course_no = 310
CONNECT BY PRIOR course_no = prerequisite
HIERARCHY
-------------------------------------------
310  Operating Systems
   130   Intro to Unix
          134   Advanced Unix Admin
              135   Unix Tips and Techniques
       330   Network Administration
   145   Internet Protocols

6 rows selected.
```

Figure 16.3 displays the scenario when the condition is moved to the CONNECT BY clause, causing the removal of a branch of the tree.

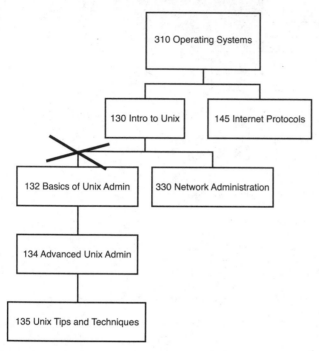

FIGURE 16.3
Using the CONNECT BY clause to eliminate an entire branch

The condition is part of the CONNECT BY clause, and when you examine the result, you find that COURSE_NO 132 and its respective descendants have been eliminated.

```
SELECT LPAD(' ', 3*(LEVEL-1)) ||course_no
       || ' ' ||description AS hierarchy
  FROM course
 START WITH course_no = 310
CONNECT BY PRIOR course_no = prerequisite
   AND course_no <> 132
HIERARCHY
-----------------------------------
310  Operating Systems
   130  Intro to Unix
      330  Network Administration
   145  Internet Protocols

4 rows selected.
```

Accessing Root Row Data with the CONNECT_BY_ROOT Operator

The CONNECT_BY_ROOT operator returns column data from the root row. The following SQL statement displays the course number of the root row in the column labeled ROOT. Note that the CONNECT_BY_ROOT operator is invalid in the START WITH and the CONNECT BY clauses.

```
SELECT description, course_no,
       CONNECT_BY_ROOT course_no AS root,
       LPAD(' ', 1*(LEVEL-1))
       ||SYS_CONNECT_BY_PATH(course_no, '/') AS "Path"
  FROM course
 START WITH course_no IN (310, 130)
 CONNECT BY PRIOR course_no = prerequisite
```

DESCRIPTION	COURSE_NO	ROOT	Path
Intro to Unix	130	130	/130
Basics of Unix Admin	132	130	/130/132
Advanced Unix Admin	134	130	/130/132/134
Unix Tips and Techniques	135	130	/130/132/134/135
Network Administration	330	130	/130/330
Operating Systems	310	310	/310
Intro to Unix	130	310	/310/130
Basics of Unix Admin	132	310	/310/130/132
Advanced Unix Admin	134	310	/310/130/132/134
Unix Tips and Techniques	135	310	/310/130/132/134/135
Network Administration	330	310	/310/130/330
Internet Protocols	145	310	/310/145

12 rows selected.

The CONNECT_BY_ISLEAF Pseudocolumn

The CONNECT_BY_ISLEAF is a pseudocolumn that displays the value 1 if the row is the last child, also referred to as the leaf, of the hierarchy tree, as defined with the CONNECT BY clause. The output of the following query displays for course numbers 135, 330, and 145 the value 1 in the LEAF column; the others show zero as they are either root or branch nodes.

```
SELECT course_no, LPAD(' ', 1*(LEVEL-1))
       ||SYS_CONNECT_BY_PATH(course_no, '/') AS "Path",
       LEVEL, CONNECT_BY_ISLEAF AS leaf
  FROM course
 START WITH course_no = 310
 CONNECT BY PRIOR course_no = prerequisite
```

COURSE_NO	Path	LEVEL	LEAF
310	/310	1	0
130	/310/130	2	0

```
132   /310/130/132                      3        0
134    /310/130/132/134                 4        0
135     /310/130/132/134/135            5        1
330   /310/130/330                      3        1
145   /310/145                          2        1
```

```
7 rows selected.
```

Joining Tables

Prior to Oracle9i, joins in hierarchical queries were not allowed. To achieve somewhat similar results, you had to write inline views or use custom-written PL/SQL functions to display any columns from related tables. The effect of a join in a hierarchical query is shown in the following example. The query joins the COURSE and SECTION tables and includes the SECTION_ID column in the result.

The join uses the common COURSE_NO column. The root rows are chosen via the START WITH clause. Here only those root rows with a COURSE_NO of 310 are selected as the root rows on which the hierarchy will be based. From the root row, the children, grandchildren, and any further descendants are determined.

You see a large number of rows because some courses have multiple sections. For example, COURSE_NO 132, Basics of Unix Admin, has two sections: SECTION_ID 139 and 138. For each section, the hierarchy is listed with the respective child sections. The individual child sections then show their child rows and so on.

```
SELECT LPAD(' ', 3*(LEVEL-1)) || c.course_no||' '||
       description AS hierarchy, s.section_id
  FROM course c, section s
 WHERE c.course_no = s.course_no
 START WITH c.course_no = 310
CONNECT BY PRIOR c.course_no = prerequisite
HIERARCHY                                SECTION_ID
---------------------------------------- ----------
310 Operating Systems                          103
   130 Intro to Unix                           107
      330 Network Administration               104
      132 Basics of Unix Admin                 139
         134 Advanced Unix Admin               110
            135 Unix Tips and Techniques       112
            135 Unix Tips and Techniques       115
            135 Unix Tips and Techniques       114
            135 Unix Tips and Techniques       113
         134 Advanced Unix Admin               111
            135 Unix Tips and Techniques       112
            135 Unix Tips and Techniques       115
            135 Unix Tips and Techniques       114
            135 Unix Tips and Techniques       113
```

```
      134 Advanced Unix Admin                  140
          135 Unix Tips and Techniques         112
          135 Unix Tips and Techniques         115
          135 Unix Tips and Techniques         114
          135 Unix Tips and Techniques         113
  132 Basics of Unix Admin                     138
    134 Advanced Unix Admin                    110
        135 Unix Tips and Techniques           112
        135 Unix Tips and Techniques           115
...
139 rows selected.
```

Sorting

The following query lists all the courses that require COURSE_NO 20 as a prerequisite. Examine the order of the rows with COURSE_NO 100, 140, 142, 147, and 204 in the following result. These five rows share the same hierarchy level (and the same parent PREREQUISITE value). The order in a hierarchy level is rather arbitrary.

```
SELECT LEVEL, LPAD(' ', 2*(LEVEL-1)) || c.course_no
       AS course_no,
       description, prerequisite AS pre
  FROM course c
 START WITH c.course_no = 20
CONNECT BY PRIOR c.course_no = prerequisite
```

LEVEL	COURSE_NO	DESCRIPTION	PRE
1	20	Intro to Information Systems	
2	100	Hands-On Windows	20
2	140	Systems Analysis	20
3	25	Intro to Programming	140
4	240	Intro to the BASIC Language	25
4	420	Database System Principles	25
5	144	Database Design	420
2	142	Project Management	20
2	147	GUI Design Lab	20
2	204	Intro to SQL	20
3	80	Programming Techniques	204
4	120	Intro to Java Programming	80
...			
5	210	Oracle Tools	220

```
20 rows selected.
```

If you want to order the result by the DESCRIPTION column, in alphabetical order, without destroying the hierarchical default order of the CONNECT BY clause, you use the ORDER SIBLINGS BY clause. It preserves the hierarchy and orders the siblings as specified in the ORDER BY clause.

```
SELECT LEVEL, LPAD(' ', 2*(LEVEL-1)) || c.course_no
       AS course_no,
       description, prerequisite AS pre
  FROM course c
 START WITH c.course_no = 20
CONNECT BY PRIOR c.course_no = prerequisite
 ORDER SIBLINGS BY description
```

LEVEL	COURSE_NO	DESCRIPTION	PRE
1	20	Intro to Information Systems	
2	147	GUI Design Lab	20
2	100	Hands-On Windows	20
2	204	Intro to SQL	20
3	80	Programming Techniques	204
4	120	Intro to Java Programming	80
5	122	Intermediate Java Programming	120
6	124	Advanced Java Programming	122
6	125	Java Developer I	122

...

20 rows selected.

Any other ORDER BY clause has the effect of the DESCRIPTION column now taking precedence over the default ordering. For example, the result of ordering by the DESCRIPTION column without the SIBLINGS keyword results in the following, where the hierarchy order is no longer intact.

```
SELECT LEVEL, LPAD(' ', 2*(LEVEL-1)) || c.course_no
       AS course_no,
       description, prerequisite AS pre
  FROM course c
 START WITH c.course_no = 20
CONNECT BY PRIOR c.course_no = prerequisite
 ORDER BY description
```

LEVEL	COURSE_NO	DESCRIPTION	PRE
6	124	Advanced Java Programming	122
8	450	DB Programming with Java	350
5	144	Database Design	420
...			
2	142	Project Management	20
2	140	Systems Analysis	20

20 rows selected.

Ordering by the LEVEL pseudocolumn results in all the parents being grouped together and then all children, all the grandchildren, and so on.

```
SELECT LEVEL, LPAD(' ', 2*(LEVEL-1)) || c.course_no
       AS course_no,
       description, prerequisite AS pre
  FROM course c
 START WITH c.course_no = 20
CONNECT BY PRIOR c.course_no = prerequisite
 ORDER BY LEVEL
```

LEVEL	COURSE_NO	DESCRIPTION	PRE
1	20	Intro to Information Systems	
2	100	Hands-On Windows	20
2	204	Intro to SQL	20
2	147	GUI Design Lab	20
...			
8	430	Java Developer III	350

20 rows selected.

▼ LAB 16.2 EXERCISES

a) Show the course number and course description of courses that have course number 310 as a prerequisite. Make these records the root of your hierarchical query. Display all the courses that can be taken after these root courses have been completed as child records. Include the LEVEL pseudocolumn as an additional column.

b) Execute the following query. What do you observe about the result?

```
SELECT LEVEL, LPAD(' ', 6*(LEVEL-1)) ||course_no
       || ' ' ||description hier
  FROM course
 START WITH course_no = 310
CONNECT BY PRIOR course_no = prerequisite
    AND LEVEL <= 3
```

c) What does the following START WITH clause accomplish?

```
SELECT LEVEL, LPAD(' ', 3*(LEVEL-1)) ||course_no
       || ' ' ||description hier
  FROM course
 START WITH prerequisite IS NULL
CONNECT BY PRIOR course_no = prerequisite
```

d) Execute the following query, placing the PRIOR operator on the PREREQUISITE column. How does the result compare to the results of the previously issued queries?

```
SELECT LEVEL, LPAD(' ', 6*(LEVEL-1)) ||course_no
       || ' ' ||description hierarchy
  FROM course
 START WITH course_no = 132
CONNECT BY course_no = PRIOR prerequisite
```

e) Write the SQL statement to display the following result.

```
LEVEL HIERARCHY
----- ------------------------------------
    5 310   Operating Systems
    4    130   Intro to Unix
    3       132   Basics of Unix Admin
    2          134   Advanced Unix Admin
    1             135   Unix Tips and Techniques

5 rows selected.
```

f) Insert the following record into the COURSE table and execute the query. What error message do you get, and why? Roll back the INSERT statement after you issue the SELECT statement.

```
INSERT INTO course
   (course_no, description, prerequisite,
    created_by, created_date, modified_by, modified_date)
VALUES
   (1000, 'Test', 1000,
    'TEST', SYSDATE, 'TEST', SYSDATE)

SELECT course_no, prerequisite
  FROM course
 START WITH course_no = 1000
CONNECT BY PRIOR course_no = prerequisite

ROLLBACK
```

▼ LAB 16.2 EXERCISE **ANSWERS**

a) Show the course number and course description of courses that have course number 310 as a prerequisite. Make these records the root of your hierarchical query. Display all the courses that can be taken after these root courses have been completed as child records. Include the LEVEL pseudocolumn as an additional column.

ANSWER: The START WITH clause starts the hierarchy with the prerequisite course number 310. The PRIOR operator identifies COURSE_NO as the parent record for which all the children are retrieved.

```
SELECT LEVEL, LPAD(' ', 6*(LEVEL-1)) ||course_no
       || ' ' ||description hierarchy
  FROM course
 START WITH prerequisite = 310
CONNECT BY PRIOR course_no = prerequisite
    LEVEL HIERARCHY
--------- ------------------------------------------------
        1 130   Intro to Unix
        2       132   Basics of Unix Admin
        3          134   Advanced Unix Admin
        4             135   Unix Tips and Techniques
        2       330   Network Administration
```

```
1 145   Internet Protocols
```

6 rows selected.

The START WITH condition returns two records, one for the Intro to Unix class and the second for Internet Protocols. These are the root records from the hierarchy.

```
START WITH prerequisite = 310
```

The PRIOR operator in the CONNECT BY clause identifies COURSE_NO as the parent. Child records are those records with the same course number in the PREREQUISITE column. The following two CONNECT BY clauses are equivalent.

```
CONNECT BY PRIOR course_no = prerequisite

CONNECT BY prerequisite = PRIOR course_no
```

If you use the PRIOR operator on the PREREQUISITE column, you reverse the hierarchy and travel in the opposite direction. You will see examples of this shortly.

Finally, you need to add the LEVEL function as a single column to display the hierarchy level of each record. If you also want to show the hierarchy visually with indentations, use the combination of LEVEL and LPAD (which has the following syntax).

```
LPAD(char1, n [, char2])
```

The LPAD function uses the first argument as a literal. If char2 is not specified, by default it is filled from the left with blanks up to the length shown as parameter n. The following SELECT clause indents each level with six additional spaces. (You can choose any number of spaces you like.)

```
SELECT LEVEL, LPAD(' ', 6*(LEVEL-1)) ||course_no
       || ' ' ||description hierarchy
```

The length for the first level is 0 (Level 1 – 1 = 0); therefore, this level is not indented. The second level is indented by 12 spaces (6 * (2 – 1) = 6), the next by 12 (6 * (3 – 1) = 12), and so on. The resulting padded spaces are then concatenated with the course number and course description.

b) Execute the following query. What do you observe about the result?

```
SELECT LEVEL, LPAD(' ', 6*(LEVEL-1)) ||course_no
       || ' ' ||description hier
  FROM course
 START WITH course_no = 310
CONNECT BY PRIOR course_no = prerequisite
    AND LEVEL <= 3
```

ANSWER: The LEVEL pseudocolumn restricts the rows in the CONNECT BY clause to show only the first three levels of the hierarchy.

```
LEVEL HIER
--------- --------------------------------------
        1 310   Operating Systems
        2     130   Intro to Unix
        3         132   Basics of Unix Admin
        3         330   Network Administration
        2     145   Internet Protocols
```

5 rows selected.

In the previous exercise, you learned that the WHERE clause eliminates the particular row but not its children. You restrict child rows with conditions in the CONNECT BY clause. Here the PRIOR operator applies to the parent row, and the other side of the equation applies to the child record. A qualifying child needs to have the correct parent, and it must have a LEVEL number of 3 or less.

c) What does the following START WITH clause accomplish?

```
SELECT LEVEL, LPAD(' ', 3*(LEVEL-1)) ||course_no
       || ' ' ||description hier
  FROM course
 START WITH prerequisite IS NULL
CONNECT BY PRIOR course_no = prerequisite
```

ANSWER: This query's START WITH clause identifies all the root rows of the COURSE table. Those are the courses that have no prerequisites.

Although START WITH is optional with hierarchical queries, you typically identify the root rows of the hierarchy. That's the starting point for all rows.

The following statement displays the result of a query that doesn't have a START WITH clause.

```
SELECT LEVEL, LPAD(' ', 3*(LEVEL-1)) ||course_no
       || ' ' ||description hier
  FROM course
CONNECT BY PRIOR course_no = prerequisite
```

```
    LEVEL HIER
--------- ---------------------------------------------
        1 10   Technology Concepts
        2    230   Intro to the Internet
...
        1 310   Operating Systems
        2    130   Intro to Unix
        3       132   Basics of Unix Admin
        4          134   Advanced Unix Admin
        5           135   Unix Tips and Techniques
        3       330   Network Administration
        2    145   Internet Protocols
        1 330   Network Administration
...
        1 130   Intro to Unix
        2    132   Basics of Unix Admin
        3       134   Advanced Unix Admin
        4      135   Unix Tips and Techniques
        2    330   Network Administration
        1 132   Basics of Unix Admin
        2    134   Advanced Unix Admin
        3          135   Unix Tips and Techniques
        1 134   Advanced Unix Admin
        2    135   Unix Tips and Techniques
        1 135   Unix Tips and Techniques
        1 350   Java Developer II
...
        1 430   Java Developer III
```

```
     1  450   DB Programming with Java
```

107 rows selected.

Although such a query is not very useful, it helps to understand why the records appear multiple times. When the START WITH clause is not specified, every record in the table is considered the root of the hierarchy. Therefore, for every record in the table, the hierarchy is displayed, and the courses are repeated multiple times.

For example, the course number 135, Unix Tips and Techniques, is returned five times. From the root 310, Operating Systems, it is five levels deep in the hierarchy. It is repeated for the root course number 130, Intro to Unix, and then for 132, Basics of Unix Admin, and then for 134, Advanced Unix Admin, and finally for itself.

d) Execute the following query, placing the PRIOR operator on the PREREQUISITE column. How does the result compare to the results of the previously issued queries?

```
SELECT LEVEL, LPAD(' ', 6*(LEVEL-1)) ||course_no
       || ' ' ||description hierarchy
  FROM course
 START WITH course_no = 132
CONNECT BY course_no = PRIOR prerequisite
```

ANSWER: The PREREQUISITE column becomes the parent, and the COURSE_NO column becomes the child. This effectively reverses the direction of the hierarchy compared to the previously issued queries.

The result of the query shows all the prerequisites a student needs to take before enrolling in course number 132, Basics of Unix Administration.

```
LEVEL HIERARCHY
--------- -----------------------------------------
    1 132    Basics of Unix Admin
    2     130   Intro to Unix
    3          310   Operating Systems
```

3 rows selected.

The student needs to take course number 310, Operating Systems, and then course number 130, Intro to Unix, before taking course number 132, Basics of Unix Admin.

e) Write the SQL statement to display the following result.

```
LEVEL HIERARCHY
----- ------------------------------------
    5 310   Operating Systems
    4    130   Intro to Unix
    3       132   Basics of Unix Admin
    2          134   Advanced Unix Admin
    1             135   Unix Tips and Techniques
```

5 rows selected.

ANSWER: The rows show you the prerequisite courses for course number 135 as a root. The ORDER BY clause orders the result by the hierarchy level.

```
SELECT LEVEL, LPAD(' ', 2*(5-LEVEL)) ||course_no
       || ' ' ||description hierarchy
  FROM course
 START WITH course_no = 135
CONNECT BY course_no = PRIOR prerequisite
 ORDER BY LEVEL DESC
```

Because the result shows the prerequisites, the PRIOR operator needs to be applied on the PREREQUISITE column. PREREQUISITE becomes the parent column.

```
CONNECT BY course_no = PRIOR prerequisite
```

The ORDER BY clause orders the records by the hierarchy level, in descending order. The indentation with the LPAD function is different from previous examples. You now subtract the number 5 from each level and multiply the result by 2, resulting in the largest indentation for the root.

f) Insert the following record into the COURSE table and execute the query. What error message do you get, and why? Roll back the INSERT statement after you issue the SELECT statement.

```
INSERT INTO course
   (course_no, description, prerequisite,
    created_by, created_date, modified_by, modified_date)
VALUES
   (1000, 'Test', 1000,
    'TEST', SYSDATE, 'TEST', SYSDATE)

SELECT course_no, prerequisite
  FROM course
 START WITH course_no = 1000
CONNECT BY PRIOR course_no = prerequisite

ROLLBACK
```

ANSWER: The INSERT statement causes the course number 1000 to be its own parent and child. This results in a loop in the hierarchy and is reported by the hierarchical query.

```
SELECT course_no, prerequisite
  FROM course
 START WITH course_no = 1000
CONNECT BY PRIOR course_no = prerequisite
```

ERROR:
ORA-01436: CONNECT BY loop in user data

no rows selected

This is quite an obvious loop; because it is in the same record, the row is both the parent and the child. However, you can run the query without any error if you use the NOCYCLE parameter following CONNECT BY.

```
SELECT course_no, prerequisite
  FROM course
 START WITH course_no = 1000
```

```
CONNECT BY NOCYCLE PRIOR course_no = prerequisite
  COURSE_NO PREREQUISITE
---------- ------------
     1000         1000
```

1 row selected.

The pseudocolumn CONNECT_BY_ISCYCLE enables you to detect the offending row by displaying the value 1; otherwise, it shows 0. The pseudocolumn works only when the NOCYCLE parameter of the CONNECT BY clause is specified.

```
SELECT CONNECT_BY_ISCYCLE, course_no, prerequisite
  FROM course
 START WITH course_no = 1000
CONNECT BY NOCYCLE PRIOR course_no = prerequisite
CONNECT_BY_ISCYCLE   COURSE_NO PREREQUISITE
------------------- ---------- ------------
                 1       1000         1000
```

1 row selected.

Loops can be buried deep within the hierarchy and can be difficult to find when many rows are involved, unless you can use the CONNECT_BY_ISCYCLE pseudocolumn.

Lab 16.2 Quiz

In order to test your progress, you should be able to answer the following questions.

1) The ORDER BY clause does not order the columns within a hierarchy, but it does order the columns in the order stated in the ORDER BY clause, unless the SIBLINGS keyword is used.

_____ a) True
_____ b) False

2) Which column is the parent in the following SQL statement?

```
CONNECT BY PRIOR emp = manager
```

_____ a) The EMP column
_____ b) The MANAGER column
_____ c) None of the above

3) You can use joins in hierarchical queries.

_____ a) True
_____ b) False

4) The pseudocolumn CONNECT_BY_ISLEAF displays 0 if the row is the last branch of the hierarchy tree.

_____ a) True
_____ b) False

ANSWERS APPEAR IN APPENDIX A.

▼ WORKSHOP

The projects in this section are meant to prompt you to utilize all the skills you have acquired throughout this chapter. The answers to these projects can be found at the companion Web site to this book, located at www.oraclesqlbyexample.com.

1) Name other hierarchical relationships you are familiar with.

2) Change the prerequisite of course number 310, Operating Systems, a root row in the hierarchy, from a null value to 145, Internet Protocols. Write the query to detect the loop in the hierarchy, using the CONNECT_BY_ISCYCLE pseudocolumn.

3) Why doesn't the following query return any rows?

```
SELECT *
  FROM instructor
 WHERE REGEXP_LIKE(instructor_id, '[:digit:]')
```

no rows selected

4) Add a Social Security number column to the STUDENT table or create a separate table with this column. Write a column check constraint that verifies that the Social Security number is entered in the correct ###-##-#### format.

CHAPTER 17

Exploring Data Warehousing Features

CHAPTER OBJECTIVES

In this chapter, you will learn about:

- ▶ Advanced SQL Concepts, Analytical Functions, and the WITH Clause
- ▶ ROLLUP and CUBE Operators

This chapter revisits some of the concepts and functionality discussed in previous chapters, including the DECODE function, the CASE expression, and aggregate functions. You will see how to use the PIVOT and UNPIVOT clauses to effortlessly produce cross-tab queries. This will help expand on your existing knowledge and enable you to solve more complex queries.

Analytical functions allow you to explore information in ways never imagined before. You can use analytical functions to determine rankings, perform complex aggregate calculations, and reveal period-to-period changes.

The WITH clause allows you to reuse a query result without having to re-execute the statement; this greatly improves execution time and resource utilization.

The CUBE and ROLLUP operators perform aggregation on multiple levels at once.

This chapter offers you a glimpse at some of the incredibly powerful capabilities of Oracle's data warehousing features, which allow users to query large volumes of summarized data.

LAB 17.1
Advanced SQL Concepts, Analytical Functions, and the WITH Clause

---

LAB OBJECTIVES

After this lab, you will be able to:

▶ Transpose a Result Set

▶ Utilize Analytical Functions and the WITH Clause

Oracle allows you to write queries to generate cross-tabular data in various ways. You've already learned about the DECODE function and the CASE expression. The PIVOT clauses introduced in Oracle 11g simplifies the writing of these queries even further.

Transposing Results

Transposing SQL results into a cross-tab is very useful when you're reporting data. End users demand this layout for improved readability of reports and analysis of data. As you will discover, there are various ways to transpose data into a cross-tab. The new PIVOT functionality to makes this task even easier.

USING THE DECODE FUNCTION

The DECODE function not only permits you to perform powerful *if-then-else* comparisons but also allows you to transpose or pivot the results of queries. For example, the following query returns a list of the number of classes held for each day of the week, with the day of the week formatted using the DY format mask.

```
SELECT TO_CHAR(start_date_time, 'DY') Day,
       COUNT(*) num_of_classes
  FROM section
 GROUP BY TO_CHAR(start_date_time, 'DY')
 ORDER BY 2
DAY  NUM_OF_CLASSES
---  --------------
FRI               4
```

```
...
MON             15
SAT             17
TUE             17
```

7 rows selected.

You can transpose the result, effectively producing a cross-tab to display the result horizontally, with the days of the week as columns and a count below. You do this by nesting the DECODE function in the COUNT function.

```
SELECT  COUNT(DECODE(
        TO_CHAR(start_date_time, 'DY'), 'MON', 1)) MON,
        COUNT(DECODE(
        TO_CHAR(start_date_time, 'DY'), 'TUE', 1)) TUE,
        COUNT(DECODE(
        TO_CHAR(start_date_time, 'DY'), 'WED', 1)) WED,
        COUNT(DECODE(
        TO_CHAR(start_date_time, 'DY'), 'THU', 1)) THU,
        COUNT(DECODE(
        TO_CHAR(start_date_time, 'DY'), 'FRI', 1)) FRI,
        COUNT(DECODE(
        TO_CHAR(start_date_time, 'DY'), 'SAT', 1)) SAT,
        COUNT(DECODE(
        TO_CHAR(start_date_time, 'DY'), 'SUN', 1)) SUN
  FROM section
   MON    TUE    WED    THU    FRI    SAT    SUN
  -----  -----  -----  -----  -----  -----  -----
    15     17      7      5      4     17     13
```

1 row selected.

The syntax of the DECODE function is as follows.

```
DECODE (if_expr, equals_search,
        then_result [,else_default])
```

 Search and result values can be repeated.

When each row of the expression TO_CHAR(start_date_time, 'DY') is evaluated, Oracle returns the day of the week, in the format DY, which is MON for Monday, TUE for Tuesday, and so on. If the DECODE expression is equal to the search value, the value 1 is returned. Because no ELSE condition is specified, a NULL value is returned.

The COUNT function without an argument does not count NULL values; NULLs are counted only with the wildcard COUNT(*). Therefore, when the COUNT function is applied to the result of either NULL or 1, it counts only records with NOT NULL values. Alternatively, you can also use the SUM function.

USING CASE

Instead of using the DECODE function, you can write the statement with the equivalent CASE expression for an identical result.

```
SELECT COUNT(CASE WHEN TO_CHAR(start_date_time, 'DY')
       = 'MON' THEN 1 END) MON,
    COUNT(CASE WHEN TO_CHAR(start_date_time, 'DY')
       = 'TUE' THEN 1 END) TUE,
    COUNT(CASE WHEN TO_CHAR(start_date_time, 'DY')
       = 'WED' THEN 1 END) WED,
    COUNT(CASE WHEN TO_CHAR(start_date_time, 'DY')
       = 'THU' THEN 1 END) THU,
    COUNT(CASE WHEN TO_CHAR(start_date_time, 'DY')
       = 'FRI' THEN 1 END) FRI,
    COUNT(CASE WHEN TO_CHAR(start_date_time, 'DY')
       = 'SAT' THEN 1 END) SAT,
    COUNT(CASE WHEN TO_CHAR(start_date_time, 'DY')
       = 'SUN' THEN 1 END) SUN
  FROM section
```

USING A SCALAR SUBQUERY

The following query shows yet another way to accomplish the same output. The drawback of this solution is that you execute seven individual queries; this is not as efficient as using DECODE or CASE, which execute only once against the table.

```
SELECT (SELECT COUNT(*)
          FROM section
         WHERE TO_CHAR(start_date_time, 'DY') = 'MON') MON,
       (SELECT COUNT(*)
          FROM section
         WHERE TO_CHAR(start_date_time, 'DY') = 'TUE') TUE,
       (SELECT COUNT(*)
          FROM section
         WHERE TO_CHAR(start_date_time, 'DY') = 'WED') WED,
       (SELECT COUNT(*)
          FROM section
         WHERE TO_CHAR(start_date_time, 'DY') = 'THU') THU,
       (SELECT COUNT(*)
          FROM section
         WHERE TO_CHAR(start_date_time, 'DY') = 'FRI') FRI,
       (SELECT COUNT(*)
          FROM section
         WHERE TO_CHAR(start_date_time, 'DY') = 'SAT') SAT,
       (SELECT COUNT(*)
          FROM section
         WHERE TO_CHAR(start_date_time, 'DY') = 'SUN') SUN
  FROM dual
```

USING THE PIVOT AND UNPIVOT CLAUSES

The new PIVOT clause in Oracle 11g greatly simplifies the writing of cross-tab queries. It rotates the rows into columns. The following example shows the same query listed in the FROM clause as in the beginning of the chapter. If you apply the PIVOT clause to this listing of sections by day of the week, Oracle creates a horizontal row by listing and summing all the values shown the specified IN list.

```
SELECT * FROM
  (
   SELECT TO_CHAR(start_date_time, 'DY') day,
          COUNT(*) num_of_sections
     FROM section
    GROUP BY TO_CHAR(start_date_time, 'DY')
   ) classes_by_day
  PIVOT (SUM(num_of_sections)
   FOR day IN ('MON','TUE', 'WED','THU',
               'FRI','SAT','SUN'))

'MON' 'TUE' 'WED' 'THU' 'FRI' 'SAT' 'SUN'
----- ----- ----- ----- ----- ----- -----
15    17    7     5     4     17    13


1 rows selected
```

The following statement creates a table called LOCATION_BY_DATE. The difference from the previous query is that this example also includes the LOCATION column in the inner query. Now the cross-tabulated result is computed not only by the days of the week but also by the location. Another difference is the removal of quotes in the column heading; the columns shown in the IN list have an alias.

```
CREATE TABLE LOCATION_BY_DAY AS
SELECT * FROM
  (
   SELECT TO_CHAR(start_date_time, 'DY') Day,
          s.location,
          COUNT(*) num_of_classes
     FROM section s
    GROUP BY TO_CHAR(start_date_time, 'DY'), location
   ) sections_by_day
  PIVOT (SUM(num_of_classes) FOR day IN
   ('MON' AS MON,'TUE' AS TUE,'WED' AS WED,'THU' AS THU,
    'FRI' AS FRI,'SAT' AS SAT,'SUN' AS SUN))
```

LOCATION	MON	TUE	WED	THU	FRI	SAT	SUN
H310		1					
L210	2	3	1		1	2	1
L214	2	2		2	1	4	4
M500						1	

...

```
L509         4    5    3    2    1    4    6
L211              1         1         1
```

12 rows selected

Using the LOCATION_BY_DAY table as a source, the UNPIVOT clause allows the rotation of columns back to rows. NUM_OF_CLASSES is a numeric column created as part of the result, and it contains the number of records for the combination of location and day of the week. The DAY column holds the values shown in the IN clause.

The default option of the UNPIVOT clause is EXCLUDE NULLS, but in this example you see the inclusion of null values through the use of the INCLUDE NULLS option. This generates null values, such as for location L210 and THU.

```
SELECT *
  FROM location_by_day
UNPIVOT INCLUDE NULLS (num_of_classes
  FOR day IN (mon, tue, wed, thu, fri, sat, sun))
LOCATION        DAY  NUM_OF_CLASSES
--------------- ---- --------------
L210            MON               2
L210            TUE               3
L210            WED               1
L210            THU
L210            FRI               1
L210            SAT               2
L210            SUN               1
L211            MON


...
M500            SUN
```

84 rows selected

For very difficult queries, where the result cannot be performed using any of the previously mentioned solutions, you might want to consider creating a temporary table to hold intermediate results. Creating temporary tables is discussed in Chapter 12, "Create, Alter, and Drop Tables."

Analytical Functions

Oracle includes a number of very useful functions that allow you to analyze, aggregate, and rank vast amounts of stored data. You can use these analytical functions to find the top-*n* revenue-generating courses, compare revenues of one course with another, or compute various statistics about students' grades.

Although this lab does not discuss all the available analytical functions, it does provide an overview of the most commonly used functions. You will gain an appreciation of their core functionality and usefulness, particularly with regard to the calculation of rankings or generation of moving averages, moving sums, and so on.

Analytical functions execute queries fairly quickly because they allow you to make one pass through the data rather than write multiple queries or complicated SQL to achieve the same result. This significantly speeds up query performance.

The general syntax of analytical functions is as follows.

```
analytic_function([arguments]) OVER (analytic_clause)
```

The OVER keyword indicates that the function operates after the results of the FROM, WHERE, GROUP BY, and HAVING clauses have been formed.

ANALYTIC_CLAUSE can contain three other clauses: QUERY_PARTITIONING, ORDER_BY, or WINDOWING.

```
[query_partition_clause] [order_by_clause [windowing_clause]]
```

There are slight variations in the general syntax for certain functions, with some requiring specific clauses and others not. The QUERY_PARTIONING clause allows you to split a result into smaller subsets on which you can apply the analytical functions. The ORDER_BY_CLAUSE is much like the familiar ordering clause; however, it is applied to the result of an analytical function. WINDOWING_CLAUSE lets you compute moving and accumulative aggregates—such as moving averages, moving sums, or cumulative sums—by choosing only certain data within a specified window.

QUERY PROCESSING WITH ANALYTICAL FUNCTIONS

You perform query processing with analytical functions in several steps (see Figure 17.1). First, joins, WHERE, GROUP BY, and HAVING clauses are carried out. The analytical functions then use these results. If any partitioning clause is listed, the rows are split into the appropriate partitions. These partitions are formed after the GROUP BY clause, so you may be able to analyze data by partition, not just the expressions of the GROUP BY clause. If a windowing clause is involved, it determines the ranges of sliding windows of rows. The analytical functions are based against the specified window and allow moving averages, sums, and so on. Analytical functions may have an ORDER BY clause as part of the function specification that allows you to order the result before the analytical function is applied. Finally, if an ORDER BY clause is present at the end of the statement, the result set is sorted accordingly.

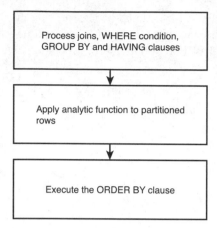

FIGURE 17.1
Query processing steps with analytical functions

ANALYTICAL FUNCTION TYPES

Analytical functions can be categorized into various types; Table 17.1 provides an overview of the different types. Ranking functions determine the ranking of a value (for example, to determine the top three students, based on their grade averages or to determine the first and last values of an ordered group). The reporting functions take the familiar aggregate function capabilities a step further, allowing you to aggregate values without the need for a GROUP BY clause. The windowing capability allows you to generate moving averages, cumulative sums, and the like. The LAG/LEAD functions allow you to easily see how much values changed from one period to another.

TABLE 17.1   Type and Purpose of Analytical Functions

FUNCTION TYPE	PURPOSE
Ranking	Compute ranking. Function examples are RANK, DENSE_RANK, NTILE, and ROW_NUMBER.
Hypothetical ranking	Determine the rank of hypothetical data values within a result set.
FIRST/LAST	Find the FIRST and LAST values in an ordered group.
Reporting	Use aggregate functions such as SUM, AVG, MIN, MAX, COUNT, VARIANCE, or STDDEV. Also calculate ratios using functions as RATIO_TO_REPORT.
Windowing	Calculate moving averages and cumulative values, using AVG, SUM, MIN, MAX, COUNT, FIRST_VALUE, and LAST_VALUE. (Note that FIRST_VALUE and LAST_VALUE, unlike the FIRST/LAST function, are available only within WINDOWING_CLAUSE.)

TABLE 17.1   Continued

FUNCTION TYPE	PURPOSE
Statistical	Calculate statistics. For example, the MEDIAN function and the STATS_MODE function allow calculation of the median and the most frequently occurring value.
LAG/LEAD	Allows you to specify an individual row relative to before or after the current row. The functionality is somewhat similar to windowing and is very useful for comparing period-to-period changes.
Inverse percentile	Determine the value in a data set that is equal to a specific percentile. This functionality is beyond the scope of this book.
Linear regression	Compute linear regression and other related statistics. These functions are beyond the scope of this book.

RANKING FUNCTIONS

Chapter 8, "Subqueries," explores the subject of top-*n* queries, using an inline view and the ROWNUM pseudocolumn. Ranking functions allow for even more advanced functionality. In this lab, you will learn about the differences between the ranking functions.

Let's look first at the DENSE_RANK ranking function. The following query shows the ranking of the grades for student ID 254 in section 87. The grades are ranked by the lowest grade first. Notice the use of the ORDER BY clause in the analytical function.

```
SELECT numeric_grade,
       DENSE_RANK() OVER (ORDER BY numeric_grade) AS rank
  FROM grade
 WHERE student_id = 254
   AND section_id = 87
NUMERIC_GRADE        RANK
------------- ----------
           71          1
           71          1
           75          2
...
           91          5
           98          6
           98          6

12 rows selected.
```

The NUMERIC_GRADE value of 71 is the lowest grade of the student; it holds rank number 1. The next highest grade, which is 75, holds rank number 2, and so on. The ORDER BY clause controls the ordering of the ranking. If you want the highest grade to have rank number 1, use DESCENDING in the ORDER BY clause. The default is ASCENDING. You might already have noticed one difference from the inline view; the DENSE_RANK function allows identical values to share the same rank.

To find out the three lowest grades of the student, rather than all the grades, you can modify the query by using the ranking function and an inline view, as in the following example.

```
SELECT *
  FROM (SELECT numeric_grade,
               DENSE_RANK() OVER (ORDER BY numeric_grade)
               AS rank
          FROM grade
         WHERE student_id = 254
           AND section_id = 87)
 WHERE rank <= 3
NUMERIC_GRADE        RANK
------------- ----------
           71          1
           71          1
           75          2
           76          3
```

4 rows selected.

The lowest grade occurs twice. The DENSE_RANK function, unlike the ROWNUM pseudocolumn (discussed in Chapter 8), does not distinguish between grades that share the same values. Therefore, the next query returns only three rows.

```
SELECT *
  FROM (SELECT numeric_grade
          FROM grade
         WHERE student_id = 254
           AND section_id = 87
         ORDER BY numeric_grade)
 WHERE rownum <=3
NUMERIC_GRADE
-------------
           71
           71
           75
```

3 rows selected.

The next query shows you the revenue generated per course. It is based on a table named COURSE_REVENUE, and its columns are defined as follows.

```
SQL> DESCR course_revenue
```

Name	Null?	Type
COURSE_NO	NOT NULL	NUMBER(8)
REVENUE		NUMBER
COURSE_FEE		NUMBER(9,2)
NUM_ENROLLED		NUMBER
NUM_OF_SECTIONS		NUMBER

The REVENUE column holds the revenue generated by the respective COURSE_NO. The COURSE_FEE column shows the amount charged for enrollment in one individual course, and the NUM_ENROLLED column stores the number of students enrolled in a specific course. The NUM_OF_SECTIONS column holds the number of sections per course.

This table is not part of the STUDENT schema but can be created from the additional script available for download from the companion Web site, located at www.oraclesqlbyexample.com.

RANK, DENSE_RANK, AND ROW_NUMBER

The following query illustrates the differences between the three ranking functions RANK, DENSE_RANK, and ROW_NUMBER. The simplest function of the three is ROW_NUMBER, which is listed as the last column in the result; it has similar functionality to the ROWNUM pseudocolumn. It sequentially assigns a unique number to each row, starting with the number 1, based on the ORDER BY clause ranking of the revenue. When rows share duplicate revenue values, such as the course numbers 20 and 350, one of them arbitrarily gets the next number assigned.

```
SELECT course_no, revenue,
       RANK() OVER (ORDER BY revenue DESC)
         rev_rank,
       DENSE_RANK() OVER (ORDER BY revenue DESC)
         rev_dense_rank,
       ROW_NUMBER() OVER (ORDER BY revenue DESC)
         row_number
  FROM course_revenue
```

COURSE_NO	REVENUE	REV_RANK	REV_DENSE_RANK	ROW_NUMBER
25	53775	1	1	1
122	28680	2	2	2
120	27485	3	3	3
...				
240	14235	7	7	7
20	10755	8	8	8
350	10755	8	8	9
124	9560	10	9	10
125	9560	10	9	11
130	9560	10	9	12
142	8365	13	10	13
147	5975	14	11	14
310	4780	15	12	15
...				
204	1195	23	16	24

```
24 rows selected.
```

The RANK function assigns each row a unique number. However, duplicate rows receive the identical ranking, and a gap appears in the sequence before the next rank. In the column labeled REV_RANK, course numbers 20 and 350 share the identical revenue and therefore obtain the same rank. You can see a gap before the next rank.

The ranking function DENSE_RANK assigns duplicate values the same rank. The result of this function is displayed in the column labeled REV_DENSE_RANK.

The syntax of the three functions is as follows.

```
ROW_NUMBER() OVER ([query_partition_clause] order_by_clause)
   RANK() OVER ([query_partition_clause] order_by_clause)
DENSE_RANK() OVER ([query_partition_clause] order_by_clause)
```

The ORDER_BY_CLAUSE is required because it determines the ordering of the rows and therefore ranking. Although in the previous example no null values were present, you should understand that a null is assumed to be equal to another null value. As with the ORDER BY clause at the end of a SQL statement, you can include the NULLS FIRST or NULLS LAST clause to indicate the position of any nulls in the ordered sequence. If you need a refresher on NULLS FIRST or NULLS LAST, refer to Lab 6.2 in Chapter 6, "Aggregate Functions, GROUP BY, and HAVING Clauses."

The syntax includes the optional QUERY_PARTITION_CLAUSE, which allows you to rank across portions of the result set, as in the following examples.

PARTITIONING THE RESULT

The previous query generated the ranking over the entire result. The optional partitioning clause lets you create independent rankings and resets the rank whenever the partitioned values change. In the following query, the COURSE_FEE column is added to show the respective fee per course number. The ranking is now partitioned by a course's fee instead of the entire result. The ranking changes after each value change in the COURSE_FEE column.

```
SELECT course_no, course_fee fee, revenue,
       RANK() OVER (PARTITION BY course_fee
          ORDER BY revenue DESC) rev_rank,
       DENSE_RANK() OVER (PARTITION BY course_fee
          ORDER BY revenue DESC) rev_dense_rank,
       ROW_NUMBER() OVER (PARTITION BY course_fee
          ORDER BY revenue DESC) row_number
  FROM course_revenue
```

COURSE_NO	FEE	REVENUE	REV_RANK	REV_DENSE_RANK	ROW_NUMBER
230	1095	15330	1	1	1
240	1095	14235	2	2	2
135	1095	4380	3	3	3
25	1195	53775	1	1	1
122	1195	28680	2	2	2
120	1195	27485	3	3	3
140	1195	17925	4	4	4
100	1195	15535	5	5	5
20	1195	10755	6	6	6
350	1195	10755	6	6	7
124	1195	9560	8	7	8

125	1195	9560	8	7	9
130	1195	9560	8	7	10
...					
204	1195	1195	20	13	21

24 rows selected.

The first step in the query execution is the formation of the partition, and then for each distinct partition value, the ORDER BY clause is executed. This example demonstrates the use of a single partitioned value, the COURSE_FEE column. You can partition over multiple values/columns by listing each individual expression and separating them with commas in the partitioning clause.

Do not confuse the partitioning clause in analytical functions with the concept of physically splitting very large tables or indexes into smaller partitioned tables and indexes. Table and index partitioning functionality is beyond the scope of this book and independent of analytical functions discussed in this lab.

NTILE

The NTILE function is another ranking function you can use to divide data into buckets of fourth, thirds, or any other groupings. The next SELECT statement shows the result split into four buckets (four quartiles, or 4×25 percent buckets). Those in the first quartile of the revenue receive the number 1 in the NTILE column. The next quartile displays the number 2, and so on.

```
SELECT course_no, revenue,
       NTILE(4) OVER (ORDER BY revenue DESC) ntile
  FROM course_revenue
```

COURSE_NO	REVENUE	NTILE
25	53775	1
122	28680	1
120	27485	1
140	17925	1
100	15535	1
230	15330	1
240	14235	2
20	10755	2
...		
204	1195	4

24 rows selected.

The syntax of the NTILE function is as follows.

```
NTILE(expr) OVER ([query_partition_clause] order_by_clause)
```

Other less frequently used ranking functions are CUME_DIST and PERCENT_RANK. CUME_DIST determines the position of a specific value relative to a set of values, and PERCENT_RANK calculates the percent rank relative to the number of rows.

HYPOTHETICAL RANKING

Sometimes, you might want to find out how a specific data value would rank if it were part of the result set. You can perform this type of what-if analysis with the hypothetical ranking syntax, which uses the WITHIN GROUP keywords. The following query determines the rank of the value 20,000 if it was present in the REVENUE column of the COURSE_REVENUE table. As you can see from the result of the query, it would have a rank of 4.

```
SELECT RANK(20000) WITHIN GROUP (ORDER BY revenue DESC)
       "Hypothetical Rank"
  FROM course_revenue
Hypothetical Rank
-----------------
                4

1 row selected.
```

The syntax for hypothetical ranking is as follows.

```
[RANK|DENSE_RANK|PERCENT_RANK|CUME_DIST](constant[, ...])
WITHIN GROUP (order_by_clause)
```

FIRST AND LAST FUNCTIONS

The FIRST and LAST functions operate on a set of values to show the lowest or highest value within a result. The syntax of these functions is as follows.

```
aggregate_function KEEP
(DENSE_RANK {LAST|FIRST} order_by_clause)
[OVER query_partitioning_clause]
```

The following query displays for the GRADE table and SECTION_ID 99 a count of the number of rows with the highest and the lowest grades.

```
SELECT COUNT(*),
       MIN(numeric_grade) min, MAX(numeric_grade) max,
       COUNT(*) KEEP (DENSE_RANK FIRST ORDER BY numeric_grade)
        lowest,
       COUNT(*) KEEP (DENSE_RANK LAST ORDER BY numeric_grade)
        highest
  FROM grade g
 WHERE section_id = 99
```

COUNT(*)	MIN	MAX	LOWEST	HIGHEST
108	73	99	2	9

```
1 row selected.
```

This result indicates a total of 108 rows, or individual grades. Of these rows, the lowest grade is 73 and the highest is 99, as computed with the familiar MIN and MAX functions. The query's last two columns apply the FIRST and LAST functions; two grade rows exist for the lowest grade of 73, and nine rows have 99 as the highest grade.

The FIRST and LAST functions allow you to order by one column but apply the aggregate to another column. This effectively eliminates the writing of a subquery that reads the same table yet again.

The following query is an equivalent statement to determine the result of the FIRST and LAST ranking functions. It makes multiple passes through the GRADE table.

```
SELECT numeric_grade, COUNT(*)
  FROM grade
 WHERE section_id = 99
   AND (numeric_grade IN (SELECT MAX(numeric_grade)
                            FROM grade
                           WHERE section_id = 99)
        OR
        numeric_grade IN (SELECT MIN(numeric_grade)
                            FROM grade
                           WHERE section_id = 99))
 GROUP BY numeric_grade
NUMERIC_GRADE    COUNT(*)
-------------  ----------
          73           2
          99           9

2 rows selected.
```

MEDIAN

The MEDIAN function returns the median, or middle, value. This function has the following syntax.

```
MEDIAN (expression) [OVER (query_partitioning_clause)]
```

As indicated by the square brackets in this syntax, the OVER partitioning clause is optional. The following statement excludes the clause. It lists all the distinct grade type codes and the respective median and works just like any other aggregate function.

```
SELECT grade_type_code, MEDIAN(numeric_grade)
  FROM grade
 GROUP BY grade_type_code
GR MEDIAN(NUMERIC_GRADE)
-- --------------------
FI                    85
HM                    85
MT                    88
PA                    87
```

```
PJ                      88
QZ                      85.5
```

6 rows selected.

The following SELECT does not use an aggregate function to compute the median. The statement returns the GRADE_TYPE_CODE and the NUMERIC_GRADE columns for section ID 150. The third column, MEDIAN, displays the median of the NUMERIC_GRADE column, partitioned by GRADE_TYPE_CODE. The median for GRADE_TYPE_CODE FI is 88 and for MT is 77 for the respective section ID.

```
SELECT grade_type_code, numeric_grade,
       MEDIAN(numeric_grade) OVER
         (PARTITION BY grade_type_code)
       AS median
  FROM grade
 WHERE section_id = 150
```

GR	NUMERIC_GRADE	MEDIAN
FI	77	88
FI	88	88
FI	99	88
MT	76	77
MT	77	77
MT	88	77

6 rows selected.

STATS_MODE

The STATS_MODE function is another useful statistical function. The following statement illustrates the use of this function, which returns the value that occurs with the greatest frequency. In this instance, the function's parameter is the COST column, and it returns the value 1195.

```
SELECT STATS_MODE(cost)
  FROM course
STATS_MODE(COST)
----------------
            1195
```

1 row selected.

To verify the result that 1195 is the most frequently occurring COST column value, you can run the following query.

```
SELECT cost, COUNT(*)
  FROM course
 GROUP BY cost
 ORDER BY COUNT(*)
```

```
    COST    COUNT(*)
---------- ----------
      1595          1
                    1
      1095          3
      1195         25
```

4 rows selected.

The syntax of the STATS_MODE function is as follows.

```
STATS_MODE(expr)
```

REPORTING FUNCTIONALITY

The reporting functionality allows you to compute aggregates for a row in a partition. The syntax is as follows.

```
{SUM|AVG|MAX|MIN|COUNT|STDDEV|VARIANCE}
    ([ALL|DISTINCT] {expression|*})
        OVER ([PARTITION BY expression2[,...]])
```

The following example lists the individual grades and the grade type for STUDENT_ID 254 enrolled in SECTION_ID 87. The last column, labeled AVG, displays the grade average for each grade type.

```
SELECT numeric_grade, grade_type_code,
       AVG(numeric_grade)
         OVER(PARTITION BY grade_type_code) AS avg
  FROM grade
 WHERE student_id = 254
   AND section_id = 87
NUMERIC_GRADE GR        AVG
------------- -- ----------
           91 FI         91
           91 HM       84.8
           75 HM       84.8
           98 HM       84.8
...
           91 HM       84.8
           76 MT         76
```

12 rows selected.

There is no GROUP BY clause, even though an aggregate function is used in the SELECT statement. The aggregate function is processed last and works over the GRADE_TYPE_CODE column partition. The partitioning clause works similarly to the GROUP BY clause, grouping together rows and building the aggregate for each of the distinct values of the partition.

If you omit the partition, as indicated in the following example by the empty set of parentheses, the aggregate is computed for all the rows of the result set.

```
SELECT numeric_grade, grade_type_code,
       AVG(numeric_grade) OVER() AS avg
  FROM grade
 WHERE student_id = 254
   AND section_id = 87
NUMERIC_GRADE GR        AVG
------------- -- ----------
          91 FI 84.5833333
          91 HM 84.5833333
          75 HM 84.5833333
          98 HM 84.5833333
...
          76 MT 84.5833333


12 rows selected.
```

RATIO_TO_REPORT

The RATIO_TO_REPORT function is a reporting function that computes the ratio of a value to the sum of a set of values. The syntax is as follows.

```
RATIO_TO_REPORT(expression) OVER ([query_partition_clause])
```

The following SQL statement illustrates the use of the RATIO_TO_REPORT function. The result of the function, displayed in the RATIO column, represents the ratio of the entire revenue because the partitioning clause is absent. The first row shows the total revenue of COURSE_NO 10 for 1195; the RATIO column indicates that the computed value represents 4.496284 percent of the entire revenue.

```
SELECT course_no, revenue,
       RATIO_TO_REPORT(revenue) OVER () AS ratio
  FROM course_revenue
 COURSE_NO    REVENUE      RATIO
---------- ---------- ----------
        10       1195 .004496284
        20      10755  .04046656
        25      53775   .2023328
       100      15535 .058451698
       120      27485 .103414542
...
       350      10755  .04046656
       420       2390 .008992569


24 rows selected.
```

WINDOWING

The WINDOWING clause allows you to compute cumulative, moving, and centered aggregates. A window has a defining starting point and ending point. The parameters in the windowing clause are always relative to the current row. A sliding window changes the starting point or ending point, depending on the definition of the window.

A window that defines a cumulative sum starts with the first row and then slides forward with each subsequent row. A moving average has sliding starting and ending rows for a constant logical or physical range.

The following SELECT statement illustrates the computation of a cumulative average and a cumulative sum that is based on the values from the first row until and including the current row. The result shows the individual course numbers and their respective revenues. The CumAvg column shows the cumulative average, and the CumSum column shows the cumulative sum.

```
SELECT course_no, revenue,
       AVG(revenue) OVER (ORDER BY course_no
          ROWS BETWEEN UNBOUNDED PRECEDING AND CURRENT ROW)
          "CumAvg",
       SUM(revenue) OVER (ORDER BY course_no
          ROWS BETWEEN UNBOUNDED PRECEDING AND CURRENT ROW)
          "CumSum"
  FROM course_revenue
```

COURSE_NO	REVENUE	CumAvg	CumSum
10	1195	1195	1195
20	10755	5975	11950
25	53775	21908.3333	65725
100	15535	20315	81260
120	27485	21749	108745
...			
350	10755	11451.5217	263385
420	2390	11073.9583	265775

24 rows selected.

Examine the third output row, where COURSE_NO is equal to 25. The average was built based on the revenue values of COURSE_NO 10, 20, and 25, which have REVENUE column values of 1195, 10755, and 53775, respectively. The average of these three values is 21908.3333. The next row builds the average from the previously mentioned values plus the current value, which is 15535; divided by four, this yields 20315. The value in the CumAvg column changes for each subsequent row.

The CumSum column is the cumulative sum, and for each subsequent row it adds the revenue value to the previously computed sum.

The next example shows a centered average; it is computed with the row preceding the current row and the row following the current row. The column is labeled CentAvg. A moving average takes the current row and the previous row, and the result is shown in the MovAvg column.

```
SELECT course_no, revenue,
       AVG(revenue) OVER (ORDER BY course_no
          ROWS BETWEEN 1 PRECEDING AND 1 FOLLOWING)
       "CentAvg",
       AVG(revenue) OVER (ORDER BY course_no
          ROWS 1 PRECEDING)
       "MovAvg"
  FROM course_revenue
```

COURSE_NO	REVENUE	CentAvg	MovAvg
10	1195	5975	1195
20	10755	21908.3333	5975
25	53775	26688.3333	32265
100	15535	32265	34655
120	27485	23900	21510
...			
420	2390	6572.5	6572.5

24 rows selected.

You can expand this functionality for any of the aggregate functions. This allows you to compute moving sums, centered sums, moving min and max values, and so on.

The syntax of the windowing clause is as follows.

```
order_by_clause {ROWS|RANGE}
{BETWEEN
  {UNBOUNDED PRECEDING|CURRENT ROW|
   expression {PRECEDING|FOLLOWING}}
AND
  {UNBOUNDED FOLLOWING|CURRENT ROW|
   expression {PRECEDING|FOLLOWING}}|
  {UNBOUNDED PRECEDING|CURRENT ROW|
   expression PRECEDING}}
```

The ROWS and RANGE keywords allow you to define a window, either *physically* through the number of rows or *logically*, such as a time interval or a positive numeric value in the RANGE keyword. The BETWEEN...AND clause defines the starting and ending points of the window, and if none are specified, Oracle defaults to RANGE BETWEEN UNBOUNDED PRECEDING AND CURRENT ROW.

UNBOUNDED PRECEDING indicates that the window starts at the first row of the partition, and UNBOUNDED FOLLOWING indicates that the window ends at the last row of the partition.

Besides the aggregate functions, such as AVG, COUNT, MIN, MAX, SUM, STDDEV, and VARIANCE, you can use the FIRST_VALUE and LAST_VALUE functions, which return the first value and last value in the window, respectively.

LOGICAL AND PHYSICAL WINDOWS

As mentioned previously, a window can be defined as either a logical window or a physical window. A physical window is defined with the ROWS keyword. A logical window uses the RANGE keyword. Table 17.2 highlights the main differences between logical and physical windows. You will explore these differences in the following exercises.

Table 17.2 Differences Between Physical and Logical Windows

PHYSICAL WINDOW	LOGICAL WINDOW
Specify window with the ROWS keyword.	Specify the window with the RANGE keyword.
Ability to specify the exact number of rows.	Logical offset that determines the starting and ending points of the window; this can be a constant (for example, RANGE 5 PRECEDING), an expression that evaluates to a constant, or an interval (for example , RANGE INTERVAL 10 DAYS PRECEDING).
Duplicate values in the ORDER BY clause do not affect the definition of the current row.	Duplicate values are considered the same for the purpose of defining the current row; therefore, the aggregate function includes all duplicate values, even if they follow the current physical row.
Allows multiple ORDER BY expressions.	Only one ORDER BY expression is allowed.

THE ORDER BY CLAUSE

ORDER BY in a windowing clause is a mandatory clause that determines the order in which the rows are sorted. Based on this order, the starting and ending points of the window are defined.

```
SELECT numeric_grade, grade_type_code,
       AVG(numeric_grade) OVER(ORDER BY grade_type_code)
       AS cumavg
  FROM grade
 WHERE student_id = 254
   AND section_id = 87
NUMERIC_GRADE GR       CUMAVG
------------- -- ----------
           91 FI           91
           91 HM 85.3636364
           75 HM 85.3636364
           98 HM 85.3636364
...
           76 MT 84.5833333

12 rows selected.
```

The SELECT statement computes the average of grades, based on the GRADE_TYPE_CODE column. The moving average changes with each change in the GRADE_TYPE_CODE value. Because no windowing clause is specified, the window defaults to RANGE BETWEEN UNBOUNDED PRECEDING AND CURRENT ROW. This is effectively a logical window. Therefore, the cumulative average value changes with the change of the value in the GRADE_TYPE_CODE column.

 One of the keys to understanding logical windows is that the current row equals all the rows with the same ORDER BY values.

In the following statement, the windowing clause is missing, but now there are four columns in the ORDER BY clause. These columns represent the primary key and make the values in the ORDER BY clause unique. In the CUMAVG_OVER_PK column, the average changes with each row. The PARTITION column is formed with a combination of the PARTITIONING clause and the WINDOWING clause. The rows are partitioned by GRADE_TYPE_CODE, and the cumulative average change is reset with each change in the partition.

```
SELECT numeric_grade, grade_type_code,
       grade_code_occurrence AS occur,
       AVG(numeric_grade) OVER(ORDER BY student_id,
         section_id, grade_type_code,
         grade_code_occurrence) AS cumavg_over_pk,
       AVG(numeric_grade) OVER(PARTITION BY
       grade_type_code
       ORDER BY student_id, section_id,
       grade_type_code, grade_code_occurrence)
       AS partition
  FROM grade
 WHERE student_id = 254
   AND section_id = 87
```

NUMERIC_GRADE	GR	OCCUR	CUMAVG_OVER_PK	PARTITION
91	FI	1	91	91
91	HM	1	91	91
75	HM	2	85.6666667	83
98	HM	3	88.75	88
98	HM	4	90.6	90.5
81	HM	5	89	88.6
71	HM	6	86.4285714	85.6666667
71	HM	7	84.5	83.5714286
81	HM	8	84.1111111	83.25
91	HM	9	84.8	84.1111111
91	HM	10	85.3636364	84.8
76	MT	1	84.5833333	76

```
12 rows selected.
```

INTERVALS AND THE LOGICAL WINDOW

The following SQL statement shows another example of the functionality of a logical window and the RANGE keyword. The resulting output of the statement lists the number of students who enrolled on specific dates. The sliding windowing functionality with the moving AVG function is applied to the last three columns, named PREV 10 DAYS, NEXT 10 DAYS, and 20-DAY WINDOW.

The column PREV 10 DAYS indicates the average number of students who enrolled 10 days prior to the listed ENROLL_DATE. The starting point of the window is 10 days prior to the ENROLL_DATE of the current row, and the ending point of the window is the current row. The next column, labeled NEXT 10 DAYS, is a window that defines itself from the current row until 10 days after ENROLL_DATE. The column 20-DAY WINDOW shows a 20-day sliding window, starting with 10 days prior to the current row and ending 10 days after the current row.

```
SELECT TRUNC(enroll_date) ENROLL_DATE, COUNT(*) "# ENROLLED",
       AVG(COUNT(*))OVER(ORDER BY TRUNC(enroll_date)
        RANGE INTERVAL '10' DAY PRECEDING) "PREV 10 DAYS",
       AVG(COUNT(*))OVER(ORDER BY TRUNC(enroll_date)
        RANGE BETWEEN CURRENT ROW
        AND INTERVAL '10' DAY FOLLOWING) "NEXT 10 DAYS",
       AVG(COUNT(*))OVER(ORDER BY TRUNC(enroll_date)
        RANGE BETWEEN INTERVAL '10' DAY PRECEDING
        AND INTERVAL '10' DAY FOLLOWING) "20-DAY WINDOW"
  FROM enrollment
 GROUP BY TRUNC(enroll_date)
```

ENROLL_DA	# ENROLLED	PREV 10 DAYS	NEXT 10 DAYS	20-DAY WINDOW
30-JAN-07	11	11	17	17
02-FEB-07	14	12.5	20.6	19
04-FEB-07	23	16	22.8	19.8571429
07-FEB-07	20	17	23.4	20.625
10-FEB-07	22	19.75	24.4	22.375
11-FEB-07	24	20.6	27.2	23.8888889
13-FEB-07	25	22.8	28	25.125
16-FEB-07	26	23.4	29	25.4285714
19-FEB-07	25	24.4	30.5	26.3333333
21-FEB-07	36	27.2	36	27.2

```
10 rows selected.
```

Examine the first row; it displays 30-JAN-07 in the ENROLL_DATE column. You see that 11 students enrolled on this date. The average number of enrollments for the previous 10 days is computed by the nested AVG(COUNT(*)) function, which computes the average of the number of enrolled students per ENROLL_DATE within the last 10 days. Because this is the first row and there are no prior values, the average is equal to the number of enrolled students. All the values in the ENROLL_DATE column are truncated to ensure that only date, not time, values are considered.

All the cumulative window values change as you move forward within each subsequent enroll-ment date. For example, the row with the ENROLL_DATE value 10-FEB-07 shows the average number of enrollments for the previous 10 days (including the current date) as 19.75. This value is computed by averaging the number of enrollments up to and including the 02-FEB-07 value. The value in the NEXT 10 DAYS column is computed once again, through the sliding window of 10 days after the current date and inclusive of the current row. This includes all the enrollments up to and including 19-FEB-07. The value in the 20-DAY WINDOW column includes the prior 10 days and the 10 days following the current date of the row.

The query shows the use of interval literals; remember that interval literals are expressed in the following format.

```
INTERVAL n DAY|MONTH|YEAR
```

If you need to compute the time interval between two dates, use the NUMTOYMINTERVAL function or the NUMTODSINTERVAL function, discussed in Chapter 5, "Date and Conversion Functions."

LAG/LEAD FUNCTIONS

The LAG and LEAD functions allow you to get values from other rows relative to the position of the current row. The syntax is as follows.

```
{LAG|LEAD}(expression[,offset][,default])
   OVER ([query_partition_clause] order_by_clause)
```

The LAG function returns one of the values of the previous rows, and the LEAD function returns one of the values of the next rows. The optional OFFSET parameter identifies the relative posi-tion of the row; if no parameter is specified, it defaults to 1. The optional default parameter returns the value if the offset falls outside the boundaries of the table or the partition, such as the last and first rows. The LAG and LEAD functions do not have a windowing clause because the offset indicates the exact row.

The following SQL statement shows a useful example of the LAG function. The This Month's Revenue column displays the revenue generated for the month in which an individual section begins. The Previous Month column is computed using the LAG function. The offset number is specified as 1, which indicates to always use the previous row's value. The Monthly Change column computes the change from the previous month by subtracting the value of the This Month's Revenue column from the value in the Previous Month column.

```
SELECT TO_CHAR(start_date_time, 'MM') "Month",
       SUM(cost) "This Month's Revenue",
       LAG(SUM(cost),1) OVER
         (ORDER BY TO_CHAR(start_date_time, 'MM'))
         "Previous Month",
       SUM(cost)-LAG(SUM(cost),1) OVER
         (ORDER BY TO_CHAR(start_date_time, 'MM'))
         "Monthly Change"
  FROM enrollment e, section s, course c
```

```
WHERE e.section_id = s.section_id
  AND s.course_no = c.course_no
  AND c.cost IS NOT NULL
GROUP BY TO_CHAR(start_date_time, 'MM')
Mo This Month's Revenue Previous Month Monthly Change
-- -------------------- -------------- --------------
04                59745
05                98780          59745          39035
06                48695          98780         -50085
07                58555          48695           9860
```

4 rows selected.

ADVANTAGES OF ANALYTICAL FUNCTIONS

Analytical functions have a number of advantages. Unlike SELECT statements containing aggregate functions and the GROUP BY clause, they allow you to display summary and detail data together rather than write separate queries. The following SELECT statements illustrate this advantage.

This query shows the average revenue per number of sections in a course.

```
SELECT num_of_sections, AVG(revenue)
  FROM course_revenue
 GROUP BY num_of_sections
 ORDER BY 1
NUM_OF_SECTIONS AVG(REVENUE)
--------------- ------------
              1       2987.5
              2   10369.2857
              3   7833.33333
              4      10157.5
              5      22107.5
              6        27485
              8        53775
```

7 rows selected.

The next statement allows you to show any of the table's columns; you are not limited to only the columns listed in the GROUP BY clause, and you avoid the ORA-00937 and ORA-00979 errors. The result shows a list of both summary and detail data.

```
SELECT course_no, revenue, num_of_sections,
       AVG(revenue) OVER (PARTITION BY
         num_of_sections) AS avg_rev_per_cour
  FROM course_revenue
COURSE_NO    REVENUE NUM_OF_SECTIONS AVG_REV_PER_COUR
---------- ---------- --------------- ----------------
       10       1195               1           2987.5
      132       2390               1           2987.5
```

145	2390	1	2987.5
...			
147	5975	1	2987.5
134	2390	2	10369.2857
350	10755	2	10369.2857
...			
146	3585	2	10369.2857
...			
135	4380	3	7833.33333
...			
25	53775	8	53775

24 rows selected.

Analytical functions perform postprocessing on the result, which makes them very efficient and simple to use. Some analytical functions cannot be duplicated using any other SQL syntax. For example, the DENSE_RANK or moving and cumulative values cannot be computed without the use of the analytical clause in a statement.

The WITH Clause

The WITH clause, also referred to as the *subquery factoring clause*, offers the benefit of reusing a query when it occurs more than once within the same statement. Instead of storing the query results in a temporary table and performing queries against this temporary table, you can use the WITH clause; it gives the query a name, and you can reference it multiple times. This avoids a reread and re-execution of the query, which improves overall query execution time and resource utilization, particularly when very large tables and/or joins are involved. The WITH clause also simplifies the writing of SQL statements. You most frequently use this type of query when querying against large volumes of data, such as in data warehouses.

The WITH keyword indicates that multiple SQL statements are involved. The following example determines the revenue generated by each instructor. The query result returns revenue for only those instructors who have revenue greater than the average generated by all instructors combined.

```
WITH
revenue_per_instructor AS
 (SELECT instructor_id, SUM(cost) AS revenue
   FROM section s, course c, enrollment e
  WHERE s.section_id = e.section_id
    AND c.course_no = s.course_no
  GROUP BY instructor_id)
SELECT *
  FROM revenue_per_instructor
 WHERE revenue > (SELECT AVG(revenue)
                    FROM revenue_per_instructor)
```

```
INSTRUCTOR_ID      REVENUE
-------------   ----------
          101       51380
          103       44215
          107       35745
          108       39235
```

4 rows selected.

The WITH clause creates a name for the "temporary" result REVENUE_PER_INSTRUCTOR. This result is then referred to in the subsequent SELECT statements in the context of the original query.

Because the REVENUE_PER_INSTRUCTOR query involves a join and an aggregate function, it is useful to examine the result of the join to ensure the accuracy of the aggregate function.

```
SELECT instructor_id, cost, s.section_id, student_id
  FROM section s, course c, enrollment e
 WHERE s.section_id = e.section_id
   AND c.course_no = s.course_no
 ORDER BY instructor_id
```

```
INSTRUCTOR_ID        COST SECTION_ID STUDENT_ID
-------------   ---------- ---------- ----------
          101        1195         87        256
...
          105        1195        152        138
          105        1195        152        144
          105        1195        152        206
          105        1195        152        207
          105        1195        144        153
          105        1195        144        200
          105        1095        113        129
          105        1195        105        202
          105        1195         91        232
          105        1195        105        263
          105        1195        105        261
          105        1195        105        259
          105        1195        105        260
          105        1195         83        124
          105        1195         91        271
...
          108        1195         86        102
```

226 rows selected.

For example, review INSTRUCTOR_ID 105. Effectively, the SUM function adds up all the individual values of the COST column, resulting in a total of 19020. Adding the GROUP BY clause and the SUM function to the joined tables produces this output, which is identical to the result achieved by the REVENUE_PER_INSTRUCTOR query.

```
SELECT instructor_id, SUM(cost)
  FROM section s, course c, enrollment e
 WHERE s.section_id = e.section_id
   AND c.course_no = s.course_no
 GROUP BY instructor_id
INSTRUCTOR_ID  SUM(COST)
-------------  ----------
          101      51380
          102      24995
          103      44215
          104      29675
          105      19020
          106      21510
          107      35745
          108      39235
```

8 rows selected.

To determine the average revenue for all instructors, you nest the two aggregate functions AVG and SUM. REVENUE_PER_INSTRUCTOR, however, reuses the previous result instead of executing the following query.

```
SELECT AVG(SUM(cost))
  FROM section s, course c, enrollment e
 WHERE s.section_id = e.section_id
   AND c.course_no = s.course_no
 GROUP BY instructor_id
AVG(SUM(COST))
--------------
     33221.875
```

1 row selected.

Without the WITH clause, you need to write the following statement, which effectively performs the reading of the tables and the join twice--once for the subquery and once for the outer query. This requires more resources and consumes more time than writing the query with the subquery factoring clause, particularly when large tables, many joins, and complex aggregations are involved.

```
SELECT instructor_id, SUM(cost) AS revenue
  FROM section s, course c, enrollment e
 WHERE s.section_id = e.section_id
   AND c.course_no = s.course_no
 GROUP BY instructor_id
HAVING SUM(cost) > (SELECT AVG(SUM(cost))
  FROM section s, course c, enrollment e
 WHERE s.section_id = e.section_id
   AND c.course_no = s.course_no
 GROUP BY instructor_id)
```

Do not confuse the WITH clause in subqueries with the START WITH clause used in hierarchical queries, discussed in Chapter 16, "Regular Expressions and Hierarchical Queries."

You can also write this query using the analytical function discussed previously. As you have discovered throughout this book, there are often many ways to formulate a SQL statement. Knowing the options is useful and allows you to choose the most efficient statement.

```
SELECT *
  FROM (SELECT instructor_id, SUM(cost) AS revenue,
               AVG(SUM(cost)) OVER() AS avg
          FROM section s, course c, enrollment e
         WHERE s.section_id = e.section_id
           AND c.course_no = s.course_no
         GROUP BY instructor_id) t
 WHERE revenue > avg
INSTRUCTOR_ID    REVENUE        AVG
------------- ---------- ----------
          101     51380  33221.875
          103     44215  33221.875
          107     35745  33221.875
          108     39235  33221.875

4 rows selected.
```

Inter-Row Calculations

Oracle can perform spreadsheet-like calculations in queries. This capability can be useful for budgeting and forecasting. It allows the display of additional rows or calculations in the query result through the application of formulas in the MODEL clause of a SELECT statement. Following is a query example based on the MODEL_EXAMPLE table, consisting of the columns COURSE, GENDER, YEAR, and ENROLL_NO, which store data about courses, gender, the enrollment year, and the enrollment figures, respectively. (This table can be created based on the additional script available from the companion Web site, located at www.oraclesqlbyexample.com.)

This table contains only data for the year 2008, but the following sample query result shows additional rows (shaded in gray) for the years 2009 and 2010. For those years, the query determines the projected enrollment numbers in the courses Spanish II and Spanish III, based on the previous year's enrollment numbers. You need to keep in mind that these rows represent a query result, and the query does not update the MODEL_EXAMPLE table.

```
SELECT course, gender, year, s
  FROM model_example
 MODEL PARTITION BY (gender)
       DIMENSION BY (year, course)
       MEASURES (enroll_no s)
   (
```

```
    s[2009,'Spanish II'] = s[2008,'Spanish I'],
    s[2010,'Spanish III'] = ROUND((s[2009, 'Spanish II'])*0.80)
    )
    ORDER BY year, gender, course
```

COURSE	G	YEAR	S
Spanish I	F	2008	37
Spanish II	F	2008	59
Spanish III	F	2008	3
Spanish I	M	2008	3
Spanish II	M	2008	35
Spanish III	M	2008	34
Spanish II	F	2009	37
Spanish II	M	2009	3
Spanish III	F	2010	30
Spanish III	M	2010	2

10 rows selected.

The MODEL clause lists a PARTITION element that is much like the familiar partition in the previously discussed analytical functions query and defines the top-level grouping. The DIMENSION element identifies the key to the MEASURES cells, which hold numeric values. In this example, the GENDER column is the partitioned column, and the DIMENSION columns YEAR and COURSE identify the groups within each partition. The MEASURE column is ENROLL_NO and is uniquely identified by the combination of partition and dimension columns.

The rule s[2009, 'Spanish II'] = s[2008, 'Spanish I'] is a definition of an assignment. A rule consists of references. The two-dimensional [2009, 'Spanish II'] reference defines a single cell for the dimensions YEAR and COURSE. The measure s is an alias, as defined in the MEASURE element. The left side of the assignment indicates the destination cell; the right side determines the values for it. In this instance, the destination cell with the year 2009 and the course Spanish II does not exist in the MODEL_EXAMPLE table and is created in the result set by default; this action is referred to as UPSERT. The right side of the assignment states that the measure cell should be the same value as the value in year 2008 and for the course Spanish I. Two rows are created for this year: one for male and another for female.

The next rule, s[2010, 'Spanish III'] = ROUND((s[2009, 'Spanish II'])*0.80), defines that the enrollment number for Spanish III in year 2010 should be 80 percent of the enrollment for Spanish II in 2009, rounded to nearest whole number.

The previous statement's calculations refer to specific individual cells. You can also specify ranges of cells, create loops, and so on. The following example illustrates the projection of enrollment figures for Spanish II for the years 2009 through 2011 (shaded in gray). The FOR loop creates these years. The measure values are based on the previous year's value of Spanish II. The CURRENTV( ) function returns the current value of the YEAR dimension column, but because the function reads CURRENTV( )-1, it looks at the previous year's value. The calculation ROUND((s[CURRENTV( )-1, 'Spanish II'])*1.1) assumes a 10 percent increase each subsequent year and is rounded to the nearest whole number.

```
SELECT course, gender, year, s
  FROM model_example
 WHERE course = 'Spanish II'
 MODEL PARTITION BY (gender)
       DIMENSION BY (year, course)
       MEASURES (enroll_no s)
 (
  s[FOR year FROM 2009 TO 2011 INCREMENT 1,
    'Spanish II']
  = ROUND((s[CURRENTV()-1,'Spanish II'])*1.1)
 )
 ORDER BY year, gender, course
COURSE             G    YEAR           S
----------------   -    ------    ----------
Spanish II         F    2008          59
Spanish II         M    2008          35
Spanish II         F    2009          65
Spanish II         M    2009          39
Spanish II         F    2010          72
Spanish II         M    2010          43
Spanish II         F    2011          79
Spanish II         M    2011          47

8 rows selected.
```

Creating Your Own Custom Function

So far, you have used a variety of the rich offerings of Oracle's built-in functions. Using the PL/SQL language, you can write your own functions. Although this book does not discuss PL/SQL in detail, this brief section offers a glimpse into what a customized PL/SQL function can accomplish when used in a SQL statement.

Why would you write your own PL/SQL function? This functionality is quite useful in the case of complicated query logic because it allows you to easily call the function that hides the complexity of the logic. The following example shows a custom function that chooses the next business day if the passed date falls on a weekend day. The function queries the HOLIDAY table to make sure the next business day does not fall on a company holiday. You can use this function much as you would any of the single-row functions you have learned about.

The next example shows how the function called NEXT_BUSINESS_DAY works. As you can see, it hides all the complexity of figuring out the date for you and simply returns the next business day.

```
SELECT next_business_day('07-AUG-2010')
  FROM dual
```

```
NEXT_BUSI
---------
09-AUG-10
```

1 row selected.

Because August 7, 2010, falls on a Saturday, the next business day is a Monday. Therefore, if you're trying to write a report to list the due dates of invoices and you must always display a business day as the due date, it is easy to use this function. Furthermore, it is simpler than writing a long CASE expression. Other statements can use the stored function and take advantage of the functionality. In addition, a stored function ensures that subsequent changes to the logic are automatically applied to any statement that calls the function.

Following is the PL/SQL code that implements and stores NEXT_BUSINESS_DAY function in the database.

```
CREATE OR REPLACE FUNCTION next_business_day(i_date DATE)
  RETURN DATE IS
  v_date DATE;
BEGIN
 v_date:=i_date;
 SELECT NVL(MAX(holiday_end_date)+1, v_date)
   INTO v_date
   FROM holiday
  WHERE v_date BETWEEN holiday_start_date AND holiday_end_date;
 IF TO_CHAR(v_date, 'DY') = 'SAT' THEN
    v_date:=v_date+2;
 ELSIF TO_CHAR(v_date, 'DY') = 'SUN' THEN
    v_date:=v_date+1;
 END IF;
 RETURN v_date;
EXCEPTION
 WHEN OTHERS THEN
   RETURN NULL;
END next_business_day;
/
```

In previous Oracle versions, functions executed from a SQL statement had to be wrapped inside a package—a type of PL/SQL object.

Clearly, writing your own custom functions simplifies the logic of complicated business rules and can overcome SQL limitations. However, you must keep in mind that a function will be executed for every row of the result set; the key is to eliminate as many rows as possible before applying the function.

To learn more about PL/SQL, refer to *Oracle PL/SQL by Example,* 4th Edition, by Benjamin Rosenzweig and Elena Silvestrova Rakhimov (Prentice Hall, 2008).

▼ LAB 17.1 EXERCISES

a) The following query result is a list of all the distinct course costs and a count of each. Write the query that achieves this result.

1095	1195	1595	NULL
3	25	1	1

1 row selected.

b) Modify the following query to display the top three revenue-generating courses. If there is a tie in the revenue, include the duplicates.

```
SELECT course_no, revenue,
       RANK() OVER (ORDER BY revenue DESC)
         rev_rank,
       DENSE_RANK() OVER (ORDER BY revenue DESC)
         rev_dense_rank,
       ROW_NUMBER() OVER (ORDER BY revenue DESC)
         row_number
  FROM course_revenue
```

c) Based on the following statement, explain how the result of the AVG column is achieved.

```
SELECT numeric_grade AS grade, grade_type_code,
       grade_code_occurrence AS occurrence,
       AVG(numeric_grade) OVER(PARTITION BY grade_type_code
       ORDER BY grade_code_occurrence) AS avg
  FROM grade
 WHERE student_id = 254
   AND section_id = 87
```

GRADE	GR	OCCURRENCE	AVG
91	FI	1	91
91	HM	1	91
75	HM	2	83
98	HM	3	88
98	HM	4	90.5
81	HM	5	88.6
71	HM	6	85.6666667
71	HM	7	83.5714286
81	HM	8	83.25
91	HM	9	84.1111111
91	HM	10	84.8
76	MT	1	76

12 rows selected.

d) How would you formulate the problem this query is attempting to solve?

```
SELECT e.*, SUM(diff) OVER (ORDER BY 1 ROWS BETWEEN
        UNBOUNDED PRECEDING AND CURRENT ROW) AS cum_sum
  FROM (SELECT TRUNC(enroll_date),
             TRUNC(enroll_date)-LAG(TRUNC(enroll_date),1)
              OVER (ORDER BY TRUNC(ENROLL_DATE)) DIFF
          FROM enrollment
          GROUP BY TRUNC(enroll_date)) e
```

TRUNC(ENR	DIFF	CUM_SUM
30-JAN-07		
02-FEB-07	3	3
04-FEB-07	2	5
07-FEB-07	3	8
10-FEB-07	3	11
11-FEB-07	1	12
13-FEB-07	2	14
16-FEB-07	3	17
19-FEB-07	3	20
21-FEB-07	2	22

10 rows selected.

e) Explain the result of the following query.

```
WITH
num_enroll AS
(SELECT COUNT(*) num_students, course_no
  FROM enrollment e JOIN section s
 USING (section_id)
 GROUP BY course_no),
avg_stud_enroll AS
(SELECT AVG(num_students) avg#_of_stud
  FROM num_enroll
 WHERE num_students <> (SELECT MAX(num_students)
                         FROM num_enroll))
SELECT course_no, num_students
  FROM num_enroll
 WHERE num_students > (SELECT avg#_of_stud
                        FROM avg_stud_enroll)
   AND num_students < (SELECT MAX(num_students)
                        FROM num_enroll)
```

COURSE_NO	NUM_STUDENTS
20	9
100	13
120	23
122	24
124	8
125	8

130	8
140	15
230	14
240	13
350	9

`11 rows selected.`

▼ LAB 17.1 EXERCISE **ANSWERS**

a) The following query result is a list of all the distinct course costs and a count of each. Write the query that achieves this result.

```
    1095       1195       1595       NULL
---------- ---------- ---------- ---------
    3          25          1          1
```

`1 row selected.`

ANSWER: There are various ways to write the query. You can use PIVOT, CASE, or DECODE to obtain the same output.

If you use the PIVOT clause, you can write the following query.

```
SELECT *
  FROM (SELECT cost, COUNT(*) num_of_rows
          FROM course
          GROUP BY cost) course_cost
 PIVOT (SUM(num_of_rows)
  FOR cost IN (1095, 1195, 1595, null))
```

Or use the CASE expression, as follows.

```
SELECT COUNT(CASE WHEN cost = 1095 THEN 1 END) "1095",
       COUNT(CASE WHEN cost = 1195 THEN 1 END) "1195",
       COUNT(CASE WHEN cost = 1595 THEN 1 END) "1595",
       COUNT(CASE WHEN cost IS NULL THEN 1 END) "NULL"
  FROM course
```

Or use the DECODE function, as follows.

```
SELECT COUNT(DECODE(cost, 1095, 1)) "1095",
       COUNT(DECODE(cost, 1195, 1)) "1195",
       COUNT(DECODE(cost, 1595, 1)) "1595",
       COUNT(DECODE(cost, NULL, 1)) "NULL"
  FROM course
```

The transposed result uses the COUNT function to count the row only if it meets the search criteria of the DECODE function or CASE expression. The first column of the SELECT statement tests for courses with a cost of 1095. If this expression is equal to 1095, the DECODE function or CASE expression returns the value 1; otherwise, it returns a NULL value. The COUNT function counts NOT NULL values; the NULL values are not included. This is different from the way the COUNT(*) function works, which includes NULL values in the count.

The last column in the SELECT statement tests for courses with a NULL cost. If this condition of a NULL course cost is true, the DECODE function or the CASE expression returns a 1, and the row is included in the count.

If your Oracle version does not support the PIVOT clause, you might want to use the CASE expression because it is easier to understand than DECODE functionality. It also has the added benefit of being ANSI compatible.

b) Modify the following query to display the top three revenue-generating courses. If there is a tie in the revenue, include the duplicates.

```
SELECT course_no, revenue,
       RANK() OVER (ORDER BY revenue DESC)
         rev_rank,
       DENSE_RANK() OVER (ORDER BY revenue DESC)
         rev_dense_rank,
       ROW_NUMBER() OVER (ORDER BY revenue DESC)
         row_number
  FROM course_revenue
```

ANSWER: Using an inline view, you restrict the rows to only those where the values in the REV_DENSE_RANK column are 3 or less. The DENSE_RANK function is the better choice, just in case some courses share the same revenue.

```
SELECT course_no, revenue, rev_dense_rank
  FROM (SELECT course_no, revenue,
               DENSE_RANK() OVER (ORDER BY revenue DESC)
                 rev_dense_rank
          FROM course_revenue) t
 WHERE rev_dense_rank <= 3
```

COURSE_NO	REVENUE	REV_DENSE_RANK
25	53775	1
122	28680	2
120	27485	3

3 rows selected.

BOTTOM-*N* RANKING

The bottom-*n* ranking is similar to top-*n* except that you change the order of the ranking. Instead of ordering the revenue in descending order, the ORDER BY clause is now in ascending order. The query to determine the bottom three revenue-ranking courses is shown here.

```
SELECT course_no, revenue, rev_dense_rank
  FROM (SELECT course_no, revenue,
               DENSE_RANK() OVER (ORDER BY revenue ASC)
                 rev_dense_rank
          FROM course_revenue) t
 WHERE rev_dense_rank <= 3
```

COURSE_NO	REVENUE	REV_DENSE_RANK
10	1195	1
204	1195	1

132	2390	2
145	2390	2
420	2390	2
134	2390	2
146	3585	3
330	3585	3

8 rows selected.

c) Based on the following statement, explain how the result of the AVG column is achieved.

```
SELECT numeric_grade AS grade, grade_type_code,
       grade_code_occurrence AS occurrence,
       AVG(numeric_grade) OVER(PARTITION BY grade_type_code
       ORDER BY grade_code_occurrence) AS avg
  FROM grade
 WHERE student_id = 254
   AND section_id = 87
```

GRADE	GR	OCCURRENCE	AVG
91	FI	1	91
91	HM	1	91
75	HM	2	83
98	HM	3	88
98	HM	4	90.5
81	HM	5	88.6
71	HM	6	85.6666667
71	HM	7	83.5714286
81	HM	8	83.25
91	HM	9	84.1111111
91	HM	10	84.8
76	MT	1	76

12 rows selected.

ANSWER: The statement computes a cumulative average for each partition. The average is reset after the values listed in the partition clause change. The ORDER BY clause determines the definition of the window.

After the WHERE clause is executed, postprocessing with the analytical function takes over. The partitions are built first. The result shows three distinct values: FI, HM, and MT, for final, homework, and midterm, respectively. After a change in partition, the average is reset.

It is easiest to follow the logic by examining the individual computations for each respective row. They are listed next to the result.

GRADE	GR	OCCURRENCE	AVG	
91	FI	1	91	/* (91)/1 */
91	HM	1	91	/* (91)/1 partition change*/
75	HM	2	83	/* (91+83)/2 */
98	HM	3	88	/* (91+83+98)/3 */
98	HM	4	90.5	/* (91+83+98+98)/4 */

```
...
   76 MT              1             76  /* (76)/1 partition change*/

12 rows selected.
```

For the HM partition there are duplicates for the NUMERIC_GRADE column values (rows 4 and 5 show 98). Because the column GRADE_CODE_OCCURRENCE is part of the ORDER BY clause and has different and ever-changing values, the cumulative average is computed for each row.

d) How would you formulate the problem this query is attempting to solve?

```
SELECT e.*, SUM(diff) OVER (ORDER BY 1 ROWS BETWEEN
       UNBOUNDED PRECEDING AND CURRENT ROW) AS cum_sum
  FROM (SELECT TRUNC(enroll_date),
               TRUNC(enroll_date)-LAG(TRUNC(enroll_date),1)
               OVER (ORDER BY TRUNC(ENROLL_DATE)) DIFF
          FROM enrollment
         GROUP BY TRUNC(enroll_date)) e
```

TRUNC(ENR	DIFF	CUM_SUM
30-JAN-07		
02-FEB-07	3	3
04-FEB-07	2	5
07-FEB-07	3	8
10-FEB-07	3	11
11-FEB-07	1	12
13-FEB-07	2	14
16-FEB-07	3	17
19-FEB-07	3	20
21-FEB-07	2	22

```
10 rows selected.
```

Answer: The query determines the difference in days between the distinct ENROLL_DATE values; it considers only the date, not the time values. In the query result, you see the distinct ENROLL_DATE values, the difference in days between each value, and the cumulative sum of days in the last column.

e) Explain the result of the following query.

```
WITH
num_enroll AS
(SELECT COUNT(*) num_students, course_no
  FROM enrollment e JOIN section s
 USING (section_id)
 GROUP BY course_no),
avg_stud_enroll AS
(SELECT AVG(num_students) avg#_of_stud
  FROM num_enroll
 WHERE num_students <> (SELECT MAX(num_students)
                          FROM num_enroll))
SELECT course_no, num_students
  FROM num_enroll
```

```
WHERE num_students > (SELECT avg#_of_stud
                        FROM avg_stud_enroll)
  AND num_students < (SELECT MAX(num_students)
                        FROM num_enroll)
```

COURSE_NO	NUM_STUDENTS
20	9
100	13
120	23
122	24
124	8
125	8
130	8
140	15
230	14
240	13
350	9

11 rows selected.

ANSWER: The query returns courses and the respective enrollments above the average enrollment per course, excluding courses with the highest enrollment.

This query uses two inline queries, NUM_ENROLL and AVG_STUD_ENROLL. The first query,
NUM_ENROLL, computes the number of enrolled students per course. The second query,
AVG_STUD_ENROLL, uses the previous query to determine the average number of students
enrolled, excluding the course with the highest enrollment. The last query shows the COURSE_NO
column together with the number of enrolled students where the course has an enrollment that
is higher than the average enrollment. Remember that this average excludes the course with the
highest enrollment. The last condition specifically excludes the course with the highest enrollment in the result, as it would otherwise be included, because it obviously has a higher-than-
average enrollment.

As you have discovered, SQL allows you to express a query in many different ways to achieve the
same result. The differences often lie in the efficiency of the statement. The result you see can also
be obtained by using the following query; several joins are required with each execution of the
condition, thus requiring more resources and time than simply reusing the temporarily stored
query result. Furthermore, the WITH clause breaks down the problem into individual pieces, therefore simplifying the writing of complex queries.

```
SELECT course_no, COUNT(*) num_students
  FROM enrollment e JOIN section s
 USING (section_id)
 GROUP BY course_no
HAVING COUNT(*) > (SELECT AVG(COUNT(*))
                     FROM enrollment e JOIN section s
                    USING (section_id)
                    GROUP BY course_no
                   HAVING COUNT(*) <> (SELECT MAX(COUNT(*))
                    FROM enrollment e JOIN section s
                   USING (section_id)
                   GROUP BY course_no))
```

```
AND COUNT(*) <>(SELECT MAX(COUNT(*))
                   FROM enrollment e JOIN section s
                USING (section_id)
                GROUP BY course_no)
```

Lab 17.1 Quiz

In order to test your progress, you should be able to answer the following questions.

1) The difference between the RANK and DENSE_RANK functions is that DENSE_RANK leaves no gaps in ranking sequence when there are ties in the values.

   _____ a) True

   _____ b) False

2) If you use the RANK function without a partitioning clause, the ranking works over the entire result set.

   _____ a) True

   _____ b) False

3) The ROWS keyword in a windowing clause defines a logical window.

   _____ a) True

   _____ b) False

4) The LAG and LEAD functions can contain a windowing clause.

   _____ a) True

   _____ b) False

5) The FIRST_VALUE and LAST_VALUE functions work only with a windowing clause.

   _____ a) True

   _____ b) False

ANSWERS APPEAR IN APPENDIX A.

LAB 17.2
ROLLUP and CUBE Operators

LAB OBJECTIVES

After this lab, you will be able to:

▶ Use the ROLLUP and CUBE Operators
▶ Understand the GROUPING and GROUPING SETS Capabilities

Oracle includes many enhancements to the GROUP BY clause, which makes aggregating data from many different perspectives simpler and more efficient. These enhancements come in the form of the ROLLUP and CUBE operators, the GROUPING function, and GROUPING SETS capability. The ROLLUP and CUBE operators allow you to create subtotals and grand totals by simply eliminating the need to run multiple queries against the data.

You will see how useful these capabilities are for analyzing data and discovering relationships between data elements. This functionality is primarily used in data warehousing environments, with the goal of providing users with reporting and decision support functionality against summarized data.

End-user access is often accomplished with various querying tools that read this summarized data and allow users to "slice and dice" the information in any way they desire. As many companies are increasingly using their databases to gain a competitive market advantage and to better support their customers as well as reduce costs, this capability allows you to uncover much information about the data.

Many software vendors offer various types of tools that present the summarized data in an easily understandable format; Oracle also supplies its own version of an end-user decision support software tool, called Oracle BI Discoverer. While we will not discuss the capabilities and merits of such tools, we illustrate the summarization capabilities of Oracle to discover relationships and information about the data. You will see that this functionality is quite powerful and extremely valuable, yet very easy to use.

The ROLLUP Operator

The ROLLUP operator allows you to create subtotals and grand totals, also referred to as *super aggregate rows*, for various groupings and for all rows.

The table used for the exercises in this lab is called INSTRUCTOR_SUMMARY and is included in the supplemental tables you can download from the companion Web site, located at www.oraclesqlbyexample.com. It contains summary data generated from the various tables in the STUDENT schema.

The DESCRIBE command lists the following columns. The primary key of the table consists of the INSTRUCTOR_ID, SEMESTER_YEAR, and SEMESTER_MONTH columns.

```
SQL> DESCR instructor_summary
Name                        Null?      Type
------------------------    --------   ---------------
INSTRUCTOR_ID               NOT NULL   NUMBER(8)
GENDER                                 CHAR(1)
CAMPUS                                 VARCHAR2(11)
SEMESTER_YEAR               NOT NULL   VARCHAR2(4)
SEMESTER_MONTH              NOT NULL   VARCHAR2(2)
NUM_OF_CLASSES                         NUMBER
NUM_OF_STUDENTS                        NUMBER
REVENUE                                NUMBER
```

INSTRUCTOR_ID is identical to the familiar column in the INSTRUCTOR table. The GENDER column identifies the gender as male (M), female (F), or unknown (U) (if the title of an instructor is different than Mr., Mrs., or Ms.). The CAMPUS column indicates the name of the campus where the instructor's office is located. The SEMESTER_YEAR and SEMESTER_MONTH columns display the year and month the instructor worked. The column NUM_OF_CLASSES holds the number of sections the instructor taught, the NUM_OF_STUDENTS shows the column number of students for all the sections, and the REVENUE column contains the revenue generated by the individual instructor for these classes.

Using the familiar GROUP BY clause, the following query produces a list of instructors, grouped by the GENDER, SEMESTER_YEAR, and SEMESTER_MONTH columns, including the total number of students taught.

```
SELECT gender, semester_year AS year,
       semester_month AS month,
       SUM(num_of_students) AS total
  FROM instructor_summary
 GROUP BY gender, semester_year, semester_month
G YEAR MO       TOTAL
- ---- --  ----------
F 2007 05           0
F 2007 06          16
F 2008 07          37
M 2007 06          45
M 2007 07          79
U 2007 05           0
U 2007 07          49

7 rows selected.
```

All the distinct occurrences of these three columns are summarized.

Instead of using the GROUP BY clause, the next query uses the ROLLUP operator. With it, you discover the formation of subtotals for each of the groups. Your individual result does not display the shading shown here; it is used here to illustrate the location of the formed super aggregate rows.

```
SELECT gender, semester_year AS year,
       semester_month AS month,
       SUM(num_of_students) AS total
  FROM instructor_summary
 GROUP BY ROLLUP(gender, semester_year, semester_month)
 G YEAR MO      TOTAL
 - ---- -- ----------
 F 2007 05          0
 F 2007 06         16
 F 2007            16 Subtotal for female in year 2007
 F 2008 07         37
 F 2008            37 Subtotal for female in year 2008
 F                 53 Subtotal for entire female gender
 M 2007 06         45
 M 2007 07         79
 M 2007           124 Subtotal for male in year 2007
 M                124 Subtotal for entire male gender
 U 2007 05          0
 U 2007 07         49
 U 2007            49 Subtotal for unknown gender 2007
 U                 49 Subtotal for entire unknown gender
                  226 Grand Total
```

15 rows selected.

In this result, you notice some of the same rows as in the previous GROUP BY query. The difference is that here you see additional rows. These additional rows indicate subtotals for the GENDER and YEAR columns, a subtotal for each GENDER column only, and a grand total column. The subtotals are formed for each change in value.

The first shaded set of summary rows indicates 16 female students in 2007, 37 females in 2008, and 53 female students total.

You needed only one query to generate different groupings of data. The individual groupings are group 1: gender, year, and month; group 2: gender and year; group 3: gender; and group 4: grand total.

The number of columns or expressions appearing in the ROLLUP clause determines the number of groupings. The formula is $n + 1$, where n is the number of columns listed in the ROLLUP clause. Without the ROLLUP clause, you would need to write four individual queries.

The first query is already listed at the beginning of this lab, but it is repeated here, and also shown with partial output. This query represents the different individual rows grouped by the columns GENDER, SEMESTER_YEAR, and SEMESTER_MONTH.

```
SELECT gender, semester_year AS year,
       semester_month AS month,
       SUM(num_of_students) AS total
  FROM instructor_summary
 GROUP BY gender, semester_year, semester_month
G YEAR MO        TOTAL
- ---- -- ----------
F 2007 05            0
F 2007 06           16
...
U 2007 07           49

7 rows selected.
```

The second query lists the GENDER and SEMESTER_YEAR columns and computes the respective summary data.

```
SELECT gender, semester_year AS year,
       SUM(num_of_students) AS total
  FROM instructor_summary
 GROUP BY gender, semester_year
G YEAR       TOTAL
- ---- ----------
F 2007          16
F 2008          37
M 2007         124
U 2007          49

4 rows selected.
```

The third query is a listing grouped to give you a subtotal for the gender.

```
SELECT gender, SUM(num_of_students) AS total
  FROM instructor_summary
 GROUP BY gender
G       TOTAL
- ----------
F          53
M         124
U          49

3 rows selected.
```

The last query is the grand total for all the rows.

```
SELECT SUM(num_of_students) AS total
  FROM instructor_summary
    TOTAL
----------
      226
```

1 row selected.

The idea of the ROLLUP operator is that you don't need to write multiple queries, and Oracle doesn't need to process the table multiple times but rather does all the necessary work in one pass through the table. This is a very efficient and quick way to accomplish the desired result.

The CUBE Operator

The CUBE operator takes the formation of super aggregates another step further: It allows you to generate all the possible combinations of groups. If you have n columns or expressions in the GROUP BY clause, the CUBE operator generates 2^n groupings. The CUBE operator gets its name from the different combinations that can be achieved from an n-dimensional cube. The following example illustrates the combinations based on the previously used query. The CUBE operator is now substituted for the ROLLUP operator.

```
SELECT gender, semester_year AS year,
       semester_month AS month,
       SUM(num_of_students) AS total
  FROM instructor_summary
 GROUP BY CUBE(gender, semester_year, semester_month)
```

G	YEAR	MO	TOTAL
-	----	--	----------
F	2007	05	0
F	2007	06	16
F	2007		16
F	2008	07	37
F	2008		37
F		05	0
F		06	16
F		07	37
F			53
M	2007	06	45
M	2008	07	79
M	2007		124
M		06	45
M		07	79
M			124
U	2007	05	0
U	2007	07	49
U	2007		49
U		05	0

U	07	49
U		49
2007	05	0
2007	06	61
2007	07	128
2007		189
2008	07	37
2008		37
	05	0
	06	61
	07	165
		226

31 rows selected.

The shading around the rows indicates the new additionally formed subtotals. You see a subtotal for GENDER and SEMESTER_MONTH, another for SEMESTER_YEAR and SEMESTER_MONTH, and another for SEMESTER_YEAR only; you also see a total by SEMESTER_MONTH.

CUBE determines the 2^3 different combinations for the three columns, which results in a total of eight different subtotals. ROLLUP already determined four, and CUBE adds four more combinations.

Determining the ROLLUP and CUBE Combinations

Assume that you have three rollup groups in your GROUP BY ROLLUP clause, listed like the following hypothetical columns named YEAR, MONTH, and WEEK.

```
GROUP BY ROLLUP (year, month, week)
```

You get the following four rollup groups, according to the $n + 1$ formula: group 1 consists of year, month, and week; group 2 shows year and month; group 3 shows year; and group 4 shows the grand total. Hierarchies such as time periods or sales territories (for example, continent, country, state, county) lend themselves naturally to the ROLLUP operator, although you can obviously create your own or use your own combination of columns to roll up.

If you use the CUBE operator instead of ROLLUP, you generate eight different combinations, all of which are listed in Table 17.3. The empty set of parentheses, ( ), indicates the grand total.

TABLE 17.3   Grouping Combinations

OPERATOR	FORMULA GROUPING	COMBINATIONS
ROLLUP (year, month, week)	$n + 1$ $3 + 1 = 4$	(year, month, week), (year, month), (year), ( )
CUBE (year, month, week)	2^n $2^3 = 8$	(year, month, week), (year, month), (year), (month, week), (year, week), (week), (month), ( )

To exclude certain subtotals from the CUBE result or the ROLLUP result, you can selectively remove columns from the CUBE or ROLLUP clause and place them into the GROUP BY clause or generate summaries based on composite columns. Although it is useful to know about these options, you can simplify this with the GROUPING SETS clause, discussed shortly.

Table 17.4 lists the partial ROLLUP and CUBE results when a column moves into the GROUP BY clause. The example uses three columns called YEAR, MONTH, and WEEK. Most notably, the summary grand total is missing from all the partial rollups.

TABLE 17.4   Partial ROLLUP and CUBE Operations

GROUP BY CLAUSE	GROUPING COMBINATIONS
year, ROLLUP (month, week)	(year, month, week), (year, month), (year)
year, month ROLLUP (week)	(year, month, week), (year, month)
year, CUBE(month, week)	(year, month, week), (year, month), (year, week), (year)
year, month, CUBE (week)	(year, month, week), (year, month)

You can further group on composite columns. A composite column defined in this context is a collection of columns and is listed within a set of parentheses. As such, a composite column is treated as a single unit; this avoids any unnecessary aggregations for specific levels. Table 17.5 lists the results of operations on composite columns.

TABLE 17.5   Composite Column ROLLUP and CUBE Operations

COMPOSITE COLUMNS	GROUPING COMBINATIONS
ROLLUP ((year, month), week)	(year, month, week), (year, month), ( )
ROLLUP (year), (month, week)	(year, month, week), (month, week)
CUBE ((year, month), week)	(year, month, week), (year, month), (week), ( )
CUBE (year), (month, week)	(year, month, week), (month, week)

GROUPING SETS

Computing and displaying only selective results can actually be simplified with the GROUPING SETS extension of the GROUP BY clause. You explicitly state which summaries you want to generate. The following query applies the GROUPING SETS functionality to the query drawn on previously.

```
SELECT gender, semester_year AS YEAR,
       semester_month AS month,
       SUM(num_of_students) AS total
  FROM instructor_summary
 GROUP BY GROUPING SETS
       ((gender, semester_year),   -- 1st Group
```

```
           (semester_month),      -- 2nd Group
           ()                      -- 3rd Group
```

G	YEAR	MO	TOTAL
F	2007		16
F	2008		37
M	2007		124
U	2007		49
		05	0
		06	61
		07	165
			226

8 rows selected.

The query produces three sets: one for the GENDER and SEMESTER_YEAR columns, a second for SEMESTER_MONTH, and the last one for the grand total. Each individual set must be enclosed in parentheses; the empty set of parentheses indicates the grand total. The GROUPING SETS clause provides the advantage of reading the table once and generating the results immediately and only for those summaries in which you are interested. GROUPING SETS functionality is very efficient and yet selective about the results you choose to report.

If you have many hierarchy groupings, you may not want to specify all the different groupings individually. You can combine multiple GROUPING SETS clauses to generate yet more combinations.

The following example lists two GROUPING SETS clauses in the GROUP BY clause.

```
GROUP BY GROUPING SETS (year, month),
         GROUPING SETS (week, day)
```

The cross-product results in the following equivalent groupings.

```
GROUP BY GROUPING SETS (
         (year, week),
         (year, day),
         (month, week),
         (month, day))
```

The GROUPING Function

One of the purposes of the GROUPING function is that it helps you distinguish summary rows from any rows that are a result of null values. The following query shows a CUBE operation on the columns SEMESTER_YEAR and CAMPUS. As it turns out, the CAMPUS column contains null values, and it is difficult to distinguish between the summary row and an individual row holding a null value.

```
SELECT semester_year AS year, campus,
       SUM(num_of_classes) AS num_of_classes
```

```
   FROM instructor_summary
  GROUP BY CUBE (semester_year, campus)
  ORDER BY 1
  YEAR CAMPUS        NUM_OF_CLASSES
  ---- ----------- --------------
  2007 DOWNTOWN              10
  2007 LIBERTY               19
  2007 MORNINGSIDE           29
  2007                       10 Summary row or null?
  2007                       68
  2008 MORNINGSIDE           10
  2008                       10
       DOWNTOWN              10
       LIBERTY               19
       MORNINGSIDE           39
                             10 Summary row or null?
                             78

12 rows selected.
```

The GROUPING function eliminates any ambiguities. Whenever you see a value of 1 in a column where the GROUPING function is applied, it indicates a super aggregate row, such as a subtotal or grand total row created by the ROLLUP or CUBE operator.

```
  SELECT semester_year AS year, campus,
         SUM(num_of_classes) AS num_of_classes,
         GROUPING (semester_year) GP_YEAR,
         GROUPING (campus) GP_CAMPUS
    from instructor_summary
   group by CUBE (semester_year, campus)
   ORDER BY 1
```

YEAR	CAMPUS	NUM_OF_CLA	GP_YEAR	GP_CAMPUS	
2007	DOWNTOWN	10	0	0	
2007	LIBERTY	19	0	0	
2007	MORNINGSIDE	29	0	0	
2007		10	0	0	NULL value GP_CAMPUS
2007		68	0	1	
2008	MORNINGSIDE	10	0	0	
2008		10	0	1	
	DOWNTOWN	10	1	0	
	LIBERTY	19	1	0	
	MORNINGSIDE	39	1	0	
		10	1	0	NULL value GP_CAMPUS
		78	1	1	

```
12 rows selected.
```

When examining the result, you observe the columns where the GROUPING function is applied and has a value of 0 or 1. The number 1 indicates that this column is a super aggregate row.

The first shaded area on the resulting output shows a 0 in the GP_CAMPUS column; this indicates that the NULL value in the CAMPUS column is indeed a NULL. The next row lists the number 1 in the GP_CAMPUS column; this designates the row as a summary row. It lists 68 classes for all campus locations in 2007.

The second shaded row shows the number 1 in the GP_YEAR column. This indicates that the SEMESTER_YEAR column is an aggregate, just like the previous three rows. That means the rows display the aggregate values for each individual campus for all years.

The last row contains the number 1 for both the GP_YEAR and the GP_CAMPUS columns. This indicates the grand total.

You can use the GROUPING function not only to determine whether it's a generated row or NULL value but to return certain rows from the result set with the HAVING clause. This is yet another way to selectively choose certain summary rows only.

```
HAVING GROUPING(campus) = 1
```

You can use the GROUPING function to add labels to the super aggregate rows. Instead of a blank column, you can display a label such as GRAND TOTAL:.

```
SELECT CASE WHEN GROUPING(semester_year) = 1
                AND GROUPING(campus) = 1 THEN 'GRAND TOTAL:'
            ELSE semester_year
        END AS year,
        CASE WHEN GROUPING(semester_year) = 1
                AND GROUPING(campus) = 1 THEN NULL
            ELSE campus
        END AS campus,
        SUM(num_of_classes) AS num_of_classes,
        GROUPING (semester_year) GP_YEAR,
        GROUPING (campus) GP_CAMPUS
    FROM instructor_summary
  GROUP BY CUBE (semester_year, campus)
  ORDER BY 4, 2, 5
```

YEAR	CAMPUS	NUM_OF_CLAS	GP_YEAR	GP_CAMPUS
2007	DOWNTOWN	10	0	0
2007	LIBERTY	19	0	0
2007	MORNINGSIDE	29	0	0
2007		10	0	0
2007		68	0	1
2008	MORNINGSIDE	10	0	0
2008		10	0	1
	DOWNTOWN	10	1	0
	LIBERTY	19	1	0
	MORNINGSIDE	39	1	0

```
                                        10      1        0
        GRAND TOTAL:                    78      1        1


    12 rows selected.
```

 Remember that you can also use the NVL or COALESCE function to test for null values and return a substitute value.

The GROUPING_ID Function

If a query includes many GROUPING functions, you might want to consider consolidating the columns with the GROUPING_ID function. This function is not only similar in name and functionality to GROUPING, it also allows multiple columns as a parameter; it returns a number indicating the level of aggregation in the rollup or cube.

The GROUPING_ID function returns a single number that identifies the exact aggregation level of every row.

```
    SELECT semester_year AS year,
           campus,
           SUM(num_of_classes) AS num_of_classes,
           GROUPING (semester_year) GP_YEAR,
           GROUPING (campus) GP_CAMPUS,
           GROUPING_ID(semester_year, campus)
           AS GROUPING_ID
      FROM instructor_summary
     GROUP BY CUBE (semester_year, campus)
```

YEAR	CAMPUS	NUM_OF_C	GP_YEAR	GP_CAMPUS	GROUPING_ID
2007	DOWNTOWN	10	0	0	0
2007	LIBERTY	19	0	0	0
2007	MORNINGSIDE	29	0	0	0
2007		10	0	0	0
2007		68	0	1	1
2008	MORNINGSIDE	10	0	0	0
2008		10	0	1	1
	DOWNTOWN	10	1	0	2
	LIBERTY	19	1	0	2
	MORNINGSIDE	39	1	0	2
		10	1	0	2
		78	1	1	3

```
    12 rows selected.
```

The GROUPING_ID function works just like the GROUPING function that generates zeros and ones. However, the GROUPING_ID function concatenates the zeros and ones and forms a bit vector, which is treated as a binary number. The GROUPING_ID function returns the binary number's base-10 value. A value of 1 for each GROUPING column indicates that this is the grand total. The binary number 11 for the two-level column aggregation represents the number 3, which is returned by the GROUPING_ID function. Zeros in all the columns of the GROUP-ING functions indicate that this is the lowest aggregation level.

Table 17.6 lists binary numbers and their numeric equivalents on the example of a four-column CUBE, representative of a GROUP BY clause such as CUBE(year, month, week, day). The column labeled GROUPING_ID displays the result of the GROUPING_ID function for each individual column; the Bit-Vector column indicates which bits are turned on and off. The BIN_TO_NUM function allows you to convert a binary value to a number. Every argument represents a bit in the bit vector.

```
SELECT BIN_TO_NUM(1,1)
  FROM dual
BIN_TO_NUM(1,1)
---------------
              3

1 row selected.
```

TABLE 17.6   Bit to Numeric Representation on the Example of a Four-Column Cube

GROUPING_ID	NUMERIC EQUIVALENT BIT-VECTOR	AGGREGATION LEVEL
0	0 0 0 0	(year, month, week, day)
1	0 0 0 1	(year, month, week)
2	0 0 1 0	(year, month, day)
3	0 0 1 1	(year, month)
4	0 1 0 0	(year, week, day)
5	0 1 0 1	(year, week)
6	0 1 1 0	(year, day)
7	0 1 1 1	(year)
8	1 0 0 0	(month, week, day)
9	1 0 0 1	(month, week)
10	1 0 1 0	(month, day)
11	1 0 1 1	(month)
12	1 1 0 0	(week, day)
13	1 1 0 1	(week)
14	1 1 1 0	(day)
15	1 1 1 1	( )

You can use the GROUPING_ID function for labeling columns, as discussed previously. However, its primary use is in *materialized views*, which are Oracle objects that allow you to create and maintain aggregate summary tables. Storing pre-aggregate summary information is an important technique for maximizing query performance in large decision support applications. The effect of the creation of this materialized view is that data is physically stored in a table. Any changes to the underlying tables are reflected in the materialized view through various refresh methods. (Unlike views, discussed in Chapter 13, "Indexes, Sequences, and Views," materialized views require physical storage.)

```
CREATE MATERIALIZED VIEW instructor_sum_mv
STORAGE(INITIAL 5 M PCTINCREASE 0)
AS
SELECT semester_year AS year,
       campus,
       SUM(num_of_classes) AS num_of_classes,
       GROUPING_ID(semester_year, campus)
       AS GROUPING_ID
  FROM instructor_summary
 GROUP BY CUBE (semester_year, campus)
Materialized view created.
```

To perform this operation, you must have the CREATE MATERIALIZED VIEW privilege.

THE GROUP_ID FUNCTION

The GROUP_ID function lets you distinguish among duplicate groupings; they may be generated as a result of combinations of columns listed in the GROUP BY clause. GROUP_ID returns the number 0 to the first row in the set that is not yet duplicated; any subsequent duplicate grouping row receives a higher number, starting with the number 1.

```
SELECT semester_year AS year, campus,
       SUM(num_of_classes) AS num_of_classes,
       GROUPING_ID(semester_year, campus) GROUPING_ID,
       GROUP_ID()
  from instructor_summary
 group by GROUPING SETS
       (semester_year, ROLLUP(semester_year, campus))
```

YEAR	CAMPUS	NUM_OF_CLASSES	GROUPING_ID	GROUP_ID()
2007	DOWNTOWN	10	0	0
2007	LIBERTY	19	0	0
2007	MORNINGSIDE	29	0	0
2007		10	0	0
2008	MORNINGSIDE	10	0	0
		78	3	0
2007		68	1	0
2008		10	1	0
2007		68	1	1
2008		10	1	1

```
10 rows selected.
```

This query illustrates the result of the GROUP_ID function, which returns a 0 for the first row; the subsequent identical group returns the number 1 in the GROUP_ID() column. You can see this in the last two rows of the result.

If you have complicated queries that may generate duplicate values, you can eliminate those rows by including the condition HAVING GROUP_ID( ) = 0.

▼ LAB 17.2 EXERCISES

a) Describe the effect of the following SQL statement and its resulting output.

```
SELECT salutation AS SALUTATION, SUBSTR(phone, 1,3)
       AS "Area Code",
       TO_CHAR(registration_date, 'MON') AS "Reg.Month",
       COUNT(*)
  FROM student
 WHERE SUBSTR(phone, 1,3) IN ('201','212','718')
   AND salutation IN ('Mr.', 'Ms.')
 GROUP BY ROLLUP (salutation, SUBSTR(phone, 1,3),
       TO_CHAR(registration_date, 'MON'))
```

SALUT	Area Code	Reg.Month	COUNT(*)
Mr.	201	FEB	34
Mr.	201	JAN	9
Mr.	201		43
Mr.	212	FEB	1
Mr.	212	JAN	1
Mr.	212		2
Mr.	718	FEB	72
Mr.	718	JAN	17
Mr.	718		89
Mr.			134
Ms.	201	FEB	27
Ms.	201	JAN	5
Ms.	201		32
Ms.	212	FEB	2
Ms.	212	JAN	1
Ms.	212		3
Ms.	718	FEB	52
Ms.	718	JAN	13
Ms.	718		65
Ms.			100
			234

21 rows selected.

b) Answer the following questions about the result set.

How many female students are there in total?

How many male students live in area code 212?

What is the total number of students?

How many female students live in the area code 718 and registered in January?

c) If the CUBE operator is used on the query in exercise a instead of ROLLUP, how many different combinations of groups do you get? List the groups.

d) Describe the result of the following query, which uses the GROUPING SET extension to the GROUP BY clause.

```
SELECT SALUTATION, SUBSTR(phone, 1,3) "Area Code",
       TO_CHAR(registration_date, 'MON') "Reg.Month",
       COUNT(*)
  FROM student
 WHERE SUBSTR(phone, 1,3) IN ('201','212','718')
   AND salutation IN ('Mr.', 'Ms.')
 GROUP BY
       GROUPING SETS
       ((SALUTATION, SUBSTR(phone, 1,3)),
        (SALUTATION, TO_CHAR(registration_date, 'MON')),
        ()
       )
```

SALUT	Are	Reg	COUNT(*)
Mr.	201		43
Mr.	212		2
Mr.	718		89
Ms.	201		32
Ms.	212		3
Ms.	718		65
Mr.		FEB	107
Mr.		JAN	27
Ms.		FEB	81
Ms.		JAN	19
			234

11 rows selected.

e) Write the individual queries to proof the numbers found in exercise d.

▼ LAB 17.2 EXERCISE ANSWERS

a) Describe the effect of the following SQL statement and its resulting output. (For space reasons, the code is not repeated here.)

ANSWER: The query generates summary totals by using the ROLLUP operator. This effectively creates groupings, which are counting rows in the STUDENT table. Four rollup groups are generated based on the columns: salutation, area code, and registration month (labeled "Reg.Month").

The first ROLLUP group is salutation, area code, and registration date; the second group is saluta-tion and area code; the third is salutation; and the last is a grand total of all the rows. Each shaded row in the following output indicates the first occurrence of a group.

SALUT	Area Code	Reg.Month	COUNT(*)	
Mr.	201	FEB	34	Group #1
Mr.	201	JAN	9	
Mr.	201		43	Group #2
Mr.	212	FEB	1	
Mr.	212	JAN	1	
Mr.	212		2	
Mr.	718	FEB	72	
Mr.	718	JAN	17	
Mr.	718		89	
Mr.			134	Group #3
Ms.	201	FEB	27	
Ms.	201	JAN	5	
Ms.	201		32	
Ms.	212	FEB	2	
Ms.	212	JAN	1	
Ms.	212		3	
Ms.	718	FEB	52	
Ms.	718	JAN	13	
Ms.	718		65	
Ms.			100	
			234	Group #4

21 rows selected.

b) Answer the following questions about the result set.

How many female students are there in total?

How many male students live in area code 212?

What is the total number of students?

How many female students live in the area code 718 and registered in January?

ANSWER: You can obtain all these answers by examining the result set.

You can easily answer the first question (How many female students are part of the result set?) by looking at the result set. The correct answer is that there are 100 female students. Following is an excerpt of the output.

SALUT	Area Code	Reg.Month	COUNT(*)
...			
Ms.			100

You can obtain the answer to the next question, about the male students living in area code 212, from the following row. As you can see, the number of students is 2.

```
SALUT Area Code Reg.Month    COUNT(*)
----- --------- ---------- ---------
...
Mr.   212                          2
```

You can obtain the total number of students satisfying the WHERE clause of the query with the last row, the grand total row. There are 234 in total.

```
SALUT Area Code Reg.Month    COUNT(*)
----- --------- ---------- ---------
...
                                 234
```

Finally, there are 13 female students who live in area code 718 and registered in January.

```
SALUT Area Code Reg.Month    COUNT(*)
----- --------- ---------- ---------
...
Ms.   718       JAN               13
```

c) If the CUBE operator is used on the query in exercise a instead of ROLLUP, how many different combinations of groups do you get? List the groups.

ANSWER: There are three columns involved; therefore, there are 2^3 possible combinations, which translates to eight different groupings.

Group 1: Salutation, area code, and registration date

Group 2: Salutation and area code

Group 3: Salutation

Group 4: Area code and registration date

Group 5: Registration date

Group 6: Salutation and registration date

Group 7: Area code

Group 8: Grand total

d) Describe the result of the following query, which uses the GROUPING SET extension to the GROUP BY clause.

```
SELECT SALUTATION, SUBSTR(phone, 1,3) "Area Code",
       TO_CHAR(registration_date, 'MON') "Reg.Month",
       COUNT(*)
  FROM student
 WHERE SUBSTR(phone, 1,3) IN ('201','212','718')
   AND salutation IN ('Mr.', 'Ms.')
 GROUP BY
       GROUPING SETS
       ((SALUTATION, SUBSTR(phone, 1,3)),
        (SALUTATION, TO_CHAR(registration_date, 'MON')),
        ()
       )
```

```
SALUT Are Reg  COUNT(*)
----- --- --- ---------
Mr.   201          43
Mr.   212           2
Mr.   718          89
Ms.   201          32
Ms.   212           3
Ms.   718          65
Mr.       FEB     107
Mr.       JAN      27
Ms.       FEB      81
Ms.       JAN      19
                  234
```

11 rows selected.

ANSWER: The query result shows students with the salutations Mr. and Ms. who live in area codes 201, 212, and 718. The GROUPING SETS extension to the GROUP BY clause allows you to selectively group specific information. There are three individual groups. The first set is salutation and area code and is indicated as a set with the enclosed parentheses. The next set is the registration month, and the salutation is again enclosed in parentheses. The final set is an empty set of parentheses, indicating the grand total. The GROUPING SETS clause is very efficient as it queries the table once to generate the result.

e) Write the individual queries to proof the numbers found in exercise d.

ANSWER: In exercise d, you already identified the three groupings, which then translate into three individual queries.

The following is query 1.

```
SELECT salutation, SUBSTR(phone, 1, 3), COUNT(*)
  FROM student
 WHERE SUBSTR(phone, 1,3) IN ('201','212','718')
   AND salutation IN ('Mr.', 'Ms.')
 GROUP BY salutation, SUBSTR(phone, 1, 3)
SALUT SUB  COUNT(*)
----- --- ---------
Mr.   201       43
Mr.   212        2
Mr.   718       89
Ms.   201       32
Ms.   212        3
Ms.   718       65
```

6 rows selected.

The following is query #2.

```
SELECT salutation, TO_CHAR(registration_date, 'MON'),
       COUNT(*)
  FROM student
 WHERE SUBSTR(phone, 1,3) IN ('201','212','718')
   AND salutation IN ('Mr.', 'Ms.')
 GROUP BY salutation, TO_CHAR(registration_date, 'MON')
SALUT TO_  COUNT(*)
----- ---  ---------
Mr.   FEB       107
Mr.   JAN        27
Ms.   FEB        81
Ms.   JAN        19

4 rows selected.
```

The following is query #3.

```
SELECT COUNT(*)
  FROM student
 WHERE SUBSTR(phone, 1,3) IN ('201','212','718')
   AND salutation IN ('Mr.', 'Ms.')
 COUNT(*)
---------
      234

1 row selected.
```

Lab 17.2 Quiz

In order to test your progress, you should be able to answer the following questions.

1) A query has the following GROUP BY clause. How many different groupings are visible in the result?

    ```
    GROUP BY CUBE (color, price, material, store_location)
    ```

    _____ a) 4

    _____ b) 5

    _____ c) 16

    _____ d) 24

    _____ e) Unknown

2) A query has the following GROUP BY clause. How many different groupings are visible in the result?

    ```
    GROUP BY ROLLUP (color, price, material, store_location)
    ```

    _____ a) 4

    _____ b) 5

    _____ c) 16

    _____ d) 24

    _____ e) Unknown

3) A return value of 1 from the GROUPING function indicates an aggregate row.

    _____ a) True

    _____ b) False

4) How many groups are generated by the following query?

    ```
    GROUP BY GROUPING SETS((color, price), material, store location)
    ```

    _____ a) 3

    _____ b) 4

    _____ c) 5

    _____ d) 16

    _____ e) Unknown

ANSWERS APPEAR IN APPENDIX A.

▼ WORKSHOP

The projects in this section are meant to prompt you to utilize all the skills you have acquired through-out this chapter. The answers to these projects can be found at the companion Web site to this book, located at www.oraclesqlbyexample.com.

1) Write the question for the following query and answer.

```
SELECT COUNT(DECODE(SIGN(total_capacity-20),
            -1, 1, 0, 1)) "<=20",
       COUNT(DECODE(SIGN(total_capacity-21),
             0, 1, -1, NULL,
             DECODE(SIGN(total_capacity-30), -1, 1)))
             "21-30",
       COUNT(DECODE(SIGN(total_capacity-30), 1, 1)) "31+"
  FROM (SELECT SUM(capacity) total_capacity, course_no
          FROM SECTION
         GROUP BY COURSE_NO)

    <=20       21-30        31+
--------- --------- ---------
      2         10          16
```

1 row selected.

2) Using an analytical function, determine the top three zip codes where most of the students live.

3) Explain the result of the following query.

```
SELECT 'Q'||TO_CHAR(start_date_time, 'Q') qtr,
       TO_CHAR(start_date_time, 'DY') day, count(*),
       DENSE_RANK() OVER (
           PARTITION BY 'Q'||TO_CHAR(start_date_time, 'Q')
           ORDER BY COUNT(*) DESC) rank_qtr,
       DENSE_RANK() OVER (ORDER BY COUNT(*) DESC) rank_all
  FROM enrollment e, section s
 WHERE s.section_id = e.section_id
 GROUP BY 'Q'||TO_CHAR(start_date_time, 'Q'),
       TO_CHAR(start_date_time, 'DY')
 ORDER BY 1, 4
```

QT	DAY	COUNT(*)	RANK_QTR	RANK_ALL
Q2	MON	42	1	1
Q2	TUE	35	2	2
Q2	SAT	30	3	3
Q2	SUN	29	4	4
Q2	WED	15	5	6
Q2	FRI	13	6	7
Q2	THU	13	6	7
Q3	SAT	29	1	4
Q3	TUE	20	2	5

9 rows selected

CHAPTER 18

SQL Optimization

CHAPTER OBJECTIVES

In this chapter, you will learn about:

▶ The Oracle Optimizerf

▶ Writing Effective SQL Statements

Throughout this book, you have seen alternate SQL statements for many solutions. This chapter focuses on helping you determine which SQL statement will most efficiently and quickly return results. It provides an overview of the workings of the Oracle optimizer and describes SQL performance tuning techniques. The list of tuning suggestions in this chapter is by no means comprehensive but merely a starting point. When you understand how to read the execution steps of SQL statements, you will have gained a better understanding of Oracle's optimization strategies and will be able to focus on tuning problem areas with alternate SQL statements and techniques.

LAB 18.1
The Oracle Optimizer and Writing Effective SQL Statements

LAB OBJECTIVES

After this lab, you will be able to:

▶ Read an Execution Plan
▶ Understand Join Operations
▶ Use Alternate SQL Statements

Poor system performance is often caused by one or a combination of problems: poor database design, improper tuning of the Oracle server, and poorly written SQL statements. A well-thought-out database design has the greatest positive impact on database performance, followed by effectively written SQL statements, and then tuning the Oracle server itself. This chapter focuses on writing effective SQL statements.

The Oracle database server provides a number of tools that help you improve the efficiency of SQL statements. This chapter shows you how to obtain an *execution plan,* which is a sequence of the steps that Oracle carries out to perform a specific SQL command. You can change the execution plan by choosing an alternate SQL statement or by adding a *hint,* which is a directive to execute the statement differently.

Using hints, you can force the use of a specific index, change the join order, or change join method. Before you learn more about the execution plan and the query tuning tools, you must understand the basics of how the Oracle database server evaluates a SQL statement.

SQL Statement Processing

Before a SQL statement returns a result set, the server performs a number of operations that are completely transparent to the user. First, Oracle creates a cursor, an area in memory where Oracle stores the SQL statement and all associated information.

Next, Oracle parses the SQL statement. This entails checking the syntax for validity, checking whether all the column and table names exist, and determining whether the user has permission to access these tables and columns. Part of the parsing operation is also the determination of the execution plan.

Because parsing requires time and resources, there are ways to eliminate parsing when repeatedly executing similar statements. Under these circumstances, the use of bind variables may be helpful. Bind variables are placeholders for values, which get substituted with different values. Oracle maintains a cache of recently executed SQL statements and their respective execution plan, so if an identical statement has been used previously, it does not need to be reparsed.

If bind variables are being used, they are associated with the appropriate values. Next, the SQL statement is executed. If the SQL statement is a query, the result needs to be fetched. Once all the rows are fetched, the cursor is closed. Figure 18.1 shows an overview of these steps.

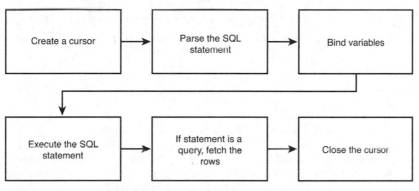

FIGURE 18.1
Overview of SQL statement processing steps

The Oracle Optimizer

The Oracle optimizer, which is part of the Oracle software, examines each SQL statement and chooses the best execution plan for it. An execution plan consists of a sequence of steps that are necessary to execute the SQL statement.

The rule-based optimizer (RBO) was Oracle's first optimizer, employed by Oracle since its beginnings. The RBO determined the execution plan through a number of rigid rules. This optimizer is no longer supported by Oracle, however, and it has been replaced by the cost-based optimizer (CBO).

The CBO considers statistics when determining the best plan, and these statistics are stored in the data dictionary. Statistics include values such as the number of rows in the table and the selectivity of columns, among many other factors.

Statistics are gathered automatically in Oracle if they become stale. In versions prior to Oracle 10g, you had to perform this step manually by using the DBMS_STATS package or the ANALYZE command. The statistics help Oracle by calculating the estimated cost of the various execution options to help determine the best and lowest-cost plan.

Choosing the Optimizer Mode

The CBO has a number of optimizer modes. You can decide whether you want to optimize for best overall throughput (ALL_ROWS) or best response (FIRST_ROWS_n). The ALL_ROWS mode is most useful for reporting and batch processing, whereas FIRST_ROWS_n is best for interactive applications, to quickly retrieve the first n rows. Based on the chosen optimizer mode, the gathered statistics, and certain database initialization parameters, the Oracle optimizer chooses the best execution plan. Table 18.1 lists the optimizer modes.

You modify the optimizer mode on the database instance level in the database initialization file with the OPTIMIZER_MODE parameter. Or, for an entire session, you use the ALTER SESSION SET OPTIMIZER_MODE command. For an individual SQL statement, you can override it with a hint.

TABLE 18.1   Optimizer Mode

OPTIMIZER MODE	EXPLANATION
FIRST_ROWS_n	This mode has the goal of retrieving the specified first n row(s). This mode is best for interactive programs that need to display n initial rows of data on a screen. (This setting differs from the FIRST_ROWS mode in that you list the number of rows. The FIRST_ROWS optimizer goal, without the specified number of rows, is supported for backward compatibility.)
ALL_ROWS	The goal of this mode is to retrieve all the rows and achieve the best performance with minimal resources. This is typically the default setting.

Keeping Statistics Up-to-Date in Oracle

Accurate statistics about the distribution of data are essential for good performance. Oracle automatically gathers statistics for objects that have stale or missing statistics and periodically updates these statistics. The statistics are stored in the data dictionary. Gathering of statistics is accomplished through a job called BSLN_MAINTAIN_STATS_JOB, which is created automatically when the database is initially created. Oracle's internal job scheduler periodically runs this job to check for stale or missing statistics. If you have access to the DBA_ dictionary views, you can check whether the job is running by executing the following statement.

```
SELECT job_name, enabled, last_start_date
  FROM dba_scheduler_jobs
 WHERE job_name = 'BSLN_MAINTAIN_STATS_JOB'
```

```
JOB_NAME                    ENABL LAST_START_DATE
--------------------------- ----- -----------------------------------
BSLN_MAINTAIN_STATS_JOB TRUE   31-JAN-09 10.00.02.109124 PM -05:00

1 row selected.
```

If you create a new index on a table or rebuild an existing one, Oracle automatically collects the statistics. However, the statistics may be stale when 10 percent or more of the rows change due to INSERT, UPDATE, or DELETE operations. Oracle keeps track of the modifications in the USER_TAB_MODIFICATIONS data dictionary.

The USER_TAB_MODIFICATIONS data dictionary view shows the tables owned by the current user that are being monitored. Furthermore, it shows the volume of data modified since the last gathering of statistics. The number found in the INSERTS, UPDATES, and DELETES columns of the view is approximate; these columns may not be populated for a few hours after the completion of the *Data Manipulation Language* (DML) operation.

```
SELECT table_name, inserts, updates, deletes,
       timestamp
  FROM user_tab_modifications
TABLE_NAME       INSERTS UPDATES DELETES TIMESTAMP
---------------- ------- ------- ------- ---------
COURSE                 1       0       0 30-JAN-09

1 row selected.
```

Gathering Statistics Manually

In case you want to manually gather statistics (which may be useful after a large data load or mass update), the following paragraphs explain some of the involved procedures you will need to execute. You can check for the presence of statistics by querying the data dictionary views ALL_TABLES and ALL_INDEXES. After statistics about a table or an index are gathered, a number of columns in these data dictionary views contain values. For example, in the USER_TABLES view, the NUM_ROWS column contains the number of rows in the table, the average row length, and the date and time the statistics were last gathered

```
SELECT table_name, num_rows, avg_row_len,
       TO_CHAR(last_analyzed, 'MM/DD/YYYY')
       AS last_analyzed
  FROM user_tables
TABLE_NAME           NUM_ROWS AVG_ROW_LEN LAST_ANALY
-------------------- -------- ----------- ----------
INSTRUCTOR                 10          85 01/23/2009
GRADE                    2004          49 01/23/2009
...
ZIPCODE                   227          53 01/23/2009

10 rows selected.
```

For indexes, you can review the number of rows, the number of distinct keys, and the date and time the statistics were last updated. Other related data dictionary views contain additional information, but querying USER_TABLES and USER_INDEXES provides you with some of the most essential information.

```
SELECT index_name, num_rows, distinct_keys,
       TO_CHAR(last_analyzed, 'MM/DD/YYYY')
       AS last_analyzed
  FROM user_indexes
INDEX_NAME         NUM_ROWS DISTINCT_KEYS LAST_ANALY
---------------- -------- ------------- ----------
INST_ZIP_FK_I            9             4 01/23/200
GR_GRTW_FK_I         2004           252 011/23/2009
...
CRSE_PK               30            30 011/23/2009

20 rows selected.
```

THE DBMS_STATS PACKAGE

The DBMS_STATS package is an Oracle-supplied PL/SQL package that generates and manages statistics for use by the CBO. Table 18.2 lists a few of the many procedures in the package for gathering statistics.

TABLE 18.2   DBMS_STATS Procedures That Gather Statistics

PROCEDURE	PURPOSE
GATHER_TABLE_STATS	Gathers table, column, and index statistics.
GATHER_INDEX_STATS	Gathers index statistics.
GATHER_SCHEMA_STATS	Gathers statistics for all objects in a schema.
GATHER_DATABASE_STATS	Gathers statistics for all objects in a database instance.
GATHER_SYSTEM_STATS	Gathers system statistics about the CPU and I/O.

Following are some examples of how to execute the procedures to collect statistics. The following statement gathers exact statistics for the COURSE table, located in the STUDENT schema. You can execute the PL/SQL procedure in SQL*Plus or SQL Developer via the Run Script icon.

```
EXEC DBMS_STATS.GATHER_TABLE_STATS(
     ownname=>'STUDENT', tabname=>'COURSE');
PL/SQL procedure successfully completed.
```

The two parameters OWNNAME for the schema name and TABNAME for the table name are required. The example uses the named notation syntax (ownname=>) to identify each parameter with the appropriate value. You do not need to list the parameter names OWNNAME and TABLENAME if you supply the parameter values in the order in which they are defined in the package.

```
EXEC DBMS_STATS.GATHER_TABLE_STATS('STUDENT', 'COURSE');
```

The procedure has additional parameters (for example, ESTIMATE_PERCENT) that let you specify the sample percentage. If you don't specify the additional parameters, default values are assigned. In the previous examples, ESTIMATE_PERCENT is not specified, so the default is to compute the exact statistics.

If the different parameters do not fit on one line or if you want to separate the parameters, write the procedure call as follows:

```
BEGIN
   DBMS_STATS.GATHER_TABLE_STATS(
      ownname=>'STUDENT',
      tabname=>'COURSE',
      cascade=>TRUE);
END;
/
```

The procedure adds a third parameter, the CASCADE parameter, and sets it to TRUE. This instructs the procedure to collect both table and index statistics simultaneously. To find out the different parameter names of a procedure, you issue the SQL*Plus DESCRIBE command in SQL*Plus. It lists all the individual procedures available and their respective parameters. The In/Out column indicates whether the procedure requires an input parameter or returns an output value. You can find out more information about each parameter and the respective default values in the *Oracle 11g PL/SQL Packages and Types References* manual.

```
SQL> DESCRIBE DBMS_STATS
...
PROCEDURE GATHER_TABLE_STATS
Argument Name           Type          In/Out  Default?
----------------------  ------------  ------  --------
   OWNNAME              VARCHAR2      IN
   TABNAME              VARCHAR2      IN
   PARTNAME             VARCHAR2      IN      DEFAULT
   ESTIMATE_PERCENT     NUMBER        IN      DEFAULT
   BLOCK_SAMPLE         BOOLEAN       IN      DEFAULT
   METHOD_OPT           VARCHAR2      IN      DEFAULT
   DEGREE               NUMBER        IN      DEFAULT
   GRANULARITY          VARCHAR2      IN      DEFAULT
   CASCADE              BOOLEAN       IN      DEFAULT
...
```

EXACT STATISTICS OR SAMPLE SIZE

As mentioned earlier, statistics can be either computed exactly or estimated. Because calculating exact statistics may take a long time on very large tables, it is sometimes more practical to estimate sufficiently accurate statistics. For large tables, a sampling percentage size of 10 to 25 percent is often sufficient, or you can let Oracle determine the size of the sample.

USING SQL DEVELOPER TO GATHER STATISTICS

The SQL Developer menu options make it easy to gather statistics (see Figure 18.2).By right-clicking on a table's node, you will be able to choose Statistics menu. From there, you can choose Gather Statistics option, which evokes the menu in Figure 18.2 where you choose the sample size and shows in the SQL tab the corresponding DBMS_STATS.GATHER_TABLE_STATS procedure to be executed. If you click a connection name instead, you can also gather statistics for the schema.

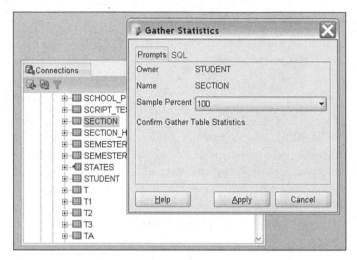

FIGURE 18.2
Gathering statistics in SQL Developer

Managing Statistics

Besides gathering statistics, the DBMS_STATS package includes procedures to modify, view, export, import, delete, lock, and restore statistics. For example, you can save the current statistics before gathering new statistics so you can restore them if the performance of the system is adversely affected. You can also copy the statistics from one database instance to another. This is useful if you want to test how your SQL statements behave in a different environment (for example, test vs. production). You can also lock the statistics so they remain unchanged. Table 18.3 shows a few of the DBMS_STATS procedures that manage statistics for an individual table.

TABLE 18.3   DBMS_STATS Procedures

PROCEDURE	PURPOSE
DELETE_TABLE_STATS	Deletes statistics for an individual table.
CREATE_STAT_TABLE	Creates a table to hold statistics for import/export.
LOCK_TABLE_STATS	Freezes the current statistics, including indexes for an individual table.

TABLE 18.3 Continued

PROCEDURE	PURPOSE
UNLOCK_TABLE_STATS	Unlocks the table and index statistics.
RESTORE_SCHEMA_STATS	Restores all the statistics for a specified schema for a particular timestamp. This is useful if performance degrades and you want to restore the previous set of statistics.
EXPORT_TABLE_STATS	Exports statistics about an individual table so it can be used for a later import.
IMPORT_TABLE_STATS	Imports table statistics into the data dictionary.

Timing the Execution of a Statement

If a SQL statement does not perform well, you need a baseline to compare the execution time of other alternative SQL statements.

 Repeated executions of the same or similar statements take less time than the initial execution because the data no longer needs to be retrieved from disk since it is cached in memory. Just because you make a minor change to the statement doesn't mean the statement is actually running faster.

In SQL Developer, you will see the execution time next to the Eraser icon. One simple way to find out the execution duration of a statement within SQL*Plus is to use the SQL*Plus command SET TIMING ON, which returns the elapsed execution time after the execution of the statement completes.

Tuning a SQL statement is effective only if your SQL statement executes against realistic data volumes and column distributions similar to what would be expected in a production environment. For instance, the execution plan for a join involving two tables varies if the data in the test environment is 100 rows but in production it is 500,000 rows. The Oracle optimizer also evolves with each subsequent version of the Oracle database, so having a test environment that closely resembles your production environment greatly aids in this process.

The Execution Plan

The optimizer creates an *execution plan*, also referred to as an *explain plan*. This plan shows the individual steps the Oracle database executes to process a statement. Oracle reads the execution plan from the inside out, meaning the most indented step is performed first. If two steps have the same level of indentation, the step listed first is the first one executed. The following shows a SQL statement and its execution plan. You'll learn how to obtain such an output shortly. (The ID column on the left is only a number identifying the step; it does not indicate the execution order in any way.)

```
SELECT student_id, last_name
  FROM student
 WHERE student_id = 123
-------------------------------------------------
| Id | Operation                    | Name    |
-------------------------------------------------
|  0 | SELECT STATEMENT             |         |
|  1 |   TABLE ACCESS BY INDEX ROWID| STUDENT |
|  2 |     INDEX UNIQUE SCAN        | STU_PK  |
-------------------------------------------------
```

The first step performed is a lookup of the value 123 in the index STU_PK. Using the index entry, the row is retrieved from the STUDENT table via ROWID, which specifies the location (data file and data block) of the row.

There are various ways to obtain an execution plan. This chapter discusses the use of SQL Developer's Explain Plan and Autotrace features together with the EXPLAIN PLAN FOR command in SQL*Plus, along with the DBMS_XPLAN.DISPLAY package.

The best way to generate an explain plan is by using SQL Developer because it involves only a mouse-click. However, most of the explain plan results in this chapter are shown in the SQL*Plus output format because it is easier to read in the printed format.

SQL DEVELOPER'S EXPLAIN PLAN

SQL Developer allows you to obtain an execution plan by clicking the Execute Explain Plan icon (or pressing F6), as shown in Figure 18.3. The result is graphically displayed in the Explain tab.

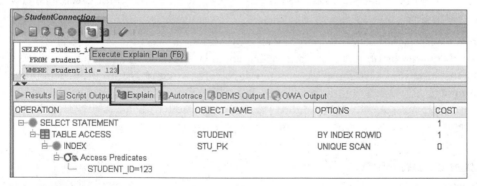

FIGURE 18.3
Explain plan output in SQL Developer

SQL DEVELOPER'S AUTOTRACE

In addition to using the Explain Plan icon, another way to generate an explain plan is with the Autotrace icon, located to the right of the Explain Plan icon. The result is shown in the Autotrace tab. In You see an explain plan as well plus you notice additional statistics that are useful for database administrators (DBAs) and advanced SQL users for further fine-tuning of SQL statements. These statistics are present because the statement is actually executed.

 You must have the SELECT_CATALOG_ROLE privilege to obtain a result using Autotrace.

DBMS_XPLAN IN SQL*PLUS

You can list the explain plan by using the EXPLAIN PLAN FOR command and the DISPLAY function of the DBMS_XPLAN package. The DISPLAY function retrieves the execution plan and runtime statistics, based on the V$SQL_PLAN and V$SQL_PLAN_STATISTICS data dictionary tables. The following statement shows how you can create an explain plan by using the EXPLAIN PLAN command.

```
SQL> EXPLAIN PLAN FOR
  2   SELECT student_id, last_name
  3     FROM student
  4    WHERE student_id = 123
  5   /
Explained.
```

Afterward, you can retrieve the plan by using the following DISPLAY function.

```
SELECT *
  FROM TABLE(DBMS_XPLAN.DISPLAY)
PLAN_TABLE_OUTPUT
-----------------------------------------------------------------------

|Id|Operation                       |Name    |Rows|Bytes|Cost (%CPU)|Time    |
-----------------------------------------------------------------------
| 0|SELECT STATEMENT                |        |   1|  12|  2 (50) |00:00:01|
| 1| TABLE ACCESS BY INDEX ROWID|STUDENT|   1|  12|  2 (50) |00:00:01|
|*2|  INDEX UNIQUE SCAN             |STU_PK  |   1|    |  1 (100)|00:00:01|
-----------------------------------------------------------------------


Predicate Information (identified by operation id):
---------------------------------------------------
PLAN_TABLE_OUTPUT
-----------------------------------------------------------
   2 - access("STUDENT_ID"=123)


13 rows selected.
```

If your result does not fit the display of your screen, you can enter the following SQL*Plus commands to increase the line size and suppress any headings.

```
SET LINESIZE 130
SET PAGESIZE 0
```

The explain plan display used in this chapter alternates between the SQL*Plus version and the SQL Developer version. One format sometimes lends itself to better readability than the other format within the text of this book. The overall steps in the execution plan do not differ.

Understanding COST, CARDINALITY, ROWS, and BYTES Values

The previous explain plan contains a number of columns that provide more detail about each individual step. The COST value is a number that represents the estimated disk I/O and amount of CPU and memory required to execute the desired action.

The COST helps you determine how involved each step is so you can focus on tuning the steps with the highest cost. The COST is determined using estimated amounts of memory, I/O, and CPU time required to execute the statement, as well as certain Oracle initialization parameters. The number of the ROWS or CARDINALITY column shows how many rows the optimizer expects to process at this step. In SQL*Plus, you can also see the BYTES column displaying the size, in bytes, expected for the step.

While a number of the explain plans in this book do not show the ROWS/CARDINALITY and COST columns for space reasons, you should display them when tuning a statement as these values provide useful details about each individual step.

SQL DEVELOPER OUTPUT PREFERENCES

In SQL Developer, you can move the columns in the Explain Plan and Autotrace tabs into the order you find most useful. You can also use the Tools/Preference menu to control which of various columns are shown in the various tabs (see Figure 18.4). The Autotrace column on the right of the screen has additional check boxes for the display.

SQL*PLUS OUTPUT PREFERENCES

If you execute the DISPLAY function without any parameter, you see the statistics. If you want to display only the minimum plan information, use the BASIC parameter, as in the next statement.

```
SELECT *
  FROM TABLE(DBMS_XPLAN.DISPLAY(null, null, 'BASIC'))
-------------------------------------------------
| Id | Operation                   | Name    |
-------------------------------------------------
|  0 | SELECT STATEMENT            |         |
|  1 |  TABLE ACCESS BY INDEX ROWID| STUDENT |
|  2 |   INDEX UNIQUE SCAN         | STU_PK  |
-------------------------------------------------

8 rows selected.
```

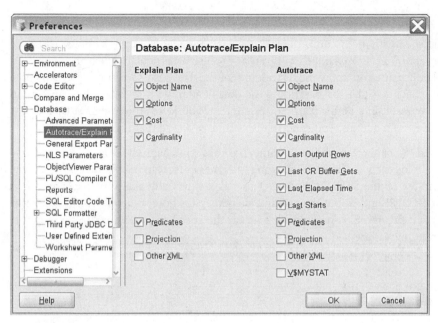

FIGURE 18.4
SQL Developer Preferences screen

The DISPLAY function has several parameters, and the syntax is as follows.

```
DBMS_XPLAN.DISPLAY
  (table_name IN VARCHAR2 DEFAULT 'PLAN_TABLE',
  statement_id IN VARCHAR2 DEFAULT NULL,
  format IN VARCHAR2 DEFAULT 'TYPICAL',
  filter_preds IN VARCHAR2 DEFAULT NULL)
```

The first parameter allows you to specify the name of the table where the plan is stored. By default, the explain plan is stored in PLAN_TABLE. The second parameter lets you include a STATEMENT_ID; this is useful if execute the EXPLAIN PLAN command with a SET STATE-MENT_ID clause to identify different statements. If you do not specify a value, the DISPLAY function returns the most recent explained statement. The third parameter permits you to change the display output of the plan. The BASIC value shows the operation ID, the operation, and the object name. The TYPICAL option is the default and includes the predicate (WHERE clause). The ALL choice displays all available data, including column information (column projection) and data related to the Oracle parallel server, if applicable. FILTER_PREDS indicates whether you want to display the predicate (that is, WHERE clause) in the result.

Hints

If you are not satisfied with the optimizer's plan, you can change it by applying hints. Hints are directives to the optimizer. For example, you can ask to use a particular index or to choose a specific join order. Because you know the distribution of the data best, sometimes you can come up with a better execution plan by overriding the default plan with specific hints. In certain instances, this may result in a better plan. For example, if you know that a particular index is more selective for certain queries, you can ask the optimizer to use that index.

A hint is enclosed by either a multiline comment with a plus sign (/*+ */) or a single line comment with a plus sign (--+). The following statement uses an index hint to scan the STU_ZIP_FK_I index on the STUDENT table. This index is actually a very poor choice when compared to the STU_PK index, but the example demonstrates how you can override the optimizer's default plan. Figure 18.5 shows a full scan on the specified index for 268 rows before the WHERE condition was applied.

```
SELECT /*+ INDEX (student stu_zip_fk_i) */
       student_id,
       last_name
  FROM student
 WHERE student_id = 123
```

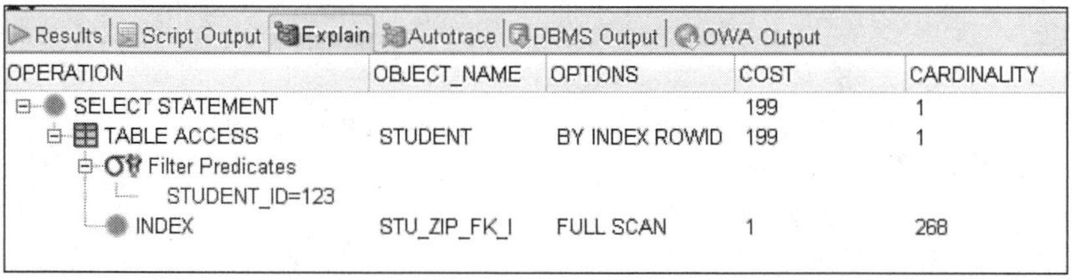

	Results	Script Output	Explain	Autotrace	DBMS Output	OWA Output			
OPERATION		OBJECT_NAME	OPTIONS	COST	CARDINALITY
⊟–● SELECT STATEMENT				199	1
⊟–▦ TABLE ACCESS		STUDENT	BY INDEX ROWID	199	1
⊟–O Filter Predicates					
└── STUDENT_ID=123					
└──● INDEX		STU_ZIP_FK_I	FULL SCAN	1	268

FIGURE 18.5
Forcing a specific index and resulting explain plan result

Table 18.4 lists some of the frequently used hints. You will use some of them in the exercises throughout this lab.

TABLE 18.4   Popular Hints

HINT	PURPOSE
FIRST_ROWS(n)	Returns the first n rows as quickly as possible.
ALL_ROWS	Returns all rows as quickly as possible.
INDEX(tablename indexname)	Uses the specified index. If an alias is used in the FROM clause of the query, be sure to list the alias instead of the table name.
ORDERED	Joins the tables as listed in the FROM clause of the query.
LEADING(tablename)	Specifies which table is the first table in the join order.

TABLE 18.4   Continued

HINT	PURPOSE
USE_MERGE(tablename)	Uses the sort-merge join method to join tables.
USE_HASH(tablename)	Uses the hash join method to join tables.
USE_NL(tablename)	Uses the nested loop join method; the specified table name is the inner table.

INCORRECTLY SPECIFYING HINTS

If you incorrectly specify a hint, the optimizer ignores it, and you are left to wonder why the hint does not work. The following is an example of the index hint specified incorrectly, and Figure 18.6 shows the resulting explain plan.

```
    SELECT /*+ INDEX (student stu_zip_fk_i) */
           student_id,
           last_name
      FROM student s
     WHERE student_id = 123
```

OPERATION	OBJECT_NAME	OPTIONS	COST	CARDINALITY
⊟ ● SELECT STATEMENT			1	1
⊟ ⊞ TABLE ACCESS	STUDENT	BY INDEX ROWID	1	1
⊟ ● INDEX ·	STU_PK	UNIQUE SCAN	0	1
⊟ ⌾ Access Predicates				
└ STUDENT_ID=123				

FIGURE 18.6
Incorrect hint

Instead of the table name STUDENT, the table alias s should be used because an alias is used in the FROM clause of the statement. This incorrect and therefore ignored hint causes the optimizer to use a different, actually more efficient index.

Your hint may also be ignored if you use the FIRST_ROWS hint in a query that contains a GROUP BY clause, an aggregate function, a set operator, the DISTINCT keyword, or an ORDER BY clause (if not supported by an index). All these Oracle keywords require that the result or sort first be determined based on all the rows before returning the first row.

Join Types

Determining the type of join and the join order of tables has a significant impact on how efficiently a SQL statement executes. Oracle chooses one of four types of join operations: sort-merge join, hash join, nested-loop join, or cluster join. This lab discusses only the first three, which are the most popular ones.

SORT-MERGE JOIN

To perform a sort-merge join, a full table scan is executed for each table. In the following SQL statement, the entire ENROLLMENT table is read and sorted by the joining column, and then the STUDENT table is scanned and sorted. The two results are then merged, and the matching rows are returned for output. The first row is returned only after all the records from both tables are processed.

This join is typically used when the majority of the rows are retrieved, when the join condition is not an equijoin, when no indexes exist on the table to support the join condition, or when a USE_MERGE hint is specified (see Figure 18.7).

```
SELECT /*+ USE_MERGE (e, s)*/ *
  FROM enrollment e, student s
 WHERE s.student_id = e.student_id
```

OPERATION	OBJECT_NAME	OPTIONS	COST	CARDINALITY
⊟ ● SELECT STATEMENT			8	226
⊟ ⋈ MERGE JOIN			8	226
⊟ ● SORT		JOIN	4	226
TABLE ACCESS	ENROLLMENT	FULL	3	226
⊟ ● SORT		JOIN	4	268
⊟ Oᴙ Access Predicates				
S.STUDENT_ID=E.STUDENT_ID				
⊟ Oᴙ Filter Predicates				
S.STUDENT_ID=E.STUDENT_ID				
TABLE ACCESS	STUDENT	FULL	3	268

FIGURE 18.7
Sort-merge join

HASH JOIN

Oracle performs a full table scan on each of the tables and splits each into many partitions in memory. Oracle then builds a hash table from one of these partitions and probes it against the partition of the other table (see Figure 18.8). A hash join typically outperforms a sort-merge join.

```
SELECT /*+ HASH_JOIN */ *
  FROM enrollment e, student s
 WHERE s.student_id = e.student_id
```

OPERATION	OBJECT_NAME	OPTIONS	COST	CARDINALITY
⊟‒● SELECT STATEMENT			7	226
⊟‒⋈ HASH JOIN			7	226
⊟‒◯⊛ Access Predicates				
└‒ S.STUDENT_ID=E.STUDENT_ID				
⊞ TABLE ACCESS	ENROLLMENT	FULL	3	226
⊞ TABLE ACCESS	STUDENT	FULL	3	268

FIGURE 18.8
Hash join

NESTED-LOOP JOIN

With a nested-loop join, the optimizer picks a driving (or outer) table that is the first table in the join chain. In this example, the driving table is the ENROLLMENT table. A full table scan is executed on the driving table and for each row in the ENROLLMENT table; the primary key index of the STUDENT table (here the inner table) is probed to see if the WHERE clause condition is satisfied. If it is, the row is returned in the result set. This probing is repeated until all the rows of the driving table, in this case the ENROLLMENT table, are tested.

In Oracle 11g, the nested-loop join has been further enhanced. Oracle can batch multiple physical reads and builds a vector. Then the explain plan for a nested loop shows two NESTED LOOPS rows instead of one. Figure 18.9 displays the execution plan of a nested-loop join with the two NESTED LOOPS rows indicating that the statement is using the enhanced Oracle 11g join functionality.

```
SELECT /*+ USE_NL(e s) */ *
   FROM enrollment e, student s
  WHERE e.student_id = s.student_id
```

OPERATION	OBJECT_NAME	OPTIONS	COST	CARDINALITY
⊟‒● SELECT STATEMENT			229	226
⊟‒⋈ NESTED LOOPS				
⊟‒⋈ NESTED LOOPS			229	226
⊞ TABLE ACCESS	ENROLLMENT	FULL	3	226
⊟‒● INDEX	STU_PK	UNIQUE SCAN	0	1
⊟‒◯⊛ Access Predicates				
└‒ E.STUDENT_ID=S.ST				
⊞ TABLE ACCESS	STUDENT	BY INDEX ROWID	1	1

FIGURE 18.9
Nested-loop join

The execution plan for a nested loop is read differently from the other execution plans because of the loop. The access to the STU_PK index, the most indented row, is not read first but rather is probed for every row of the driving ENROLLMENT table.

The nested-loop join is typically the fastest join when the goal is to retrieve the first row as quickly as possible. It is also the best join to use when you access approximately 1 to 10 percent of the total rows from the tables involved. This percentage varies, depending on the total number of rows returned, the total number of rows in the table, various parameters in your Oracle initialization file, and the Oracle version. It gives you a general idea of when this join is useful.

> The selection of the driving table is essential to good performance of a nested-loop join. Making the driving table return the least number of rows is critical for probing fewer records in subsequent joins to other tables. Therefore, you should eliminate as many rows as possible from the driving table.

Bind Variables and the Optimizer

If you repeatedly execute the same statement, with only slightly different values in the WHERE clause, you can eliminate the parsing with the use of *bind variables,* also referred to as *host variables.* For example, if the users of your program repeatedly issue this query but substitute a different phone number each time, you should consider substituting a bind variable for the literal value.

```
SELECT last_name, first_name
  FROM student
 WHERE phone = '614-555-5555'
```

The use of a bind variable eliminates the parsing of the SQL statement. This overhead is significant when you have many users on a system. Bind variables are prefixed with a colon. The new statement with a bind variable looks as follows.

```
SELECT last_name, first_name
  FROM student
 WHERE phone = :phone_no
```

The :PHONE_NO bind variable gets a new value assigned whenever the user issues the statement. The statement with the bind variable is already parsed, and the execution plan is determined and therefore ready for execution.

The following example illustrates the use of a bind variable in SQL*Plus. The VARIABLE command creates a bind variable. The next PL/SQL block assigns the variable the value 914-555-5555.

```
SQL> VARIABLE phone_no VARCHAR2(20)
SQL> BEGIN
  2    :phone_no :='914-555-5555';
  3  END;
  4  .
SQL> /

PL/SQL procedure successfully completed.
```

The subsequent execution of the SQL statement using the bind variable associates the assigned value with the variable and returns the correct row.

```
SQL> SELECT last_name, first_name
  2    FROM student
  3   WHERE phone = :phone_no
  4  /
LAST_NAME                       FIRST_NAME
------------------------------  ------------------------------
Mwangi                          Paula

1 row selected.
```

Bind variables are advantageous in applications where the same statement is executed repeatedly. At the first invocation of the statement with the bind variables, the optimizer looks at the selectivity of the value and determines the best possible execution plan. This assumes that every value associated with the bind variable has the same selectivity.

Starting with Oracle 11g, the database observes and checks whether the different bind values passed can alter the execution plan, and it may modify the execution plan accordingly. This new feature referred to as *adaptive cursor sharing*, means that Oracle may perform a modification of the execution plan, depending on the value.

In general, you will find frequent use of bind variables if the same statements are executed repeatedly. This is typically the case in transaction processing–oriented environments; the use of bind variable results in time and resource savings due to the elimination of the parsing step.

In contrast, in data warehousing environments, the queries are long running or of an ad hoc nature. Therefore, the use of literals is typically preferred because the optimizer can make an accurate determination about the most efficient execution plan. Also, the parsing time is negligible in comparison to the execution time.

For table columns where the data is not uniformly distributed, Oracle automatically creates histograms. For example, Oracle may determine that the values of a particular column are distributed as 10 percent for values of >=500 and 90 percent for values of <500. The histogram for this skewed data allows the optimizer to better understand the distribution of data.

Tips for Improving SQL Performance

There are several good habits to adopt when you write SQL statements. Keep the following guidelines in mind when diagnosing performance problems and when writing or rewriting SQL statements.

- ▶ Functions applied to indexed columns in the WHERE clause do not take advantage of the index unless you use the MIN or MAX function. For example, a function-based index based on the UPPER function, is useful for case-independent searches on the search column. If you always apply the TRUNC function to columns of the DATE data type, consider not storing the time portion in the column as this information is probably irrelevant. Implicit data type conversions can also cause Oracle to cast a value to another data type, thus preventing the use of the index, as you will see in the exercises.

▶ Use analytical functions, where possible, instead of multiple SQL statements as doing so simplifies the query writing and requires only a single pass through the table.

▶ Build indexes on columns you frequently use in the WHERE clause but keep in mind the performance trade-offs of DML statements. Adding an index can also adversely affect the performance of other SQL statements accessing the table. Be sure to test your scenarios carefully.

▶ Drop indexes that are never or very infrequently used. If you find that a specific index is used only for month-end processing, it may be advantageous to drop the index and rebuild it only shortly before the month-end job. You can also consider marking certain indexes invisible, so they are not used by the optimizer, but any related DML will continue to update them.

▶ Consider restructuring existing indexes. You can improve the selectivity by adding additional columns to an index. Alternatively, you can change the order of columns in a composite index.

▶ Full-table scans may at times be more efficient than indexes if the table is relatively small in size, as Oracle can read all the data with one I/O operation.

▶ If you are retrieving more than 5 to 20 percent of the rows, doing a full table scan may also be more efficient than retrieving the rows from an index.

▶ When joining tables using a nested-loop join, make sure to choose the table that returns the fewest number of rows as the driving table. You can enforce this with the ORDERED hint.

▶ Consider replacing the NOT IN operator with the NOT EXISTS operator and eliminating as many rows as possible in the outer query of a correlated subquery.

▶ If you have very large tables, consider partitioning them. This is a feature found only in Oracle Enterprise Edition.

▶ If your queries involve aggregates and joins against large tables, you can use materialized views to pre-store results and refresh them at set intervals. Oracle has a set of advisor procedures that help you design and evaluate the benefits of materialized views.

▶ Make sure you did not forget the joining criteria so as to avoid the building of a Cartesian product.

▶ Rebuild or coalesce indexes periodically to improve their performance. You do this with the ALTER INDEX indexname command and the REBUILD or COALESCE option. This is particularly useful after many DELETE statements have been issued.

▶ Make sure statistics for your tables and indexes are periodically gathered, especially after heavy DML activity. Inaccurate statistics are a common source of performance problems. Sometimes volume and distribution of your data change and your statistics may require updating.

▶ Review the result of the execution plan carefully to determine the cause of any performance problem; examine execution steps involving a large number of rows/cardinality or high cost. Use hints to tune the statement and make sure the hints are valid. Do not use hints that have no effect, such as a FIRST_ROWS_n hint on a statement with an GROUP BY clause because the GROUP BY operation needs to be processed first before any rows are returned.

▶ Use the CASE expression to avoid visiting tables multiple times. For example, if you need to aggregate rows that have different WHERE conditions within the same table, you can use the CASE expression in your SELECT list to aggregate only those rows that satisfy the necessary condition.

▶ SQL optimization is not just useful for queries, but also for DELETE, UPDATE, and INSERT operations. Too many indexes can slow down DML as the indexed column(s) need to be deleted or updated (if the indexed column values change) or values need to be inserted. However, indexes are beneficial for updates and deletions, particularly if the WHERE clause refers to an indexed column because the row is retrieved quickly. Missing foreign key indexes are a frequently overlooked problem; foreign key indexes are needed not only because they are frequently used in queries but also because they can cause locking issues, as discussed in Chapter 13, "Indexes, Sequences, and Views."

▶ Make sure you test your SQL statements carefully in a representative test environment where the data distribution, data volume, and hardware setup is similar to a production environment. Be sure to make a copy of your statistics with the DBMS_STATS.EXPORT_SCHEMA_STATS procedure. In case the performance degrades after analyzing, you can restore the old statistics with the DBMS_STATS.IMPORT_SCHEMA_STATS.

The SQL Tuning Advisor

Oracle provides the SQL Tuning Advisor to aid in the tuning process. This advisor is accessible through the Oracle Web-based Enterprise Manager and is part of Oracle's strategy to simplify many complex database administration and tuning tasks.

The SQL Tuning Advisor offers an automated approach to tuning, and it removes some of the guesswork by recommending specific actions that will benefit an individual statement or set of statements. The SQL Tuning Advisor incorporates the previously mentioned tips and recommends suggestions to improve the statement. You will see that having the background knowledge acquired from the beginning of this chapter helps you evaluate the recommendations of the tool and provides you with a better understanding of the Oracle functionality. The URL to log in to the Enterprise Manager is in the format `https://machine_name:1158/em`.

Figure 18.10 shows the login screen that connects with the STUDENT user and the SYSDBA privilege.

 The SYSDBA privilege is not required to perform SQL statement tuning tasks. Alternatively, you can login with SYSMAN account and the password you set up during the installation.

Your DBA needs to set up the appropriate privileges for you to use Enterprise Manager.

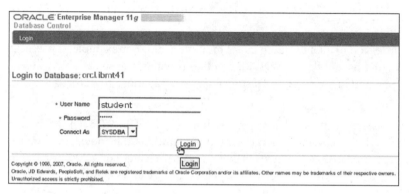

FIGURE 18.10
The Enterprise Manager login screen

After the successful login, you are presented with a screen similar to Figure 18.11. It shows the Enterprise Manager home page, from which you can access the Advisor Central link located on the bottom of the page, below the heading Related Links.

FIGURE 18.11
Enterprise Manager home page

Select the SQL Tuning Advisor Links link and then choose the sources for SQL statements to tune. For example, you can pick the top SQL statements to review and tune.

The SQL Tuning Advisor takes one or multiple statement and returns recommendations for the statements. You can choose between a limited or comprehensive scope. The comprehensive scope includes a SQL profile, and you can specify a time limit for the task. When the task is complete, you can view the changes to the statement. You can accept the tuning recommendation by creating a SQL profile.

A SQL profile is for an individual statement, and it consists of additional statistics. The profile is stored in the data dictionary and is used together with the regular statistics the next time the statement is invoked. The advantage of SQL profiles is that you avoid modifying the underlying statement, which is particularly valuable with packaged applications, where you do not have the ability to access and change the SQL statement.

The SQL Access Advisor

Another advisor in the Oracle Enterprise Manager is the SQL Access Advisor. It suggests schema modifications, such as adding or dropping materialized views or indexes based on hypothetical or actual workload. The sources of the workload can be collected through Enterprise Manager. Both DBAs and application developers will find this advisor very helpful because it offers additional suggestions to further optimize an individual application.

▼ **LAB 18.1 EXERCISES**

a) Describe the result of the following query.

```
SELECT index_name, column_name, column_position
  FROM user_ind_columns
 WHERE table_name = 'STUDENT'
 ORDER BY 1, 3
```

b) Generate an explain plan for the following SQL statement. What do you observe about the use of the index?

```
SELECT *
  FROM student
 WHERE student_id <> 101
```

c) Create an index called STU_FIRST_I on the FIRST_NAME column of the STUDENT table. Then execute the following SQL statement and describe the result of the execution plan.

```
SELECT student_id, first_name
  FROM student
 WHERE first_name IS NULL
```

d) Execute the following SQL query and describe the result of the execution plan.

```
SELECT student_id, first_name
  FROM student
 WHERE UPPER(first_name) = 'MARY'
```

e) Examine the following SQL queries and their respective execution plans. What do you notice about the use of the index? Drop the index STU_FIRST_I when you are finished.

```
SELECT student_id, first_name
  FROM student
 WHERE first_name LIKE '%oh%'
```

```
-------------------------------------------
| Id | Operation       | Name    |
-------------------------------------------
|  0 | SELECT STATEMENT |        |
|  1 |   TABLE ACCESS FULL| STUDENT |
-------------------------------------------
```

```
SELECT student_id, first_name
  FROM student
 WHERE first_name LIKE 'Joh%'
```

```
-----------------------------------------------------------
| Id | Operation                   | Name         |
-----------------------------------------------------------
|  0 | SELECT STATEMENT            |              |
|  1 |   TABLE ACCESS BY INDEX ROWID| STUDENT      |
|  2 |    INDEX RANGE SCAN          | STU_FIRST_I  |
-----------------------------------------------------------
```

f) Execute the following SQL query and describe the result of the execution plan.

```
SELECT *
  FROM zipcode
 WHERE zip = 10025
```

g) Explain why the following query does not use an index.

```
SELECT *
  FROM grade
 WHERE grade_type_code = 'HW'
```

h) Given the following SELECT statement and the resulting execution plan, determine the driving table and the type of join performed.

```
SELECT --+ FIRST_ROWS(10)
       i.last_name, c.description, c.course_no
  FROM course c, section s, instructor i
 WHERE c.course_no = s.course_no
   AND s.instructor_id = i.instructor_id
   AND s.section_id = 133
```

```
-----------------------------------------------------------
| Id | Operation                   | Name     |
-----------------------------------------------------------
|  0 | SELECT STATEMENT            |          |
|  1 |   NESTED LOOPS              |          |
|  2 |    NESTED LOOPS             |          |
|  3 |     TABLE ACCESS BY INDEX ROWID| SECTION  |
-----------------------------------------------------------
```

```
| 4 |       INDEX UNIQUE SCAN        | SECT_PK    |
| 5 | TABLE ACCESS BY INDEX ROWID| COURSE     |
| 6 |       INDEX UNIQUE SCAN        | CRSE_PK    |
| 7 | TABLE ACCESS BY INDEX ROWID | INSTRUCTOR |
| 8 |       INDEX UNIQUE SCAN        | INST_PK    |
--------------------------------------------------
```

i) The following SQL statements result in different execution plans. What differences, do you observe?

```
SELECT *
  FROM student
 WHERE student_id NOT IN
       (SELECT student_id
          FROM enrollment)


SELECT *
  FROM student s
 WHERE NOT EXISTS
       (SELECT 'X'
          FROM enrollment
         WHERE s.student_id = student_id)


SELECT student_id
  FROM student
MINUS
SELECT student_id
  FROM enrollment
```

j) Show the execution plans for the following SELECT statements and describe the difference.

```
SELECT student_id, last_name, 'student'
  FROM student
UNION
SELECT instructor_id, last_name, 'instructor'
  FROM instructor


SELECT student_id, last_name, 'student'
  FROM student
UNION ALL
SELECT instructor_id, last_name, 'instructor'
  FROM instructor
```

▼ LAB 18.1 EXERCISE ANSWERS

a) Describe the result of the following query.

```
SELECT index_name, column_name, column_position
  FROM user_ind_columns
 WHERE table_name = 'STUDENT'
 ORDER BY 1, 3
```

ANSWER: The result of the query shows a listing of all indexes on the STUDENT table and the order in which the columns are indexed. In this example, both indexes are single-column indexes.

INDEX_NAME	COLUMN_NAME	COLUMN_POSITION
STU_ZIP_FK_I	ZIP	1
STU_PK	STUDENT_ID	1

```
2 rows selected.
```

b) Generate an explain plan for the following SQL statement. What do you observe about the use of the index?

```
SELECT *
  FROM student
 WHERE student_id <> 101
```

ANSWER: The index is not used in this query; every record is examined with the full table scan instead.

```
------------------------------------
| Id | Operation       | Name    |
------------------------------------
|  0 | SELECT STATEMENT |        |
|  1 |  TABLE ACCESS FULL| STUDENT |
------------------------------------
```

Inequality conditions, such as <>, !=, or any negation using NOT, typically do not make use of an index.

c) Create an index called STU_FIRST_I on the FIRST_NAME column of the STUDENT table. Then execute the following SQL statement and describe the result of the execution plan.

```
SELECT student_id, first_name
  FROM student
 WHERE first_name IS NULL
```

ANSWER: The query does not make use of the index on the FIRST_NAME column because NULL values are not stored in the index. Therefore, a full table scan is executed.

```
CREATE INDEX stu_first_i ON student(first_name)
Index created.
```

The subsequently issued query results in the following execution plan.

```
--------------------------------------
| Id | Operation        | Name     |
--------------------------------------
|  0 | SELECT STATEMENT |          |
|  1 |   TABLE ACCESS FULL| STUDENT |
--------------------------------------
```

If you expect to execute this query frequently and want to avoid a full table scan, you might want to consider adding a row with a default value for FIRST_NAME, such as 'Unknown'. When this value is inserted in the index, a subsequently issued query, such as the following, uses the index.

```
SELECT student_id, first_name
  FROM student
 WHERE first_name = 'Unknown'
```

The index is not efficient, however, if you expect a significantly large number of the values to be 'Unknown'. In this case, retrieving values through the index rather than the full table scan may take longer.

d) Execute the following SQL query and describe the result of the execution plan.

```
SELECT student_id, first_name
  FROM student
 WHERE UPPER(first_name) = 'MARY'
```

ANSWER: The query does not make use of the index on the FIRST_NAME column.

```
--------------------------------------
| Id | Operation        | Name     |
--------------------------------------
|  0 | SELECT STATEMENT |          |
|  1 |   TABLE ACCESS FULL| STUDENT |
--------------------------------------
```

You can use the UPPER function in the SQL statement if you are unsure in which case the first name was entered.

The query returns records with the values MARY, Mary, or combinations thereof. Each time you modify an indexed column, the use of the index is disabled. The solution is to create a function-based index. For more information on this topic, refer to Chapter 13.

e) Examine the following SQL queries and their respective execution plans. What do you notice about the use of the index? Drop the index STU_FIRST_I.

```
SELECT student_id, first_name
  FROM student
 WHERE first_name LIKE '%oh%'
```

```
--------------------------------------
| Id | Operation        | Name     |
--------------------------------------
|  0 | SELECT STATEMENT |          |
|  1 |   TABLE ACCESS FULL| STUDENT |
--------------------------------------
```

```
SELECT student_id, first_name
   FROM student
  WHERE first_name LIKE 'Joh%'
-----------------------------------------------------
| Id | Operation                    | Name            |
-----------------------------------------------------
|  0 | SELECT STATEMENT             |                 |
|  1 |   TABLE ACCESS BY INDEX ROWID| STUDENT         |
|  2 |    INDEX RANGE SCAN          | STU_FIRST_I     |
-----------------------------------------------------
```

ANSWER: The first query does not make use of the index on the FIRST_NAME column because the index cannot determine the index entries. The second query allows the use of the index.

You may find that the second query does not use an index. The optimizer may determine that the table is so small that it is more efficient to read the entire table. However, if the table contains a larger data set, the optimizer will make use of the index.

You may also see an execution plan that takes advantage of both the STU_FIRST_I index and the STU_PK primary key index. If the columns in the query can be satisfied by using both indexes, you may not see any table access. For example, you might get an execution plan that retrieves the ROWIDs based on the WHERE clause. These ROWIDS are then joined to ROWIDs of the primary key index to obtain the STUDENT_ID column values.

Drop the index from the schema to restore the schema to its original state.

```
DROP INDEX stu_first_i
Index dropped.
```

f) Execute the following SQL query and describe the result of the execution plan.

```
SELECT *
   FROM zipcode
  WHERE zip = 10025
```

ANSWER: The query does not make use of the primary key index on the ZIP column.

```
--------------------------------------------
| Id | Operation         | Name            |
--------------------------------------------
|  0 | SELECT STATEMENT  |                 |
|  1 |   TABLE ACCESS FULL| ZIPCODE        |
--------------------------------------------
```

The full table access is used because the data types between the ZIP column and the number literal do not agree. The ZIP column is of VARCHAR2 data type to store leading zeros for zip codes such as 00706, and the literal in the WHERE clause is a NUMBER data type. The following query is an example of Oracle performing an implicit conversion. Oracle converts the ZIP column to a NUMBER data type and, therefore, disables the use of the index. If the WHERE clause is written as follows, it uses the index.

```
WHERE zip = '10025'
-----------------------------------------------
| Id | Operation                     | Name     |
-----------------------------------------------
|  0 | SELECT STATEMENT              |          |
|  1 |   TABLE ACCESS BY INDEX ROWID| ZIPCODE  |
|  2 |     INDEX UNIQUE SCAN         | ZIP_PK   |
-----------------------------------------------
```

g) Explain why the following query does not use an index.

```
SELECT *
  FROM grade
 WHERE grade_type_code = 'HW'
```

ANSWER: The GRADE_TYPE_CODE column is not the leading column on any index of the GRADE table.

```
-----------------------------------------
| Id | Operation          | Name  |
-----------------------------------------
|  0 | SELECT STATEMENT   |       |
|  1 |   TABLE ACCESS FULL| GRADE |
-----------------------------------------
```

The following query shows the indexes on the GRADE table. The GRADE_TYPE_CODE is a column in two different indexes but is never the leading column, nor are any of the leading columns in the WHERE clause of the query.

```
SELECT index_name, column_name, column_position
  FROM user_ind_columns
 WHERE table_name = 'GRADE'
 ORDER BY 1, 3
```

INDEX_NAME	COLUMN_NAME	COLUMN_POSITION
GR_GRTW_FK_I	SECTION_ID	1
GR_GRTW_FK_I	GRADE_TYPE_CODE	2
GR_PK	STUDENT_ID	1
GR_PK	SECTION_ID	2
GR_PK	GRADE_TYPE_CODE	3
GR_PK	GRADE_CODE_OCCURRENCE	4

6 rows selected.

The following query makes use of the index GR_GRTW_FK_I because the leading edge of the index is in the WHERE clause.

```
SELECT *
  FROM grade
 WHERE grade_type_code = 'HW'
   AND section_id = 123
```

And the following query uses the primary key index GR_PK.

```
SELECT *
  FROM grade
 WHERE grade_type_code = 'HW'
   AND section_id = 123
   AND student_id = 567
```

Oracle's skip scan feature improves index scans when the leading portion of the index is not specified. Essentially, scanning an index is faster than scanning the table, and the skip scanning feature splits the index into smaller sub-indexes. These different sub-indexes show the number of distinct values in the leading index. The feature is most useful when there are few distinct values in the leading column of the index. The explain plan indicates whether Oracle took advantage of the skip scan feature to access the data.

h) Given the following SELECT statement and the resulting execution plan, determine the driving table and the type of join performed.

```
SELECT --+ FIRST_ROWS(10)
         i.last_name, c.description, c.course_no
  FROM course c, section s, instructor i
 WHERE c.course_no = s.course_no
   AND s.instructor_id = i.instructor_id
   AND s.section_id = 133
```

```
-------------------------------------------------------
| Id | Operation                      | Name          |
-------------------------------------------------------
|  0 | SELECT STATEMENT               |               |
|  1 |  NESTED LOOPS                  |               |
|  2 |   NESTED LOOPS                 |               |
|  3 |    TABLE ACCESS BY INDEX ROWID| SECTION        |
|  4 |     INDEX UNIQUE SCAN          | SECT_PK       |
|  5 |    TABLE ACCESS BY INDEX ROWID| INSTRUCTOR     |
|  6 |     INDEX UNIQUE SCAN          | INST_PK       |
|  7 |   TABLE ACCESS BY INDEX ROWID  | COURSE        |
|  8 |    INDEX UNIQUE SCAN           | CRSE_PK       |
-------------------------------------------------------
```

ANSWER: The driving table of this nested-loop join is the SECTION table.

The query performs the following steps: The index SECT_PK is probed for the SECTION_ID 133, and one record in the SECTION table is accessed. Then the index INST_PK on the INSTRUCTOR table is checked for the matching INSTRUCTOR_ID. The LAST_NAME column value is retrieved from INSTRUCTOR. Finally, the COURSE index CRSE_PK is used to find a match for the COURSE_NO values, based on the initial result set of the SECTION table and the desired DESCRIPTION column from the COURSE table retrieved.

You can influence the join order with the ORDERED hint or the LEADING hint. This can have a significant impact on performance, depending on the size and WHERE conditions of the join. Try to eliminate as many rows as possible from the driving table to avoid probing many subsequent inner tables.

Comparing the execution time of a nested-loop join to a sort-merge join or a hash join probably will not show a great variance for the data within the STUDENT schema, but if you are joining larger tables, the differences may be significant.

i) The following SQL statements result in different execution plans. What differences do you observe?

```
SELECT *
  FROM student
 WHERE student_id NOT IN
       (SELECT student_id
          FROM enrollment)
```

```
SELECT *
  FROM student s
 WHERE NOT EXISTS
       (SELECT 'X'
          FROM enrollment
         WHERE s.student_id = student_id)
```

```
SELECT student_id
  FROM student
MINUS
SELECT student_id
  FROM enrollment
```

ANSWER: Each query has a different explain plan.

The NOT IN subquery does not take advantage of the index on the ENROLLMENT table, resulting in a full table scan.

```
-------------------------------------------------
| Id | Operation            | Name        |
-------------------------------------------------
|  0 | SELECT STATEMENT     |             |
|  1 |  FILTER              |             |
|  2 |   TABLE ACCESS FULL  | STUDENT     |
|  3 |   TABLE ACCESS FULL  | ENROLLMENT  |
-------------------------------------------------
```

The NOT IN operator can be very inefficient. Consider replacing it with NOT EXISTS, particularly because the NOT EXISTS operator takes advantage of the index on the ENROLLMENT table (see the following explain plan). You should keep in mind that you want to eliminate as many rows as possible in the outer query of the NOT EXISTS correlated subquery in order to minimize the repeated execution of the inner query.

```
-------------------------------------------------
| Id | Operation            | Name        |
-------------------------------------------------
|  0 | SELECT STATEMENT     |             |
|  1 |  FILTER              |             |
|  2 |   TABLE ACCESS FULL  | STUDENT     |
|  3 |   INDEX RANGE SCAN   | ENR_PK      |
-------------------------------------------------
```

Depending on the Oracle version, you may get different results from the listed explain plans in this book. With each new Oracle version, modifications are made to the optimizer that frequently result in more efficient execution plans.

The execution plan of the MINUS operator does not look very impressive, but using it can actually be one of the fastest ways to retrieve the result, especially when a large number of records are involved.

```
-------------------------------------------
| Id | Operation              | Name    |
-------------------------------------------
|  0 | SELECT STATEMENT       |         |
|  1 |  MINUS                 |         |
|  2 |   SORT UNIQUE NOSORT   |         |
|  3 |    INDEX FULL SCAN     | STU_PK  |
|  4 |   SORT UNIQUE NOSORT   |         |
|  5 |    INDEX FULL SCAN     | ENR_PK  |
-------------------------------------------
```

Always consider alternative SQL syntax when writing queries and tune your SQL statements with a representative data set. If the distribution of the data changes, so will the statistics, and the optimizer may favor a different execution plan.

j) Show the execution plans for the following SELECT statements and describe the difference.

```
SELECT student_id, last_name, 'student'
  FROM student
UNION
SELECT instructor_id, last_name, 'instructor'
  FROM instructor


SELECT student_id, last_name, 'student'
  FROM student
UNION ALL
SELECT instructor_id, last_name, 'instructor'
  FROM instructor
```

ANSWER: The UNION statement involves an additional sort that is not performed on the UNION ALL statement.

```
SELECT student_id, last_name, 'student'
  FROM student
UNION
SELECT instructor_id, last_name, 'instructor'
  FROM instructor
```

```
---------------------------------------------
| Id  | Operation            | Name          |
---------------------------------------------
|  0  | SELECT STATEMENT     |               |
|  1  |   SORT UNIQUE        |               |
|  2  |    UNION             |               |
|  3  |     TABLE ACCESS FULL| STUDENT       |
|  4  |     TABLE ACCESS FULL| INSTRUCTOR    |
---------------------------------------------
```

```
SELECT student_id, last_name, 'student'
  FROM student
UNION ALL
SELECT instructor_id, last_name, 'instructor'
  FROM instructor
```

```
--------------------------------------------
| Id  | Operation            | Name         |
--------------------------------------------
|  0  | SELECT STATEMENT     |              |
|  1  |  UNION-ALL           |              |
|  2  |    TABLE ACCESS FULL| STUDENT       |
|  3  |    TABLE ACCESS FULL| INSTRUCTOR    |
--------------------------------------------
```

Whenever possible, avoid any unnecessary sorts required by the use of UNION or DISTINCT.

Lab 18.1 Quiz

In order to test your progress, you should be able to answer the following questions.

1) The optimizer chooses from among many possible execution plans the one with the lowest cost.

_____ a) True
_____ b) False

2) An ORDERED hint can influence the join order of SQL statements using the CBO.

_____ a) True
_____ b) False

3) The join order of tables is irrelevant to the performance of the nested-loop join.

_____ a) True
_____ b) False

4) Incorrectly written hints are treated as comments and ignored.

_____ a) True
_____ b) False

5) The gathered statistics are stored in the data dictionary.

_____ a) True
_____ b) False

ANSWERS APPEAR IN APPENDIX A.

▼ WORKSHOP

The projects in this section are meant to prompt you to utilize all the skills you have acquired throughout this chapter. The answers to these projects can be found at the companion Web site to this book, located at www.oraclesqlbyexample.com.

1) Given the following execution plan, describe the steps and their order of execution.

```
SELECT c.course_no, c.description,
       i.instructor_id
  FROM course c, section s, instructor i
 WHERE prerequisite = 30
   AND c.course_no = s.course_no
   AND s.instructor_id - i.instructor_id
```

```
-----------------------------------------------------------
| Id | Operation                     | Name           |
-----------------------------------------------------------
|  0 | SELECT STATEMENT              |                |
|  1 |   NESTED LOOPS                |                |
|  2 |    NESTED LOOPS               |                |
|  3 |     TABLE ACCESS BY INDEX ROWID| COURSE        |
|  4 |      INDEX RANGE SCAN         | CRSE_CRSE_FK_I |
|  5 |     TABLE ACCESS BY INDEX ROWID| SECTION       |
|  6 |      INDEX RANGE SCAN         | SECT_CRSE_FK_I |
|  7 |    INDEX UNIQUE SCAN          | INST_PK        |
-----------------------------------------------------------
```

2) Describe the steps of the following execution plan.

```
UPDATE enrollment e
   SET final_grade =
       (SELECT NVL(AVG(numeric_grade),0)
          FROM grade
         WHERE e.student_id = student_id
           AND e.section_id = section_id)
 WHERE student_id = 1000
   AND section_id = 2000
0 rows updated.
```

```
-----------------------------------------------------------
| Id | Operation                     | Name          |
-----------------------------------------------------------
|  0 | UPDATE STATEMENT              |               |
|  1 |   UPDATE                      | ENROLLMENT    |
|  2 |    INDEX UNIQUE SCAN          | ENR_PK        |
|  3 |     SORT AGGREGATE            |               |
|  4 |      TABLE ACCESS BY INDEX ROWID| GRADE       |
|  5 |       INDEX RANGE SCAN        | GR_PK         |
-----------------------------------------------------------
```

3) The following SQL statement has an error in the hint. Correct the statement so Oracle can use the hint.

```
SELECT /*+ INDEX (student stu_pk) */ *
  FROM student s
 WHERE last_name = 'Smith'
```

Answers to Quiz Questions

Chapter 1

LAB 1.1 THE RELATIONAL DATABASE

Question	Answer	Comments
1)	a	
2)	b	A table must always have at least one column. Rows are not required.
3)	a	
4)	a	

LAB 1.2 DATA NORMALIZATION AND TABLE RELATIONSHIPS

Question	Answer	Comments
1)	b	The entity relationship diagram is a logical model that doesn't deal with physical tables; rather, it deals with entities and attributes.
2)	a	Another cardinality notation used to depict a one-to-many relationship is 1:M or 1:N.
3)	a	
4)	b	The schema diagram or physical model is derived from the logical data model.
5)	b	Actually, when you denormalize, you reintroduce redundancy.
6)	b	Logical database design is a phase in the database development life cycle, and it ends with the physical database implementation. SQL works with the physical database implementation.
7)	a	
8)	a	

LAB 1.3 THE STUDENT SCHEMA DIAGRAM

Question	Answer	Comments
1)	a, c	
2)	a	
3)	b	The number of rows is independent of the number of columns in a table.
4)	b	The SECTION table has the COURSE_NO and INSTRUCTOR_ID columns as foreign keys.
5)	a	Each individual database software may have limits constrained by the hardware and software. It is not uncommon to have tables exceeding 10 million rows.
6)	b	A primary key can never contain NULL values.
7)	a	
8)	c	The table has at least three foreign key columns. Some foreign keys may consist of multiple columns.
9)	a	
10)	a	An example of a foreign key that allows null values is the zip column on the instructor table.
11)	a	The prevention of orphan rows, thereby preserving the parent–child relationship between tables, is key to the success of a relational database design.

Chapter 2

LAB 2.1 THE SQL EXECUTION ENVIRONMENT

Question	Answer	Comments
1)	b	To establish a database connection, you need a valid user ID and password. You do not have to use SQL*Plus or SQL Developer to connect to Oracle. You can use other types of software that allows database connectivity.
2)	a	
3)	a	
4)	a	
5)	a	
6)	a	This answer is correct unless you use Oracle version 7 and below, where the limit was 2,000 bytes/characters.

LAB 2.2 THE ANATOMY OF A SELECT STATEMENT

Question	Answer	Comments
1)	a	
2)	a	To show all the columns, it is easiest to use the asterisk (*) wildcard character.
3)	b	The asterisk is used for the column list only.
4)	a	A column named COURSENO does not exist in the COURSE table.
5)	a	
6)	a	
7)	a	

LAB 2.2 THE ANATOMY OF A SELECT STATEMENT

Question	Answer	Comments
8)	b	SQL commands are not case-sensitive. You use uppercase to distinguish SQL commands easily.
9)	b	If the command is a SQL*Plus command or if you execute multiple statements, the result will be displayed in the Script Output tab instead.

LAB 2.3 AN INTRODUCTION TO SQL*PLUS

Question	Answer	Comments
1)	b	You can use the Easy Connect syntax if you do not want to create an entry in the TNSNAMES.ORA file. The Oracle Names server in a site that has many Oracle databases does not require an individual machine to have a TNSNAMES.ORA file.
2)	b	SQL*Plus works only against an Oracle database.
3)	a	
4)	b	SQL*Plus does not require this; only SQL commands do.

Chapter 3

LAB 3.1 THE WHERE CLAUSE

Question	Answer	Comments
1)	b	Comparison operators can compare multiple values, such as the IN operator, which compares against a list of values.
2)	b	The BETWEEN operator is inclusive of the two values specified.
3)	a	You must test for nulls, using the IS NULL operator. This query does not return any rows!
4)	a	The LIKE operator cannot compare against a list of values.
5)	b	This query is valid. Alternatively, the <> operator or the WHERE clause NOT state = 'NY' can be used.
6)	b	Because the comparison operator is the equal sign (=), not the LIKE operator, it looks for a last name exactly equal to SM%, including the % sign. If you use the LIKE operator instead, then last names beginning with the uppercase letters SM are returned.

LAB 3.2 THE ORDER BY CLAUSE

Question	Answer	Comments
1)	b	The order should be SELECT, FROM, WHERE, ORDER BY.
2)	b	The default ORDER BY sort order is ascending.
3)	a	There is no error in this statement.
4)	b	The query does not contain an error.
5)	a	Typically, yes, the exception is the use of the DISTINCT keyword in the SELECT clause.

Chapter 4

LAB 4.1 CHARACTER FUNCTIONS

Question	Answer	Comments
1)	b	For example, the INSTR function, which converts single values, requires two parameters and may have optional parameters.
2)	a	You will see other uses of the DUAL table throughout this book.
3)	a	
4)	a	You may not apply a function to the table name in the FROM clause of a SQL statement.
5)	a	The RTRIM right trims characters. If a parameter is not specified, it trims spaces.
6)	c	The LENGTH function returns the length of a string.
7)	b	The extra spaces between Mary and Jones are not trimmed. Only the spaces at the beginning and end of the string are trimmed.
8)	a	This is in contrast to the aggregate functions where one or more rows are involved. Aggregate functions are discussed in Chapter 6, "Aggregate Functions, GROUP BY, and HAVING Clauses."
9)	c	The SUBSTR function returns a specified portion of a character string.
10)	b	Usually, character functions return a data type of CHAR or VARCHAR2; however, the INSTR and LENGTH functions return a number.

LAB 4.2 NUMBER FUNCTIONS

Question	Answer	Comments
1)	a	
2)	b	The ROUND function works on DATE, NUMBER, and the floating-point data types. It can also take a string consisting of numbers as a parameter, provided that it can be implicitly converted into a NUMBER data type.
3)	b	This SELECT statement subtracts the capacity columns from each other. It is perfectly valid to use another column rather than a literal, as we have used in most other examples. The result of the query does not make much sense in this case, resulting in zero values. If any of the capacity column values contains a null value, the result is another null.
4)	c	Most functions return a null with a null argument. There are a few exceptions, such as the REPLACE and NVL functions.

LAB 4.3 MISCELLANEOUS SINGLE-ROW FUNCTIONS

Question	Answer	Comments
1)	a	Any calculation with a null always yields null. If you want to avoid this behavior, you can use the NVL function to substitute another value.
2)	b	If the data types are different, Oracle attempts to convert the substitution expression's data type to the input expression's data type. If this is not possible, the function returns an error, as in this example. The text literal 'None', which is the substitution expression, cannot be converted into the input expression's NUMBER data type. The corrected statement looks like this: SELECT NVL(TO_CHAR(cost),'None') FROM course.

LAB 4.3 MISCELLANEOUS SINGLE-ROW FUNCTIONS

Question	Answer	Comments
3)	b	The UPDATE command (discussed in Chapter 11, "Insert, Update, and Delete"), updates data in the database. None of the functions you have learned about so far will modify the value in the database.
4)	a	
5)	b	The DECODE function is permitted in any SQL statement where functions are allowed.
6)	a	The CASE expression is allowed anywhere expressions are allowed, including in ORDER BY clauses and inside functions.
7)	b	The functions in this lab can be used on most data types. For example, the NVL function is most frequently used on DATE, NUMBER, and VARCHAR2 data types.

Chapter 5

LAB 5.1 APPLYING ORACLE'S DATE FORMAT MODELS

Question	Answer	Comments
1)	a	The TRUNC function, without a format model, sets the timestamp to midnight. TRUNC can also take a NUMBER data type as a parameter.
2)	b	The TO_DATE function is required instead (for example, SELECT TO_DATE('01/12/2000','MM/DD/YYYY') FROM dual).
3)	d	The case is identical to the case of the format mask. The format mask DY returns MON, Day returns Monday and padded to nine spaces, and DAY returns MONDAY.
4)	e	The fill mode (fm) prevents any blank padding between December and 31. The date format element suffix th adds the ordinal number.
5)	b	The minutes (MI) are displayed as months (MM) instead. This is a mistake beginners often make by confusing the month (MM) format with the minutes (MI) format.

LAB 5.2 PERFORMING DATE AND TIME MATH

Question	Answer	Comments
1)	a	You need to supply a negative value as a parameter. For example, the following statement subtracts one month from the current date: SELECT ADD_MONTHS (SYSDATE,-1) FROM dual.
2)	a	You compute this by multiplying 24 hours by the 4 quarters of every hour. You can verify this with the following query: SELECT TO_CHAR(SYSDATE, 'HH24: MI'), TO_CHAR(SYSDATE+1/96, 'HH24:MI') FROM dual.
3)	c	The NEXT_DAY function takes two parameters: a date and a day of the week. Sunday, January 9, is the next Sunday after January 2, 2000.
4)	c	The ROUND function rounds not just numbers but also dates. Here the ROUND function's format model is not listed; therefore, it rounds to the nearest date. Because the time is before noon, it rounds to the current date. If the time is after noon, the next day is returned.

LAB 5.3 UNDERSTANDING THE TIMESTAMP AND TIME ZONE DATA TYPES

Question	Answer	Comments
1)	c	The FROM_TZ function returns a TIMESTAMP WITH TIME ZONE data type.
2)	a	The ALTER SESSION command can, among other things, change the individual's session time zone.
3)	a	The date and time are stored in the database server's own time zone, but the result is displayed in the individual user's time zone.
4)	a	The time zone displacement value, also called the time zone offset value, is the difference, in hours and minutes, between the local time and UTC (Coordinated Universal Time).
5)	a	
6)	a	

LAB 5.4 PERFORMING CALCULATIONS WITH THE INTERVAL DATA TYPES

Question	Answer	Comments
1)	b	The TO_YMINTERVAL function converts the text literal to an INTERVAL YEAR TO MONTH data type.
2)	b	The NUMTODSINTERVAL function returns an INTERVAL DAY TO SECOND data type.
3)	b	You can use the EXTRACT function on INTERVAL data types.
4)	b	The interval literal is correct. For example, you can execute the following query. Note that a common mistake is to misspell DAY TO SECOND by adding an S at the end of DAY.

```
SELECT TO_CHAR(SYSDATE,  'DD-MON-YYYY HH24:MI:SS')
          TO_CHAR(SYSDATE +
             INTERVAL '5 10:30:10.00' DAY TO SECOND,
             'DD-MON-YYYY HH24:MI:SS')
  FROM dual
```

LAB 5.5 CONVERTING FROM ONE DATA TYPE TO ANOTHER

Question	Answer	Comments
1)	d	Answer d results in an error because 'A123' cannot be converted to a NUMBER. (Oracle versions prior to 9i may return an error message on Answer e because the TO_CHAR function expects a NUMBER or DATE data type, not a character data type. The passed literal 'A123' is assumed to be a NUMBER data type, and Oracle attempts to implicitly convert the literal to a NUMBER; therefore, an error is returned.)
2)	c, d, e	These are all valid, including Answer e, but Answer e does not show all the digits because the passed parameter exceeds the specified precision. Answers a and b are invalid NUMBER masks; Answer b is also missing a single quote at the end of the format mask.
3)	a	It is always best to explicitly specify the data type and not to rely on Oracle's implicit conversion.
4)	a	Conversion functions operate on a single row at a time.

LAB 5.5 CONVERTING FROM ONE DATA TYPE TO ANOTHER

Question	Answer	Comments
5)	b	Changing the query as follows corrects the error.

```
SELECT *
  FROM conversion_example
 WHERE course_no = CAST(123 AS VARCHAR2(3))
```

Chapter 6

LAB 6.1 AGGREGATE FUNCTIONS

Question	Answer	Comments
1)	c	Only AVG, COUNT, and SUM are aggregate functions. ROUND is a single-row function.
2)	c	The aggregate function MAX determines the most recently modified record for the enrollment table. If a null value is returned, the value March 12, 20012, is substituted.
3)	a	Typically, aggregate functions work on groups of rows, but they can also be applied to a single row. For example, the following two statements return the same result.

```
SELECT MAX(modified_date) FROM zipcode WHERE zip =
'10025'

SELECT modified_date FROM zipcode WHERE zip = '10025'.
```

Question	Answer	Comments
4)	a	The asterisk is not a permissible argument for the AVG function.
5)	b	It computes the average capacity of only the unique (or distinct) capacities within the SECTION table.
6)	b	The statement is correct and shows an example of an expression as an argument of an aggregate function. The values in the capacity columns are multiplied by 1.5, and then the aggregate function SUM is applied.

LAB 6.2 THE GROUP BY AND HAVING CLAUSES

Question	Answer	Comments
1)	b	
2)	a	It is syntactically correct but redundant to do this because GROUP BY implies distinct values.
3)	a	Aggregate functions are not allowed in the WHERE clause unless they are part of a subquery. (See Chapter 8, "Subqueries.")
4)	b	One row will return a null prerequisite because all the NULL values are grouped together. Although one NULL does not equal another, in a GROUP BY clause, they are grouped together.

LAB 6.2 THE GROUP BY AND HAVING CLAUSES

Question	Answer	Comments
5)	a	The SQL statement is correct. You do not need to list the columns of the GROUP BY clause in the SELECT list as well. This type of query is typically not very useful because this individual example displays only the value of the COUNT function and not the column by which the group is formed. The result of the query looks like the following output.

```
   COUNT(*)
----------
         1
...
         1

28 rows selected.
```

Chapter 7

LAB 7.1 THE TWO-TABLE JOIN

Question	Answer	Comments
1)	f	The alias is incorrect on the STUDENT table's ZIP column.
2)	d	Lines 2 and 5 are incorrect. In line 5, the STUD.ZIP column does not exist; it needs to be changed to S.ZIP to correspond to the STUDENT table's alias, as listed in the FROM clause. Line 2 lists a nonexistent SZIP column. You need to change it to S.ZIP for the query to work.
3)	b	The table alias is just another name to reference the table.
4)	a	The equijoin tests for equality of values in one or multiple columns.
5)	c	The column W.GRADE_TYPE_CODE_CD is misspelled and needs to be changed to W.GRADE_TYPE_CODE for the query to work.
6)	b	The NULL value from one table does not match the NULL value from another table; therefore, the records are not included in the result.
7)	a	The USING clause assumes the equality of the values and identical column names. If you want to specify inequality or if the join columns do not share the same name, use the traditional WHERE clause or use the ON clause. For more on inequality in joins, refer to Chapter 10, "Complex Joins."
8)	a	The natural join does not allow any USING or ON clause. The common column names are assumed to be the joining criteria.
9)	b	This is not required but is often included to understand the result set.

LAB 7.2 JOINING THREE OR MORE TABLES

Question	Answer	Comments
1)	b	This statement has the correct join criteria between the SECTION, COURSE, and INSTRUCTOR tables. However, the COURSE table is not necessary to show the instructors assigned to sections.

LAB 7.2 JOINING THREE OR MORE TABLES

Question	Answer	Comments
2)	c	You get this error if you list two columns with the same name. Resolve it by prefixing the column with a table name or a table alias.
3)	b	Multicolumn joins need to have all the common columns listed. Some joins do not follow the primary/foreign key path because either a foreign key relationship does not exist or a shortcut is used to obtain the information.
4)	a	The SECTION_ID column has the wrong table alias; change it to E.SECTION_ID or G.SECTION_ID.
5)	a	The most common type of join is the equijoin, which is based on the equality of values. This is typically expressed with the equal (=) sign, or, in ANSI syntax, with the NATURAL JOIN or INNER JOIN, together with the USING clause or the ON condition. Chapter 10 covers nonequijoin conditions, self-joins, and outer joins in
6)	a	Remember the n − 1 formula? In the case of multicolumn keys, you may have additional conditions in your WHERE clause or multiple columns in your ANSI join ON or USING clause.

Chapter 8

LAB 8.1 SIMPLE SUBQUERIES

Question	Answer	Comments
1)	a	A subquery with the ORDER BY clause results in an error, except for inline views discussed in Lab 8.3.
2)	b	Subqueries can also be used in other types of SQL statements. Most frequently, they are used in SELECT statements or in INSERT, DELETE, or UPDATE statements.
3)	a	The most deeply nested subquery is executed first. This is in contrast to the correlated subquery, which executes the outer query first and then repeatedly executes the inner subquery for every row of the outer query.
4)	c	The IN operator allows multiple rows.
5)	a	You can compare column pairs by enclosing them in parentheses and comparing them to the subquery using the IN operator. Make sure the data type and column pairs match on both sides of the IN operator.

LAB 8.2 CORRELATED SUBQUERIES

Question	Answer	Comments
1)	a	The NOT EXISTS operator tests for NULL values; the NOT IN operator does not.
2)	a	For every row of the outer query, the inner query is executed.
3)	a	They result in the same output, although one may execute more efficiently than the other.
4)	b	The query looks only for enrolled students that have no corresponding record in the GRADE table for the particular section.
5)	a	The join may repeat some of the values from the child table, and applying the aggregate function to these rows may not yield the correct result. Therefore, check the result of the join!

LAB 8.3 INLINE VIEWS AND SCALAR SUBQUERY EXPRESSIONS

Question	Answer	Comments
1)	a	Just like other types of views, this is allowed.
2)	b	A scalar subquery returns a single column and single row.
3)	b	Inline views, unlike regular views, are not stored in the data dictionary.
4)	b	It is a pseudocolumn, appearing as though it were an actual column in the table, but it is not.

LAB 8.4 ANY, SOME, AND ALL OPERATORS IN SUBQUERIES

Question	Answer	Comments
1)	b	The first query tests whether the number 6 is unequal to any of the values in the list. It is unequal to the number 9, and therefore the query returns the value True. The second query checks whether the number 6 is not in the list of values. The value is included, and the query returns no rows.
2)	a	The two queries return the identical result.
3)	a	These operators can be used interchangeably.
4)	a	You can use the comparison operators and the ANY, SOME, and ALL operators to compare a list of values. The IN operator tests for equivalency of values only.

Chapter 9

LAB 9.1 THE POWER OF UNION AND UNION ALL

Question	Answer	Comments
1)	a	The UNION set operator performs a sort and lists only distinct values.
2)	b	The ORDER BY clause is always the last clause in a set operation.
3)	b	A UNION set operation does not eliminate rows; rather, it combines rows from each SELECT statement, eliminating duplicates only. An equijoin returns only rows where values from each table are equal.
4)	b	You can UNION any tables, as long as you conform to the rules of the UNION operation—that is, the same number of columns and the same data type.
5)	a	One of the rules of set operations is that the number of columns must be the same, as must the data types of those columns.

LAB 9.2 THE MINUS AND INTERSECT SET OPERATORS

Question	Answer	Comments
1)	b	The two SELECT statements result in two different sets of data.
2)	a	The SELECT statements in a set operation can be any SELECT statements.
3)	b	The data types of the columns must agree.
4)	a	All set operators, except UNION ALL, eliminate duplicate values, so DISTINCT is not needed.

Chapter 10
LAB 10.1 OUTER JOINS

Question	Answer	Comments
1)	a	The OR operator is not allowed in the outer join. The result is an error message such as "ORA-01719: outer join operator (+) not allowed in operand of OR or IN").
2)	a	The IN operator may not be used. The error message is identical to the one in Answer 1. The new ANSI join syntax overcomes some of these limitations.
3)	a	The Oracle outer join operator indicates from which table you want to display NULLs for nonmatching values. Alternatively, this can be expressed with the ANSI outer join syntax or a UNION.
4)	d	You cannot write a full outer join with two outer join operators (+). You need to write two outer join statements and combine the result with the UNION set operator or use the ANSI full outer join syntax.

LAB 10.2 SELF-JOINS

Question	Answer	Comments
1)	b	Joins do not have to follow the foreign/primary key path. But you have to carefully examine the result to make sure it is correct. A many-to-many-join relationship can result in a Cartesian product.
2)	b	You can join a table to itself without a recursive relationship (for example, to determine data inconsistencies).
3)	b	Such restrictions do not exist.
4)	a	Yes, an alias is required.

Chapter 11
LAB 11.1 CREATING DATA AND TRANSACTION CONTROL

Question	Answer	Comments
1)	b	Only DDL or DCL commands issue implicit commits.
2)	b	
3)	b	You can insert multiple rows by selecting from another table.
4)	a	
5)	b	Only committed changes can be seen by all users. The session issuing the change can always see the change.
6)	a	

LAB 11.2 UPDATING AND DELETING DATA

Question	Answer	Comments
1)	a	If the rows have not been committed to the database, you can restore them by using the ROLLBACK command. Starting with Oracle 10g, you can attempt to restore data with the FLASHBACK command. A last resort is to restore the data from a previous backup.
2)	a	

LAB 11.2 UPDATING AND DELETING DATA

Question	Answer	Comments
3)	b	Queries never place locks on rows. The exception is the SELECT FOR UPDATE command, which retrieves the rows and explicitly locks them.
4)	b	A read of uncommitted data is called a "dirty read." Oracle shows only data that has been committed, and it achieves read consistency by reading old data from the rollback (or undo) segments to present the user a picture of how the data looked at the time the query started.
5)	a	If the same session issues a DCL or DDL command instead of a ROLLBACK or COMMIT, it will force an implicit commit and therefore release the lock on the row.

LAB 11.3 THE SQL DEVELOPER DATA TAB

Question	Answer	Comments
1)	a	
2)	a	
3)	a	
4)	b	
5)	a	

Chapter 12

LAB 12.1 CREATING AND DROPPING TABLES

Question	Answer	Comments
1)	a	The primary key consists of multiple columns.
2)	a	When the CREATE TABLE statement uses the AS SELECT keywords to select from another table or tables, the SELECT statement can contain a join of multiple tables.
3)	b	The foreign key constraints of the child tables are dropped, but the child tables themselves are not.
4)	a	
5)	b	You can create a table from another, regardless of whether the table has rows.
6)	a	Any DDL command, such as CREATE TABLE, ALTER TABLE, or TRUNCATE TABLE, issues an implicit commit.
7)	a	If the foreign key column is defined as allowing nulls, a null value is also acceptable.
8)	b	Ideally, primary key values should be generic and never subject to changes; otherwise, the corresponding foreign key columns require updates.
9)	a	The INITIAL extent specifies the storage allocation when the table is initially created. Once the data is entered and the space filled, Oracle automatically allocates another extent, in a size indicated with the NEXT parameter.
10)	a	
11)	b	The maximum allowable value is 9.99. For a column defined as NUMBER(3,0), the largest value can be 999.

LAB 12.2 ALTERING TABLES AND MANIPULATING CONSTRAINTS

Question	Answer	Comments
1)	a	The syntax should not include both the keywords CONSTRAINT and PRIMARY KEY. The correct syntax is either ALTER TABLE tablename DROP CONSTRAINT followed by the constraint name or ALTER TABLE tablename DROP PRIMARY KEY.
2)	b	You use the ADD keyword to add columns or constraints to a table, whereas you use the MODIFY keyword to change characteristics of a column.
3)	b	You can add a NOT NULL constraint only if the referenced column contains values or the table is empty. With Oracle 11g, you can add a default value for the column in order to avoid having to update all the values.
4)	b	The ALTER TABLE...DISABLE Primary KEY command is an example of the command used without the name of the constraint.
5)	b	A column's data type can also be changed to a compatible data type, such as from VARCHAR2 to CHAR.
6)	a	

Chapter 13

LAB 13.1 INDEXES

Question	Answer	Comments
1)	c, d	A concatenated index typically outperforms individual column indexes. However, as with any other query, you need to know how many rows you expect to retrieve with the criteria. If you retrieve a large number of records, the full table scan may outperform the retrieval from the index. Oracle's optimizer automatically makes this determination. If you create a concatenated index, choose the column order carefully. If you have a choice, choose the most selective column first—that is, the column with the most distinct values. Starting with Oracle 9i, a new feature called skip scan can overturn these "old" rules. Be sure to test your options carefully to determine the best performance.
2)	b	Indexes can slow down INSERT, UPDATE, and DELETE operations. Retrieving data from an index may take more time if the retrieved data set is relatively large because both table and index need to be accessed.
3)	a	These columns are often listed in the WHERE clause and are therefore accessed frequently. Indexing these columns improves the performance of joins and locking during DML operations.
4)	a	
5)	b	Nulls are not stored in a B-tree index; therefore, a search for null values does not use the index. However, a concatenated index stores nulls as long as the leading column of the concatenated index is not null.
6)	a	Indexes are not useful only for SELECT statements but also for UPDATE and DELETE statements to quickly locate the record. INSERT, UPDATE, and DELETE operations on columns containing indexes are much slower because the index needs to be updated with the changed or newly inserted values.

LAB 13.2 SEQUENCES

Question	Answer	Comments
1)	a	
2)	b	It is best to use a generated value for a primary key, such as from a sequence, because it is generic, it is not subject to change, and it prevents duplicates or null values.
3)	a	
4)	b	These two objects are independent of each other. For example, you can use the same sequence for multiple tables.
5)	a	

LAB 13.3 VIEWS

Question	Answer	Comments
1)	a	
2)	a, b	
3)	e	
4)	a	Views must follow a number of rules in order to be updatable. This view allows inserts and updates and deletes referencing the state column, but not to the modified_date column. If you are in doubt, query the data dictionary view called user_updatable_columns.
5)	a	You can list only certain columns in a view, and/or you can restrict the view with the WHERE clause for specific rows.
6)	a	You can choose to keep the name or create a different name; however, an expression requires a column alias.

Chapter 14

LAB 14.1 THE ORACLE DATA DICTIONARY VIEWS

Question	Answer	Comments
1)	a	
2)	a	Other object types are also listed in this view.
3)	a	
4)	b	The all_tables view shows only the tables that are accessible to a user.
5)	a	

LAB 14.2 SCRIPTING AND REPORTING

Question	Answer	Comments
1)	a	
2)	b	The CHR(10) function issues a line feed.
3)	a	Rather than retype the same commands over again, you can use dynamic SQL scripts, also referred to as master/slave scripts or SQL to generate SQL, to simplify this task.
4)	a	
5)	a	

Chapter 15
LAB 15.1 USERS, PRIVILEGES, ROLES, AND SYNONYMS

Question	Answer	Comments
1)	b	A user's objects can be dropped with the CASCADE keyword at the end of the DROP USER statement.
2)	a	
3)	a	System and object privileges cannot be granted or revoked in the same statement. However, system and object privileges, in separate statements, can be granted to or revoked from a single role.
4)	b	Both system and object privileges can be granted to a user through a role.
5)	b	Dropping a role has no effect on the underlying objects.
6)	a	
7)	b	DCL commands implicitly issue a COMMIT, much like DDL commands.
8)	a	

Chapter 16
LAB 16.1 REGULAR EXPRESSIONS

Question	Answer	Comments
1)	b	You can't use the REGEXP_LIKE operator in the SELECT clause of a statement, or you get error message ORA-00904: "REGEXP_LIKE": invalid identifier.
2)	e	The quantifier is invalid because the minimum value 4 is greater than the maximum value 1.
3)	b	The regular expression is looking for characters that are not digits, with a minimum length of at least 1 character and a maximum of 5 characters. This pattern must end the expression. The nondigit characters are ABC, and the replacement does not occur because the pattern is not found in the supplied input string.
4)	a	
5)	a	The query results in error ORA-12729: invalid character class in regular expression error message. The POSIX classes are case-sensitive and must be spelled exactly as listed.
6)	a	The query shows CD as a result because the + operator looks for the one or more uppercase letters. The query specifies no starting position or occurrence; therefore, the default is the first starting position and the first occurrence.
7)	a	The two regular expressions are equivalent for Latin numbers. However, if you need to support other characters sets, this does not hold true.

LAB 16.2 HIERARCHICAL QUERIES

Question	Answer	Comments
1)	a	
2)	a	The PRIOR operator determines the parent.

LAB 16.2 HIERARCHICAL QUERIES

Question	Answer	Comments
3)	a	Starting with Oracle 9i, joins are allowed.
4)	b	The CONNECT_BY_ISLEAF pseudocolumn displays the value 1, if it's a leaf of the hierarchy tree; otherwise, it displays 0.

Chapter 17

LAB 17.1 ADVANCED SQL CONCEPTS, ANALYTICAL FUNCTIONS, AND THE WITH CLAUSE

Question	Answer	Comments
1)	a	
2)	a	
3)	b	The ROWS keyword defines a physical window.
4)	b	LAG and LEAD do not need a windowing clause; the position is defined with the offset value.
5)	a	

LAB 17.2 ROLLUP AND CUBE OPERATORS

Question	Answer	Comments
1)	c	The formula for determining the number of different combinations for the CUBE operator is 2^n. With four columns, the answer is 2^4, which equals 16.
2)	b	The formula for ROLLUP is $n + 1$. With four columns, there will be a total of five groupings.
3)	a	A super aggregate row generated by the CUBE or ROLLUP operator returns the number 1 with the GROUPING function.
4)	a	There are three sets. The first set is a combination of the columns color and price, as indicated by the parentheses around the columns. The second group is material, and the last group store_location.

Chapter 18

LAB 18.1 THE ORACLE OPTIMIZER AND WRITING EFFECTIVE SQL STATEMENTS

Question	Answer	Comments
1)	a	
2)	a	
3)	b	The join order has a significant impact on performance.
4)	a	
5)	a	

SQL Formatting Guide

SQL formatting guidelines are a set of written instructions, similar to a style sheet in publishing, that help programmers determine what the program code should look like. The main rule is *consistency:* Once you have decided on the style, use it rigorously.

Why have guidelines? The major benefit of standardized formatting is ease of reading. This is particularly important if someone else has to maintain, upgrade, or fix your programs. The easier a program is to read, the easier it is to understand, and the faster changes can be made. This ultimately saves time and money.

Case

SQL is case-insensitive. However, there are guidelines to follow when writing SQL in order to improve readability:

- Use uppercase for SQL commands and keywords (SELECT, INSERT, UPDATE, DELETE, ALTER, and so on), data types (VARCHAR2, DATE, NUMBER, and so on), functions (COUNT, TO_DATE, SUBSTR, and so on), and SQL*Plus commands (CONNECT, SET, and so on).

- Use lowercase for column and tables names, as well as variable names.

Formatting SQL Code

White space is important for readability. Put spaces on both sides of an equal sign or a comparison operator. All examples in this book use a monospaced font (Courier), or fixed-width font, that makes the formatting easier to read. Proportionally spaced fonts can hide spaces and make it difficult to line up clauses. Most text and programming editors use monospaced fonts by default.

Placing the various clauses of a statement in separate lines helps outline the structure of a statement. Following are formatting examples used throughout this book.

IN QUERIES

For SELECT statements, right align keywords (for example, SELECT, FROM, WHERE, ORDER BY), as in this example.

```
SELECT *
  FROM course
 WHERE prerequisite IS NULL
 ORDER BY course_no
```

IN DML STATEMENTS

For DML statements, right align keywords (for example, INSERT in INSERT INTO, VALUES, SELECT). List columns on a separate line, indenting the open parentheses two spaces. Align columns underneath each other, putting only a few columns on each line, as in this example.

```
INSERT INTO zipcode
  (zip, created_by, created_date,
   modified_by, modified_date)
VALUES
  ('11111', USER, SYSDATE,
   USER, SYSDATE)
```

IN DDL STATEMENTS

When using CREATE TABLE and defining columns, or when using ALTER to alter a table, indent the second line and all other lines thereafter two spaces, as in this example.

```
CREATE TABLE toy
  (description          VARCHAR2(15) NOT NULL,
   last_purchase_date   DATE,
   remaining_quantity   NUMBER(6))
```

When creating a table from another, right align keywords (for example, CREATE, SELECT, FROM, WHERE), as in this example.

```
CREATE TABLE jan_99_enrollment AS
SELECT *
  FROM enrollment
 WHERE 1 = 2
```

COMMENTS

Comments are very important in SQL code. Comments should explain the main sections of a program or SQL statement and any major logic or business rules that are involved or nontrivial.

I suggest that you use the -- comments instead of /* comments. You cannot embed /* comments within /* comments, so it is easier to comment out a set of code for debugging by using the /* comments if the code has only -- comments.

SQL Developer

You can configure SQL Developer to automatically comply with the guidelines you set by selecting Tools, Preferences, SQL Formatter, and then changing the appropriate settings. Then, when you choose the Format menu (or press Ctrl+F7), your code is formatted automatically.

SQL*Plus Command Reference

SQL*Plus commands are particularly useful when you write scripts. The most commonly used SQL*Plus commands are explained in this appendix so you can gain a better understanding of their value in the context of SQL scripts. This appendix also lists the SQL*Plus commands supported in SQL Developer.

A section on formatting in SQL*Plus provides an overview of the fundamental report and result output capabilities. In Chapter 2, "SQL: The Basics," you learned about editing statements using Windows Notepad; this appendix explains some of the features of the SQL*Plus line editor to round out your understanding of SQL*Plus.

SQL*Plus Commands Supported in SQL Developer

SQL Developer emulates SQL*Plus as much as possible; any unsupported command is ignored. Table C.1 lists the currently supported commands. Some of these commands behave differently in SQL Developer than in SQL*Plus. For more details on the individual commands, refer to the alphabetical listing of commands in the section, "SQL*Plus Commands."

TABLE C.1   SQL*Plus Commands Supported in SQL Developer

COMMAND	PURPOSE
@ and @@	Runs script and runs nested script respectively.
ACC[EPT]	Requires input of a variable for later reuse in the script.
CLEAR SCREEN	Clears the screen.
CONN[ECT]	Connects to another user. When executing using the Run Script icon, the commands after CONNECT are run in the new schema, but the SQL Worksheet is remains with the original connection.
DEF[INE]	Defines a variable. Also used in SET DEFINE ON|OFF to redefine substitution values.
DESC[RIBE]	Describes the structure of the object; not all object types are supported in SQL Developer.

TABLE C.1 Continued

COMMAND	PURPOSE
SET ECHO	Controls whether commands are displayed while the script is executing.
EXEC[UTE]	Executes a PL/SQL program.
EXIT	Disconnects the user and exits SQL*Plus back to the operating system. Within SQL Developer, does not end session or exit SQL Developer. Both SQL*Plus and SQL Developer issues an implicit COMMIT.
HO[ST]	In SQL Developer, executes an operating system batch file.
PRINT	Displays the bind variable's current value.
PROMPT	Sends a message to the user's screen
QUIT	See EXIT.
REM[ARK]	SQL*Plus script comment.
SET AUTOTRACE	Captures tuning information.
SET FEED[BACK]	Displays the number of records returned by the query.
SET NULL text	Substitutes the given text for any null value to help distinguish null values.
SET PAU[SE]	Controls the display of text and execution of commands by prompting the user.
SET TERM[OUT]	Controls the display of output.
SET TIMI[NG]	Turns on/off the timing statistics.
SET VER[IFY]	Controls substitution variables.
START	See @and @@.
UNDEF[INE]	Undefines a SQL*Plus variable.
SHOW USER	Displays the current user with the SHOW USER command.
VAR[IABLE]	Declares a bind variable.
WHENEVER	Performs an action on an error condition in a script.

SQL*Plus Commands

The following are some of the most commonly used commands available with SQL*Plus. Some of them are discussed in Chapter 2 and Chapter 14, "The Data Dictionary, Scripting, and Reporting." This list is not intended to be a thorough guide to SQL*Plus commands, and some of the listed commands take additional parameters beyond what this appendix describes.

Note that certain SQL*Plus commands can be toggled on or off (for example, ECHO, FEED-BACK) or changed from one value to another with the SET command (for example, LINESIZE). You can see all the current values of the variables and settings by typing SHOW ALL at the SQL*Plus prompt. All letters that appear in square brackets are optional.

@ ("AT") AND @@ (DOUBLE "AT" SIGN)

The "at" symbol (@) precedes a file name to run a SQL script. It is equivalent to the START command.

An @@ command runs a nested command file and runs in the same directory path as the calling script (for example, @@filename[.ext]).

> Do not confuse the @ START command with the connect identifier. The @ connect identifier is used in conjunction with the CONNECT command mentioned in Chaper 2 and Chapter 15, "Security."

&VARIABLENAME

The ampersand (&) symbol is used as a substitution variable. Use the SET DEFINE OFF command to turn off the use of the ampersand as the substitution variable.

&&VARIABLENAME

The double ampersand symbol (&&) is a substitution variable, but it avoids reprompting. The variable is declared for the duration of a SQL*Plus session. Use UNDEFINE to undefine a variable and allow for reprompting.

/

The forward slash is entered at the SQL*Plus prompt to execute the current SQL statement or PL/SQL block in the buffer. It must be in the first column of the line. (See also "RUN.")

ACC[EPT] VARIABLENAME

The ACCEPT command reads a line of input and stores it in a user variable.

A[PPEND]

The APPEND command appends text at the end of a line. This is a SQL*Plus line editor command.

C[HANGE]

The CHANGE command changes text on the line, indicated by following the CHANGE command with a forward slash, the old text, another forward slash, and the new text. This is a SQL*Plus line editor command.

CL[EAR] BUF[FER]

The CLEAR BUFFER command clears all lines of a SQL statement from the buffer.

CL[EAR] COL[UMNS]

The CLEAR COLUMNS command clears all formatting of columns issued previously during the current session.

CL[EAR] SCR[EEN]

The CLEAR SCREEN command clears the entire screen of all commands.

COL[UMN]

The COLUMN command shows the display attributes for all columns. To show a specific column, use COLUMN columnname. To reset the attributes, use COLUMN columnname CLEAR command. (See also "FOR[MAT] formatmodel.")

CONN[ECT]

When the CONNECT command is followed by a user ID, password, and the connect identifier (if any), it allows you to connect to the Oracle database as another user, and it closes the active session for the current user. You can also use the DISCONNECT command to close an active session.

COPY

COPY allows you to copy results between tables or databases. You can create or append rows to existing tables or create new tables.

DEF[INE] [VARIABLENAME]

The DEFINE command defines a SQL*Plus variable and stores it in a CHAR data type variable. You can use a number of predefined variables. For example, _USER shows the current user name, _CONNECT_IDENTIFIER displays the connect identifier (DB name), and _DATE displays the current date. These predefined variables are useful in SQL scripts and in the SET SQLPROMPT command. Without a variable name, DEFINE shows all the defined variables. SET DEFINE defines the substitution character—by default, the ampersand symbol (&). SET DEFINE OFF turns off the use of the substitution character.

DEL

The DEL command deletes the current line in the buffer. This command is applicable to the SQL*Plus line editor.

DESC[RIBE]

The DESCRIBE command describes the structure of a table, view, or stored object, detailing its columns and their data types and lengths.

ED[IT] [FILENAME.EXT]

The EDIT command invokes the editor specified in SQL*Plus, opening a file with the current SQL statement. You can edit a specific file by executing the EDIT command followed by a file-name.

EXE[CUTE] STATEMENT

The EXECUTE command executes a single PL/SQL statement, such as a packaged or stand-alone procedure.

EXIT

The EXIT command disconnects the current user from the database and closes the SQL*Plus software. The EXIT command returns control to the operating system in SQL*Plus. This command does not end your session in SQL Developer. The EXIT command in both programs issues an implicit commit.

FOR[MAT] FORMATMODEL

The FORMAT command, together with the COLUMN command, specifies the display format of a column. The following are examples.

```
COL "Last Name" FORMAT A30
COL cost FORMAT $999.99
COL description FORMAT A20
```

GET FILENAME[.EXT]

The GET command loads a file into the SQL*Plus buffer.

HELP [TOPIC]

The HELP command accesses the SQL*Plus help system.

HO[ST]

The HOST command switches to the operating system directory, where you can run an operating system command. When the operating system command is complete, HOST returns you to SQL*Plus. Depending on the operating system, you can specify ! or $ instead of the HOST command.

I[NPUT]

The INPUT command adds one or more lines to the current SQL statement. This command is applicable to the SQL*Plus line editor.

L[IST] [N|N M|N *|N LAST|*|*N| *LAST|LAST]

The LIST command lists the contents of the buffer. L n lists line n; n m lists lines n through m; n* lists lines n through the current line (as indicated by an asterisk); n LAST lists line n through the last line; * lists the current line; *n lists the current line through line n; and * LAST lists the current line through the last line.

PASSWORD [USERNAME]

The PASSWORD command changes the password without displaying it.

PRI[NT] [VARIABLE]

The PRINT command displays a bind variable created with the VARIABLE command.

PROMPT [TEXT]

The PROMPT command sends the specified message or a blank line to the user's screen.

REM[ARK]

The REMARK command begins a comment in a command file.

REP[LACE]

The REPLACE command is used in conjunction with the SAVE command to save a SQL statement to an existing file and overwrite it. The syntax is as follows.

```
SAVE filename[.sql] REPLACE
```

RUN

The RUN command lists and executes a SQL command in the SQL buffer. (See also "/.")

SAV[E] FILENAME[.EXT]

When followed by a file name, the SAVE command saves the file to the operating system.

SET AUTO[COMMIT]

You can set the AUTOCOMMIT command for a session to automatically commit all DML statements rather than having to issue an explicit COMMIT command.

SET DEFINE [ON|OFF]

The SET DEFINE command turns the use of the substitution character on and off. See also "DEF[INE] [variablename]."

SET ECHO [OFF|ON]

The SET ECHO command controls whether the commands in a SQL*Plus script are shown when the script is executed.

SET FEED[BACK] [6|N|OFF|ON]

The SET FEEDBACK command displays the number of records returned by a query when a query selects at least n records.

SET LIN[ESIZE] [80|N]

The SET LINESIZE command sets the number of characters that SQL*Plus displays on a line before beginning a new line.

SET MARKUP HTML ON SPOOL ON

The SET MARKUP command indicates that the output is formatted in HTML and places the appropriate tags in the output file.

SET PAGES[IZE] [14|N]

The SET PAGESIZE command sets the number of lines from the top title to the end of the page. The value 0 suppresses SQL*Plus formatting information, such as headings.

SET PAU[SE] [OFF|ON|TEXT]

The SET PAUSE command allows control of scrolling and text displayed during a pause.

SET SQLPROMPT

The SET SQLPROMPT command changes the SQL*Plus prompt. You may find it convenient to change the prompt, for example, if you frequently switch user accounts and want to set it to the current login account with SET SQLPROMPT _USER> . To include the instance name, use SET SQLPROMPT _USER'@'_CONNECT_IDENTIFIER>.

SET TERM[OUT] [OFF|ON]

The SET TERMOUT command controls the display of output.

SET TIME [ON|OFF]

The SET TIME command shows the current time.

SET TIMING [ON|OFF]

The SET TIMING command turns on or off the display of timing statistics.

SET VER[IFY] [OFF|ON]

The SET VERIFY command controls whether SQL*Plus lists text of a command before and after SQL*Plus replaces substitution variables with values.

SHO[W] ALL

The SHOW command lists the values of all SQL*Plus system variables.

SHO[W] USER

The SHOW USER command is also useful for displaying the current login name.

SHUTDOWN

The SHUTDOWN command shuts down an Oracle database instance.

SPO[OL] {FILENAME[.EXT] [CRE[ATE]|REP[LACE]|APP[END]]|OFF|OUT}

When you issue the SPOOL command followed by a file name, all commands subsequently issued in SQL*Plus are written to the file. The SPOOL OFF command stops writing to the file. If you do not specify an extension, the default extension is LIS or LST.

START {FILENAME[.EXT]|URL}

When followed by a file name, the START command executes the file. This is the same as the @ symbol.

STARTUP

The STARTUP command starts up an Oracle instance and optionally mounts and opens the database.

UNDEFINE VARIABLENAME

The UNDEFINE command deletes a user variable that was explicitly defined with the DEFINE command or implicitly with the & or && substitution variables.

WHENEVER OSERROR

The OSERROR command exits SQL*Plus if an operating system command generates an error.

WHENEVER SQLERROR

The SQLERROR command exits SQL*Plus if a SQL command generates an error.

Predefined SQL*Plus Variables

Oracle has a number of predefined system variables. You can reference these variables during a SQL*Plus session or during the execution of a script. The following DEFINE command shows all the system variables available in Oracle 11g.

```
SQL> DEFINE
DEFINE _DATE            = "27-MAR-08" (CHAR)
DEFINE _CONNECT_IDENTIFIER = "orcl" (CHAR)
DEFINE _USER            = "STUDENT" (CHAR)
DEFINE _PRIVILEGE       = "" (CHAR)
DEFINE _SQLPLUS_RELEASE = "1101000600" (CHAR)
DEFINE _EDITOR          = "Notepad" (CHAR)
DEFINE _O_VERSION       = "Oracle 11g Enterprise Edition
                          Release 11.1.0.6.0 - Production
   With the Partitioning, OLAP, Data Mining and Real Application
   Testing options" (CHAR)
DEFINE _O_RELEASE       = "1101000600" (CHAR)
DEFINE _RC              = "0" (CHAR)
```

These predefined variables are also useful if you want to change your SQL*Plus prompt from the default SQL> prompt. For example, if you want to always see which user account and instance you are connected to, you can change the default prompt with the SET SQLPROMPT command and the _USER and _CONNECT_IDENTIFIER system variables. In the following example, the prompt displays the current user followed by the @ symbol, the instance name, and the > symbol.

```
SQL> SET SQLPROMPT _USER'@'_CONNECT_IDENTIFIER>
STUDENT@orcl>
```

If you change login during your SQL*Plus session to a different user account, the login automatically reflects the new value. This is useful if you frequently switch user accounts and database instances; it helps you keep track of where you are currently logged in.

The LOGIN.SQL and GLOGIN.SQL Files

If you would like to always keep certain SQL*Plus settings in effect, you can place those commands in either a login.sql or glogin.sql (global login file for all users) file. These files work much like other SQL*Plus scripts. You find the login.sql or glogin.sql file in the sqlplus\admin subdirectory of your Oracle home directory.

Formatting Output in SQL*Plus

The SQL*Plus COLUMN command allows you to change the column heading and format the query result. These formatting options are useful in SQL*Plus and improve readability.

FORMATTING THE QUERY RESULT

To allow better viewing of the query result, you can use the COLUMN command with the FORMAT clause to change the formatting of the column. The syntax of the COLUMN command is as follows.

```
COLUMN columnname FORMAT formatmodel
```

The COLUMN keyword can be abbreviated as COL. columnname indicates the name of the column or the column alias. If you choose a mixed-case column alias or one that contains spaces, you must enclose it in double quotation marks.

formatmodel allows for formatting of numeric and alphanumeric columns. For alphanumeric columns, it consists of the letter A and a column width. Numeric columns allow formatting for $ signs and commas.

To format the alphanumeric LAST_NAME column of the STUDENT table to a width of 20 characters, you would issue the following command.

```
COLUMN last_name FORMAT A20
```

The A20 formatmodel indicates that you want the column formatted in alphanumeric format, with a maximum width of 20 characters. If any value does not fit within the column, it will wrap. If you prefer that the values get truncated, use the SET WRAP OFF command or the TRUNCATED option of the FORMAT command.

```
COLUMN last_name FORMAT A5 TRUNCATED
```

Optionally, you can wrap whole words with the COLUMN command.

```
COLUMN description FORMAT A20 WORD_WRAPPED
```

The effect on text such as "Intro to the BASIC Language" is as follows.

```
Intro to the BASIC
Language
```

Following is an example of a numeric format model that formats the COST column with a leading dollar sign and separates the thousands with a comma.

```
COL cost FORMAT $9,999.99
```

The following are some of the results of using this formatmodel on different values.

```
   945.99    $945.99
  1945.99  $1,945.99
 10945.99 ##########
```

Notice that the last value cannot fit within the specified column width of the formatmodel, and SQL*Plus indicates this overflow with a pound (#) symbol for each allowed digit.

Alphanumeric values are displayed left justified, and numeric values are shown right justified.

To display the current attributes of a column, you use the COLUMN command with the column name.

```
COLUMN cost
COLUMN    cost ON
FORMAT    $9,999.99
```

To show the attributes of all columns, enter the COLUMN command without a column name or alias. To reset the display attributes to their default, use the following syntax.

```
COL cost CLEAR
```

To reset the display attributes for all columns, issue the CLEAR COLUMNS command.

You can temporarily suppress the display attributes and return them to the default values with the following syntax.

```
COL cost OFF
```

To restore the attributes, use the COL cost ON command.

To give another column the same attributes as an existing column, you can copy the attributes with the LIKE clause of the COLUMN command. The FIRST_NAME column obtains the identical display attributes.

```
COL last_name FORMAT A10
COL first_name LIKE last_name
```

CHANGING THE COLUMN HEADING

You can change the column heading with the HEADING clause of the COLUMN command. The syntax is as follows.

```
COLUMN columnname HEADING columnheading
```

To display a heading over more than one line, you use the vertical bar (|) where a new line begins.

```
COL last_name HEADING STUDENT|LAST|NAME
```

```
STUDENT
LAST
NAME
--------
Crocitto
Landry
```

Editing in SQL*Plus

To use your default operating system editor, type EDIT at the SQL*Plus prompt. EDIT loads the contents of the SQL*Plus buffer into the default editor.

You can start and create a new file with the EDIT command, which invokes the editor.

```
SQL> EDIT
```

If you load an existing file with the user-supplied file name, that file is opened for editing. SQL*Plus supplies the extension .sql by default.

```
SQL> EDIT create_table_cat
```

 To load the SQL*Plus buffer contents into a text editor other than the SQL*Plus default editor, use the SQL*Plus DEFINE _EDITOR command. For example, the following command makes Notepad your default editor.

```
SQL> DEFINE _EDITOR = notepad
```

SQL*Plus Line Editor Editing Commands

You can edit SQL commands that have been stored in the SQL*Plus buffer from within SQL*Plus by using the SQL*Plus line editor. Editing statements one line at a time is arcane but occasionally comes in handy. To modify a statement, you need to indicate which line to change and then use an editing command to execute the change. For example, at the SQL prompt, type and execute the following statement to retrieve a list of course numbers.

```
SELECT course_no
  FROM course
```

SQL*Plus stores the last SQL command you typed in the *SQL buffer*. You can re-execute a statement by just pressing /. The statement stays in the buffer until you enter another SQL command. You can use the SQL*Plus LIST command, or simply the letter L, to list the contents of the buffer.

```
SQL>LIST
  1 SELECT course_no
  2*  FROM course
```

The semicolon and the forward slash, both of which execute the statement, are not stored in the buffer. The asterisk next to the number 2 indicates this is the current line in the buffer.

For example, if you want to retrieve a list of descriptions instead courses, change the column course_no to description, using the line editor. To make a change, indicate to the line editor which line to make current. To change it to the first line, type the number 1 at the SQL prompt.

```
SQL> 1
  1* SELECT course_no
```

Just the first line of the two-line statement is displayed, and the asterisk indicates that this is now the current line in the buffer. You can make a change to that line with the CHANGE command.

```
SQL>CHANGE /course_no/description
```

The newly changed line is presented back to you.

```
  1* SELECT description
```

The CHANGE command is followed by a forward slash, followed by the text you want to change and separated from the new text with another forward slash. The abbreviated command for the CHANGE command is the letter C.

You are now ready to execute your statement to produce the new result set. Because you are not typing the statement for the first time, you cannot use the semicolon. Type a forward slash to execute the statement instead. The forward slash always executes the current SQL statement in the buffer.

Certain commands you have learned so far, such as the LIST command, are not SQL, but SQL*Plus commands. Only SQL statements—never SQL*Plus commands—are saved in the buffer. Table C.2 lists SQL*Plus line editor commands.

TABLE C.2   SQL*Plus Line Editor Commands

COMMAND	ABBREVIATION	PURPOSE
Append text	A text	Adds text at the end of a line
Change /old/new	C /old/new	Changes old to new in a line
Change /text	C /text	Deletes text from a line
Clear Buffer	CL Buff	Deletes all lines
Del	(none)	Deletes a line
Input	I	Adds one or more lines
Input text	I text	Adds a line that consists of text
List	L	Lists all lines in the SQL buffer
List n	L n or n	Lists n line
List *	L *	Lists the current line
List last	L last	Lists the last line
List m n	L m n	Lists a range of lines (m to n)

Using the SQL*Plus Line Editor to Save and Retrieve Files

To save the current contents of the SQL*Plus buffer to a command script, use the SAVE command. The .sql extension is attached to the file name by default.

```
SQL> SAVE create_table_cat
```

To save the contents of the SQL*Plus buffer to a file that already exists, use the SAVE command with the REPLACE option.

```
SQL> SAVE create_table_cat REPLACE
```

If you want to retrieve a file and place the contents of a command script into the SQL*Plus buffer, use the SQL*Plus GET command.

```
SQL> GET create_table_cat
```

Command Scripts in SQL*Plus

If you have a set of commands (SQL*Plus, SQL, or a combination of the two) that may be used more than once, you can store them in a command script. A *command script* is a text file that can be run from the SQL*Plus command prompt as follows.

```
SQL> @create_table_cat.sql
```

Alternatively, the script can be executed from the operating system command prompt. The following command invokes SQL*Plus from the Windows operating system command line and connects via the STUDENT account and the learn password. It executes the file CREATE_TABLE_CAT.SQL, located in the c:\guest directory. The .sql extension is optional.

```
C:\>sqlplus student/learn @c:\guest\create_table_cat.sql
```

STUDENT Database Schema

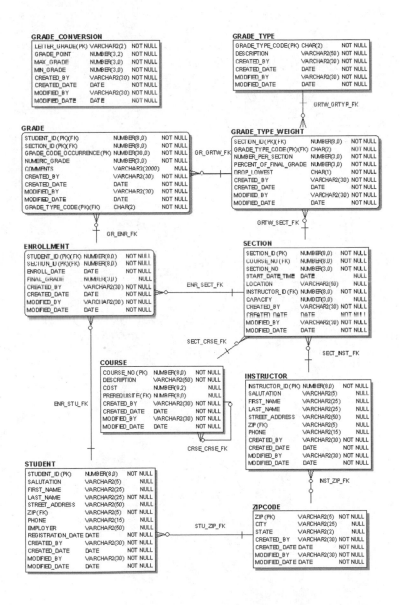

GRADE_CONVERSION

LETTER_GRADE(PK)	VARCHAR2(2)	NOT NULL
GRADE_POINT	NUMBER(3,2)	NOT NULL
MAX_GRADE	NUMBER(3,0)	NOT NULL
MIN_GRADE	NUMBER(3,0)	NOT NULL
CREATED_BY	VARCHAR2(30)	NOT NULL
CREATED_DATE	DATE	NOT NULL
MODIFIED_BY	VARCHAR2(30)	NOT NULL
MODIFIED_DATE	DATE	NOT NULL

GRADE_TYPE

GRADE_TYPE_CODE(PK)	CHAR(2)	NOT NULL
DESCRIPTION	VARCHAR2(50)	NOT NULL
CREATED_BY	VARCHAR2(30)	NOT NULL
CREATED_DATE	DATE	NOT NULL
MODIFIED_BY	VARCHAR2(30)	NOT NULL
MODIFIED_DATE	DATE	NOT NULL

GRTW_GRTYP_FK

GRADE

STUDENT_ID (PK)(FK)	NUMBER(8,0)	NOT NULL
SECTION_ID (PK)(FK)	NUMBER(8,0)	NOT NULL
GRADE_CODE_OCCURRENCE(PK)	NUMBER(30,0)	NOT NULL
NUMERIC_GRADE	NUMBER(3,0)	NOT NULL
COMMENTS	VARCHAR2(2000)	NULL
CREATED_BY	VARCHAR2(30)	NOT NULL
CREATED_DATE	DATE	NOT NULL
MODIFIED_BY	VARCHAR2(30)	NOT NULL
MODIFIED_DATE	DATE	NOT NULL
GRADE_TYPE_CODE(PK)(FK)	CHAR(2)	NOT NULL

GR_GRTW_FK

GRADE_TYPE_WEIGHT

SECTION_ID (PK)(FK)	NUMBER(8,0)	NOT NULL
GRADE_TYPE_CODE(PK)(FK)	CHAR(2)	NOT NULL
NUMBER_PER_SECTION	NUMBER(3,0)	NOT NULL
PERCENT_OF_FINAL_GRADE	NUMBER(3,0)	NOT NULL
DROP_LOWEST	CHAR(1)	NOT NULL
CREATED_BY	VARCHAR2(30)	NOT NULL
CREATED_DATE	DATE	NOT NULL
MODIFIED_BY	VARCHAR2(30)	NOT NULL
MODIFIED_DATE	DATE	NOT NULL

GR_ENR_FK

GRTW_SECT_FK

ENROLLMENT

STUDENT_ID (PK)(FK)	NUMBER(8,0)	NOT NULL
SECTION_ID (PK)(FK)	NUMBER(8,0)	NOT NULL
ENROLL_DATE	DATE	NOT NULL
FINAL_GRADE	NUMBER(3,0)	NULL
CREATED_BY	VARCHAR2(30)	NOT NULL
CREATED_DATE	DATE	NOT NULL
MODIFIED_BY	VARCHAR2(30)	NOT NULL
MODIFIED_DATE	DATE	NOT NULL

ENR_SECT_FK

SECTION

SECTION_ID (PK)	NUMBER(8,0)	NOT NULL
COURSE_NO (FK)	NUMBER(8,0)	NOT NULL
SECTION_NO	NUMBER(3,0)	NOT NULL
START_DATE_TIME	DATE	NULL
LOCATION	VARCHAR2(50)	NULL
INSTRUCTOR_ID (FK)	NUMBER(8,0)	NOT NULL
CAPACITY	NUMBER(3,0)	NULL
CREATED_BY	VARCHAR2(30)	NOT NULL
CREATED_DATE	DATE	NOT NULL
MODIFIED_BY	VARCHAR2(30)	NOT NULL
MODIFIED_DATE	DATE	NOT NULL

SECT_CRSE_FK

SECT_NST_FK

COURSE

COURSE_NO (PK)	NUMBER(8,0)	NOT NULL
DESCRIPTION	VARCHAR2(50)	NOT NULL
COST	NUMBER(9,2)	NULL
PREREQUISITE(FK)	NUMBER(8,0)	NULL
CREATED_BY	VARCHAR2(30)	NOT NULL
CREATED_DATE	DATE	NOT NULL
MODIFIED_BY	VARCHAR2(30)	NOT NULL
MODIFIED_DATE	DATE	NOT NULL

ENR_STU_FK

CRSE_CRSE_FK

INSTRUCTOR

INSTRUCTOR_ID(PK)	NUMBER(8,0)	NOT NULL
SALUTATION	VARCHAR2(5)	NULL
FIRST_NAME	VARCHAR2(25)	NULL
LAST_NAME	VARCHAR2(25)	NULL
STREET_ADDRESS	VARCHAR2(50)	NULL
ZIP (FK)	VARCHAR2(5)	NULL
PHONE	VARCHAR2(15)	NULL
CREATED_BY	VARCHAR2(30)	NOT NULL
CREATED_DATE	DATE	NOT NULL
MODIFIED_BY	VARCHAR2(30)	NOT NULL
MODIFIED_DATE	DATE	NOT NULL

NST_ZIP_FK

STUDENT

STUDENT_ID (PK)	NUMBER(8,0)	NOT NULL
SALUTATION	VARCHAR2(5)	NULL
FIRST_NAME	VARCHAR2(25)	NULL
LAST_NAME	VARCHAR2(25)	NOT NULL
STREET_ADDRESS	VARCHAR2(50)	NULL
ZIP (FK)	VARCHAR2(5)	NOT NULL
PHONE	VARCHAR2(15)	NULL
EMPLOYER	VARCHAR2(50)	NULL
REGISTRATION_DATE	DATE	NOT NULL
CREATED_BY	VARCHAR2(30)	NOT NULL
CREATED_DATE	DATE	NOT NULL
MODIFIED_BY	VARCHAR2(30)	NOT NULL
MODIFIED_DATE	DATE	NOT NULL

STU_ZIP_FK

ZIPCODE

ZIP (PK)	VARCHAR2(5)	NOT NULL
CITY	VARCHAR2(25)	NULL
STATE	VARCHAR2(2)	NULL
CREATED_BY	VARCHAR2(30)	NOT NULL
CREATED_DATE	DATE	NOT NULL
MODIFIED_BY	VARCHAR2(30)	NOT NULL
MODIFIED_DATE	DATE	NOT NULL

Table and Column Descriptions

COURSE: Information for a course

COLUMN NAME	NULL	DATA TYPE	COMMENTS
COURSE_NO	NOT NULL	NUMBER(8, 0)	The unique ID for a course
DESCRIPTION	NULL	VARCHAR2(50)	The full name for this course
COST	NULL	NUMBER(9,2)	The dollar amount charged for enrollment in this course
PREREQUISITE	NULL	NUMBER(8, 0)	The ID number of the course that must be taken as a prerequisite to this course
CREATED_BY	NOT NULL	VARCHAR2(30)	Audit column—indicates the user who inserted the data
CREATED_DATE	NOT NULL	DATE	Audit column—indicates the date of the insertion
MODIFIED_BY	NOT NULL	VARCHAR2(30)	Audit column—indicates who made the last update
MODIFIED_DATE	NOT NULL	DATE	Audit column—the date of the last update

SECTION: Information for an individual section (class) of a particular course

COLUMN NAME	NULL	DATA TYPE	COMMENTS
SECTION_ID	NOT NULL	NUMBER(8,0)	The unique ID for a section
COURSE_NO	NOT NULL	NUMBER(8,0)	The course number for which this is a section
SECTION_NO	NOT NULL	NUMBER(3)	The individual section number within this course
START_DATE_TIME	NULL	DATE	The date and time when this section meets
LOCATION	NULL	VARCHAR2(50)	The meeting room for the section
INSTRUCTOR_ID	NOT NULL	NUMBER(8,0)	The ID number of the instructor who teaches this section
CAPACITY	NULL	NUMBER(3,0)	The maximum number of students allowed in this section
CREATED_BY	NOT NULL	VARCHAR2(30)	Audit column—indicates the user who inserted the data
CREATED_DATE	NOT NULL	DATE	Audit column—indicates the date of the insertion
MODIFIED_BY	NOT NULL	VARCHAR2(30)	Audit column—indicates who made the last update
MODIFIED_DATE	NOT NULL	DATE	Audit column—the date of the last update

STUDENT: Profile information for a student

COLUMN NAME	NULL	DATA TYPE	COMMENTS
STUDENT_ID	NOT NULL	NUMBER(8,0)	The unique ID for a student
SALUTATION	NULL	VARCHAR2(5)	This student's title (for example, Ms., Mr., Dr.)
FIRST_NAME	NULL	VARCHAR2(25)	This student's first name
LAST_NAME	NOT NULL	VARCHAR2(25)	This student's last name
STREET_ADDRESS	NULL	VARCHAR2(50)	This student's street address
ZIP	NOT NULL	VARCHAR2(5)	The zip code for this student
PHONE	NULL	VARCHAR2(15)	The phone number for this student, including area code
EMPLOYER	NULL	VARCHAR2(50)	The name of the company where this student is employed
REGISTRATION_DATE	NOT NULL	DATE	The date this student registered in the program
CREATED_BY	NOT NULL	VARCHAR2(30)	Audit column—indicates the user who inserted the data

COLUMN NAME	NULL	DATA TYPE	COMMENTS
CREATED_DATE	NOT NULL	DATE	Audit column—indicates the date of the insertion
MODIFIED_BY	NOT NULL	VARCHAR2(30)	Audit column—indicates who made the last update
MODIFIED_DATE	NOT NULL	DATE	Audit column—the date of the last update

ENROLLMENT: Information for a student registered for a particular section (class)

COLUMN NAME	NULL	DATA TYPE	COMMENTS
STUDENT_ID	NOT NULL	NUMBER(8,0)	The unique ID for a student
SECTION_ID	NOT NULL	NUMBER(8,0)	The unique ID for a section
ENROLL_DATE	NOT NULL	DATE	The date this student registered for this section
FINAL_GRADE	NULL	NUMBER(3,0)	The final grade given to this student for all work in this section (class)
CREATED_BY	NOT NULL	VARCHAR2(30)	Audit column—indicates the user who inserted the data
CREATED_DATE	NOT NULL	DATE	Audit column—indicates the date of the insertion
MODIFIED_BY	NOT NULL	VARCHAR2(30)	Audit column—indicates who made the last update
MODIFIED_DATE	NOT NULL	DATE	Audit column—the date of the last update

INSTRUCTOR: Profile information for an instructor

COLUMN NAME	NULL	DATA TYPE	COMMENTS
INSTRUCTOR_ID	NOT NULL	NUMBER(8)	The unique ID for an instructor
SALUTATION	NULL	VARCHAR2(5)	This instructor's title (for example, Mr., Ms., Dr., Rev.)
FIRST_NAME	NULL	VARCHAR2(25)	This instructor's first name
LAST_NAME	NULL	VARCHAR2(25)	This instructor's last name
STREET_ADDRESS	NULL	VARCHAR2(50)	This instructor's street address
ZIP	NULL	VARCHAR2(5)	The zip code for this instructor
PHONE	NULL	VARCHAR2(15)	The phone number for this instructor, including area code
CREATED_BY	NOT NULL	VARCHAR2(30)	Audit column—indicates the user who inserted the data

COLUMN NAME	NULL	DATA TYPE	COMMENTS
CREATED_DATE	NOT NULL	DATE	Audit column—indicates the date of the insertion
MODIFIED_BY	NOT NULL	VARCHAR2(30)	Audit column—indicates who made the last update
MODIFIED_DATE	NOT NULL	DATE	Audit column—the date of the last update

ZIPCODE: City, state, and zip code information

COLUMN NAME	NULL	DATA TYPE	COMMENTS
ZIP	NOT NULL	VARCHAR2(5)	The zip code, unique for a city and state
CITY	NULL	VARCHAR2(25)	The city name for this zip code
STATE	NULL	VARCHAR2(2)	The postal abbreviation for the U.S. state
CREATED_BY	NOT NULL	VARCHAR2(30)	Audit column—indicates the user who inserted the data
CREATED_DATE	NOT NULL	DATE	Audit column—indicates the date of the insertion
MODIFIED_BY	NOT NULL	VARCHAR2(30)	Audit column—indicates who made the last update
MODIFIED_DATE	NOT NULL	DATE	Audit column—the date of the last update

GRADE_TYPE: Lookup table of a grade type (code) and its description

COLUMN NAME	NULL	DATA TYPE	COMMENTS
GRADE_TYPE_ CODE	NOT NULL	CHAR(2)	The unique code that identifies a category of grade (for example, MT, HW)
DESCRIPTION	NOT NULL	VARCHAR2(50)	The description for this code (for example, Midterm, Homework)
CREATED_BY	NOT NULL	VARCHAR2(30)	Audit column—indicates the user who inserted the data
CREATED_DATE	NOT NULL	DATE	Audit column—indicates the date of the insertion
MODIFIED_BY	NOT NULL	VARCHAR2(30)	Audit column—indicates who made the last update
MODIFIED_DATE	NOT NULL	DATE	Audit column—the date of the last update

GRADE_TYPE_WEIGHT: Information on how the final grade for a particular section is computed (for example, the midterm constitutes 50 percent, the quiz 10 percent, and the final examination 40 percent of the final grade).

COLUMN NAME	NULL	DATA TYPE	COMMENTS
SECTION_ID	NOT NULL	NUMBER(8)	The unique ID for a section
GRADE_TYPE_CODE	NOT NULL	CHAR(2)	The code that identifies a category of grade
NUMBER_PER_SECTION	NOT NULL	NUMBER(3)	Identifies how many of these grade types can be used in this section (for example, there may be three quizzes)
PERCENT_OF_FINAL_GRADE	NOT NULL	NUMBER(3)	The percentage this category of grade contributes to the final grade
DROP_LOWEST	NOT NULL	CHAR(1)	Is the lowest grade in this type removed when determining the final grade? (Y/N)
CREATED_BY	NOT NULL	VARCHAR2(30)	Audit column—indicates the user who inserted the data
CREATED_DATE	NOT NULL	DATE	Audit column—indicates the date of the insertion
MODIFIED_BY	NOT NULL	VARCHAR2(30)	Audit column—indicates who made the last update
MODIFIED_DATE	NOT NULL	DATE	Audit column—the date of the last update

GRADE: The individual grades a student received for a particular section (class)

COLUMN NAME	NULL	DATA TYPE	COMMENTS
STUDENT_ID	NOT NULL	NUMBER(8)	The unique ID for a student
SECTION_ID	NOT NULL	NUMBER(8)	The unique ID for a section
GRADE_TYPE_CODE	NOT NULL	CHAR(2)	The code that identifies a category of grade
GRADE_CODE_OCCURRENCE	NOT NULL	NUMBER(38)	The sequence number of one grade type for one section (for example, for multiple assignments numbered 1, 2, 3, and so on)
NUMERIC_GRADE	NOT NULL	NUMBER(3)	Numeric grade value (for example, 70, 75)
COMMENTS	NULL	VARCHAR2(2000)	Instructor's comments on this grade
CREATED_BY	NOT NULL	VARCHAR2(30)	Audit column—indicates the user who inserted the data
CREATED_DATE	NOT NULL	DATE	Audit column—indicates the date of the insertion

COLUMN NAME	NULL	DATA TYPE	COMMENTS
MODIFIED_BY	NOT NULL	VARCHAR2(30)	Audit column—indicates who made the last update
MODIFIED_DATE	NOT NULL	DATE	Audit column—the date of the last update

GRADE_CONVERSION: Converts a number grade to a letter grade

COLUMN NAME	NULL	DATA TYPE	COMMENTS
LETTER_GRADE	NOT NULL	VARCHAR(2)	The unique grade, as a letter (A, A?, B, B+, and so on)
GRADE_POINT	NOT NULL	NUMBER(3,2)	The number grade, on a scale from 0 (F) to 4 (A)
MAX_GRADE	NOT NULL	NUMBER(3)	The highest grade number that makes this letter grade
MIN_GRADE	NOT NULL	NUMBER(3)	The lowest grade number that makes this letter grade
CREATED_BY	NOT NULL	VARCHAR2(30)	Audit column—indicates the user who inserted the data
CREATED_DATE	NOT NULL	DATE	Audit column—indicates the date of the insertion
MODIFIED_BY	NOT NULL	VARCHAR2(30)	Audit column—indicates who made the last update
MODIFIED_DATE	NOT NULL	DATE	Audit column—the date of the last update

Additional Example Tables

Throughout this book, some exercises make use of tables that are not part of the STUDENT schema diagram listed in Appendix D, "STUDENT Database Schema." You can create these additional tables in your STUDENT schema by downloading the script sql_book_add_tables.sql from the companion Web site, located at www.oraclesqlbyexample.com. The purpose of these additional tables is to illustrate SQL concepts that could otherwise not be shown within the available data and data types in the STUDENT schema.

Chapter 4: Character, Number, and Miscellaneous Functions

GRADE_SUMMARY: Shows the use of the COALESCE function

COLUMN NAME	NULL	DATA TYPE	COMMENTS
STUDENT_ID	NULL	NUMBER(8,0)	The unique ID for a student
MIDTERM_GRADE	NULL	NUMBER(3)	The midterm grade of a student
FINALEXAM_GRADE	NULL	NUMBER(3)	The final grade of a student
QUIZ_GRADE	NULL	NUMBER(3)	The quiz grade of a student

FLOAT_TEST: Helps demonstrate the use of the BINARY_FLOAT data type

COLUMN NAME	NULL	DATA TYPE	COMMENTS
TEST	NULL	BINARY_FLOAT	The test column

Chapter 5: Date and Conversion Functions

DATE_EXAMPLE: Holds data to illustrate the use of datetime-related data types

COLUMN NAME	NULL	DATA TYPE	COMMENTS
COL_DATE	NULL	DATE	Holds data in the DATE data type
COL_TIMESTAMP	NULL	TIMESTAMP(6)	Holds data in the TIMESTAMP data type with a six-digit precision for fractional seconds
COL_TIMESTAMP_W_TZ	NULL	TIMESTAMP(6) WITH TIME ZONE	Holds data in the TIMESTAMP WITH TIME ZONE data type
COL_TIMESTAMP_W_LOCAL_TZ	NULL	TIMESTAMP(6) WITH LOCAL TIMES ZONE	Holds data in the TIMESTAMP WITH LOCAL TIME ZONE data type

CONVERSION_EXAMPLE: Helps demonstrate the effect of Oracle's implicit data type conversion

COLUMN NAME	NULL	DATA TYPE	COMMENTS
COURSE_NO	NULL	VARCHAR2(9)	The course number

MEETING: Shows the use of the OVERLAP operator

COLUMN NAME	NULL	DATA TYPE	COMMENTS
MEETING_ID	NULL	NUMBER(10)	The unique ID for a meeting
MEETING_START_DATE	NULL	DATE	The meeting's starting date and time
MEETING_END_DATE	NULL	DATE	The meeting's ending date and time

Chapter 10: Complex Joins

T1: Illustrates outer joins and full outer joins

COLUMN NAME	NULL	DATA TYPE	COMMENTS
COL1	NULL	NUMBER	Holds numeric data

T2: Illustrates outer joins and full outer joins

COLUMN NAME	NULL	DATA TYPE	COMMENTS
COL2	NULL	NUMBER	Holds numeric data

Chapter 11: Insert, Update, and Delete

INTRO_COURSE: Similar in structure to the course table and used to show examples of insert statements

COLUMN NAME	NULL	DATA TYPE	COMMENTS
COURSE_NO	NULL	NUMBER(8, 0)	The unique ID for a course
DESCRIPTION	NULL	VARCHAR2(50)	The full name for this course
COST	NULL	NUMBER(9,2)	The dollar amount charged for enrollment in this course
PREREQ_NO	NULL	NUMBER(8, 0)	The ID number of the course that must be taken as a prerequisite to this course
CREATED_BY	NULL	VARCHAR2(30)	Audit column—indicates user who inserted data
CREATED_DATE	NULL	DATE	Audit column—indicates date of insert
MODIFIED_BY	NULL	VARCHAR2(30)	Audit column—indicates who made last update
MODIFIED_DATE	NULL	DATE	Audit column—date of last update

GRADE_DISTRIBUTION: Demonstrates multitable INSERT statements

COLUMN NAME	NULL	DATA TYPE	COMMENTS
SECTION_ID	NULL	NUMBER(8)	The unique ID for a section
GRADE_A	NULL	NUMBER(4)	The number of students with grade of A
GRADE_B	NULL	NUMBER(4)	The number of students with a grade of B
GRADE_C	NULL	NUMBER(4)	The number of students with a grade of C
GRADE_D	NULL	NUMBER(4)	The number of students with a grade of D
GRADE_F	NULL	NUMBER(4)	The number of students with a grade of F

GRADE_DISTRIBUTION_NORMALIZED: Helps illustrate the use of the multitable INSERT statements

COLUMN NAME	NULL	DATA TYPE	COMMENTS
SECTION_ID	NULL	NUMBER(8)	The unique ID for a section
LETTER_GRADE	NULL	VARCHAR(2)	The unique grade as a letter (A, A-, B, B+, etc.)
NUM_OF_STUDENTS	NULL	NUMBER(4)	The number of students

EMPLOYEE: Holds employee information

COLUMN NAME	NULL	DATA TYPE	COMMENTS
EMPLOYEE_ID	NULL	NUMBER	The unique ID for an employee
NAME	NULL	VARCHAR2(10)	The employee's name
SALARY	NULL	NUMBER	The employee's salary
TITLE	NULL	VARCHAR2(10)	The employee's job title

EMPLOYEE_CHANGE: Contains changes to the EMPLOYEE table for the purpose of showing INSERT/MERGE functionality

COLUMN NAME	NULL	DATA TYPE	COMMENTS
EMPLOYEE_ID	NULL	NUMBER	The unique ID for an employee
NAME	NULL	VARCHAR2(10)	The employee's name
SALARY	NULL	NUMBER	The employee's salary
TITLE	NULL	VARCHAR2(10)	The employee's job title

SECTION_HISTORY: Lists historical data from the SECTION table to help illustrate the use of the multitable INSERT command

COLUMN NAME	NULL	DATA TYPE	COMMENTS
SECTION_ID	NOT NULL	NUMBER(8,0)	The unique ID for a section
START_DATE_TIME	NULL	DATE	The date and time on which this section meets
COURSE_NO	NOT NULL	NUMBER(8,0)	The course number for which this is a section
SECTION_NO	NOT NULL	NUMBER(3)	The individual section number within this course

CAPACITY_HISTORY: Holds historical data from the SECTION table related to the CAPACITY column; used to show the use of the multitable INSERT command

COLUMN NAME	NULL	DATA TYPE	COMMENTS
SECTION_ID	NOT NULL	NUMBER(8,0)	The unique ID for a section
LOCATION	NULL	VARCHAR2(50)	The meeting room for the section
CAPACITY	NULL	NUMBER(3,0)	The maximum number of students that can be enrolled in this section

TA: Helps illustrate a correlated update problem

COLUMN NAME	NULL	DATA TYPE	COMMENTS
ID	NULL	NUMBER	The unique ID of the table
COL1	NULL	VARCHAR2(4)	Holds alphanumeric data

TB: Helps illustrate a correlated update problem

COLUMN NAME	NULL	DATA TYPE	COMMENTS
ID	NULL	NUMBER	The unique ID the table
COL2	NULL	VARCHAR2(4)	Holds alphanumeric data

Chapter 16: Regular Expressions and Hierarchical Queries

ZIPCODE_EXAMPLE: Helps illustrate regular expression examples

COLUMN NAME	NULL	DATA TYPE	COMMENTS
ZIP	NULL	VARCHAR2(5)	The zip code

Chapter 17: Exploring Data Warehousing Features

COURSE_REVENUE: Contains data about the total revenue per course, the total number of students enrolled, and the number of sections for this course

COLUMN NAME	NULL	DATA TYPE	COMMENTS
COURSE_NO	NULL	NUMBER(8, 0)	The unique ID for a course
REVENUE	NULL	NUMBER	The revenue for this course
COURSE_FEE	NULL	NUMBER(9,2)	The course fee (course cost) of this course
NUM_ENROLLED	NULL	NUMBER	The number of students enrolled in this course
NUM_OF_SECTIONS	NULL	NUMBER	The number of sections for this course

INSTRUCTOR_SUMMARY: Holds revenue and enrollment information by instructor, year, and month

COLUMN NAME	NULL	DATA TYPE	COMMENTS
INSTRUCTOR_ID	NOT NULL	NUMBER(8,0)	The ID number of the instructor who teaches this section
SEMESTER_YEAR	NOT NULL	VARCHAR2(4)	The semester year in which this instructor teaches
SEMESTER_MONTH	NOT NULL	VARCHAR2(2)	The month in which the instructor teaches
GENDER	NULL	CHAR(1)	Gender
CAMPUS	NULL	VARCHAR2(11)	Campus location
NUM_OF_CLASSES	NULL	NUMBER	Number of sections
NUM_OF_STUDENTS	NULL	NUMBER	The number of enrolled students
REVENUE	NULL	NUMBER	Holds the generated revenue amount, computed by multiplying the course cost by number of enrolled students

MODEL_EXAMPLE: Contains data that helps illustrate inter-row calculation examples

COLUMN NAME	NULL	DATA TYPE	COMMENTS
COURSE	NULL	VARCHAR2(30)	The name of a course
GENDER	NULL	CHAR(1)	The gender of a student enrolled in course
YEAR	NULL	NUMBER	The year enrolled
ENROLL_NO	NULL	NUMBER	The number of enrolled students

Navigating the Oracle Documentation

After reading this book and performing the exercises, you will have gained significant experience and knowledge with the Oracle database. Congratulations! This book can't discuss every topic and syntax option; if it did, it would have several thousand pages. The emphasis is on highlighting the most commonly used features. What do you do to learn more about a particular topic, or what if you have further questions? One of the ways to research answers is to consult the Oracle-supplied documentation.

You might need to refer to the Oracle documentation when versions change (an inevitable fact of software development). Additional features are often added and existing functionality enhanced. Perhaps you are working with a previous Oracle version and want to check whether certain features are available. Sometimes, consulting the documentation is simply unavoidable.

Where Do You Find the Oracle Documentation?

You can download the Oracle documentation or you can look up the documentation on the Oracle Technology Network (OTN) Web site. The OTN site is Oracle's own site that contains a wealth of information, including the documentation, and it is geared toward developers and database administrators (DBAs). Before you can access the site, you must register (registration is free), at http://otn.oracle.com. After you register, you can find all Oracle documentation (including previous Oracle versions) at http://otn.oracle.com/documentation/index.html. You can also use this link: http://tahiti.oracle.com.

Figure G.1 shows the Oracle Documentation screen. This page lists all Oracle documentation and is organized by Oracle product and version. For SQL-related information, choose Oracle Database 11g.

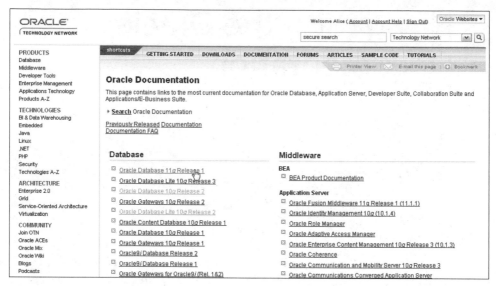

FIGURE G.1
Oracle documentation page

Navigating the Library

You can choose to download the documentation or view the library online. The library is divided into two distinct panes (see Figure G.2). The left side shows a Search box on the top to search the library for specified keywords. Alternatively, you can search in specific documentation in the Master Book List, review the Master Index and Master Glossary, or look up error messages. To search for a specific topic, review the categories below the Expand All/Collapse All links. You will find the SQL, SQL Developer, and SQL*Plus Reference manuals when you expand the Application Development, SQL and PL/SQL Languages categories.

The right side of Documentation Library highlights the useful 2 Day guides of topics in database administration and application development. On the bottom of the screen is the Supporting Documentation section, where you will also find a link to the SQL Reference manual. An additional section (not shown in Figure G.2) is a section on Database Development Clients, which contains links to SQL Developer and SQL*Plus.

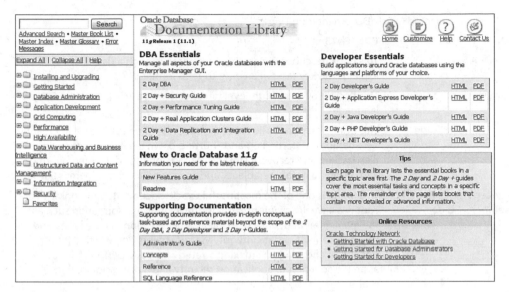

FIGURE G.2
Oracle Documentation Library page

Jump-Starting Your Search

If you do not know in which manual to look for the desired subject, the simplest thing to do is to click on the Search tab. The left side of the search tab presents a Search box that allows you to enter a word or phrase. Alternatively, you can search via the Advanced Search link, which lets you be more specific with your criteria and topic so you avoid retrieving too many matches.

The search result presents the matches considered most relevant. You can refine the results by choosing only certain books. On top of the Search result is a Help icon. When you click this icon, you find valuable tips on using the search features.

Oracle Documentation Titles

It is useful to know what topics are covered in the various Oracle manuals. This helps you evaluate the search results from the Oracle Web site or restrict the search criteria to certain manuals. Table G.1 lists of the most commonly used manuals and the notable topics covered in each.

TABLE G.1   Selected Oracle Documentation Titles

BOOK	CONTENTS
2 Day DBA	This book describes the essentials of administering a database. It explains the key tasks in an easy-to-read format.
2 Day Developer's Guide	This book provides a high-level introduction to the SQL and PL/SQL languages.
Administrator's Guide	This book describes basic database administration tasks, such as creating new databases; starting up and shutting down a database, managing files, backup and recovery, storage management; and creating, altering, and dropping database objects, and managing users and permissions.
Advanced Application Developer's Guide	This guide is one of the most useful Oracle documentation books. It contains a wealth of information for developers—information such as the management of database objects, the selection of data types, and the enforcement of data integrity via constraints. You will find information about choosing an indexing strategy for good performance as well as an introduction to application security and a discussion of PL/SQL topics.
Backup and Recovery Reference & User's Guide	These books detail backup and recovery strategies to ensure adequate protection of your database.
Concepts	This manual discusses the Oracle architecture and its core concepts and is intended for database administrators and database application developers. It explains the details of data blocks, tablespaces, the data dictionary, the database instance with startup and shutdown, the different types of database objects, data types, triggers, dependency among objects, data integrity, and security.
Data Warehousing Guide	This book covers the issues involved in designing, building, and maintaining a data warehouse. It explains the analytical functions and discusses data transformation and loading.
Error Messages	You will find most error messages in this manual, except for SQL*Plus SP2 errors. (You find those in the SQL*Plus User's Guide and Reference.) Other product-specific errors are also found in the respective Oracle product manuals.
Database Installation Guide for Windows or Installation Guide for UNIX Systems	An installation guide to installing the Oracle database software for the individual operating system environment (for example, Windows, UNIX).
Performance Tuning Guide	This manual is concerned with tuning SQL statements and the Oracle database for optimal performance. The various methods illustrate how you can collect performance statistics on your database and how to tune SQL statements.
Reference	The dynamic and static data dictionary views are listed in this book, along with the Oracle initialization parameters for the initialization file (init.ora).

TABLE G.1　Continued

BOOK	CONTENTS
SQL Language Reference	This is an alphabetical reference to all SQL commands. Furthermore, it contains a list of all functions, operators, and expressions. Diagrams show and explain the different syntax options. If you are unsure of a command's syntax options, this is the manual to consult.
Platform Guide for Windows	This text discusses the implementation of Oracle on Windows platforms.
PL/SQL Packages and Types Reference	This manual provides information about the procedures and functions of Oracle-supplied packages. For example, it provides examples and parameter listings about collecting statistics with the DBMS_STATS package.
SQL Developer User's Guide	This guide discusses the SQL Developer tool and its features.
SQL*Plus User's Guide and Reference	This guide to SQL*Plus includes all SP2 error messages, as well as a list of all SQL*Plus commands and formatting options.

Error Messages

The Oracle Error Messages manual, together with the SQL*Plus User's Guide and Reference manual, lists the most common error messages. Error messages are usually prefixed with a three-letter code that indicates the program that issued the error. It also gives you an indication of the manual in which to look for the error or which of Oracle's products causes the error. Most error messages are found in the Oracle Error Messages manual; however, some product-specific errors are found in each product's individual manual (for example, SP2 errors are found in the SQL*Plus User's Guide and Reference manual). Table G.2 lists the most common error message codes.

TABLE G.2　Common Oracle Error Message Codes

MESSAGE PREFIX	ORACLE SOFTWARE
ORA	Oracle server message
TNS	Oracle Net messages
SP2	SQL*Plus message
EXP	Export utility message
IMP	Import utility message
SQL*Loader	SQL*Loader message
KUP	External table message
RMAN	Recovery Manager message
PLS	PL/SQL message

Reading Oracle Syntax Diagrams

In Chapter 4, "Character, Number, and Miscellaneous Functions," you were introduced to a variant of BNF (Backus-Naur Form)-style syntax (refer to Table 4.1).

Most of Oracle's manuals now show the graphic syntax diagrams. To read such a diagram, you follow the path of the line, moving from the left to the right. Keywords such as commands are in uppercase and inside rectangular boxes. Required syntax always appears on the main path; an optional choice is listed above the main path. Multiple choices are indicated through multiple paths either on or above the main path.

Figure G.3 lists the partial syntax diagram of the CREATE INDEX command. As you see, the CREATE INDEX command allows for a number of choices. You can choose between the syntax options CREATE INDEX, CREATE UNIQUE INDEX, and CREATE BITMAP INDEX. The UNIQUE and BITMAP keywords are optional and let you create different types of indexes.

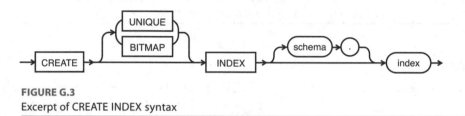

FIGURE G.3
Excerpt of CREATE INDEX syntax

Figure G.4 shows additional syntax conventions, using the example of the VALUES clause of the INSERT command. Inside circles, you find punctuation, operators, and delimiters such as commas or parentheses. Object names, expressions, parameters, and variables appear in lowercase and inside ovals. Where you are allowed to choose more than one option, the diagram has a loopback path that lets you repeat the choices. In this example, expression or the DEFAULT keyword within the set of parentheses may be repeated, but they are separated from each other by a comma.

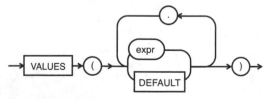

FIGURE G.4
The VALUES clause on an INSERT command

Resources

This appendix lists Oracle-related Web sites where you can explore topics in greater detail and find information beyond the scope of this book. Because Web links change frequently, also refer to the companion Web site, located at www.oraclesqlbyexample.com, for up-to-date lists and additions.

Useful Oracle-Related Web Sites

Oracle's home page is located at www.oracle.com.

The Oracle Technology Network (OTN) offers free product downloads, discussion forums, white papers, sample code, documentation, and technical articles on a variety of Oracle-related issues. You can find the site at http://otn.oracle.com. The site requires registration but is free. You will also see various forums on OTN where you can pose questions; see www.oracle.com/forums/.

Tom Kyte at Oracle runs a forum for frequently asked questions, located at http://asktom.oracle.com.

The Oracle by Example (OBE) series offers tutorial type instruction for real world problems, at http://otn.oracle.com/obe/start/index.html. Along with it, you will find the *Oracle 2 Day DBA* manual, useful for beginning DBA topics—located at http://otn.oracle.com/obe/2day_dba/index.html.

Oracle support via Metalink (also called "My Oracle Support") is available only if you purchase an Oracle support contract. The Web sites are www.oracle.com/support and http://metalink.oracle.com/index.html.

For information related to SQL Developer, see the forum at http://forums.oracle.com/forums/main.jspa?categoryID=84. The SQL Developer Exchange Web site, at www.oracle.com/technology/products/database/sql_developer/index.html, is a good resource for finding and sharing tips.

Sue Harper, Oracle's SQL Developer product manager, blogs about new features at http://sueharper.blogspot.com.

An informative Web portal called *Oracle FAQ* features extensive links to many useful Oracle-related sites. This independently run Web site is useful for further research on Oracle topics. You can find it at www.orafaq.com.

Alternative SQL Execution Tools

This book uses SQL Developer and SQL*Plus as execution environments because they are available with every Oracle installation. SQL Developer has incorporated many of the features previously available only from third-party vendors, but there are still many excellent tools on the market that make you wonder how you could have ever lived without them.

You might want to download a trial version or two to help determine the suitability for you individual needs. Following is a list of popular vendors. The ORAFAQ Web site, located at www.orafaq.com/tools/index.htm, lists many more and includes a comparison chart.

> PL/SQL Developer by Allaround Automations:
> www.allroundautomations.nl/plsqldevaddons.html
>
> Rapid SQL by Embarcadero Technologies: www.embarcadero.com
>
> SQL Navigator and Toad by Quest Software: www.quest.com

Database Design Software

The next version of SQL Developer is slated to include a data modeling extension. Many vendors offer tools that allow you to create logical and physical data models for Oracle databases. Following are a few popular vendors.

> DeZign by Datanamic: www.datanamic.com
>
> ER/Studio by Embarcadero Technologies: www.embarcadero.com
>
> ERwin Data Modeler by Computer Associates: www.cai.com

Oracle released a database design software package. You can find a trial version named Oracle SQL Developer Data Modeling at www.oracle.com/technology/products/database/sql_developer/files/Modeling.html.

User Groups

Joining a user group is one of the best ways to gain knowledge and experience using Oracle. Be sure to check out the group in your geographic area.

> International Oracle Users Group (IOUG): www.ioug.org
>
> Oracle Users Group Center:
> www.oracle.com/technology/community/user_groups/index.htm
>
> Oracle Development Tools User Group: http://odtug.com

Oracle-Related Publications

Subscribing to a magazine is a great way to stay on top of the latest Oracle news and features.

> SELECT Journal Magazine, a publication of the IOUG: www.ioug.org/selectjournal
>
> Oracle Magazine Online, a free Oracle publication that contains technology articles as well as tips and techniques: www.oramag.com/publications

Academic Resources

There are a number of Web sites related to the academic teaching environments. www.aisnet.org provides many useful links and information. For database-related teaching materials, visit www.magal.com/iswn/teaching/database/.

Oracle offers its own program geared toward academia. Review the following Web sites.

Oracle Academy: https://academy.oracle.com/index.html

Oracle Workforce: http://workforce.oracle.com

Books

Following is a list of books you can use to explore advanced subjects in further detail.

SQL for Smarties: Advanced SQL Programming by Joe Celko; Morgan Kaufman Publishers, Inc., 2005. This book provides excellent coverage of many advanced SQL topics.

SQL Puzzles & Answers by Joe Celko; Morgan Kaufman Publishers, Inc., 2006. This book contains many clever and humorous real-life examples and solutions.

Oracle PL/SQL by Example, 4th Edition, by Benjamin Rosenzweig and Elena Silvestrova Rakhimov; Prentice Hall, 2008. This book is the logical choice to take you to the next level of Oracle knowledge. It is based on the same workbook pedagogy as this book, with exercises and labs. It is a perfect introduction into PL/SQL.

Expert Oracle Database Architecture: 9i and 10g Programming Techniques and Solutions by Thomas Kyte; Apress, 2005. The book covers architecture, along with many useful SQL and PL/SQL features.

Oracle Essentials: Oracle Database 11g, 4th Edition, by Rick Greenwald, Robert Stackowiak, and Jonathan Stern; O'Reilly Media, Inc. This is a useful book for expanding your understanding of Oracle's database architecture.

Physical Database Design Using Oracle by Donald K. Burleson; CRC, 2004. This book describes how to map a logical model to an Oracle physical model.

Mastering Regular Expressions by Jeffrey E. F. Friedl; O'Reilly, 2006. This book provides detailed explanations of regular expressions.

Oracle Performance Survival Guide by Jeffrey Guy Harrison; Prentice Hall, 2009. The book includes many tuning and design tips.

Oracle Data Types

This appendix lists Oracle's most commonly used built-in data types. Note that some of the data types mentioned have additional data types to support specific national character sets, such as NCLOB or NVARCHAR2.

Oracle supports intermedia data types (images, audio, video), spacial (geographic) data, the ANY type where a data type is not known and can be dynamically configured, and the XML types. These data types can be used in conjunction with C/C++, Java, or PL/SQL.

Oracle's PL/SQL language has some of the same data types as listed in Table I.1, but in some cases, PL/SQL places certain restrictions on manipulation and size. If you are working with data types within PL/SQL, refer to *Oracle PL/SQL by Example*, 4th Edition, by Benjamin Rosenzweig and Elena Silvestrova Rakhimov (Prentice Hall, 2008) for more details.

TABLE I.1 Oracle's Most Commonly Used Built-in Data Types

DATA TYPE	EXPLANATION
NUMBER [(optional precision,[optional scale])]	Stores zero, positive, and negative fixed- and floating-point numbers. The allowable values for precision are 1 to 38 and for the scale –84 to 127.
BINARY_FLOAT	Holds floating-point numbers in 32-bit format. Floating-point numbers support infinity and NaN (not a number).
BINARY_DOUBLE	Is the 64-bit double-precision floating data point number implementation. Floating-point computation using the BINARY_FLOAT and BINARY_DOUBLE data types is more efficient than with the NUMBER data type.
VARCHAR2 (size bytes|char)	Is a variable-length character string with a maximum size of 4,000 characters or bytes. A length must always be specified. (If your database encoding scheme is single byte, the numbers of bytes and characters are identical. If you use multi-bytes to support certain foreign languages, a character may consists of more than one byte. In this case, consider using NCHAR and NVARCHAR2 data types.)
CHAR [optional size]	Holds fixed character length data with a maximum size of 2,000 characters; the default size is 1. Any space not used by the stored text is padded with blanks.

TABLE I.1   Continued

DATA TYPE	EXPLANATION
LONG	Character data type with a maximum storage capacity of 2GB. LONGs are subject to a number of restrictions, and Oracle recommends that you convert data from this data type to CLOBs.
CLOB	Stores large text objects. Use this instead of the LONG data type. Also useful for storing XML objects.
DATE	Stores date and time, including seconds, from January 1, 4712 B.C., to December 31, 9999 A.D.
TIMESTAMP [optional seconds precision]	Same as DATE but includes fractional seconds precision from 0 to 9 digits. The default is 6.
TIMESTAMP [optional seconds precision] WITH TIME ZONE	Same as TIMESTAMP, including the time zone displacement value.
TIMESTAMP [optional seconds precision] WITH LOCAL TIME ZONE	Same as TIMESTAMP WITH TIME ZONE, except time is displayed in the session's time zone and stored in the database's time zone.
INTERVAL YEAR [optional year precision] TO MONTH	Stores a period of time in years and months. The optional precision may range from 0 to 9, with a default value of 2.
INTERVAL DAY [optional day precision] TO SECOND [optional fractional seconds precision]	Stores a period of time in days, hours, minutes, and seconds. The default day precision is 2, with acceptable values from 0 to 9. The default fractional seconds precision is 6, with acceptable values from 0 to 9.
ROWID	Represents the unique address of a row in a table, displayed in hexadecimal format. Typically used in conjunction with the ROWID pseudocolumn. See Chapter 13, "Indexes, Sequences, and Views," for more information on ROWID.
RAW (size)	Holds raw binary data, with a maximum length of 2,000 bytes. Useful for small binary data such as graphics.
LONG RAW	Same as RAW except holds up to 2GB. Used for binary data such as graphics, sounds, or documents. Oracle recommends that you convert LONG RAWs to binary BLOB columns as they have fewer restrictions than LONG RAW.
BLOB	Stores unstructured binary large objects. Often used for graphic images, video clips, and sounds.
BFILE	Similar to BLOB but points to large binary file stored outside the database. Oracle can read the file only, not modify it. Oracle requires appropriate operating system–level read permissions on the file.

INDEX

Harrison

Oracle® Performance Survival Guide

A Systematic Approach to Database Optimization

- ▶ Shows how to tune performance efficiently by addressing causes rather than symptoms

- ▶ Addresses all facets of performance, including application design, SQL tuning, content management, memory, physical IO, and more

- ▶ Helps tuners focus on the areas where the greatest gains can be found

- ▶ By Guy Harrison, author of the top-selling *Oracle SQL High Performance Tuning*

AVAILABLE OCTOBER, 2009
ISBN-13: 9780137011957

Oracle Performance Survival Guide offers a structured methodology for optimizing Oracle performance in the most systematic and efficient manner possible. Authored by leading Oracle expert Guy Harrison, this is the first book to contain up-to-the-minute guidance for optimizing the performance of the new Oracle 11*g* Release 2. Harrison helps DBAs and developers quickly and efficiently optimize performance by focusing on causes rather than symptoms and identifying the areas that will deliver the greatest "bang for the buck" in their applications and environments. He covers every area of Oracle performance management, from application design through SQL tuning—content management through memory and physical IO management.

FOR MORE INFORMATION VISIT:
www.informit.com/title/ 9780137011957

The complete, systematic, expert guide to Oracle 11*g* Release 2 performance tuning— for all DBAs and developers, regardless of experience

PRENTICE HALL

informit.com/oracleseries

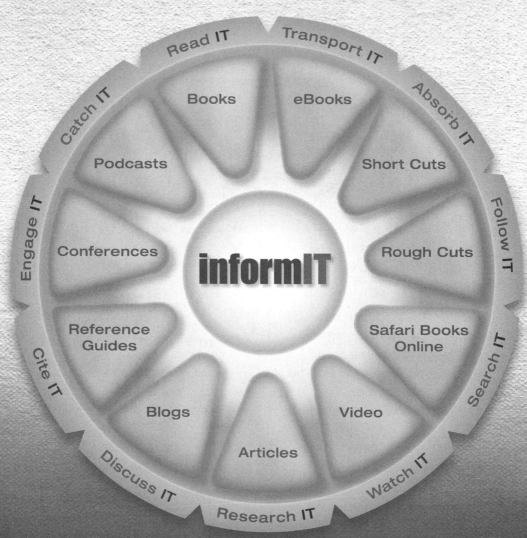

FREE Online Edition

Your purchase of **Oracle® SQL by Example** includes access to a free online edition for 45 days through the Safari Books Online subscription service. Nearly every Prentice Hall book is available online through Safari Books Online, along with more than 5,000 other technical books and videos from publishers such as Addison-Wesley Professional, Cisco Press, Exam Cram, IBM Press, O'Reilly, Que, and Sams.

SAFARI BOOKS ONLINE allows you to search for a specific answer, cut and paste code, download chapters, and stay current with emerging technologies.

Activate your FREE Online Edition at
www.informit.com/safarifree

> **STEP 1:** Enter the coupon code: FZEXAZG.

> **STEP 2:** New Safari users, complete the brief registration form.
> Safari subscribers, just log in.

If you have difficulty registering on Safari or accessing the online edition,
please e-mail customer-service@safaribooksonline.com